Macworld®
Mac® OS 8
Bible

Macworld®
Mac® OS 8
Bible

Lon Poole

IDG Books Worldwide, Inc.
An International Data Group Company

Foster City, CA ✦ Chicago, IL ✦ Indianapolis, IN ✦ Southlake, TX

Macworld® Mac® OS 8 Bible

Published by
IDG Books Worldwide, Inc.
An International Data Group Company
919 E. Hillsdale Blvd., Suite 400
Foster City, CA 94404

http://www.idgbooks.com (IDG Books Worldwide Web site)

Library of Congress Catalog Card No.: 97-074811

ISBN: 0-7645-4036-X

Printed in the United States of America

10 9 8 7 6 5 4 3 2 1

1DD/QR/RQ/ZX/FC

Distributed in the United States by IDG Books Worldwide, Inc.

Distributed by Macmillan Canada for Canada; by Transworld Publishers Limited in the United Kingdom; by IDG Norge Books for Norway; by IDG Sweden Books for Sweden; by Woodslane Pty. Ltd. for Australia; by Woodslane Enterprises Ltd. for New Zealand; by Longman Singapore Publishers Ltd. for Singapore, Malaysia, Thailand, and Indonesia; by Simron Pty. Ltd. for South Africa; by Toppan Company Ltd. for Japan; by Distribuidora Cuspide for Argentina; by Livraria Cultura for Brazil; by Ediciencia S.A. for Ecuador; by Addison-Wesley Publishing Company for Korea; by Ediciones ZETA S.C.R. Ltda. for Peru; by WS Computer Publishing Corporation, Inc., for the Philippines; by Unalis Corporation for Taiwan; by Contemporanea de Ediciones for Venezuela; by Computer Book & Magazine Store for Puerto Rico; by Express Computer Distributors for the Caribbean and West Indies. Authorized Sales Agent: Anthony Rudkin Associates for the Middle East and North Africa.

For general information on IDG Books Worldwide's books in the U.S., please call our Consumer Customer Service department at 800-762-2974. For reseller information, including discounts and premium sales, please call our Reseller Customer Service department at 800-434-3422.

For information on where to purchase IDG Books Worldwide's books outside the U.S., please contact our International Sales department at 415-655-3200 or fax 415-655-3295.

For information on foreign language translations, please contact our Foreign & Subsidiary Rights department at 415-655-3021 or fax 415-655-3281.

For sales inquiries and special prices for bulk quantities, please contact our Sales department at 415-655-3200 or write to the address above.

For information on using IDG Books Worldwide's books in the classroom or for ordering examination copies, please contact our Educational Sales department at 800-434-2086 or fax 817-251-8174.

For press review copies, author interviews, or other publicity information, please contact our Public Relations department at 415-655-3000 or fax 415-655-3299.

For authorization to photocopy items for corporate, personal, or educational use, please contact Copyright Clearance Center, 222 Rosewood Drive, Danvers, MA 01923, or fax 508-750-4470.

The IDG Books Worldwide logo is a trademark under exclusive license to IDG Books Worldwide, Inc., from International Data Group, Inc.

ABOUT IDG BOOKS WORLDWIDE

Welcome to the world of IDG Books Worldwide.

IDG Books Worldwide, Inc., is a subsidiary of International Data Group, the world's largest publisher of computer-related information and the leading global provider of information services on information technology. IDG was founded more than 25 years ago and now employs more than 8,500 people worldwide. IDG publishes more than 275 computer publications in over 75 countries (see listing below). More than 60 million people read one or more IDG publications each month.

Launched in 1990, IDG Books Worldwide is today the #1 publisher of best-selling computer books in the United States. We are proud to have received eight awards from the Computer Press Association in recognition of editorial excellence and three from *Computer Currents'* First Annual Readers' Choice Awards. Our best-selling ...*For Dummies*® series has more than 30 million copies in print with translations in 30 languages. IDG Books Worldwide, through a joint venture with IDG's Hi-Tech Beijing, became the first U.S. publisher to publish a computer book in the People's Republic of China. In record time, IDG Books Worldwide has become the first choice for millions of readers around the world who want to learn how to better manage their businesses.

Our mission is simple: Every one of our books is designed to bring extra value and skill-building instructions to the reader. Our books are written by experts who understand and care about our readers. The knowledge base of our editorial staff comes from years of experience in publishing, education, and journalism — experience we use to produce books for the '90s. In short, we care about books, so we attract the best people. We devote special attention to details such as audience, interior design, use of icons, and illustrations. And because we use an efficient process of authoring, editing, and desktop publishing our books electronically, we can spend more time ensuring superior content and spend less time on the technicalities of making books.

You can count on our commitment to deliver high-quality books at competitive prices on topics you want to read about. At IDG Books Worldwide, we continue in the IDG tradition of delivering quality for more than 25 years. You'll find no better book on a subject than one from IDG Books Worldwide.

John Kilcullen
CEO
IDG Books Worldwide, Inc.

Steven Berkowitz
President and Publisher
IDG Books Worldwide, Inc.

Eighth Annual Computer Press Awards ≥1992

Ninth Annual Computer Press Awards ≥1993

Tenth Annual Computer Press Awards ≥1994

Eleventh Annual Computer Press Awards ≥1995

IDG Books Worldwide, Inc., is a subsidiary of International Data Group, the world's largest publisher of computer-related information and the leading global provider of information services on information technology. International Data Group publishes over 275 computer publications in over 75 countries. Sixty million people read one or more International Data Group publications each month. International Data Group's publications include: **ARGENTINA:** Buyer's Guide, Computerworld Argentina, PC World Argentina; **AUSTRALIA:** Australian Macworld, Australian PC World, Australian Reseller News, Computerworld, IT Casebook, Network World, Publish, Webmaster, **AUSTRIA:** Computerwelt Osterreich, Networks Austria, PC Tip Austria; **BANGLADESH:** PC World Bangladesh; **BELARUS:** PC World Belarus; **BELGIUM:** Data News; **BRAZIL:** Annuário de Informática, Computerworld, Connections, Macworld, PC Player, PC World, Publish, Reseller News, Supergamepower; **BULGARIA:** Computerworld Bulgaria, Network World Bulgaria, PC & MacWorld Bulgaria; **CANADA:** CIO Canada, Client/Server World, ComputerWorld Canada, InfoWorld Canada, NetworkWorld Canada, WebWorld; **CHILE:** Computerworld Chile, PC World Chile; **COLOMBIA:** Computerworld Colombia, PC World Colombia; **COSTA RICA:** PC World Centro America; **THE CZECH AND SLOVAK REPUBLICS:** Computerworld Czechoslovakia, Macworld Czech Republic, PC World Czechoslovakia; **DENMARK:** Communications World Danmark, Computerworld Danmark, Macworld Danmark, PC World Danmark, Techworld Denmark; **DOMINICAN REPUBLIC:** PC World Republica Dominicana; **ECUADOR:** PC World Ecuador; **EGYPT:** PC World Middle East, PC World Middle East; **EL SALVADOR:** PC World Centro America; **FINLAND:** MikroPC, Tietoverkko, Tietoviikko; **FRANCE:** Distributique, Hebdo, Info PC, Le Monde Informatique, Macworld, Reseaux & Telecoms, WebMaster France; **GERMANY:** Computer Partner, Computerwoche, Computerwoche Extra, Computerwoche FOCUS, Global Online, Macwelt, PC Welt; **GREECE:** Amiga Computing, GamePro Greece, Multimedia World; **GUATEMALA:** PC World Centro America; **HONDURAS:** PC World Centro America; **HONG KONG:** Computerworld Hong Kong, PC World Hong Kong, Publish in Asia; **HUNGARY:** ABCD CD-ROM, Computerworld Szamitastechnika, Internetto online Magazine, PC World Hungary, PC-X Magazin Hungary; **ICELAND:** Tolvuheimur PC World Island; **INDIA:** Information Communications World, Information Systems Computerworld, PC World India, Publish in Asia; **INDONESIA:** InfoKomputer PC World, Komputek Computerworld, Publish in Asia; **IRELAND:** ComputerScope, PC Live!; **ISRAEL:** Macworld Israel, People & Computers/Computerworld; **ITALY:** Computerworld Italia, Macworld Italia, Networking Italia, PC World Italia; **JAPAN:** DTP World, Macworld Japan, Nikkei Personal Computing, OS/2 World Japan, SunWorld Japan, Windows NT World, Windows World Japan; **KENYA:** PC World East African; **KOREA:** Hi-Tech Information, Macworld Korea, PC World Korea; **MACEDONIA:** PC World Macedonia; **MALAYSIA:** Computerworld Malaysia, PC World Malaysia, Publish in Asia; **MALTA:** PC World Malta; **MEXICO:** Computerworld Mexico, PC World Mexico; **MYANMAR:** PC World Myanmar; **NETHERLANDS:** Computer! Totaal, LAN Internetworking Magazine, LAN World Buyers Guide, Macworld Netherlands, Net, WebWereld; **NEW ZEALAND:** Absolute Beginners Guide and Plain & Simple Series, Computer Buyer, Computer Industry Directory, Computerworld New Zealand, MTB, Network World, PC World New Zealand; **NICARAGUA:** PC World Centro America; **NORWAY:** Computerworld Norge, CW Rapport, Datamagasinet, Financial Rapport, Kursguide Norge, Macworld Norge, Multimediaworld Norge, PC World Ekspress Norge, PC World Nettverk, PC World Norge, PC World ProduktGuide Norge; **PAKISTAN:** Computerworld Pakistan; **PANAMA:** PC World Panama; **PEOPLE'S REPUBLIC OF CHINA:** China Computer Users, China Computerworld, China InfoWorld, China Telecom World Weekly, Computer & Communication, Electronic Design China, Electronics Today, Electronics Weekly, Game Software, PC World China, Popular Computer Week, Software Weekly, Software World, Telecom World; **PERU:** Computerworld Peru, PC World Profesional Peru, PC World SoHo Peru; **PHILIPPINES:** Click!, Computerworld Philippines, PC World Philippines, Publish in Asia; **POLAND:** Computerworld Poland, Computerworld Special Report Poland, Cyber, Macworld Poland, Networld Poland, PC World Komputer; **PORTUGAL:** Cerebro/PC World, Computerworld/Correio Informático, Dealer World Portugal, Mac*In/PC*In Portugal, Multimedia World; **PUERTO RICO:** PC World Puerto Rico; **ROMANIA:** Computerworld Romania, PC World Romania, Telecom Romania; **RUSSIA:** Computerworld Russia, Mir PK, Publish, Seti; **SINGAPORE:** Computerworld Singapore, PC World Singapore, Publish in Asia; **SLOVENIA:** Monitor; **SOUTH AFRICA:** Computing SA, Network World SA, Software World SA; **SPAIN:** Communicaciones World España, Computerworld España, Dealer World España, Macworld España, PC World España; **SRI LANKA:** Infolink PC World; **SWEDEN:** CAP&Design, Computer Sweden, Corporate Computing Sweden, Internetworld Sweden, it.branschen, Macworld Sweden, MaxiData Sweden, MikroDatorn, Nätverk & Kommunikation, PC World Sweden, PCaktiv, Windows World Sweden; **SWITZERLAND:** Computerworld Schweiz, Macworld Schweiz, PCtip; **TAIWAN:** Computerworld Taiwan, Macworld Taiwan, NEW ViSiON/Publish, PC World Taiwan, Windows World Taiwan; **THAILAND:** Publish in Asia, Thai Computerworld; **TURKEY:** Computerworld Turkiye, Macworld Turkiye, Network World Turkiye, PC World Turkiye; **UKRAINE:** Computerworld Kiev, Multimedia World Ukraine, PC World Ukraine; **UNITED KINGDOM:** Acorn User UK, Amiga Action UK, Amiga Computing UK, Apple Talk UK, Computing, Macworld, Parents and Computers UK, PC Advisor, PC Home, PSX Pro, The WEB; **UNITED STATES:** Cable in the Classroom, CIO Magazine, Computerworld, DOS World, Federal Computer Week, GamePro Magazine, InfoWorld, I-Way, Macworld, Network World, PC Games, PC World, Publish, Video Event, THE WEB Magazine, and WebMaster; online webzines: JavaWorld, NetscapeWorld, and SunWorld Online; **URUGUAY:** InfoWorld Uruguay; **VENEZUELA:** Computerworld Venezuela, PC World Venezuela; and **VIETNAM:** PC World Vietnam.   3/24/97

Credits

Acquisitions Editor
Andy Cummings

Development Editors
Kathi Duggan
Earl Jackson, Jr.

Technical Editor
Dennis R. Cohen

Copy Editor
Kathi Duggan

Production Coordinator
Tom Debolski

Graphics & Production Specialist
Vincent F. Burns
Renée Dunn
Linda Marousek
Shannon Miller
Maureen Moore
Andreas F. Schueller
Mark Schumann
Trevor Wilson
Elsie Yim

Quality Control Specialist
Mick Arellano

Proofreader
Christine Sabooni

Indexer
Ty Koontz

About the Author

Lon Poole, based in Kensington, California, is a contributing editor to *Macworld* magazine who answers readers' questions every month in his "Quick Tips" column. Lon helped create *Macworld* magazine in 1983, and writes feature articles for the publication regularly. His 1988 article entitled "Installing Memory" won a Maggie Award for Best How-To Article in a Consumer Publication. His feature article, "Here Comes System 7," was a finalist in the 1990 Excellence in Technology Communications competition. His three-part series, "How It Works," won First Place, Best In-Depth Technical Feature Article 1993 from the American Society of Business Press Editors.

Lon has been writing books about personal computers and their practical applications since 1976. He has authored five Macintosh books, including the best-selling *Macworld Guide to System 7*, as well as the now-classic *Apple II User's Guide*, which sold over a half million copies worldwide. Lon has a BA in Computer Science from the University of California, Berkeley.

Foreword

If you are like a great many Mac users, you understand the critical importance of your system software. After all, it's the first thing that's loaded or preloaded in your Mac. Plus, you're constantly being told to place new items in the system folders or find things within those folders. And when you find yourself troubleshooting, you're often digging around in the system software.

Alas, many people who use a Macintosh aren't sure why the system software works the way it does. Yet, having an understanding of the system software and how to work with it efficiently is one of the greatest boons to anyone's computing productivity. Since the system software underlies every application program you use, its mastery can augment nearly every aspect of your work.

Now, thanks to the expertise of Lon Poole and his *Macworld Mac OS 8 Bible*, our path to a productive Mac life is made easier. Lon has created the most thorough, accurate, and useful guide to the many recent incarnations of the Mac OS. I can personally and professionally attest to the Mac wizardry of Lon Poole. Lon writes the highly read "Quick Tips" column for *Macworld*. As an editor, I appreciate Lon's attention to detail, devotion to technical accuracy, and focus on providing Mac users with the most helpful tips and guidance. He accomplishes all of this in an entertaining and readable manner, belying the wealth of technical information contained within the text.

Lon is well equipped to provide comprehensive coverage of Mac OS 8 (and more!). He has been a devotee of Apple and contributor to *Macworld* from the very beginning. He helped found the magazine way back in 1983 and continues to be one of the key reasons *Macworld* is recognized as the Macintosh authority. Lon's own authority is well established in volumes of issues and books in which he provides highly specific and truly useful guidance that addresses a wide range of Macintosh computing solutions — making Lon one of the most knowledgeable Mac experts around.

Enjoy this excursion through the system software tour. Lon will tell you which system version is best for your needs, and he will tell you how to use your system software in order to work faster, smarter, and more efficiently.

Adrian Mello
former Editor-in-Chief
Macworld

Preface

According to popular legend, a Mac is so easy to use that you don't need to read books about it. Alas, if only that were true. In fact, discovering all the power that even the original version of System 7 gives your computer — let alone Mac OS 8 — would take months of exploring and experimenting. Yes, exploring and experimenting can be fun; you should do some of it. But do you really have months to devote to your computer's operating system? No! Save your time for having fun with games and multimedia, exploring the Internet, or maybe getting some work done. Benefit from the experience of others (in this case, the author and his collaborators). Read this book so you can put the full power of the Mac OS to work for you without a lot of poking around the Mac desktop.

Maybe you think you don't need this book because you have Apple's manuals and on screen help. It's true these are good sources of information. But the *Macworld Mac OS 8 Bible* contains a great deal of information you won't find in the manuals or help screens. This book also provides a different perspective on subjects you may not quite understand after reading the manuals. And because this book describes the Mac OS completely, you can use it instead of Apple's manuals if you don't happen to have them.

Who Should Read This Book

This book is aimed at people who already know Mac OS fundamentals such as choosing commands from menus, moving icons on the desktop, and selecting and editing text. If you have spent more than a few days with any Mac OS computer, you know how to do these things and are ready for what's inside this book.

Read this book to learn all about Mac OS 8 — how to use it if you have it, and why to get it if you don't. Actually, this book tells you how to use all the recent versions of the system software from 7.5 on. (If you have System 7.1.2 or earlier, read this book to find out what you're missing and why you should upgrade.)

You can stick to the basics if you're new to the Mac OS. When you're ready to go beyond the basics, you can learn how to take advantage of the power in your version of the Mac OS.

What's Inside

Macworld Mac OS 8 Bible covers Mac OS 8 and recent earlier versions progressively in six parts. Here's an overview of each part:

❖ **Part I** (Chapters 1–4) takes a quick look at the features of the Mac OS. Use it to get started right away or to get the big picture. You'll get an overview of what's special about Mac OS 8, as well as what's hot and what's cool in all recent versions of the system software. In addition, you'll see how the various recent system software versions stack up, so you can decide whether to stick with the system version you have or upgrade it.

❖ **Part II** (Chapters 5–11) describes in depth what you'll encounter when you first start using the Mac OS. Windows, icons, and menus are in your face from the moment you start up a Mac OS computer, but look closely and you may find some new and useful aspects of these elements. When you get beyond looking around the desktop, you can organize your disks, folders, and files with the Finder. You get to work by opening programs and documents (including documents from Windows and DOS computers), moving document contents around, and saving documents. Your work is sure to involve the special System Folder and its contents. You'll want to fine-tune how the system works by adjusting a multitude of settings in software control panels, and you'll also find that the accessory programs included with the Mac OS come in handy on occasion.

❖ **Part III** (Chapters 12–18) tells you how to use some important Mac OS capabilities. You discover how handy aliases can be. You learn to deal with fonts and typography, and also learn to get printing under control. You get comfortable with managing your Mac's memory (though you never truly enjoy doing it). You also learn how to set up a simple network of computers, share your files with others on the network, and use their shared files.

❖ **Part IV** (Chapters 19–23) takes you beyond System 7 basics — way beyond. You find out why the Mac OS deserves its reputation as the multimedia leader among personal computer operating systems. You learn how the Mac OS makes it easy to explore the Internet, including the Web and e-mail. You get to know how any Mac can speak and how some can listen, and how the Mac OS works with multiple languages. This part of the book also introduces AppleScript, and teaches you how to use it to automate repetitive tasks. In addition, you learn to create compound documents with OpenDoc plug-in software, or learn how to publish and subscribe.

❖ **Part V** (Chapters 24–26) presents many ways to make the most of the Mac OS. In this part of the book, a whole chapter is devoted to describing almost 100 low-cost software utilities you can use to enhance the Mac OS. Two more chapters reveal over 100 Mac OS tips and secrets.

❖ **Part VI** (Chapters 27–30) details how to upgrade or install the Mac OS, including how to install a clean copy. You find out how to get ready to install, and you can follow step-by-step instructions for installing Mac OS 8, Mac OS 7.6 and 7.6.1, System 7.5–7.5.5, and add-on system software.

❖ **Appendixes** include a glossary and cover major features of System 7.5–Mac OS 7.6.1 that Apple dropped from Mac OS 8, QuickDraw GX printing, and PowerTalk collaboration services.

If you read this book from front to back, you will find that some information appears in more than one place. In particular, everything that Part I covers in summary appears elsewhere in the book, in more detail. Also, some of the tips and secrets in Chapters 25 and 26 appear first amidst relevant subject matter throughout earlier chapters. This duplication is intentional and is meant for your benefit.

Conventions Used in This Book

This book makes use of established conventions in an effort to help guide you through the material.

Mac OS version references

As you may have realized from reading this preface, this book uses the terms *Mac OS* and *system software* to include all versions of the Macintosh system software unless a specific version number is stated, such as Mac OS 8. References to specific versions apply only to the version number cited, such as 7.5.3. In general, this book refers to versions of system software prior to 7.6 as "System" and to versions 7.6 and later as "Mac OS" because that's the terminology that Apple uses. Occasionally, the book deviates from this convention to improve readability — for example, "Mac OS 7.5–7.6.1." Just remember that *Mac OS* and *System* are two terms for the Mac system software.

Sidebars

Certain discussions in this book are expanded with sidebars. These are shaded boxes that contain background information, expert tips and advice, areas where caution is needed, and other helpful information.

All sidebars feature an icon, or symbol, that categorizes the information contained in the sidebar. These icons are designed to alert you to the type of information you will find. Here's what to look for:

The information in a **Backgrounder** sidebar provides background detail about an issue under discussion.

The information in a **Quick Tips** sidebar points out a useful tip (or tips) that can save you a great deal of time and trouble.

The information in a **Caution** sidebar alerts you to potential problems with an issue under discussion. Solutions and ways to avoid the scary situations are also included.

A **Secrets** sidebar includes concepts and ideas missing from or not easily found in Apple's documentation of the Mac OS. The information is the result of countless hours of tinkering, troubleshooting, and asking questions of expert sources.

A **Step-By-Step** sidebar provides detailed instructions that show how to perform tasks with the Mac OS. Many issues in the Mac OS can be complex, but these sidebars help break the desired goal into manageable components.

Feedback, Please

The author and publisher appreciate your feedback on this book. Please feel free to contact us, in care of IDG Books Worldwide, with questions or comments.

Acknowledgments

Once upon a time, when computer technology was so much simpler than it is today, I actually managed to write a couple of books on my own. Well, those days are gone. Several people made major contributions to earlier editions of this book, and their work lives on in the *Macworld Mac OS 8 Bible*. David Angell and Brent Heslop researched and wrote first drafts of material that appears in Chapters 12, 18, and 23 in this edition. Nancy Dunn and Rita Lewis helped reorganize and update an earlier edition of the book, and much of their work survives in Chapters 13, 14, 15, and 21, and in Appendixes A and B of this edition. Derrick Schneider applied his AppleScript expertise to Chapter 18. I most gratefully acknowledge all of their contributions.

For the *Macworld Mac OS 8 Bible*, I wish to thank Roxanne Gentile, the curator of the software library on the *Macworld Online* Web site, for putting together the updated collection of utility software in Chapter 24. Thanks also to Suzanne Courteau, the editor of my "Quick Tips" column in *Macworld*, for compiling and revising the tips in Chapters 25 and 26. I also want to acknowledge Rob Terrell for bringing Chapters 10 and 11 up to date and for reorganizing and supplementing the installation instructions in Chapters 27–30. And thank you, Tom Negrino, for working so long and hard, through much hardship, to compress the entire Internet into Chapter 20.

I also want to express my appreciation to the editorial and production team, whose diligence made all the difference. In particular, Dennis Cohen as technical reviewer did a great job of straining out technical impurities. I also want especially to thank Andy Cummings, who does not take "slow" for an answer, for moving this book along faster than I thought possible. My head is still spinning. In addition, I want to thank Kathi Duggan, who inherited the job of development editor about half way through the writing of the book, and despite that handicap, did a terrific job.

I reserve my deepest gratitude for my wife Karin, and sons Ethan and Adam, without whose love and support this work would have been impossible and pointless.

Contents at a Glance

Contents

CHAPTER

3

CHAPTER

6

Get Organized with the Finder 107

CHAPTER

7

Get More Organized with the Finder. 127

CHAPTER

8

CHAPTER

11

Put Accessory Programs to Work. 271

Introducing Accessory Programs. 271
Accessory Program Encyclopedia 272
  Apple System Profiler. 272
  AppleCD Audio Player. 274
  Apple Video Player. 275
  Calculator and Graphing Calculator. 275
  Chooser 276
  Connect To. 276
  Disk First Aid 277
  Find File 278
  Graphing Calculator. 278
  Jigsaw Puzzle 279
  Key Caps 280
  Movie Player 281
  Note Pad 282
  Scrapbook. 283
  Script Editor. 284
  SimpleSound. 284
  Stickies 286

Part III: At Work with the Mac OS. 289

CHAPTER

12

Make Aliases Hop. 291

Understanding Aliases. 291
Making an Alias. 292
Changing an Alias. 294
Keeping Track of Original Items. 295
Finding an Original Item 297
Discovering the Many Uses of Aliases. 298
  Aliases in the Apple menu. 298
  A Launcher menu. 299
  Universal Show Clipboard 300
  Aliases on the desktop. 300
  Multiple Trash cans 301
  "Remove disk" icon 301
  Open and Save shortcuts. 302
  Aliases as startup items 303

CHAPTER

13

Take Charge of Your Fonts 313

CHAPTER

18

Part IV: Beyond the Basics of the Mac OS . . . 487

Introduction

When it comes to working on a personal computer, nothing quite equals working on an Apple Macintosh or Mac-compatible computer. What creates this unique working environment is the Macintosh system software. The system software is now called the Mac OS or Mac OS X (where X is a version number such as 8), particularly when referring to Mac OS 7.6 and later. You also hear the Mac system software called System X (where X is the version number), especially when referring to System 7.5.5 and earlier.

The Mac OS displays the windows, icons, menus, pointer, and other elements of the graphical user interface (GUI, pronounced "gooey"), and the Mac OS responds to your input through the keyboard and mouse. And that's just the beginning. The Mac OS provides a raft of other services; the following is a partial list:

❖ Filing electronic documents and software items

❖ Opening application programs and documents and saving document changes

❖ Implementing basic text editing (inserting, deleting, replacing, and so on)

❖ Drawing two- and three-dimensional graphics on screen

❖ Composing text in a variety of typefaces, styles, and sizes

❖ Printing graphics and typeset text

❖ Managing the computer's memory

❖ Participating in a network of computers

❖ Accessing the Internet — e-mail, the Web, and more

❖ Working with documents from the MS DOS and Windows operating systems

❖ Displaying movies and 360-degree panoramas

❖ Playing sounds and music

❖ Synthesizing and recognizing speech

❖ Handling text in dozens of languages and writing systems

❖ Facilitating data exchange and communication among application programs

❖ Automating tasks with scripts

The Mac OS is not nearly as simple today as it was when Apple released the first Mac system software in 1984. Over the years, Apple has added many improvements: a better filing system in 1985, color in 1987, and multitasking in 1988, to name a few. The system software entered a new realm of complexity in 1990 with the release of System 7.0.

Apple continues to revise the system software, adding more features and capabilities with each new version. System 7.5, introduced in October 1994 and the earliest version covered in this book, has more than 50 features not found in its predecessor. Some of System 7.5's new features are simple, such as a digital clock in the menu bar, and some are sophisticated, such as the ability to automate tasks with AppleScript. Mac OS 7.6, released in January 1997, integrates some software updates with many system software enhancements that were first distributed separately as add-ons. The major enhancements include Desktop Printing, Open Transport networking, QuickDraw 3D graphics, and the OpenDoc plug-in software infrastructure. Six months later, Apple delivered Mac OS 8, the biggest upgrade to the Mac system software since System 7.0. Its improvements include a sleek, three-dimensional appearance; new ways of working with windows, files, folders, and disks; integrated Internet access; better performance; and more stability.

No matter how much or how little experience you have with the Mac OS, this book can show you something useful about it that you don't already know. The book describes both basic and advanced Mac OS features, and explains how you can use them to make working with your computer more productive and fun. Sure, you can discover a lot about the Mac OS by exploring it on your own, but your exploration will go faster and you'll find out more with this book as your guide.

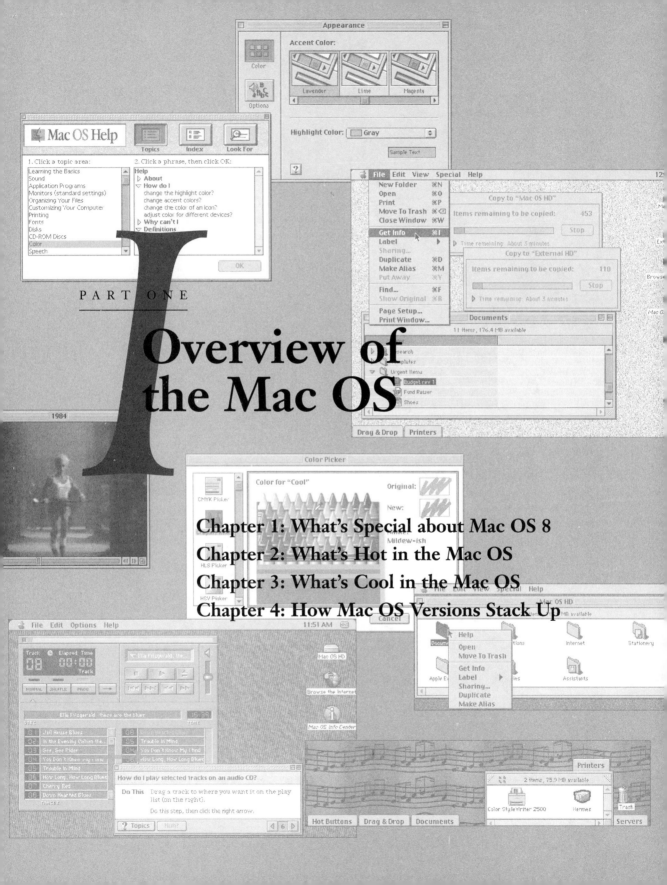

PART ONE

Overview of the Mac OS

What's Special about Mac OS 8

Mac OS 8 brings more changes to the Mac system software than any version since System 7.0. Some of the changes are very obvious, such as the look of windows, icons, and other interface elements. More changes come to light as you start using Mac OS 8. Many improved methods make it easier to work with disks and their contents — collapsible windows, pop-up windows, view options for each window, spring-loaded folders, contextual menus, and sticky menus to name a few.

What's more, Mac OS 8 comes with far more software for accessing the Internet than any previous version of the Mac system software. For starters, a setup assistant program leads you through the confusing process of getting the computer ready to use the Internet for the first time. You also get top-notch programs for sending and receiving e-mail, browsing the Web, and publishing a simple Web site from your own computer.

This chapter gives you an overview of the improvements that Mac OS 8 brings to the Mac system software. After reading this chapter, be sure to look at the next two chapters for overviews of features and capabilities that Mac OS 8 shares with earlier system software versions.

Appearance

If you've ever seen a Mac before, you can't help noticing that Mac OS 8 looks different from earlier system software versions. This section previews the first redesign of the Mac OS interface since 1991. (For the complete story on the Mac OS 8 appearance, see Chapter 5.)

Platinum appearance

There's a lot less pasty white and a lot more healthy gray glow in the *platinum appearance* of Mac OS 8. The menu bar, the menus themselves, and the background color of many windows have all acquired a platinum tan. Buttons, pop-up menus, check boxes, radio buttons, and other controls have also gone platinum.

In addition, the platinum appearance has more finely wrought three-dimensional shading than the previous look. You can see 3D shading in the menu bar and menus, but nowhere is it more evident than in the restyled controls and window borders. Many icons also got a 3D facelift in Mac OS 8. Figure 1-1 shows some examples of how the platinum appearance differs from the old look.

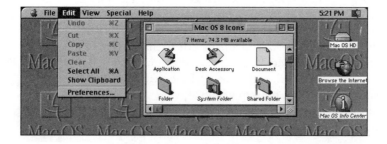

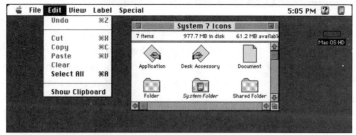

Figure 1-1: Check out the extensive use of gray and fine 3D shading in the platinum appearance of Mac OS 8 (top).

If you look closely at the menus and window titles, you'll notice that Mac OS 8 normally uses a different system font. It's called Charcoal. However, you do have the option of reverting to the Chicago font used since 1984.

The platinum appearance also involves the use of an accent color for menu highlighting and scroll boxes, although it isn't apparent in this book's monochrome illustrations.

Appearance control panel

You can fine-tune some aspects of the platinum appearance with the Appearance control panel. It gives you a choice of accent colors, a text highlight color, and a system font. In addition, you can turn off the platinum appearance in applications that don't use it explicitly. If you don't turn it off, the Mac OS applies the platinum appearance system wide. Figure 1-2 shows some of the options in the Appearance control panel.

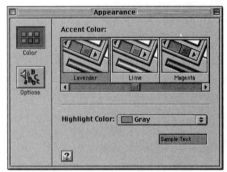

Figure 1-2: Set appearance options in the Appearance control panel.

Desktop picture or pattern

Nothing affects the look of the screen like the desktop's background. Mac OS 8 gives you a wider choice of background patterns than ever before, and it lets you cover the pattern with a picture. You select a pattern or a picture with the Desktop Pictures control panel. Figure 1-3 shows the section of the Desktop Pictures control panel in which you select a desktop picture.

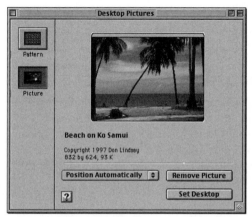

Figure 1-3: Select a desktop picture or pattern with the Desktop Pictures control panel.

Ease of Use

There's more to Mac OS 8 than its sleek platinum appearance. It's also loaded with improved features and capabilities that make it easier to use than earlier system software versions.

Working with windows

Many windows in Mac OS 8 have controls not present in earlier system software. One of these is the collapse box, which you click to hide all of a window except its title bar and click again to expand the window. The collapse box sits at the far right end of a window title bar, bumping the zoom box to the left. You can still collapse and expand a window by double-clicking its title bar, although you have the option of disabling that action (as described in "Appearance and Behavior Modification" in Chapter 5).

Another control not present prior to Mac OS 8 is the window frame, which you can drag with the mouse to move the window. It does the same job as the title bar, effectively giving you a bigger handle to grab and drag.

Viewing folder and disk contents

In Mac OS 8, you change the view of a folder or disk window with a revamped View menu. You can choose to view files and folders as icons, buttons, or a list of names and other facts. If you're viewing icons or buttons, you can choose View menu commands that clean them up by aligning them to an invisible grid or that arrange them by name, date, kind, and so on. If you're viewing a list, you can sort it by those same criteria. Figure 1-4 shows the View menu for icons and buttons.

Figure 1-4: Choose the view for a folder or disk window from a revamped View menu.

Button views

If you choose "as Buttons" from the View menu, you see files and folders represented by square buttons. You open a button by clicking it once, drag it by its name, and select it by dragging across it. Figure 1-5 shows an example of a folder window viewed as buttons.

Figure 1-5: View files and folders as buttons, and open one by clicking it once.

Pop-up windows

You can make a pop-up window from a regular window by choosing "as Pop-up Window" from the View menu. This anchors the window at the bottom of the screen and changes its title bar into a tab. Clicking the tab at the top of a window closes it and leaves the tab at the bottom of the screen. Clicking a tab at the bottom of the screen makes the window pop up from there. (To find out more about pop-up windows, see "Using Pop-up Windows" in Chapter 7.) Figure 1-6 shows an open pop-up window and the tabs of closed pop-ups.

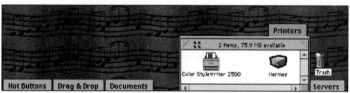

Figure 1-6: Click a pop-up window's tab to open and close it.

View options

By choosing View Options from the View menu, you can adjust several aspects of a window's appearance. For a window viewed as icons or buttons, you can select an icon or button size and a forced arrangement. You can force icons or buttons to always snap to a grid when you move them, or you can keep them arranged by name, date, and so on. If you select any of the forced arrangement options, a small icon in the upper left corner of the window indicates which arrangement is in force. All these options are available not only for folder and disk windows, but for the desktop as well.

For a window viewed as a list, you can select an icon size, select which columns to show, specify whether to take the time to calculate folder sizes, and specify whether to display relative dates such as "today" and "yesterday." You can also display a Date Created column in Mac OS 8 (which you couldn't do in earlier system software versions).

Note that the View Options command adjusts each window or the desktop individually unlike the Views control panel it mostly replaces. (You'll find more information about view options in "Fine-tuning Views" in Chapter 7.) Figure 1-7 shows the View Options dialog boxes for an icon view, a button view, and a list view.

Figure 1-7: Adjust each window's appearance
individually with the View Options command.

Finder preferences

The Finder in Mac OS 8 has a Preferences command that you can use to set
appearance and behavior options for all Finder icons and windows. For the
first time in any Finder, you can simplify the menus to see just the essential
commands. You can also configure spring-loaded opening of folders and disks
(as described next). Other options replace similar options formerly found in
the Views and Labels control panels. Figure 1-8 shows the Finder Preferences
dialog box.

For more information on Finder Preferences, see "Simple Finder" in
Chapter 6 and "Fine-tuning Views," "Folder Ins and Outs," and "Labeling
Items" in Chapter 7.

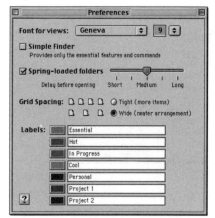

Figure 1-8: Set appearance and behavior
options for all Finder icons and windows
with the Preferences command.

Spring-loaded opening

You no longer have to do a lot of double-clicking to travel through layers of
folders in the Finder. Disks and folders spring open when you pause briefly
over them with the mouse button held down. This behavior comes in handy
when you're moving or copying items to a folder that's buried inside other
folders. You can also make a disk or folder spring open by clicking it one-and-
a-half times (like double-clicking, but hold down the mouse button on the
second click). As long as you keep pressing the mouse button, you can open
any folder or disk by pausing over its icon. You can adjust the delay factor with
the Finder Preferences command.

Contextual menus

Mac OS 8 brings menu commands closer to hand with contextual menus. You
see a contextual menu of commands that can affect an icon, a window, or some
text in the Finder when you press the Control key while clicking the object. If
you Control-click a group of selected items, the contextual menu lists commands
that pertain to all of them. Figure 1-9 shows an example of a contextual menu.

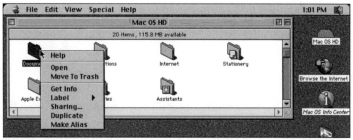

Figure 1-9: See a contextual menu by Control-clicking an icon, a window, or some text in the Finder.

Sticky menus

When you open any menu on the Mac OS 8 menu bar, or any contextual or pop-up menu, it stays open even if you release the mouse button. You can then choose a menu item by clicking it, or you can open a different menu by moving the pointer to the menu title. The menu goes away if you click outside it or if you don't move the mouse for 15 seconds. You can also operate menus the old way, by holding down the mouse button.

File menu commands

The Finder's File menu has some additional commands in Mac OS 8, and several of them have useful keyboard shortcuts. The Move To Trash command disposes of items you have selected. The Show Original command locates an alias's original item and brings it into view in the window that contains it. You use the items in the Label submenu to apply a colored label to the items you have selected (like the Labels menu prior to Mac OS 8). In addition, the Sharing command's window is improved. Figure 1-10 shows the File menu.

Figure 1-10: Use the additional commands in the Finder's File menu.

You'll find more information on labeling items in Chapter 7, aliases in Chapter 12, and sharing in Chapter 18.

The Internet

Mac OS 8 goes a lot further than previous system software versions in helping you get connected to the Internet and access Internet services. This section gives you an overview of what Mac OS 8 provides. (For the full story, see Chapter 20.)

Setting up

Setting up an Internet connection can be an incredible nightmare, but not if you use the Internet Setup Assistant program that comes with Mac OS 8. It interviews you to get the necessary information and then makes all the control panel settings behind the scenes. You don't have to open the control panels to get started, although you can always tweak them later. Figure 1-11 shows the Internet Setup Assistant's first screen.

Figure 1-11: Set up an Internet connection with the Internet Setup Assistant program.

E-mail

Exchange electronic mail with people around the world or across the street by using any of the three e-mail programs that come with Mac OS 8. More people use the Internet for sending and receiving e-mail than any other purpose. Claris Emailer Lite is the best of the bunch, although you can also use the e-mail capabilities of Netscape Navigator or Cyberdog if you prefer.

Web browsing

It may not be as utilitarian as e-mail, but the World Wide Web is the flashiest part of the Internet. You can view text, pictures, and movies and hear sounds from Web sites around the world with the Web browser programs you get with Mac OS 8. Netscape Navigator is part of a standard installation of Mac OS 8, and you can also install Cyberdog and Microsoft Internet Explorer along with it. With any of these Web browsers, you can seek out information that's published on the Web. Alternatively, you can use Castanet Tuner and the PointCast Network to receive information that's broadcast over the Web, so you don't have to find it on your own. Microsoft Internet Explorer, Castanet Tuner, and the PointCast Network are bonus items on the Mac OS 8 CD-ROM, meaning you have to install them after installing the system software.

Connect To

Mac OS 8 includes a bare-bones program, Connect To, for quickly accessing any Internet site whose URL (Uniform Resource Locator) you know. You choose Connect To from the Apple menu, type or paste the URL, and click the Connect button. Connect To accomplishes this magic by using system-wide preferences set in the Internet Config program. These preferences are preset during a standard installation of Mac OS 8, but you can change them later. Figure 1-12 shows the Connect To program's dialog box.

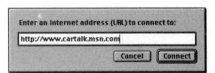

Figure 1-12: Access an Internet site quickly by typing its URL into the Connect To program's dialog box.

Personal Web Sharing

The Personal Web Sharing software included with Mac OS 8 makes it easy to host a Web site on your computer. You place your prepared Web pages in the Web Pages folder on your startup disk and click the Start button in the Web Sharing control panel. While you're connected to the Internet, anyone with an Internet connection and a Web browser can see your pages. The Web browser can be running on any kind of computer or even on an Internet connection device that hooks up to a TV. If you're connected to an intranet (TCP/IP network), anyone on the intranet can see your pages with a Web browser running on any kind of computer. Figure 1-13 shows the Web Sharing control panel.

Figure 1-13: Share your Web pages on the Internet or an intranet with the Web Sharing control panel.

Mac OS Runtime for Java

Your computer can run programs written in the popular Java programming language with the Mac OS Runtime for Java software that's part of a standard installation of Mac OS 8. Small Java programs called *applets* are often embedded in Web pages to make the pages more interesting or useful. When you view a Web page with an embedded Java applet, the applet runs automatically. You can also run Java applets outside of Web browsers. The Apple Applet Runner is an application program that runs Java applets, and the Apple Applet Viewer is an OpenDoc part that lets you put Java applets in an OpenDoc document. Both are included with Mac OS Runtime for Java.

Performance

Every new Mac OS has better performance than the previous version. In Mac OS 8, Apple completely rewrote the Finder so it doesn't keep you waiting like earlier versions. This section describes the main improvements.

Simultaneous operations

The Finder in Mac OS 8 is more responsive than earlier versions. After opening a folder or disk that contains a large number of files and folders, you no longer have to wait for every item to appear in the folder or disk window before doing anything else. The Finder continues updating the window while you proceed with other work, such as opening a program or making an alias. What's more, you can do other work in the Finder while it copies files or empties the Trash. Figure 1-14 shows two batches of files being copied at the same time.

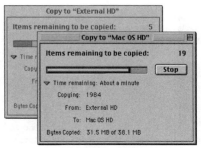

Figure 1-14: Keep working in the Finder while it copies files or empties the Trash.

Live scrolling

While you drag a scroll box in a folder or disk window in Mac OS 8, you see the items in the window scroll past continuously. In earlier Finder versions, you see only the scroll box move while you drag it; the items displayed in the window don't change until you release the mouse button after moving the scroll box to a new position.

Multimedia

In addition to all its other improvements, Mac OS 8 is the first system software version to include QuickTime VR and the ability to play MPEG movies. This section previews these features.

Interacting with QuickTime VR scenes

With Mac OS 8 you also get QuickTime VR 2.0.1, which lets you turn 360 degrees to view panoramas and turn objects to view them from different angles. You can view a QuickTime VR panorama or object anywhere you can view a linear QuickTime movie if you have QuickTime 2.5 or later installed.

When you view a QuickTime VR panorama, you can look up, look down, scan left, or scan right by dragging the pointer with the mouse. You can zoom in or out by pressing the Option or Control key. In addition, a VR controller appears across the bottom of the window if you have QuickTime VR 2.0 or later installed. Figure 1-15 shows a QuickTime VR panorama being scanned to the right.

Figure 1-15: Drag the mouse to see another view of a QuickTime VR panorama.

When you view a QuickTime VR object, you can manipulate it to see a different view of it. You click the object and drag up, down, or sideways, and the object or some part of it moves. For example, it may turn around so you can see all sides of it, or it may open and close. With QuickTime VR 2.0 and later, you can also zoom an object in and out by pressing the Option or Control key. Figure 1-16 shows a QuickTime VR object being turned to the left.

Figure 1-16: Drag the mouse to see a QuickTime VR object from other angles.

MPEG movies

The QuickTime MPEG Extension that comes with Mac OS 8 enables QuickTime to display MPEG movies on a PowerPC computer without any special equipment. MPEG (Motion Picture Experts Group) is a worldwide industry standard for compressing video.

Summary

This chapter introduced the platinum appearance of Mac OS 8, which is accompanied by a wider variety of desktop patterns and the ability to cover the pattern with a desktop picture. In addition, this chapter previewed what makes Mac OS 8 easier to use than earlier system software versions. There are additional controls for moving and collapsing windows. The Finder's View menu is revamped, making it simpler to set the view of each folder and disk window and to keep it arranged. You can view files and folders as one-click buttons, and you can make any disk or folder window into a pop-up window. Many view options that previously applied to all folder and disk windows can now be set for each window separately. The Finder Preferences command offers a Simple Finder option plus options that were formerly part of the Views and Labels control panels. You can make disks and folders spring open without lifting a finger. You can see a contextual menu of relevant commands by Control-clicking an icon, a window, or some text in the Finder. All menus stay open even if you release the mouse button. And several commands have been added to the Finder's File menu.

This chapter also gave you an overview of what Mac OS 8 provides for getting connected to the Internet and accessing Internet services. The Internet Setup Assistant simplifies setting up an Internet connection. You can use any of three programs to exchange e-mail. You also have three choices of Web browsers, and the Connect To program quickly connects you to any Internet location if you know its URL. The Personal Web Sharing software makes it easy to publish your own Web pages on the Internet or an intranet. In addition, you can run Java applets that are embedded in Web pages and run Java programs outside Web pages with the Mac OS Runtime for Java software.

Finally, this chapter told you about Mac OS 8's improved performance and enhanced multimedia capabilities. The Finder is more responsive thanks to its live scrolling of windows and its ability to perform simultaneous operations. The multimedia enhancements include QuickTime VR 2.0.1 and MPEG movie playback.

CHAPTER TWO

What's Hot in the Mac OS

IN THIS CHAPTER

- **Icons:** editing by mouse alone, translucent icon dragging, and dragging to open

- **Menus:** tooling around with the Apple menu, multitasking with the Application menu, and checking the menubar clock

- **Desktop:** saving time with stationery pads, printing with desktop printer icons, and getting onscreen help

- **Files and folders:** outlining in Finder windows, finding files fast, creating custom icons, categorizing with item labels, using aliases, and sharing files

- **Multimedia:** watching QuickTime movies and manipulating QuickDraw 3D graphics

Despite all the innovation in Mac OS 8, it has plenty in common with earlier versions of the Mac system software. This chapter and the next give you an overview of notable features and capabilities present in all Mac OS versions since System 7.5. This chapter draws your attention to some of the more powerful mousing techniques available with the Mac OS. You'll also read here about distinctive elements of the Mac OS menu bar, the two kinds of help available onscreen, aliases, and desktop printing. Other basic features noted in this chapter include stationery pads, hierarchical outlines of disk contents, file searching, file sharing, custom icons, and item labels.

Those capabilities are basic compared with what the Mac OS can do with multimedia. This chapter introduces the system software extensions you get for watching movies, and manipulating three-dimensional graphics: QuickTime and QuickDraw 3D.

After reading this chapter, be sure to look through the next chapter for an overview of more essential Mac OS features.

Basics

The Mac OS has essential features and capabilities to help you with everyday tasks on your computer. This section takes a look at fifteen you're sure to find useful.

Editing by mouse alone

Instead of using the venerable Cut, Copy, and Paste commands to move text, graphics, or other material in document windows, you can simply drag it from one place to another. You can drag within a document, between documents, and between applications. You can drag material from a document to a Finder window or the desktop, and it becomes a clipping file. Conversely, you can drag a clipping file to a document window. This capability, called *drag-and-drop editing*, works only with applications that are designed to take advantage of it. (For more information, see "Moving Document Contents Around" in Chapter 8.) Figure 2-1 shows an example of drag-and-drop editing.

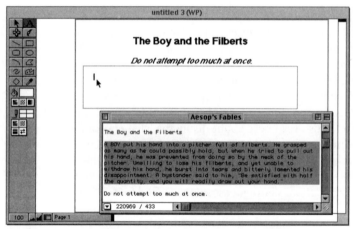

Figure 2-1: Dragging text from place to place within a document.

Translucent icon dragging

When you drag an icon on a PowerPC computer, the icon becomes translucent so you can still identify the icon while you look through it to see where you're dragging. If you drag a group of icons, only the icon under the pointer is translucent; the others in the group are outlines. Translucent icon dragging is a feature of Mac OS 7.5.3 and later. (In earlier system software versions, you always see icons' outlines when you drag them.) Figure 2-2 illustrates translucent icon dragging.

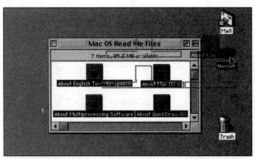

Figure 2-2: An icon appears translucent when you drag it on a PowerPC computer with Mac OS 7.5.3 and later.

Dragging to open

You can open a document not only with the application that created it, but with any compatible application you have. Drag the document icon to an application icon, and if they're compatible, the application icon is highlighted. Release the mouse button and the highlighted application opens the document. For example, you can drag a diverse collection of documents to an application that compresses them so that they consume less disk space. This drag-and-drop capability speeds up your work, and you can use it with aliases of documents and applications as well as the actual items. (For more information, check out "Opening Programs, Documents, and More" in Chapter 8.)

Tooling around with the Apple menu

The Apple menu is like the tool belt a carpenter wears. It doesn't hold all of his tools and equipment, but it holds the things he needs most often and special things for the work he's currently doing. With the Mac OS, you can customize the Apple menu so that it gives you immediate access to programs, documents, folders, and anything else you use frequently or need for a current job. When you choose an item from the Apple menu, it opens right away. You don't have to root around a cluttered desktop or scrounge through folders with the Finder. The Apple menu is available in almost every program. It lists items conveniently in alphabetical order and even shows their icons.

You put an item in the Apple menu by dragging its icon into the Apple Menu Items folder in the System Folder. The item becomes instantly available in the Apple menu — there is no need to restart your computer. To remove an item from the Apple menu, drag its icon out of the Apple Menu Items folder. (For more information on the Apple Menu, see "Opening Programs, Documents, and More" in Chapter 8.) Figure 2-3 shows an example of the Apple menu and its special folder.

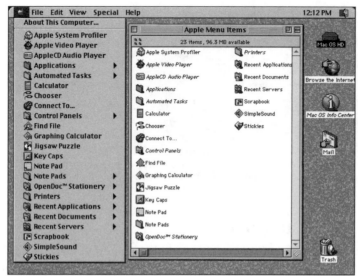

Figure 2-3: Open anything from the Apple menu, which lists whatever you put in the Apple Menu Items folder.

Multitasking with the Application menu

The Mac OS lets you keep more than one program open at a time and switch between the open programs. This capability is known as *multitasking*. You can have as many programs open simultaneously as fit in your computer's memory. You can switch to any open program, including the Finder, by clicking its window or by choosing it from the Application menu at the right end of the menu bar. You can copy and paste among documents of open programs without closing documents and quitting programs. By switching to the Finder, you can open other programs, find documents, organize folders and disks, and so on. Figure 2-4 shows the Application menu and several programs open at once.

Having multiple programs open leads to a confusion of windows. You can eliminate window clutter by using Application menu commands to hide windows temporarily.

Some programs can use the Mac OS multitasking capabilities to operate in the background while you work with another program. *Background programs* operate during the intervals — only split seconds long — when the active program isn't using the computer. Programs working in the background can print documents, send and receive e-mail, get files from the Internet, copy items in the Finder, back up disks to tape, and so on.

Figure 2-4: Keep multiple programs open at the same time and switch to one with the Application menu.

For more information about multitasking, background operations, and hiding windows, see "Managing Multiple Open Programs" in Chapter 8.

Checking the menubar clock

You have the option of displaying a digital clock near the right end of the menu bar. Clicking the clock alternates between a display of the time and the date. You set the format of this clock with the Date & Time control panel and can set the clock to chime on the hour, at quarter past, at half past, and at quarter 'til. (For more information on the clock options, see "Date & Time" in Chapter 10.) Figure 2-5 shows the clock settings in the Date & Time control panel.

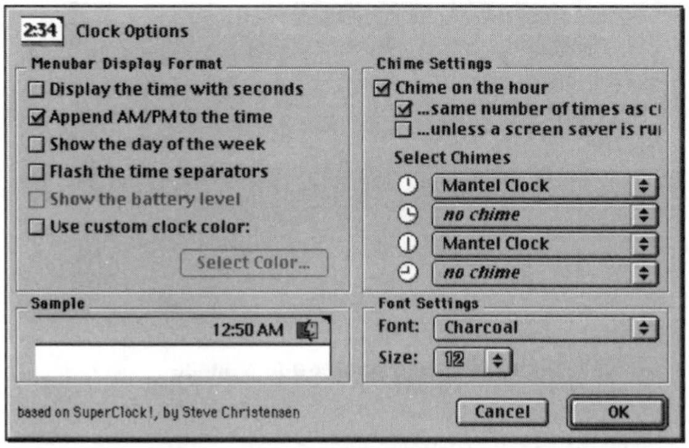

Figure 2-5: Configure the optional menubar clock to display the time and more.

Saving time with stationery pads

If you regularly create new documents with common formatting, contents, and so on, you can save time with stationery pad documents. Opening a stationery pad is like tearing off a page from a pad of preprinted forms — you get a new document with all common elements preset. Stationery pads have a distinctive icon that looks like a stack of document icons. You can make any document a stationery pad by setting the Stationery Pad option in its Info window. (For more details about making and using stationery pads, see "Creating Documents" in Chapter 8.) Figure 2-6 shows some sample stationery pad icons.

Figure 2-6: Open a stationery pad to get a new document with preset contents and formatting.

Printing with desktop printer icons

If you use more than one printer, you can choose one without using the Chooser. The Mac OS desktop printing software (optional prior to Mac OS 7.6) creates desktop icons for each of your printers. You make one the default printer with the Finder's Printing menu, which appears when you select a desktop printer icon. Desktop printers queue documents to be printed and print them in the background while you do other work. You can open a desktop printer to see and manage the queue. (For more information on desktop printing, see "Using Printers with Desktop Icons" in Chapter 14.) Figure 2-7 shows desktop printer icons and a desktop printer window.

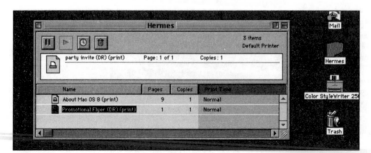

Figure 2-7: Use desktop printer icons to choose a printer and manage background printing.

Getting onscreen help

Although the Mac OS graphical interface is easier to learn and remember than a bunch of cryptic command words, it's hard to remember what every icon and graphical doodad means. Optional balloon help can assist your memory. Here's how it works: You choose Show Balloons from the Help menu (called the Guide menu in system software versions earlier than Mac OS 7.6). This action turns on balloon help, which works from any application, not just the Finder. Then you use the mouse to point to something — an icon, menu, part of a window, or some other object. A cartoon-style balloon pops up next to the object. Words inside the balloon describe the object to which the balloon points. The message usually tells you what the object is, what it does, or what happens when you click it. Figure 2-8 shows an example of a help balloon.

Figure 2-8: A help balloon describes an object and how it's used.

The Mac OS includes an interactive help system, called *Apple Guide*, that shows and tells you how to get things done while you actually do them. Step-by-step instructions appear in a guide window, which floats above all other windows. As you move from step to step, the guide may coach you by marking an object on-screen with a circle, arrow, or underline. Figure 2-9 shows an example of Apple Guide.

Apple Guide watches what you do and can adjust its steps if you work ahead or make a mistake. It can even perform a step for you, such as opening a control panel.

For more information on balloon help and Apple Guide, see "Getting Onscreen Help" in Chapter 5.

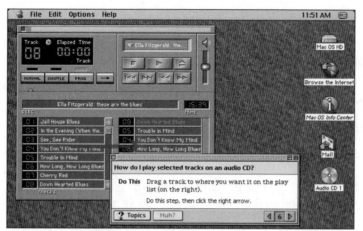

Figure 2-9: Apple Guide displays step-by-step instructions in a floating window and points out objects onscreen.

Outlining in Finder windows

The Finder can display the contents of a folder or disk in a window as a list of item names and other information. Some of the items in a list may be folders, which may contain more folders, and so on. You can see the contents of all the enclosed folders as part of one list in an indented outline format. The levels of indentation in the outline clearly diagram the layers of folders listed in the window. You can expand or collapse any level in the outline to show or hide the corresponding folder's contents by clicking a small triangle next to the folder's icon. With folders expanded, you can select items from more than one folder at a time. (For more information, see "Viewing Folder and Disk Contents" in Chapter 6.) Figure 2-10 shows an example of the outline structure of a list view.

QUICK TIPS

Folder Path Menus

The title of a Finder window appears to be static, but when you press ⌘ while clicking the window title, a folder path menu pops up. The pop-up folder menu reveals the path through your folder structure from the active window to the disk containing it. You can open any folder along the path by choosing the folder from the pop-up menu. To close the active window while opening a folder along the path, press Option while choosing the folder from the pop-up menu.

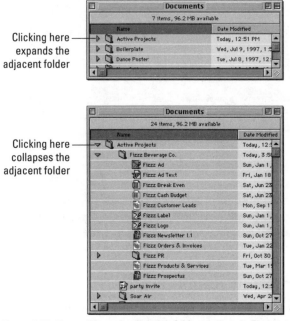

Clicking here expands the adjacent folder

Clicking here collapses the adjacent folder

Figure 2-10: Expanding and collapsing folder outlines in Finder windows.

Finding files fast

No more hunting through folders and disks for lost items — a chore even with list view outlines. The Find command finds and fetches lost items for you quickly. Choosing Find from the Finder's File menu opens the Find File window. The simplest form of the Find File window allows you to specify where you want to search and one attribute you want to match. For example, you can search all disks for items whose names contain the text you specify. You can change where Find File looks for items and specify that it look at an attribute other than the item's name. You can also add more search criteria to the Find File window by clicking the More Choices button.

Find File displays the results of a search in an Items Found window. You can open a found item or the folder that encloses it. You can also drag found items to the desktop. In addition, you can change the file sharing privileges, set the label, and open Info windows for found items. (You'll find a full description of Find File under "Finding Items" in Chapter 7.) Figure 2-11 shows the results of a Find File search.

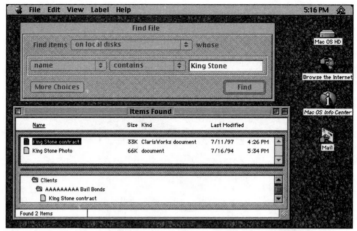

Figure 2-11: Find items that match one or more criteria with Find File.

Creating custom icons

Tired of the same old icons? You can replace individual full-size icons with your own designs. First you copy a picture you want to use as an icon. Then you select the icon you want to customize, choose Get Info from the File menu, select the icon in the Info window, and paste. (For more information, see "Appearance and Behavior Modification" in Chapter 5.) Figure 2-12 shows an example of a custom icon in an Info window.

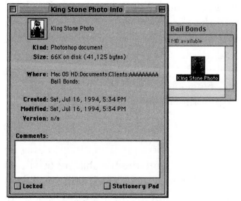

Figure 2-12: Customize an icon by pasting a picture into its Info window.

Categorizing with item labels

Just as people use colored file folder labels to categorize folders of paper documents, the Mac OS can categorize folders or other items with color. Each color has an associated text label. You label an item with the Label submenu of the Finder's File menu (Mac OS 8) or the Label menu (Mac OS 7.6 and earlier). After labeling items, you can arrange a folder or disk window by label. You can also use Find File to search for items by label and apply labels to found items. Label colors and text are not fixed; you can change them by using the Labels control panel. (For a complete explanation of using and changing labels, see "Labeling Items" in Chapter 7.) Figure 2-13 shows some labeled items and a label being applied to another item.

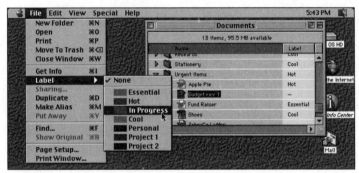

Figure 2-13: Setting an item's label.

Using aliases

You can't be in two places at once, but your documents, applications, and folders can be in many places at one time. Mac OS aliases make this virtual omnipresence possible. An *alias* is a small file (1K to 20K, depending on total disk capacity) that points to another file. When you open an alias, the item it points to opens automatically. When you drag an item to the alias of a folder, the item you drag goes into the folder to which the alias points. You can put aliases anywhere — on the desktop, in the Apple menu, or in other accessible places — and leave the original items buried deep within nested folders. An alias looks exactly like the original item except that its name is in italics, and its name may end with the word *alias*. Figure 2-14 shows an alias and its original item.

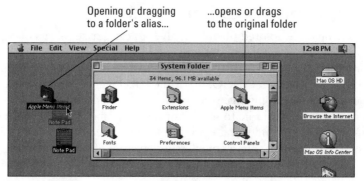

Figure 2-14: Things you do to an alias happen to its original item.

Aliases have a variety of uses, which include the following:

❖ Opening frequently used programs, documents, and folders from the desktop while the real items remain buried in nested folders.

❖ Adding items to the Apple menu without moving the original items from their folders.

❖ Organizing documents and folders according to multiple filing schemes without duplicating items. For example, you can file documents by project, addressee, date, and topic.

❖ Simplifying access to file servers and individual items on servers. Opening an alias of an item on a server makes an automatic connection with the server (except for providing the password, which you must type unless you gained access to the original item as a guest).

❖ Getting nearly automatic access to your computer's hard disks from another computer on the same network.

To learn how to make aliases and discover more strategies for their use, see Chapter 12.

Sharing files

If your computer is connected to other Macs in a network, the Mac OS makes it possible to share any of your folders, even whole disks, and their contents with other network users. Of course, you can access folders and disks others have made available to you, too. The remainder of this section briefly introduces file sharing on the Mac OS; Chapter 18 covers file sharing in detail.

Using someone else's folders

To use another computer's folder or disk, open the Chooser desk accessory. It lists as AppleShare *file servers* the names of all computers that are sharing their folders and disks. After you choose one, the Chooser asks you to connect as a guest or registered user and then presents a list of items you may share, as shown in Figure 2-15.

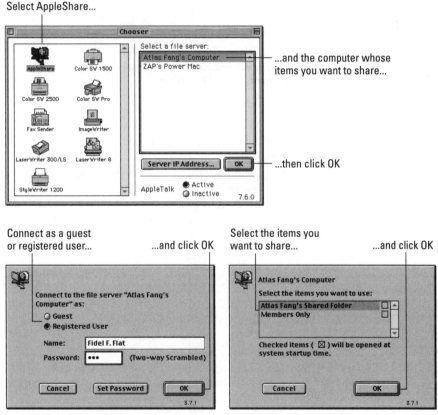

Figure 2-15: Selecting folders to share.

Sharing your folders with others

Before you can share your own folders or disks with other network users, you must start file sharing with the File Sharing control panel (Mac OS 8) or the Sharing Setup control panel (prior to Mac OS 8). Your computer then shows up as an AppleShare file server in the Choosers of other network users. Figure 2-16 shows the File Sharing control panel.

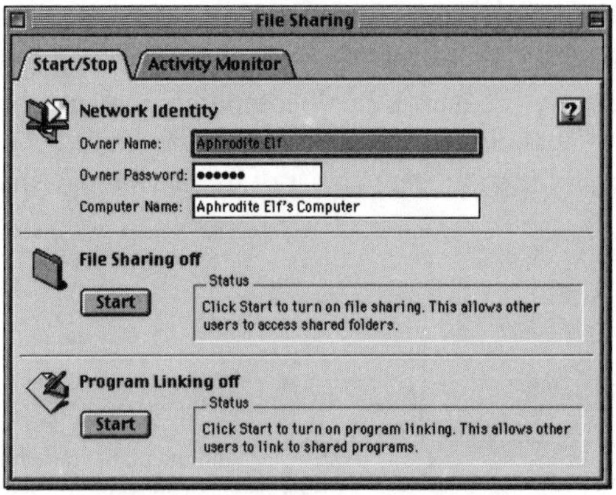

**Figure 2-16: Set up file sharing in the File Sharing
control panel.**

To share one of your disks or folders with others, select it and then use the
Finder's Sharing command to display the item's sharing window. There you
specify who can see the item's folders, view its files, and make changes to them.
You can grant different access privileges to the owner of the item (usually you),
to one other registered user or a group of registered users you designate, and
to everyone else. Figure 2-17 shows a sharing window in Mac OS 8.

**Figure 2-17: Use the Sharing command to
share an item and set its access privileges.**

You identify registered users, set their passwords, and create groups of users
with the Users & Groups control panel. You can see who is sharing what and
how busy they're keeping your computer with the File Sharing control panel
(Mac OS 8) or the File Sharing Activity Monitor control panel (prior to Mac

OS 8). You can also use either of these control panels to disconnect individual users who are sharing your folders and disks. Figure 2-18 shows an example of the Users & Groups and the File Sharing control panels in Mac OS 8.

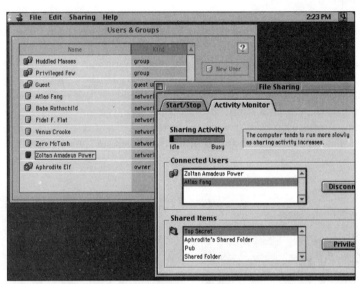

Figure 2-18: Identify who can use your shared items and see who's currently using them.

Multimedia

The Mac OS gives you many ways to enjoy audio and video on your computer. You can watch digital movies, interactively view "virtual reality" panoramas and objects, and manipulate three-dimensional objects displayed on the computer screen. You can play audio CDs in your computer's CD-ROM drive, and if your computer has video input capability it can display video from a camcorder or other video equipment. This section introduces you to movies and 3D graphics; Chapter 19 covers all the Mac OS multimedia capabilities in detail.

Watching QuickTime movies

With a standard installation of the Mac OS, your computer can play digital video and audio — movies — from its hard disk or CD-ROM. The QuickTime system extension not only makes that possible, it makes movies ubiquitous. You don't need a special program to watch QuickTime movies. Most applications let you copy and paste movies as easily as you copy and paste graphics, and you can play a QuickTime movie wherever you encounter one.

What's more, the version of QuickTime included with Mac OS 7.6 and later enables the computer to play CD-quality digital sound and MIDI soundtracks. It can display closed-caption text along with the movie. It can also overlay the regular video track of a movie with independently animated sprites and three-dimensional graphics.

Applications use two methods for controlling movie playback. They can display a standard VCR-like controller just below the movie. You use this play bar to play, stop, browse, or step through the movie and adjust its sound level. Applications can also display movies without controllers. In this case, a badge in the lower left corner of the movie distinguishes it from a still graphic. To play a movie that has a badge and no controller, you double-click the movie. Clicking a playing movie stops it. Figure 2-19 shows one QuickTime movie with a playback controller and another movie with a QuickTime badge.

Figure 2-19: Play back a QuickTime movie by manipulating the controller along its bottom edge (left) or by double-clicking a movie with a badge in its lower left corner (right).

Because movies involve so much data, they are invariably compressed to save space on disk. QuickTime can display movies that have been saved using a variety of compression methods.

Manipulating QuickDraw 3D graphics

It takes a lot of work to draw and shade graphic objects to give them a three-dimensional appearance, but the QuickDraw 3D software enables the Mac OS to render 3D graphic objects that are in motion. In some cases, you watch 3D animation that someone else created. In other cases, you provide the motion by rotating, moving, and zooming a 3D graphic object with the mouse. QuickDraw 3D provides a standard viewer with controls for zooming, rotating, and moving a 3D object, and for viewing it from various preset angles. Because QuickDraw 3D renders at the Mac OS level, it's easy for any application to incorporate dynamic 3D graphics. The 3D graphics all have the same format so you can cut, copy, paste, drag, and drop them in any participating application. Figure 2-20 shows an example of the standard QuickDraw 3D viewer in the Scrapbook.

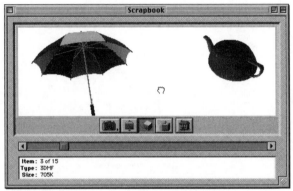

Figure 2-20: Change the view of a 3D graphic with the controls at the bottom of a standard QuickDraw 3D viewer.

Summary

This chapter introduced you to special Mac OS features and capabilities that help you with everyday tasks on your computer. They include drag-and-drop editing, translucent icon dragging on a PowerPC computer, and dragging documents to open them with applications that didn't create them. The Mac OS also provides the Apple menu for opening your favorite items quickly and the Application menu for switching between open applications. You can check the time and date with the menubar clock. Stationery pads save you time when you need to create duplicate documents with consistent formatting and content. Desktop printer icons make it easy to choose a printer and manage background printing. If you need help while using the Mac OS, you can use balloon help to get descriptions of items.

There are several ways the Mac OS makes it easier to work with your disks, files, and folders. You can see indented outlines of your layers of folders. You can find files fast with the Find File program. You can give items custom icons so they're easier to recognize. You can categorize items with colored labels. For all practical purposes, you can keep items in more than one place at the same time by making aliases of them. And you can share files with other computer users on a network.

In addition to those basic capabilities, the Mac OS gives you many ways to enjoy audio and video on your computer. They include watching QuickTime movies and manipulating QuickDraw 3D graphic objects displayed on the computer screen.

3 What's Cool in the Mac OS

The Mac OS has more features and capabilities worth noting besides the ones introduced in the previous chapters. This chapter continues the overview, first pointing out a couple more ways you can open documents. You'll also read here about the organization of the System Folder, three kinds of fonts, and what virtual memory does for you. These features are available in all system software versions.

Moving beyond the basics, this chapter introduces software that comes with Mac OS 8 and some earlier system software versions for networking and Internet access. You'll also read here about the powerful Mac OS capabilities for managing system extensions, automating tasks with AppleScript, hearing the computer read text aloud, giving the computer spoken commands, and more. This chapter concludes by presenting the ways the Mac OS lets you work with documents created by applications you don't have, including documents created with Windows and DOS computers.

Essential Mac OS Features

Of the many essential features and capabilities that the Mac OS provides for your everyday work, this section singles out a couple of ways in which you open documents and programs that you want to use, the organization of the system software, the three kinds of fonts you can use, and the benefits of virtual memory.

Opening items quickly from the Launcher

To save yourself the trouble of hunting for applications, documents, and other items that you use often, you can use the Launcher control panel as a central launching pad. It displays a window that contains up to eight panels of large buttons for opening items. You open any item in the Launcher window by clicking its button. (You'll find the complete story on the Launcher under "Opening Programs, Documents, and More" in Chapter 8.) Figure 3-1 shows an example of the Launcher.

Figure 3-1: One click opens an item displayed in the Launcher window.

Opening and saving in applications

You don't always want to use the Finder or the Launcher to open document files, and you never use the Finder or the Launcher to save documents. When you're working in an application program, you use its Open, Save, and Save As commands to open and save documents. Those commands all have similar dialog boxes. The Open and Save dialog boxes list the contents of one folder at a time and have buttons for moving through folders and disks. Figure 3-2 shows examples of the Open and Save dialog boxes.

You don't have to use the mouse to open items and move through folders in an Open or Save dialog box. You can use the keyboard as well. For example, you can select an item in the contents list by typing the first part of its name. In a Save dialog box, a heavy black border around the contents list signifies that typing will affect it. Conversely, if the document name is highlighted or contains a flashing text insertion point, then typing will affect it.

For the details on Open and Save dialog boxes, see "Opening Programs, Documents, and More" and "Saving Documents" in Chapter 8.

Contents of folder named above

Disk that contains this folder

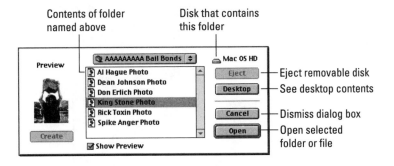

Eject removable disk
See desktop contents
Dismiss dialog box
Open selected folder or file

Choose enclosing folder to see its contents

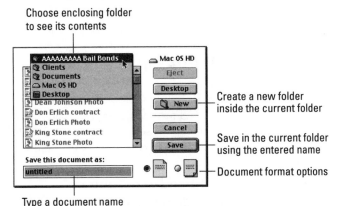

Create a new folder inside the current folder

Save in the current folder using the entered name

Document format options

Type a document name

Figure 3-2: Open and save documents from any application by using a standard dialog box.

Organizing the System Folder

The system software consists of hundreds of files — system extensions, control panels, fonts, preference files, and many other kinds. The Mac OS organizes system software files in a number of special folders inside the System Folder. There's a Control Panels folder, a Preferences folder, an Extensions folder, a Fonts folder, and so on. Most of the special folders have distinctive icons. Moreover, the Mac OS Finder knows which special folder to put many items in when you drag them to the System Folder icon. (To learn more about the System Folder's special folders, see Chapter 9.) Figure 3-3 shows an example of the System Folder.

Figure 3-3: Special folders subdivide the System Folder.

Tackling fonts and typography

The Mac OS works with three kinds of fonts: fixed-size, TrueType variable-size, and PostScript variable-size. Installing the optional QuickDraw GX software that comes with the Mac OS provides advanced typography in all applications that take advantage of it. This section introduces the different kinds of fonts and typography. (Chapter 13 covers fonts in detail.)

TrueType, PostScript, and fixed-size fonts

Thanks to the TrueType font technology built into the Mac OS, text looks smooth at any size onscreen or on any printing device. *TrueType fonts* are variable-size outline fonts similar to the PostScript fonts that look so sharp on PostScript printers (and onscreen if you have installed the Adobe Type Manager software, which is not included with Mac OS 8). The Mac OS smoothly scales TrueType fonts to any size. Fixed-size fonts also look good on the screen and a printer at their prescribed sizes, but they appear lumpy when scaled to other sizes. Figure 3-4 shows how smoothly TrueType scales 36-point Times text compared with a scaled-up 18-point fixed-size font.

Xylophone   Xylophone

Figure 3-4: The Mac OS scales TrueType fonts
(left) more smoothly than fixed-size fonts (right).

QuickDraw GX typography

If you install QuickDraw GX, application programs that take advantage of GX typography let you stretch, rotate, skew, and manipulate text around objects. In addition, you can manage such type controls as line weights, tracking, and kerning for your fonts — just like a professional typographer. With GX fonts, QuickDraw GX automatically substitutes ligatures by merging two characters into one (such as *a* and *e* into *æ*) as you enter text normally. In addition, QuickDraw GX can automatically form rational fractions like ⅞.

Extending memory

Application programs are becoming more memory hungry all the time, and the Mac OS has a large memory appetite itself. Seems like a computer can never have too much memory. The Mac OS can increase the amount of memory available by using part of a hard disk transparently as additional memory. This extra memory, called *virtual memory*, lets you keep more programs open simultaneously and increase the amount of memory each program gets when you open it. Given more memory, programs may allow you to open additional or larger documents. Furthermore, on PowerPC computers, having virtual memory turned on substantially reduces the amount of memory that programs need. (For more information on memory management, see Chapter 16.)

Networking and the Internet

In response to the phenomenal popularity of the Internet, Apple modernized the Mac OS networking software to make the Internet's TCP/IP networking protocol used on the Internet a full peer of the AppleTalk networking protocol used on Mac OS and other Apple computers. In addition, Apple started bundling its Cyberdog software for accessing the Internet. Apple also extended the usefulness of AppleTalk networking by including software for accessing a network remotely by modem. This section introduces these networking and Internet features of the Mac OS. (Chapter 17 has the details on setting up TCP/IP and AppleTalk networking, and Chapter 20 has more information on Cyberdog.)

Open Transport

The Mac OS has long been able to connect to different types of networks, but until Apple developed the Open Transport networking software, AppleTalk was the chief networking protocol and other types of networks such as the Internet's TCP/IP were subordinate. (A *networking protocol* is a set of rules for exchanging data.) Open Transport puts AppleTalk and TCP/IP on an equal footing and lays the groundwork for putting other networking protocols on that same equal footing. With Open Transport, you set up an AppleTalk connection with the AppleTalk control panel and a TCP/IP connection with the TCP/IP control panel. Open Transport is required with Mac OS 7.6 and later and is optional with earlier system software versions on some computer models.

To take full advantage of Open Transport networking for dial-up connections to the Internet (or any TCP/IP network), Apple developed the Open Transport PPP software and includes it with Mac OS 7.6 and later. With Open Transport PPP, you set up a modem connection using the Modem and PPP control panels.

Cyberdog

Taking advantage of high interest in the Internet, Apple created a unique software package called Cyberdog as a demonstration of the company's OpenDoc plug-in software system. Cyberdog has acquired a cult following among savvy Internet users who appreciate how easy it makes customizing their use of the Internet. Cyberdog is a suite of software components (OpenDoc Live Object parts) for accessing the Web, sending and receiving e-mail, following discussions in Usenet newsgroups (electronic bulletin boards), exchanging files with FTP file servers, and connecting as a Telnet terminal to computers on the Internet. Cyberdog lets you view text, pictures, audio, movies, and QuickTime VR scenes on the Internet without helper applications. In addition, Cyberdog can take the place of the more traditional Chooser desk accessory in connecting to AppleShare file servers, including computers with file sharing turned on. Figure 3-5 shows one starting point for accessing the Web, e-mail, newsgroup discussions, your AppleTalk network, and more through Cyberdog 2.0.

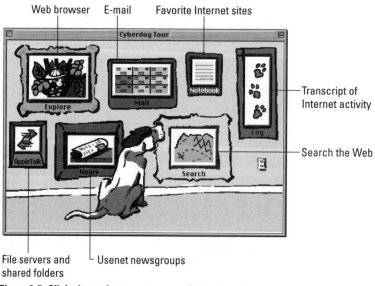

Figure 3-5: Click picture buttons to access Internet services and your AppleTalk network through Cyberdog.

To keep track of Web sites plus individual pictures, movies, text, and sounds that you find on the Web, you can use Cyberdog's Notebook. But that's not all the Notebook can help you organize — it can also store e-mail addresses, newsgroups, FTP sites, Telnet sessions, and more. In addition, a Cyberdog log gives you three ways to view a history of your Internet and AppleTalk activities: chronologically, alphabetically, and hierarchically. Figure 3-6 shows a Cyberdog Notebook.

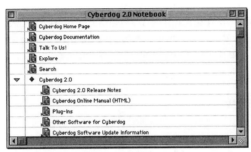

Figure 3-6: Organize your favorite Internet stuff with Cyberdog's Notebook.

Apple Remote Access

The Apple Remote Access Client software included with Mac OS 7.6 and later lets your computer connect to a remote network by modem. When connected, you can access shared files on the remote computer or network exactly as though you were connected to the computer or network locally (as described in Chapter 17), but someone using the remote computer or network can't access files on your computer. In addition, you may be able to use other services on the remote network, such as network printers and file servers.

Advanced Mac OS Features

When you're ready to go beyond the basics, the Mac OS has many powerful features and capabilities to help you work more efficiently. This section takes a look at managing startup items, automating tasks, speech, writing with multiple languages, matching colors among input and output devices, working with OpenDoc compound documents, incorporating live data from one document into other documents, and taking advantage of multiple processors.

Managing startup items

To help you manage the large number of items that load when you start up your computer, the Mac OS includes the Extensions Manager control panel. You can use it to disable and enable control panels, extensions, and other startup items either individually or in sets. An improved Extensions Manager comes with Mac OS 7.6 and later. For each item, it displays its status (enabled or disabled), name, size, and version, and the package it was installed with. You can also display each item's type and creator codes. You can view items grouped by the folders they're in, grouped by the package they were installed with (but generally only for packages created by Apple), or ungrouped. You can enlarge the Extensions Manager window to display detailed information about a particular item. Figure 3-7 shows an example of the improved Extensions Manager.

Figure 3-7: Disable and enable startup items with the Extensions Manager control panel.

Scripting across the system

With the AppleScript extension to the Mac OS, you can automate multistep tasks involving one or many applications, such as locking a batch of documents in the Finder or placing a batch of graphics files into a page layout document. You can create a *script,* or a set of instructions, by performing the task once manually while the AppleScript system watches and records your actions. Then you modify the script with a script editing program. (To learn the basics of creating scripts with AppleScript, see Chapter 22.) Figure 3-8 shows an example of a script created with the Script Editor program that comes with the Mac OS.

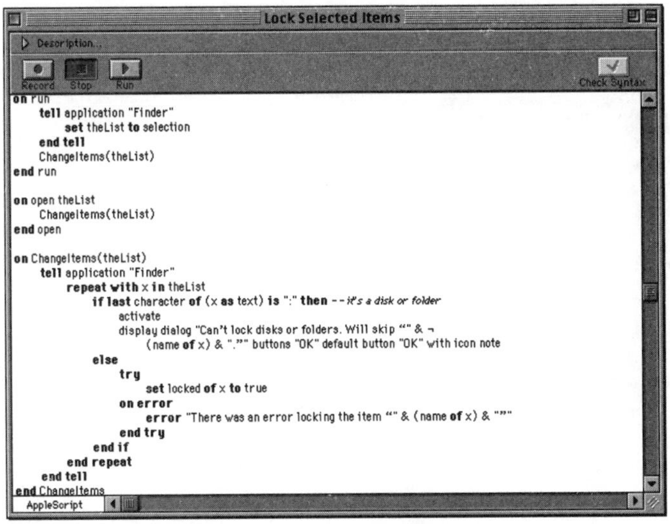

```
                         Lock Selected Items
 ▷ Description...
  ●      ■      ▶                                              ☑
 Record  Stop   Run                                        Check Syntax
on run
     tell application "Finder"
          set theList to selection
     end tell
     ChangeItems(theList)
end run

on open theList
     ChangeItems(theList)
end open

on ChangeItems(theList)
     tell application "Finder"
          repeat with x in theList
               if last character of (x as text) is ":" then  --it's a disk or folder
                    activate
                    display dialog "Can't lock disks or folders. Will skip "" & ¬
                         (name of x) & "."" buttons "OK" default button "OK" with icon note
               else
                    try
                         set locked of x to true
                    on error
                         error "There was an error locking the item "" & (name of x) & """
                    end try
               end if
          end repeat
     end tell
end ChangeItems
AppleScript  ◀
```

Figure 3-8: Automate tasks with AppleScript scripts.

Listening and speaking with PlainTalk

The very first Macintosh could speak in 1984 — at its debut it thanked Steve Jobs for being "like a father to me." Its voice, created by the MacinTalk system extension, had a heavy robot accent. Today, Apple's PlainTalk text-to-speech software can give your computer a clearer voice in English or Mexican Spanish. In addition, many computers can use PlainTalk speech recognition software to recognize spoken commands. You configure speech options with the Speech control panel, which is shown in Figure 3-9.

There are several ways to get your computer to speak. With English Text-to-Speech 1.5, which comes with Mac OS 7.6 and later, you can have the computer announce its alert messages. Some application programs use the text-to-speech software to read text aloud. And you can write AppleScript scripts that speak. The text-to-speech software synthesizes a variety of voices, male and female, with good inflection. It is quite accurate and can correctly pronounce most words and punctuation — even abbreviations. Almost any Mac OS computer can synthesize speech, although computers with a PowerPC or 68040 processor sound most natural.

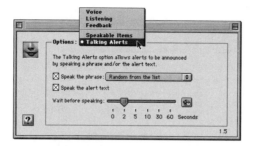

Figure 3-9: Set speech options with different sections of the Speech control panel.

English Speech Recognition enables the Mac OS to take spoken commands from anyone who speaks North American English. Applications can also take advantage of speech recognition software, but few do. When you speak commands, you just speak normally, without intense pauses, unnatural diction, or special intonation. You don't have to train the computer to recognize your voice. Speech recognition works on a computer with a PowerPC processor and 16-bit sound input (the Centris and Quadra AV models can also recognize spoken commands).

For more information on speech and languages, see Chapter 21.

Writing foreign languages with WorldScript

Mac system software enhanced its position as an international operating system with the inclusion of WorldScript software in System 7.1. WorldScript puts Asian, Middle-Eastern, and other non-Roman languages on an equal footing with English and other Roman languages. WorldScript deals with differences in language structure, writing direction, alphabetical sorting, calendar, date and time display, and currency. The software that defines all that is called a *language script system*. One language script system can be used by multiple languages. For example, the Roman script is used for English, French, Italian, Spanish, and German.

Associated with each language script system are one or more keyboard layouts. A keyboard layout defines the relationship between keys you press and characters that appear on screen. You can select a keyboard layout by opening the Keyboard control panel and selecting one or more from a list. If you select more than one keyboard layout, a Keyboard menu appears near the right end of the menu bar. Figure 3-10 shows the Keyboard control panel and Keyboard menu.

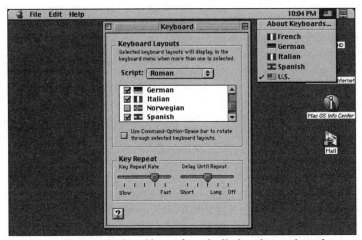

Figure 3-10: Choose a keyboard layout from the Keyboard control panel or menu.

The WorldScript software is available for custom installation with Mac OS 7.5.3 and later, and the Roman script system is built into the Mac OS together with a variety of keyboard layouts for European languages. Apple sells additional packaged script systems and keyboard layouts for these languages: Arabic & Persian, Chinese, Cyrillic, Hebrew, Indian, Japanese, and Korean.

To write in multiple languages, you also need application software that takes advantage of WorldScript, such as ClarisWorks, WordPerfect, Nisus Writer, or WorldWrite.

For more information on using multiple languages, see Chapter 21.

Matching colors with ColorSync

Apple has developed a color management system called ColorSync that minimizes the problem of mismatched color input and output. It gives you more predictable and accurate color from your applications, scanners, digital cameras, displays, and printers. Each device has a color profile, and ColorSync quickly adjusts colors in an image as it goes from scanner or camera to display screen and then to print. ColorSync works with a variety of preset color sets, including Toyo and Pantone, and with color management systems, such as Efi Color and the Kodak Color Management System. ColorSync is part of a standard installation of Mac OS 7.6 and later and is included with earlier system software as part of QuickDraw GX.

Working with OpenDoc plug-in software

The Mac OS (7.5.3 and later) includes OpenDoc, which makes it possible to create documents that contain any kind of material. You're not limited to the types of material allowed by a particular application. Every OpenDoc document can contain standard text and graphics as well as spreadsheets, graphs, database records, QuickTime media, sounds, styled text, live Web pages, and so forth. That doesn't mean OpenDoc is a colossal integrated application. OpenDoc by itself can't work with any kind of material. Instead it provides an endless number of software sockets for a new kind of general-purpose plug-in software, and each plug-in software part gives you the ability to work with a particular type of material.

OpenDoc changes how you think about working with documents. Instead of thinking in terms of applications, you think in terms of content. Instead of switching applications to work on a different kind of content, you just select the content you want to work on and the appropriate menus appear automatically in the menu bar. You can use the menu commands to view or edit the selected content.

For each type of data you want to include in an OpenDoc document, you need an editor. You can think of an OpenDoc editor as a small, focused application that specializes in a particular kind of data.

To get you started with OpenDoc, Mac OS 7.6 and later system software versions give you the option of installing Cyberdog. Although Cyberdog focuses on Internet services such as the Web, e-mail, and FTP (file transfer), there are also parts for basic text editing, viewing graphics, and viewing QuickTime movies. Apple also distributes a collection of basic OpenDoc parts known as the OpenDoc Essentials Kit. Figure 3-11 shows an example of an OpenDoc document that was created with parts from Cyberdog and the OpenDoc Essentials Kit.

The full story on OpenDoc is in Chapter 23.

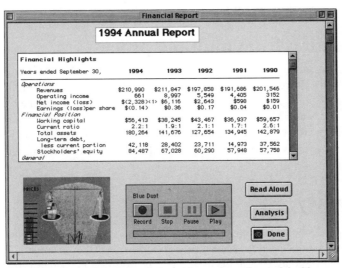

Figure 3-11: Create documents that contain any type of material with OpenDoc plug-in software.

Sharing live data

The Mac OS enables you to share information dynamically from one document to other documents. Because the sharing is dynamic, changes made to the original information are automatically reflected in copies of it, wherever they are. Think of it as live copy and paste. The automatic updating extends to computers interconnected on a network, so a document on your computer can dynamically share information from a document on another networked computer. By contrast, copying and pasting shares information statically and only one computer is involved.

You make a live copy of information by *publishing* an *edition* of it. You include copies of the information in a document by *subscribing* to the edition. Publishing material from a document creates a live copy of the material in an edition file on disk. Any number of other documents (on your computer or other computers networked to yours) include live copies of the material by subscribing to the edition. When you change the original material and save the document that contains it, the edition is automatically updated. Each subscribing document learns of the update the next time it is opened (unless you set it to update only one request).

Information can only be shared dynamically among documents created by programs that include Edit menu commands for publishing and subscribing. You don't find these commands in all programs.

To learn more about Publish and Subscribe, see Chapter 23.

Benefiting from multiple processors

Multiprocessor support can deliver blazing speed on a Mac OS computer with two or more PowerPC processors, but like multiprocessor environments on any operating system, applications must be designed to take advantage of multiple processors. Some Mac OS programs are designed for multiprocessing, including Adobe Photoshop, Adobe Premiere, QuickTime 2.5 (if MP Movie Pack from DayStar Digital is present), Kodak Color Processors, and Strata StudioPro Blitz.

Compatibility

The Mac OS helps you open documents created with programs you don't have. They may be documents created on a Windows, DOS, or Apple II (ProDOS) computer. You may be able to use an application that can open foreign documents itself, or you may need translation software to convert the foreign document to a format your application can open. This section gives you an overview of the Mac OS file and disk compatibility software. (For more detailed information, see "Translating Documents" in Chapter 8.)

Using DOS disks with PC Exchange

The Mac OS can access floppy disks from Windows, DOS, and Apple II (ProDOS) computers if the PC Exchange control panel is installed. The foreign disk's icon appears on the desktop, and you can open it to see its contents. If you have Mac programs that can open DOS or Windows documents, you can use PC Exchange to assign DOS filename extensions to specific Mac applications. Figure 3-12 shows an example of the PC Exchange control panel.

**Figure 3-12: Assign Mac applications to open
Windows and DOS files by using PC Exchange.**

Opening strange items with Easy Open

The Easy Open software relieves your frustration in trying to open a document when you don't have the application that created it. Instead of seeing a message that the document can't be opened, you see a list of applications that can open that kind of document either with or without file translation. Easy Open knows which file translators you have installed on your Mac and which kinds of documents your applications can open. Easy Open works with translation software such as Data Viz's MacLinkPlus, which comes with Mac OS 7.6 and later. Figure 3-13 shows an example of an Easy Open translator list.

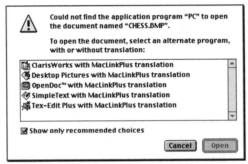

Figure 3-13: Open a document when you don't have the application that created it with the help of Easy Open and MacLinkPlus.

An Easy Open utility program, Document Converter, creates document converter icons that can be used to convert documents without opening them. You simply drop a document onto the appropriate converter icon to perform the translation.

Summary

This chapter introduced you to more Mac OS features and capabilities that you're sure to find indispensable. They include the Open and Save dialog boxes for opening and saving documents from within programs, special folders for organizing the contents of the System Folder, and virtual memory for reducing program memory needs on PowerPC computers and making more memory available on all computers.

You're likely to use all three kinds of fonts that the Mac OS works with — fixed-size, TrueType variable-size, and PostScript variable-size. You may also use the advanced typography made available by QuickDraw GX.

You'll use some of the other Mac OS features and capabilities previewed in this chapter, but you probably won't use them all. The Launcher provides a convenient central launching pad for all the documents, programs, folders, and other items that you open frequently. Open Transport lets you connect your computer to other computers on an AppleTalk network or a TCP/IP network such as the Internet. If you connect to the Internet, you can use Cyberdog to access the Web, e-mail, newsgroups, FTP file servers, and other Internet services. You can also use Cyberdog instead of the more traditional Chooser to access shared files and file servers if you're connected to an AppleTalk network. If you need to access an AppleTalk network remotely by modem, you can use the Apple Remote Access software.

To make the most of the Mac OS, you can manage your startup items with the Extensions Manager control panel, automate repetitive tasks with AppleScript, and minimize mismatched colors with ColorSync. In addition, with English or Mexican Spanish text-to-speech software, you can hear your computer announce its alert messages and read other text aloud. With speech recognition software, you can speak commands. The WorldScript software enhances the Mac OS so you can write in multiple languages. OpenDoc lets you create documents with all kinds of content, limited only by the variety of OpenDoc plug-in software your computer has. You can share live data from one document with any number of others by using the Publish and Subscribe commands. And if your computer has multiple PowerPC processors, the Mac OS lets applications use them to deliver blazing speed.

And finally, when you need to open documents created by applications you don't have, the Mac OS can help. The PC Exchange control panel lets the Mac OS use Windows and DOS disks and assign specific applications to open documents according to their DOS filename extensions. The Mac OS Easy Open and MacLinkPlus software can translate documents to formats that your applications can open.

CHAPTER FOUR

How Mac OS Versions Stack Up

IN THIS CHAPTER

- **Comparing system versions** from System 7.5 to Mac OS 8

- **Checking system enablers** that are required for certain computers

- **Assessing equipment requirements** for processor, RAM, and hard disk space

- **Switching systems** when more than one is present on a hard disk

If you're using an old version of the Mac OS, should you upgrade to the latest? To answer that question, this chapter explains the key features of various versions of the Mac system software, focusing on System 7.5 through Mac OS 8. If you want to upgrade but have applications that require an older version of system software, this chapter explains how you can switch between the two versions of system software on one Mac. Finally, the chapter details the hardware requirements for using various versions of the Mac system software. (For information on where to get the Mac OS and how to install or upgrade it, see Chapters 27–30.)

Comparing System Versions

Well over 90 percent of all Macintosh computers use System 7.0 or later, and over 40 percent use System 7.5 or later. Many Mac OS users are using the version of system software that came with their computers. Apple began shipping System 7.0 on all new Macs in the middle of 1991, changed to System 7.1 in October 1992, upgraded to System 7.5 in November 1994, moved to Mac OS 7.6 in the beginning of 1997, and stepped up to Mac OS 8.0 in July 1997. During those years millions of people upgraded older Macs to newer versions of the system software on their own. If you use an old version of the system software, you may be wondering how it compares with newer versions and whether you should upgrade.

If you're not sure which version of the system software is currently installed on your computer, you can find out by choosing About This Computer (Mac

OS 7.6 and later) or About This Macintosh (System 7.5.5 and earlier) from the Apple menu when the Finder is the active application. The About This Computer window or the About This Macintosh window reports the system software version number in the upper right corner, as shown in Figure 4-1.

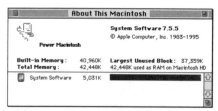

Figure 4-1: Determine the system software version with About This Computer (top) or About This Macintosh (bottom).

Before System 7.5

Although System 7.5 and later are best for the majority of Mac OS computers, earlier versions are viable options for old, low-powered (by today's standards) Mac models. If your Mac has a 68020 or 68000 processor, less than 8MB of RAM, and 80MB or less of hard disk capacity, there's probably no point in upgrading to System 7.5 or later. In so doing, you won't have System 7.5's faster file finding, submenus in the Apple menu, menubar clock, or Audio CD support, although several of those capabilities are available as system extensions from independent software authors. For other features and capabilities such as AppleScript, Open Transport, and OpenDoc, you need more computing power, and practically speaking you need System 7.5 or later.

If your Mac has a 68000 processor and less than 2MB of RAM, System 6.0.8 may be your best bet. You won't have System 7's file sharing, aliases, or virtual memory, but your computer will have more pep and more memory available for opening programs. If you want to spruce up System 6.0.8, you can install TrueType fonts for smoothly scaled text and QuickTime for watching digital movies.

You can get System 6.0.8 and System 7.0.1 free from Apple's online software library (http://www.info.apple.com). If you use System 7.0.1, it's important that you install the System 7.1.1 Tune-Up extension (also available from the Apple online software library) as well. The tune-up fixes a major bug in System 7.0.1 that causes files and folders to disappear from the desktop, and it improves performance.

System 7.5

System 7.5 makes the computer easier to use in many small ways. It speeds disk searches with the Find File program, makes submenus an option in the Apple menu, adds a clock to the menu bar, and provides the Launcher control panel. Two of the numerous utilities in System 7.5, Macintosh Easy Open and PC Exchange, help you find translators for documents created by applications that you don't have. These utilities also allow you to work with disks from DOS and Windows computers. System 7.5 also increases the limit on hard disk size from 2GB to 4GB.

On a grander scale, System 7.5 introduces Apple Guide for step-by-step interactive help and incorporates AppleScript for system-wide automation of repetitive tasks. Also included for optional installation are QuickDraw GX for advanced typography, advanced graphics, and a new way of printing; and PowerTalk for e-mail, contact management, and password management.

System 7.5.1

In System 7.5.1, an improved Launcher control panel lets you drag-and-drop to add, remove, and reorganize items. You can turn off the computer by pressing the Power key on the keyboard. The General Controls control panel has a new option for saving documents. With file sharing on, you can eject removable disks and CD-ROMs without turning off file sharing, and a removable disk or CD-ROM is shared automatically when you insert it. If a file server (including a shared disk or folder) disconnects unexpectedly and you have documents open from it, you can usually save them.

System 7.5.2

System 7.5.2 works only on the following computers: the Power Mac 7200/75, 7200/90, 7500/100, 8500/120, 9500/120, and 9500/132; and the PowerBook 190, 2300, and 5300. Other Mac OS computers use System 7.5.3 to get everything System 7.5.2 has to offer and more. In addition, System 7.5.3 is more reliable, so System 7.5.2 users should upgrade to it.

System 7.5.3

System 7.5.3 includes all the improvements of System 7.5.1 and 7.5.2. In addition, the Finder turns an icon translucent when you drag it on a PowerPC computer, displays long item names better, copies small files faster, and generally retains Get Info comments when rebuilding the desktop. The Close View control panel has new keyboard shortcuts, Find File has a new preference for displaying the kinds of found items, and Memory has a larger standard Disk Cache size. System 7.5.3 also improves performance and fixes countless problems.

Open Transport 1.1, the first reliable version of Apple's modern networking software, comes with System 7.5.3. So does QuickTime 2.1 and English Text-to-speech software. You have the option of installing Desktop Printing 1.0.3 and the digital signatures portion of PowerTalk by itself. The System 7.5.3 CD-ROM includes several bonus items: Mexican Spanish text-to-speech, QuickDraw 3D 1.0.3, and OpenDoc 1.0.4.

System 7.5.4

Apple never distributed System 7.5.4 widely. After distributing it to a small number of software developers, a problem was discovered in System 7.5.4. The fixed version was named System 7.5.5.

System 7.5.5

System 7.5.5 doesn't add any new features. It simply upgrades system software version 7.5.3 or 7.5.4 to improve reliability and performance. In particular, System 7.5.5 is faster than earlier versions of system software when virtual memory is turned on.

Mac OS 7.6

Mac OS 7.6 delivers a few minor improvements, fixes some problems, and incorporates a number of system software add-ons that were (and still are) available separately. The core Mac OS 7.6 includes QuickTime 2.5, LaserWriter 8.4.2, Open Transport 1.1.1, multiprocessor support, Desktop Printing 2.0.2, ColorSync 2.1.1, Extensions Manager 7.6, and additional screen capture options. You also get the performance increases and bug fixes first made in System 7.5.5, 7.5.3, and earlier versions of the system software.

There are also some technologies and capabilities that Mac OS 7.6 can't use. PowerTalk is incompatible with Mac OS 7.6, and Classic AppleTalk networking is no longer an option with Mac OS 7.6 (you must use Open Transport). Also, Mac OS 7.6 does not let you turn off the Modern Memory Manager feature in the Memory control panel.

Apple overhauled the installation software for Mac OS 7.6, making it easy to add more items in a standard installation, including OpenDoc 1.1.2, OpenDoc Essentials Kit 1.0.1, QuickDraw 3D 1.0.6, MacLinkPlus 8.1, Apple Remote Access Client 2.1, Cyberdog 1.2, Open Transport PPP 1.0, English Text-to-Speech 1.5, and QuickDraw GX 1.1.5.

Some computers can't use everything that comes with Mac OS 7.6, and some can't use Mac OS 7.6 at all. You can only install QuickDraw 3D on a PowerPC computer. OpenDoc, OpenDoc Essentials, Cyberdog, and LaserWriter 8.4.2 require the CFM 68K Runtime Enabler version 4.0, which is not included with Mac OS 7.6, for use on computers with 68030 and 68040 processors.

Some computers can't use Mac OS 7.6 but can use Mac OS 7.6.1 and later. They are the Power Mac 4400, 5500, 6500, 7300, 7600, 8600, and 9600, and the PowerBook 3400. The following Macs can't use anything later than System 7.5.5: Plus, SE, SE/30, II, IIx, IIcx, Portable, PowerBook 100, original Classic, and original LC.

Mac OS 7.6.1

Mac OS 7.6.1 is a minor upgrade that fixes errors in Mac OS 7.6. You get fewer Type 11 crashes with Mac OS 7.6.1 because 7.6.1 reports serious program errors more accurately than earlier versions. Mac OS 7.6.1 also reports other errors less frequently, including Type 12 and Type 112 errors. You still get most of the system errors, but they get reported with more accurate numbers.

Beginning with 7.6.1, the Mac OS also reserves itself 300K more temporary memory any time you open an application that uses up all the remaining memory available. As a result, that application has 300K less memory, and in some cases, the lesser amount of memory isn't enough to open the application.

Mac OS 7.6.1 also removes the first of the three PowerBook low-battery warnings because it was showing up way too soon on PowerBook 1400 computers. Now one message appears 2 to 4 minutes before the battery runs out, and another message appears about 10 seconds before the Mac OS forces the computer to sleep. About a dozen lesser bugs are fixed by Mac OS 7.6.1.

Besides bug fixes, Mac OS 7.6.1 includes the CFM 68K Runtime Enabler version 4.0 missing from Mac OS 7.6. Mac OS 7.6.1 also updates a number of system software files for compatibility with the Power Mac 4400, 5500, 6500, 7300, 7600, 8600, and 9600, and the PowerBook 3400.

BACKGROUNDER

Coping with Type 11 Errors

Mac OS 7.6.1 doesn't actually stop any Type 11 errors from happening, but it does report them more accurately. This is the first Mac OS version to properly classify specific system errors occurring in PowerPC-native programs as well as 68K programs running on 68K machines or emulated on PowerPC machines. Previously, the Mac OS classified all system errors in PowerPC-native code as "miscellaneous hardware exceptions," reported them as Type 11 errors, and forced a restart. Mac OS 7.6.1 reports the true errors — a bus error (Type 1) when a program tries to access non-existent memory, an address error (Type 2) when a program tries to execute instructions at odd memory addresses, an illegal instruction error (Type 3) when a program gets lost and tries to execute data as if it were instructions, and so on — and for most of them it forces the active application to "unexpectedly quit." You have a chance to save your work before restarting or shutting down to restore maximum stability.

Mac OS 8.0

Mac OS 8.0 brings substantial changes to the system software. The Finder was rewritten from scratch and is fully native on PowerPC computers. (You'll find a rundown on all the Finder improvements in Chapter 1.)

A number of other software modules have been upgraded to fix errors and provide more features. A standard installation of Mac OS 8 includes the core Mac OS 8 module, Mac OS Info Center, Internet Access, and Open Transport PPP 1.0.1. Additional software modules are part of a standard installation of Mac OS 8, although you can decline installation of any of them. They are Mac OS Runtime for Java 1.0.2, Personal Web Sharing 1.1, QuickDraw 3D 1.5.1, OpenDoc 1.2.1, and MacLinkPlus 9.0. Along with the standard installation items, you can also install any of the following: Apple Location Manager, Cyberdog 2.0, QuickDraw GX 1.1.6, English Text-to-Speech 1.5, and Apple Remote Access 2.1. Note that QuickDraw GX 1.1.6 provides advanced typography and graphics, but does not provide any printing services. Mac OS 8 cannot use QuickDraw GX printing software.

The core Mac OS 8 software includes the following new or revised control panels: Appearance 1.0, Apple Menu Options 1.1.3, Desktop Pictures 1.0, Extensions Manager 4.0.1, File Sharing 8.0, General Controls 7.5.8, Keyboard 7.7, Memory 7.5.8, Monitors 7.6.6, Monitors & Sound 1.3, Startup Disk 7.5.4, and Users & Groups 8.0.

With Mac OS 8 you also get the following new or improved system extensions: Apple CD-ROM 5.3.3, Apple Guide 2.2, AppleScript 1.1.2, AppleShare Workstation Client 3.7, Color Picker 2.1, ObjectSupportLib 1.2, Open Transport 1.2, QuickTime 2.5, QuickTime MPEG Extension 1.0, QuickTime Musical Instruments Extension 2.5, and QuickTime VR 2.0.

Mac OS 8 also includes numerous corrections and additions to the System file, which contains much of the basic system software. The CFM 68K Runtime Enabler version 4.0 and the WorldScript Power Adapter 7.5.3 are now part of the System file. The screen capture capabilities were fixed to work when At Ease is installed but inactive. Virtual memory performance has been improved yet again. Font menus are created faster. Hard disks that take a long time to spin up after being switched on are no longer missed during startup. Sound output is no longer incorrectly suppressed on Power Mac and Performa 5200, 5300, 6200, and 6300 computers.

A lot of the changes in the control panels, extensions, and the System file have to do with the platinum appearance added in Mac OS 8.

Feature summary

Table 4-1 lists the major new features and capabilities added to or removed from the Mac system software beginning with version 7.0.

Table 4-1 Mac OS Features at a Glance					
Feature	*8.0*	*7.6 – 7.6.1*	*7.5.3 – 7.5.5*	*7.5 – 7.5.1*	*7.0 – 7.1.2*
TrueType	●	●	●	●	●
Aliases	●	●	●	●	●
File sharing	●	●	●	●	●
Virtual memory	●	●	●	●	●
Multitasking (cooperative)	●	●	●	●	●
Stationery	●	●	●	●	●
Publish and Subscribe	●	●	●	●	●
Balloon Help	●	●	●	●	●
Custom icons	●	●	●	●	●
Icon labels	●	●	●	●	●

(continued)

Feature	8.0	7.6 – 7.6.1	7.5.3 – 7.5.5	7.5 – 7.5.1	7.0 – 7.1.2
Drag to open	●	●	●	●	●
Outlined list views	●	●	●	●	●
Specialized folders	●	●	●	●	●
Fonts folder	●	●	●	●	○[1]
QuickTime	●	●	●	●	○[1,3]
Mac OS PC Exchange	●	●	●	●	○[1,2,3]
PowerTalk	○	○	●	●	○[1]
AppleScript	●	●	●	●	○[1]
Scriptable Finder	●	●	●	●	○[1]
Improved file finding	●	●	●	●	○
Apple Guide	●	●	●	●	○
Easy Open	●	●	●	●	○[3]
Big desktop patterns	●	●	●	●	○[3]
Documents folder	●	●	●	●	○
Finder hiding	●	●	●	●	○
Apple-menu submenus	●	●	●	●	○[3]
Launcher	●	●	●	●	○
Drag-and-drop editing	●	●	●	●	○[1]
MacTCP	●	●	●	●	○[3]
Control Strip	●	●	●	●	○[2]
QuickDraw GX printing	○	●	●	●	○
QuickDraw GX typography	●	●	●	●	○
Stickies	●	●	●	●	○[3]
Menu bar clock	●	●	●	●	○[3]
Collapsible windows	●	●	●	●	○[3]
Improved Scrapbook and Note Pad	●	●	●	●	○

(continued)

Feature	8.0	7.6 – 7.6.1	7.5.3 – 7.5.5	7.5 – 7.5.1	7.0 – 7.1.2
Power key turns off	●	●	●	○	○
Smarter file sharing	●	●	●	○	○
Open Transport	●	●	●	○[3]	○[1]
Desktop printing	●	●	●	○[3]	○[1]
Text-to-speech	●	●	●	●	○[3]
Translucent icon drag	●	●	●	○	○
Multiprocessing	●	●	○[3]	○[3]	○[1]
ColorSync	●	●	○[3]	○[3]	○
OpenDoc	●	●	○[3]	○[3]	○[1]
Cyberdog	●	●	○[3]	○	○
QuickDraw 3D	●	●	○[3]	○[3]	○[1]
Apple Remote Access	●	●	○[3]	○[3]	○[1]
MacLinkPlus	●	●	○[3]	○[3]	○[3]
Platinum appearance	●	○	○	○	○
Charcoal system font	●	○	○	○	○
Desktop picture	●	○[3]	○[3]	○[3]	○[3]
Window collapse box	●	○	○	○	○
Draggable window frame	●	○	○	○	○
Button views	●	○	○	○	○
Pop-up windows	●	○	○	○	○
Improved View menu	●	○	○	○	○
View options for each folder	●	○	○	○	○
Simple Finder	●	○	○	○	○
Spring-loaded folders	●	○	○	○	○
Contextual menus	●	○	○	○	○
Sticky menus	●	○[3]	○[3]	○[3]	○[3]
Move To Trash command	●	○	○	○	○

(continued)

Table 4-1 *(continued)*					
Feature	*8.0*	*7.6 – 7.6.1*	*7.5.3 – 7.5.5*	*7.5 – 7.5.1*	*7.0 – 7.1.2*
Show Original (of alias)	●	○[3]	○[3]	○[3]	○
Improved Sharing window	●	○	○	○	○
Simultaneous Finder operations	●	○	○	○	○
Apple Location Manager	●	○[3]	○	○	○
Internet Setup Assistant	●	○[3]	○[3]	○[3]	○
Internet applications	●	○[3]	○[3]	○[3]	○[3]
Personal Web Sharing	●	○[3]	○[3]	○	○
Mac OS Runtime for Java	●	○[3]	○[3]	○[3]	○

● *Included with this version of the Mac OS.*   ○ *Not included with this version of the Mac OS.*

[1] *Fonts folder and QuickTime are included with System 7.1–7.1.2. AppleScript is included with System 7.1.1 Pro and 7.1.2. PowerTalk is included with System 7.1.1 Pro and can be added to 7.1.2. The Scriptable Finder can be added to System 7.1.1 Pro and 7.1.2. Macintosh PC Exchange is included with System 7.1.2. Drag-and-drop editing, Open Transport, Desktop printing, OpenDoc, and Apple Remote Access can be added to System 7.1–7.1.2. Multiprocessing and QuickDraw 3D can be added to System 7.1.2.*

[2] *The feature is not included with this version of system software except on certain Mac models (such as 660AV and 840AV models and PowerBooks).*

[3] *The feature is not included with this version of system software, but is available from Apple or an independent software developer.*

Checking System Enablers

Prior to System 7.1, Apple brought out a new version of system software to accommodate each new batch of Macintosh models. Now Apple supports a new model or a new series with a plug-in software component called a *system enabler*. A system enabler contains software that modifies the system software to work with a particular kind of Macintosh. The enabler for a particular Mac model must be in the System Folder or the computer will not start up. For example, a Power Mac 8600 requires System Enabler 702 to start up with System 7.5.5.

Periodically Apple eliminates the need for any of the existing system enablers by combining them all together with other system improvements in a new version of the system software. All the Mac models then in existence when a new system software version comes out don't need enablers if they use that new system software version (though they still need enablers if they use the older system version). Macs introduced later will need system enablers until Apple rolls them into the next new system software version. For example, a Power Mac 6100/66, 7100/80, 8100/100, or 8100/110 requires the PowerPC Enabler with System 7.5.1, but doesn't need an enabler with System 7.5.3 and later.

Table 4-2 lists the Mac models that require an enabler with System 7.5 or later, the system enabler each model requires, the earliest system software version the enabler can be used with, and the earliest system software version that eliminates the need for the enabler. The following Mac models do not require a system enabler with System 7.5 or later: Centris series, Classic series, Color Classic, II series, LC series, Mac TV, Performa 200, Performa 400 series, Performa 500 series, Performa 600 series, Performa 6110 series, Plus, Portable, Power Mac 6100/60, Power Mac 7100/66, Power Mac 8100/80, Power Macintosh Upgrade card, PowerBook 100 series except 190, PowerBook 200 series, PowerBook 500 series, Quadra series, and SE series.

Table 4-2
System Enablers for System 7.5–Mac OS 8

Macintosh Model	Enabler Name and Version	Earliest Mac OS version	
		With enabler	Without enabler
Performa 5200, 5300, 6200, 6300	System Enabler 406 v. 1.0	7.5.1	7.5.3
Performa 5400, 6400	System Enabler 410 v. 1.1	7.5.3	7.5.5
PowerBook 190	PowerBook 5300/2300/190 Enabler v. 1.2.4	7.5.2	7.5.3
PowerBook 2300, 5300	PowerBook 5300/2300/190 Enabler v. 1.2.1	7.5.2	7.5.3
Power Mac 5200/75, 5300/100 LC	System Enabler 406 v. 1.0	7.5.1	7.5.3
Power Mac 6100/66, 7100/80, 8100/100, 8100/110	PowerPC Enabler v. 1.1.1	7.5.1	7.5.3
Power Mac 7200/75, 7200/90, 7500/100, 8500/120, 9500/120, 9500/132	System Enabler 701 v. 1.1	7.5.2	7.5.3
Power Mac 4400/200	System Enabler 827	7.5.3	7.6.1*
Power Mac 5400	System Enabler 410 v. 1.1	7.5.3	7.5.5
Power Mac 6400	System Enabler 410 v. 1.1	7.5.3	7.5.5

(continued)

		Earliest Mac OS version	
Macintosh Model	Enabler Name and Version	With enabler	Without enabler
Power Mac 6500 Series	System Enabler 411	7.5.5	7.6.1*
Power Mac 7300	System Enabler 702	7.5.5	7.6.1*
Power Mac 8600/200	System Enabler 702	7.5.5	7.6.1*
Power Mac 9600/200	System Enabler 702	7.5.5	7.6.1*
Power Mac 9600/200MP	System Enabler 702	7.5.5	7.6.1*
Power Mac 9600/233	System Enabler 702	7.5.5	7.6.1*

Table 4-2 *(continued)*

* Does not work with Mac OS 7.6 but does work with 7.6.1.

Assessing Equipment Requirements

Mac OS 8 requires a computer with a 68040 or PowerPC processor, at least 8MB of RAM (16MB or more highly recommended), and 95MB to 110MB of hard disk space, depending on which modules you install. On a computer with less than 16MB of RAM, you must turn on virtual memory and set it to 16MB.

Mac OS 7.6 works on all computers with 68040 and PowerPC processors and on most computers with 68030 processors. It requires 8MB of RAM (16MB or more preferred), and 40MB to 120MB of hard disk space. On a computer with less than 16MB of RAM, you must turn on virtual memory and set it to 16MB. You can't use Mac OS 7.6 on a Mac Plus, SE, SE/30, II, IIx, IIcx, Portable, PowerBook 100, original Classic, or original LC. System 7.5.5 is the latest version those models can use.

Systems 7.5–7.5.5 work on any computer that can use the Mac OS except the three oldest Macintosh models. Only the original Mac 128K, the Mac 512K, and the Mac XL lack the necessary software in their *ROM* (read-only memory) to use System 7.5. To use Systems 7.5–7.5.5, a computer with a PowerPC processor needs at least 8MB of RAM; 16MB minimum if you install everything. A computer with any 68K processor needs half that much RAM. System 7.5 needs 13MB to 20MB of hard disk space.

If you're not sure how much RAM your computer has, you can tell by choosing About This Computer (Mac OS 7.6 and later) or About This Macintosh (System 7.5.5 and earlier) from the Finder's Apple menu. If you see an amount

labeled Built-in Memory, that's how much RAM your computer has. If you
don't see an amount labeled Built-in Memory, then the amount labeled Total
Memory tells how much RAM your computer has. Prior to Mac OS 7.6, the
Built-in Memory amount isn't reported if it's the same as Total Memory, which
happens when virtual memory is turned off in the Memory control panel.
Figure 4-1 at the beginning of this chapter shows the About This Computer
and the About This Macintosh windows.

To check the amount of hard disk space available, open the icon of the hard
disk where you want to install the system software. The available space is
reported at the top of the disk's window.

If the amount of memory or hard disk space is reported in K (kilobytes), you
can convert to MB (megabytes) by dividing the number of K by 1,024 (for
example, 2048K ÷ 1024 = 2MB).

Switching Systems

You can switch between two versions of system software if necessary, even if
you have only one hard disk. To install a second System Folder on a disk, use
the Installer program's Clean Install option (see "Performing a Clean
Installation" in Chapter 27). Alternatively, you can drag the System file from
the existing System Folder to the Startup Items folder, and rename that System
Folder. If you don't remove the System file, the Installer program updates the
existing System Folder instead of creating a new System Folder. After
installation, move the old System file back to its previous location, either by
dragging it there or by selecting it and then choosing the Put Away command.
Leave the older System Folder renamed. A System Folder can have any name;
having a System file and a Finder together in the same folder qualifies that
folder as being a System Folder, regardless of its name.

Apple ordinarily advises against installing two System Folders on the same disk,
claiming you can't be sure which System Folder will be used during startup and
become the active (or *blessed*) System Folder. Although multiple System Folders
can lead to confusion, they don't have to lead to disaster. You can designate
which System Folder will be the blessed one during the next startup or restart
by using the System Picker utility (described in Chapter 24). Mac OS 8
requires System Picker 1.5 or later.

If you can't get System Picker, you can switch to a System Folder by *de-blessing*
all the others. To de-bless a System Folder, open it and drag the System file
into the Startup Items folder. If you want to switch System Folders, first

de-bless the current System Folder (the one with a small system icon on it).
Then bless another System Folder by opening it, opening its Startup Items
folder, and dragging the System file from the Startup Items folder to the
System Folder. Close the System Folder window and make sure the System
Folder icon now has a badge, indicating it's currently blessed.

Summary

After reading this chapter, you know which features and capabilities were added
to and in a few cases removed from successive versions of the Mac system
software. Table 4-1 summarized the feature differences among versions 7.0
through 8.0. You also know that some computer models require a system
enabler file in the System Folder until they are upgraded with a version of the
system software that integrates the enabler file.

From reading this chapter you also know what kind of processor, how much
RAM, and how much hard disk space the various system software versions require.

This chapter concluded by telling you how to switch systems when more than
one is installed on your hard disk.

Start on the Desktop

The desktop, with its windows, icons, and menus, serves as a home base for everything you do with your Macintosh. Because you see so much of it, how it looks and operates is important. Mac OS 8 introduces a sleek redesign of the menu bar, menus, and windows called the *platinum appearance*. The menu bar and menus have 3D shading and color accents. Windows have the same basic structure in all system software versions, but Apple enhanced their 3D shading and restyled their controls for Mac OS 8 windows. Icons also get a 3D facelift in Mac OS 8.

Windows, icons, and menus not only look different in Mac OS 8, they are easier to use than in earlier system software versions. You can drag windows by their borders and collapse them with a special control. Menus stay open on their own, and you can pop up a contextual menu when you point at objects on the screen.

You also have even more ways to customize windows, menus, icons, and the desktop itself in Mac OS 8. You have more choices of accent color for windows and menus. You can choose between two fonts for menus, window titles, and so on. You have more desktop pattern choices, and you can cover the pattern with a picture. In addition to these improvements, you can still change the text highlight color and customize icons just as in Mac OS 7.0–7.6.1.

All versions of the Mac OS let you adjust the sensitivity of the keyboard and mouse or trackball. Get the keyboard to repeat characters when it feels right to you. And get the mouse or trackball to respond the way you like when you move and click it.

And hey, you may never need to do this, but the Mac OS makes it easy to take a picture of the screen, a window, or a selected area.

This chapter describes and illustrates the basic features of the Mac OS *interface* and how to fine-tune them. And be sure to see the remaining chapters in Part II for detailed information about other aspects of the Mac OS, such as the Finder and the System Folder.

Menus

The Mac OS has always used menus to present commands and attributes from which you can choose. The menu titles appear across the top of the screen in a menu bar in the form of words and icons, and clicking a menu title pulls down a list of commands and attributes in that category. The Mac OS 8 menu bar has the same five standard menus as all system software versions since 7.0 — Apple, File, Edit, Help, and Application — and it has the optional menu-bar clock that was first included with System 7.5.

However, Apple has changed the look of menus in Mac OS 8 as part of its platinum appearance. Apple has also enhanced menu behavior so that you no longer have to hold down the mouse button to use a menu and added contextual menus that list commands and attributes relevant to an object when you click it while holding down the Control key.

Menu appearance

After 13 years of flat black and white, the Mac OS 8 menu bar and menus have color accents and 3D shading. The background color of the menu bar and menus is light gray, and 3D shading makes their edges look rounded and menu separator lines look engraved. In addition, menu titles and commands are highlighted in an accent color when you select them. The platinum appearance's 3D shading requires a monitor set to display at least 16 levels of gray or 256 colors, and the color highlighting requires at least 256 colors. Figure 5-1 shows an example of a menu bar and menu with the Mac OS 8 platinum appearance.

On monitors displaying at least four grays or 16 colors, system software versions 7.0 and later use true gray text to display inactive menu titles and inactive menu items and gray lines to divide sections of menus. On a monitor displaying fewer than 16 colors, the system software simulates gray text by alternating black and white dots.

You can choose the accent color that the platinum appearance uses for menu highlighting. The Appearance control panel gives you a choice of 17 colors and black and white (which effectively turns off the platinum appearance). (See "Windows" later in this chapter for more information on the Appearance control panel.)

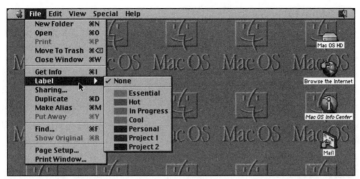

Figure 5-1: Platinum appearance's color highlighting and 3-D shading enhance the menu bar and the menus.

The platinum menu appearance normally applies to all application programs. However, the platinum appearance causes harmless cosmetic flaws in the menus of some programs. If these flaws bother you, you can eliminate them by turning off the "System-wide platinum appearance" option in the Options section of the Appearance control panel.

Menu symbols

A menu item may be accompanied by a variety of symbols. A triangle pointing to the right indicates the menu item has a submenu. An ellipsis at the end of the item name indicates that choosing the item brings up a dialog box in which you must supply additional information before the command can be completed.

The following symbols indicate the status of a menu item:

✓ designates an attribute that applies to everything that is currently selected

– designates an attribute that applies only to some things that are currently selected

▶ designates a menu item with a submenu

◆ designates a program that's running in the background and requires attention; to find out why, make it the active, foreground application

Other symbols are used to specify keyboard shortcuts for menu items. Pressing a specified combination of keys has the same effect as choosing the menu item. For example, pressing the ⌘ key and the X key is equivalent to choosing the Cut command from the Edit menu. The following symbols represent keys:

⌘ represents the Command key

⇧ represents the Shift key

⌥ represents the Option key

⌃ represents the Control (or Ctrl) key

⌦ represents the Delete key

When you use a keyboard shortcut for a command in a menu, the title of the menu flashes briefly to signal that the command has been issued. You can change how many times the title flashes or turn off the signal altogether in the Menu Blinking section of the General Controls control panel.

Sticky menus

Beginning with Mac OS 8, menus are sticky. You do not have to hold down the mouse button to keep a menu displayed, although you can if you want to. To use a menu, you position the pointer over its title in the menu bar and either click or press the mouse button. If you click, the menu sticks open. You can leave your finger off the mouse button and move the pointer up and down the menu, highlighting each menu item as the pointer passes over it. The menu disappears if you move the pointer to the menu bar. You can display the same menu or another menu by moving the pointer over the menu title. You don't have to click again unless it's been more than 15 seconds since you last moved the mouse. To choose a menu item, you position the pointer over it and click. If you click outside a menu, or if you don't move the mouse for 15 seconds, the menu disappears and you have to click a menu title again to make menus stick open. Sticky menus also work with menus outside the menu bar — a pop-up menu stays open if you click it, and so does a contextual menu (more about contextual menus later).

You can use menus the non-sticky traditional way with any version of the system software. Position the pointer over a menu title and press the mouse button to display the menu. The menu disappears if you release the mouse button. To choose a menu item, hold down the mouse button as you drag the pointer to the menu item, and then release the button to choose the item.

Standard menus

The menu bar includes the following five standard menus in most Mac OS applications:

❖ **Apple menu** is at the left end of the menu and has an Apple logo for its title. This menu usually includes an About item, which describes the application you're currently using, followed by an alphabetical list of programs, documents, and other items you can open. For information on using and customizing the Apple menu, see "Opening Programs and Documents" in Chapter 9.

❖ **File menu** is next to the Apple menu and contains commands that affect a whole document, such as New, Open, Close, Save, and Print. The last item is usually Quit, which you use when you're done working with an application.

❖ **Edit menu** is to the right of the File menu and contains commands that you can use to change a document's contents, such as Undo, Cut, Copy, Paste, and Clear.

❖ **Help menu** gives you access to onscreen help. The menu title and its location are different in Mac OS 8 than in earlier system software versions. In Mac OS 8, the help menu is labeled "Help," and the menu is immediately to the right of the last application menu in the menu bar. In earlier versions, the help menu is labeled with a question mark icon and the menu is near the right end of the menu bar. In addition, the help menu is referred to as the Guide menu in Mac OS 7.5–7.6.1. For more information about onscreen help, see "Getting Onscreen Help" later in this chapter.

❖ **Application menu,** located at the right end of the menu bar, displays an alphabetical list of the applications that are currently running on the computer. Choosing a listed application makes it the active application so you can use it.

Each application may add its own menus between the Edit menu and the Help menu.

Contextual menus

If you're using Mac OS 8 or later, you may not have to look through the menus on the menu bar to find a command or attribute. You can display a *contextual menu* by holding down the Control key while clicking an icon, a window, or some selected text for which you want to choose a command or attribute. The contextual menu lists commands that are relevant to the item that you Control-click. Figure 5-2 shows an example of a contextual menu for a window.

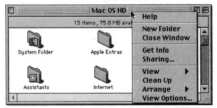

Figure 5-2: Control-clicking an item displays a contextual menu in the Mac OS 8 Finder.

You can Control-click one icon or a selection of several icons. When several icons are selected, Control-clicking any one of them displays a contextual menu of commands that pertain to the whole group. For example, if you Control-click a folder icon, the contextual menu includes the Sharing command. But if you select a folder and a document and then Control-click either one, the contextual menu does not include the Sharing command because it does not apply to the document. (For more information on selecting items, see "Icons" later in this chapter.)

Contextual menus are available in the Finder with Mac OS 8 (unless the Simple Finder option is turned on with the Preferences command, as described in the next chapter), and other applications can adopt them. In addition, some applications have contextual menus that work with earlier versions of system software, although you may do something other than Control-clicking to display one of those contextual menus. For example, you display a contextual menu in Netscape Navigator by moving the pointer over an object in the browser window and pressing the mouse button for a few seconds.

Windows

All the windows that you use to view and interact with the stuff on your Mac get a face-lift as part of the Mac OS 8 platinum appearance. The basic structure is the same in all Mac OS versions for each type of window — regular window, movable dialog box, immovable dialog or alert box, and so on. But Apple designed a new look for Mac OS 8 windows and added some new ways of working with them.

Window appearance

Windows with the platinum appearance have a more finely wrought 3-D look than windows in Mac OS 7.0–7.6.1. Figure 5-3 compares the look of movable windows and stationary alert boxes in Mac OS 7.6.1 with their platinum appearance in Mac OS 8.

Only the active window has 3D shading. It stands out from the inactive windows behind it because the Mac OS displays inactive windows with flat gray borders and a gray title. To make an inactive window active, click any part of it you can see. This brings it to the front and sends the former active window to the background. Figure 5-4 shows an active window and inactive windows in Mac OS 8.

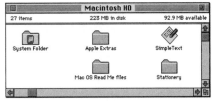
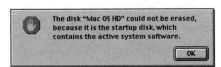
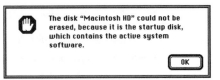

Figure 5-3: Windows and alert boxes are grayer and have a more pronounced 3D look in Mac OS 8 (left column) in earlier system software versions (right column).

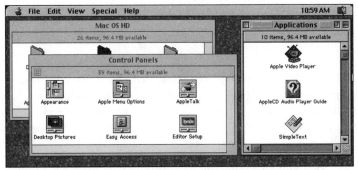

Figure 5-4: Embossed window detail helps the active window stand out.

To see the 3D shading of the platinum appearance or the less pronounced shading of Mac OS 7.0–7.6.1, your monitor must be set for at least 16 grays or 256 colors. If the monitor's color depth is set below that, your windows and dialog boxes lack 3D shading. (For more information on setting the monitor's color depth, see "Monitors & Sound" in Chapter 10.)

Window controls

The design of a window has as much to do with function as with form. Many parts of a window's frame are actually control surfaces that you can use to move the window, size it, close it, or change the view of its contents. Figure 5-5 shows how window controls appear in Mac OS 8.

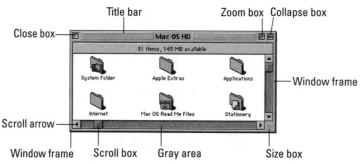

Figure 5-5: Manipulate windows with their many controls.

Mac OS 8 windows have all the controls that were in earlier system software versions as well as two new controls. You won't find all the window controls on every kind of window, though. Document windows have all or most of the available controls, movable dialog boxes have fewer controls, and immovable dialog or alert boxes have no controls.

The window controls have the following effects:

❖ **Title bar:** Drag to move the window. With Mac OS 7.5 and later, double-clicking the title bar may collapse or expand the window and Option-double-clicking may collapse or expand all windows like clicking and Option-clicking the Collapse box. (To set up this option, see "Appearance and Behavior Modification" later in this chapter.)

❖ **Close box:** Click to make the window go away. Press the Option key and click to close all windows.

❖ **Zoom box:** Click to make the window as large as it needs to be to show all its contents, up to the size of the screen. Click again to make the window resume its previous size and location. Press the Option key and click to force the window to fill the screen. (The zoom box usually leaves a margin on the right side of the screen.)

❖ **Collapse box:** Click to hide all but the window's title bar, or if the window is collapsed, click to show the entire window. Press the Option key and click to collapse (or expand) all windows. (This control is not included in system versions prior to Mac OS 8.)

❖ **Scroll bar arrow, box, gray area:** Click or press the arrow to scroll the window's contents smoothly; click or press the gray area to scroll in chunks; drag the box to quickly bring another part of the window's contents into view. The scroll bar controls do not appear if scrolling would not bring anything else into view.

❖ **Size box:** Drag to adjust the size of the window.

❖ **Window frame:** Drag to move the window. (This function is not included in system versions prior to Mac OS 8.)

Window Tricks

Although background windows don't have visible controls, you can move and collapse or expand them while they're in the background. If you have more than one program open at the same time, these tricks only work with windows of the program you're currently using.

To move a background window, press the ⌘ key while you drag the window's title bar, or in Mac OS 8 while you drag the window's frame.

To collapse or expand a background window, press the ⌘ key while double-clicking the window's title bar. Pressing ⌘ keeps the window from coming to the front.

To collapse or expand all windows, press the Option key while double-clicking any window's title bar. Option-clicking a collapse button does the same thing in Mac OS 8.

Other controls

The platinum appearance of Mac OS 8 extends to many of the controls you manipulate in windows, dialog boxes, and alert boxes. Examples include buttons with text or picture labels, check boxes, radio buttons, sliders, the little arrows used for increasing or decreasing numeric values, and pop-up menus (described previously). The restyling gives them a 3D look without changing the way they work. Figure 5-6 compares the platinum appearance of buttons, check boxes, radio buttons, and pop-up menus in Mac OS 8 with their flat appearance in Mac OS 7.6.1.

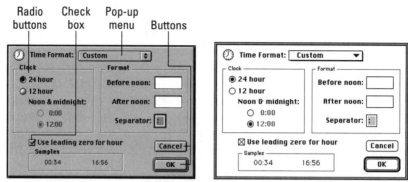

Figure 5-6: Embossing enhances buttons, check boxes, and radio buttons in Mac OS 8 (left).

Icons

Not only windows get a 3D face-lift in Mac OS 8; so do the icons that are inside them and on the desktop. The icons may look different, but you select them and rename them the same way in all system software versions (7.0 and later).

Icon appearance

As part of the Mac OS 8 desktop redesign, Apple restyled the icons that represent folders, disks, and some files to give them the appearance of depth. Several system files have this 3D appearance, and so do the generic icons used for programs and documents that don't have unique icons. However, most programs and documents look the same in all system software versions (7.0 and later). Figure 5-7 shows examples of the restyled icons in Mac OS 8 and their counterparts in Mac OS 7.6.1.

Selecting icons

The look of an icon has no bearing on how you use it. Everyone who uses a Mac quickly learns how to select icons by clicking, but even some seasoned veterans don't know that in windows and on the desktop you can select more than one icon at a time. In addition, you can select icons individually by typing instead of clicking.

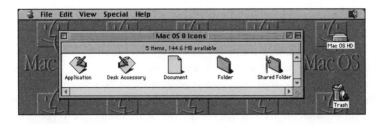

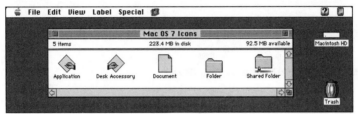

Figure 5-7: Folder, disk, and some file icons have a 3D look in Mac OS 8 (top) and a flat look in earlier system software versions (bottom).

When you select an icon, the Mac OS highlights it by making it darker and displaying its name in white type on a black background. If the icon you select is on a monitor that's set to display black and white, the Mac OS highlights the icon by inverting its colors; white becomes black and black becomes white. Figure 5-8 shows examples of icons that are highlighted and icons that aren't.

Figure 5-8: Icon highlighting on a color or grayscale monitor (left) and a black-and-white monitor (right).

Multiple selection by Shift-clicking

Ordinarily, clicking an icon selects it (highlights it) and deselects the icon that was highlighted. You can select a group of icons in the same window or a group of icons on the desktop by pressing the Shift key while clicking each icon in turn. At any time, you can deselect a selected icon by pressing the Shift key and clicking it again.

Multiple selection by dragging

In addition to Shift-clicking to select multiple icons, you can select adjacent icons by dragging across them. As you drag, the Mac OS displays a rectangle, called a *selection rectangle*, and every icon it touches or encloses is selected. Icons are highlighted one-by-one as you drag over them, not en masse after you stop dragging. All items must be on the desktop or in a single window. Figure 5-9 shows an example of selecting several icons with a selection rectangle.

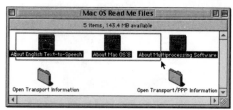

Figure 5-9: Selecting adjacent items by dragging a selection rectangle.

You can combine dragging with the Shift key. Pressing Shift while dragging a selection rectangle across unselected icons adds the enclosed icons to the current selection. Conversely, pressing Shift while dragging a selection rectangle across selected icons deselects the enclosed group without deselecting other icons (if any).

Selection by typing

When you know the name of an icon you want to select but aren't sure where it is in a window, you can select it more quickly by typing than by clicking. Typing also may be faster than clicking if the icon you want to select requires lots of scrolling to bring into view.

To select an icon by typing, simply type the first part of its name. You need to type only enough of the name to uniquely identify the icon you want. In a window in which every icon has a completely different name, for example, you need to type only the first letter of a name to select an icon. By contrast, in a folder where every icon begins with *Power*, you have to type those five letters plus enough additional letters to single out the icon you want. When selecting by typing, uppercase and lowercase letters are interchangeable.

While typing, you can select the next item alphabetically by pressing Tab or the previous item alphabetically by pressing Shift-Tab. Pressing an arrow key selects the icon nearest the currently selected icon in the direction that the arrow key points. To select the icon of the startup disk, press ⌘-Shift-up arrow. Table 5-1 summarizes keyboard selection techniques.

Table 5-1	
Selecting Icons by Typing	
To Select This	*Do This*
An icon	Type the icon's partial or full name
Next icon alphabetically	Press Tab
Previous icon alphabetically	Press Shift-Tab
Next icon up	Press up arrow
Next icon down	Press down arrow
Next icon left	Press left arrow
Next icon right	Press right arrow
Startup disk icon	Press ⌘-Shift-up arrow
Multiple icons	Press Shift while clicking each icon or while dragging to enclose them

Renaming icons

Clicking an icon highlights the icon and its name but does not select the icon name for editing. This behavior protects your icons from being accidentally renamed by your cat walking across your keyboard (which has actually happened to people using system software older than System 7.0). If you select an icon and begin typing, expecting your typing to rename the selected icon, you may be surprised to discover that your typing selects another icon whose name most closely matches what you're typing (as described previously).

To rename a disk, folder, program, document, or other item, you must explicitly select its name. Either click the name directly, or click the item's icon and then press Return or Enter. An icon whose name is selected for editing has a distinctive look: the icon is highlighted as usual, and the name has a box around it. The box does not appear when you just click the icon. Figure 5-10 shows an icon with its name selected and another icon with its name not selected.

Tip: For an additional visual cue that you have selected a name on a color or gray-scale monitor, make sure the text highlight color is something other than black and white. Then you know that a name highlighted in color (or gray) is ready for editing, whereas a name highlighted in black and white is not. To set the text highlight color, use the Appearance control panel (in Mac OS 8) or the Colors control panel (in Mac OS 7.0–7.6.1) as described in "Appearance and Behavior Modification" later in this chapter.

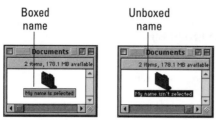

Figure 5-10: A boxed icon name is ready for editing.

Selecting all or part of an icon name

Right after you select an icon name, the whole name is selected. While the whole name is selected, you can replace it completely by typing a new name. If instead you want to select part of the name or an insertion point in the name, be sure you wait until the selection box appears around the name. The Finder may think you're double-clicking an icon and open it if you click the name and then immediately click, double-click, or drag in the name to select part of it.

Stop Waiting for the Editing Box

After clicking an icon name to edit it, you have to wait and wait for the editing box to appear around the name. To cut the wait short, just twitch the mouse and the name is highlighted for editing. You don't have to wait after clicking an icon's name if you immediately move the pointer. Another way to avoid waiting after clicking an icon's name is to move the insertion point by pressing the arrow keys. Click the name and immediately press the up arrow or the left arrow to move the insertion point to the beginning of the name, or immediately press the down arrow or the right arrow to move the selection point to the end. Once the selection point is established, pressing the left arrow moves it left and pressing the right arrow moves it right.

The length of time you must wait for the editing box to appear around an icon name you clicked depends on the duration of a double-click interval — approximately 1.9 seconds, 1.3 seconds, or 0.9 second, as set in the Mouse control panel. If you have trouble editing icon names without opening the item, try setting a briefer double-click speed with the Mouse control panel.

Copy, Paste, and Undo

While editing a name, you can use the Undo, Cut, Copy, and Paste commands in the Edit menu. Use the same methods for editing an icon name as you use to edit text in the Note Pad or Stickies programs (which come with Mac OS 8 and some earlier system software versions).

Besides selecting all or part of a name and copying it, you can also copy the entire name of any item by selecting its icon and choosing Copy from the Edit menu. Note that you do not have to select the name to copy it; you can just select the icon. Then you can choose the name of another icon (not just the icon this time) that's not in the same folder and choose Paste from the Edit menu to give it the copied name.

You can copy the names of multiple icons by selecting the icons and using the Copy command. If the total length of all selected icon names exceeds 256 characters, the Finder copies only the first 256 characters.

The Undo command works only as long as the icon name remains selected for editing. You cannot undo your changes to a name after you finish editing it. If you change your mind while editing a name and want to revert to the name the icon had before you began editing, simply delete the entire name and press Return or Enter. If an icon has no name when you press Return or Enter (ending the editing of the name), the Finder uses the icon's former name.

Renaming locked items

You can't change the name of a locked item or an item that you are sharing on a network. However, you can copy its entire name as just described. (For information on locking and unlocking items, see "Protecting Files, Folders, and Disks" in Chapter 7. For information on sharing items on a network, see "Designating Your Shared Items" in Chapter 18.)

Appearance and Behavior Modification

If you don't like the way icons, windows, and menus look and act, there are a few things you can do about it.

In the looks department, you can change the accent color that Mac OS 8 uses for menu selection, scroll boxes, and the like. You can change the system font that Mac OS 8 uses in menus, window titles, button names, dialog box messages, and elsewhere. You can control whether the platinum appearance introduced with Mac OS 8 applies to all applications or just to the ones that have adopted it. You can change the color that the Mac OS (version 7.0 or later) uses to highlight an icon name or other text that you select. You can change the color that Mac OS versions 7.0–7.6.1 use to shade window borders and scroll bars. And you can replace individual icons with your own pictures.

In the behavior department, you can change what action makes the Mac OS collapse or expand a window, and whether it plays a sound when it does that.

Accent and highlight color for Mac OS 8

You can choose an accent color or a highlight color with Mac OS 8's Appearance control panel. Mac OS 8 uses the accent color to highlight a menu item when you point at it and to decorate scroll boxes and other interface items. The highlight color is used to highlight text when you select it.

After opening the Appearance control panel, you click the Color button to see a sample of the current accent color and two other possibilities. You also see a sample of the current highlight color. You can scroll the sample accent colors to see a total of 17 available colors plus black and white; click any one you see to make it the accent color. A pop-up menu lists possible highlight colors; choose the one you want to use. Figure 5-11 shows the Color panel of the Appearance control panel.

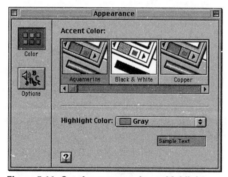

Figure 5-11: Set the accent color or highlight
color with the Appearance control panel in Mac OS 8.

Setting the accent color to Black & White effectively disables the normal platinum appearance of Mac OS 8. The resulting high-contrast display is easier for some visually impaired people to see.

Platinum appearance and system font for Mac OS 8

When Mac OS 8 applies the platinum appearance to all programs, you may notice some cosmetic flaws. They're harmless, but if you don't want to see them, you can turn off system-wide platinum appearance with the Appearance control panel.

Furthermore, the system font that Mac OS 8 uses for window titles, menus, buttons, and dialog boxes may cause problems in some applications. Some programs may actually refuse to open when the system font is set to anything but Chicago. To work around this problem, you can change the system font to Chicago with the Appearance control panel.

To change the system font or turn the system-wide platinum appearance on or off, click the Options button on the right side of the Appearance control panel. Then make your changes in the Appearances section on the right side of the control panel. You must restart your computer for changes to the system font or the system-wide platinum appearance to take effect.

Figure 5-12 shows the Options panel of the Appearance control panel.

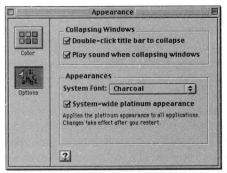

Figure 5-12: Set the system font or the system-wide platinum appearance with the Appearance control panel in Mac OS 8.

If you make changes to the system font or the system-wide platinum appearance because they cause problems with an program, contact the program's manufacturer to see if an updated version is available.

Window and highlight color for Mac OS 7.0–7.6.1

You can choose a window color or text highlight color with the Color control panel in Mac OS versions 7.0–7.6.1. For windows, a pop-up menu lists eight colors and black and white. Another pop-up menu lists eight colors, black and white, and the option to mix your own text highlight color. Figure 5-13 shows the choices in the Color control panel.

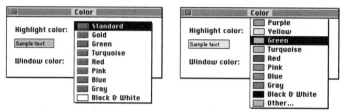

Figure 5-13: Set the window color (left) or highlight color (right) with the Color control panel in Mac OS 7.0–7.6.1.

The window color you choose does not apply to tool palettes and special-purpose windows created by some application programs. Although you can create your own text highlight color, you can't create your own window-shading color by using the Color control panel.

Collapsing windows

It's up to you whether windows expand and collapse when you double-click their title bars. It's also up to you whether the Mac OS plays a little sound effect whenever you collapse or expand a window. You control the collapsing window behavior of Mac OS 8 with clearly labeled check boxes in the Options section of the Appearance control panel (previously shown in Figure 5-12).

With Mac OS 7.5–7.6.1, you control collapsing window behavior with the WindowShade control panel. In this control panel, you can set the number of times you must click a window's title bar to hide the window (or show the window if it's already hidden). You can designate one or more keys that you must press while clicking a window's title bar for WindowShade to do its work. You can also turn sound effects on or off. Figure 5-14 shows the WindowShade control panel in System 7.5.

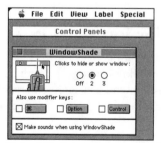

Figure 5-14: Setup window collapsing with the WindowShade control Panel in Mac OS 7.5–7.6.1.

Custom icons

Would you like to see dinosaurs or hummingbirds on your desktop instead of
ordinary icons? The Mac OS (versions 7.0 and later) lets you replace the icons
of individual documents, programs, folders, and disks with your own pictures.
Figure 5-15 shows some examples of custom icons.

There are icon collections available free on the Internet, from online information
services such as America Online, and from user groups. You can also make icons
from clip-art that you get from those sources or on disk. You can even create your
own icons with a graphics program.

Figure 5-15: Icons your way.

Installing a custom icon

To replace an icon with a picture, first select the picture you want to use for the
icon and copy it with the Copy command (in the Edit menu). Then go to the
Finder and find the icon you want to replace. Select the icon (click it once) and
choose Get Info from the Finder's File menu. In the Info window, click the
icon to select it and use the Paste command (in the Edit menu) to replace it
with the picture you just copied. You can also copy an icon from an Info
window and paste it into a different Info window. Figure 5-16 shows an Info
window with a custom icon pasted in.

For best results, the picture you use for a custom icon should measure 32 by 32
pixels (dots). Multiples of this size, such as 64 by 64, 128 by 128, or 256 by 256,
may also yield acceptable results. If your picture is larger than 32 by 32, the
Finder reduces it proportionally to fit that amount of space when you replace
an icon with it. Reducing a picture distorts it, especially if the original size is an
odd or fractional multiple of the final size. If your picture is smaller than 32 by
32, the Finder centers it on a white 32 by 32 square.

Boxed icon selected for
cut, copy, or paste

**Figure 5-16: A custom icon pasted
into an item's Info window.**

If you duplicate or make an alias of an item with a custom icon, the duplicate or alias inherits the custom icon. (To learn about duplicating items, see Chapter 7. To learn about making an alias, see Chapter 12.)

You cannot replace the icon of a locked item, open document, or open program. Nor can you replace system software icons such as the System Folder, Finder, Control Panels Folder, and Trash. (You can replace individual control panel icons, however.)

Reverting to a standard icon

To revert to an item's standard icon, select the item, choose Get Info from the Finder's File menu, select the icon in the Info window, and choose Clear or Cut from the Edit menu.

Desktop Background

When it comes to the overall appearance of the screen, nothing has more impact than changing the desktop's background. In addition to changing the background pattern, with Mac OS 8 you have the option of covering the pattern with a picture. Depending on your system software version, you use the Desktop Picture control panel (Mac OS 8 and later) or the Desktop Patterns control panel (Mac OS 7.5–7.6.1).

Desktop pictures and patterns with Mac OS 8

With Mac OS 8, you change the look of the desktop by selecting a background picture or pattern in the Desktop Picture control panel. After opening the control panel, you click a button that corresponds to the type of desktop background you want to see, pattern or picture, and then pick the specific background you want.

Mac OS 8 desktop pattern

If you click the Pattern button in the Desktop Pictures control panel, the control panel shows one pattern from the set of available patterns. You can page through the available patterns by clicking the scroll arrows. When you see a pattern you like, click the Set Desktop button to make that pattern the desktop pattern. Figure 5-17 shows the desktop pattern controls in the Mac OS 8 Desktop Picture control panel.

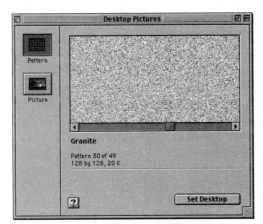

Figure 5-17: Set a desktop pattern with the Desktop Pictures control panel in Mac OS 8.

You can remove the pattern currently displayed in the control panel by choosing Cut or Clear from the Edit menu. After cutting a pattern, you can use the Paste command to store it in the Scrapbook.

To modify one of the patterns, first copy it by choosing the Copy command from the Edit menu. Then open a paint program and paste the copied image into it by choosing Paste from the Edit menu. Make changes to the pasted pattern with the program's painting tools and commands. Select the modified pattern in the paint program, and use the Copy command to make a copy of it. Finally, open the Desktop Pictures control panel and use the Paste command to add the copied pattern to the set of available desktop patterns.

You can create a new desktop pattern with a graphics program, a scanner, or other graphics source. Select the image you want to use as a desktop pattern, copy it, switch to the Desktop Picture control panel, and paste.

After pasting a pattern into the Desktop Pictures control panel, you can name it with the Edit Pattern Name command in the Edit menu. (You can't use this command to change the name of a preinstalled pattern.)

Mac OS 8 desktop picture

If you click the Picture button in the Desktop Pictures control panel, the control panel shows a reduced view of the current desktop picture or a sample of the current desktop pattern if there is currently no desktop picture. You use the controls at the bottom of the control panel to set a picture as the desktop background. Figure 5-18 shows a sample picture in the Desktop Picture control panel.

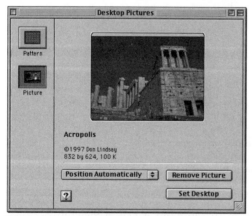

Figure 5-18: Set a desktop picture with the Desktop Pictures control panel in Mac OS 8.

If the control panel shows a reduced view of a desktop picture that you don't want to use, click the Remove Picture button. The Remove Picture button then changes to a Select Picture button, and the control panel displays a sample of the desktop pattern that's currently set.

When the control panel shows a sample of the current desktop pattern, you can select a picture to overlay it by clicking the Select Picture button. The control panel displays a standard Open dialog box in which you select a picture file that you want to use as a desktop picture. A check box at the bottom of the dialog box controls the display of picture previews on the left side of the dialog box. (For more information on the Open dialog box, see "Opening Documents" in Chapter 8.) Figure 5-19 shows an example of the dialog box in which you select a desktop picture file.

Figure 5-19: Selecting a desktop picture file.

You can adjust the position of the currently selected picture on the screen by using the pop-up menu next to the Remove Picture button in the Desktop Pictures control panel. This setting compensates for any difference between the size of the screen and the size of the selected picture. The setting Position Automatically uses optional alignment and positioning information stored in the picture file by the person who created the picture. If the picture doesn't have that information, the control panel scales the picture to fit the screen without changing the picture's aspect ratio. If you choose a different setting, you can see the effect by looking at the reduced view in the control panel.

Tip: To have the Mac OS randomly choose a different desktop picture each time you restart the computer, drag a folder of pictures to the sample desktop area of the Desktop Pictures control panel.

If the picture you select for a desktop picture is on a CD or other removable disk that is not available the next time you start up or restart the computer, the desktop pattern will be displayed instead. If you want your desktop picture to always be available, copy it to your hard disk and select that copy with the Desktop Picture control panel.

If you have selected a desktop picture and your computer runs low on memory, you may notice the screen redrawing slowly after you close a window. If this happens, try using a desktop pattern instead of the desktop picture.

Desktop patterns with Mac OS 7.5–7.6.1

With Mac OS 7.5 through 7.6.1, you can select a desktop pattern from the Desktop Patterns control panel. It displays a sample of one desktop pattern from a set of available patterns, and you can scroll through the available patterns. Two numbers below the large sample of the pattern tell you which of the total number of available patterns you are seeing. When you see a pattern you want to use, click the Set Desktop Pattern button at the bottom of the window. Figure 5-20 shows the Desktop Pattern control panel in Mac OS 7.6.1.

Figure 5-20: Set a desktop pattern with the Desktop Patterns control panel in Mac OS 7.5–7.6.1.

You can use the Cut, Copy, and Paste commands from the Edit menu to remove a pattern, copy it to a painting program for editing, or insert a new pattern copied from a graphics program.

Tip: With the Desktop Patterns control panel, you can also change the pattern that appears in the background of utility program windows such as Find File, Calculator, and Scrapbook. Here's how: Open the Desktop Patterns control panel, and scroll to find a pattern you like. Press Option to change the Set Desktop Pattern button to Set Utilities Pattern, and click the button. Whatever pattern you set will be the same for all the utility windows; you can't set a different pattern for each utility.

Keyboard and Mouse Adjustments

Another part of the basic Mac OS interface isn't something you look at. It's something, actually two things, you touch — namely the keyboard and the mouse, trackpad, or trackball. Like many aspects of the Mac OS, the behavior of the keyboard and the mouse, trackpad, or trackball is adjustable to allow for differences among users. If you find yourself becoming frustrated or impatient as you use the mouse, trackball, or trackpad, you may be able to solve the problem by changing its sensitivity. Similarly, if you type a character repeatedly when you mean to type it only once, you can adjust the keyboard sensitivity.

Setting keyboard sensitivity

When you press almost any key on the keyboard and hold it down, the computer types that character repeatedly as long as you keep the key down. (The ⌘, Option, Control, Caps Lock, and Esc keys don't repeat.) In the Keyboard control panel, you can change how quickly the characters repeat and how long you must hold down a key before the repeat feature kicks in. If you find repeating keys annoying rather than handy, you can disable the repeat by selecting Off in the Delay Until Repeat section of the control panel. Figure 5-21 shows the Keyboard control panel as it looks in Mac OS 8 and Mac OS 7.6.

The Keyboard control panel also allows you to choose a keyboard layout. You use this option when you want to type in a different language. (For more information on using different languages with your computer, see "WorldScript" in Chapter 21.)

The Easy Access control panel gives you some other ways to adjust how your keyboard responds to your typing. It's especially helpful for people with disabilities. (For detailed information on Easy Access, see Chapter 10.)

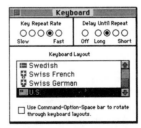

Figure 5-21: Set keyboard sensitivity in the Keyboard control panel of Mac OS 8 (left) and earlier system software versions (right).

Setting mouse, trackpad, or trackball sensitivity

You can change the way the Mac OS responds to your manipulation of your computer's mouse or trackball by setting options in the Mouse control panel. On a PowerBook with a trackpad, you adjust its responsiveness with the Trackpad control panel. Figure 5-22 shows the Mouse and Trackpad control panels as they look in Mac OS 8.

Figure 5-22: Set mouse or trackball sensitivity in the Mouse control panel and trackpad sensitivity in the Trackpad control panel.

The Mouse Tracking option (Mouse control panel) or Tracking Speed option (Trackpad control panel) determines the *tracking speed* — how fast the pointer moves as you glide the mouse, trackpad, or trackball. This setting is a matter of personal taste. If you feel that the pointer doesn't keep up, try a faster setting. If you often lose track of the pointer as you move it, try a slower one. Often, when you switch from a small monitor to a large one, you need to switch to a faster tracking speed because the pointer has a longer distance to travel from the menu bar to the Trash.

The Double-Click Speed option determines how quickly you must double-click for the Mac OS to perceive your two clicks as one double-click rather than two separate, unrelated clicks. When you select a double-click speed, the mouse button pictured in the Mouse control panel or the trackpad button pictured in the Trackpad control panel flashes to demonstrate the double-click interval you've selected.

In addition, the Double-Click Speed option determines how long you can hold down the mouse, trackpad, or trackball button when you click a menu title and still have Mac OS 8 interpret the gesture as a click so that the menu stays displayed after you release the mouse button. The shorter the double-click speed, the more quickly you must press and release. If you don't release within the allotted time, Mac OS 8 interprets the gesture as a press instead of a click and puts away the menu when you release.

Getting Onscreen Help

If you have a question about an object in the Finder or another part of the Mac OS software, or you aren't sure how to accomplish a task, the Mac OS itself provides a source of advice as close as the Help menu (referred to as the Guide menu in Mac OS 7.5–7.6.1). Through the Help menu, you can access two onscreen help systems, one that briefly explains objects you point at on the screen and another that interactively guides you step-by-step through tasks. Plus, if you're using a program that includes a help system of its own, the Help menu may include commands for reaching that more extensive information. Figure 5-23 shows the Help menu in the Finder of Mac OS 8 and System 7.5.

 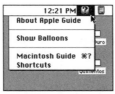

Figure 5-23: The Finder's Help menu in Mac OS 8 (left) and its Guide menu in earlier system Software versions (right).

Balloon help

When you need immediate information about objects you see onscreen, you can turn on Mac OS *balloon help*. With balloon help on, you position the pointer over an object and a concise description of it appears in a cartoon-style balloon. The balloon points to the object and tells you what the object is, what it does, what happens when you click it, or some portion of this information. You do not have to press any keys or click anything to make help balloons appear. Figure 5-24 shows an example of balloon help.

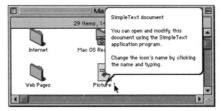

Figure 5-24: A help balloon describes the object under the pointer.

All system software versions 7.0 and later have the balloon help capability. However, not all objects have help balloons, especially objects in application programs (more on that shortly).

Turning balloon help on and off

You turn on balloon help by choosing Show Balloons from the Help menu. That command then changes to Hide Balloons, and choosing it again turns off balloon help.

Working with balloon help on

Everything works normally when balloon help is on. Using balloon help does not put the Mac OS into help-only mode. It's like someone is standing over your shoulder and describing onscreen objects to you.

Help balloons appear whether or not you press the mouse button. You click, double-click, and otherwise use programs normally, except you may perceive a slight delay as help balloons come and go when you move the pointer slowly across items that have balloon help descriptions.

The object that a help balloon describes may be large or small and individual or collective. For example, the Close box in the active window's title bar has its own help balloon. In contrast, an inactive window has one balloon for the whole window. Sometimes a help balloon describes a whole group, as in the Mouse control panel, where one balloon tells you about the seven settings for the Mouse Tracking option. Figure 5-25 shows the help balloons for a Close box and the Mouse Tracking option.

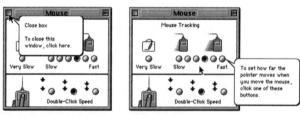

Figure 5-25: Help balloons vary in scope.

Moving the pointer slowly over several objects that have help balloons opens and closes balloons in sequence. To prevent excessive flashing of help balloons, they do not appear when you move the pointer quickly. For a help balloon to appear, the pointer must be in the same area for about one-tenth of a second or longer. You cannot change this timing.

What balloon help knows

Balloon help knows about all standard objects in the Macintosh interface. They include windows in general, system software icons, the Apple menu, the Help menu, the Application menu, standard parts of Open and Save dialog boxes (described in Chapter 8), and the Page Setup and Print dialog boxes (described in Chapter 15). Balloon help cannot describe a specific program's menu commands, window contents, dialog boxes, and so on unless the program's developer or publisher has included the necessary information. For example, Apple has provided complete balloon help for the Finder, standard control panels, and many of the accessory and utility programs that come with the Mac OS.

Apple Guide

The Mac OS (versions 7.5 and later) includes a help system that goes far beyond balloon help's answers to your "What is this?" questions. Called *Apple Guide*, this help system answers your "How do I . . . ?" and "Why can't I . . . ?" questions. It shows and tells you how to get things done while you actually do them. Step-by-step instructions appear in a guide window, which floats above all other windows. As you move from step to step, Apple Guide may coach you by marking an object onscreen with a circle, arrow, or underline. Figure 5-26 shows an example of an Apple Guide instruction and coaching mark.

Apple Guide watches what you do and can adjust its steps if you work ahead or make a mistake. In some cases, Apple Guide will actually perform a simple operation for you, such as opening a control panel.

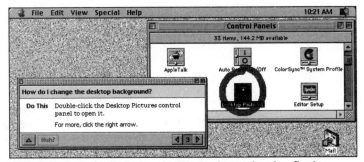

Figure 5-26: Apple Guide displays step-by-step instructions in a floating window and draws coaching marks to point out objects onscreen.

Notice that the Apple Guide window has a Zoom box, and in Mac OS 8 it also has a Collapse box. You can use these controls to temporarily shrink the window so you can see what's underneath it, and then use them again to restore the window.

Bringing up Apple Guide

You can bring up Apple Guide by choosing a command from the Help menu. For example, in the Mac OS 8 Finder you choose the Help command. In earlier versions of the Finder, you choose Mac OS Guide or Macintosh Guide. While you're using another program, look for a Help menu command that begins with the name of the program and ends with the word Guide, such as SimpleText Guide. If the Help menu lists only the About Help and Show Balloons commands, then the program you're using doesn't have Apple Guide help.

You can also bring up Apple Guide help from some control panels by clicking a button labeled with a question mark in the control panel.

When you bring up Apple Guide by choosing a Help menu command or clicking a help button, you initially see the Apple Guide topics window. A title at the top of the window tells you what software the help covers. For example, Mac OS Help covers a broad variety of system software topics but SimpleText Guide covers only topics related to SimpleText.

The Apple Guide topics window usually includes three large buttons labeled Topics, Index, and Look For. You click one of those buttons to choose how you want to find help on a task or a term: by scanning a list of topics, by browsing an index, or by looking for words in the guide. One of the three methods probably suits you better than the others, but try them all if you have trouble finding a task or term by using your favorite method.

The Apple Guide help that comes with some software doesn't offer choices for finding help. An example is the AppleCD Audio Player program, which comes with the Mac OS 8 and some earlier system software versions, and which offers only scanning by topic.

Scanning help topics

To see a list of help topics, click the Topics button at the top of the Apple Guide topics window. Clicking a topic on the left side of the topics window displays a list of specific tasks and terms on the right side. If the list on the right includes headings in bold, you can show and hide a heading's subordinate phrases by clicking the triangle next to the heading. Figure 5-27 shows an example of scanning Apple Guide topics with some headings expanded and others collapsed.

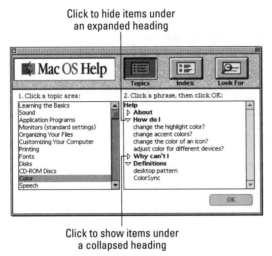

Figure 5-27: Scanning the list of topics in Apple Guide.

Browsing the help index

To browse an Apple Guide index, click the Index button in the Apple Guide topics window. Apple Guide displays an alphabetical list of key terms used in the guide. You can scroll through the index with the scroll bar. You can type the first part of a term you want to look up in the index, and the index instantly scrolls to the index entry that most closely matches what you typed. You can also scroll the index to entries starting with a particular letter of the alphabet by dragging the pointer at the top of the index list to that letter or by simply clicking that letter. You can't see all 26 letters of the alphabet at the top of the index list, but you can see more by clicking and dragging the pointer slightly past the last letter you can see. Clicking an entry in the index displays a list of tasks in which that entry appears. Figure 5-28 shows an example of browsing an Apple Guide index.

Drag the marker
or click a letter to
go to that letter

Drag the marker to
either end of the letter
bar to see more letters

Figure 5-28: Browsing an index in Apple Guide.

Searching help for key words

To have Apple Guide look for words you specify, click the Look For button in
the Apple Guide topics window. Then on the left side of the window click the
arrow button and type a key word or two that describe the step-by-step
instructions you want to see. When you click the Search button (or press
Return or Enter) a list of relevant tasks appears. Figure 5-29 shows an example
of searching Apple Guide for a key word.

Figure 5-29: Searching for help in Apple Guide.

Following step-by-step instructions

When you double-click an item on the right side of the Apple Guide topics window (or select the item and click OK), the topics window goes away. After a brief pause, another Guide window appears with an introduction to the task or a definition of the term you selected in the topics window. Figure 5-30 shows an example of the step-by-step window.

Figure 5-30: The first Apple Guide step describes the task or defines the term.

Read the information in the Guide window and follow any instructions it gives you. To go to the next step in a multiple-step task, click the right-pointing arrow at the bottom right of the Guide window. To back up one step, click the left-pointing arrow.

If you decide that you have selected the wrong task or term, you can return to the topics window by clicking the Topics button at the bottom of the Guide window. The Topics button may be labeled with an up-pointing arrow, a question mark, or the word Topics. You can also put away Apple Guide altogether by closing all guide windows.

At each new step, the guide may draw a circle, line, or arrow onscreen to point out a menu title or other object you must use to complete the step. These coaching marks appear in red or another color on a color monitor. If the step calls for you to choose from a menu, Apple Guide colors the menu item you should choose as well. On a black-and-white screen, it underlines the menu item.

If the Guide window mentions something you don't understand, try clicking the Huh? button at the bottom of the Guide window for clarification. (This button may be labeled I'm Stuck.) Clicking this button brings up another Guide window that may contain a definition of a term or begin step-by-step instructions for accomplishing a task related to the task you initially chose. For example, clicking Huh? in Step 2 of the task "How do I bring a window to the front?" brings up the task "How do I hide or show windows?"

If you work ahead of the step currently displayed in the Guide window, Apple Guide can adjust itself to catch up. When you click the right-pointing arrow to go to the next step, Apple Guide skips ahead to the next step that matches your location in the task.

While you're following the steps in Apple Guide, you can still use your computer normally. If the Guide window is in your way, you can drag it somewhere else or click its zoom box to make it smaller; click again to make it larger. If you're using Mac OS 8, you can collapse a Guide window into its title bar by clicking its Collapse box. If you're using Mac OS 7.5–7.6.1, you can collapse the Guide window according to the setup in the WindowShade control panel (described in "Appearance and Behavior Modification" in Chapter 5).

If you have not properly completed a step when you click the right-pointing arrow at the bottom of the Guide window, Apple Guide explains what you need to do to get back on track.

What Apple Guide knows

The Mac OS (versions 7.5 and later) comes with step-by-step help for system-level tasks such as printing, file sharing, control panel use, and troubleshooting. Mac OS 8 and some earlier system software versions also include Apple Guide help for SimpleText, AppleCD Audio Player, Apple Video Player, and OpenDoc. Developers and system administrators can create additional help, which can cover tasks that involve multiple applications. Apple Guide's usefulness depends greatly on how well crafted the help procedures for individual tasks are. Apple has set a good example with its system-level help procedures.

Putting away Apple Guide

When you are finished with Apple Guide, you put it away by closing the Guide window.

Other help

Many programs add how-to help, onscreen reference material, or other items to the Help menu. For example, many Claris and Microsoft products list onscreen help commands in the Help menu.

Taking a Screen Picture

You can take a picture of the whole screen at any time by pressing ⌘-Shift-3. Each picture you take appears at the root level of your startup disk as a file named Picture 1, Picture 2, and so on. You can view the screen pictures with SimpleText.

Rather than taking a picture of the whole screen, you can take a picture of a window or any rectangular portion of the screen if you are using Mac OS 7.6 or later. Use the following keystrokes:

❖ **Rectangular region:** Press ⌘-Shift-4 and then drag to select a rectangular region that you want to take a picture of (omits the pointer from the picture).

❖ **Window:** Press ⌘-Shift-4-Caps Lock and then click a window that you want to take a picture of (omits the pointer from the picture).

❖ **Cancel:** Press the Space bar to cancel a ⌘-Shift-4 combination.

❖ **Picture on Clipboard:** Add the Control key to any of the screen capture keystrokes to copy the picture to the Clipboard instead of saving it as a picture file on the startup disk. With the ⌘-Shift-4 combinations, you can alternatively press the Control key while selecting the region or window you want to take a picture of.

When using step-by-step onscreen help with system software versions 7.5.3 and later, you can copy a picture of the help window to the Clipboard by pressing the Option key and clicking the panel. This function does not work in all help windows, and it does not apply to items in the Help (or Guide) menu that are not based on Apple Guide. Examples of help based on Apple Guide include Mac OS Help (Mac OS 8 and later), Mac OS Guide (Mac OS 7.6 and 7.6.1), and Macintosh Guide (Mac OS 7.5–7.5.5). Most application-specific online help is not based on Apple Guide.

Summary

After reading this chapter, you know about the changes that Mac OS 8 brings to menus, windows, buttons and other controls, icons in the Finder, and the desktop background. The platinum appearance of Mac OS 8 makes menus, windows, controls, and many icons look more three dimensional. In addition, menus are gray with color accents instead of black and white. You can change the background pattern with any version of the system software, but Mac OS 8 gives you more elaborate choices and it lets you cover the pattern with a picture. You can take a picture of all or part of the screen by pressing a combination of keys.

The function of menus, windows, and icons work has improved along with the appearance. You can hold menus open the traditional way, or let Mac OS 8 hold them open for you. In addition to the standard menus in the menu bar, the Mac OS 8 Finder can display contextual menus. Mac OS 8 also gives you two more windows controls than earlier system versions: the collapse box and window frames you can drag.

The methods for selecting icons individually or in a group are the same in Mac OS 8 as in earlier systems. The procedure for editing an icon's name also hasn't changed since System 7.0.

If you don't like the way icons, windows, and menus look and act, you can change some aspects of their appearance and behavior. You can give each file, folder, and disk a custom icon. You can change other appearances and behaviors with the Appearance control panel in Mac OS 8 or the Color and WindowShade control panels prior to Mac OS 8.

Besides fine-tuning the things you look at, you can also adjust the responsiveness of the keyboard and either the mouse, trackpad, or trackball with the Keyboard, Mouse, and Trackpad control panels.

In addition, you now know that you can get two kinds of onscreen help: Balloon Help and Apple Guide.

The Mac OS 8 innovations described in this chapter are just the beginning. Many more improvements are covered in the next two chapters.

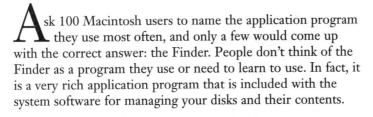

CHAPTER SIX

Get Organized with the Finder

IN THIS CHAPTER

- **Simplifying the Finder** in Mac OS 8

- **Opening and closing disks**, folders, and files

- **Viewing folder and disk contents** in different formats and levels of detail

- **Working with files and folders**: creating a new folder, copying and moving items, duplicating an item, and deleting files and folders

- **Working with disks**: removing and erasing disks

Ask 100 Macintosh users to name the application program they use most often, and only a few would come up with the correct answer: the Finder. People don't think of the Finder as a program they use or need to learn to use. In fact, it is a very rich application program that is included with the system software for managing your disks and their contents.

This chapter describes the simple ways you can organize the stuff on your computer with the Finder. You can open and close disks, folders, and files. You can view the contents of each folder and disk as icons, as a list, and in Mac OS 8 as buttons. You can create folders and you can copy, move, duplicate, and delete folders and files. You can also remove or erase disks, if you have more than one on your desktop.

Once you've mastered the skills presented in this chapter, you're ready for the advanced techniques covered in other chapters. The next chapter gets into the more elaborate ways you can organize your disks and their contents. Chapter 8 discusses opening and saving programs and documents. Chapter 9 describes the organization of the System Folder. Aliases are covered in Chapter 12 and file sharing in Chapter 18.

Simple Finder

A quick scan of the Finder's menus gives you an idea of its capabilities. Not all of them are essential. If you'd rather not bother with the Finder's more advanced capabilities, you can simplify its menus in the Finder's Preferences dialog box. To do this, choose Preferences from the Edit menu to bring up the Finder's Preferences dialog box, and then click the Simple Finder option to turn it on. (The option is turned on when you see a check mark in the option's check box.) Figure 6-1 shows the Preferences dialog box with the Simple Finder option turned off.

Figure 6-1: Setting the Simple Finder option.

In the interest of simplicity, you can ignore the other options in the Preferences dialog box. For more information about them, see Chapter 7.

The Preferences command and the Simple Finder option are available only in Mac OS 8. If you're using an earlier system software version, you can't suppress the Finder's more advanced features and commands, you can only ignore them.

Opening and Closing Disks, Folders, and Files

When you want to see what's in a disk, folder, or file, you open it. You open a program when you want to use it to view or edit the kinds of documents it can create. Opening a disk, a folder, or a file that is a document displays its contents in a window. Opening a file that is a program displays its menus in the menu bar and may display a document window for that program (not all programs automatically display a document window). When you don't want to see a window any more, you can close it. (You can also make a window into a pop-up window in the title bar, as described in Chapter 7.)

There are two ways to open a disk, folder, or file. You can select its icon and choose Open from the File menu, or you can simply double-click the icon. Instead of double-clicking an icon, you click it once if it's part of a square button in a Mac OS 8 window (more about these buttons in the next section). Note that the File menu shows a keyboard shortcut for the Open command, ⌘-O, which means you can also open an icon by selecting it and pressing ⌘-O.

There are also two ways to close a window. You can choose Close from the File menu (its keyboard shortcut is ⌘-W), or you can simply click the window's close box. To close all open windows at once, press the Option key while closing one of the windows you want to close. This shortcut works with the Close command and the close box.

The Open and Close commands also appear in the contextual menu that pops up when you hold down the Control key and click an icon in Mac OS 8, as described in the previous chapter. (To see contextual menus, the Simple Finder option must be turned off with the Preferences command in Mac OS 8's Finder.)

Tip: You can open a folder or file and close the window it's in at the same time. Just press the Option key while opening the item. This trick works whether you double-click or choose the Open command.

Viewing Folder and Disk Contents

After opening a folder or disk, you see in its window the files and folders it contains. You can choose to see the contents of a folder or disk window as icons that you can move around or as an ordered list of item names and other facts. If you're using Mac OS 8, you can also choose to see the contents of a folder or disk window as buttons that you open by clicking once (instead of double-clicking).

Regardless of a window's view format, you can scroll or size the window to see more of its contents.

Choosing a view

You choose a view format from the View menu. With Mac OS 8, you choose one of three basic formats: icons, buttons, or list. (The Views menu has additional commands for choosing variations of the basic formats if the Simple Finder option is turned off in the Preferences dialog box, as described in the next chapter.) Figure 6-2 shows examples of the three basic view formats.

In system versions earlier than Mac OS 8, you choose one of seven specific formats from the View menu: icon, small icon, name, size, kind, label, or date. The icon view is the same as the icon view in Mac OS 8, and the small icon view is a variation of it. The other views are all variations of the list view in Mac OS 8. You can't view a folder or disk window as buttons in earlier system versions. A window set to button view in Mac OS 8 appears in icon view if you display it in an earlier version of system software.

Figure 6-2: Window contents viewed as icons (top), as buttons (middle), or as a list (bottom).

Working with list views

List views can pack a lot of information into a window, and you can use that information to organize the list view. You can sort the list by any of the column headings at the top of the view. You can see the contents of enclosed folders in an indented outline format. Also, you can select items contained in more than one enclosed folder.

Changing the sort order

When you initially view a window as a list, the items are arranged alphabetically by name. You can sort the list in a different order by clicking one of the column headings near the top of the window. For example, to list the items in the order they were last modified, click the Date Modified heading.

A quick glance at the column headings tells you the sort order. The dark heading indicates the sort order in a Mac OS 8 window. In system versions earlier than Mac OS 8, the heading that indicates sort order is underlined.

Expanding and collapsing folders

You can open folders to see what's inside, but if you layer lots of folders within folders, windows clutter your screen by the time you reach the innermost folder. There is a faster and easier way. The Finder displays list views in an indented outline format. The levels of indentation in the outline show how folders are nested. The indented outline provides a graphical representation of a folder's organization. You can look through and reorganize folders without opening additional windows. Figure 6-3 shows an example of a list view with both expanded and collapsed folders.

Internet			
14 items, 141.7 MB available			
Name	Date Modified	Size	Kind
About Internet Access	Fri, May 30, 1997, 12:00 PM	33K	SimpleText read-
Claris Emailer Lite 1.1 v4	Mon, Jun 30, 1997, 2:20 PM	17K	alias
▷ Internet Applications	Mon, Jun 30, 1997, 2:13 PM	–	folder
Internet Dialer	Mon, Jun 30, 1997, 2:20 PM	17K	alias
Internet Setup Assistant	Mon, Jun 30, 1997, 2:20 PM	17K	alias
▽ Internet Utilities	Mon, Jun 30, 1997, 2:13 PM	–	folder
▽ Aladdin	Mon, Jun 30, 1997, 2:59 PM	–	folder
DropStuff w/EE™ 4.0 Installer	Mon, Mar 17, 1997, 12:00 PM	512K	application progra
▷ DropStuff™ 4.0 Folder	Mon, Jun 30, 1997, 2:59 PM	–	folder
▷ Stuffit Expander™	Mon, Jun 30, 1997, 2:16 PM	–	folder
▷ Client Access	Mon, Jun 30, 1997, 2:17 PM	–	folder
▷ Internet Config	Mon, Jun 30, 1997, 2:17 PM	–	folder
Internet Setup Utility	Fri, May 30, 1997, 12:00 PM	347K	application progra
Netscape Navigator™ 3.01	Mon, Jun 30, 1997, 2:20 PM	17K	alias

Figure 6-3: A list view with expanded and collapsed folders.

Triangles next to folder names tell you whether the folders are expanded or collapsed. If a triangle points to the right, the folder next to it is collapsed and you cannot see its contents. If the triangle points down, the folder is expanded and you can see a list of the items in the folder indented below the folder name.

To expand a folder, click the triangle to the left of the folder's icon. When you expand a folder, the Finder remembers whether folders nested within it were previously expanded or collapsed and restores each to its former state. Figure 6-4 shows a folder before and after expanding it.

To collapse a folder, click the triangle to the left of the folder's icon. Figure 6-5 shows a folder before and after collapsing it.

Tip: To collapse a folder and all the folders nested within it, press Option while clicking the triangle of the outer folder. To expand a folder and all the folders nested within it, press Option while you click.

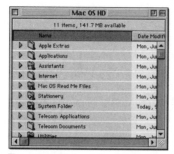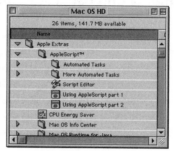

Figure 6-4: Click a left-pointing triangle to expand a folder.

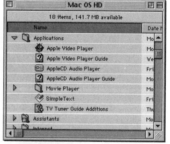

Figure 6-5: Click a down-pointing triangle to collapse a folder.

Selecting from multiple folders

After expanding several folders in a list view, you can select items from more than one of the expanded folders. To select an additional item, press Shift while clicking it. You can also select consecutive items by pressing Shift while dragging a selection rectangle across them. If you need to deselect a few items, Shift-click each item or Shift-drag across consecutive items. Figure 6-6 shows a window with items selected from several folders.

Mac OS HD			
23 items, 141.7 MB available			
Name	Date Modified	Size	Kind
▷ 📁 Assistants	Mon, Jun 30, 1997, 2:20 PM	–	folder
▽ 📁 Internet	Mon, Jun 30, 1997, 2:20 PM	–	folder
📄 About Internet Access	Fri, May 30, 1997, 12:00 PM	33K	SimpleTe
📄 Claris Emailer Lite 1.1 v4	Mon, Jun 30, 1997, 2:20 PM	17K	alias
▷ 📁 Internet Applications	Mon, Jun 30, 1997, 2:13 PM	–	folder
📄 Internet Dialer	Mon, Jun 30, 1997, 2:20 PM	17K	alias
📄 Internet Setup Assistant	Mon, Jun 30, 1997, 2:20 PM	17K	alias
▷ 📁 Internet Utilities	Mon, Jun 30, 1997, 2:13 PM	–	folder
📄 Netscape Navigator™ 3.01	Mon, Jun 30, 1997, 2:20 PM	17K	alias
▽ 📁 Mac OS Read Me Files	Mon, Jun 30, 1997, 2:01 PM	–	folder
📄 About English Text-to-Speech	Sun, Apr 20, 1997, 12:00 PM	33K	SimpleTe
📄 About Mac OS 8	Tue, Jun 3, 1997, 12:00 PM	50K	SimpleTe
📄 About Multiprocessing Software	Mon, May 19, 1997, 12:00 PM	50K	SimpleTe
📄 Open Transport Information	Mon, Jun 30, 1997, 2:01 PM	–	folder

Figure 6-6: Items selected from multiple folders.

Selected items remain selected if you expand folders in the same window. Selected items also remain selected if you collapse folders in the same window, except that any selected items in a folder you collapse are no longer selected.

QUICK TIPS

Finder Keyboard Shortcuts

Much of what you do with the mouse you can do with keyboard shortcuts instead. For instance, you can select an item in a folder or disk window (or the desktop, if no window is active) without using the mouse by typing the item's name or the first part of its name. Other keystrokes select an item near the currently selected item, open the item, and so on. The following table gives the details.

Objective	Action
Select an item by name	Type the item's full or partial name
Select the next item alphabetically	Tab
Select the previous item alphabetically	Shift-Tab
Select next item up, down, left, or right	Up arrow, down arrow, left arrow, or right arrow
Select the startup disk	⌘-Shift-up arrow
Select multiple items	Shift-click each item or Shift-drag across the items

(continued)

Objective	Action
Begin editing the selected item's name	Return or Enter
Insert at the beginning of a selected item name	Up arrow
Insert at the end of a selected item name	Down arrow
Move the insertion point in a selected item name	Left arrow or right arrow
Align (or don't align) icons or buttons (countermands Views control panel setting)	⌘-drag icon or button, Options, or Views
Copy an item to the desktop or another folder	Option-drag on the same disk
Make an alias (Mac OS 8 only)	⌘-Option-drag
Move selected items to the Trash (Mac OS 8 only)	⌘-Delete
Open the selected item	⌘-O or ⌘-down arrow
Open the selected item and close the active window	⌘-Option-O or ⌘-Option-down arrow or Option-double-click
Open the selected item's enclosing folder or disk	⌘-Up arrow
Open the selected item's enclosing folder or disk	⌘-Option-up arrow and close the active window
Open an enclosing folder or disk of the active window	⌘-click the window title and then choose from the pop-up menu
Zoom window to full size	Option-click zoom box
Expand the selected folder in a list view	⌘-right arrow
Expand the selected folder and its enclosed folders	⌘-Option-right arrow or Option-click the triangle
Expand all folders in the active window	⌘-A and then ⌘-right arrow
Expand all folders and their enclosed folders	⌘-A and then ⌘-Option-right arrow
Collapse the selected folder in a list view	⌘-Left arrow
Collapse the selected folder and its enclosed folders	⌘-Option-left arrow or Option-click the triangle
Collapse all folders in the active window	⌘-A and then ⌘-right arrow
Collapse all folders and their enclosed folders	⌘-A and then ⌘-Option-right arrow
Close a window	⌘-W
Close all windows	⌘-Option-W or Option-click the close box
Close a window while opening the selected item	⌘-Option-O or ⌘-Option-down arrow
Close a window and make the desktop active	⌘-Option-up arrow

(continued)

Objective	Action
Move a background window	⌘-drag
Hide the active program's windows	Option while making another program active
Make the desktop active	⌘-Shift-up arrow
Skip Trash warnings	Option while choosing Empty Trash
Erase a floppy disk	⌘-Option-Tab as you insert the disk
Cancel the operation in progress	⌘-period
Start up without extensions	Shift while starting up
Start up with Extensions Manager open	Space bar while starting up
Start up without internal hard disk	⌘-Option-Shift-Delete
Start up from a CD-ROM	C while starting up
Sleep mode (PowerBook only)	⌘-Shift-0 or Control-click menu bar clock
Sleep mode (System 7.5.1 and later)	Power or ⌘-Option-Power
Restart safely (System 7.5.1 and later)	Power or ⌘-Shift-Power
Shut down safely (System 7.5.1 and later)	Power or ⌘-Option-Shift-Power
Force active program to quit (lose unsaved work)	⌘-Option-Escape
Restart a crashed computer (lose unsaved work)	⌘-Control-Power
Rebuild the desktop	⌘-Option during startup or while inserting a disk
Reset Chooser and control panel settings stored	⌘-Option-P-R while starting up in parameter RAM (PRAM)

Seeing more contents

If you can't see everything in a window, you can scroll the window or change its size to see more. Each scroll bar becomes active only if using it would bring more into view.

Smart zooming

A window may not fit its content optimally after you expand or collapse folders in a list view, rearrange icons or buttons in an icon or button view, or simply change from one view to another. You can quickly size a window up or down to fit its contents and view format by clicking the zoom box. The Mac OS makes the window just as large as it needs to be to show as much of the window's contents as will fit on the screen. This smart zooming helps you make best use of your screen real estate.

Tip: If you do want to zoom a window to fill the screen (instead of just large enough to show the window's contents), press Option while clicking the zoom box.

Working with Files and Folders

There's a lot you can do with the Finder besides fiddling with the way you view the content of folders and disks. You can create a new folder. You can copy or move an item to another folder or disk. You can duplicate a file or folder in the same folder. You can also get rid of files and folders you don't want to keep.

Creating a new folder

You create a new folder with the New Folder command in the File menu. The new folder is created in the active window, or on the desktop if no window is active. This means you must open a disk or folder before you can create a folder inside it. If the disk or folder is already open but its window is covered by another window, click the window in which you want to create the folder to bring that window to the front. To create a folder on the desktop, click the startup disk icon (or any other desktop icon) to make the desktop active.

If you create a folder in the wrong place, don't sweat it. You can move it as described next.

Copying and moving items

To move an item to a different folder on the same disk, you just drag it to the window or icon of the destination folder. Similarly, you move an item to the *root level* (main level) of a disk by dragging it to the disk icon or window. To drag an item, you position the pointer over it, press the mouse button, and continue pressing while you move the mouse. The pointer moves across the screen and drags the item you pointed at along with it. You release the mouse button when you get the item positioned over the destination folder icon, disk icon, or window. You can tell when you have the item positioned over the destination because the Finder highlights it. The Finder highlights an icon by making it darker, and it highlights a window by drawing a gray or colored border inside the window frame.

You can move an item by dragging its icon or its name. In a list view, you can also drag an item by any text on the same line as the item's icon, such as its modification date or kind. In a Mac OS 8 window viewed as buttons, you can drag an item only by its name.

Tip: If you're working in a list view and want to move an item from an enclosed folder to the main level of the window, just drag the item to the window's status area. That's the space just below the title bar where the number of items in the window is reported.

Tip: If you change your mind while dragging and want to return the item you're dragging to its original location, just drag it up to the menu bar and release the mouse button. The Finder puts it back where you got it from.

To copy an item to another folder on the same disk, press Option while you drag the item to the destination folder. If you're using Mac OS 8, the pointer has a little plus sign when you Option-drag, reminding you that you're making a copy.

The Finder always copies an item when you drag it to a folder that's on another disk (or to another disk itself). Again, the Mac OS 8 Finder displays a little plus sign on the pointer when you drag an item over a folder (or a folder window) of a different disk. When you drag an item to another folder, the Finder figures out whether the destination folder is on the same disk as the source folder. If so, the Finder moves the items you're dragging to the destination folder. If the items you're dragging come from a different disk than the destination folder, the Finder copies the items you're dragging.

When you copy an item to a disk or folder that already contains an item by the same name, an alert box asks whether you want to replace the item at the destination. The alert tells you which of the like-named items is newer. If you copy a group of items and more than one of them has the same name as items at the destination, the alert doesn't name the duplicates. Figure 6-7 shows examples of the alerts that the Finder displays to verify replacement.

Figure 6-7: Confirm imminent replacement of an item (left) or items (right).

The Finder is also smart about copying an entire floppy disk to a hard disk. It puts the floppy disk's contents into a new folder on the hard disk and gives the folder the same name as the floppy. You can also copy a hard disk to a larger hard disk. You can even copy a disk to a folder on another disk.

Autoscrolling While Moving

You can scroll a window in the Finder without using the scroll bars. Simply place the pointer in the window, press the mouse button, and drag toward the area you want to view, as shown in the figure. Drag the pointer up, down, left, or right past the window's active area to begin scrolling. Dragging past a window corner scrolls diagonally.

As you drag, you can vary the scrolling speed. To scroll slowly, drag just to the window's edge (and continue pressing the mouse button). Increase scrolling speed by dragging beyond the window's edge. You can use this scrolling technique, known as *autoscrolling,* while performing the following operations:

❖ Moving an icon or group of icons to a new place in any visible window (Mac OS 7.6.1 and earlier autoscroll only the active window)

❖ Moving an item or group of items into a folder in any visible window (Mac OS 7.6.1 and earlier autoscroll only the active window)

❖ Dragging a selection rectangle around adjacent items in the active window to select them all

Be careful when autoscrolling while dragging a selected item or items, especially when autoscrolling to the left. If you accidentally move the pointer completely out of the window and release the mouse button, the Finder places the selected items on the desktop. You can return items from the desktop to their original folder by selecting them and using the Finder's Put Away command.

Drag past any edge
or corner of the window

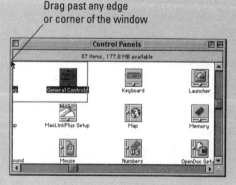

Duplicating an item

You can duplicate an item in the same folder by selecting it and choosing Duplicate from the File menu. If the item is a folder, the duplicate contains duplicates of everything in the original folder. You can also duplicate an item by Option-dragging it to another place in the same window. One more way to duplicate an item: choose Duplicate from the contextual menu that pops up when you Control-click the item. (To see contextual menus in Mac OS 8, the Simple Finder option must be turned off with the Preferences command.)

Copy Fitting

When copying batches of files from your hard drive to a floppy disk or other removable with little space available, you must do heavy mental addition to figure out which files will fit on the destination disk. If you try to copy too much, the Finder barks, "There is not enough room on the disk...." The Finder can help you figure out how many files fit on the destination disk. You'll need to use the Get Info command, and it's not available if you have turned on the Simple Finder option with the Mac OS 8 Finder's Preferences command. Here are the steps:

1. Create a new folder on the hard drive.

   In system versions earlier than Mac OS 8, the new folder must be in a window, not directly on the desktop.

2. Select the new folder and choose Get Info from the File menu to bring up the folder's Info window.

   Get Info also appears in the contextual menu that pops up when you Control-click a folder in Mac OS 8.

3. Begin dragging files into the folder.

   As you drag, the Finder updates the folder's size in its Info window. When the folder size approaches the amount of space available on the destination disk (1400K for a high-density floppy), you know that you've got enough to fill the disk and no more.

If the Trash is empty, you can collect items in it instead of in a specially created folder. This method has two advantages: you can quickly return all items to their original places with the Put Away command in the File menu (this command is not available in Mac OS 8 if you have turned on the Simple Finder option), and you don't have to wait for the Finder to make copies of items that come from several disks. (The Finder doesn't copy items to the Trash, but it must copy items you drag from one disk to a folder on another disk.) The Get Info command only reports the size of the Trash to the nearest K, however, whereas it gives you the exact number of bytes in a folder.

The Finder constructs the name of a duplicate item you create with the Duplicate command by suffixing the name with the word *copy*. Additional copies of the same item also have a serial number suffixed. Figure 6-8 shows an example of several duplicates of an item in the same folder.

Figure 6-8: How the Finder names duplicated items.

If any suffixes result in a name longer than 31 characters, the Finder removes characters from the end of the original item's name. For example, duplicating an item named June Income and Expense Report results in an item named June Income and Expense Re copy.

Colons Are Special

Icon names can't include colons because the Mac OS uses colons internally to specify the path through your folder structure to a file. A path name consists of a disk name, a succession of folder names, and a file name, with a colon between each pair of names. For example, the path name "Mac OS HD:System Folder:Control Panels:Memory" specifies the location of the Memory control panel on a startup disk named Mac OS HD. Putting a colon in a file name would confound the scheme for specifying paths, so the Finder won't let you do it.

Deleting files and folders

You get rid of files and folders you no longer want by dragging them to the Trash icon. When you drag a folder to the Trash, everything inside that folder goes to the Trash as well. You can also move an item to the Trash by choosing Move To Trash from the contextual menu that pops up when you Control-click the item. (To see contextual menus in Mac OS 8, you must have turned off the Simple Finder option with the Preferences command in the Finder.)

Tip: If you've turned off the Simple Finder option in Mac OS 8, you don't have to drag things to the Trash with the mouse. Pressing ⌘-Delete moves all selected items to the Trash. (This shortcut doesn't work prior to Mac OS 8 unless you install the free control panel Finder Options or an equivalent, as described in Chapter 25.)

Emptying the Trash

Your junk accumulates in the Trash until you explicitly tell the Finder to delete it. You do that by choosing Empty Trash from the Special menu or from the contextual menu that pops up when you Control-click the Trash.

The Finder does not remove locked items. If it encounters one while it is emptying the Trash, it displays an alert advising you that the Trash contains locked items and asking whether you want to delete the other items or stop deleting. To get rid of locked items in the Trash, press Option while choosing the Empty Trash command.

Back from the Trash

When you delete files by emptying the Trash, the disk space occupied by deleted files becomes immediately available for other files. The Empty Trash command removes a file's entry from the relevant disk's file directory. It also changes the disk's sector-allocation table to indicate that the disk sectors the file occupied are available for use by another file.

To save time, the command does not erase file contents in the now-available sectors. Until the system writes a new file over the deleted file's data, the Norton Utilities program from Symantec (408-253-9600, http://www.symantec.com) can resurrect the deleted file. Any blackguard with disk-utility software can retrieve files you deleted — or view any fragment of deleted files' contents — unless you erase their contents with Norton Utilities, Super Tools (described in Chapter 24), or equivalent software. There are actually companies that specialize in sifting through e-mail and other documents that unwary computer users thought they had eliminated by emptying the Trash.

Trash warnings

When you choose the Empty Trash command, the Finder tells you how many items the Trash contains and how much disk space they occupy. You decide whether to discard them all or cancel. Figure 6-9 shows an example of the alert that appears when you empty the Trash.

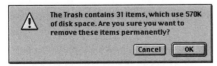

Figure 6-9: Confirm emptying the Trash.

Tip: You can disable the Trash warning by pressing Option while choosing the Empty Trash command.

Disable Trash Warning

If you always suppress the Trash warning by pressing the Option key when you choose the Empty Trash command, you may prefer to disable the warnings more permanently. To do that, select the Trash icon and choose Get Info from the File menu. This brings up the Trash Info window. At the bottom of that window, turn off the "Warn before emptying" option and close the Trash Info window. The figure shows the Trash Info window.

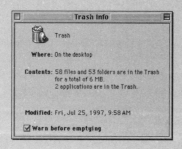

Trash contents

If an item you move to the Trash has the same name as an item already there, the Finder renames the item that's already there. Suppose, for example, that the Trash contains an item named Untitled and you dragged another like-named item there. The Finder renames the item already there to Untitled copy. If you later add another item named Untitled, the Finder changes Untitled copy to Untitled copy 2, changes Untitled to Untitled copy, and leaves the name of the item you just added unchanged. In other words, the item most recently added has the plain name and the least recently added has the highest number suffix.

The Trash contains all the items that you have dragged to it from all the disks whose icons are on the desktop. The Empty Trash command deletes the items from all disks involved. If there's a disk whose trashed items you don't want deleted yet, remove the disk from the desktop as described in the next section. The Empty Trash command doesn't affect disks whose icons are not on the desktop. If you can't remove the disk, you have no choice but to open the Trash and drag the items you don't want deleted onto the desktop or into a folder. Then use the Empty Trash command.

If you eject a floppy disk (and put away its icon) after dragging items from that disk to the Trash, those items disappear from the Trash, but the Finder does not delete them. They reappear in the Trash the next time you insert that disk. If you insert that floppy disk in another Mac, they appear in its Trash.

Tip: Sometimes the Trash contains a folder named Rescued Items. That folder contains former temporary files found when you started up your Macintosh. The Rescued Items folder appears only after a system crash. Although it's unlikely, you may be able to recreate your work up to the time of the system crash by opening the contents of the Rescued Items folder.

Shared Trash

If you're sharing someone else's disk or folder over a network and you drag an item from the shared disk to the Trash on your desktop, the item goes into your Trash, not into the Trash on the computer where the shared disk or folder resides. The item is removed from that computer if you use the Empty Trash command. From the opposite viewpoint, you do not know when someone sharing your folder drags items from it to his or her Trash. (The owner of a shared disk or folder can set access privileges to keep unauthorized people from dragging items from it to their Trash. For more information on file sharing, see Chapter 18.)

Working with Disks

There are two things you do with disks that you don't do with files or folders: remove them without deleting their contents, and erase them so they can be reused.

Removing disks

There are two ways to remove a disk: one is to use the Eject or Put Away menu command, and the other is to drag the disk to the Trash. With either method, you can eject a removable disk and remove its icon from the desktop, or you can eject and leave the icon behind.

Eject and Put Away commands

The official way to remove a floppy disk, CD-ROM disc, or other removable disk from your desktop in Mac OS 8 is to select its icon and choose Eject from the Special menu. You can also Control-click the disk icon to pop-up its contextual menu and choose Eject from it. (To see contextual menus in Mac OS 8, the Simple Finder option must be turned off with the Preferences command in the Finder.)

With Mac OS 7.0–7.6.1, you use the Put Away command in the File menu to remove a disk from the desktop. These commands remove the disk's icon from the desktop and make its contents unavailable. If the disk is a floppy disk, CD-ROM, or Zip disk, dragging its icon to the Trash ejects the disk from the disk drive. With other types of removable disks, you may have to push a button or flip a lever on the disk drive to remove the disk.

If you eject a disk with open windows in Mac OS 8 and later use the disk with an earlier system software version, the windows will be closed.

Dragging a disk to the Trash

The shortcut for removing a disk icon is to drag it to the Trash. Lots of people use this shortcut because it's so convenient, even though it doesn't exactly make sense. If you think about it, dragging a disk to the Trash could just easily mean you never want to use it again — erase it. By convention, dragging a disk to the Trash means you want to get rid of its icon, not its contents.

If you have more than one hard disk icon, you may be able to remove one that's not your startup disk by dragging the icon to the Trash. The Eject command doesn't work with most hard disk icons. This process, called *unmounting* the disk, makes its contents unavailable. The reverse process, called *mounting* the disk, happens every time you start up the computer. You can also mount disks using the Drive Setup utility program that comes with Mac OS 8, or a disk utility such as Mt. Everything (described in Chapter 24).

Ejecting a disk and leaving behind the icon

It's also possible to eject a disk without removing its icon from the desktop. To do this with Mac OS 8, you select the icon and press the Option key while choosing the Eject command. With Mac OS 7.0–7.6.1, you don't have to press the Option key.

When you eject a disk and leave its icon on the desktop, the icon turns gray to signify that the disk itself isn't available. You can insert a different disk in the same disk drive and the second disk's icon also appears on the desktop.

Because both icons are on the desktop, it's possible to copy items from the now-inserted disk to the ejected disk's gray icon. This involves a lot of disk swapping as the Finder reads a little bit from the source disk, ejects it, asks you to insert the destination disk, writes a little bit to the destination disk, ejects it, asks you to insert the source disk, and repeat. It's a very tedious process left over from the days when everyone used a Mac with one floppy disk drive and no hard disk.

Erasing disks

Erasing a disk removes all of the files and folders it contains. When you open a disk after erasing it, you see no folders and no files in its window. Be sure this is what you want to happen before you erase a disk.

To erase a disk, you select its icon and choose Erase Disk from the Special menu. The Finder displays a dialog box asking you to confirm that you really want to erase the disk and includes a space where you can edit the disk name. The ability to change the name is purely for your convenience. You can always edit the disk icon's name later, as described in the previous chapter.

Erasing a disk creates a blank disk directory, a process called *initialization*, which wipes out the means of accessing the existing files on the disk without actually touching the files themselves. The contents of all your old files are still on a disk after you erase it, but there's no easy way to get at them any more. It's sort of like someone erased the catalog of a library. The books would still be on the shelves, but you would have no way to look them up.

In fact you can recover deleted files after erasing a disk by using the Norton Utilities program from Symantec (408-253-9600, http://www.symantec.com). The same program can erase a disk such that no one can recover files from it.

Summary

After reading this chapter, you know how to boil down the Finder to its essential commands by turning on the Simple Finder option with the Preferences command in Mac OS 8. You know that double-clicking or using the Open command with a disk, folder, or file displays its contents in a window. Conversely, the Close command or close box puts a window away when you don't want to see it any more. While a window is open, you can use the View menu to see the window's contents as icons, buttons, or a list. In a list view, you can change the sort order by clicking a column heading. Also, you can expand and collapse folders in a list view by clicking the triangles next to their names.

With enclosed folders expanded, you can select items from multiple folders at the same time.

You also found out in this chapter that you can do more with the Finder than view the contents of your disks and folders. You can create a new folder with the New Folder command; drag items to copy or move them; duplicate items with the Duplicate command; and delete items by dragging them to the Trash and eventually emptying the Trash with the Empty Trash command. If there's more than one disk on your desktop, you can remove a disk by dragging it to the Trash or by using the Eject command (Mac OS 8) or the Put Away command (Mac OS 7.0–7.6.1). You can erase a disk with the Erase disk command.

Get More Organized with the Finder

Once you master the simple ways of organizing your disks, folders, and files with the Finder that were presented in the previous chapter, you're ready for the advanced techniques covered in this chapter. Here you learn how to make and use pop-up windows. You learn how to fine-tune the view in a folder or disk window by aligning icons, arranging items in a different order, setting a view font, and selecting an icon or button size for a view. You learn how to search for items by name and other criteria.

Using techniques described in this chapter, you can make your way continuously into a folder's enclosed folders or out the other direction through enclosing folders toward the disk or desktop. You can return items from the desktop or the Trash to their previous locations. You can categorize items with text and color labels, and you can attach comments to an item. This chapter also tells you how to lock or otherwise protect files, folders, and disks. You learn how to make the Finder do more than one thing at a time. Finally, you find out why you might want to partition your hard disk and how to do it.

To use most of the techniques described in this chapter with Mac OS 8, the Simple Finder option must be turned off with the Finder's Preferences command. If the Finder's menus don't contain commands mentioned in this chapter, such as the Put Away command in the File menu, turn off the Simple Finder option as described in the previous chapter. (Prior to Mac OS 8, there is no Simple Finder option to turn on or off.)

To learn even more ways to organize your disks and their contents, be sure to read the coverage of opening and saving programs and documents in the next chapter, the System Folder in Chapter 9, aliases in Chapter 12, and file sharing in Chapter 18.

Using Pop-up Windows

With Mac OS 8, you can change any folder or disk window to a pop-up window. A pop-up window is anchored to the bottom of the screen, and in place of a title bar it has a tab labeled with the window title. Clicking the tab at the top of a window closes the window and leaves the tab at the bottom of the screen. Clicking a tab at the bottom of the screen makes the window pop up from there. Figure 7-1 shows both states of a pop-up window.

Figure 7-1: Clicking a tab at the bottom of the screen (left) displays a pop-up window (right), and clicking the tab of an open window (top) closes it and leaves its tab showing (bottom).

Pop-up windows are easy to find and open, so they're great places to keep stuff you use often. You can move or copy items into a pop-up window by dragging them to its tab. This works whether the pop-up window is open or closed. When you drag an item to the tab of a closed window, the window pops up. If the window is set for icon or button view, then you can continue dragging inside the window to place the icon or button where you want it.

When you drag something out of a pop-up window, the Finder automatically closes the window when you release the mouse button. If you need to drag several items from a pop-up window to a common destination, select them all and drag them as a group. If you drag them individually, you have to pop up the window for each one. That would be a real drag.

Pop-up windows are not available in system versions earlier than Mac OS 8.

Making a pop-up window

You can make a regular disk or folder window into a pop-up window by choosing "as Pop-up Window" from the View menu while the window is active (front-most). Another method is to drag the window's title bar to the bottom of the screen, where it changes into the tab of a collapsed pop-up window.

If you already have several pop-up windows and you try to make another one whose tab won't fit in the available space at the bottom of the screen, the Finder displays an alert explaining why you can't make another pop-up window. Keep in mind that the length of a pop-up window's name directly affects the size of the window's tab. You can make room for more tabs by abbreviating the names of existing pop-up windows and by moving tabs as close together as possible at the bottom of the screen, as described in the following subsection.

To make a pop-up window into a regular window, you can choose "as Window" from the View menu while the pop-up window is active; the pop-up window must be open to be active. You can also make a pop-up window into a regular window by dragging its tab up toward the top of the screen. As you drag, you see the outline of the window, and eventually the outline changes to the rectangular shape of a regular window.

Moving a pop-up window

You can move a pop-up window left and right by dragging its tab along the bottom of the screen. This allows you to arrange pop-up window tabs in any order you like. Be sure to drag a pop-up window's tab while the window is closed. If you drag the tab while the window is open, it becomes a regular window.

A pop-up window is always anchored to the bottom of the screen. If you drag it off the bottom of the screen, it becomes a regular window.

To move a tab as close to its neighbor as possible, drag the tab so that it partially overlaps its neighbor and release the mouse button. When you drag, don't let the pointer touch the neighbor or the tab you're dragging will snap back to its former location when you release the mouse button.

Sizing a pop-up window

You can change the size of a pop-up window by dragging one of the two size boxes at its top corners. The size boxes can adjust the width and height of the window. You can also adjust the height alone by dragging the pop-up window's tab up or down. Keep in mind that if you drag the tab high enough, you make the pop-up into a regular window.

Fine-tuning Views

There are lots of ways to fine-tune the basic icon, button, and list views described in the previous chapter. You can clean up icons or buttons by aligning them to an invisible grid whenever you want, or you can have the Finder keep them aligned automatically. You can arrange or sort items by name, kind, or other criterion. You can select an icon or button size for any view. In a list view, you can select which columns of information are displayed about items in the view. An additional option in Mac OS 8 lets you force the contents of an icon or button view to stay arranged in a particular order, such as by name.

With Mac OS 8, you fine-tune each window individually. With earlier system software versions, some options apply to individual windows but others apply to all windows. The options that apply to all windows are clearly identified in this section.

Cleaning up icons or buttons

When icons or buttons are in disarray, you can have the Finder align them in neat rows and columns. You clean up the active window by choosing Clean Up from the View menu in Mac OS 8. Prior to Mac OS 8, you choose Clean Up Window from the Special menu. If no window is open or active, the Finder cleans up the desktop icons. Figure 7-2 shows a window before and after being cleaned up.

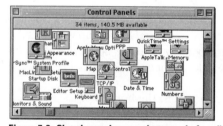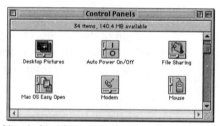

Figure 7-2: Cleaning up icons or buttons: before (left) and after (right) using the Clean Up command.

You can clean up individual icons by holding down the ⌘ key while dragging them singly or in groups — unless the Snap to Grid option is turned on (as described later in this section). If that option is turned on, the Finder aligns icons when you drag them without pressing the ⌘ key.

In system software versions earlier than OS 8, you can also use the Finder's Clean Up command to align only the icons you select in a window or on the desktop. Pressing Shift changes Clean Up to Clean Up Selection.

Arranging icons or buttons

While the Finder is cleaning up icons or buttons, you can have it arrange them in a particular order, such as by name or modification date. The Finder arranges icons first by the attribute you choose and second by name if necessary. For example, if you arrange by kind, then all application icons will come before all the folder icons; the application icons will be arranged alphabetically by name before the alphabetically arranged folder icons. The first icon goes in the upper left corner, and remaining icons fill the window from left to right and top to bottom.

The procedure for arranging icons is different in Mac OS 8 than in earlier system software versions.

Arrange in Mac OS 8

You arrange and clean up icons in Mac OS 8 by choosing the order you want from the Arrange submenu of the View menu. Note that you do not need to choose Clean Up as well. Figure 7-3 shows a window before and after being arranged (and simultaneously cleaned up) by icon name.

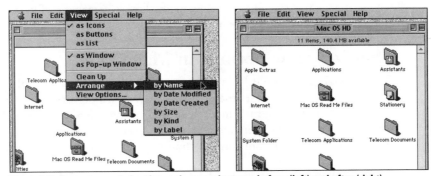

Figure 7-3: Arranging and cleaning up icons or buttons: before (left) and after (right).

You can clean up the desktop by clicking any desktop icon to make the desktop active and then choosing the order you want from the Arrange submenu. In this case, the Finder puts the startup disk icon in the upper right corner and fills the desktop from top to bottom and right to left. No matter which order you choose, the Finder always arranges desktop icons in groups in the following order: hard disk volumes, desktop printers, floppy disks and other removable disks, shared disks and folders, and all other icons. The Trash icon always goes in the bottom right corner of the desktop.

Arrange in Mac OS 7.0–7.6.1

You can use the Clean Up command in Mac OS 7.6.1 and earlier to arrange icons by any of the choices in the View menu. First you must set the order you want by choosing it from the View menu. This has the side effect of temporarily changing to a list view. Change back to an icon view by choosing "by Icon" or "by Small Icon" from the View menu. Now press the Option key while you choose the Clean Up command, and the Finder rearranges all icons in the window.

If you press Option while cleaning up the desktop (instead of a window), the Finder aligns all desktop icons in a standard configuration. It moves the startup disk's icon to the upper-right corner of the desktop, lines up other disk icons below it, puts the Trash in the lower-right corner, and arranges all other desktop icons in rows and columns next to the disk icons.

Sorting a list view

Much as you can have the Finder arrange icons in a window, you can have it sort a list view. The most direct method is to click the heading of the column by which you want to sort the list, as mentioned in the previous chapter. Alternatively, you can choose a sort order from the Sort submenu of the View menu in Mac OS 8. In earlier system software versions, you choose the sort order directly from the View menu. You may find the menu method more convenient if the window isn't wide enough to show the column by which you want to sort.

Setting view options in Mac OS 8

Additional view options let you change the format and contents of folder and disk windows. You can set the icon size for each window, regardless of the type of view. You can have the Finder keep icons arranged automatically. You can set the spacing between icons and buttons. You can determine which columns appear in a list view. And you can choose a font for the text in all windows.

You set these view options in Mac OS 8 with the Finder's View Options and Preferences commands. In earlier system software versions, you use the Views control panel (as described later in this section). Figure 7-4 shows the View Options dialog box and the Preferences dialog box in Mac OS 8.

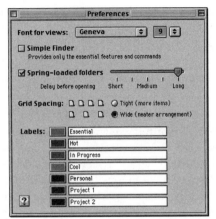

Figure 7-4: Setting view options with the View Options and Preferences commands in Mac OS 8.

Text font and size in Mac OS 8

To choose the font and size used for text in all disk and folder windows in Mac OS 8, choose Preferences from the Finder's Edit menu. Choose a font and a size from the pop-up menus at the top of the Preferences dialog box. If you want to use a size that isn't listed, you can enter any size between 6 and 72 in the space provided. Figure 7-5 shows the font and size settings in the Preferences dialog box.

Figure 7-5: Choosing a font and size for all icon names and list view text in Mac OS 8.

The Finder uses the font and size settings for icon names, the window information header (number of items in the window and space available on the disk), and all the text in list views. The settings for font and size affect all windows.

After changing the font or the size, you may want to use the Clean Up command to adjust the spacing of icons on the desktop and in windows. You must clean up each window separately.

Tip: Although the standard font and size in Mac OS 8 is Geneva 10, you should try Geneva 9. The italic style used for alias names looks better and is easier to edit in Geneva 9 because there is a special italic Geneva 9 font installed in the system. (For more information on aliases, see Chapter 12, and for more information on fonts, see Chapter 13.)

Icon or button view options in Mac OS 8

You can set the size and automatic arrangement of icons or buttons on the desktop and in each Mac OS 8 window whose contents you view as icons or buttons. To set these view options for a window, bring it to the front and choose View Options from the View menu. To set these options for the desktop, click any desktop icon to make the desktop active and then choose View Options from the View menu. Figure 7-6 shows the View Options dialog box for icon and button views.

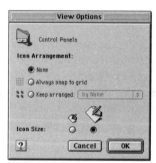
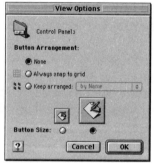

Figure 7-6: Setting view options for an icon view (left) or button view (right) in Mac OS 8.

Setting the Icon Arrangement or the Button Arrangement option to "Always snap to grid" or "Keep arranged" makes icons you drag in the window align to the same grid as the Clean Up command. When either of these settings is in effect for a window, you see an icon at the left end of the window's status bar, just below the close box. The icon in the window matches the current setting of the Icon Arrangement or the Button Arrangement option in the View options dialog box.

Tip: You can temporarily reverse the state of an "Always snap to grid" or "Keep arranged" setting by pressing ⌘ while dragging. If either of those settings is selected, ⌘-dragging temporarily disables forced grid alignment.
If neither of those settings is selected, then ⌘-dragging temporarily enables forced grid alignment.

The distance between aligned icons or buttons in Mac OS 8 is determined by the Grid Spacing option of the Preferences command. This option applies to all windows and the desktop, but affects each window only when you next make a change to it. Figure 7-7 shows the Grid Spacing option in the Preferences dialog box.

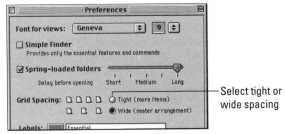

Figure 7-7: Setting the grid spacing for all windows and the desktop in Mac OS 8.

No-Icon View of the Desktop

If you keep lots of items on the desktop, you may want to reduce the space some of them take up by eliminating their icons. You can do this selectively — leaving some items with icons and others without — by replacing the icons you don't want to see with blank custom icons.

First you need to copy some white space to the Clipboard. With Mac OS 7.6 or later, you can do that by pressing ⌘-Shift-Control-4 and then dragging a selection rectangle across any small white area on the screen. Alternatively, with any system software version you can copy some white space from a paint program.

Then select a desktop icon you want to eliminate, use the Finder's Get Info command to bring up the icon's Info window, and paste the white space over the icon in the Info window. Repeat with each of the other icons you want to eliminate.

Pasting white space as a custom icon leaves only the item name visible. Six items without icons fit in the space previously occupied by two items with icons.

List view options in Mac OS 8

You can set the icon size and select what information you want shown in each Mac OS 8 window viewed as a list. To set these view options for a window, bring it to the front and choose View Options from the View menu. Figure 7-8 shows the View Options dialog box for list views.

Figure 7-8: Setting view options for a list view in Mac OS 8.

A list view includes an icon and a name for every item in the window. You can select which of seven other columns of information you want displayed. By selecting just the columns you need to see in a window, you can see most or all columns without scrolling the window. Click a window's zoom box to make it just wide enough to show all the columns you selected for display. If the window can't be made wide enough to show all the columns you selected for display, the window fills the screen and you have to scroll to see some columns. (You cannot change the order of the columns or their individual widths.)

You can set the icon size in each window to standard (large), small, or tiny. Standard icons are the size you usually see on the desktop. Small icons are the size you see in the Apple and Application menus. Tiny icons are so small you don't see any unique detail, just a generic folder, application, or document icon.

The Comments column shows the first 25 characters of the comments entered into each item's Info window. (For more information, see "Attaching Comments to Items" later in this chapter.)

The option "Use relative date" has the Finder display "today" instead of today's date or "yesterday" instead of yesterday's date in the Date Created and the Date Modified columns. For other dates, the Finder uses the date format set in the Date & Time control panel (as described in Chapter 10).

The option "Calculate folder sizes" has the Finder display the size of each folder in the window. It takes a while for the Finder to add up the sizes of items in a large folder. You can keep working on other tasks while the Finder calculates folder sizes, but calculating folder sizes reduces the performance for doing other work.

Setting view options in Mac OS 7.0–7.6.1

Prior to Mac OS 8, you set view options with the Views control panel. You can choose a font and size for text, set icon alignment rules, and determine list view contents. All these options affect every disk and folder window as well as the desktop. You can't set any of these options separately for each window as you can with Mac OS 8. Figure 7-9 shows the Views control panel in Mac OS 7.6.

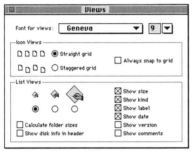

Figure 7-9: Setting view options with the Views control panel prior to Mac OS 8.

Text font and size in Mac OS 7.0–7.6.1

With Mac OS 7.6.1 and earlier, you choose a text font and a text size for windows and the desktop from the pop-up menus at the top of the Views control panel. If the text size you want isn't listed, you can enter any size between 6 and 36. The Finder uses the font and size settings for icon names, the disk information header (number of items, disk space used, and disk space available), and all the text in list views. Your font and size settings affect all windows and icons.

Icon alignment in Mac OS 7.0–7.6.1

Other settings in the Views control panel determine how the Finder aligns icons in Mac OS 7.6.1 and earlier. You can set the type of grid the Clean Up command uses and decide whether icons automatically align with that grid when you drag them. The settings affect icons on the desktop and in all windows with icon or small-icon views. You cannot set icon alignment options separately for each window as you can with Mac OS 8.

The "Staggered grid" option makes it possible to arrange icons close together without their names overlapping. Turning on the "Always snap to grid" option makes icons you have dragged align to the Clean Up command's grid. You can temporarily reverse the "Always snap to grid" setting by pressing ⌘ while dragging icons.

List view options in Mac OS 7.0–7.6.1

With Mac OS 7.6.1 and earlier, you determine how much information the Finder shows in all windows with list views (name, size, kind, and so on) by setting numerous options at the bottom of the Views control panel. You cannot set list view options separately for each window as you can with Mac OS 8.

List views always include an icon and name for every item in the window. In addition, you select which of six other columns of information to include: size, kind, label, date, version, and comments. Your selections appear as choices in the Finder's Views menu. You cannot change the order of the columns or their widths, only whether each appears or not.

Judicious setting of list view options keeps your list view windows as small as possible. You can make a list view window narrower by reducing the number of items checked in the Views control panel and then clicking the window's zoom box.

You can set the icon size for all list views to standard, small, or tiny. Standard icons are like desktop icons. Small icons are like the icons in the Apple and Application menus. With tiny icons you see only generic folder, application, and document icons.

You can also set an option to have the Finder calculate and display folder sizes. Adding up the sizes of items in a large folder can take quite a while. Fortunately, the Finder only calculates sizes of folders you can see and does this work in the background so that you can get on with other tasks. But other tasks may slow down if the Finder is concurrently calculating folder sizes.

Another list view option has the Finder show disk information in the header of all list view windows. The disk information includes the number of items in the window, the amount of disk space in use, and the amount of disk space available. This information is standard in icon and small-icon views.

Finding Items

No matter how carefully you organize your folders and disks, there comes a time when you can't find a file or folder without a lot of digging through layers of folders. The Finder's Find command fetches lost or buried items with less effort. Choosing Find from the Finder's File menu opens a utility program named Find File. You can also open Find File by choosing it from the Apple menu. You can use Find File to search for items that match a single criterion or up to eight criteria.

Making a simple search

The simplest form of the Find File window allows you to specify where you want to search and one attribute you want to match. Find File is preset to look on all disks for items whose names contain the text you specify. You can change where Find File looks for items and specify that it look at an attribute other than the item's name. Figure 7-10 shows the Find File window set up to search by name.

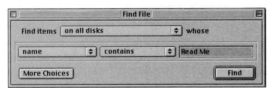

Figure 7-10: Setting up a simple search in the Find File window.

You use the pop-up menus in the Find File window to specify which attribute you want Find File to look at and how you want Find File to compare that attribute with a value or a state you specify. Table 7-1 lists the possible combinations.

You can have Find File look in the following places: on all disks, on all local disks (not including file servers), on mounted servers (whose icons appear on the desktop), on the desktop, in the Finder selection (the items currently selected), or on a specific disk by name. Find File does not look inside the System file or suitcase files for fonts, sounds, or desk accessories. It can find those kinds of items in folders and on the desktop, though.

Find File can search for items based on any of 16 attributes, 4 of which are ordinarily hidden. The 12 attributes you can always see are name, size, kind, label, date created, date modified, version, comments, lock attribute, folder attribute, file type, and creator. The other four attributes are contents, name/icon lock, custom icon, and visibility. To see the extra four attributes, you press the Option key when you first click the left-most pop-up menu in the Find File window.

	Table 7-1 Find File Criteria	
Search By	***Search How***	***Search For***
Name	Contains/starts with/ends with/ is/is not/doesn't contain	Text you enter
Size	Is less than/is greater than	Amount you enter, in kilo-bytes
Kind	Is/is not	Alias/application/clipping file/control panel*/docu-ment/extension*/folder/font/ letter/sound/stationery
Label	Is/is not	Label you choose from pop-up menu
Date created	Is/is before/is after/is not, is within 1/2/3 days of, is within 1/2/3 weeks of, or is within 1/2/3/6 months of	Date you specify
Date modified	Is/is before/is after/is not, is within 1/2/3 days of, is within 1/2/3 weeks of, or is within 1/2/3/6 months of	Date you specify
Version	Is/is not	Text you enter
Comments	Contain/do not contain	Text you enter
Lock attribute	Is	Locked/unlocked
Folder attribute	Is/is not	Empty/shared/mounted
File type	Is/is not	4 characters you enter
Creator	Is/is not	4 characters you enter
Contents	Contain/do not contain	Text you enter
Name/icon lock	is	Locked/unlocked
Custom icon	is	Present/not present
Visibility	is	Invisible/visible

*Available only in Mac OS 7.5.3 and later

Find and Find Again

Although the Finder's Find command ordinarily opens the Find File utility, you can have it bring up the Find dialog box of System 7.1 by pressing Shift while choosing the Find command. The Find dialog box has a simple form and an expanded form. The simple form of the Find dialog box sets up a search by name of all disks. The Finder displays the first item it finds, opening the folder that contains the item and selecting the item. The figure below shows the simple form of the old Find dialog box.

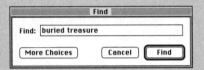

To find another match, use the Find Again command. If the active window contains another matching item, the Finder selects it and scrolls it into view. Otherwise the Finder looks in other folders and disks.

Clicking the More Choices button in the Find dialog box extends your search options. You specify what you want to search for and where you want to search. The old Find and Find Again commands can find by two criteria not available in the Find File utility: a kind that contains or doesn't contain the text you enter, and a version number that is less than or greater than the text you enter. In addition, you can restrict Find and Find Again to searching just the active window. If you restrict the search to one disk, you can have the Finder select all the items it finds at once in a list view. The figure below shows an example of the old expanded Find dialog box.

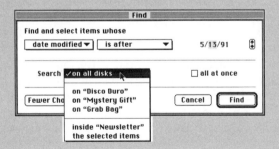

Making an expanded search

You can add more search criteria to the Find File window. Clicking the More Choices button adds a criterion at the bottom of the window. Clicking the Fewer Choices button removes a criterion. Alternatively, you can use the More Choices and Fewer Choices commands in Find File's File menu. Figure 7-11 shows a Find File window with two criteria.

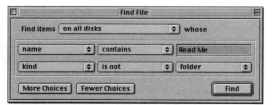

Figure 7-11: Setting up an expanded search in the Find File window.

Using search results

The search begins when you click the Find button in the Find File window. While the search progresses, a count of the number of items found appears in the window. When the search ends, Find File displays all the found items in the Items Found window. Figure 7-12 shows an example of the Items Found window.

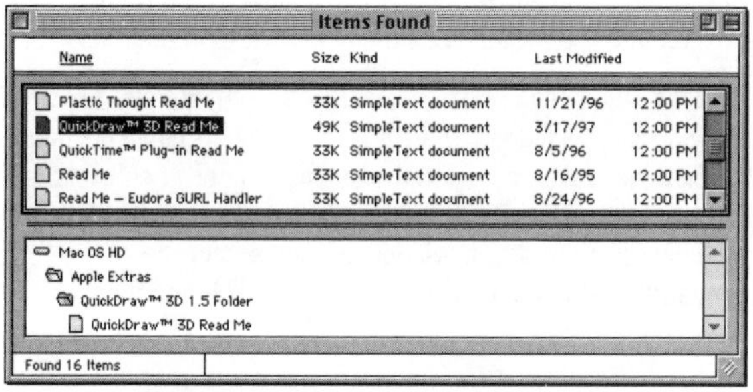

Figure 7-12: Viewing the results of a Find File search.

You can sort the list of found items, which appears at the top of the Items Found window, by name, size, kind, or modification date. To change the order, use the View menu in the Find File program or click the column heading in the Items Found window. To sort in reverse order, press Option and click a column heading or press Option while you choose from the Find File's View menu.

Selecting an item (by clicking it) in the list of found items at the top of the Items Found window displays the item's folder location at the bottom of the window. If you'd like to see more of a lengthy folder location without scrolling, you can make the bottom part of the window taller (and the top part shorter) by dragging the two parallel lines that separate the top and bottom parts of the window.

You can select multiple items in the list of found items as you do in the Finder: by Shift-clicking or dragging a selection rectangle across them. To select all items, use the Select All command in Find File's Edit menu. When you select multiple items at the top of the Items Found window, no folder location is displayed at the bottom of the window.

You can open an item in the Items Found window by double-clicking it. If more than one item is selected, double-clicking any of them opens them all. In addition, you can open selected items by choosing Open from Find File's File menu.

To open a selected item's enclosing folder, use the Open Enclosing Folder command. The Finder automatically becomes active, the folder opens, and the Finder scrolls to and selects the item in the folder window.

The Trash is another place you can drag one or more found items. However, due to an error, dragging multiple items as a group from the Items Found window to the Trash has no effect in the initial version of Mac OS 8. You can work around this problem by dragging the selected items from the Items Found window to an alias of the Trash. (To make an alias of the Trash, select the Trash and choose Make Alias from the Finder's File menu.)

In addition to opening found items and their enclosing folders, you can also drag found items from the top of the Items Found window to the desktop or to any folder or disk visible in the Finder. If the destination is on the same disk as the found item you drag, the found item moves to the destination. If the destination is on a different disk, the found item is copied to it.

Besides opening and dragging found items, you can use other commands in Find File's File menu as follows:

❖ **Print Item** prints selected documents just as the Finder's Print command does.

❖ **Get Info** displays the Info windows of selected items.

❖ **Sharing** allows you to share selected folders (as described in Chapter 18) and link selected programs (as described in Chapter 22).

With one item selected at the top of the Items Found window, you can also select one item at the bottom of the window. Menu commands affect either one item or the other, but not both. The affected item is the one in the section of the window that has a heavy border. You can alternate this rectangle between the top and bottom sections of the window by pressing Tab.

Find File Shortcuts

You can quit Find File while opening a found item by holding down the Option key and double-clicking the item in the Find File's Items Found window. This trick saves you the trouble of reactivating Find File to quit it. The Option-key shortcut also works with the Get Info, Sharing, Open Enclosing Item, and Print commands in the version of Find File that comes with Mac OS 7.5.3 and later. You can read several pages of additional shortcuts by choosing Find File Shortcuts from the Help menu while Find File is active.

Folder Ins and Outs

Getting to a folder where you want to move or copy an item can take a lot of double-clicking of folder icons as you travel in and out of folders on the way. Mac OS 8 has a couple of features that make it possible to traverse a folder hierarchy without a lot of double-clicking. You can make folders spring open as you delve deeper through layers of folders, and you can zip up through folder layers toward the enclosing disk. (The ability to zip up through folder layers is also available in earlier system software versions.)

Spring-open folders

With Mac OS 8, you can make a folder or disk spring open when you pause briefly over it. This behavior is normally turned on, but you can use the Finder's Preferences command to adjust the amount of time you must pause until a folder or disk springs open or to turn off spring-loaded opening altogether. (Spring-loaded opening is not available in system software versions earlier than OS 8.)

Making folders and disks spring open

A disk or folder springs open automatically if you drag an item to its icon and pause briefly with the pointer positioned over the icon and the mouse button held down. The folder or disk icon flashes twice and opens. This will also occur if you pause while dragging a group of items.

If you continue holding down the mouse button, you can then drag to a folder icon in the window that just opened and continue deeper into the layers of folders. You may need to travel through a folder that's already open to get into a folder it encloses. Go ahead and drag to the folder's open icon; its open window springs to the front so you can make a folder in it spring open. If you make the wrong disk or folder spring open by accident, simply drag the pointer out of its window and the window closes automatically.

When you release the mouse button, the Finder moves or copies the item or items you were dragging into the active window. The active window does not close, but all other windows of folders that you made spring open do close automatically. If any of the folders you made spring open were already open, their windows do not close either.

If you change your mind about moving or copying the item you're dragging, just drag it to the menu bar and release the mouse button. The Finder returns the item to the place you got it from.

Actually, folders spring open even if you're not dragging anything but the pointer. To make this happen, begin to double-click the first disk or folder you want to spring open, but don't release the mouse button after pressing it the second time. This gesture is called a *click-and-a-half*, because you make one click and half of a second click. After a brief pause while you continue to hold down the mouse button, the pointer changes to a magnifying glass, the icon flashes twice, and opens.

Setting spring-open options

To adjust the amount of time you must pause until a folder or disk springs open or to turn off spring-loaded opening altogether, choose Preferences from the Finder's Edit menu. Figure 7-13 shows the "Spring-loaded folders" option in the Preferences dialog box.

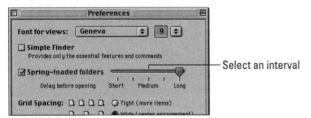

Figure 7-13: Setting options for spring-loaded opening in Mac OS 8.

Finding enclosing folders

Rather than go deeper into your layers of folders, you can go the other direction and open a folder that encloses an open folder. If the open folder is nested inside several layers of folders, you can quickly open any of those enclosing folders or the disk that encloses them all. You can do this in Mac OS 8 and in other versions of the Mac OS (7.0 and later).

To open any of the nested folders or the disk that encloses an open folder, make the open folder's window active (bring it to the front) and then press ⌘ while clicking the window title. A menu pops up showing the layers of nested folders and the disk that all enclose the open folder. You open one of the folders or the disk by choosing it from the pop-up menu. If the outermost folder is on the desktop, the pop-up menu doesn't list an enclosing disk. Figure 7-14 shows an example of a folder window's pop-up menu.

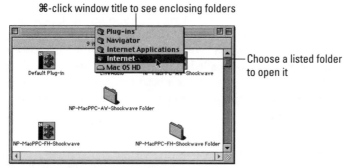

Figure 7-14: Opening an enclosing folder.

While opening one of the folders or the disk that encloses an open folder, you can simultaneously close the open folder's window. Simply hold down Option and ⌘, click the menu title, and choose a folder or the disk from the pop-up menu. You must start holding down Option and ⌘ before clicking the window title. If you ⌘-click the window title and then press Option while choosing from the pop-up menu, the window opens for the folder you chose but the previously active window doesn't close.

Putting Stuff Back

From time to time you may find that your desktop has become cluttered with files and folders you no longer need to have there. You could drag these items back to some folder, but if you just want to put them back where they came from, there's an easier way. Just select the items you want to put back and use the Put Away command. The Finder returns the selected items to their former locations without opening any folders.

The Put Away command also works with items in the Trash. You can open the Trash, select items you don't want to delete, and use the Put Away command to return them to their former locations.

The Put Away command returns items to the folders they were last in, but does not necessarily return items in their original order within the window.

Labeling Items

The Finder enables you to classify folders, programs, and documents by labeling them with a word or phrase. On monitors displaying at least 16 colors, labeling an item also colorizes it.

Applying labels

To label an item with Mac OS 8, select it and choose a label from the Label submenu of the Finder's File menu. In earlier system software versions, use the Label menu. Figure 7-15 shows the Label submenu in Mac OS 8.

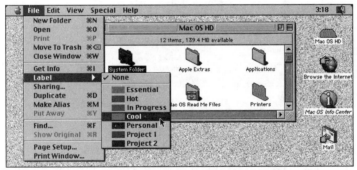

Figure 7-15: Specifying a label for selected icons with Mac OS 8.

You can also label items found by Find File in Mac OS 7.5 and later. Select items in the Items Found window that you want labeled alike, and choose a label from Find File's Label menu.

When you label a color icon, the Finder blends the label color as if you covered the icon with a piece of acetate that is the same color as the label. To label an item without colorizing it, change the label color to solid black, as described later.

Using labels

After labeling items, you can view a folder or disk window's contents arranged by label. You can also search for items by label with the Finder's Find command. Label colors also show up in the Apple menu and in the directory dialog boxes used by many programs' Open and Save commands. Figure 7-16 shows a folder window sorted by label, and Figure 7-17 shows how you search by label.

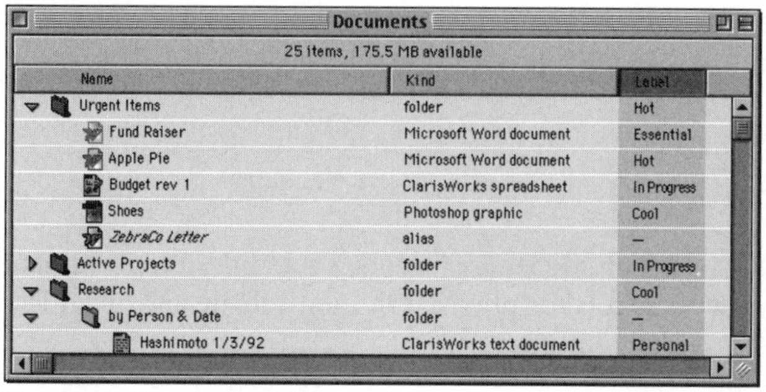

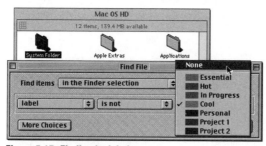

Figure 7-16: Viewing by label.

Figure 7-17: Finding by label.

Changing label names and colors

You change the standard label names and colors in Mac OS 8 with the Finder's Preferences command. In earlier system software versions, you use the Labels control panel. Figure 7-18 shows the Labels settings in the Preferences dialog box of Mac OS 8 and the Labels control panel of Mac OS 7.6.

If you click a label color to change it, the Finder displays the standard Color Picker dialog box. You can select the type of color picker you want to use from the list on the left side of the dialog box. (In system software versions earlier than Mac OS 8, you may have to click a More Choices button at the bottom of the dialog box to see this list.)

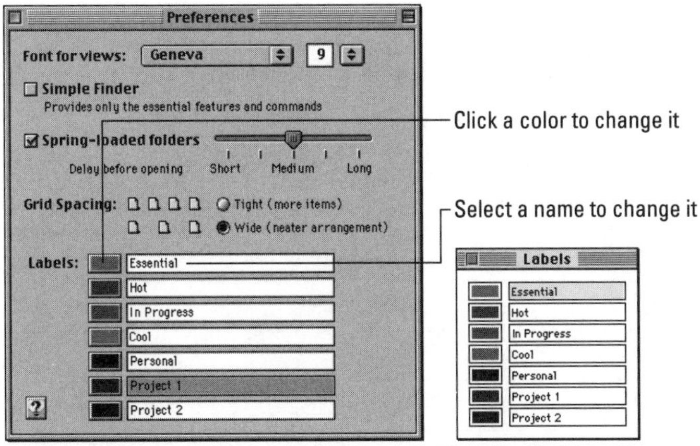

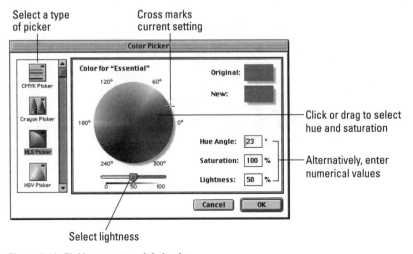

Figure 7-18: Changing label colors or names in Mac OS 8 (left) and in earlier system software versions (right).

You pick a new color by clicking a color wheel, adjusting sliders, typing numbers, or clicking a color swatch, depending on the color picker you selected. For example, the Crayon Picker uses swatches that look like crayons, and the HLS Picker uses a wheel, a slider, and a numeric entry. With Mac OS 8, you can also pick up any color displayed on the screen by holding down the Option key, which turns the pointer into an eyedropper, and clicking the color you want to pick up. Figure 7-19 shows the HLS picker in the Color Picker dialog box of Mac OS 8, and Table 7-2 lists the HLS settings for the standard label colors (in case you want to reset them after experimenting).

Figure 7-19: Picking a custom label color.

Table 7-2			
Values for Standard Label Colors			
Label	*Hue Angle*	*Saturation*	*Lightness*
Essential	23°	100%	50%
Hot	1°	94%	45%
In Progress	328°	93%	49%
Cool	196°	98%	46%
Personal	240°	100%	41%
Project 1	131°	100%	20%
Project 2	29°	89%	18%

A Mildew-ish Green Label

Select the Crayon Picker in Mac OS 8 and you see a box of 60 crayons in various premixed colors with fanciful names such as Obsidian, Marigold, and Dirt. Instead of clicking each crayon to see a sample of its color and its name on the right side of the dialog box, you can drag across the crayons and watch the color sample and the name change. Hold down the Option key and click the edge of a crayon to pick up a lighter or darker shade of color, which is appropriately named with the suffix "-ish."

Transparent Labels

If you've avoided icon labels because they discolor your beautiful color icons, you need shun them no longer. You can label a color icon without changing its color — provided the label color is black, white, or any shade of gray. (On a color monitor, icons with white labels are invisible unless they are selected.) You can still view Finder windows by label, find items by label, and so on. To make a label transparent, open the Labels control panel and click the color of a label you want to use. The standard Color Picker dialog box appears. Select the HSL Picker (named the Apple HSL Picker prior to Mac OS 8) on the left side of the dialog box. Then set the Hue Angle and Saturation to 0, and set the Lightness to 100 for white, 0 for black, or a number between 0.01 and 99.99 for a shade of gray. You can type the three values in the spaces provided, or you can click the center of the color wheel and adjust the slider.

Attaching Comments to Items

You can attach notes or comments to folders, files, and some disks in their Info window. To bring up an item's Info window, select it and use the Get Info command. Type anything you want (up to a maximum of 199 characters) in the space provided at the bottom of the Info window. Although the window has no scroll bar to see lengthy comments, you can scroll by pressing the arrow keys or by dragging the pointer past the borders of the entry box. Figure 7-20 shows comments in an Info window.

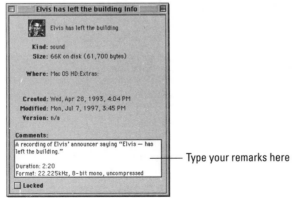

Type your remarks here

Figure 7-20: Viewing comments in an Info window.

In Mac OS 8, you can't attach comments to floppy disks. The part of the floppy disk where comments are located in earlier system software versions is used by Mac OS 8 to store view options for the disk and its folders.

Protecting Files, Folders, and Disks

The Mac OS lets you protect files and folders individually so they can't be changed. You can lock a file with the Get Info command, lock folders with the Sharing command, and specially protect the System Folder and Applications folder with the General Controls control panel. In addition, you can lock a disk so it can't be erased and its contents can't be changed.

Locking a file

To lock a file, select its icon and use the Get Info command to bring up the file's Info window. At the bottom of the Info window is a Locked option. If you turn it on, you will be able to open the file and copy its contents, but you won't be able to change its contents or its name. In addition, the Finder does not delete locked files that are in the Trash unless you press Option while choosing the Empty Trash command (as discussed in the previous chapter). A locked file has a small lock icon near its name in a list view. Figure 7-21 shows a locked file's Info window and several locked files in a list view.

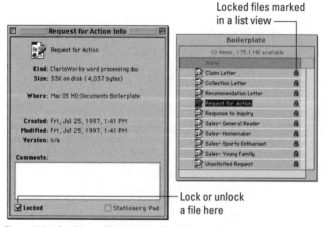

Figure 7-21: Locking a file with the Get Info command.

Locking a folder

You can protect against moving, renaming, or deleting a folder by using the Finder's Sharing command. Normally you use the Sharing command to control who can access your folder over a network (as described in Chapter 18), but you can also use the Sharing command for simple folder protection.

To lock a folder, select its icon and choose Sharing from the Finder's File menu to bring up the folder's Sharing window. In that window, turn on the option labeled "Can't be moved, renamed or deleted." You don't have to actually share the folder or change any other settings in the Sharing window. A locked folder has a small lock icon near its name in a list view. Figure 7-22 shows the Sharing window of a locked folder and some locked folders in a list view.

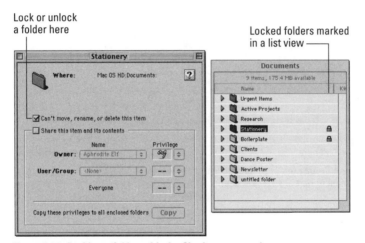

Figure 7-22: Locking a folder with the Sharing command.

You Can't Lock a Folder without File Sharing

The Sharing command only locks folders while file sharing is turned on in the File Sharing control panel (Mac OS 8) or the Sharing Setup control panel (Mac OS 7.6.1 and earlier). In fact, you can't even bring up a Sharing window while file sharing is off. If you try, the Sharing command displays an alert saying you must turn on file sharing and offers to open the appropriate control panel so you can do so. If you lock some folders while file sharing is on and later turn file sharing off, the folders become unlocked until you turn file sharing on again.

Protecting the System Folder and Applications folder

The Mac OS can protect the contents of two special folders in the startup disk, the System Folder and the Applications folder. You set this protection with the option "Protect System Folder" and the option "Protect Applications folder" in the General Controls control panel. You can use these options only if file sharing is turned off (as detailed in Chapter 18). Figure 7-23 shows the General Controls control panel.

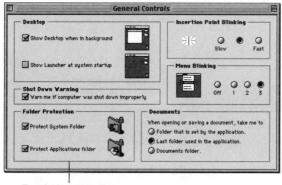

Turn folder protection
on and off here

Figure 7-23: Setting folder protection with the General Controls control panel in Mac OS 7.5 and later.

Turning on folder protection prevents anyone from moving, renaming, or deleting items directly enclosed by the protected folder. The protection does not extend to items in folders enclosed by the protected folder. For example, with System Folder protection turned on, you cannot move, rename, or delete the Control Panels folder, but you can do all those things to individual control panels inside the Control Panels folder.

Locking a disk

You can lock floppy disks and some other disks. After locking a disk, you can't erase it, change its name, copy files onto it, duplicate files on it, or move files and folders it contains to the desktop or the Trash. A locked disk is said to be *write protected*.

To lock a floppy disk, you slide the tab in the corner of the disk so that the square hole is open. You unlock a floppy disk by sliding the tab so that the square hole is closed.

Some other removable disks have locking mechanisms on their cases. Check the instructions that came with your removable disks or disk drive for specific information about locking them.

You may be able to lock or write-protect your hard disk using the setup program that came with it. For example, you can write-protect an Apple hard disk with the Drive Setup program that comes with Mac OS 8 and some earlier system software versions.

Doing Background Work

The Mac OS 8 Finder can perform most of its time-consuming work in the background, while you continue doing other work in the Finder or other programs. For example, you can copy files or empty the Trash while opening folders, renaming icons, setting view options, or editing notes with Stickies. You can open control panels and applications while the Finder works in the background. You can even start copying a batch of files before an ongoing copy operation finishes. Figure 7-24 shows two copy operations under way simultaneously while the Get Info command is being used.

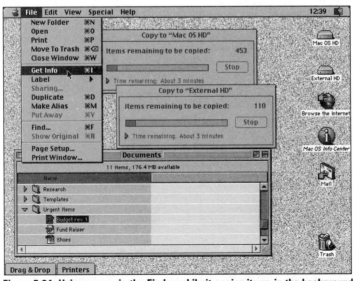

Figure 7-24: Using menus in the Finder while it copies items in the background.

The performance of your computer suffers while the Finder works on a task in the background. Furthermore, a background task proceeds more slowly than it does in the foreground. If the computer gets really busy with the background task, the mouse and keyboard may seem to stop working for a few seconds. If you type faster than the screen can display the characters, the system remembers the most recent 20 characters you type (about five seconds of typing at 40 words per minute). The system can also remember one click or double-click and can catch up with your dragging as long as you don't release the mouse button.

In system software versions earlier than Mac OS 8, the Finder's multitasking capabilities are limited to copying items, duplicating items, or emptying the Trash while you work in another application (not the Finder). After one of those operations, you can switch to another program by clicking in any of its windows or by choosing it from the Application menu or the Apple menu. You can't open a program or document by double-clicking its icon or using the Finder's Open command while the Finder copies, duplicates, empties Trash, or finds, but you can open programs and documents listed in the Apple menu. Also, you can't use most control panels while the Finder works in the background. None of these limitations applies with Mac OS 8.

Partitioning Hard Disks

If you work with lots of small files, you can save a significant amount of disk space by dividing a large hard drive into several smaller disk volumes, a process called *partitioning*. For example, a small preference file that takes 16.5K on a 1GB hard drive would take only 4K on a 250MB partition, saving 12.5K per small file. If you have lots of small files, the savings can literally add up to megabytes.

Each partitioned volume looks and acts exactly like a hard disk. Every volume has its own disk icon on the desktop, and all volumes appear at the desktop level of Open and Save dialog boxes (which are described in the next chapter). Think of volumes as individual disks that happen to be stored on the same mechanism.

Partitioning has other advantages besides using disk space more efficiently. Here are three:

❖ Items can be easier to find.

❖ You can secure an individual volume's contents with a password or lock it against overwriting.

❖ Accidental corruption of one volume is unlikely to affect other volumes.

On the down side, partitioning reduces storage flexibility. Each volume has a separate amount of available space. If you fill one volume, you can't store any more on it even though other volumes on the same drive have plenty of space available. Also, making multiple volumes increases the clutter of icons on the desktop. But these disadvantages are minor. Unless you work with a lot of files larger than 8K, it generally makes sense to partition a hard disk whose capacity is larger than 500MB.

Partitioning a hard disk

Before partitioning a hard disk you must back it up. You won't be able to access any of your existing files after partitioning until you have restored them from a backup. Make sure your backup program allows you to restore folders individually, because after partitioning you will have smaller disk volumes and all your folders may not fit on one volume.

You partition a disk with a disk setup program. You can probably use the disk setup program that came with your computer, or with your hard disk if you have added another hard disk or replaced your original hard disk. For example, Apple's Drive Setup program, which comes with Mac OS 8 and some earlier system software versions, can partition an Apple hard disk but not other brands. You can also buy a disk setup utility, such as Hard Disk ToolKit from FWB (415-482-4800, http://www.fwb.com).

Optimum volume size

The hardest part about partitioning a hard disk is deciding how many volumes to create and what size to make each one. Generally, you want to make a volume large enough to hold all related items and leave room to add items in the future. For example, you can create one volume to hold all your software — application programs and system software — and another volume to hold all your documents. Unless you create very large documents (in which case you may be better off not partitioning), the volume for applications and the System Folder probably needs to be bigger than the volume for documents.

The size of a volume determines the minimum size of a file on that volume. The smallest amount of space that can be allocated to a file on a volume is called the *allocation block size*. Larger volumes have larger allocation block sizes. For example, a 100-word memo needs only about 600 bytes of storage space, but it uses up to 16.5K (16,896 bytes) on a 1GB volume or 8K (8,192 bytes) on a 500MB volume. In Mac OS 7.5 and later, the Finder rounds file sizes up to the nearest whole number, so a list view would report the size of a 16.5K file as 17K.

Some documents, and all programs, get a minimum of two blocks. One of these blocks is for the file's data and the other block is for the file's resources. For example, a SimpleText document always occupies at least 33K on a 1GB hard disk.

Minimum allocation block size grows by 0.5K for every 32MB in volume capacity, as tabulated in Table 7-3.

	Table 7-3				
Smallest File Sizes for Various Volume Sizes					
Volume Size	**Smallest File**	**Volume Size**	**Smallest File**	**Volume Size**	**Smallest File**
0 to 31MB	0.5K	832 to 863MB	13.5K	1664 to 1695MB	26.5K
32 to 63MB	1K	864 to 895MB	14K	1696 to 1727MB	27K
64 to 95MB	1.5K	896 to 927MB	14.5K	1728 to 1759MB	27.5K
96 to 127MB	2K	928 to 959MB	15K	1760 to 1791MB	28K
128 to 159MB	2.5K	960 to 991MB	15.5K	1792 to 1823MB	28.5K
160 to 191MB	3K	992 to 1023MB	16K	1824 to 1855MB	29K
192 to 223MB	3.5K	1024 to 1055MB	16.5K	1856 to 1887MB	29.5K
224 to 255MB	4K	1056 to 1087MB	17K	1888 to 1919MB	30K
256 to 287MB	4.5K	1088 to 1119MB	17.5K	1920 to 1951MB	30.5K
288 to 319MB	5K	1120 to 1151MB	18K	1952 to 1983MB	31K
320 to 351MB	5.5K	1152 to 1183MB	18.5K	1984 to 2015MB	31.5K
352 to 383MB	6K	1184 to 1215MB	19K	2016 to 2047MB	32K
384 to 415MB	6.5K	1216 to 1247MB	19.5K	2048 to 2079MB	32.5K
416 to 447MB	7K	1248 to 1279MB	20K	2080 to 2111MB	33K
448 to 479MB	7.5K	1280 to 1311MB	20.5K	2112 to 2143MB	33.5K
480 to 511MB	8K	1312 to 1343MB	21K	2144 to 2175MB	34K
512 to 543MB	8.5K	1344 to 1375MB	21.5K	2176 to 2207MB	34.5K
544 to 575MB	9K	1376 to 1407MB	22K	2208 to 2239MB	35K
576 to 607MB	9.5K	1408 to 1439MB	22.5K	2240 to 2271MB	35.5K
608 to 639MB	10K	1440 to 1471MB	23K	2272 to 2303MB	36K
640 to 671MB	10.5K	1472 to 1503MB	23.5K	2304 to 2335MB	36.5K
672 to 703MB	11K	1504 to 1535MB	24K	2336 to 2367MB	37K
704 to 735MB	11.5K	1536 to 1567MB	24.5K	2368 to 2399MB	37.5K
736 to 767MB	12K	1568 to 1599MB	25K	2400 to 2431MB	38K
768 to 799MB	12.5K	1600 to 1631MB	25.5K	2432 to 2463MB	38.5K
800 to 831MB	13K	1632 to 1663MB	26K	2464 to 2495MB	39K

Summary

After reading this chapter, you know how to make a pop-up window with the View menu or by dragging any window to the bottom of the screen. You know how to move a pop-up window by dragging its tab, and how to change its size with its two size boxes.

You also know how to clean up icons and buttons in folder and disk windows. You can arrange icons or buttons and sort a list view with the View menu. Also, you know you can use the View Options and Preferences commands in Mac OS 8 to set the icon size for each window, have the Finder keep icons arranged automatically, and choose a font for the text in all windows. In earlier system software versions, you use the Views control panel to choose a font and size for text, set icon alignment rules, and determine list view contents.

When you need to find items, you know how to use the Finder's Find command. With Mac OS 7.5 and later, that command opens the Find File program, which lets you specify a simple search with one condition or an elaborate search with up to eight conditions.

You know it's not necessary to do a lot of double-clicking to traverse layers of folders. In Mac OS 8, you can make folders spring open as you delve deeper through layers of folders, and in any Mac OS version (7.0 or later) you can zip up through folder layers toward the enclosing disk.

If you find your desktop has become cluttered with files and folders, you know the Put Away command returns them to their former locations. It also works with items in the Trash.

You know how to classify folders, programs, and documents by applying labels with the Labels submenu (or the Labels menu prior to Mac OS 8). You can arrange a list view by label, and you can search for items by label with the Finder's Find command. To change label names or colors, you use the Preferences command in Mac OS 8 or the Labels control panel in earlier system software versions.

In addition, you know how to attach comments to items and lock files with the Get Info command. You can lock folders with the Sharing command, protect the System Folder and the Applications folder with the General Controls control panel, and lock disks with locking mechanisms on their cases or with their disk setup programs.

You know the Finder can copy files, empty the Trash, and do other work in the background while you work with the Finder or another program at the same time. And you know that partitioning a hard disk can save storage space if you have a lot of small files.

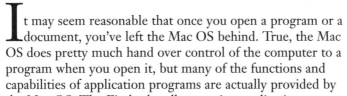

CHAPTER EIGHT

Work with Programs and Documents

IN THIS CHAPTER

- **Opening programs and documents** from the Finder, the Apple menu, the Launcher, and applications

- **Managing multiple open programs**

- **Moving document contents around** with drag-and-drop editing as well as Cut, Copy, and Paste

- **Creating documents** from scratch, by duplication, or from stationery pads

- **Saving documents** from applications

- **Translating documents** from programs you don't have, including Windows and DOS programs

It may seem reasonable that once you open a program or a document, you've left the Mac OS behind. True, the Mac OS does pretty much hand over control of the computer to a program when you open it, but many of the functions and capabilities of application programs are actually provided by the Mac OS. The Finder handles opening application programs, and the Mac OS manages to let you have more than one program open at the same time. The Finder can also open documents, and you can open them from applications using a standard dialog box provided by the Mac OS. A similar dialog box shows up when you save a document from any application.

Many programs rely on the Mac OS for basic document editing, such as the Cut, Copy, and Paste commands. You don't need those editing commands as much in programs that adopt the Mac OS drag-and-drop editing technology, which lets you move material around in a document and between documents by dragging it with the mouse.

The Mac OS also makes it possible for you to open documents created by programs you don't have, including not only Mac programs but programs on Windows, DOS, and Apple II computers. You can even use removable disks from those foreign systems in your Mac.

161

Opening Programs, Documents, and More

You can open programs, documents, other kinds of files, and folders with the Finder, the Apple menu, the Launcher control panel, or the Startup Items or Shutdown Items folders. In addition, you can open a document from the application that created it or any compatible application.

Opening from the Finder

You already know the basic methods for opening a program from the Finder (assuming you read Chapter 6). To review: you either double-click the program's icon, or in a Mac OS 8 button view, click the program's button. If you prefer a more formal approach, you can select the icon by clicking it once and then use the Open command. The Open command is in the File menu, and also appears in the contextual menu that pops up when you Control-click a program in Mac OS 8.

You can also open a program from the Finder by opening a document. When you open a document by double-clicking its icon, clicking its button, or using the Open command, the Finder figures out which application created it, opens that application, and tells the application to open the document. Quite a chain of events you start by double-clicking a document.

Suppose you want to open a bunch of documents. No problem, just select them all and then double-click one of the selected icons or use the Open command. If the documents were created by different applications, the Finder doesn't get ruffled. It opens each application and gives it a list of the documents you want opened.

Drag-and-drop opening

You can open a document from the Finder by dragging its icon to the icon of any application program that can open it. The program need not have created the document, but it must be compatible with it. For example, many Read Me documents are plain text documents that any word processor can open. Dragging a document over a compatible program without releasing the mouse button highlights the program's icon, as if you had dragged the document over a folder. Releasing the mouse button removes the highlighting, opens the program (unless it's already open), and opens the document. If a program can't open a document you drag to it, nothing happens — no highlighting, no opening. Figure 8-1 shows how an application icon looks if it can open a document that you drag to it.

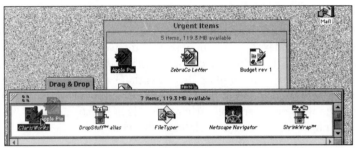

Figure 8-1: Opening a document by dragging it to a compatible application.

SECRETS

Multiple Drag

In system software versions earlier than Mac OS 8, you can drag multiple items at once to an overlapping window without moving or resizing the windows. Start by selecting the items in the source window. Next, activate the destination window by clicking along its right edge or its bottom edge (where its scroll bars would be if it were active). You can also click just below the title bar, where the column headings or disk information appear. But don't click anywhere inside the destination window or in its title bar, or you will deselect the items in the source window. Finally, drag the selected items from the now-inactive source window to the now-active destination window. You can drag the whole group of selected items by dragging any one of them, even if the target window covers some of them in the inactive source window. Unfortunately, this trick does not work in Mac OS 8. The following figure shows an example of dragging several items at once from an inactive window to the active window.

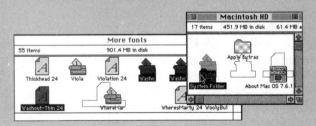

Opening the unknown

If you try to open a document and the Finder can't find the application that created it, the Finder displays an alert. If you have the Mac OS Easy Open software installed (it's part of a standard installation of Mac OS 7.5 and later), the alert gives you a choice of applications that can handle the kind of document you tried to open. (Mac OS Easy Open, which is called Macintosh Easy Open in system versions earlier than Mac OS 7.6, is covered in detail under "Translating Documents" later in this chapter.)

Things are different if you don't have Mac OS Easy Open installed or if it's turned off. The Finder displays an alert telling you it couldn't find the application that created the document you want to open. If the document is a type that SimpleText can open, the Finder asks whether you want to have SimpleText open the document. SimpleText can open documents saved in plain text format by another program (but not word processing documents saved in a proprietary format). In addition, SimpleText can open pictures saved in the PICT format, movies saved in the QuickTime format, and 3D graphics saved in the QuickDraw 3D format (for details on viewing movies and 3D graphics, see Chapter 19). The PICT, QuickTime, and QuickDraw 3D formats are all standard Mac OS formats. Figure 8-2 shows examples of the alerts that the Finder displays when it can't find the application to open a document.

The Microsoft Word document "Fictitious Names" could not be opened, because the application program that created it could not be found.

`OK`

The document "Thuvia, Maid of Mars" could not be opened, because the application program that created it could not be found. Do you want to open it using "SimpleText"?

`Cancel` `OK`

Figure 8-2: Attempting to open the document of a missing application (Mac OS Easy Open not active).

You may notice that sometimes the Finder's alert names an application that created a document, yet the Finder can't find the application. That can happen if the application is on a disk that's not on the desktop, such as an ejected CD-ROM or other removable disk. The Finder may also know the name of the application but not where to find it if the document you're trying to open is on a shared disk or file server that you're accessing on a network. And the Finder naturally can't find an application that you have deleted, though it remembers the application's name until you rebuild the desktop (as described in the next chapter).

Opening with the Apple Menu

The Apple menu expedites opening items you use frequently. Anything you can double-click in the Finder, including documents, application programs, desk accessories, folders, control panels, and even fonts and sounds, you can also put in the Apple menu and open by choosing it there. Figure 8-3 shows an example of the Apple menu.

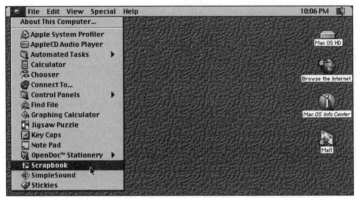

Figure 8-3: Opening an item by choosing it from the Apple menu.

Adding and removing Apple menu items

You put an item in the Apple menu by dragging it into the Apple Menu Items folder, which is inside the System Folder. The item becomes instantly available in the Apple menu (no need to restart your computer). Figure 8-4 shows how you add items to the Apple menu.

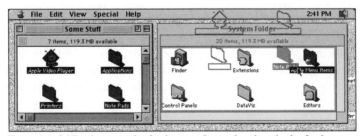

Figure 8-4: Adding items to the Apple menu by putting them in the Apple Menu Items folder.

To remove an item from the Apple menu, drag its icon out of the Apple Menu Items folder onto the desktop or into another folder.

Organizing the Apple menu

The Apple menu always lists items alphabetically in plain text. Names of aliases are not italicized in the menu even though they are italicized in the Apple Menu Items folder (for the complete story on aliases, see Chapter 12). You don't affect the Apple menu when you rearrange the contents of the Apple Menu Items folder by dragging icons in its window, clicking column headings in a list view, or using the Finder's View menu.

You can make an item appear at the top of the Apple menu by prefixing its name with a blank space. Prefixing a name with an Apple logo or solid diamond (♦) symbol makes the name appear below names prefixed with a space but above names without prefixes. To prefix a name with an Apple logo or solid diamond, open the Key Caps desk accessory and set it to the Charcoal font or the Chicago font. Press Control-T for the Apple logo or Control-S for the solid diamond, and use the Copy command to put the symbol on the Clipboard. Switch to the Finder, select an insertion point at the beginning of the item name, and paste. The Apple logo and the solid diamond look like boxes in the Apple Menu Items window because they're not part of the Geneva font, which the Finder uses for text in windows unless you specify another font with the Views control panel. They look right in the Apple menu, however, which uses the Charcoal font or the Chicago font.

To make items appear at the bottom of the Apple menu, prefix them with a hollow diamond (◊) or a bullet (•). Press Shift-Option-V for the hollow diamond or Option-8 for the bullet.

Grouping and separating items

You can group different types of items by prefixing different numbers of blank spaces to their names. The more blank spaces, the higher on the Apple menu the item appears. For example, you can prefix, two blanks to the name of the most important item in your Apple menu, one blank to names of less important items, and none to other items. Figure 8-5 shows an Apple menu where multiple blank spaces force some items higher in the menu than items with a single blank space.

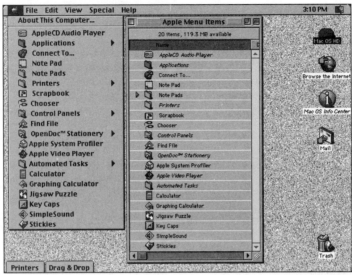

Figure 8-5: Grouping Apple menu items by prefixing names with multiple blank spaces.

QUICK TIPS

Dividing Apple Menu Items

A giant list arranged by group can be difficult to scan quickly. It helps to visually separate the different groups of items. You can make separators for the Apple menu by naming empty folders with hyphens and prefixing the right number of blank spaces to the names so that each one appears between two different groups of items.

To further refine your Apple menu, you can hide the icons of the separators you make. First, you copy some white space. If you're using Mac OS 7.6 or later, press Control-⌘-Shift-4 to copy an area of the screen that you select, and select a small amount of white anywhere on the screen. In earlier system software versions, use a paint program to copy some white space. With white space copied, select a separator item and use the Finder's Get Info command to display the item's Info window. Then select the icon in that window and paste the white space over it. The following figure shows an example of an Apple menu with separators made from folders with blank custom icons.

(continued)

(continued)

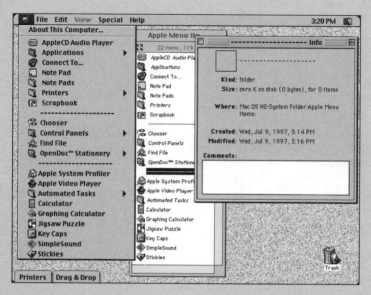

Instead of using ordinary empty folders to make separators in the Apple menu, you can use aliases. Aliases of the Finder work well as Apple menu separators because opening one (by accidentally choosing it from the Apple menu) results in a message saying that the item can't be opened. Another possible Apple menu separator is a sound or alias of a sound. Choosing a separator that's based on a sound file simply plays the sound.

STEP-BY-STEP

Forcing Order Invisibly

Forcibly reordering items in the Apple menu by putting spaces or special symbols at the beginning of the items' names has side effects you may dislike. The spaces or symbols visibly alter the names and conspicuously shift the names to the right. Here's how to invisibly force the order you want:

1. Open the Note Pad or a new document in SimpleText.

2. Press Return to create a blank line, select the blank line, and copy it to the Clipboard.

3. Switch to the Finder. Open the Apple Menu Items folder, and click the name of an item that you want to appear at the top of the Apple menu to select the name for editing.

4. Press the up-arrow key to move the insertion point to the beginning of the selected name and paste. The whole name goes blank, but don't fret.

5. Press Enter or click outside the name, and the name springs back into view. The renamed item jumps to the top of the window if you're viewing by name.

To increase an item's alphabetic buoyancy, paste the blank line two or more times at the beginning of the item's name.

Warning: Some applications don't work properly with files or folders whose names contain blank lines (blank spaces are okay). Specifically, some versions of QuarkXPress and PageMaker generate an undefined PostScript error if you try to print a document that's in a folder whose name begins with a blank line (not a blank space). If you encounter problems after pasting blank lines at the beginning of file or folder names, you'll have to use blank spaces instead.

Making submenus in the Apple menu

If your Apple menu has so many items that you must scroll to see them all, consider consolidating the less-used items in a folder or two within the Apple Menu Items folder. In Mac OS 7.5 and later, you can make the contents of folders within the Apple Menu Items folder appear as submenus of the Apple menu by using the Apple Menu Options control panel. You can also use this control panel to create submenus that list the items you have used recently. Figure 8-6 shows the Apple Menu Options control panel.

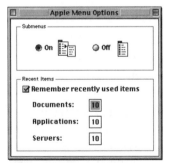

Figure 8-6: Adding submenus to the Apple menu and tracking recently used items.

The Launcher

Another way to open items is with the Launcher control panel. The Launcher displays a window of large buttons, and clicking a button (once) opens the item it represents. The Launcher is similar to a folder window viewed as buttons in Mac OS 8, but the Launcher has features a folder window doesn't have. Moreover, you don't need Mac OS 8 to use the Launcher; it comes with Mac OS 7.5 and later. Figure 8-7 shows an example of the Launcher window.

Click one of these to see another category of items

Click one of these to open an item

Figure 8-7: Opening an item by clicking its button in the Launcher control panel.

Items in the Launcher window are aliases in the Launcher Items folder inside the System Folder. (For detailed information on aliases, see Chapter 12.)

Launcher categories

You can categorize items in the Launcher by placing their aliases in specially named folders within the Launcher Items folder. The name of a category folder must begin with a bullet (press Option-8 to type a bullet). The names of up to eight category folders appear as button names in a panel at the top of the Launcher window, and clicking a category button displays the items in the corresponding category folder.

Tip: Here is a shortcut for opening a category folder: press Option and click the folder's button in the Launcher window. To open the Launcher Items folder itself, Option-click the Applications button in the Launcher window.

Adding, moving, and removing Launcher buttons

In the Launcher that comes with system software versions 7.5.1 and later, you can choose one of three sizes for icons in the Launcher window. You can also drag icons to, from, and within the Launcher window (without opening the Launcher Items folder or its subfolders) and open a document by dragging it to a compatible application in the Launcher. Specifically, you can do the following:

❖ Add an item by dragging its icon to the Launcher window, including to a category button in the Launcher window.

❖ Move an item in the Launcher by pressing the Option key and dragging the item.

❖ Open a document by dragging its icon to a compatible application's icon in the Launcher. (An application icon becomes highlighted when you drag a document icon over it in the Launcher if the application is able to open the document.)

❖ Move or copy an item to a folder by dragging the item's icon to the folder's icon in the Launcher.

❖ Remove an item from the Launcher by pressing the Option key and dragging the item to the Trash. (Do not Option-drag an item from the Launcher over a desktop printer icon, or your computer may crash.)

❖ Change the icon size for the visible Launcher category by pressing the ⌘ key, clicking inside the Launcher window, and choosing from the menu that pops up.

Startup and shutdown items

If you want to have a program, document, or anything else open every time you start up your computer, or every time you shut it down, the Finder can do that for you. Just put the items you want to open during startup into the Startup Items folder, which is inside the System Folder. Put the items you want to open during shutdown into the Shutdown Items folder, which is also inside the System Folder. Actually, to avoid disorganizing your disk you should generally put aliases (not original items) in the Startup Items and Shutdown Items folders. (For more information on these special folders, see "Investigating the System Folder" in the next chapter. For information on creating aliases, see Chapter 12.)

The Open command

Yet another way to open items is with the Open command in most applications. Choosing the Open command from any program's File menu (except the Finder's) displays a standard Open dialog box. It shows items from the desktop, the main level of one disk, or one folder at a time. The Open dialog box also has buttons and a pop-up menu for opening disks, folders, and ultimately the document you want. In some programs, the Open dialog box includes a place to display a preview of the document that's currently selected in the dialog box. Each application can also add its own unique controls to assist in opening documents. Figure 8-8 shows an example of an Open dialog box.

Figure 8-8: Opening an item using a standard dialog box.

Opening a document

You open a document that's listed in the Open dialog box by selecting it (click it once) and clicking the Open button. You can also double-click the document to open it. Either way, the Open dialog box goes away and the document appears in a window.

If you realize while double-clicking an item in an Open dialog box that you are pointing at the wrong item, continue pressing the mouse button and drag the pointer to the item you want to open. When you release the mouse button, the currently selected item opens. To cancel a double-click in an Open dialog box, hold down the mouse button on the second click and drag the pointer outside the dialog box before releasing the mouse button.

Opening a folder

To open a document that's not listed in the Open dialog box, you must open the folder that contains the document. You can open a folder by double-clicking it or by selecting it and clicking the Open button. You may have to open several folders to find the document you want to open. Each time you open a folder, the Open dialog box displays a list of its contents. The name of the folder appears above the list as part of a pop-up menu.

You can use the pop-up menu to go back through the folder layers toward the desktop. At the end of the pop-up menu is the desktop, and just ahead of it is the disk that contains the folder you currently see in the dialog box. Choosing an item from the pop-up menu takes you to that item, displaying its contents in the dialog box. As a shortcut, you can move back one folder to the folder that contains the currently listed folder by clicking the name of the disk where it is displayed above the Eject button in the dialog box.

Changing disks

To see a different disk in the dialog box, click the Desktop button to see the disks and other items on the desktop, and then double-click the disk you want to see. You can also go to the desktop by choosing it from the pop-up menu at the top of the dialog box.

If you're using a removable disk, you can eject it by clicking the Eject button in the dialog box. When you insert another removable disk, its contents appear in the dialog box. You don't have to go to the desktop before clicking the Eject button.

Navigating by keyboard

You can move through folders and open items by using the keyboard as well as the mouse. In an Open dialog box, typing an item's full name or the first part of it selects the item. For example, pressing *m* selects the first item that begins with the letter *M* or *m*. Typing several letters quickly specifies a longer name to be selected, but pausing between keys starts the selection process all over again. The Key Repeat Rate setting in the Keyboard control panel determines how long you must pause to make a fresh start. After you have selected an item in an Open dialog box (by any means), pressing Return or Enter opens the item. The Open dialog box recognizes many other keyboard shortcuts. Table 8-1 has the details.

Table 8-1
Open Dialog Box Keyboard Shortcuts

Objective	Keystroke
Select a listed document, folder, or disk	Type the item's full or partial name
Scroll up in the list of items	Up arrow
Scroll down in the list of items	Down arrow
Open the selected item	Return, Enter, ⌘-down arrow, or ⌘-O
Open the enclosing folder, disk, or volume	⌘-up arrow
Go to the next disk or volume	⌘-right arrow
Go to the previous disk or volume	⌘-left arrow
Go to the desktop	⌘-Shift-up arrow or ⌘-D
Eject the current disk	⌘-E
Eject the floppy disk in drive 1	⌘-Shift-1
Eject the floppy disk in drive 2	⌘-Shift-2
Click the Open button	Return or Enter
Click the Cancel button	Escape or ⌘-period (.)
Show the original of an alias (instead of opening it)	Option-⌘-O, Option-double-click, or Option-click Open

Managing Multiple Open Programs

With the Mac OS, you can have more than one program open at a time. When you open a program, the Finder remains open in the background. You can switch to the Finder without quitting the program you just opened. If your computer has enough memory, you can open additional programs without quitting. You can have as many programs open simultaneously as fit in your computer's memory. Figure 8-9 shows a desktop with windows from several programs open at the same time.

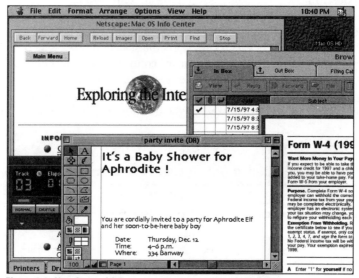

Figure 8-9: Keeping multiple programs open at the same time.

The capability of having multiple programs open simultaneously, called *multitasking*, can be very convenient. For example, you can copy and paste among documents of open programs without closing documents and quitting programs.

Multitasking's convenience has disorienting side effects. For example, a stray mouse click may make another open application active, bringing its windows to the front and covering the windows of the program you were using. If this happens unexpectedly, you may think that the program you're using has crashed when it is actually open and well in the background. You must get used to having multiple layers of open programs like piles of paper on a desk.

No matter how many programs you have open, only one has control of the menu bar. The program currently in control is called the *active program*, and its icon appears at the right end of the menu bar. You can tell which open program is currently active by looking at that icon and at the titles of the other menus on the menu bar.

Switching programs

Not only does the icon at the right end of the menu bar tell you which application is active, but it also marks the Application menu. The Application menu lists all open programs by name and small icon. You use the Application menu to switch from one open program to another. Figure 8-10 shows an example of the Application menu.

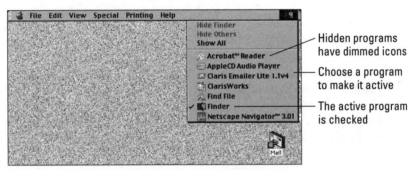

Figure 8-10: Switch applications with the Application menu.

To make a program in the Application menu the active program, choose it from the menu. When you do, that program takes over the menu bar and the program's windows come to the front. The program that was active becomes inactive. Its windows drop back but remain visible except for the parts covered by other open programs' windows.

You can also make a program the active program by clicking in any of its windows or by opening its icon or any of its document icons in the Finder. Clicking the desktop or a Finder icon makes the Finder active. On one hand, being able to bring the Finder to the front with a single mouse click can be very handy. On the other hand, it can be disorienting to have the application you're using suddenly disappear behind the Finder's windows due to a misplaced click.

Reducing window clutter

With many programs open, the desktop quickly becomes a visual Tower of Babel. You can eliminate the clutter by choosing the Application menu's Hide Others command. It hides the windows of all programs except the currently active one. The icons of hidden programs are dimmed in the Application menu. To make the windows of all programs visible, choose Show All from the Application menu.

You can hide the active program's windows and simultaneously switch to the most recently active program by choosing the first command from the Application menu. The command's name begins with the word Hide and ends with the name of the currently active program.

Tip: To hide the active program's windows as you switch to a particular program, press Option while choosing the other program from the Application menu. Or press Option while clicking the other program's window. You hide windows and switch to the Finder by pressing Option while clicking the desktop, a Finder icon, or a Finder window.

You can have the Mac OS hide the Finder's desktop automatically whenever you are working in another program. With the Finder's desktop hidden, you can't accidentally activate the Finder by clicking the desktop. To keep the Finder hidden, turn off the "Show Desktop when in background" option in the General Controls control panel, as shown in Figure 8-11.

Figure 8-11: Keep the Finder hidden with the General Controls control panel.

Memory partitions

Every application program and desk accessory you open has its own layer on the desktop and its own part of memory. You can see how your computer's memory is partitioned at any time. Just switch to the Finder and choose About This Computer (or About This Macintosh if you're using System 7.5.5 or earlier) from the Apple menu. Figure 8-12 shows an example of the About This Computer window.

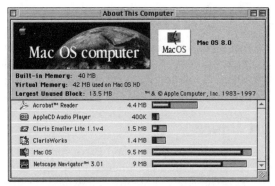

Figure 8-12: Checking memory used by open programs.

Background operations

Some programs can operate in the background by using Mac OS multitasking capabilities. Background programs run during the intervals (typically less than ⅛ of a second long) when the active program isn't using the computer. They usually work while the active program waits for you to do something.

Interacting with Background Programs

A background program can't use the menu bar and shouldn't interact directly with you in any way. It can, however, ask you to activate it by some or all of the following means:

❖ Displaying a diamond symbol next to its name in the Application menu

❖ Flashing its icon on top of the Application menu's icon or the Apple menu's icon

❖ Playing the system alert sound (commonly a beep)

❖ Displaying a brief alert message which you must dismiss before continuing

In addition, a program in the background can interact with other open programs by sending them Apple Events messages (as described in Chapter 22).

Moving Document Contents Around

While you have a document open, you can generally move its contents to different places in the same document or other documents. The classic way to move contents is with the Cut, Copy, and Paste commands in the Edit menu. Many programs also let you drag content from one place and drop it in another.

Cut, Copy, and Paste

Everyone quickly learns to use the Cut, Copy, and Paste commands to transfer material within a document and between documents. First you select the content you want to move — some text, a picture, a movie, or whatever kind of data the document contains. Then you choose Cut or Copy from the Edit menu to place the selected data on the Clipboard, which is a holding area for data in transit. The Cut command removes the selected data from its original location, but the Copy command doesn't. Next you select the location where you want to place the contents of the Clipboard, and choose Paste from the Edit menu to put it there.

The Paste command does not empty the Clipboard. After pasting once, you can paste again. The Clipboard doesn't change until you copy or cut again (or until you shut down the computer).

You can copy-and-paste or cut-and-paste within the same document, between documents in the same application, or between documents in different applications. With a little practice, cut-and-paste and copy-and-paste become second nature, especially if you use the keyboard shortcuts (⌘-X for Cut, ⌘-C for Copy, and ⌘-V for Paste).

Drag-and-drop

The Mac OS (7.5 and later) provides a more direct way to copy text, graphics, and other material within a document, between documents, and between applications. This capability, called *drag-and-drop editing*, works only with applications that are designed to take advantage of it. Several programs that come with the Mac OS (7.5 and later) work with drag-and-drop editing, including SimpleText, Stickies, Note Pad, and Scrapbook.

To move material within a document, open the document and select the text, graphic, or other material that you want to copy. Then position the mouse pointer over the selected material, press the mouse button, and drag to the place where you want to move it. As you drag, an outline of the selected material follows the pointer, and if you're dragging text, an insertion point shows where the copy will appear when you stop dragging. If you want to copy selected material within a document rather than move it, press the Option key before releasing the mouse button. Figure 8-13 shows some text being moved within a document.

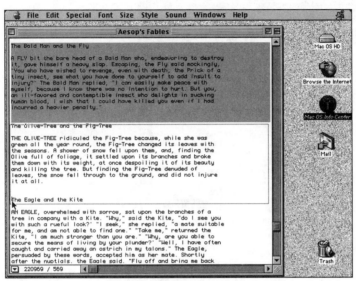

Figure 8-13: Drag-and-drop editing within a document.

To copy material between documents, first open both documents and position them so that you can see the source material and the place where you want to drop a copy of it. Select the text, graphic, or other source material and then drag the selected material to the place in the second document where you want the copy. As you drag, an outline of the selected material follows the mouse pointer. When the pointer enters the destination window, a border appears around the content area of the window, and if you're dragging text, an insertion point shows where the copy will appear when you stop dragging. Note that you do not have to press the Option key to make a copy when dragging between documents. You can use the same method to copy between two documents in the same application or between documents in different applications. Figure 8-14 shows some text being copied from one application to another.

You can also drag selected material from a document to the desktop or a folder window, where the Finder creates a *clipping file* that contains a copy of the dragged material. You can open a clipping file to see it in the Finder, but you can't select anything in a clipping file. You can copy the contents of a clipping file to a document by dragging the clipping-file icon to the open document's window. Clipping files can contain text, pictures, QuickTime movies, and sound.

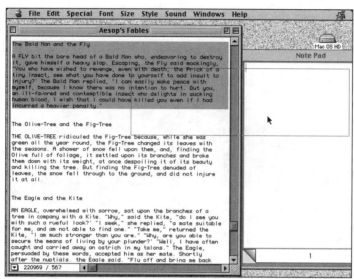

Figure 8-14: Drag-and-drop editing between documents.

You can use a clipping file over and over. For example, you can keep handy clippings that contain your letterhead, the company logo, a list of your e-mail addresses, and any other element that you use frequently.

Some people prefer drag-and-drop to cut-and-paste editing because they find it easier to use. Drag-and-drop has one clear advantage: It doesn't wipe out the contents of the Clipboard, so it's a good method to use when the Clipboard contains important material that you're not ready to replace.

Creating Documents

You can't always be opening documents that already exist. Sometimes you need to create new ones. Many application programs automatically create a new, untitled document when you double-click the application icon, but not when you open the application by double-clicking a document icon. If an application doesn't create a new document automatically, you can usually create one by choosing New from the File menu.

You can also create a new document by making a copy of an existing document. This method is especially useful if the existing document contains something you want to include in a new document, such as a letterhead or some boilerplate. To make a copy of a document, use the Finder's Duplicate command or one of the other methods described in "Working with Files and Folders" in Chapter 6.

Rather than duplicating a document every time you want a copy of it, you can make it a stationery pad. Opening a stationery pad — whether from the Finder directly, from the Apple menu, from the Launcher, or with the Open command in many applications — is like tearing a page from a pad of preprinted forms. You get a new document with a preset format and contents. Stationery pads generally have a distinctive icon that looks like a stack of document icons, although some types of stationery have generic (blank) stationery pad icons. Figure 8-15 shows some examples of stationery pad icons.

Figure 8-15: Stationery pad icons resemble pads of paper.

You can make any document a stationery pad by selecting the document in the Finder, choosing the Get Info command, and setting the Stationery Pad option in the Info window. Some applications enable you to directly save a document as a stationery pad (more about that in the next section, "Saving Documents"). Figure 8-16 shows the Stationery Pad option in an Info window.

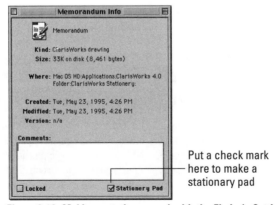

Put a check mark here to make a stationary pad

Figure 8-16: Making a stationery pad with the Finder's Get Info command.

What happens when you open a stationery pad depends on whether the application that opens it knows the difference between stationery pads and regular documents and may also depend on how you open it. If an application knows about stationery pads, it always creates a new untitled document with the format and content of the stationery pad. In this case, it doesn't matter how you open the stationery pad. If you use the Finder, the Apple menu, or the Launcher, the Mac OS figures out which application creates the type of stationery you're opening and tells that application to open the stationery. If you use the application's Open command, the application opens the stationery directly.

What happens when you open a stationery pad created by an application that does not know about stationery pads depends on whether you open the stationery in the Finder or in the program.

If you open a stationery pad for a type of document created by an application that doesn't know about stationery, the Mac OS creates a new document by making a copy from the stationery pad and has the application open the new document. With Mac OS 8, the Finder automatically names the new document. In earlier system software versions, you may get a dialog box asking you to enter a document name before opening the document. The dialog box appears only if you're using Mac OS 7.6.1 or earlier and the application that created the stationery document doesn't know how to open stationery properly itself.

If you open a stationery pad with the Open command of an application that doesn't know about stationery, the application opens the stationery pad itself, not a copy of it. A message warns you that you are opening a stationery pad. If you make changes, they will be saved into the stationery pad itself.

QUICK TIPS

When Locks Are Better Than Stationery

Opening a stationery pad creates a new document file. If you want to make a template that doesn't create a new file every time you open the template, don't make the template a stationery pad. Instead, make the template an ordinary document, but lock it by using the Finder's Get Info command. You may want to use this method with templates for single envelopes and mailing labels, for example. Then you can open the locked template, type or paste the recipient's address, print, and close without saving.

Saving Documents

After creating a new document or making changes to a document you opened, you need to save the document on disk so the changes persist. You save a changed document by choosing Save or Save As from the File menu. Either command brings up a standard Save dialog box if the document has never been saved. The Save As command always brings up the Save dialog box so you can save a copy of the document. If the document has been saved previously, the Save command does not bring up a dialog box; the application automatically saves the changed document in place of the previously saved document.

The Save dialog box looks and works much like the Open dialog box. It displays the contents of the desktop, the main level of one disk, or one folder at a time, and has controls for opening a different disk or folder in the dialog box. In addition, the Save dialog box has a space where you enter a name for the document. The Save dialog box may have other controls for setting document format options. Figure 8-17 shows an example of a Save dialog box.

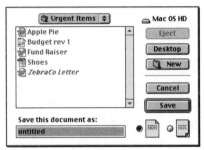

Figure 8-17: Save a document using a standard dialog box.

Specifying a name and location

The first time you save a document and every time you use the Save As command, you need to type a name for the document in the space provided, and you need to specify where you want the document saved. You do that by opening a folder, the main level of a disk, or the desktop in the dialog box. All the same methods described earlier in this chapter for opening folders, disks, and the desktop in an Open dialog box also work in a Save dialog box. You can open folders and disks by double-clicking them or by selecting one and clicking the Open button. You can use the pop-up menu or click the disk name to go back through the folder layers toward the desktop. You can eject a removable disk with the Eject button.

When you select a folder or disk in the Save dialog box, there is an Open button but no Save button. To change the Open button to a Save button so you can save the document, select the document name at the bottom of the dialog box by clicking it or pressing the Tab key.

Copy and Paste in the Save Dialog

While you are editing the name of the item you're saving, the Cut, Copy, and Paste commands are available from the Edit menu. This means you can copy a name for a document from within the document before choosing the Save command, and then paste the copied name into the Save dialog box. When pasting a document name, only the first 31 characters are used; the rest are omitted. In some programs, you must use the keyboard equivalents: ⌘-X for Cut, ⌘-C for Copy, and ⌘-V for Paste.

Saving a stationery pad

In many applications you can designate in the Save dialog box whether to save a document as a stationery pad or a regular document. Some applications offer this choice with two radio buttons, one labeled with a regular document icon and the other labeled with a stationery pad icon. Other documents offer more document format options in a pop-up menu at the bottom of the Save dialog box.

Creating a new folder

The Save dialog box usually includes a button you can click to create a new folder. Clicking the New Folder button displays a small dialog box in which you type the name of the folder you want to create and click. The new folder is created in the folder, disk, or desktop whose contents are currently displayed in the Save dialog box. Figure 8-18 shows the dialog box in which you enter a new folder name.

Navigating by keyboard

You can use the Open dialog box keyboard shortcuts previously listed in Table 8-1 to move through folders and disks in a Save dialog box as well. You can also press ⌘-N to create a new folder. However, there is a trick to navigating by keyboard in a Save dialog box. You must select the contents list in the dialog box so your keystrokes don't end up as part of the document name. You alternate between the contents list and the name entry area by pressing the Tab key. Clicking in either area also makes it the keyboard target. The Mac OS lets you know when your typing affects a contents list by outlining it with a heavy black border. A flashing insertion point or highlighted text in the document name indicates that your typing goes there. Figure 8-19 shows a Save dialog box where the contents list is the keyboard target and another where the document name is the target.

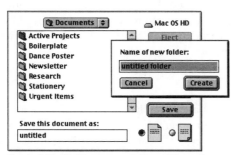

Figure 8-18: Making a new folder while saving.

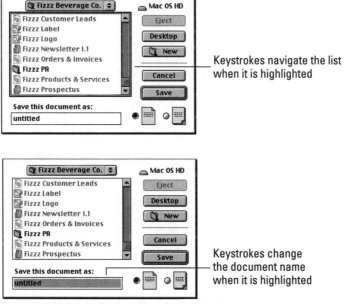

Figure 8-19: Using the keyboard in a Save dialog box to navigate the contents list (top) or edit the document name (bottom).

Translating Documents

As the Mac OS has evolved, it has gradually simplified the process of opening documents created with programs you don't have. Someone else may have created the documents on another Mac OS computer or a Windows, DOS, or Apple II (ProDOS) computer. You may have created the document with an application you don't have any more. In any case, you need to open the document with an application you do have. You may be able to use an application that can open foreign documents itself, or you may need translation software to convert the foreign document to a format your application can open. The Mac OS comes with several pieces of file compatibility and document translation software: PC Exchange, Mac OS Easy Open, and MacLinkPlus.

PC Exchange

With the PC Exchange control panel installed, the Mac OS can access floppy disks from Windows or DOS computers. When you insert a disk from one of those computers into your computer, the foreign disk's icon appears on the Finder's desktop. You can open the foreign disk and see its files and folders (which are called *subdirectories* in DOS and Windows). You can open folders by double-clicking them, and you can open document files if you have compatible Mac programs or document translation software. For example, most Mac applications from Adobe, Claris, and Microsoft can open documents created by their Windows counterparts.

When you double-click a document file on a foreign disk, the Finder can determine which Mac program to have open the file by looking up the DOS *file name suffix* (the three characters following the period) in PC Exchange. PC Exchange contains a list that correlates DOS file name suffixes, which are also known as *file name extensions*, with Mac programs and document types. A file whose name ends with .TXT, for example, is opened by SimpleText as a text document. Table 8-2 lists several common DOS file name extensions. Figure 8-20 shows an example of the PC Exchange control panel.

To add a DOS extension and corresponding Mac application and document type, you click the Add button in the PC Exchange control panel. This action brings up a suffix-assignment dialog box, in which you type a suffix, select a Mac program, and choose a document type. Figure 8-21 shows the suffix-assignment dialog box.

Figure 8-20: Matching DOS file name suffixes to Mac programs with PC Exchange.

	Table 8-2
	DOS File Name Suffixes

Suffix	Application and Document Type
.AI	Adobe Illustrator 4.1 document
.BMP	Windows or OS/2 bitmap graphic
.CDR	Corel Draw document
.COM	An application program
.DBF	Database file (various spreadsheet and database applications)
.DOC	Microsoft Word document
.DOT	Microsoft Word template
.EPS	Encapsulated Postscript file
.EXE	Self-extracting compressed file (PkZip format) or an application
.GIF	GIF graphic
.HTM	Web page (HTML file)
.IL5	Illustrator document (number is the application version)
.JPG	JPEG compressed graphic
.P65	Adobe PageMaker 6.5 publication files
.PCT	PICT graphic

(continued)

	Table 8-2 *(continued)*
.PCX	PC Paintbrush graphic
.PDF	Adobe Acrobat document
.PM6	PageMaker 6 document (number is the application version)
.PPT	Microsoft PowerPoint document
.PRN	Any print-to-disk file from many applications, including PostScript, PCL (HP LaserJet), or ASCII (for line printers)
.PS	PostScript files
.PSD	Adobe Photoshop document
.PT6	PageMaker 6 template (number is the application version)
.PUB	Microsoft Publisher document
.QXD	QuarkXPress document
.RTF	Rich Text Format word processing document (which can be opened in a word processor or placed in PageMaker)
.SAM	AmiPro document
.T65	Adobe PageMaker 6.5 template files
.TBL	Adobe table editor document
.TIF	TIFF graphic
.TXT	Plain text document
.WK1	Lotus 1-2-3 spreadsheet (the number is the application version)
.WKS	Microsoft Works document
.WMF	Windows Meta File graphic
.WP	WordPerfect document
.WPD	WordPerfect document (version 6.1 and higher)
.WPG	WordPerfect graphic
.WQ1	Quattro Pro spreadsheet (the number is the application version)
.WRI	Microsoft Write document
.WS2	WordStar document (the number is the application version)
.XLS	Microsoft Excel spreadsheet
.ZIP	Compressed file (PkZip format)

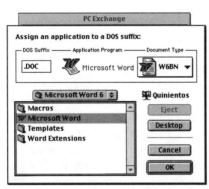

Figure 8-21: Assigning a DOS suffix to a Mac application and file type with PC Exchange.

To change a DOS extension assignment, click the Change button in the PC Exchange control panel to bring up the suffix-assignment dialog box. There you can edit the suffix, select a different Mac program, and select a document type from the ones that the selected application can open.

Clicking the Remove button in the PC Exchange control panel removes the currently selected DOS assignment from the list. Before clicking Remove, you can select multiple items in the list by ⌘-clicking them (to select them individually) or Shift-clicking (to select a range).

Mac OS Easy Open and MacLinkPlus

The Mac OS Easy Open control panel can automatically translate documents created by programs you don't have, and can then have a program you do have open the translated document. MacLinkPlus enhances Mac OS Easy Open so that it can translate many more types of documents. Mac OS Easy Open comes with Mac OS 7.5 and later (it's called Macintosh Easy Open in system software versions earlier than 7.6), and MacLinkPlus is included with Mac OS 7.6 and later.

In addition to helping you open documents, Easy Open enhances the Open and Save dialog boxes and list views in the Finder. Without Easy Open, the Open and Save dialog boxes display tiny generic icons for documents, applications, folders, and disks. With Easy Open, those dialog boxes display small color icons like the ones you see in the Finder. Easy Open also provides more detailed information in the Kind column of list views in folder and disk windows. Rather than see every file listed as "document," you usually see the name of the program that created the document.

Translation choices

Easy Open and MacLinkPlus go to work whenever you open a document that wasn't created by any of the applications you have. It doesn't matter how you open the document — by double-clicking its icon in the Finder, choosing it from the Apple menu, or using the Open command in an application.

When you open a document created by an unknown application, Easy Open displays a dialog box that lists your alternatives for opening the document. Each alternative identifies a program you have and may also specify an available translator that can translate the document you're opening for that program. A program may be listed more than once, each time with a different translator. For example, if you try to open an old PICT (picture) document created by MacDraw, which you no longer have, Easy Open might list ClarisWorks three times, once with no translator (ClarisWorks can open PICT documents directly), once with MacLinkPlus translation, and once with QuickTime translation. Figure 8-22 shows an example of Easy Open's translation choices dialog box.

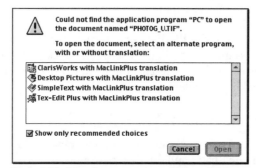

Figure 8-22: Choosing a program and a translator to open a document created by an application you don't have.

In Easy Open's translation choices dialog box, you select a translation alternative that looks promising (ideally a translation for a program closely related to the document) and click the Open button. You can alternatively just double-click a translation alternative. Easy Open applies the translator you selected (if any) and has the program you selected open the translated document.

You can see more choices in the translation choices dialog box by turning off the "Show only recommended choices" option. With this option turned off, you see a list of all the programs you have that can conceivably open the file. If you choose an alternative that's not on the short recommended list, the file probably won't translate well. For example, America Online can open a Word for Windows document, but the document comes across as unformatted text with a bunch of extraneous box characters. Some of the programs in Easy Open's long list won't even open the file, so in general you save time when you stick with the recommended translations.

Easy Open keeps track of the program and translator that you choose to open each type of document. If you subsequently open another document of the same type, Easy Open automatically selects the same program and translator for you.

Easy Open setup

You can set several options in the Mac OS Easy Open control panel that affect how Easy Open behaves. You can also use the control panel to turn off Easy Open. Figure 8-23 shows the Mac OS Easy Open control panel.

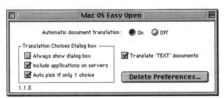

Figure 8-23: Setting Easy Open options.

If you want Easy Open to display its translation choices dialog box only the first time that you open a particular type of document, turn off the "Always show dialog box" option in the control panel. Turn on this option if you want Easy Open to display the list of alternative programs and translators every time you open a document that wasn't created by a program you have. Easy Open does not waste your time with the list of alternative programs if you have only one program that can open a document and the "Auto pick if only 1 choice" option is turned on.

If you want the list of alternative programs to include programs from file servers, which operate more slowly than programs on your local disks, turn on the option "Include applications on file servers."

Turning on the "Translate 'TEXT' documents" option tells Easy Open to look at the contents of the text documents you open to see whether those contents can be translated to some type of formatted document. Turning off this option speeds the opening of plain-text documents, but also causes many Windows and DOS documents to be opened as unformatted text documents by SimpleText. (Many formatted Windows and DOS documents look like plain text documents to the Mac OS.) If you want to translate any Windows or DOS documents, you should leave this option turned on.

Translating without opening

You don't have to open a document to translate it. The Document Converter program that comes with Mac OS 7.6 and later can use the MacLinkPlus translators to translate a document without opening it. Look for Document Converter in the MacLinkPlus folder on the startup disk.

You use Document Converter to make a separate converter for each type of conversion you want to have on tap. Once you have the right converter, you can drag and drop files onto it to translate them in one step. When you drag a file to a converter, it automatically adds the word *converted* to the name of the translated file.

To make a converter, first locate the Document Converter and make a duplicate of it. Double-click the duplicate to see a long list of translation options. Scroll through the list to look for the combination of program and translator that you want to make a converter for. Select the program and translator combination you want and click the Set button. You can also just double-click the program and translator combination. Doing so creates a customized converter, renamed to indicate which file format it translates to. Figure 8-24 shows a few of the dozens of choices.

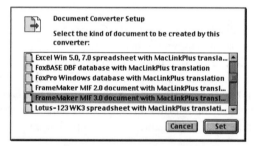

Figure 8-24: Setting up a document converter.

Reducing translation overhead

You can speed up Document Converter setup, decrease the startup time for your computer, and reduce the amount of memory used for system software by disabling MacLinkPlus translators you never use. The MacLinkPlus translators are in the Data Viz folder, which is in the System Folder. You can create a folder named Unused Translators in the Data Viz folder and drag unneeded translators into it to disable them.

Summary

After reading this chapter, you know how to open documents in the Finder by dragging them to any compatible program. You know how to open anything from the Apple menu and the Launcher control panel, and how to have items opened during startup or shutdown. You are familiar with the Open dialog box used by all applications for opening documents and with the similar Save dialog box used by applications for saving new documents and document changes.

When you have more than one program open at the same time, you know how to make any of them active. You can deal with window clutter, and you understand how multiple programs share your computer's memory and work in the background.

You know several ways to create new documents. You can duplicate existing documents or create new ones from scratch with an application's New command. You can also make and use stationery pads for creating new documents.

Finally, you know how the Mac OS helps you open documents created by applications you don't have. The PC Exchange control panel enables your computer to use removable disks from Windows, DOS, and Apple II computers, and you can configure the control panel to have your applications automatically open compatible foreign documents according to their DOS file extensions. The Mac OS Easy Open control panel and the MacLinkPlus translation software enable you to open documents that aren't directly compatible with any of your applications.

CHAPTER NINE

9

Dig into the System Folder

IN THIS CHAPTER

- **Probing the System Folder:** what's inside the System, Fonts, Apple Menu Items, Startup Items, Shutdown Items, Control Panels, Extensions, and Preferences folders, and more

- **Adding to and removing from the System Folder** and dealing with conflicts between system extensions

- **Uncovering more special items:** the Trash, Desktop, Temporary Items, and Rescued Items folders

- **Maintaining the desktop database** that links documents to their creator applications

Your computer has a special folder that contains all the essential software that gives the Mac OS its unique appearance and behavior. That folder is normally named System Folder, although the name is not mandatory. You can always spot the System Folder by its distinctive icon, which looks like a folder emblazoned with a miniature Mac OS logo (or with a miniature Finder icon prior to Mac OS 8).

The Mac OS uses additional special folders and files, several of them invisible, to keep track of items in the Trash, items on the desktop, and temporary files used by application programs. A desktop database matches documents with the applications that created them so they all have the right icons and you can open documents from the Finder.

Investigating the System Folder

The System Folder contains several additional special folders, each with a distinctive icon, a unique name, and particular contents. The System Folder also contains a few files, such as the System file, which you can open like a folder, and the Finder. In addition, there may be some ordinary folders in the System Folder. Figure 9-1 shows an example of a System Folder in Mac OS 8.

Figure 9-1: Inside a typical System Folder.

Here's a brief rundown on the items in a typical Mac OS 8 System Folder:

❖ **Finder** is the application for organizing files, folders, and disks (see Chapters 6 and 7).

❖ **Extensions** contains software that extends the capabilities of the Mac OS and application programs (covered later in this section).

❖ **Apple Menu Items** contains items listed in the Apple menu (see Chapter 8).

❖ **Application Support** contains items used by some application programs.

❖ **Claris** contains items used by applications from Claris Corp. and by other applications that use the Claris XTND file translation software.

❖ **Control Panels** contains small programs for setting options (see Chapters 10 and 11).

❖ **Control Strip Modules** contains the modules that appear in the Control Strip (see Chapter 10).

❖ **DataViz** contains file translation software (see Chapter 8).

❖ **Editors** contains OpenDoc editors (see Chapter 23).

❖ **Fonts** contains fixed-size, TrueType, and PostScript fonts (see Chapter 13).

❖ **Launcher Items** contains items to be displayed in the Launcher window (see Chapter 8).

❖ **MacTCP DNR** is mostly obsolete in Mac OS 7.6 and later, but some applications that use a TCP/IP network may require it.

❖ **Preferences** contains settings, status, and other information used by various programs (covered later in this section).

❖ **Scrapbook File** contains the items you can copy with the Scrapbook program (see Chapter 10).

❖ **Scripting Additions** contains files that extend the AppleScript language (see Chapter 22).

❖ **Shutdown Items** contains items to be opened as the computer shuts down (covered later in this section).

❖ **Startup Items** contains items to be opened as the computer starts up (covered later in this section).

❖ **System** contains much of the basic system software as well as sounds, keyboard layouts, and language script systems (covered next in this section).

❖ **Text Encodings** contains software that enables displaying and editing multiple languages.

❖ **Clipboard** temporarily stores what you copy or cut.

This list is not meant to be definitive. Earlier system software versions may not have all of the above items, yet may have other items not listed above. Furthermore, additional items may show up in your System Folder after you install applications or other software.

System file

Of all the items in the System Folder, there are two that must be present for the computer to start up. One is the Finder and the other is the System file. The System file has long been terra incognita to all but the most intrepid resource-hacking Mac OS users. Although a large part of it remains an uncharted wilderness of basic system software, the Finder lets you see and work with some of the System file's contents.

Seeing System file contents

You can open the System file as if it were a folder and see which alert sounds, keyboard layouts, and script systems for foreign languages it contains. Several items do not appear when you open the System file because they are permanently installed in every computer that can use the Mac OS. These items include the simple beep sound, the U.S. keyboard layout, and the Roman script system for Western languages. Figure 9-2 shows examples of the items you can see by opening a System file.

Figure 9-2: The System file contains sounds and keyboard layouts.

Working with System file contents

Not only can you see the contents of the System file, you can also drag items in and out of it as if it were a folder. Changes to sounds take effect as soon as you close the System file, but changes to other items require restarting your computer first. The Finder doesn't allow you to drag items in or out of the System file when other programs are open. You must quit all open programs except the Finder, make your changes to the System file contents, and then open the programs again.

Items you drag out of the System file become independent files. You can move them to any folder or the desktop and copy them to other disks. You can rename sounds but not other items in the System file. You can open a sound that's in or out of the System file, which makes the computer play it.

Installing sounds in the System file makes them candidates for the system alert sound, which you choose with the Monitors & Sound control panel or the Sound control panel. There are several kinds of sound files, but you can put only one kind into the System file. The kind of sound file that can go in the System file is called a *System 7 Sound* or sometimes an *snd*. Specifically, you can't put HyperCard sounds or AIFF sounds in the System file.

The keyboard layouts you install appear as choices in the Keyboard control panel. Selecting a different keyboard layout there changes your Mac's arrangement of the keys on your keyboard. Selecting the Español (Spanish) layout, for example, makes the semicolon key on a U.S. keyboard produce an ñ (Chapter 21 includes more details about foreign-language keyboard arrangements).

Fonts folder

The Mac OS simplifies font organization by keeping all fonts — TrueType, fixed-size, and PostScript — in a special Fonts folder inside the System Folder. Installing fonts in the Fonts folder makes them available in programs that let you choose fonts. Newly installed fonts may not be available in programs that are already open until you quit and reopen the programs. A Fonts folder can contain up to 128 items — fonts, suitcases, or a combination. Each suitcase in the Fonts folder can contain any number of fixed-size and TrueType fonts up to a maximum of 16MB, so if you need room for more than 128 fonts, you can group fonts together in suitcases. (For more information about fonts, see Chapter 13.) Figure 9-3 shows examples of font files and font suitcases in the Fonts folder.

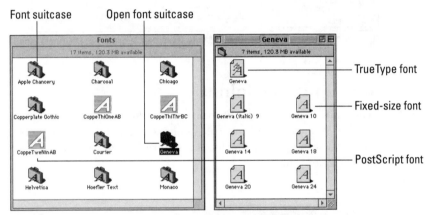

Figure 9-3: The Fonts folder contains font suitcases and font files.

Some old applications that use PostScript fonts do not look for them in the Fonts folder. For more information on this situation, see "Managing Fonts" in Chapter 13.

Apple Menu Items folder

The Apple Menu Items folder enables you to quickly open anything you use often. All the items in the folder appear on the Apple menu, and choosing an item from the menu has the same effect as opening (double-clicking) the corresponding item in the folder. (For information on using the Apple menu, see the previous chapter.) Figure 9-4 shows an example of the Apple Menu Items folder and the resulting Apple menu.

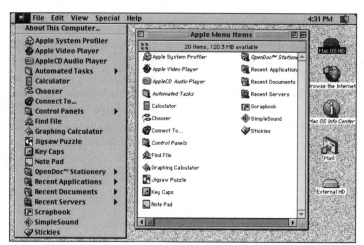

Figure 9-4: The contents of the Apple Menu Items folder appear in the Apple menu.

Startup Items folder

Everything you put in the Startup Items folder — application programs, desk accessories, documents, control panels, sounds, and so on — gets opened when you start up your Macintosh. Figure 9-5 shows an example of the Startup items folder.

Figure 9-5: Items in the Startup Items folder open when the computer starts up.

To have your computer open an item at startup time, drag it or an alias of it to the Startup Items folder. Dragging an item out of that folder removes it from the startup sequence.

Although any kind of item that can be opened can be a startup item, it's usually best to place aliases of items and not the items themselves in the Startup Items folder. That way if you need to open an item again without starting up, you don't have to remember that you made it a startup item and go digging into the System Folder for it. Moreover, some applications don't work at all if you move them out of the folder that contains their support files. (For information on making aliases, see Chapter 12.)

QUICK TIPS

Arranging Startup Items

If you open several application programs during startup, you may have to quit some of them later to free up memory for opening another. Naturally, you'll want to quit the applications least important to you. You'll free up the most memory by quitting the applications opened last during startup. To make that easy, rename the items in your Startup Items folder so that the most important application comes first alphabetically, the next most important comes second, and so on. One way to do that is by putting a sequence number (01, 02, 03, and so on) at the beginning of the startup item name. This trick works only for ordering items of the same kind — aliases, application programs, control panels, documents, and so forth — because the Finder opens all of one kind of an item before opening any of another kind.

Shutdown Items folder

Besides having items open automatically during startup, you can have items open automatically when you shut down or restart your computer. For example, you could have the computer play a sound or start a backup program. To make an item open during the shutdown process, add the item or an alias of it to the Shutdown Items folder. (Chapter 12 explains how to make aliases.) Figure 9-6 shows an example of the Shutdown Items folder.

Figure 9-6: Items in the Shutdown Items folder open when the computer shuts down.

Any item you can open from the Finder you can put into the Shutdown Items folder, but aliases have advantages over original items. When you no longer want an original item opened at startup, you have to figure out where to put it. In contrast, when you no longer want an alias opened during shutdown, you can just discard the alias. Furthermore, putting original items into the Shutdown Items folder tends to disorganize your disk, and some applications won't work if you remove them from the folders that contain their support files.

Control Panels folder

The items in the Control Panels folder give you control over system appearance and behavior. The folder contains small programs called *control panels*. Each affects one aspect of the system. Some control panels also add functions to the basic system software during startup. (For information about using individual control panels, see Chapter 10.) Figure 9-7 shows an example of the Control Panels folder.

Figure 9-7: Items in the Control Panels folder add functionality and options to the system software.

Extensions folder

The items in the Extensions folder are small software modules called *system extensions*. They customize your Macintosh by extending the services and functions of system software. Figure 9-8 shows an example of the Extensions folder.

Figure 9-8: Items inside the Extensions folder extend the capabilities of the system software.

Adding and removing extensions

Most system extensions are placed in the Extensions folder by installation software, and other software may be installed elsewhere at the same time. Generally you don't have to drag files into the Extensions folder. However, you can drag files out of the Extensions folder if you don't want or need the capabilities they provide. For example, if you don't have an AudioVision 14 monitor, you don't need the PowerPC Monitors Extension. Removing unnecessary extensions can reduce startup time, reduce system memory use, and increase system reliability. You may find it easier to manage extensions with the Extensions Manager control panel (described in Chapter 10). After removing or adding items to the Extensions folder, you typically must restart your computer for the changes to take effect.

Extension and Control Panel Loading Sequence

System extensions may be in the Extensions folder, the Control Panels folder (where they are built into some control panels), or the System Folder itself. During startup, the Mac OS loads extensions in three groups. First, it goes through the Extensions folder in alphabetical order. Then it loads the extensions that are built into items in the Control Panels folder, again alphabetically. Finally, it checks the System Folder itself and alphabetically loads system extensions it finds there. This loading sequence can cause problems for old system extensions and control panels created before System 7 existed.

Some system extensions and control panels have peculiar names that put the items first or last in the loading sequence. Names of items meant to come first usually begin with blank spaces. Names meant to come last often begin with a tilde (~) or a diamond (◊).

To have control panels whose names begin with blank spaces load first during startup, put them in the Extensions folder. To have control panels whose names start with tildes or diamonds loaded last during startup, put them in the System Folder. For convenient access to the control panels you move out of the Control Panels folder, make aliases for them, and put the aliases in the Control Panels folder. (See Chapter 12 for instructions on making aliases.)

Common extensions

The version of system software and the options you have installed affect the contents of your Extensions folder. A typical installation of the Mac OS includes the following:

❖ **Appearance Extension** provides the platinum appearance first included with Mac OS 8 (as described in Chapter 5).

❖ **Apple Built-in Ethernet, Apple Ethernet NB,** and **EtherTalk Phase 2** enable you to connect the computer to an Ethernet network (as described in Chapter 17).

❖ **Apple CD-ROM, Apple Photo Access, Audio CD Access, Foreign File Access, High Sierra File Access,** and **ISO 9660 File Access** enable the Mac to read CD-ROMs in a variety of formats, including audio CDs and Kodak Photo CDs.

❖ **Apple Guide, About Apple Guide, Macintosh Guide, the Global Guides folder,** and other Apple Guide documents provide step-by-step interactive help for various tasks (as described in Chapter 5).

❖ **AppleScript, AppleScript Lib,** and **Scripting Additions,** make it possible to automate tasks in one application or many (as described in Chapter 22). Note that beginning with Mac OS 7.5.5, the preferred location for scripting addition files is the Scripting Additions folder at the main level of the System Folder.

❖ **AppleShare,** a Chooser extension, enables you to use folders and disks from other computers connected to yours (as described in Chapter 18).

❖ **Color Picker** improves the dialog box in which you select a custom color (as described in Chapter 7).

❖ **ColorSync** ensures that color input from scanners and graphics programs matches color output on monitors, printers, and plotters (as described in Chapters 10 and 15). ColorSync is optional in System 7.5–7.5.5.

❖ **Contextual Menu Extension** enables the Mac OS 8 contextual menus (as described in Chapter 5).

❖ **Desktop Printer Spooler, Desktop PrintMonitor, Desktop Printer Extension, Desktop Printer Menu,** and **PrintingLib** enable you to work with desktop printer icons (as described in Chapter 14). Mac OS 8 has only the first two of these. The desktop printing software is optional in System 7.5.3–7.5.5, and must be obtained separately for System 7.5–7.5.2.

❖ **EM Extension** enables you to open the Extensions Manager control panel by holding down the spacebar during startup (as described in Chapter 10).

❖ **File Sharing Extension, File Sharing Library,** and **Network Extension** enable you to share your folders and disks with other people in your network (as described in Chapter 18). The function of Network Extension is built into the Mac OS 8 System File.

❖ **GXGraphics** provides advanced QuickDraw GX typography in Mac OS 8 (as described in Chapter 13).

❖ **Internet Access** and **Internet Config Extension** assist in connecting to the Internet and sharing Internet preference settings among applications in Mac OS 8 (as described in Chapter 20).

❖ **LaserWriter, StyleWriter, ImageWriter,** and other Chooser extensions (also called *printer drivers*) enable your system to print on a specific type of printer (as described in Chapter 14).

❖ **MacinTalk Pro, MacinTalk 3, Speech Manager,** and the **Voices** folder enable text-to-speech synthesis (as described in Chapter 21).

❖ **Modem Scripts** folder contains documents that enable communicating through a modem (as described in Chapters 17 and 20). Prior to Mac OS 7.6, the individual modem script documents may be loose in the Extensions folder.

❖ **MRJ Libraries** folder provides support for Java applications in Mac OS 8 (as described in Chapter 20). MRJ is optional in Mac OS 7.6.1 and earlier.

❖ **Multiprocessing** folder lets Mac OS 7.6 and later take advantage of multiple central processors on computers that have them.

❖ **OpenDoc Libraries** folder, **Memory Manager,** and **SOMobjects for Mac OS** are part of the OpenDoc component software (described in Chapter 23). OpenDoc is optional in System 7.5.5 and earlier.

❖ **Open Transport Library** and all other files whose name begin **Open Transport, Open Tpt,** or **OpenTpt** provide Open Transport networking (described in Chapter 17).

❖ **PowerPC Monitors Extension** supports the AudioVision 14 monitor.

❖ **Printer Descriptions** contain information about specific printers for use with version 8.0 and later of the LaserWriter extension (as described in Chapter 14).

❖ **Printer Share** makes it possible to share more types of printers on a network (as described in Chapter 14).

❖ **PrintMonitor** prints documents in the background while you continue working (as described in Chapter 14).

❖ **QuickDraw 3D** and other files whose names begin with QuickDraw 3D or **Apple QD3D** enable the Mac OS to draw three-dimensional graphics in real time (as described in Chapter 19).

❖ **QuickTime, QuickTime MPEG Extension, QuickTime Musical Instruments, QuickTime PowerPlug,** and **QuickTime VR** make it possible to watch digital movies, decompress compressed pictures, hear MIDI music, and manipulate panoramas as described in Chapter 19.

❖ **Shared Library Manager** and **Shared Library Manager PPC** manage shared libraries of program code for the Mac OS and applications.

❖ **Web Sharing Extension** makes it easy to host a Web site from your computer with Mac OS 8 (as described in Chapter 20).

Additional extensions (System 7.5–Mac OS 7.6.1)

System 7.5–Mac OS 7.6.1 have still more items in the Extensions folder:

❖ **Clipping Extension** enables drag-and-drop editing within and between documents and applications (as described in Chapter 8).

❖ **Find File Extension** enables the Finder's Find command to open the Find File program (as described in Chapter 7).

❖ **Finder Help** and **Shortcuts** provide onscreen help for the Finder (as described in Chapter 5).

❖ **Finder Scripting Extension** enables you to automate Finder tasks with AppleScript (as described in Chapter 22).

❖ **WorldScript Power Adapter** accelerates text processing on all PowerPC computers. It is not just for multiple-language systems.

Prior to Mac OS 8, the Extensions folder may also include some of the following items:

❖ **System Update** (old versions are called **Hardware System Update**) fixes bugs and makes minor improvements in the system software (as described in Chapter 4).

❖ **Sound Manager** upgrades system software to improve the handling of sound.

❖ **PowerTalk Extension, PowerTalk Manager, Mailbox Extension, Catalogs Extension, Business Card Templates,** and **AppleTalk Service** provide PowerTalk collaboration services (described in Appendix B) — if you choose to install PowerTalk with System 7.1.1 Pro through 7.5.5.

QuickDraw GX extensions (System 7.1.1 Pro–Mac OS 7.6.1)

If you install QuickDraw GX with System 7.1.1 Pro–Mac OS 7.6.1, the Extensions folder also contains the following:

❖ **LaserWriter GX, StyleWriter GX, ImageWriter GX, PDD Maker GX,** and other printer drivers enable QuickDraw GX printing on specific types of printers (as described in Appendix A).

❖ **QuickDraw GX Helper** enables GX desktop printing to be turned off in individual applications (as described in Appendix A).

❖ **QuickDraw GX** provides advanced typography (described in Chapter 13) and simplified printing (described in Appendix A).

QUICK TIPS

Finding and Fixing Extension Conflicts

If your computer crashes and freezes more frequently after you add new extensions or control panels, or if your Macintosh refuses to start up, then system extensions may be in conflict. Sometimes changing the order in which the Mac OS loads system extensions resolves the conflict.

Fixing other conflicts between system extensions and control panels involves experimenting. Start by removing all the items you have added to the System Folder and its inner folders since the trouble began. Then drag half the extensions and control panels to the desktop and restart. If this solves the problem, the offending item is among the half you removed to the desktop; if not, it is among the other half. In either case, leave only half the group containing the offending item (one quarter of all extensions and control panels) on the desktop and restart. If the problem occurs again, the offender is among the group you just put back; if not, it is among the group on the desktop. Continue halving the offending group until you reduce it to a single item (the troublemaker). Instead of dragging control panels and extensions to and from the desktop, you can drag them to and from a new folder you create for that purpose. Alternatively, you can use an extension management utility such as Extension Manager to turn them on and off individually without dragging them in and out of folders (see "Extensions Manager" in Chapter 10).

When you find an item that causes a conflict, try renaming it so that it comes before or after other system extensions in the same folder. By experimenting with names, you may find a startup sequence that works.

As a last resort, move all system extensions and control panels to the desktop. Then put them in the System Folder (not the Extensions or Control Panels folders) one at a time, from most important to least. Restart your computer each time you add another item to the System Folder. When you find an item that causes a conflict, discard it and try the next item you previously moved to the desktop. You may be able to resume using the items you discarded when they are next upgraded.

If a conflict prevents you from starting up from your hard disk, start from a floppy disk or a CD-ROM that contains a System Folder, such as a Mac OS installation CD-ROM. Then you can make a change to the System Folder on the hard disk and try restarting from it.

Preferences folder

What you see in your Preferences folder depends on what you have installed on your hard disk. Many application programs save files of preference settings in the Preferences folder. Also, the Mac OS saves a plethora of preference files in the Preferences folder. Figure 9-9 shows an example of the Preferences folder.

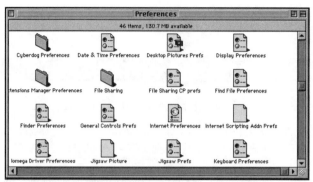

**Figure 9-9: Items inside the Preferences folder keep track of settings
and status information for specific programs.**

It's generally pretty easy to figure out which preferences file goes with what
program by looking at the name of the preferences file. See if you can guess
which control panels save settings in the following preferences files:
Appearance Preferences, Desktop Pictures Prefs, and Keyboard Preferences.
Here are descriptions of some items you'll find in the Preferences folder:

❖ The **File Sharing** folder contains file-sharing access privileges for your disks
   and folders (as described in Chapter 18). You don't have this folder if File
   Sharing has never been turned on.

❖ **Finder Preferences** contains many of the settings you make with the
   Finder's Preferences command in Mac OS 8 (as described in Chapters 6
   and 7). In earlier system software versions, this file contains settings you
   make with various control panels.

❖ **Appearances Preferences, Apple Menu Options Prefs, AppleTalk
   Preferences, Control Strip Preferences, Desktop Picture Prefs** or
   **Desktop Pattern Prefs, Extensions Manager Preferences, Find File
   Preferences, General Controls Prefs, Keyboard Preferences, Launcher
   Preferences, Mac OS Easy Open Preferences, PC Exchange Preferences,
   QuickTime Preferences, Sound Preferences, TCP/IP Preferences,** and
   WindowShade Preferences all contain additional settings you make with
   control panels in Mac OS 7.5 and later (as described in Chapter 10). Your
   Preferences folder may not include them all.

❖ The **Users & Groups Data File** contains names and privileges for
   registered users and groups to whom you have given access to your
   computer (as described in Chapter 18).

❖ **ColorSync Profiles** stores color matching information for specific scanners,
   monitors, and printers (as described in Chapters 10 and 15).

❖ **AppleMail Letterheads, PowerTalk Setup Preferences,** and **PowerTalk Startup Preferences** contain e-mail forms and control panel settings for PowerTalk, if you install it in System 7.1.1 Pro–7.5.5 (as described in Appendix B).

❖ **AppleCD Audio Player Prefs** and **CD Remote Programs** contain album and song titles that you enter for individual audio CDs together with other settings for the AppleCD Audio Player program (as described in Chapter 19).

❖ **QuickDraw GX Helper Prefs** identifies the applications in which you have turned off GX desktop printing, if you have installed QuickDraw GX with System 7.1.1. Pro–Mac OS 7.6.1 (as described in Appendix A).

❖ **Jigsaw Picture** contains the picture that the Jigsaw Puzzle program uses to make its puzzles (as described in Chapter 11).

❖ **Stickies file** contains the text of notes you post on your screen with the Stickies program in Mac OS 7.5 and later.

Adding Items to the System Folder

Putting control panels, system extensions, fonts, sounds, keyboard layouts, or language scripts where they belong is just as easy as putting them all in the System Folder. You simply drag the items to the System Folder icon. The Finder recognizes items that go in many of the special folders or the System file and asks whether you want the items put into their proper places. Figure 9-10 shows the alert that appears when you drag items to the System Folder icon if the Finder recognizes them.

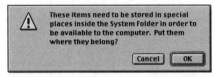

These items need to be stored in special places inside the System Folder in order to be available to the computer. Put them where they belong?

Cancel   OK

Figure 9-10: The Finder knows where to put some items you drag to the System Folder.

If you consent, the Finder distributes items as follows:

❖ **Control panels** go to the Control Panels folder.

❖ **Apple Guide documents, Chooser extensions, communications tools, libraries, Modem LinkTools, network extensions, PowerTalk extensions, the PrintMonitor program**, and **system extensions** are placed in the Extensions folder.

❖ **OpenDoc editors** may go in the Extensions folder. This is an error. They belong in the Editors folder.

❖ **Desk accessories** go to the Apple Menu Items folder.

❖ **TrueType, fixed-size**, and **PostScript** fonts are moved to the Fonts folder.

❖ **Sounds, keyboard layouts**, and **language script systems** go to the System file.

❖ All other items go into the main level of the System Folder.

When you drag folders to the System Folder, the Finder looks inside them and puts items it recognizes in the Control Panels, Extensions, Fonts, or Apple Menu Items folders. If a folder you drag contains items the Finder doesn't recognize, the Finder leaves them in the folder and puts the folder loose in the System Folder. If an item you drag to the System Folder has the same name as an item already there, the Finder not only asks whether you want to replace the latter with the former, but also tells you which is newer.

Overriding the Finder

The Finder sometimes makes mistakes when it puts items in special folders for you. It may put some items in the correct places and incorrectly leave others in the System Folder itself. For example, it may put a control panel in the Control Panels folder but leave that control panel's auxiliary folder in the System Folder. That control panel won't work right because it expects to find its auxiliary folder in the same folder. You must open the System Folder and drag the auxiliary folder to the Control Panels folder yourself, as shown in the figure.

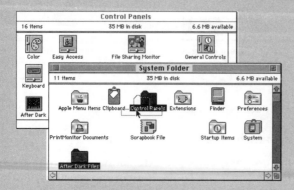

Moreover, the Finder never puts anything you drag to the System Folder icon into the Preferences folder or the Startup Items folder. You must open the System Folder and drag items to those folders directly.

When you drag items to the System Folder window instead of the System Folder icon, the Finder does not put them in the inner folders for you.

Removing Items from the System Folder

Before you can remove an item from the System Folder, you must know which inner folder contains it. If you're not sure, use the Finder's Find command to locate the item (see "Finding Items" in Chapter 7). Be sure to drag items from the special folders onto the desktop or into an ordinary folder. Many items you drag out of special folders remain installed if you merely drag them to the System Folder window.

If you happen to discard a special folder, you can make a replacement by using the Finder's New Folder command (in the File menu). After creating a new folder, change its name to that of the special folder you want. Wait a few seconds and you'll see its icon get the distinctive look of the special folder you're creating.

Uncovering More Special Folders

The Mac OS further organizes your disks with additional special folders outside the System Folder. The Finder creates the following special folders as needed on each disk:

❖ The invisible Temporary Items folder contains temporary files created by the programs you are using. A program normally deletes its temporary files automatically when you quit it.

❖ The Trash folder contains the items you drag from the disk to the Trash icon. Your disks' Trash folders are invisible, but you see their consolidated contents when you open the Trash icon. A visible Trash folder in a shared disk contains items from the disk that are located in the owner's Trash.

❖ The Network Trash folder contains items from your shared disk or folder that network users have dragged to the Trash — but have not yet permanently removed — on their computers. The discarded items appear in the network users' Trash, not yours.

❖ The Rescued Items folder contains items the Finder finds in the Temporary Items folder when you restart after a system crash (or after switching off the power without using the Shut Down command — tsk, tsk!). You may be able to reconstruct your work by opening them. If a Rescued Items folder exists, you can always see it by opening the Trash.

❖ The Desktop folder contains items located on the desktop. Although it is invisible on your disks, the Desktop folder of a shared disk is visible to others and contains items from the disk that are on the owner's desktop.

Maintaining the Desktop Database

Something you don't see in the System Folder is the invisible desktop database that the Finder uses to keep track of the following:

❖ Which icons to use for documents created by all your applications (unless you have customized them, as described under "Custom icons" in Chapter 5)

❖ What kind of file each icon refers to

❖ Where programs are

❖ What comments you enter with the Finder's Get Info command

The Mac OS keeps this database hidden so users don't alter it inadvertently, but you can see some of the information the database contains by selecting a file in the Finder and choosing Get Info from the Finder's File menu.

The Finder creates and maintains a desktop database on every disk. On disks larger than 2MB, the desktop database consists of two invisible files named Desktop DB and Desktop DF. On smaller disks, the desktop database is kept in one file named Desktop. The Finder creates these files automatically on new disks and updates them with new information whenever you install another application.

Rebuilding the desktop database

You can force the Finder to rebuild the desktop database by holding down the Option and ⌘ keys while starting up the computer. After the Mac OS has loaded all system extensions, the Finder displays an alert asking if you want to rebuild the desktop file on the startup disk. After rebuilding the startup disk, the Finder asks if you want to rebuild the next disk on the desktop, if you have more than one disk. The Finder asks separately about each disk on the desktop, even if you stop holding down the ⌘ and Option keys (so give your fingers a rest). Figure 9-11 shows an example of the alert box that asks whether you want to rebuild the desktop.

You can rebuild the desktop database on floppy disks and other removable disks by pressing ⌘ and Option while inserting the disk. The Finder displays its confirmation alert before rebuilding.

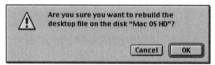

Figure 9-11: Confirming that you want to rebuild a disk's desktop database.

Some Mac OS experts advocate rebuilding the desktop database once a month, and some even suggest rebuilding weekly. They claim folder and disk windows open faster if you rebuild the desktop database frequently. You probably won't hurt anything by rebuilding frequently but it may be a waste of your time, because rebuilding can take several minutes per disk depending on the number of applications and files you have. You can try rebuilding once a month, and keep up with that schedule if you feel it improves the performance of the Finder. If you don't notice any performance benefit, don't bother rebuilding until something goes wrong.

Warning: On system software versions earlier than Mac OS 8, rebuilding the desktop erases all comments you have entered in Get Info windows for items on the disks involved. See Chapter 24 for a description of Super Comments software, which you can use to retain Get Info window comments while rebuilding the desktop.

QUICK TIPS

Rebuilding Without Restarting — A Dubious Practice

It's possible to rebuild the desktop on your startup disk without restarting the computer, although there is some risk involved. What you do is close all folder and disk windows, close all control panels, put away any open dialog boxes, and then force the Finder to quit by pressing ⌘-Option-Escape. That brings up an alert box in which you click the Force Quit button if you're sure you want to go through with this. Then all the desktop icons, the folder and disk windows, and the Finder menus go away as the Finder quits. Now hold down the ⌘ and Option keys until the Finder displays its alert asking you to confirm rebuilding the desktop. The risk in forcing the Finder to quit is that you're not giving it a chance to clean up after itself, for example by closing the desktop database in an orderly fashion. That's right, forcing the Finder to quit could induce problems with the desktop database! You face even more weirdness if you leave control panels or dialog boxes open when you force the Finder to quit, because the Finder won't be able to save any changes you've made to settings in those windows.

Detecting and fixing a corrupt desktop database

When something goes wrong with the desktop database, you may see generic (blank) icons instead of the distinctive icons that tell you what kind of file you're looking at. Another symptom of desktop database trouble is being unable to open documents by double-clicking their icons, even if the icons are not generic. Also, problems with the desktop database can cause folder and disk icons to display slowly, although the type of view and the view options you have selected also have an effect on performance. Figure 9-12 shows some generic icons.

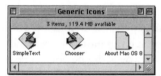

Figure 9-12: Time to rebuild the desktop if you see generic icons like these.

If you suspect problems with the desktop database, try rebuilding it as described previously. If the problems persist, you need to bring in the heavy equipment. Use the free TechTool program (described in Chapter 24) to delete the desktop database files and force the Finder to rebuild them from scratch. (There are other programs that do the same thing.)

There is a risk that something could go wrong during the rebuilding, such as a power failure, that would corrupt the desktop database. Corruption can also just happen during the normal course of events, as a result of otherwise undetectable program errors. The symptoms of a corrupt desktop database include generic icons, the inability to open documents by double-clicking their icons, a sluggish Finder, or documents that open with the wrong application. Again, these symptoms can have other causes. For instance, you'll have trouble opening a document if the application that created it is on an ejected disk or if you don't have the application. The cure for a corrupted desktop database is to rebuild it from scratch using TechTool or an equivalent.

Summary

After reading this chapter, you know what's in the System Folder and why. You know the Finder is there along with the System file, which contains much of the basic system software as well as sounds, keyboard layouts, and language script systems. The Apple Menu Items folder contains items listed in the Apple menu. The Startup Items folder contains items to be opened as the computer starts up, and the Shutdown Items folder contains items to be opened as the computer shuts down. The Extensions folder contains software that extends the capabilities of the Mac OS, and the Control Panels folder contains small programs for setting options. The Fonts folder contains fixed-size, TrueType, and PostScript fonts. The Editors folder contains OpenDoc editors, and the DataViz folder contains file translation software. The Preferences folder contains settings, status, and other information used by various programs. The System Folder may contain many other items as well.

You read here about many of the items in a typical Extensions folder, and how to add and remove items in it. You also read about other special folders and files that the Mac OS uses to keep track of items in the Trash, items on the desktop, and temporary files used by application programs.

Finally, after reading this chapter, you know that the Finder maintains a desktop database to match documents with the applications that created them so they all have the right icons and you can open documents from the Finder. You also know how to rebuild the desktop database as needed.

CHAPTER TEN

Put Control Panels to Work

IN THIS CHAPTER

- **Introducing control panels:** what they have in common

- **Investigating an encyclopedia of control panels,** which describes the ones that come with the Mac OS

Y our computer is highly configurable. You can set numerous options that affect various aspects of its appearance and behavior, including the color it uses to highlight text, the way it uses energy, the alert sound it makes, how it connects to a network, and the voice it speaks with. All these options and many, many more are set with control panels.

Introducing Control Panels

The inner workings of each control panel are different, but all control panels have some things in common. This section describes the similarities — where they are and the basics of how you use them.

Where control panels are

By convention, control panel icons go into the special Control Panels folder inside the System Folder. So that you can open the Control Panels folder easily, it is listed in the Apple menu. (The Apple Menu Items folder contains an alias of the Control Panels folder.)

Normally the Control Panels item in the Apple menu is a submenu, and you can see all the control panels listed in it. (You can turn off submenus in the Apple menu with the Apple Menu Options control panel, which is described later in this chapter.)

You can open the Control Panels folder and use its window as a master control panel. You can rearrange the individual control panel icons in this window by dragging them or by using the Finder's View menu. Figure 10-1 shows an example of the Control Panels folder.

Figure 10-1: An open Control Panels folder.

Some control panels work just fine if you move them out of the Control Panels folder, while others must remain there. The control panels that must remain in the Control Panels folder contain software that extends the system software during startup, just like System extensions in the Extensions folder. These control panels won't work unless they're located in the Control Panels folder, the Extensions folder, or the System Folder. During startup, the system looks in those places for system software extensions. To tell whether a control panel extends the system software, watch to see whether its icon appears at the bottom of the screen during startup. A few control panels that extend system software don't display their icons during startup (notably Close View, Easy Access, and in some cases Memory), but most do.

How to use a control panel

To use a control panel, you open it as you would open any program — choose it from the Apple menu, double-click its icon, and so forth. Each open control panel has its own window, which contains an assortment of options you can set. (You'll find more information on setting each control panel's options in the next section of this chapter.) When you're done with a control panel, you simply close its window to put it away.

While open, many control panels act like Finder documents. They don't have their own menus in the menu bar. They aren't listed in the Application menu because they aren't application programs or desk accessories. Their windows hide along with folder and disk windows if you hide the Finder. If you have several of these control panels open and you Option-click the close box of any one of them, they all close along with folder and disk windows. Likewise,

Option-clicking the collapse box in any of their windows collapses them all (or expands them all if they are already collapsed). In the past all control panels behaved like Finder documents.

Nowadays some control panels are actually application programs that are in the Control Panels folder because of their function. You'll notice these control panel applications have their own menus in the menu bar and are listed individually in the Applications menu when they are open. You hide, close, or collapse their windows separately.

There is one way control panel applications behave like other control panels. When you close the window of a control panel application it quits automatically. In contrast, a typical application does not quit until you use its Quit command.

One reason for making a control panel an application is so it can be controlled by AppleScript scripts (as described in Chapter 22). Only application programs can be controlled by AppleScript scripts.

Control Panels Encyclopedia

Each control panel contains a unique set of options that you set by clicking buttons, turning check boxes on or off, clicking radio buttons, adjusting sliders, choosing from pop-up menus, selecting from a list of items, or typing text. This section describes the options available in the control panels that come with the Mac OS. The control panels are listed here in alphabetical order.

As you go through this section, you will notice that some control panels have brief descriptions and others have detailed descriptions. Control panels that are covered in depth elsewhere in this book have brief descriptions here that refer you to another chapter for details. The descriptions here for control panels not covered elsewhere tell you in detail how to use the control panels.

Appearance

You can use the Appearance control panel to set several options that affect how Mac OS 8 looks and how collapsing windows work. These options are divided into two sets, Color and Options, and you can work with one set at a time. You bring up a set of options by clicking its button on the left side of the control panel window. Figure 10-2 shows the Color set of options in the Appearance control panel.

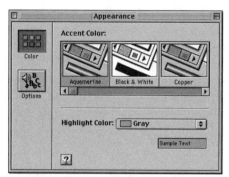

Figure 10-2: The Appearance control panel.

When you click the Colors button, you can make changes to the following options:

❖ **Accent Color** changes the color of scroll boxes, the highlight color of a selected menu item, and the progress bar.

❖ **Highlight color** changes the color used to highlight text that you have selected.

When you click the Options button, you can make changes to the following options:

❖ **Double-click title bar to collapse** determines whether double-clicking a window's title bar collapses it (or expands it, if it is already collapsed) just like clicking the window's collapse box.

❖ **Play sound when collapsing windows** determines whether you hear a nifty "whoosh" sound when a window collapses or expands.

❖ **System Font** lets you choose a font for menus, window titles, buttons, and dialog boxes. Charcoal is the preferred font for the new Mac OS 8 look, but some programs made before Mac OS 8 may refuse to open unless System Font is set to Chicago.

❖ **System-Wide Platinum appearance**, when checked, applies the color and 3D shading of the Mac OS 8 platinum appearance to windows and menus in all applications. You may notice harmless cosmetic flaws in some programs. If they bother you, you can turn off this option.

If you're familiar with system software earlier than Mac OS 8, you'll notice that the Appearance control panel in Mac OS 8 replaces the Color and WindowShade control panels found in Mac OS 7.5–7.6.1.

You'll find more information on using the Appearance control panel in "Appearance and Behavior Modification" in Chapter 5.

Apple Menu Options

Apple Menu Options activates the hierarchical menus used in the Apple menu, as well as creating and enabling the Recent Documents, Recent Applications, and Recent Server menu items. (The Apple Menu is covered in detail in "Opening Programs, Documents, and More" in Chapter 8.) Figure 10-3 shows the Apple Menu Options control panel.

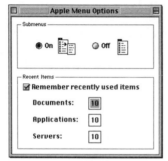

Figure 10-3: The Apple Menu Options control panel.

Turning on the Submenus option creates a hierarchy of submenus in the Apple menu. After turning on the Submenus option, you see submenus whenever you highlight a folder listed in the Apple menu. A submenu lists the contents of the highlighted folder. Highlighting a folder listed in a submenu displays another submenu, up to five levels deep.

Turning on the Recent Items option creates folders in the Apple menu for tracking the documents, applications, and servers that you most recently used. You can set the number of documents, applications, and servers that you want to track. The control panel tracks recent items by creating aliases of those items and placing the aliases in the Recent Applications folder, Recent Documents folder, or Recent Servers folder (where appropriate) in the Apple Menu Items folder (inside the System Folder). If you wish to suppress tracking of one type of item, set the number to be remembered to 0 (zero) and discard the appropriate recent items folder if it exists.

AppleTalk

If your computer is connected to an AppleTalk network, you use the AppleTalk control panel to specify the type of connection, such as Ethernet or LocalTalk cabling. The AppleTalk control panel is part of the Open Transport networking software, which is mandatory with Mac OS 7.6 and later and optional with earlier system software. This control panel replaces the Network control panel. (See "Configuring an AppleTalk Connection" in Chapter 17 for details.) Figure 10-4 shows the AppleTalk control panel.

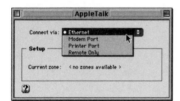

Figure 10-4: The AppleTalk control panel.

ATM GX

The Adobe Type Manager GX (ATM GX) control panel controls the smooth scaling of PostScript Type 1 fonts onscreen and on non-PostScript printers. ATM GX is installed when QuickDraw GX is installed with system software versions 7.5–7.6.1. It also works without QuickDraw GX, and you can install it separately by using the QuickDraw GX installer's Custom Install option. The version of QuickDraw GX that comes with Mac OS 8 does not include ATM GX. Figure 10-5 shows the ATM GX control panel.

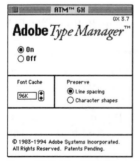

Figure 10-5: The ATM GX control panel (System 7.5–Mac OS 7.6.1 only).

The Font Cache option affects performance. If applications seem to scroll more slowly with ATM GX turned on, try increasing the Font Cache size.

The Preserve option determines whether ATM GX preserves line spacing or character shapes when it scales text. Preserving line spacing keeps line breaks and page breaks from changing with and without ATM, but this setting may clip the bottoms of some letters and vertically compress some accented capital letters. Preserving character shapes reduces the clipping but may change line breaks. The clipping occurs only onscreen and on output devices that don't use PostScript. No clipping occurs on a PostScript printer. (For more information on QuickDraw GX, see "QuickDraw GX Typography" in Chapter 13 and all of Appendix A.)

AutoRemounter

Use the AutoRemounter control panel to determine whether — and when — your PowerBook automatically reconnects to shared disks and folders, as shown in Figure 10-6.

Figure 10-6: The AutoRemounter control panel.

Select the After Sleep option to have the computer reconnect upon waking up. Select the Off option if you don't want the computer to reconnect automatically. If you want the computer to insist that each shared item's password (if any) be entered before reconnecting to the item, select the Always Entering Passwords option. If you want the computer to reconnect without asking for passwords, select the Automatically Remounting option.

The AutoRemounter control panel works only on PowerBook computers. It is not needed on desktop computers that can sleep, because shared disks and other network volumes remain mounted while a desktop computer sleeps.

Cache Switch

On a Mac with a 68040 processor, you use the Cache Switch control panel to enable or disable the processor's internal caches. The setting of this control panel provides a trade-off between performance and compatibility. Figure 10-7 shows the Cache Switch control panel.

Figure 10-7: The Cache Switch control panel.

Selecting the Faster option improves performance by enabling the processor to store frequently used instructions and data in its internal caches. If you have programs that don't work correctly when the processor's caches are enabled, select the More Compatible option. It makes your computer run slower because the processor has to fetch all instructions and data from the computer's main memory.

CloseView

You can use the CloseView control panel to magnify your screen 2 to 16 times and to invert the displayed colors. Several of the control panel options have keyboard shortcuts. The keystrokes are displayed in the control panel, and they changed beginning with System 7.5.3 because some of the older shortcuts were used by the Finder. Figure 10-8 shows the CloseView control panel in Mac OS 8.

Figure 10-8: The CloseView control panel.

CloseView is not installed automatically with the rest of the control panels. With some system software installations, you will find CloseView in the Universal Access folder, which is in the Apple Extras folder on your startup disk. You can drag the control panel from there to your Control Panels folder. If it's not on your hard disk anywhere, you can install it by doing a custom installation of the system software — the Mac OS 8 or Mac OS 7.6 module — and select the Universal Access component group in the Custom Install section of the Installer program (as described in Chapters 28–30).

Color

The Color control panel sets the text-highlighting color and window-shading color in Mac OS 7.6.1 and earlier. With Mac OS 8, you use the Appearance control panel instead. (For more information, see "Appearance and Behavior Modification" in Chapter 5.) Figure 10-9 shows the Color control panel.

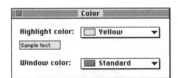

Figure 10-9: The Color control panel (Mac OS 7.6.1 and earlier).

ColorSync System Profile

On a Mac with ColorSync, Apple's color-matching software, you use the ColorSync System Profile control panel to specify a color profile for your display screen. The profile specifies the range of colors that a particular type of monitor can display. Other types of input and output devices, such as scanners and printers, have unique color profiles, and the ColorSync software uses the profiles to shift colors so that they look the same on all compatible devices. Figure 10-10 shows the ColorSync System Profile control panel.

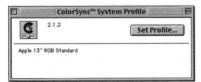

Figure 10-10: The ColorSync System Profile control panel.

The ColorSync software, including the ColorSync System Profile control panel and profiles for several Apple monitors, is installed when you install Mac OS 8, Mac OS 7.6, or QuickDraw GX and Systems 7.5–7.5.5. Profiles for other devices come with the devices.

Control Strip

The modular Control Strip control panel provides quick access to commonly adjusted features. Clicking a button in the Control Strip pops up a menu of related settings. Each button in the Control Strip corresponds to a module in the Control Strip Modules folder (inside the System Folder). The modules initially appear in the Control Strip in alphabetical order, from left to right. You can change a module's position by dragging it in the Control Strip while pressing the Option key. Figure 10-11 shows the Control Strip on a PowerBook with Mac OS 8.

Figure 10-11: The Control Strip control panel.

The Control Strip floats above all application windows. You can collapse and expand the strip by clicking or dragging the tab at the end nearest the center of the screen. To collapse the strip to its smallest size, click the box at the opposite end. You can move the strip by pressing the Option key and dragging the tab, but the strip must touch the left or right edge of the screen.

The Control Strip comes with the following modules:

❖ **AppleTalk Switch** shows whether AppleTalk is active (network wires on Mac icon) or inactive (no network wires). You also can use this module to activate and deactivate AppleTalk. (Deactivating AppleTalk conserves battery power.)

❖ **CD Strip** controls the playing of audio compact discs. You can start, stop, or play any track of a CD. You can also set the CD player to automatically play CDs when they are inserted, or to eject a CD that's already in the drive. If your computer is without a CD drive, this item will not appear.

❖ **File Sharing** shows the status of file sharing and the identity of connected users (if any). You also can use this module to open the File Sharing control panel (Sharing Setup prior to Mac OS 8) and to turn file sharing on and off. An icon on the File Sharing module's button indicates whether file sharing is turned on and people are connected (two faces); file sharing is turned on and no one is connected (a folder icon with network wires); file sharing is off (a folder icon with no network wires); or file sharing is starting up (a folder icon with blinking network wires).

❖ **Monitor BitDepth** shows the number of colors being used by the main monitor. You can switch between color depths by choosing a different setting in the pop-up menu. Typical settings include 256 colors, Thousands of colors (16-bit color), and Millions of colors (32-bit color). Some video hardware cannot use color settings below 256 colors; some video hardware can use Thousands or Millions only when additional video RAM (VRAM) is installed.

❖ **Monitor Resolution** shows the dimension of the monitor or monitors, in pixels. If your monitor can display more than one resolution, you can choose one from the pop-up menu. Some monitors can use more resolutions than others. For example, a standard 14-inch monitor has a resolution of 640 × 480 pixels, a standard 19-inch monitor has a resolution of 1280 × 1024, and an AppleVision 1710 can display either of those and several resolutions between.

❖ **Printer Selector** lets you quickly switch between printers on your local area network. To appear in the menu, a printer must have an icon on the desktop (or a desktop icon that has been moved to a folder).

❖ **Sound Volume** allows you to adjust the sound level.

Additional items appear only on PowerBooks:

❖ **Battery Monitor** shows the battery level for your PowerBook and indicates whether the power adapter is plugged in. You can use this module to hide and show the battery-level indicator in the Control Strip.

❖ **HD Spin Down** shows whether the internal hard disk is spinning. You can use this module to spin down the hard disk, which conserves battery power.

❖ **Location Manager** lets you switch to a different group of settings (a location) or open the Location Manager control panel.

❖ **Power Settings** allows you to change the battery-conservation setting or open the PowerBook control panel.

❖ **Sleep Now** allows you to put the PowerBook to sleep.

❖ **Video Mirroring** enables you to set an external monitor to mirror the built-in monitor (present only on a PowerBook with an external display connected).

Date & Time

You use the Date & Time control panel to set the current date and the current time. Through the Date Formats and Time Formats buttons, this control panel also enables you to set how the date and time are displayed to suit your preference or the language that you're using. The control panel offers you a choice of preset formats for the language script system used by your version of the Mac OS, which for North American and Western European users is the Roman script system. You don't see any additional preset formats after installing Apple Language Kit software so that you can write in additional languages. You can set your own custom format, however. (For more information on using multiple languages, see "WorldScript" in Chapter 21.) Figure 10-12 shows the Date & Time control panel

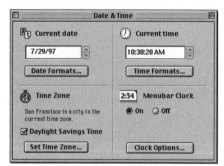

Figure 10-12: The Date & Time control panel.

In the Time Zone section of the control panel, you can see and set the time zone in which you are using your computer. You also can adjust the computer's clock for Daylight Savings Time. Clicking the Set Time Zone button brings up a list of city names; select one in your time zone. (You can find out what time it is in a different zone by selecting a city in that time zone.)

Changing the current time zone in the Date & Time control panel also changes the computer's location as set in the Map control panel (described later in this chapter). Likewise, setting a new location in the Map control panel may change the time zone reported in the Date & Time control panel. Turning on the Daylight Savings Time option sets the Mac's clock ahead one hour; turning off this option sets the Mac's clock back one hour, returning it to standard time. The first time you set this option, you may have to adjust the hour displayed at the top of the control panel.

In the Menubar Clock section of the control panel, you can turn on and off an optional digital clock near the right end of the menu bar. Clicking the Clock Options button in this section brings up a dialog box in which you can set the display format of the clock and set the clock to chime on the hour, half-hour, and quarter-hour. On a battery-powered Mac, you also can turn on or off a battery-level indicator, which appears next to the clock.

Clicking the clock in the menu bar shows the date, and clicking again shows the time. Option-clicking hides the clock, or shows the clock if it is hidden. With Mac OS 7.6.1 and earlier, Control-clicking the battery indicator (if present) puts the computer to sleep.

Desktop Pattern

Desktop Pattern sets the background pattern for the desktop in Mac OS 7.6.1 and earlier. With Mac OS 8, you use the Desktop Pictures control panel instead. (See "Desktop Background" in Chapter 5 for more information.) Figure 10-13 shows the Desktop Pattern control program.

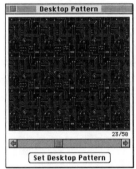

Figure 10-13: The Desktop Pattern control program (Mac OS 7.6.1 and earlier).

Desktop Pictures

Desktop Pictures lets you change the background pattern displayed on the desktop so you can get away from the fresh-from-the-factory look. Many cool patterns and nifty designs are available to choose from. You can even cover the desktop pattern with a color picture. You use Desktop Pictures with Mac OS 8, and Desktop Pattern with earlier system software. (See "Desktop Background" in Chapter 5 for more details.) Figure 10-14 shows the part of Desktop Pictures used for setting a desktop picture.

Figure 10-14: The Desktop Pictures control program.

Although Desktop Pictures appears in the Control Panels folder, it actually is an application program. If you leave Desktop Pictures open, you can switch to it by choosing it from the Application menu.

Easy Access

The Easy Access control panel sets up three alternative methods of using the keyboard and mouse: Mouse Keys, Slow Keys, and Sticky Keys. Easy Access whistles when you turn any of these features on or off. You can silence the whistle by turning off the audio-feedback option at the top of the Easy Access control panel. To work, Easy Access must be in the Control Panels folder at startup time. Figure 10-15 shows the Easy Access control panel.

Figure 10-15: The Easy Access control panel.

Mouse Keys

Mouse Keys enables you to click, drag, and move the pointer with the keypad instead of the mouse, trackpad, or trackball. Mouse Keys is very handy for moving graphic objects precisely. You can turn on Mouse Keys by pressing ⌘-Shift-Clear instead of using the Easy Access control panel. You also can turn it off by pressing Clear. When Mouse Keys is on, the 5 key in the keypad acts like a mouse button. Press once to click; press twice to double-click; or hold it down. The eight keys around 5 move the pointer left, right, up, down, and diagonally. Pressing 0 locks the mouse button down until you press the period key in the keypad.

Slow Keys

Slow Keys makes the Mac OS wait before it accepts a keystroke, thereby filtering out accidental keystrokes. You can turn Slow Keys on or off from the keyboard by holding down the Return key for about 10 seconds. No icon indicates whether Slow Keys is on or off, but about five seconds after you begin holding down the Return key, the computer makes three short, quiet beeps; about four seconds after that, the computer whistles to confirm that Slow Keys is being turned on or off. You don't hear these sounds if you use the Easy Access control panel, however, and some applications (such as Microsoft Word) may mute the sounds.

Sticky Keys

Sticky Keys enables you to type combination keystrokes such as ⌘-Shift-3 (which puts a snapshot of your screen in a picture document that most graphics programs can open) one key at a time. Sticky Keys also enables you to lock down any modifier key by pressing it two times in a row. You can turn on Sticky Keys by pressing Shift five times in succession. You can turn Sticky Keys off by pressing Shift five times again or by pressing any two modifier keys simultaneously. When Sticky Keys is on, an icon at the right end of the menu bar shows its status. Figure 10-16 shows the four states of the Sticky Keys status icon.

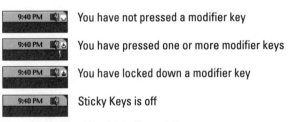

9:40 PM   You have not pressed a modifier key

9:40 PM   You have pressed one or more modifier keys

9:40 PM   You have locked down a modifier key

9:40 PM   Sticky Keys is off

Figure 10-16: Checking Sticky Keys status.

SECRETS

PowerBook Mouse Keys

You can't use Mouse Keys to point and click on a PowerBook, because PowerBooks have no numeric keypad. The System extension Mouse Keys modifies the Easy Access control panel to recognize different keys instead of the numeric keypad. It substitutes the *K* key and the keys next to it for the 5 key and the keys next to it on the keypad. The Escape key substitutes for the Clear key. Thus, after installing the Mouse Keys extension, you turn on Mouse Keys by pressing ⌘-Shift-Escape, and you turn it off by pressing Escape.

When Mouse Keys is on, the *K* acts like a trackball or trackpad button. Press once to click; press twice to double-click; or hold it down. The eight keys around *K* move the pointer left, right, up, down, and diagonally. Pressing the spacebar locks the mouse button down until you press Enter.

Be careful not to press ⌘-Option-Escape, which, instead of activating Mouse Keys, brings up a dialog box that asks whether you want to force the active program to quit.

Editor Setup

Editor Setup is used to set which editor software you want to use by default for viewing and editing a particular kind of content in an OpenDoc document. For example, you could specify that you want to use the Apple QuickTime Viewer editor for viewing QuickTime movies that you add to your OpenDoc documents. If you have other editors for the same type of content, they may be used when you open documents created by other people. For example, if you open a document created by someone who has selected the Cyberdog QuickTime Viewer editor and you also have that editor, then the movies in that document will be displayed by that editor. (See "OpenDoc Compound Documents" in Chapter 23 for more information.) Figure 10-17 shows the Editor Setup control panel and the dialog box in which it lists the OpenDoc editors available on your computer for a particular type of document content.

Energy Saver

Energy Saver version 2.0 and later helps keep your computer from running up your power bill. You can set your monitor and computer to go to sleep, which is a low-power mode, or shut down after a specified period of inactivity. You can also use Energy Saver to schedule startup and shutdown times for your computer. Buttons at the top of the Energy Saver window control whether you see sleep options or scheduling options. Figure 10-18 shows Energy Saver's basic sleep options.

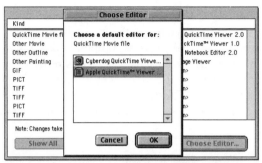

Figure 10-17: The Editor Setup control panel and its Choose Editor dialog box.

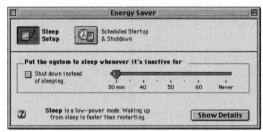

Figure 10-18: The Energy Saver control program's basic sleep options.

The Energy Saver control panel version 2.0 and later works only on computers with PCI expansion slots and requires System 7.5.2 or later.

Sleep setup

To set the amount of time before your computer goes to sleep or shuts down, adjust the slider labeled "Put the system to sleep whenever it's inactive for." If you want the computer to shut down instead of going to sleep, turn on the option labeled "Shut down instead of sleeping."

You can set separate times for the computer, monitor, and hard disk to go to sleep by clicking the Show Details button. Hard disk sleep spins down the hard disk, reducing your computer's energy use even more. If you decide you don't want separate timings for display sleep and hard disk sleep, click the Hide Details button. Figure 10-19 shows Energy Saver's detailed sleep options.

Part II: Getting Started with the Mac OS

Scheduled Startup & Shutdown

You can also use Energy Saver to set your computer to turn on or off at specified times. This is a handy feature, especially if your computer takes a while to start up. You could set your Mac to turn on automatically so it's ready when you get to work in the morning, or to make sure it's off at night in case you forget. To see Energy Saver's scheduling options, click the Scheduled Startup & Shutdown button at the top of the control panel window, as shown in Figure 10-20.

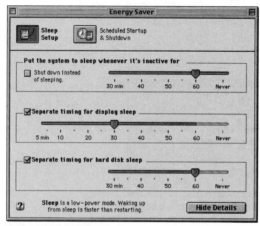

Figure 10-19: The Energy Saver control program's detailed sleep options.

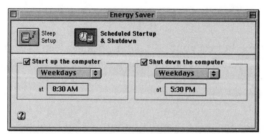

Figure 10-20: The Energy Saver control program's scheduling options.

To set a time for the computer to start up or shut down, turn on the "Start up the computer" option or the "Shut down the computer" option and enter a time in the space provided. Use the pop-up menu to choose the day or days you want the schedule to be effective: a specific day of the week, weekdays only, weekends only, or every day.

Energy Savings

A Mac OS computer and monitor that bear the logo of the EPA's Energy Star program can use the Energy Saver control panel to automatically reduce their power consumption to 60 watts or less (30 watts for the computer and 30 watts for the monitor) when they're inactive. For example, a 150-watt Energy Star computer and monitor that are inactive half of each 10-hour weekday and are on all the time would cost $62 less per year to operate (at $0.10 per kWh) than a conventional system. Turning off an Energy Star computer nights and weekends would save another $42 per year.

Even more important than the cost savings is the reduction in air pollution that's a byproduct of generating electricity. According to the Rocky Mountain Institute (970-927-3851, http://www.rmi.org), "Computers and other electronic office equipment represent the fastest-growing electrical load in the United States, keeping at least a dozen 1,000-megawatt power plants fully occupied." In an office, using the Energy Saver control panel and turning off your computer at night and over weekends also decreases the demand for air conditioning, saving even more energy and pollution.

Extensions Manager (Mac OS 7.6 and later)

The Extensions Manager control panel can individually disable System extensions, control panels that contain System extensions, and Chooser extensions. Disabled startup items don't use RAM and can't conflict with other startup items. A list of the startup items that are present in your System Folder appears in the Extensions Manager window, which has several improvements in Mac OS 7.6 and later. For each listed item, the newer Extensions Manager displays its status (enabled or disabled), name, size, version, and the package it was installed with. You can also display each item's type and creator codes by selecting options with the Preferences command (in the Edit menu). Figure 10-21 shows the Extensions Manager in Mac OS 8.

Reorganizing the Extensions Manager list

You can reorganize the Extensions Manager list as follows:

❖ View items grouped by the folders they're in, grouped by the package they were installed with, or ungrouped by choosing from the View menu.

❖ Collapse and expand a group by clicking the triangle next to the group name or by double-clicking the name.

❖ Sort the list within each group by clicking any column heading to set the sort order.

❖ Adjust the widths of the Name and Package columns by dragging the right boundary line of the Name column heading or the left boundary line of the Package column heading. You can't adjust the other column widths.

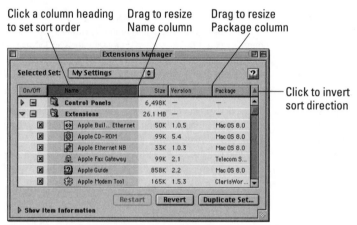

Figure 10-21: The Extensions Manager (Mac OS 7.6 and later).

Seeing detailed information about an item

To see more information about a particular item, you click its name to select it and then click the triangle labeled Show Item Information at the bottom left corner of the Extensions Manager window. You can also select an item and choose Get Info from the Extensions Manager's File menu to open the item's Get Info window in the Finder, or choose Find Item to open the folder that contains the item and select the item. Figure 10-22 shows the Extensions Manager expanded to show item information.

Enabling and disabling items

You disable or enable an extension or other item by clicking the check box next to the item's name. Enabling or disabling a group affects all the items in the group. You can save the current configuration of the Extensions Manager as a named set by choosing New Set from the File menu. Your named sets appear in the Selected Set pop-up in alphabetical order, and choosing a set from that pop-up changes Extensions Manager to the configuration saved for that set. To enable or disable all items, use the All On or All Off commands in the Edit menu.

Figure 10-22: The Extensions Manager expanded to show item information (Mac OS 7.6 and later).

Mac OS 8 comes with two preconfigured sets, Mac OS All and Mac OS Base. Choosing the Mac OS All set turns on only the startup items that are installed by the Mac OS Installer for Mac OS 8. Choosing the Mac OS Base set turns on only the most essential startup items.

Changes you make to the status of any items take place when you restart. To restart immediately, click the Restart button. To restart later, quit Extensions Manager and use the Restart command in the Finder's Special menu when you are ready to restart. To cancel the changes you've made, click the Revert button in the Extensions Manager window.

Extensions Manager puts disabled items from the Extensions folder in a folder named Extensions (disabled). Disabled control panels are stored in a folder named Control Panels (disabled). Disabled items from the System Folder go into a folder named System Extensions (disabled).

Using Extensions Manager during startup

You can enable or disable startup items while your computer is starting up. To bring up the Extensions Manager control panel at the beginning of the startup process, hold down the Spacebar. Holding down the Shift key at the beginning of the startup process temporarily disables all extensions, without affecting settings in the Extensions Manager control panel.

Extensions Manager (Systems 7.5–7.5.5)

The Extensions Manager control panel included with Systems 7.5–7.5.5 has the same basic function as the improved version in Mac OS 7.6 and later. You use it to individually disable and enable control panels, extensions, and other software that's loaded during startup. Disabled startup items don't use RAM and can't conflict with other startup items. A list of the startup items that are present in your System Folder appears in the Extensions Manager window, as shown in Figure 10-23.

Figure 10-23: The Extensions Manager control panel (Systems 7.5–7.5.5).

First in the list are items in the Extensions folder; second are items in the Control Panels folder; and third are items stored loose in the System Folder. A check mark next to an item means that the item is enabled. Items without check marks are disabled and will not be loaded the next time the Mac starts. To change the state of an item — enabled or disabled — you click it. The Undo button in the Extensions Manager window reverts all items to the states they were in when you opened the control panel.

You can save the current state of all items as a set by choosing Save Set from the Sets pop-up menu. After you save a set, it appears in the Sets pop-up menu. Choosing a set from the pop-up menu sets the state of all items to match their state when the set was saved. Choosing All On from the pop-up enables all items, and choosing All Off disables all items. Choosing the predefined set whose name is the same as the system software version, such as System 7.5.5, enables only the items that are installed as part of the system software.

Extensions Manager puts disabled System extensions in a folder named Extensions (disabled). Disabled control panels are stored in a folder named Control Panels (disabled). Disabled items from the System Folder go into a folder named System Extensions (disabled).

You can bring up the Extensions Manager control panel at the beginning of the startup process by holding down the Spacebar. Holding down the Shift key at the beginning of the startup process temporarily disables all extensions, without affecting settings in the Extensions Manager control panel.

File Sharing

You use the File Sharing program with Mac OS 8 to identify your computer and its owner (probably you) on your local area network. You can also use the File Sharing program to start and stop file sharing and program linking. In addition, you can use the File Sharing program to monitor file sharing activity on your computer — who is connected to your computer for file sharing, which folders and disks you have made available for sharing, and how busy your computer is with handling file sharing. You can also use File Sharing to disconnect anyone who is connected. File Sharing is an application program, not a true control panel, so it is listed in the Applications menu when it is open. (For complete information on these settings, see "Identifying Your Computer" and "Turning File Sharing On and Off" in Chapter 18 and "Linking Programs" in Chapter 22.) Figure 10-24 shows the section of the File Sharing program where you start and stop file sharing and program linking.

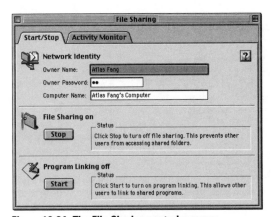

Figure 10-24: The File Sharing control program.

File Sharing Monitor

With system software earlier than Mac OS 8, File Sharing Monitor shows who is connected to your computer for file sharing, which folders and disks you have made available for sharing, and how busy your computer is with handling file sharing. You can also disconnect people from your computer if you need to.

With Mac OS 8, you use the File Sharing control panel instead. (See "Monitoring File Sharing Activity" in Chapter 18 for more information.) Figure 10-25 shows the File Sharing Monitor control panel.

Figure 10-25: The File Sharing Monitor control panel (Mac OS 7.6.1 and earlier).

General Controls

The General Controls control panel sets a number of system options. Figure 10-26 shows the options you can set in the General Controls control panel.

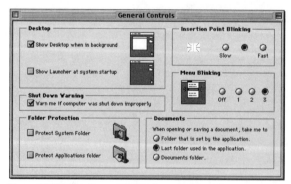

Figure 10-26: The General Controls control panel.

On the left side of the General Controls window, you can show or hide the Finder's desktop when the Finder is not the active application, and you can have the Launcher control panel open automatically during startup. You can have the Mac OS display a warning during startup if the computer crashed or was not shut down properly. In addition, you can individually protect the System Folder and the Applications folder on the startup disk, preventing items in them from being renamed or removed; to use these options, file sharing must be turned off in the File Sharing or Sharing Setup control panel, whichever your computer has.

On the right side of the General Controls window, you can set blinking rates for the text insertion point and menus. Another option determines which folder you see first in a Save or Open dialog box. The first setting, "Folder that is set by the application," specifies the folder that contains the document you opened to launch the application, which is the application's folder if you opened the application directly instead of opening one of its documents. (In Systems 7.5–7.5.2, the first setting is "Folder which contains the application.") The second setting specifies the most recent folder used in the application. The third setting specifies the Documents folder on the startup disk.

Keyboard

The Keyboard control panel sets the key repeat rate and the delay time until key repeating begins. (These options are detailed in "Keyboard and Mouse Adjustments" in Chapter 5.) In addition, you can select foreign language keyboard layouts that you'd like to use. If you select more than one keyboard layout, a keyboard menu appears next to the Applications menu, and you choose the keyboard layout you want to use from it. (For more information on using multiple languages, see "WorldScript" in Chapter 21.) Figure 10-27 shows the Keyboard control panel in Mac OS 8 and in Mac OS 7.6.1.

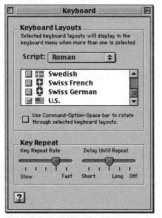
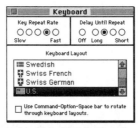

Figure 10-27: The Keyboard control panel in Mac OS 8 (left) and earlier system software versions (right).

Launcher

The Launcher control panel displays a window that contains buttons for opening programs, documents, folders, or anything else you can open from the Finder. You open an item in the Launcher window by clicking its button. In Mac OS 8, the Launcher control panel is similar to an ordinary folder window whose contents are viewed as buttons, but the Launcher has more features. Figure 10-28 shows an example of the Launcher control panel.

Figure 10-28: The Launcher control panel.

Items in the Launcher window are aliases in the Launcher Items folder inside the System Folder. You can categorize items in the Launcher by placing their aliases in specially named folders within the Launcher Items folder. The name of a category folder must begin with a bullet (press Option-8). The names of up to eight category folders appear as button names in a panel at the top of the Launcher window, and clicking a category button displays the items in the corresponding category folder.

In the Launcher that comes with System 7.5.1 and later, you can choose the button size. You can also add icons to the Launcher by dragging them to its window; remove icons from it by Option-dragging them out; and open a document by dragging it to the button of a compatible application.

For more information on the Launcher, see "Opening Programs, Documents, and More" in Chapter 8.

Location Manager

The Location Manager is useful for computers that are often transported to different locations. If you have a PowerBook that you use at home and at the office, for instance, you'll often need to change the settings for your printer, network connection, or Internet connection each time you wake the computer from sleep. The Location Manager takes care of that by saving a group of settings for each location and letting you switch to any location's settings all at once. The settings for a location can include sound volume, default printer, Extensions Manager configuration, file sharing on or off, AppleTalk and TCP/IP network configurations, time zone, and one or more items to be opened automatically. Figure 10-29 shows an example of the Location Manager's window.

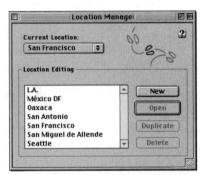

Figure 10-29: The Location Manager control panel.

Changing to a different location

To switch to the settings for another location, simply choose the location from the pop-up menu at the top of the Location Manager window. If you have the Control Strip turned on, you can also choose a location from the Location control strip module.

Choosing a location during startup

If you want to choose a location when you start up the computer, you can set the Location Manager to display a pop-up menu of available locations in a dialog box during startup. You can have the Location Manager display this dialog box every time you start up the computer, only when you hold down the Spacebar, or never. You select one of these options in the dialog box displayed by the Preferences command in the Location Manager's Edit menu. Figure 10-30 shows the Location Manager's Preferences dialog box.

Figure 10-30: Startup preference
for the Location Manager control panel.

Creating a new location

To create a new location you click the Location Manager's New button, which brings up a new location window. You enter a name for the new location in the space provided at the top of the location window. Then one by one you add system settings from a list on the left side of the location window to a list of location settings on the right. To add a setting, select it in the list of system settings and click the Add button. You can remove a setting by selecting it in the list of location settings and clicking the Delete button. When the list of location settings contains everything you want remembered for the location, you save changes and close the location window. Figure 10-31 shows a location window.

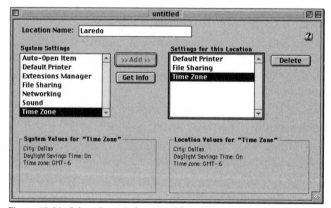

Figure 10-31: A location window specifies the settings saved for a particular location.

When you add a setting to a location, the Location Manager stores the current value of that setting as part of the location. For instance, if the computer's sound volume is set to 3 when you add the Sound setting to a location, then the Location Manager stores a sound volume of 3 for that location; whenever you switch to that location, your computer's sound volume will be set to 3.

If you add an Auto-Open Item to a location, the Location Manager displays a standard Open dialog box in which you select the item that you want automatically opened for that location. You can add more than one Auto-Open Item to a location.

Changing settings used for a location

You can change a location by adding, removing, or changing settings. Start by selecting the location in the list on the left side of the Location Manager window and clicking the Open button (or double-click the location) to display the location window. To add a setting, select it in the list of available system settings on the left side of the location window and click the Add button. To remove a setting, select it in the list of location settings on the right side of the Location window and click the Delete button.

To change the value of a setting for a location, you must change the actual value for the system with the applicable control panel or other software. Then you select the setting in the list of system settings on the left side of the Location Manager window and click the Update button. For example, to change the sound volume stored for a location, you open the location with the Location Manager's Open button, set the system volume with the Monitors & Sound control panel or the Sound control strip module, then select the Sound setting in the location window, and click the Update button in that window.

If you're not sure how to change the value of a setting, select the setting in the location window and click the Get Info button there. This displays a dialog box that explains how you change the value of the selected setting.

Removing a location

To remove a location, you select it in the list of locations on the left side of the Location Manager window and click the Delete button.

Mac OS Easy Open

The Mac OS Easy Open control panel (called Macintosh Easy Open in system software versions earlier than Mac OS 8) automates the opening of documents created by applications that you do not have. The documents may have been created by someone else on another computer, or you may have created them with applications you no longer have. Easy Open works hand-in-hand with translation software installed on your computer, such as the DataViz MacLinkPlus translators included with the system software.

You use the Easy Open control panel to turn automatic file translation on or off and to set several options. Figure 10-32 shows the Mac OS Easy Open control panel.

Figure 10-32: The Mac OS Easy Open control panel.

For a complete description of the control panel options as well as how Easy Open helps you open documents created by applications you don't have, see "Translating Documents" in Chapter 8.

MacLinkPlus Setup

Let's face it: not everyone uses the Mac OS. And often, Mac OS users have to trade files with people who use Windows and DOS computers. In olden times, swapping files with a PC user was a difficult task. Nowadays, Apple makes that task easier by including the DataViz MacLinkPlus translation software with the Mac system software. MacLinkPlus can translate documents created by Windows, DOS, and Apple II applications to formats that Mac OS applications can open. In addition, MacLinkPlus can translate documents from one Mac format to another. The MacLinkPlus translators are used automatically by the Mac OS Easy Open control panel, and you can use them to translate documents on demand. You'll find a detailed description in "Translating Documents" in Chapter 8.

You can set several MacLinkPlus options with the MacLinkPlus control panel. You choose an option from the Category pop-up menu at the top of the control panel, and then choose a setting for the option from the Preference pop-up menu lower in the control panel. A description of the current Category choice appears in the middle of the control panel. Figure 10-33 shows the MacLinkPlus Setup control panel.

MacLinkPlus Setup
MacLink®Plus Translator Preferences
©DataViz, Inc.   V: 9.0.2
Category: **PC Text Translations**
Preference: **Windows Text**
When MacLinkPlus translates PC text documents into word processing or other text formats, there is no way to tell whether the document is DOS or Windows text. Please indicate whether you would like the text to be treated as DOS or Windows text. Note: This will only affect the document when you are using extended ASCII characters.
Registration Number: #00823051-8795
Apple Bundle
DataViz, Inc.

Figure 10-33: The MacLinkPlus Setup control panel.

These are the options you can set with the MacLinkPlus Setup control panel:

❖ **Languages** lets you specify the language used in the documents you are going to translate. This option determines the set of characters available in the document.

❖ **Graphic Clipboard** lets you have the translator automatically place a copy of a converted graphics file onto the Clipboard so that you can simply paste it into a document.

❖ **PCX Color Output** lets you pick the number of colors — 256, 16, or monochrome — in documents you are going to translate to PCX format.

❖ **Drawing Size** lets you choose the size of PICT graphics translated from vector-based CGM, CDF, GEM, PIC, and WPG files.

❖ **Bitmap Compression** lets you decide if you want bitmaps to be compressed (using whatever compressor is normally used for the file format being used) or uncompressed.

❖ **Text Translations** lets you specify whether the PC text files you are going to translate use the DOS or Windows character set. If a text file contains extended-ASCII characters (for example, accent marks and symbols) the translator needs to know whether the file came from DOS or Windows, because they have different character sets.

❖ **AutoBullet, AutoNumber & Outlines** lets you indicate whether you want paragraphs that have been formatted for automatic renumbering, automatic bullets, or outlining to be converted to plain text with numbers or bullets, or to retain their original formatting attributes.

MacTCP

The MacTCP control panel enables you to connect a computer that uses System 7.5.5 or earlier to a TCP/IP network such as the Internet. Clicking the More button in the MacTCP control panel brings up a large dialog box full of network settings. Configuring this dialog box requires specific information about your network connection and is best done with the help of the person who administers your TCP/IP network or Internet connection. Figure 10-34 shows the MacTCP control panel.

Figure 10-34: The MacTCP control panel (System 7.5.5 and earlier).

MacTCP has been replaced by the Open Transport networking software's TCP/IP control panel in Mac OS 7.6 and later. Also, computers with PCI slots must use TCP/IP instead of MacTCP. (You'll find detailed information in "Configuring a TCP/IP Connection" in Chapter 17.)

Map

The Map control panel sets the world location (latitude and longitude) and the time zone of your computer. These settings duplicate the Time Zone setting in the Date & Time control panel (described earlier in this chapter). Even if you never move your computer, you should set its location so that people receiving your e-mail in a different time zone can tell what time you sent the e-mail. The Map control panel can also compute the time difference and distance between any two places. Figure 10-35 shows the Map control panel.

Figure 10-35: The Map control panel.

Tiny flashing dots on the map mark known places; the preset locations include an idiosyncratic mix of major cities and obscure locations, among them the Middle of Nowhere. Click a dot or drag across one to see its name. You can type a place name in the space provided and click the Find button, or go through the list of known places alphabetically by pressing Option while clicking Find. The latitude, longitude, and time zone entries pertain to the most recently selected location, which Map marks with a flashing star. The map scrolls if you drag beyond its boundaries.

To add a new place, specify its latitude and longitude by clicking, by dragging, or by typing the coordinates in the spaces provided. Then type the place name and click the Add City button. After adding a new place, verify the estimated time zone and correct it, if necessary.

Color Map

In system versions older than Mac OS 7.6, the Map control panel normally displays a black-and-white map of the world, but you can replace it with a color map from the Scrapbook. Simply scroll in the Scrapbook to the color world map, copy it, open the Map control panel, and paste. If you can't find a color map in your Scrapbook, you don't have the standard Scrapbook file. To get it, temporarily move the Scrapbook file from your System Folder to the desktop. Next, do a custom installation of the system software (as described in Chapters 28–30), selecting only the Scrapbook for installation. After installation, copy the color map and paste it into the Map control panel. Finally, select the Scrapbook file on the desktop, choose Put Away from the Finder's File menu, and click OK when the Finder asks whether it's OK to replace the Scrapbook file in the System Folder with the one that you're moving (putting away) from the desktop.

Map marks the location of your computer with a flashing dark cross. Set this fact by finding or adding the proper location and then clicking the Set button, or by choosing a new location for your time zone in the Date & Time control panel and then closing and reopening Map. Map automatically adjusts the time and date of your system's clock according to the difference between the old and new locations. Your computer stores its location in battery-powered memory, along with the time of day and other semipermanent settings.

The distance or compass direction from your Macintosh to the place marked with the flashing star appears at the bottom of the control panel, along with the time at the distant place. Change from distance in miles to distance in kilometers or direction in degrees by clicking the unit of measurement in the lower-left corner of the control panel. To see the time difference between that place and your location, click the words Time Differ in the control panel. (If you don't see the words Time Differ, first click the words Time Zone.)

You can enlarge the map by pressing Option while opening the Map control panel. To magnify more, press Shift-Option while opening.

Memory

The Memory control panel sets the size of the disk cache, turns virtual memory on and off, and makes it possible to set aside part of memory as a very speedy RAM disk. With System 7.5.5 and earlier, the 32-Bit Addressing option appears in the Memory control panel for some Mac models. (For detailed information about the Memory control panel settings, see "Adjusting System Memory Use" and "Increasing Total Memory" in Chapter 16.) Figure 10-36 shows an example of the Memory control panel.

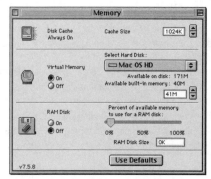

Figure 10-36: The Memory control panel.

What's Your Time?

If you deal with people in multiple time zones, you can use the Map control panel to keep track of local times for various people and offices without having to remember the names of their cities. Here's what you do:

1. Open the Map control panel.

2. Have Map locate the person's city by typing the name of the city and clicking the Find button.

3. Type the person's name over the city name, and click the Add City button.

Now you need only type a person's name in Map and click the Find button to determine whether it is a polite time to call.

If you want Map to remember a person whose city isn't on the map, you can substitute a known city in the same time zone or add the unknown city.

Whenever you add a new place or person to Map, verify the time zone and correct it, if necessary. Map estimates the time zone of a new place based on its latitude and longitude, but time-zone boundaries have many irregularities. Also, Map does not know about Daylight Savings Time. If you are on Daylight Savings Time and someone else is not (or vice versa), Map will be off by one hour in computing the other person's local time.

Modem

The Modem control panel works with the PPP control panel to let you connect by modem or ISDN terminal adapter to the Internet or any other TCP/IP network. You can use this control panel to set which serial port your modem is connected to, what kind of modem you have, and what kind of dialing your phone line uses. You can also set the modem to have its speaker turned off, or to ignore the fact that there may be no dial tone on the line (which might happen on some PBX systems, or when dialing out on a phone line in a country outside the United States). If your particular brand of modem isn't listed in the Modem pop-up menu, try the "Hayes Optima 288" for a connection speed of 28.8 Kbps or the "Hayes Optima 14.4" for a connection speed of 14.4 Kbps. Most modems attempt to imitate these kinds of modems. (See "Making a Dial-up TCP/IP Connection" in Chapter 17 for detailed information.) Figure 10-37 shows the Modem control panel.

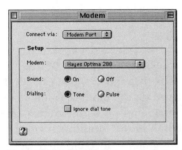

Figure 10-37: The Modem control panel.

Monitors

The Monitors control panel sets the number of colors or grays of one or more monitors. It's primarily used with system software versions earlier than Mac OS 8 on computers without PCI expansion slots. The Monitors control panel is replaced in Mac OS 8 by Monitors & Sound (described later in this chapter), although Monitors is available in the Apple Extras folder on the Mac OS 8 startup disk. Figure 10-38 shows the Monitors control panel on a system with two monitors.

If your computer has multiple monitors, you can drag little images of those monitors around the Monitors control panel to determine their relative positions. You can set which monitor has the menu bar by dragging the little menu bar to the appropriate little monitor in the control panel. You also can designate which monitor displays startup messages and icons. Press the Option

key to display a tiny Macintosh icon; then drag this icon to the monitor that
you want to use during startup. Normally these changes take effect when you
close the control panel. You can make them take effect immediately by pressing
Option when you drag the monitors, menu bar, or startup icon.

**Figure 10-38: The Monitors control
panel (Mac OS 7.6.1 and earlier).**

You can set other monitor options by clicking the Options button in the
Monitors control panel. In the dialog box that appears, you can set the monitor
resolution (the number of pixels displayed on the monitor) and choose a
gamma correction method. (To see gamma options with Systems 7.5 and 7.5.1,
you must Option-click the Options button in the Monitors control panel.)
Depending on the capabilities of the computer's video circuitry, you may see
other options in the dialog box. Figure 10-39 shows the dialog box of
additional options.

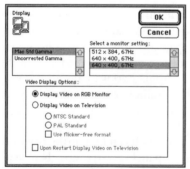

**Figure 10-39: Additional options of the
Monitors control panel.**

Monitors & Sound

Monitors & Sound lets you change the number of colors (or grays) your monitor is displaying and its resolution. Some types of monitors have additional options that you can set with Monitors & Sound. In addition, you use Monitors & Sound to set options for the system alert sound and sound input and output. You select a group of options by clicking a button at the top of the Monitors & Sound window. Figure 10-40 shows the monitor options in Monitors & Sound.

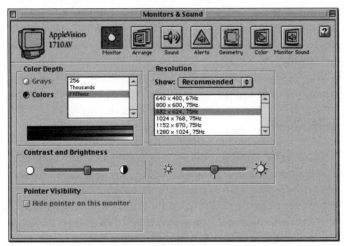

Figure 10-40: The Monitor options in Monitors & Sound.

Beginning with Mac OS 8, Monitors & Sound replaces the separate Monitors control panel and Sound control panel. Monitors & Sound also replaces the Sound & Displays control panel on computers with PCI expansion slots.

The individual Monitors and Sound control panels are still included in the Apple Extras folder on the startup disk in case you need to use them. For example, the only way to add a new alert sound by copy-and-paste is with the Sound control panel. Also, some video and sound devices can't be controlled from the Monitors & Sound control panel. If you have such a device, use the old Monitors control panel or Sound control panel as appropriate.

Monitor options

To set general monitor options, you click the Monitor button at the top of the Monitors & Sound window. The possible settings for the Color Depth option can range from black and white to millions of colors (32-bit color), depending on

the capabilities of your monitor and your computer's video-output circuitry. The
settings for the Resolution option also depend on your monitor and video-output
circuitry, but in general can range from 512×384 pixels (the nominal size of a
12-inch monitor) up to 1280×1024 pixels (the size of a 19-inch monitor).

The Monitor panel of Monitors & Sound includes additional options for some
monitors. For example, you may be able to select a gamma correction setting
or adjust the monitor's brightness and contrast.

You access more options for some monitors by clicking other buttons at the top
of the Monitors & Sound window. For example, the following buttons display
additional options for an AppleVision 1710 or AppleVision 1710AV monitor:

❖ **Geometry** includes options for changing how the monitor draws the screen
   picture. You can expand the display area, so that there is less of a black
   border around the visible area. You can also change the pincushion (how
   concave the sides of the picture are) and the rotation of the display. A Recall
   Factory Settings button resets the monitor to its presets.

❖ **Color** includes options for white point, gamma curve, and ambient light:

   • The white point of a monitor is, in essence, what color the monitor is
     displaying when it's displaying white. There are three standard settings
     for white point: D50 is used mainly for graphic arts and attempts to
     match the white seen in printed matter. 6500 + 8 MPCD is a white
     that is the same as the sun. 9300 + 8 MPCD is the white point used by
     most computer monitors and is the brightest white setting.

   • Gamma curve refers to the way your monitor displays brightness
     relative to the input value from the computer. The Mac OS has
     traditionally used a gamma setting of 1.8.

   • The Ambient Light option adjusts for the way surrounding room light
     affects how colors appear on the screen.

You can save a collection of Color settings and switch back and forth
between them using the buttons and the list on the right side of the window.
Once you've changed some settings, you can save and name the set by
clicking the Save button. The Import and Export buttons are handy if you
want to share your settings with others.

❖ **Monitor Sound** options control the level and tone of sound played through
   the speakers of a monitor that has them, such as the AppleVision 1710AV
   monitor. If the monitor has a built-in microphone, the Monitor Sound
   options control whether it is on or off, its routing, and the amount of gain
   (amplification or attenuation) applied to it.

Gamma Options

Gamma options in Monitors & Sound (and in the options dialog box of the Monitors control panel) provide alternative color balancing for a video display with a picture tube. Color balancing is necessary because the intensity of color on a picture tube does not correspond uniformly to the intensity of the electron beam that traces the video picture on the phosphor coating inside the tube. The computer's video circuitry compensates to provide the most accurate color possible. This compensation commonly is called *gamma correction.* Changing the gamma correction has no effect on video performance, only on color balance.

Sound options

To set sound input and output options for the computer, you click the Sound button at the top of the Monitors & Sound window. Sliders let you adjust the overall output level and the relative volume of the computer's built-in speaker. You can also mute all sound output or the sound played through the built-in speaker. Computers that output stereo sound also have sliders for overall channel balance (left and right) and the channel balance heard through the built-in speaker. Computers with other sound output capabilities, such as stereo surround sound, have options for controlling those capabilities. You may also be able to choose a sound output quality. The options for sound input let you choose a source, such as the computer's microphone port, an internal CD-ROM drive, or the line input jacks if the computer has them. In addition, you can switch to other sound input or output hardware (NuBus or PCI card) if you have such a thing installed. Figure 10-41 shows typical sound input and output options in Monitors & Sound.

Alerts options

To set the system alert sound and its volume, click the Alerts button at the top of the Monitors & Sound control panel. Figure 10-42 shows the system alert options in Monitors & Sound.

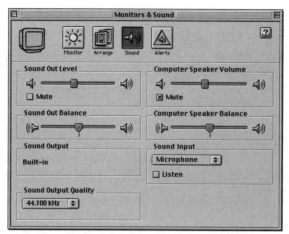

Figure 10-41: The sound options in Monitors & Sound.

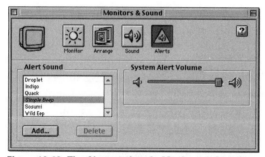

Figure 10-42: The Alerts options in Monitors & Sound.

If you don't like any of the sounds offered, you can record your own by clicking the Add button in the Alerts section of Monitors & Sound. This action brings up a dialog box that has buttons for controlling recording and playback, and a gauge that measures the duration of the recorded sound. Click the Record button to record or re-record up to 10 seconds of sound from the computer's microphone or another audio source. (You set the sound input source in the Sound section of this control panel.) Then Click the Play button to hear your recording. When you're satisfied with your recording, click the Save button, and type a name for the new alert sound when you're asked. Figure 10-43 shows the dialog box in which you record an alert sound.

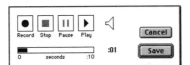

Figure 10-43: The dialog box for recording an alert sound.

The Add button is not available in versions of Monitors & Sound distributed prior to Mac OS 8. But you can record new alert sounds with the SimpleSound accessory program (described in the next chapter). You can also add new alert sounds by dragging sound files into the System file (as described in "Investigating the System Folder" in Chapter 9).

Arrange options

If your computer has two or more monitors, you adjust their relative positions and other options by clicking the Arrange button at the top of the Monitors & Sound window. You adjust the relative positions of the monitors by dragging little images of them around the Monitors & Sound window. You can set which monitor has the menu bar by dragging the little menu bar to the appropriate little monitor in the control panel. You can also designate which monitor displays startup messages and icons. Press the Option key to display a tiny Macintosh icon; then drag this icon to the monitor that you want to use during startup.

Mouse

The Mouse control panel sets the mouse-to-pointer (or trackball-to-pointer) tracking speed and the double-click interval. The double-click interval also determines how long you have to wait after selecting an icon name before it is ready for editing. (See "Keyboard and Mouse Adjustments" in Chapter 5 for more details.) Figure 10-44 shows the Mouse control panel.

Figure 10-44: The Mouse control panel.

Network

The Network control panel determines which network connection to use if more than one is available to a computer with System 7.5.5 or earlier. This control panel has been supplanted by the AppleTalk control panel that comes with Open Transport in Mac OS 7.6 and later. Also, computers with PCI slots must use the AppleTalk control panel instead of Network. (For details, see "Configuring an AppleTalk Connection" in Chapter 17.) Figure 10-45 shows the Network control panel.

Figure 10-45: The Network control panel (System 7.5.5 and earlier).

Numbers

The Numbers control panel sets the number format — decimal separator, thousand separators, and currency symbol — for a region of the world that you choose from a pop-up menu of the languages installed in the System file. Figure 10-46 shows the Numbers control panel.

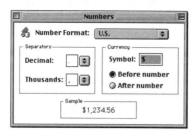

Figure 10-46: The Numbers control panel.

OpenDoc Setup

OpenDoc Setup lets you set the least amount of memory that each OpenDoc document uses when it's open. You can also set when OpenDoc starts up, so that it's either always on or only on when OpenDoc documents are open.

(See "OpenDoc Compound Documents" in Chapter 23 for more details.)
Figure 10-47 shows the OpenDoc Setup window.

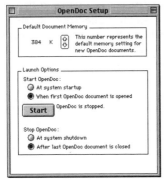

Figure 10-47: The OpenDoc Setup control program.

PC Exchange

With the PC Exchange control panel installed, your computer can access floppy disks from Windows, OS/2, DOS, and Apple II (ProDOS) computers. When you insert a disk from one of those computers into a Mac, the foreign disk's icon appears on the Finder's desktop. You can open the foreign disk and see its files and folders (which are called *sub-directories* in DOS, Windows, and OS/2). You can open folders by double-clicking them, and you can open document files if you have compatible Mac programs. (More information on PC Exchange can be found in "Translating Documents" in Chapter 8.) Figure 10-48 shows the PC Exchange control panel.

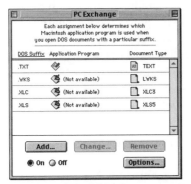

Figure 10-48: The PC Exchange control panel.

PowerBook

The PowerBook control panel sets battery conservation and system responsiveness for PowerBook computers. When the PowerBook control panel's Easy/Custom switch is set to Easy, the control panel collapses to show only the single conservation-performance slider. When the switch is set to Custom, the control panel expands to display all its options. Figure 10-49 shows the expanded PowerBook control panel.

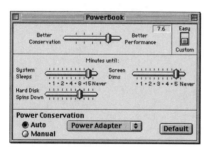

Figure 10-49: The PowerBook control panel.

Moving the main conservation-performance slider to the left conserves battery power by making the computer sleep, the hard disk spin down, the screen dim, and the processor cycle after shorter periods of inactivity. Moving the conservation-performance slider to the right increases system responsiveness by lengthening the period of inactivity before the computer sleeps, the hard disk spins down, the screen dims, and the processor cycles.

The expanded control panel has three sliders for individually setting the idle time until system sleep, hard-disk spin-down, and screen dimming. Also, you can turn processor cycling on or off. You can set the three sliders and the processor-cycling option differently for battery operation than for operation with the power adapter plugged into the computer. You choose the power mode from the pop-up menu in the Power Conservation section of the control panel. The computer determines whether to use the battery settings or the power-adapter settings as long as power conservation is set to Auto. When power conservation is set to Manual, the settings in the expanded section of the control panel stay in effect indefinitely.

PowerBook Setup

The PowerBook Setup control panel sets up special features that some PowerBooks have and others don't. PowerBook Setup configures the Modem port for a PowerBook that has an internal modem. You can set the PowerBook to use the internal modem or a device connected to the external Modem port. When the internal modem is selected, a "Wake On Ring" option determines whether the modem wakes the computer to receive an incoming call. In addition, PowerBook Setup lets you set a SCSI ID number for a PowerBook that has SCSI Disk Mode, which enables connecting the PowerBook to another computer as an external SCSI disk. Another PowerBook Setup option available on some PowerBook models lets you set a time and date for the computer to wake itself up. Figure 10-50 shows an example of the PowerBook Setup control panel.

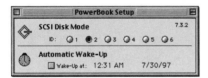

Figure 10-50: The PowerBook Setup control panel.

PowerTalk Setup

The PowerTalk Setup control panel has configuration settings for PowerTalk collaboration services that come with Systems 7.5–7.5.5. Besides turning all collaboration services off or on, you can set your PowerTalk Key Chain to lock itself automatically after a period of inactivity whose duration you specify. You also can set PowerTalk to require entry of your Key Chain access code during startup. PowerTalk is not compatible with Mac OS 8, and you lose access to the Key Chain and other PowerTalk services after installing Mac OS 8. (For details on PowerTalk, see Appendix B.) Figure 10-51 shows the PowerTalk control panel.

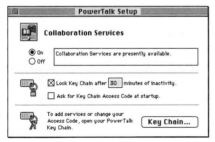

Figure 10-51: The PowerTalk Setup control panel (System 7.5.5 and earlier).

PPP

The PPP control panel is an adjunct to the Open Transport networking software used by Mac OS 7.6 and later (optional with earlier system software). PPP makes a connection to the Internet or another TCP/IP network through the modem or ISDN adapter specified in the Modem control panel. (For more information, see "Making a Dial-up TCP/IP Connection" in Chapter 17.) Figure 10-52 shows the PPP control panel.

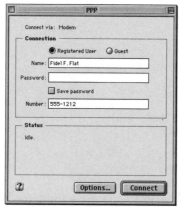

Figure 10-52: The PPP control panel.

QuickTime Settings

QuickTime settings fall into two categories: AutoPlay and Music. You select a category from the pop-up menu at the top of the control panel. The AutoPlay options specify whether to automatically play an audio CD when inserted and whether to automatically start up a CD-ROM when inserted. (Not all CD-ROMs support this feature.) Figure 10-53 shows the AutoPlay options of the QuickTime Settings control panel.

Music settings route MIDI music. You always have the option of routing MIDI music through the QuickTime Music Synthesizer (which can play MIDI files through the SimplePlayer application). You may have other routing options if you have added MIDI devices or software to your computer. For example, you could have a MIDI device connected to the modem port or the printer port. Another possibility is a plug-in synthesizer program to replace the QuickTime synthesizer. In addition, you could have professional music software that uses the Opcode Music System (OMS). Figure 10-54 shows the Music options of the QuickTime Settings control panel.

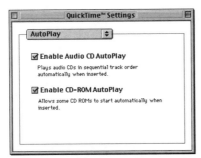

Figure 10-53: The AutoPlay options of the QuickTime Settings control panel.

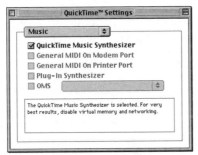

Figure 10-54: The Music options of the QuickTime settings control panel.

Sharing Setup

You use the Sharing Setup control panel with Mac OS 7.6.1 and earlier to name your computer and its owner on its network, set the owner's network password, and start or stop file sharing and program linking. With Mac OS 8, you use the File Sharing control panel instead. (For complete information on these settings, see "Identifying Your Computer" and "Turning File Sharing On and Off" in Chapter 18 and "Linking Programs" in Chapter 22.) Figure 10-55 shows the Sharing Setup control panel.

Figure 10-55: The Sharing Setup control panel
(Mac OS 7.6.1 and earlier).

Sound

The Sound control panel sets sound input and output options, primarily with
system software versions earlier than Mac OS 8 on computers without PCI
expansion slots. The Sound control panel is replaced in Mac OS 8 by Monitors
& Sound (described earlier in this chapter), although the Sound control panel
is available in the Apple Extras folder on the Mac OS 8 startup disk.

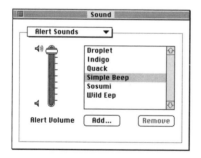
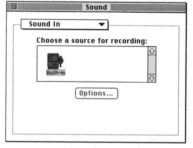

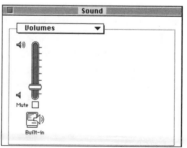

Figure 10-56: Sections of the Sound control panel (Mac OS 7.6.1 and earlier);
the specific options depend on the computer's sound capabilities.

The Sound control panel has four groups of sound options: alert sounds, sound in, sound out, and volumes. You choose a group from the pop-up menu at the top of the control panel. Figure 10-56 shows the four groups of options in the Sound control panel.

In the Alert Sounds group of options, there are two ways to add and remove system alert sounds. One way is to use the Edit menu's Cut, Copy, and Paste commands. For example, you can copy a sound from the Scrapbook (described in the next chapter) and paste it into the Sound control panel. You can also record a new system alert sound by clicking the Add button, or remove an alert sound by selecting it and clicking the Remove button.

It's also possible to add and remove alert sounds by dragging them in and out of the System file (as described in "Investigating the System Folder" in Chapter 9).

Speech

The Speech control panel lets you choose the voice your computer uses to speak text aloud, as well as determine when your computer will use this voice. You can set your computer to use any available voice to speak the alerts that appear on your screen. If you have installed speech recognition software on a computer capable of using it, you configure that with the Speech control panel as well. (For more information on computer speech, see "Text-to-Speech" and "Speech Recognition" in Chapter 21.) Figure 10-57 shows the Talking Alerts options of the Speech control panel.

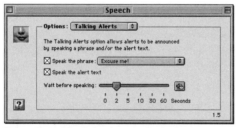

Figure 10-57: The Speech control panel.

Speech Setup

The Speech Setup control panel sets speech recognition options for the PlainTalk Speech Recognition software version 1.3, which Quadra and Centris 660AV and 840AV computers must use. All Power Mac computers should use PlainTalk 1.5 and its Speech control panel. (See "Speech Recognition" in Chapter 21 for more information.) Figure 10-58 shows the Speech Setup control panel.

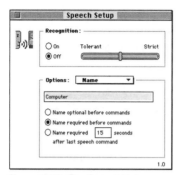

Figure 10-58: The Speech Setup control panel.

Startup Disk

If your computer has more than one disk drive, the Startup Disk control panel sets which one will be used when you start up the computer. This control panel doesn't work with a Macintosh Plus, and it has no effect unless your computer has more than one hard disk that contains a System Folder. And in some cases, Startup Disk won't enable you to choose among multiple volumes from a single partitioned hard disk. Figure 10-59 shows the Startup Disk control panel.

Figure 10-59: The Startup Disk control panel.

TCP/IP

The TCP/IP control panel regulates the way your computer works over a TCP/IP network. You can use this control panel to set the IP address, domain name server, router address, and other settings for your TCP/IP network or Internet connection. TCP/IP is part of the Open Transport networking software that's mandatory with Mac OS 7.6 and later and optional with earlier system software. It replaces the MacTCP control panel. (See "Configuring a TCP/IP Connection" in Chapter 17 for more details.) Figure 10-60 shows the TCP/IP control panel.

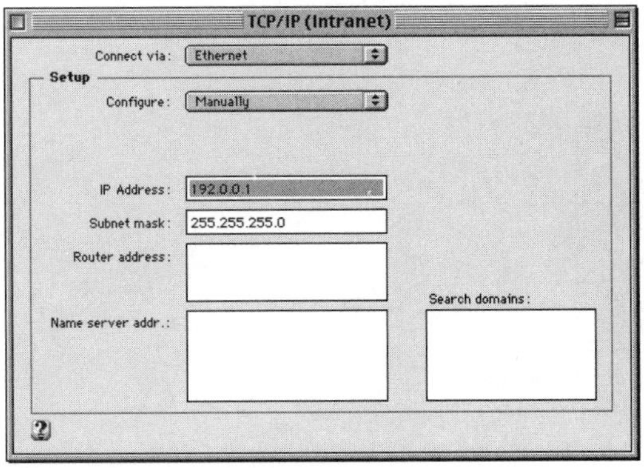

Figure 10-60: The TCP/IP control panel.

Text

The Text control panel enables you to specify a set of rules for alphabetizing, capitalizing, and distinguishing words. First you choose among the installed language-script systems, such as Roman, Cyrillic, Arabic, Japanese, and Chinese. Then you choose among the regional rules for text behavior that the chosen script system supports. For example, the Roman script system has text behavior rules for Brasil, Danish, Dutch, English, Finnish, French, French Canadian, German, Italian, Norwegian, Spanish, and Swedish. Figure 10-61 shows the Text control panel.

Figure 10-61: The Text control panel.

Trackpad

The Trackpad control panel sets the trackpad-to-pointer tracking speed and the double-click interval. The double-click interval also determines how long you have to wait after selecting an icon name before it is ready for editing. (See "Keyboard and Mouse Adjustments" in Chapter 5 for more details.) Figure 10-62 shows the Trackpad control panel.

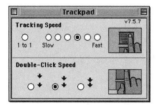

Figure 10-62: The Trackpad control panel.

Users & Groups

Users & Groups identifies people and groups to whom you give specific access privileges for file sharing and program linking. Mac OS 8 has an improved version of Users & Groups that has a different look and method of operation. (For complete information on both versions of Users & Groups, see "Identifying Who Can Access Your Shared Items" in Chapter 18.) Figure 10-63 shows the Users & Groups control panel in Mac OS 8.

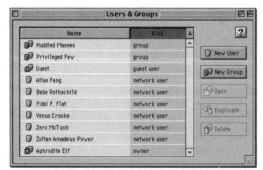

Figure 10-63: The Users & Groups control program.

Views

The Views control panel sets format and content options for Finder windows in Mac OS 7.6.1 and earlier. In Mac OS 8, you set these options with the Appearance control panel and with the Finder's View Options and Preferences commands. (See "Appearance and Behavior Modification" in Chapter 5 for a detailed description.) Figure 10-64 shows the Views control panel.

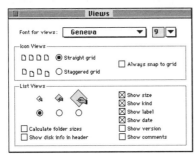

Figure 10-64: The Views control panel (Mac OS 7.6.1 and earlier).

Web Sharing

The Web Sharing control panel lets you serve Web pages from your Mac. You can choose any folder on your hard disk to be shared over the Web. All you need to do is to create the HTML files that go inside. Practically speaking, you also need a fixed IP address on the Internet (not a dial-up connection), since other people on the Web can't find your Web site while you are disconnected from the Internet. (For more information, see "Web Sharing" in Chapter 20.) Figure 10-65 shows the Web Sharing control panel.

Figure 10-65: The Web Sharing control panel.

WindowShade

With System 7.5–Mac OS 7.6.1, the WindowShade control panel gives you the
option of collapsing a window into its title bar. The effect, which is like rolling
up a window shade, works with all windows and palettes (not just Finder
windows). In the control panel, you designate the combination of mouse clicks
and modifier keys that triggers window collapsing and expanding. You also can
turn roller-shade sound effects on and off. With Mac OS 8, you get the same
effect by clicking a window's collapse box, and you set window collapsing
options in the Appearance control panel (described earlier in this chapter).
Figure 10-66 shows the WindowShade control panel.

Figure 10-66: The WindowShade
control panel (System 7.5–Mac OS 7.6.1).

Summary

This chapter told you what all control panels have in common. They're located
in the Control Panels folder. Also, even though some control panels are
applications and others are essentially Finder documents, you open and close
them all the same way.

This chapter also described the control panels that come with the Mac system
software, from Appearance to WindowShade. Some descriptions were brief and
referred you to other chapters where particular control panels are covered in
depth. Other descriptions told you in detail how to use the control panels.

CHAPTER ELEVEN

Put Accessory Programs to Work

IN THIS CHAPTER

- **Introducing accessory programs:** desk accessories and application programs

- **Investigating an encyclopedia of accessory programs,** which describes the ones that come with the Mac OS

A pple has always included accessory programs with the Mac system software. Accessory programs enhance the features and capabilities of the system software. Each accessory is a small, focused program that provides a narrowly defined set of features and capabilities. Some are indispensable, such as the Chooser, which you use to set up or select a printer and to access files over a network. Others are more diversionary, such as the Jigsaw Puzzle or the AppleCD Audio Player, which plays music CDs. Some you will use all the time, such as Find File, which quickly searches your disks for items you can't find by browsing. Others you'll hardly ever use, but will be mighty glad to have them when you need them, such as Disk First Aid.

Introducing Accessory Programs

In the old days, accessory programs were all desk accessories, and you could open them only from the Apple menu. These days some accessories are application programs and others are desk accessories, and very little differentiates them. You can put both kinds of programs in folders, on the desktop, or in the Apple menu. Each desk accessory can have its own unique icon, although some use the generic desk accessory icon, which looks like a backwards generic application icon.

You move and copy desk accessories by dragging their icons in the Finder, just as you would with an application. If you want to install a desk accessory in the Apple menu, simply drag it to the System Folder icon; you don't have to use the Font/DA Mover utility program. For historical reasons, desk accessories can also exist in suitcase files, like fonts.

You can open a desk accessory all the ways you can an application program but one. For example, you can open a desk accessory by double-clicking it or by choosing it from the Apple menu. But unlike an application program, you can't open a desk accessory by opening one of its documents because desk accessories don't have documents. Thus, you can't open a desk accessory by double-clicking a document or by dragging a document to the desk accessory icon.

Another difference between most desk accessories and applications is the way you quit them. Like application programs, desk accessories have a Quit command in the File menu. In addition, most desk accessories quit automatically when you close their windows.

Accessory Program Encyclopedia

Each accessory program has a unique set of features and capabilities that enhance the Mac OS. This section describes the features and capabilities of the accessory programs that come with the Mac OS. The accessory programs are listed here in alphabetical order.

As you go through this section, you will notice that most accessory programs have detailed descriptions but a few have only brief descriptions. Accessory programs that are covered in depth elsewhere in this book have brief descriptions here that refer you to another chapter for details. The descriptions here for accessory programs not covered elsewhere tell you in detail how to use the programs.

Apple System Profiler

If you ever need to call Apple for technical support for your computer, you may be asked all kinds of questions you don't know the answer to. What's your processor type? Exactly which version of the system are you running? Which SCSI bus is your startup drive on? And so on.

The Apple System Profiler answers these questions, and more. Just by running this program you can find out the details of your computers' setup in several categories. Figure 11-1 shows the system overview category in Mac OS 8.

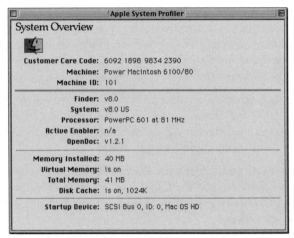

Figure 11-1: The Apple System Profiler can tell you all of the hidden little details about your machine.

The number of categories depends on the version of System Profiler you have. The version of System Profiler that comes with Mac OS 8 has the following seven categories:

❖ **System Overview** displays basic information about your computer; including your personal customer number for the computer; the name and identification number of your computer model; the Finder and System versions; the type of processor and its speed; the active system enabler version (if any); the OpenDoc version; the amount of RAM installed; virtual memory status; the total amount of memory; the size of the disk cache; and the SCSI ID of the startup disk.

❖ **Network/Communication Overview** displays file sharing status; the name of the AppleTalk network zone (if any); the chosen printer's name, software version, and network location (if it's on a network); the active network port; a list of the networking software currently installed; and the current TCP/IP address information if you're connected to the Internet or another TCP/IP network.

❖ **Volume Information** displays a list of hard disk, shared disk, and other storage volumes. For a volume you select from the list, you see the volume's name and kind (such as hard disk); its capacity and space available; its SCSI ID and bus number; whether the volume is mounted on the desktop and write-protected (locked); and where the volume is located.

❖ **Device Information** displays a list of SCSI devices connected to the computer. For a device you select from a list, you see the device type; SCSI ID and bus number; make and model; version of the device's read-only memory (ROM); the type of SCSI interface; whether the device has removable media; and the number of volumes on the device.

❖ **Control Panel Information** displays a list of control panels in the System Folder, both enabled and disabled, and the folder location of the one currently selected in the list. You can restrict the list to show only Apple control panels or only non-Apple control panels.

❖ **Extension Information** displays a list of extensions in the System Folder, both enabled and disabled, and the folder location of the one currently selected in the list. You can restrict the list to show only Apple extensions or only non-Apple extensions.

❖ **System Folder Information** displays a list of System Folders on the startup disk.

❖ **Application Information** displays a list of application programs on the startup disk, and the folder location of the one currently selected in the list.

If you ever do call for technical support, you may be asked to run this program and switch to one of the information categories. It's easy to do: just use the Select menu to choose the information you want to see.

Sometimes it's easier to get a report that has all of the system information in a single file. You can use the Create Report item in the File menu to do just that. When selected, Create Report asks you for a file name, and saves a complete listing of your system details to it. You can examine reports you have previously saved with the Open Report command.

AppleCD Audio Player

The AppleCD Audio Player application plays audio CDs in your CD-ROM drive. You can play, pause, stop, skip back, skip forward, scan back, and scan forward by clicking the buttons on the right side of the control panel. What's more, you can program a custom play list for every CD, and Audio Player remembers each play list you create. You can also enter CD and track titles, which Audio Player remembers as well. (See "Audio CDs" in Chapter 19 for more details on using this accessory.) Figure 11-2 shows the AppleCD Audio Player program.

Figure 11-2: The AppleCD Audio Player program.

Apple Video Player

The Apple Video Player application plays video and audio from a VCR, camcorder, or other video equipment on a computer with video inputs. The application can also display TV shows on a computer with a TV tuner installed. In addition, you the Video Player can capture the video and save it in a movie file on disk. (For detailed information, see "Apple Video Player" in Chapter 19.) Figure 11-3 shows the Apple Video Player's main window and its Controls window.

Figure 11-3: The Apple Video Player and its controls.

Calculator and Graphing Calculator

The Calculator desk accessory adds, subtracts, multiplies, and divides numbers that you enter. You can type numbers and operation symbols or click the keys in the desk accessory. In addition, you can copy the text of a calculation — for example, 69.95+26.98+14.99*.0725— and paste it into the Calculator. Figure 11-4 shows the Calculator desk accessory.

Figure 11-4: The Calculator desk accessory.

Chooser

The Chooser desk accessory enables you to select a printer or other output device, or to create a desktop printer icon if your computer has desktop printing software installed (it's standard with Mac OS 7.6 and later and optional with earlier systems). You also use the Chooser to access file servers and shared folders from other computers on the same network as your computer. (For more information on the Chooser, see "Using Printers with Desktop Icons" and "Using Printers Without Desktop Icons" in Chapter 14 and "Sharing Someone Else's Folders and Disks" in Chapter 18.) Figure 11-5 shows the Chooser desk accessory.

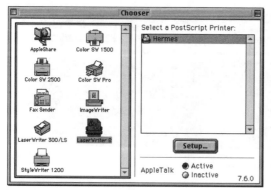

Figure 11-5: The Chooser desk accessory.

Connect To

The Connect To program quickly connects you to any Internet location whose URL (uniform resource locator) you know. You enter the URL in the space provided, and Connect To sends the URL to the appropriate Internet application. For example, Connect To sends a URL that begins with http:// to your Web browser application. (For more details, see "Your Internet Connection" in Chapter 20.) Figure 11-6 shows the Connect To program.

Figure 11-6: The Connect To program.

Disk First Aid

The Disk First Aid program checks the condition of a disk's directory, which keeps track of where files are stored on the disk, and can often repair any problem it finds. A directory can become damaged when the computer crashes or freezes. To use Disk First Aid, you select one or more disks in its window and click the Verify button or the Repair button. Figure 11-7 shows the Disk First Aid window.

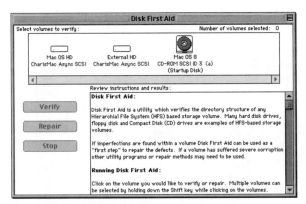

Figure 11-7: The Disk First Aid program.

Disk First Aid can't repair damage on the startup disk or on any disk when file sharing is turned on. If you need to repair the startup disk, start up from a system software installation CD-ROM or from a Disk Tools floppy disk.

Disk First Aid is in the Apple Extras folder on the startup disk. (For more information on Disk First Aid, see "Preparing for Installation" in Chapter 27.)

Find File

The Find File utility program finds files, folders, and disks that match up to eight criteria. (Find File is described fully in "Finding Items" in Chapter 7.) Figure 11-8 shows the Find File program.

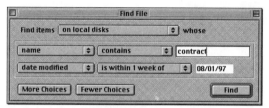

Figure 11-8: The Find File program.

Graphing Calculator

PowerPC computers come with an special calculator program, the Graphing Calculator, to show off their processing power. It can graph an equation in the same time that it takes the ordinary Calculator to perform arithmetic on a lesser Mac. Figure 11-9 shows the Graphing Calculator and its full keypad.

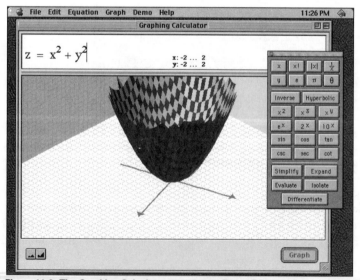

Figure 11-9: The Graphing Calculator program on PowerPC computers.

You can enter equations in the Graphing Calculator and it will draw the graph the equation represents. For example, enter "$z = x^2 + y^2$" into the space above the graph. For exponents, press the caret (Shift-6) to move the cursor up above the line; when you're done entering an exponent, press the Right Arrow to return to normal.

You will see the graph of this equation — a three-dimensional parabola — drawn. Using the mouse, you can spin the graph about an axis and see it from another angle. Hold down the mouse over the image and move left or right. The graph will spin in the direction you move the mouse.

The Graphing Calculator knows how to draw in two or three dimensions and knows about the variables x, y, and z. You can use these variables in your equations. You can also use constants like pi, infinity, and e.

Unlike many calculators, the Graphing Calculator understands equations as you've learned them in math class. If you need help entering parts of your equation, use the Full Keypad or Small Keypad from the Equation menu. Both provide a floating window with buttons for things like sine, cosine, exponents, and other commonly used functions. Other useful functions such as Square Root and Derivative are available in the Equation menu as well.

The Edit menu lets you copy the graph to the Clipboard, so you can paste it into other documents — very handy for school reports. And you can use the Preferences menu item to change the size of the graph grid, or the font and size of the typefaces used.

The Demo menu steps through the graphing of a set of equations. It's useful when trying to learn all that the Graphing Calculator can do, but it's probably best used to impress folks with the power and speed of your PowerPC computer.

Jigsaw Puzzle

The Jigsaw Puzzle program can create endless numbers of jigsaw puzzles with large, medium, or small pieces from any graphics file that is compatible with SimpleText (that is, in a format that QuickTime can open). You can have the program show the picture on which the puzzle is based (like the box top of a conventional puzzle), and you can also have it solve the puzzle for you. Figure 11-10 shows the Jigsaw Puzzle program with a puzzle made from one of the pictures from the Extra Desktop Pictures folder in the CD Extras folder on the Mac OS 8 installation CD-ROM.

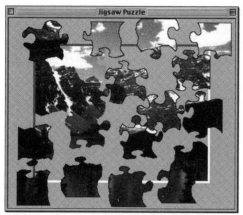

Figure 11-10: The Jigsaw Puzzle program, with medium-size pieces.

Key Caps

The Key Caps program shows all the characters that you can type in any font installed in your system. You choose the font from the Key Caps menu, which appears to the right of the Edit menu when the Key Caps desk accessory is active. Key Caps changes to show the effect of pressing Shift, Option, or Control separately or in combination. Figure 11-11 shows an example of the Key Caps program.

Figure 11-11: The Key Caps program.

In Key Caps, pressing Option outlines the keys that, when pressed along with Option, don't directly produce a character. Each of those Option-key combinations, called *dead keys*, adds an accent or other diacritic to certain subsequently typed keys. Pressing a dead key — for example, Option-E for an accent — outlines the keys that can have that diacritic added. Figure 11-12 shows how dead keys appear in Key Caps.

Pressing Option outlines keys that can add a diacritic, and pressing one of them while pressing Option . . .

. . . outlines the keys that can have that diacritic added

Figure 11-12: Reviewing dead keys and their effects.

QUICK TIPS

Printing Key Caps

You may want to print Key Caps as a handy reference, but it has no Print command. To work around this situation, take a picture of the screen and print that picture, as follows:

Open Key Caps, choose the font that you want it to show, and press any modifier keys (Shift, Option, Control, or ⌘) that you want to be in effect. Move the mouse pointer to an empty area of the menu bar; hold down the mouse button; temporarily release the modifier keys; press ⌘-Shift-3; again press the modifier keys that you released temporarily; and, finally, release the mouse button. Your gyrations should be rewarded by the sound of a camera shutter as the system snaps a picture of the screen.

Now open your startup disk, and look for a document named Picture 1. Print this document, using SimpleText or any graphics program. Cut out the Key Caps window with scissors after printing, or crop it out with a graphics program before printing. If you take additional snapshots, those snapshots are numbered sequentially.

Movie Player

Movie Player is used to play QuickTime movies. You have more control over a movie in Movie Player than in ordinary applications such as SimpleText and ClarisWorks. For example, you can present a movie centered on a completely black screen. In addition, Movie Player has commands for simple movie editing. For instance, you can turn off the video, audio, or other tracks, and you can extract individual tracks as new movies. You can also get detailed information about a movie in a separate window. Figure 11-13 shows the Movie Player information window for a movie.

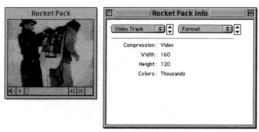

Figure 11-13: The information window for a movie in Movie Player.

Movie Player is located in the Applications folder on a Mac OS 8 startup disk. With earlier system software it's in the Apple Extras folder on the startup disk. (For more information on Movie Player, see "QuickTime Movies" in Chapter 19.)

Note Pad

The Note Pad records brief messages that you type or paste into it. You can print notes, go to any note by number, and find text in one note or all notes. Each note can contain up to 32K (about 32,000) characters. You can drag text between the Note Pad and another application that has adopted Mac OS drag-and-drop editing, such as ClarisWorks, the Scrapbook, and SimpleText (see "Moving Document Contents Around" in Chapter 8). You can scroll and resize the Note Pad window. In addition, you can set the font and size of the text in the notes. Figure 11-14 shows the Note Pad.

Figure 11-14: The Note Pad program.

To create a new Note, use the New command from the File menu, or press ⌘-N. Click the dog-ear in the lower-left corner to flip forward or back through the notes.

Scrapbook

The Scrapbook stores and retrieves text, pictures, sounds, movies, and other types of information that you paste into it, one item at a time. You can copy an item to or from the Scrapbook by dragging from or to another application that has adopted Mac OS drag-and-drop editing, such as ClarisWorks, SimpleText, or the Finder (see "Moving Document Contents Around" in Chapter 8 for details). Figure 11-15 shows a movie pasted into the Scrapbook.

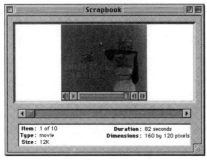

Figure 11-15: The Scrapbook.

You can resize the window of the Scrapbook. As you scroll through items, the Scrapbook reports the number of the item, the type of the item, and its size. For picture items, the Scrapbook also reports the item's dimensions and the amount (if any) by which the item is reduced for display in the Scrapbook. The Scrapbook also reports the duration of sound items.

QUICK TIPS

Relieving Scrapbook Clutter

After extensive use, your Scrapbook may become cluttered with old clippings. If you can't bear to throw them out, make a copy of the Scrapbook file in your System Folder (use the Finder's Duplicate command and store the copy in some other folder) before you start weeding. Later, you can use the old copy that you made by double-clicking it. To get the standard Mac OS Scrapbook file, you must install System 7 on a disk that has no Scrapbook file in its System Folder. The Installer does not replace a Scrapbook file that it finds in the System Folder when you install or upgrade the system software.

Script Editor

The Script Editor is used to write, record, and edit AppleScript scripts. You'll find it in the AppleScript folder inside the Apple Extras folder on the startup disk. (For more information on AppleScript and Script Editor, see Chapter 22.) Figure 11-16 shows an example script in a Script Editor window.

Figure 11-16: An AppleScript script in the Script Editor program.

SimpleSound

SimpleSound is a small application that you can use to record sound. You can record sound files and new system alert sounds. The Alert Sounds window shows a list of all alert sounds currently in your System file. You can also open sound files, each in its own window. Figure 11-17 shows the Alert Sounds window and the windows of two sound files.

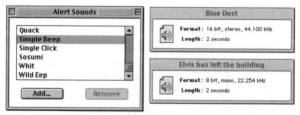

Figure 11-17: The Alert sounds window and the windows of two sound files in the SimpleSound program.

Playing sounds

You can play an alert sound by clicking its name in the Alert Sounds window. Selecting an alert sound in the Alert Sounds window also makes it the system alert sound, just like selecting it in the Monitors & Sound control panel or the Sound control panel (described in Chapter 10).

To play an open sound file, make its window active and use the Play command in the Sound menu, or double-click the icon in the sound's window. You can stop a playing sound with the Stop command in the Sound menu, by clicking the icon in the sound's window once, or by pressing ⌘-period.

Making sounds

Before making a new sound, you can set the sound quality by choosing a quality level from the Sound menu. Higher quality sound requires more storage space on disk. You have the following four choices:

❖ **CD Quality** records in stereo with 16-bit samples and a 44.1kHz sampling rate.

❖ **Music Quality** records in mono with 8-bit samples and a 22kHz sample rate.

❖ **Speech Quality** records in mono with 3-to-1 compression and a 22kHz sampling rate.

❖ **Phone Quality** records in mono with 6-to-1 compression and a 22kHz sampling rate.

To make a new alert sound, click the Add button in the Alert Sounds window. To make a new sound file, use the New command in the File menu. Either action brings up a dialog box with buttons that work like a traditional tape recorder. The dialog box also shows the elapsed recording time and the remaining time available. Click the Record button to record or re-record sound from the computer's microphone or another audio source. (You set the sound input source in the Sound section of the Monitors & Sound control panel or the Sound In section of the Sound control panel, as described in the Chapter 10.) Then click the Play button to hear your recording. When you're satisfied with your recording, click the Save button, and type a name for the new sound when you're asked. Figure 11-18 shows the dialog box in which you record a sound.

Figure 11-18: The dialog box for recording a new sound.

New alert sounds are saved in the Finder sound format (also known as the snd format) and are put in the System file. You can open the System file and drag sounds to the desktop.

New sound files are saved in the audio interchange file format (AIFF), and each goes in the folder that you select when you save the sound.

Stickies

The Stickies application displays notes similar to Post-it Notes on your screen. You can set the color and the text font, size, and style for each note. You can drag selected text to move it within a note, copy it between notes, or copy it between a note and another application that has adopted Mac OS drag-and-drop editing, such as SimpleText and the Note Pad. Stickies windows have no scroll bars, but you can scroll by pressing the arrow keys or by dragging inside the note. Figure 11-19 shows examples of Stickies notes.

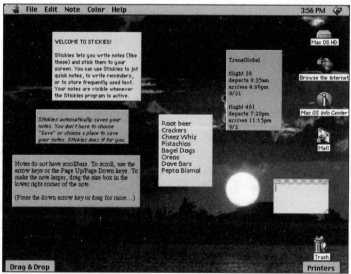

Figure 11-19: The Stickies program's note windows.

Summary

After reading this chapter, you know that a number of accessory programs come with the Mac system software. Each is a small, focused program that provides very specific features and capabilities. Accessory programs range from the indispensable Chooser, which you use to set up or select a printer and to access files over a network, to the diversionary Jigsaw Puzzle. You'll use some of them all the time, such as Find File, which quickly searches disks for items you can't seem to find. Others, such as Disk First Aid, you'll use only in case of trouble. Some accessory programs are desk accessories and others are application programs, although the difference between them is minimal.

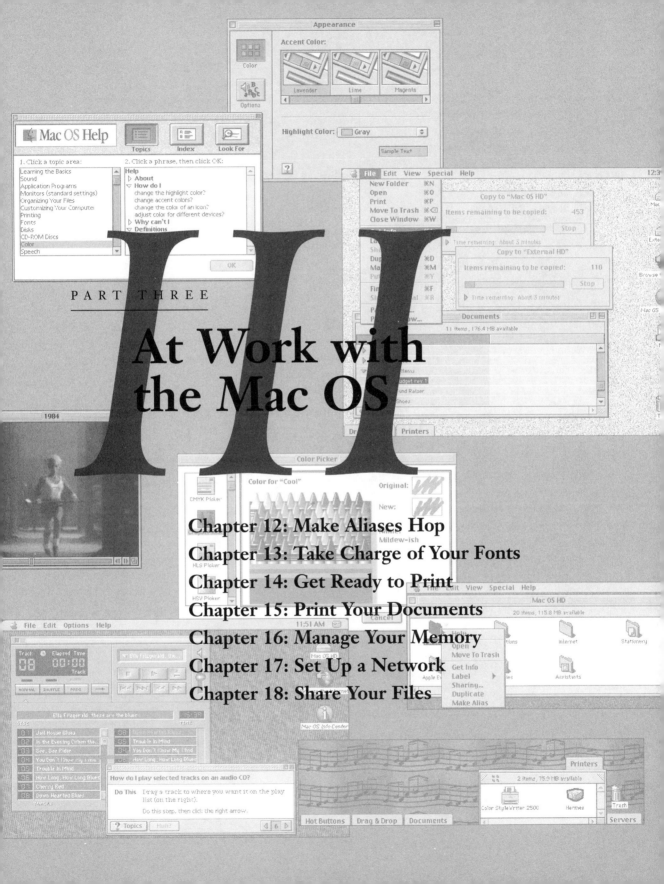

PART THREE

At Work with the Mac OS

Make Aliases Hop

12

D id you ever wish a file or folder could be in more than one place? You want to keep the contents of your disk organized by putting programs and documents in folders, and putting those folders in other folders. But when you want to open an item, you end up digging through folders to find what you want to open. *Aliases* cut through the organizational red tape. Think of an alias as a stand-in or an agent for a real program, document, folder, or disk. Aliases act like real items when you open them or drag items to them. You can place these agents at your beck and call in any handy location, such as on the desktop or in the Apple menu. Aliases even look like the items they represent, except that their names are italicized.

Understanding Aliases

Like the documents, programs, and other files on your disks, aliases are files that contain information. Aliases contain a different kind of information than other files. Where a document file contains text, pictures, or other data and a program file contains code, an alias file contains a pointer to a document, program, other file, folder, or disk. Figure 12-1 shows how aliases point to other items.

By analyzing the information in an alias, the system software can locate the alias's *original item*. This process is called *resolving* an alias. The system software can successfully resolve an alias to locate the alias's original item, even if you move or rename the original item or move the original item to a different folder. The only way you can break the connection between an alias and its original item is to drag the original item to the Trash and empty the Trash. The system software cannot successfully resolve an alias whose original item no longer exists.

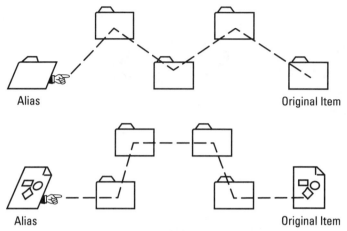

Figure 12-1: An alias points to its original item.

When you open an alias, the system software uses the information in the alias to locate the original item and then opens the original. Dragging an item to the alias of a folder or disk in the Finder has the same effect as dragging it to the original folder or disk — the Finder uses the information in the alias to locate the original folder or disk and places the item you dragged there. Likewise, dragging a document to an alias of a compatible program opens the document. You can even drag an alias of a document to an alias of a compatible application; the Finder uses the information in both aliases to have the application open the document.

Making an Alias

You can make an alias for any item you can open from the Finder. That category includes documents, application programs, desk accessories, folders, disks, control panels, and even fonts and sounds. Making an alias is a simple procedure. In the Finder, select the item for which you want to create an alias and choose Make Alias from the File menu. A new item appears with the same icon as the original item. The alias has an italicized name that matches that of the original item plus the suffix *alias*. Figure 12-2 illustrates the procedure.

In addition to the File menu, if your Mac has Mac OS 8 or later you can control-click an item to pop-up its contextual menu and then choose Make Alias from there. For more information using contextual menus, see "Contextual Menus" in Chapter 5.

Figure 12-2: Using the Make Alias command (left) and newly made alias with the original item (right).

Mac OS 8 provides a convenient shortcut for making an alias at a location different from the original — for example, in another folder or on another disk. Just drag the original item to the place you want the alias, and press ⌘-Option before releasing the mouse button. You can start pressing those keys any time while dragging, but you must hold them down while you release the mouse button if you want to make an alias. The pointer changes shape when you ⌘-Option-drag an item to a place where the Finder can make an alias, such as a folder, a disk, or the desktop. The pointer acquires a small right-pointing arrow in addition to its normal large left-pointing arrow. Figure 12-3 shows the pointer shape that means "make alias" in Mac OS 8 and later.

Figure 12-3: The pointer has a special shape when you ⌘-Option-drag to create an alias.

It normally takes two or three steps to make an alias at a location different from the original if you're using system software version 7.6.1 or earlier. First you make an alias at the same location as the original item. Then you drag the alias to the place you want it. If that place is on a different disk than the original item, you'll probably want to delete the alias you made next to the original.

If you want to make an alias anywhere in one step using system software version 7.6.1 or earlier, you need to install the free utility software Finder Options (described in Chapter 24).

Same Alias, Different Size

Aliases vary in size from 1K to 17K or more, depending on the capacity of the disk they're on. For example, an alias takes up 1K of a floppy disk, 20MB hard disk, or 40MB hard disk. On a 100MB disk, an alias takes up 2K, and aliases on a 1GB disk occupy 17K each. If a hard disk is partitioned into multiple volumes (each having its own icon on the desktop), the volume capacity determines the size of the aliases on it. For details on the relationship between partition size and file size, see "Partitioning Hard Disks" in Chapter 7.

Changing an Alias

After you make an alias, you can manipulate it as you would any other item. You can move it, copy it, rename it. You can change its icon, comments, or locked status in its Get Info window.

If you move an alias to another folder on the same disk or to the desktop, the alias still knows where to find its original item.

You can copy an alias by using the Finder's Duplicate command or by dragging the alias to another disk or to a folder on another disk. To copy an alias or other item to another folder on the same disk, press Option while dragging. All copies of the alias point to the same original item.

You rename an alias as you would any other item on the desktop or in a Finder window. Immediately after you create an alias, its name is selected for editing. You can change the name by typing a replacement or by using other standard text-editing techniques (see "Renaming Icons" in Chapter 5). For example, you might want to shorten "Microsoft Word alias" to "Word" before adding the alias to the Apple menu or the Launcher. To keep the name as is, click anywhere outside the name or press Return or Enter.

If you want an alias to have exactly the same name as its original item, the two cannot be in the same folder. You must move one out. For example, if you make an alias with the idea of moving it to another folder and you don't want the alias to have the suffix "alias," you have to move the alias before editing its name. Of course an alias and its original can be in the same folder if their names are very similar but not identical. For example, the alias name could have an extra blank space at the end.

Like any item, you remove an alias by dragging it to the Trash. Remember, throwing away an alias doesn't affect the original item. You're only throwing away the alias, not the item to which it points.

An alias inherits its icon from the original item. If you subsequently change the original item's icon, the alias icon is updated automatically the next time you open it. Like most other icons, you can customize an alias icon in its Info window. You bring up the Info window by using the Finder's Get Info command (see "Custom Icons" in Chapter 5). The alias's custom icon won't be affected by changes to the icon of the original item. You can also type comments about the alias and lock the alias in its Info window. Locking an alias in its Info window prevents changing the name or icon of the alias — the same as locking any file. Locking an alias does not lock its original item.

QUICK TIPS

Oodles of Aliases

You can create multiple aliases for the same original item so that you can access the original from different locations. Only disk space limits the number of aliases you can create. To make aliases for several items in the same window at once, select them all and ⌘-Option-drag the group where you want the aliases (Mac OS 8 and later) or use the Make Alias command. An alias appears for every item you selected. All the new aliases are automatically selected so that you can immediately drag them to another place without having to manually select them one by one.

Keeping Track of Original Items

Aliases are truly amazing at keeping track of their original items. Not only can you rename and move an alias's original item, but you also can replace it with another file that has the same name, all without breaking the link to the alias. You may wonder how the system software can find an alias's original item after you rename or move the original item. If the system software cannot find an item that has the same name and folder location as the original, it searches for the original item's unique *file ID number*, which the system software internally assigns to each file. Once the system software finds the item by using this ID number, it updates the alias with the original item's current name and folder location.

QUICK TIPS

Removing the Suffix 'Alias'

To remove the word *alias* quickly from the end of an alias's name, click the name once to select it for editing, pause briefly (or avoid the pause by moving the mouse slightly to the right after you click the alias name), double-click the last word of the name, and then press Delete twice (once to delete the selected word *alias* and a second time to delete the space before that word). If you double-click too soon after selecting the name, the Finder opens the item to which the alias points rather than selecting the last word of the name.

Alternatively, you can select the name for editing, press the down-arrow key or right-arrow key to move the insertion point to the end of the name, and press Delete six times to erase the last word and the space preceding it. To conclude your name editing, click anywhere outside the name or press Return or Enter. If you want the Finder never to add the word *alias* as a suffix, you can modify the Finder as described in "Removing the alias from aliases" in Chapter 25.

You can prevent the system software from updating an alias with the current name and folder location of the alias's original item. To do this, lock the alias by turning on the Locked option in its Info window. Locking an alias does not prevent the system software from finding its original item, only from updating the alias if the original item's name or folder location have changed.

When you copy the original item referenced by an alias, the alias still points to the original item (not to the copy you just made). Sounds reasonable, but it doesn't feel reasonable when you want to move an alias's original item to a different disk. That's because in general, moving and copying involve the same action — dragging an item. If you drag to a folder on the same disk, the Finder moves the item and the item's alias knows where to find the moved item. If you drag to a folder on another disk, the Finder copies the item. The alias knows where the original item is, but not the copy. If you then delete the original item (on the alias's disk), you break the alias's link to the item, even though a copy of the item exists on another disk.

If you use an alias for which the original item has been deleted, the system software tells you that it can't find the original item. Although an orphaned alias may seem utterly useless, "Confirming Startup Items" later in this chapter proves otherwise. Figure 12-4 shows the alert you see if the system can't resolve an alias.

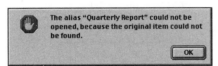

The alias "Quarterly Report" could not be opened, because the original item could not be found.

OK

Figure 12-4: The message you see when the system software can't find an alias's original item.

You can use utility software to connect an orphaned alias to its original file or to a copy of the original (see "Alias Crony" in Chapter 24). But it's often easier just to create a new alias and throw out the broken one.

Finding an Original Item

You can find an alias's original item by choosing Show Original (in Mac OS 8 and later) or Get Info (Mac OS 7.6.1 and earlier) from the Finder's File menu. The Show Original command brings up the window that contains the original item, scrolls the original item into view, and selects it. The Get Info command displays the alias's Info window. In Mac OS 7.6.1 and earlier, an alias's Info window includes a Find Original button, and clicking that button brings up the window that contains the original item, scrolls the original item into view, and selects it. In all Mac OS versions, an alias's Info window reports the disk and folder path to the original. Figure 12-5 shows examples of Info windows in Mac OS 8 and in an earlier version of the system software.

If you try to find an original item on a removable disk that's not currently inserted, the Finder usually asks you to insert that disk. The Finder also ejects any currently inserted disk of the same type (floppy disk, Zip disk, and so forth). This can lead to a vicious bout of disk swapping, which you can cut short by pressing ⌘-period repeatedly until the Finder stops asking you to insert disks. Then put away the currently inserted disk (by dragging it to the Trash or using Mac OS 8's Move to Trash command), insert the disk that contains the alias's original item, and try the Show Original command (Mac OS 8 and later) or Find Original button (Mac OS 7.6.1 and earlier) again.

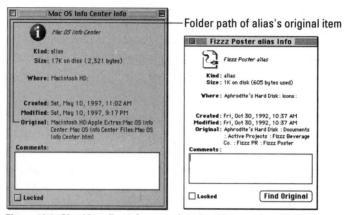

Figure 12-5: Checking alias information in Mac OS 8 and later (left) or Mac OS 7.6.1 and earlier (right).

Instead of asking you to insert a missing disk that contains an alias's original item, the Finder may display a message saying the original item couldn't be found. That happens with some types of removable hard disks, including some 44MB SyQuest cartridges, unless some hard disk of the same type has been inserted since you started up or restarted your computer.

Discovering the Many Uses of Aliases

There are many useful applications for aliases. The most common is quick access to programs and documents you work with frequently. For example, you can make an alias of a spreadsheet you use regularly to update sales figures and place the alias in a convenient location, such as the desktop. Some of the most important uses of aliases include adding items to the Apple menu or to the Startup Items folder; adding desktop convenience for accessing items; accessing archived information from removable disks; and streamlining access to shared items. The following sections provide a collection of scenarios to leverage the power of aliases, providing express service to a wide range of items.

Aliases in the Apple menu

The most convenient place from which to open application programs, desk accessories, control panels, documents, folders, and other items is the Apple menu. Because the Apple menu is always on the menu bar, items in the Apple menu are never more than a mouse click away. You can add to the Apple menu any item that you can open by using the Finder, including aliases.

Placing an alias in the Apple menu is as easy as dragging the alias icon to the Apple Menu Items folder, which is in the System Folder. The name of the alias appears instantly in the Apple menu in plain (not italic) text. Choosing the alias from the Apple menu opens the alias's original item. (You don't have to restart your computer for changes to the Apple Menu Items folder to take place.)

You can add as many aliases as you want to the Apple Menu Items folder. However, it's a good idea to keep the number within a reasonable range to avoid having to scroll through an extra-long menu. To remove an alias from the Apple menu, drag its icon out of the Apple Menu Items folder.

One way to shorten the Apple menu is to put some related aliases in a submenu. You do this by putting the aliases in a folder inside the Apple Menu Items folder, or by putting the alias of a folder (or a disk) into the Apple Menu Items folder. For example, during installation of the system software, an alias of the Control Panels folder is placed in the Apple Menu Items folder, making all the control panels appear in a Control Panels submenu of the Apple menu. Another example: the Finder places folders named Recent Applications, Recent Documents, and Recent Servers in the Apple Menu Items folder and puts aliases of recently used items in those folders. To see submenus in the Apple menu and track recent items in submenus, you must have these features turned on in the Apple Menu Options control panel (as described in "Opening Programs, Documents, and More" in Chapter 8).

Adjusting an alias's position in the Apple menu

Items in the Apple menu appear alphabetically by name. You may want to change the name of your alias to adjust its position in the Apple menu. You can force an item to the top of the menu by putting a blank space at the beginning of its name or force it to the bottom of the list by beginning its name with a bullet (•). These and other techniques for organizing the Apple menu are described in more detail in "Opening Programs, Documents, and More" in Chapter 8.

Fast access to the Apple Menu Items folder

One useful alias you can add to the Apple menu is an alias of the Apple Menu Items folder. Adding this alias allows you to open the Apple Menu Items folder quickly and easily customize the Apple menu.

A Launcher menu

You can organize aliases in submenus of the Apple menu by putting the aliases in folders inside the Apple Menu Items folder. For example, you might have folders named Applications, Utilities, and Documents. The problem with this scheme is the time it takes to make aliases and place them in the appropriate folders. One efficient way to organize the Apple menu is to place an alias of the Launcher Items folder in the Apple Menu Items folder. In this way, adding aliases to the Apple menu is as simple as dragging the original items to the proper categories in the Launcher window, as described in "Opening Programs, Documents, and More" in Chapter 8.

Universal Show Clipboard

Some application programs lack a Show Clipboard command, and others that have one use a private clipboard whose contents may look different when pasted into another program. With an alias, you can put a Show Clipboard command in your Apple menu for reviewing the standard Clipboard contents from any application program. First, make an alias of the Clipboard file, which is in the System Folder. Then place the alias in the Apple Menu Items folder and rename the alias Show Clipboard. Now, choosing Show Clipboard from the Apple menu switches to the Finder and opens the Clipboard.

Aliases on the desktop

Other than the Apple menu, the desktop is the most accessible place for opening items and the most accessible place for folders to which you want to drag items. Rather than drag frequently used programs, control panels, documents, and folders themselves onto the desktop, make aliases of them and put the aliases on the desktop. Putting aliases on the desktop of items that are nested several folders deep gives you quick access to the folders without digging through other folders to find them.

Putting aliases of programs on the desktop avoids problems that can occur when you move the programs themselves onto the desktop. Such programs depend on support files being with them in the same folder (or on the desktop). For example, a word processor may also need a dictionary file on the desktop in order to check spelling. Aliases save you the hassle of guessing which support files a program needs in order to run correctly and avoid the mess that may result when you place those support files on the desktop. By creating an alias for an application, the alias accesses the original application in its folder, saving you from moving the application and its supporting files to get full access to the application.

By making aliases of documents and programs you use frequently and putting the aliases on the desktop, you never have to remember where you put the original items. Also, you can open several related items at the same time, even if the original items happen to be in different folders or on different disks, by opening aliases on the desktop.

Getting at buried desktop aliases

When windows of open programs obscure desktop aliases, you can hide those windows by choosing Hide Others from the Application menu while the Finder is active. When a folder or disk window covers desktop icons with Mac OS 8 and later, click the window's Collapse box to shrink the window to its title bar. With system software 7.5–7.6.1, you can collapse a window with the WindowShade control panel. In all versions of the system software, you can also close all windows in the Finder at once by pressing Option while clicking the Close box of any Finder window.

Clearing the desktop of alias clutter

If your desktop becomes too cluttered with aliases, you can put related aliases together in folders on the desktop. For example, you can make aliases of the Trash and hard disk, put the aliases in a folder, and put the folder in your Apple menu for instant access. Leave that folder open and its window comes to the front along with the other Finder windows whenever you switch to the Finder. If you want that folder of aliases open all the time, put an alias of the folder in the Startup Items folder (located in the System Folder).

You don't have to create your own special folder for frequently used aliases. Instead you can use the Launcher control panel, whose window displays the aliases you put in the Launcher Items folder, as described in "Opening Programs, Documents, and More" in Chapter 8.

Multiple Trash cans

If you're lucky enough to have a big monitor, put aliases of the Trash in the upper and lower left corners of the desktop. The extra Trash icons expedite discarding items when you're working on the left side of the desktop. Extending this idea, if you have two monitors, put a Trash alias on the desktop of the second monitor. That way, you never have to drag icons across two screens to throw them away.

"Remove disk" icon

In a few minutes you can solve a problem that has plagued Mac OS users since day one — the customary but dumb method of removing a disk from the Mac by dragging the disk icon to the Trash. You simply make an alias of the Trash, change the alias's name to Remove Disk, and paste a custom icon in the alias's Get Info window. Make the custom icon look like a hand removing a disk or a disk with an arrow pointing in the direction of ejection. Figure 12-6 shows an example of a "remove disk" icon.

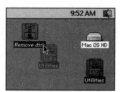

Figure 12-6: For removing disks, try an alias of the Trash with a custom icon.

Open and Save shortcuts

Alias names appear in italics in Open and Save dialog boxes, and opening an alias there (by double-clicking it, for instance) opens its original item. Instead of opening an alias's original item, you can quickly select the original item in an Open or Save dialog box by pressing Option while opening the alias. In this case, the system opens the folder containing the original item and selects the original item (but does not open the original item). Figure 12-7 shows an example of an alias in the Open dialog box.

Figure 12-7: Alias names are italicized in Open and Save dialog boxes.

To make an alias appear near the top of the list in Open and Save dialog boxes, put a blank space at the beginning of the alias's name. Items having initial blank spaces in their names float alphabetically to the top of an Open or Save dialog box's list. (When you view the desktop level in an Open or Save dialog box, disks always appear at the top of the list above all other items.)

If you don't like how initial spaces look, you can paste a blank line at the beginning of each name that you want to appear at the top of the list. Create the blank line by pressing Return in the Note Pad or any word processor. For step-by-step instructions and a caveat, see "Opening Programs, Documents, and More" in Chapter 8.

Quick Access to Favorite Folders

For quick access to a favorite folder in Open and Save dialog boxes, put an alias of the folder on the desktop. In an Open or Save dialog box, you can quickly get to aliases of favorite folders at the desktop level by clicking the Desktop button. Instead of working your way down through one branch of your folder structure and then working your way up another branch to the folder you want, you zip to the desktop level and there open the alias of the folder you want. It's as if you can jump from one branch of a tree to root level and then jump to a spot on another branch on another tree without having to crawl up the trunk and along the other branch.

Chances are you will only use this folder alias in Open and Save dialog boxes, never in the Finder. The specially named folder alias doesn't have to clutter up your desktop to appear at the desktop level of Open and Save dialog boxes. You can hide the folder alias behind another icon. Follow these steps:

1. Copy some white space to the Clipboard. You can do that in Mac OS 7.6 and later by pressing ⌘-Shift-4, and then pressing the Control key while dragging a selection rectangle over a small amount of white space. In System 7.5.5 and earlier press ⌘-Shift-3 to make a screen shot file (named Picture 1 at the root level of the startup disk) and open the screen shot file. Select some white space in it, and choose Copy from the Edit menu.

2. In the Finder, select your specially named folder alias on the desktop. Use the Get Info command to bring up the alias's Info window.

3. In the alias's Info window, select the icon image and choose Paste from the Edit menu to replace the alias's icon with white space. Close the alias's Info window.

4. On the desktop, align the icon behind which you want to hide the alias. You can align the icon by holding down the ⌘ key while dragging the icon slightly. Still pressing ⌘, drag the alias's name (it no longer has a visible icon) near the icon that will cover it. Release the mouse button and the alias's name should snap to the same position as the other icon. Abbreviate the alias's name if it is longer than the coverup icon's name.

5. Click the desktop anywhere to deselect the alias, and then type the first part of the coverup icon's name to select it and bring it to the front, hiding the alias's name.

Aliases as startup items

Every time you start up (or restart) your computer, the Finder automatically opens everything in the Startup Items folder. For example, if you regularly use a particular program, you may want it ready to go immediately after you start up your computer. But some programs must remain in a folder with other auxiliary files, and the programs won't work correctly if you move their icons to the Startup Items folder. Furthermore, returning items to their previous locations when you no longer want them opened at startup time can be a drag.

Moving an alias of a program, document, or other item to the Startup Items folder causes the original item to open during startup. To remove an alias from the startup sequence, drag the alias out of the folder.

Application programs in the Startup Items folder open in alphabetical order, so you can rename the alias of an application program to determine when it starts relative to other application programs in that folder. Aliases of desk accessories, control panels, and folders open alphabetically after all application programs have opened. For more information about the Startup Items folder, see "Startup Items Folder" in Chapter 9.

Confirming Startup Items

Here's a trick if you use Mac OS 7.6.1 or earlier and want to open items in the Startup Items folder only some of the time:

1. Make a duplicate of an application (such as SimpleText).

2. Make an alias of the duplicate.

3. Drag the duplicate application to the Trash.

4. Empty the Trash.

5. Place the alias of the application you just deleted in the Startup Items folder.

6. Give the alias a name that alphabetically precedes all other items in that folder.

When the Finder encounters the alias, it displays an alert telling you that it cannot find the alias's original item, as shown in the figure below. Click Stop to cancel opening the startup items, or click Continue to finish opening5 them.

This trick does not work with Mac OS 8.

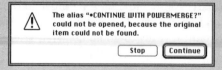

Startup messages

Do you like to have reminders at start-up, but don't want to use Stickies? Create a clipping file of your notes, and place an alias of it in the Startup Items folder. Rename it to be alphabetically last, for example zzNotes, so it opens after other startup items. At startup the Finder does not have to launch an application to display the note, which you can easily dismiss by pressing ⌘-W. If you keep the clipping on your desktop, you will be able to view it anytime you want, within seconds. You can use a startup clipping in a lab setting where many people use a single Mac to display general notes, update information, disclaimers, warnings, and so on. For information on creating clipping files, see "Creating Documents" in Chapter 8.

Audio CD autoplay

Would you like to have an audio CD play when you start up your Mac? Putting an alias of any track from any audio CD into the Startup Items folder has the Finder automatically launch AppleCD Audio Player during startup and begin playing whatever CD is in the drive at that track. The track alias works with any audio CD, not just the one used to make the alias. If there's no CD in the drive, the Mac requests one. If you have QuickTime 2.5 or later, you can get a similar effect with the Enable Audio CD AutoPlay option in the QuickTime Settings control panel (see "Audio CDs" in Chapter 19). The control panel option always starts at track 1, but you can make an alias to start with any track.

Abridged System Folder

Aliases can help you quickly find folders in the System Folder whose contents you need to get at, such as the Startup Items folder and the Fonts folder. Here's how you do it: Make aliases for the System Folder items you access often — including the System Folder itself — and put all those aliases in a new folder. You can open and find an item in that new folder faster than in the System Folder. To make the new folder look like a System Folder, copy the icon from the System Folder's Info window and paste it into the new folder's Info window.

System Folder annex

If you need more space on your startup disk and you have another hard disk with space available, you can move large items such as the After Dark Files folder (which can easily be over 15MB) from the System Folder to a non-startup disk. After copying an item from the System Folder to the non-startup disk, make an alias of the copy (not of the original in the System Folder). Drag the original item from the System Folder to the Trash, drag the alias from the non-startup disk to the location that the original item formerly occupied in the

System Folder, and rename the alias so it has exactly the same name as the original item. For example, an alias of the After Dark Files folder must be named After Dark Files and put in the Control Panels folder.

This technique doesn't work with all System Folder items. You'll have to experiment to see if it helps you.

Aliases of items on removable disks

You can use aliases to keep track of and quickly open items on removable disks — even the ones that aren't currently inserted. For example, you can keep the installation software for applications that you download from the Internet on removable hard disks and make an alias of each installation folder or installer program in a folder named Installers on your main hard drive. Then when you need to reinstall some software, you can quickly open the appropriate alias in your Installers folder. The system tells you the name of the disk to insert so that it can open the alias's original item.

Be sure to make aliases of archived items *after* copying them to removable disks, not before. If you make aliases of the items while they are still on the hard disk, the aliases stop working when you delete the original items from the hard disk after copying them to a removable disk. (Remember, aliases point to the original items, not to copies of the originals on other disks.)

Personal Icon Library

A single floppy disk can use aliases to store hundreds of interesting icons for later use as custom icons for any file, folder, or disk. Just make aliases of files, folders, or disks having icons you want to save and copy the aliases to a floppy named Personal Icon Library. Whenever you want to use one of the custom icons from the floppy disk, copy the icon from the alias's Info window and paste it into the Info window of the file, folder, or disk whose icon you want to customize (as described in "Icons" in Chapter 5).

Server access from Save dialog

Don't you hate it when you get into a Save dialog box only to realize that you
want to save on a server volume that you're not connected to? You don't have
to cancel the Save dialog box, mount the server volume, and choose Save again
if you take the time to make an alias of your Recent Servers folder and put it
on your desktop. You can open that alias and get at recently used servers quite
easily from within any Save dialog box. (Click the Desktop button in the Save
dialog box for fast access to the Recent Servers alias.) If you find that the server
you want to use is not included in the Recent Servers folder because you have
not accessed it as recently as the servers that are included, you need to increase
the number of servers that the Finder keeps track of in this folder. To do that,
use the Apple Menu Options control panel (described in Chapter 10).

Aliases of Shared Items

The file sharing capabilities of the Mac OS enable you to share items from someone else's computer that
is connected to the same network as yours. But getting access to shared items involves wading through
a fair amount of bureaucracy in the Chooser.

Aliases cut through the red tape. Here's how: You access a shared disk or folder once by using the Chooser
(see "Sharing Someone Else's Folders and Disks" in Chapter 18). Next, select the shared item or any folder
or file in it and make an alias of it on your hard disk. An alias keeps track of its original item even when the
original item is on another networked Mac. The figure below shows some aliases of shared items.

Once you make an alias of a shared item, you can get to the shared item by opening the alias either from
the Finder or from an Open command's directory dialog box. Dragging something to the alias of a shared
disk or folder also automatically accesses that shared item. You still must enter a password unless you
initially access the original item as a guest. If the shared item is not available — for example, because the
Mac in which it resides is turned off — then the Finder tells you that it cannot find the item on the network.

Aliases of remote shared items

Not only do aliases work across a local network, they also work across a remote network connection made with Apple Remote Access (ARA, described in "Making a Remote AppleTalk Connection" in Chapter 17). If you create an alias of a remote file, folder, or disk, disconnect the remote network, and then open the alias, the system software tries to make the remote network connection again automatically.

Instead of locating the alias's original item on the remote network as it should, the system software may locate another item that coincidentally has the same name on your local network. Sound far-fetched? Suppose the alias's original item is a shared disk with a common name such as Macintosh HD on a remote Mac with a common name such as Power Mac 7600. Further suppose your Mac is connected to a local network on which someone is sharing a hard disk named Macintosh HD from a Mac named Power Mac 7600. If you double-click the alias, the system software will open the Macintosh HD on your local network, not the one on the remote network. A similar situation can occur if you sometimes connect to two remote Macs that are named alike and have shared hard disks with the same names.

Situations like these can develop unexpectedly when someone changes the name of a Mac or a shared disk; suddenly you discover that double-clicking an alias opens the wrong item. What's worse, the system software updates the alias so that the information in it now points to the wrong item. Even after you fix the conflicting aliases by changing one of the original item's names, the alias will continue representing the wrong item.

Your Office on Disk

Aliases can give you nearly automatic access to your computer's hard disks by using a floppy disk in any other computer on the same network. To set up access to your office from a floppy disk, follow these steps:

1. Make sure that file sharing is turned on (see Chapter 18).

2. Select all your hard disk icons and choose Sharing from the File menu, opening a Sharing Info window for each disk.

3. In each window set the options as shown in the figure. These settings restrict access to your disks so that only you can make changes or see files or folders.

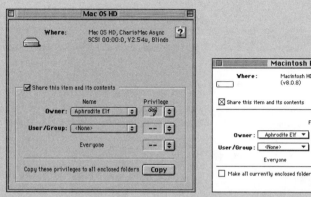

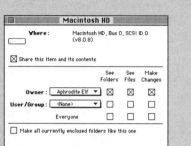

4. Make an alias of each hard disk and copy the aliases to a floppy disk.

Now you can use that floppy disk to access your hard disk from any Mac on your network, as long as file sharing is active on your Mac. You simply insert the disk, open the alias for the disk you want to use, and enter your password when asked. Correctly entering your password allows you access to all applications, folders, and documents on your disk from any remote computer. You don't have to bother opening the Chooser, selecting AppleShare, selecting your computer, and typing your name as the registered user.

You can prevent the system software from updating an alias by locking the alias. It's a good idea to lock aliases of items on remote file servers, especially if you use ARA to connect to more than one Mac. A locked alias works as long as all the file servers you access have unique names. To lock an alias, select it, choose Get Info from the Finder's File menu, and set the Locked option in the alias's Info window.

Aliases keep shared documents current

Besides providing easy access to shared items from other computers, aliases can help you make sure that others who share your documents have the latest versions.

Suppose, for example, that you create a letter template that you want the rest of your group to use. By making an alias of the template and copying it to a shared folder, other users can copy the alias to their disks and use the alias to open the original template. If you later replace the original template with a version having the same name, the aliases that people already copied will open the new version. Users who share the alias always get the newest version of the original item it represents, even when the original frequently changes.

STEP-BY-STEP

An Alias's Alias

When you move a drive from one AppleShare file server to another, network users have to tediously search all servers (by using the Chooser) for the moved drive unless you inform them of its new location. For example, that may happen if you have to move a shared drive from a busy server to an idle server or from a server needing repair to a temporary substitute.

You can solve this problem by creating an alias of an alias of every shared hard disk. Follow these steps:

1. Working from a shared hard disk that is always available to everyone, create an alias of every shared hard disk on the network.

2. Create aliases of those hard-drive aliases and copy the second set of aliases to each user's Mac.

With the double aliases in place, a shared hard disk named Crown Jewels, for example, can be accessed by double-clicking the alias named "Crown Jewels alias alias" on any user's Mac. That alias points to the alias "Crown Jewels alias" on the always-available shared drive, which in turn points to Crown Jewels itself.

Now, if you move Crown Jewels to a different file server, you merely make a new alias to replace the old Crown Jewels alias on the always-available shared drive. You do not have to update users' copies of "Crown Jewels alias alias," and users do not need to know that Crown Jewels has been moved.

This example uses the initial alias names that the Mac generates, but you can rename aliases freely. For example, both the alias and the alias's alias could be named Crown Jewels like the hard disk.

The only drawback to using an alias to share a template is that unless you're using a program that allows more than one person to open the same document, only one person can access the template document at a time. However, anyone who opens the template can quickly and easily save it with a different name and then close it to free it for someone else to open.

Summary

In this chapter, you learned that an alias is a file that represents another item such as a program, document, folder, or disk. Opening an alias or dragging something to an alias in the Finder has the same effect as opening or dragging to the alias's original item. But you can rename, move, or copy an alias or give it a custom icon without affecting its original item and without breaking the link between the alias and its original. An alias stays linked to its original item even if you move or rename the original. To see an alias's original item, you can use the Finder's Show Original command (Mac OS 8 and later) or the Find Original button in the alias's Info window (Mac OS 7.6.1 and earlier).

Aliases have a multitude of uses, some of which this chapter describes. You can use aliases to add items to the Apple menu and Startup Items folder. You can use an alias to make a universal Show Clipboard command. An alias can be a "remove disk" icon on the desktop and can provide shortcuts in Open and Save dialog boxes. Aliases are also useful for archiving files on removable disks and easily accessing shared disks and folders. This chapter describes 16 other uses of aliases.

CHAPTER THIRTEEN

Take Charge of Your Fonts

With the original Mac OS font technology, text looks great when displayed or printed as long as you stick to a half-dozen font sizes — usually 9, 10, 12, 14, 18, and 24 points. Apple's TrueType font technology, a standard part of Mac system software versions 7.0 and later, makes odd sizes and big sizes like 11, 13, 36, 100, and 197 look just as good. The optional QuickDraw GX software provides much more refined control of type, as long as the typefaces and programs that you're using take advantage of the advanced capabilities.

Introducing Fonts

Your computer can display and print text in three types of fonts: fixed-size, TrueType, and PostScript. Which looks best depends on the font size and the output device (display screen or type of printer).

Fixed-size fonts

Originally all Macs used fixed-size fonts to display text onscreen and to print on many types of printers. A *fixed-size font* contains exact pictures of every letter, digit, and symbol for one size of a font. Fixed-size fonts often are called *bitmapped fonts* because each picture precisely maps the dots, or *bits*, to be displayed or printed for one character. Figure 13-1 shows the dots in an enlarged view of a couple of fixed-size letters.

Figure 13-1: Times capital A
and G bit maps at fixed sizes
12, 14, and 18 (enlarged to
show detail).

Each fixed-size font looks great in one size only, so fixed-size fonts usually are installed in sets. A typical set includes 9-, 10-, 11-, 14-, 18-, and 24-point sizes. If you need text in a size for which no fixed-size font is installed, the system software must scale a fixed-size font's character bit maps up or down to the size you want. The results are lumpy, misshapen, or blocky, as shown in Figure 13-2.

Times 9. ABC D EFG HIJKL MNO PQRSTUV WX YZ abcdefghijklmnopqrstuvwxyz 123
Times 10. ABCDEFGHIJKLMNOPQRSTUVWXYZabcdefghijklmnopqrstu
Times 11. ABCDEFGHIJKLMNOPQRSTUV WXY Zabcdefghijklmn
Times 12. ABCDEFGHIJKLMNOPQRSTUV WXY Zabcdefghij
Times 13. ABCDEFGHIJKLMNOPQRSTUVWXYZabcde
Times 14. ABCDEFGHIJKLMNOPQRSTUVWXYZa
Times 16. ABCDEFGHIJKLMNOPQRSUVW
Times 18. ABCDEFGHIJKLMNOPQRST
Times 20. ABCDEFGHIJKLMNOPQ
Times 24. ABCDEFGHIJKLM
Times 30. ABCDEFGHIJ

Figure 13-2: Fixed-size fonts look best at installed sizes — shown here for 9-, 10-,
12-, 18-, and 24-points at 72 dots per inch.

TrueType fonts

TrueType is a variable-size font technology. Instead of fixed-size bitmaps, TrueType fonts use curves and straight lines to outline each character's shape. Because TrueType fonts are based on outlines, they sometimes are called *outline fonts*. Figure 13-3 shows the outline for an example TrueType letter.

Figure 13-3: Outline for TrueType Times capital G.

TrueType fonts look good at all sizes, and they work with all Mac OS applications and all types of printers, including PostScript printers. The system software smoothly scales a TrueType font's character outlines to any size on a display screen and on printers of any resolution, all with equally good results. The system software also lets you mix TrueType fonts with fixed-size and PostScript fonts. Figure 13-4 shows an example of TrueType font scaling.

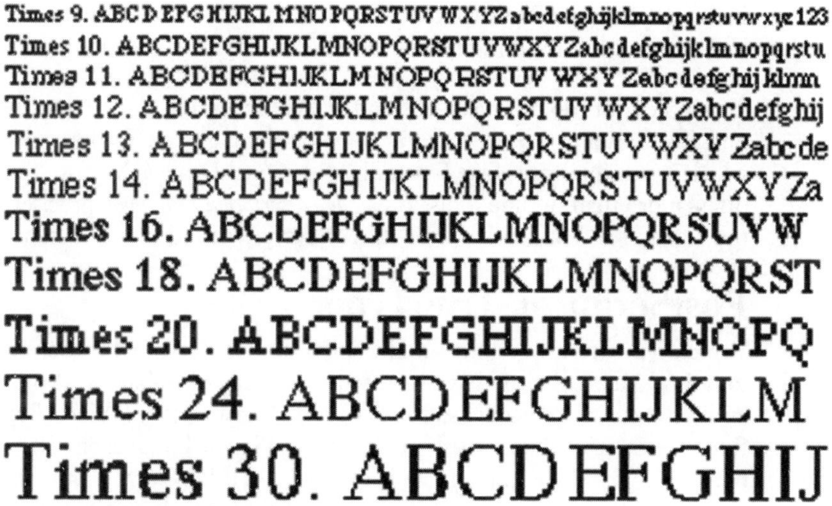

Times 9. ABCD EFG HIJKL MNO PQRSTUV WX YZ abcdefghijklmnopqrstuvwxyz 123
Times 10. ABCDEFGHIJKLMNOPQRSTUVWXYZabcdefghijklmnopqrstu
Times 11. ABCDEFGHIJKLMNOPQRSTUVWXYZabcdefghijklmn
Times 12. ABCDEFGHIJKLMNOPQRSTUVWXYZabcdefghij
Times 13. ABCDEFGHIJKLMNOPQRSTUVWXYZabcde
Times 14. ABCDEFGHIJKLMNOPQRSTUVWXYZa
Times 16. ABCDEFGHIJKLMNOPQRSUVW
Times 18. ABCDEFGHIJKLMNOPQRST
Times 20. ABCDEFGHIJKLMNOPQ
Times 24. ABCDEFGHIJKLM
Times 30. ABCDEFGHIJ

Figure 13-4: TrueType fonts scale smoothly to all sizes and resolutions (Times shown at 72 dots per inch).

An enhanced form of TrueType fonts, known as TrueType GX fonts, accommodates much larger sets of characters and provides advanced typographic control that otherwise requires special application programs. You'll find the details in "QuickDraw GX Typography" later in this chapter.

PostScript fonts

TrueType fonts look great in any size onscreen or output on any printer, but they are not alone. *PostScript* fonts were the first to look great at any size and any resolution. They use an outline font technology invented by Adobe Systems. It's similar to TrueType but differs in how it mathematically specifies font outlines and how it adjusts the outlines for small font sizes.

Although PostScript fonts originally were designed for printing on LaserWriters and other PostScript output devices, the Adobe Type Manager (ATM) software smoothly scales PostScript fonts to any size for non-PostScript printers and the display screen, just like TrueType. With ATM and PostScript fonts, you don't need a set of fixed-size or TrueType fonts for the screen display. Apple includes ATM with QuickDraw GX. If you don't install QuickDraw GX, you can obtain ATM separately from Adobe (408-536-6000, http://www.adobe.com).

To make use of ATM, you must buy PostScript fonts for your System Folder; fonts built into your printer don't help. Adobe includes the four basic LaserWriter fonts — Times, Helvetica, Courier, and Symbol — with the purchase of ATM. The Adobe Type Basics package includes all 11 standard LaserWriter font families — Avant Garde, Bookman, Courier, Helvetica, Helvetica Narrow, New Century Schoolbook, Palatino, Symbol, Times, Zapf Chancery, and Zapf Dingbats — along with 16 other font families and ATM.

TrueType fonts do not mean the end of PostScript for a number of reasons. For one, PostScript can set text at any angle or along a curve or other nonlinear path, which is possible with TrueType only with QuickDraw GX. Also, PostScript offers more than outline fonts. It's a *page description language*, precisely specifying the location and other characteristics of every text and graphics item on the page.

PostScript or TrueType?

Which type of outline font should you use, TrueType or PostScript? Many longtime Mac OS users have invested thousands of dollars in PostScript fonts, and for them, it makes sense to stick with PostScript and ATM. But PostScript fonts are messier than TrueType. With PostScript fonts, each style of a font — bold, italic, bold italic, plain, and so on — is a different file on your hard disk. Moreover, PostScript font file names can be hard to figure out because they're a contraction of the full font name plus style name. For example, Helvetica Bold Italic has the file name HelveBolIta, and Garamond Demi Book comes out GaramDemBoo. So just to have the basic four font styles of a font you must have four PostScript font files. But that's not all. In addition, for each PostScript font family such as Times or Helvetica, you must also have at least one size of the same fixed-size font installed. ATM can't jigger the system without that fixed-size font. For example, to go with the four PostScript fonts AGarBol, AGarBolIta, AGarIta, and AGarReg you must also have one Adobe Garamond fixed-size font such as AGaramond 12.

In contrast, with most TrueType fonts you have one item to deal with, a font suitcase. (Font suitcases are described in detail later in this chapter.)

If you don't already have a collection of PostScript fonts, and especially if you don't print on PostScript printers, go with TrueType. More PostScript fonts are available than TrueType, but TrueType fonts sometimes cost less, and some are even free. (For example, every version of Mac system software from 7.0 onward includes TrueType versions of at least the Times, Helvetica, Courier, and Symbol fonts. Also, many applications from Claris and Microsoft come with an assortment of TrueType fonts.)

Font Styles and Families

Text varies by style as well as size. The system software can display and print four basic styles — plain, bold, italic, and bold italic — and many others (as listed in your friendly Style menu). The system software can derive various styles by modifying the plain style, but you get better-looking results by installing separate styled versions of fonts, as shown in the figure. Many fixed-size, TrueType, and PostScript fonts come in the four basic styles. Some PostScript font families include 20 or more styled versions. Collectively, the styled versions together with the plain version of a font are known as a *font family*. The following figure illustrates the difference between installed styles and derived styles with enlarged type samples of text at display resolution (72 dots per inch).

Times, Times italic, Times bold italic, and Times bold	Only plain Times installed; other styles derived from it
Necessity never made a good bargain.	Necessity never made a good bargain.
Three may keep a secret, if two of them are dead.	*Three may keep a secret, if two of them are dead.*
Lost time is never found again.	**Lost time is never found again.**
He that lives upon hope will die fasting.	**He that lives upon hope will die fasting.**

How to recognize the best font sizes

You can usually tell which font sizes will look good onscreen by inspecting the Font menu of a program that you're using. The program highlights the best-looking sizes with outline-style numbers. All sizes of a TrueType font are highlighted (If you have PostScript fonts and ATM installed, all the sizes also look good.) Only the installed sizes of fixed-size fonts are highlighted, as shown in Figure 13-5.

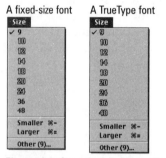

Figure 13-5: Smooth sizes are outlined.

Managing Fonts

All fonts can exist as individual items, each with its own icon. A single capital *A* appears on the icons of fixed-size fonts. The icons of TrueType fonts have three capital *A*s, each a different size to suggest the variable sizing of the font. The icons of PostScript fonts may look like a generic laser printer, or they may have custom graphics designed by the companies that make the fonts. Figure 13-6 shows examples of different types of font files.

Figure 13-6: Each type of font file has a different icon. From left: TrueType, fixed-size, Adobe PostScript, and two other PostScript font files.

Where fonts are kept

You'll probably find your fonts in the Fonts folder (inside the System Folder). For convenience, TrueType and fixed-size fonts are usually kept in *font suitcases*, which you can think of as special folders for holding fonts. Generally each font suitcase holds related fonts, such as the different sizes of a fixed-size font or the different styles of a TrueType font family. You can create a new font suitcase file by duplicating an existing font suitcase, opening the duplicate, and dragging the contents of the duplicate to the Trash.

Besides the Fonts folder, you may find PostScript fonts in the Extensions folder or loose in the System Folder. Some old applications that use PostScript fonts do not look for them in the Fonts folder or even in the Extensions folder. For example, Aldus PageMaker versions 4.01 and earlier and ATM versions 2 and earlier can't find PostScript fonts in the Extensions folder. ATM versions 2.0.2 and 2.0.3 look in the Extensions folder (and the System Folder) but not in the Fonts folder, and ATM versions 3.0 and later look in the Fonts folder (and in the Extensions folder and the System Folder). If your text prints in the wrong font on a PostScript printer or looks lumpy onscreen, try putting PostScript fonts in the System Folder itself (not the Fonts folder or the Extensions folder).

Reviewing Fonts

You can see a sample of any TrueType or fixed-size font by opening the font file. Note that when you open a font suitcase you see not a font sample, but a window of font files. Opening one of those font files shows you a sample of it. You can't see a sample of a PostScript font by opening a PostScript font file. Figure 13-7 shows examples of TrueType and fixed-size font samples.

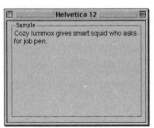

Figure 13-7: TrueType and fixed-size font samples.

Adding Fonts

You get a basic set of TrueType fonts and fixed-size fonts with the Mac system software. You can add or remove both types of fonts at any time by dragging icons in the Finder. The simplest way to add fonts is to drag their icons to the System Folder icon (not the System Folder window). You can drag font suitcases, folders containing fonts, or loose fonts to the System Folder icon. The Finder knows to put the fonts in the Fonts folder. However, the Finder does not distribute items for you if you drag them to the System Folder window instead of the System Folder icon. Figure 13-8 shows some fonts being dragged to the System Folder icon.

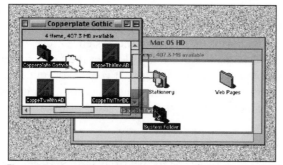

Figure 13-8: Install fonts by dragging them to the System Folder icon.

Before putting the fonts where they belong, the Finder displays an alert asking if that's what you want to do. This alert lets you know the Finder has recognized the items you dragged to the System Folder icon, and it gets your OK before putting them in their places. Figure 13-9 shows an example of the alert in Mac OS 8.

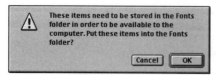

Figure 13-9: The Finder knows where fonts go.

The Finder automatically extracts fonts and font suitcases from folders that you drag to the System Folder icon. If a folder contains items other than fonts or font suitcases, the Finder puts the other items in the places where they belong (see "Adding Items to the System Folder" in Chapter 9).

Newly added fonts become available right away, except that TrueType and fixed-size are not available in any applications that are open when you add the fonts. Newly added TrueType and fixed-size fonts become available to an open application after you quit the application and open it again.

If you prefer, you can drag TrueType, PostScript, and fixed-size fonts directly to the Fonts folder icon. You also can open the Fonts folder and drag TrueType, PostScript, and fixed-size fonts to its window.

Removing Fonts

To remove fonts from your system, open the Fonts folder and drag the fonts or suitcases to another folder, the desktop, or the Trash. All applications except the Finder must be closed before you can remove any TrueType or fixed-size fonts from the Fonts folder. You can remove PostScript fonts any time. If you want to remove PostScript fonts but can't find them in the Fonts folder, look in the Extensions folder and the System folder. Figure 13-10 shows some fonts being removed to a folder on the desktop.

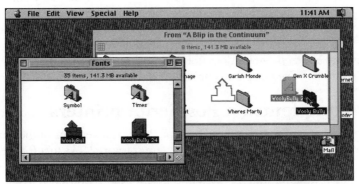

Figure 13-10: Remove fonts by dragging them out of the Fonts folder.

Determining Font Priorities

You may be wondering how the system software decides which type of font to use — fixed-size, TrueType, or PostScript — when you have all three types installed for one font such as Helvetica. The particular font that the system software displays or prints depends on the type of output device (display screen or type of printer).

Displaying fonts onscreen

For screen display, the system software first tries to find a bitmapped font in the exact size needed. If it can't find that, it looks for a TrueType version of the font that it can scale to the needed size. Lacking that, it tries to have the Adobe Type Manager (ATM) software, if installed, scale a PostScript font to the needed size. Some versions of ATM can even use Adobe Multiple Master fonts to display temporary substitutes that closely match PostScript fonts not installed on your computer. If no other font is available, the system software scales the best-available fixed-size font.

Curiously, when both fixed-size and TrueType versions of the same font are present, the system software always derives styled fonts from the fixed-size version, even if a styled TrueType version is installed. For example, if you have a fixed-size 12-point Times plain and a TrueType Times italic installed (but no fixed-size 12-point Times italic), the system software derives a 12-point Times italic by slanting the fixed-size 12-point Times.

Individual programs can tell the system software to ignore fixed-size fonts if a TrueType equivalent is available, and current versions of many popular programs now work this way. You may be able to turn this behavior on and off in some of your programs. Check each program's preference settings for one that tells the program that you prefer outline fonts. A decision to ignore fixed-size fonts in one program does not affect other programs; the system software always prefers fixed-size fonts unless an application specifically overrides it.

Printing fonts on PostScript printers

When choosing fixed-size, TrueType, or PostScript versions of the same font for printing on a PostScript printer, the system software looks first for a PostScript font from the printer's ROM, RAM, or hard disk (if any). If the printer doesn't have the PostScript font, the system software tries to download (copy) it from the computer's Fonts folder, Extensions folder, or System Folder. Failing that, the system software tries to use a TrueType font, and as a last resort a fixed-size font.

If the system software can find no PostScript equivalent for a TrueType font, it sends the TrueType font to the printer before sending the document to be printed. If the printer is one that can't handle TrueType fonts, the system software converts the TrueType font to PostScript, with some loss of quality at small point sizes, and sends that. Either way, sending fonts causes a significant delay on many printers. If you use TrueType-only fonts with a PostScript printer that has its own hard disk or a large amount of memory, you may be able to reduce printing time by downloading (sending) the TrueType fonts to the printer in advance of printing documents. Fonts you download to a printer's hard disk remain there unless you remove them. Fonts you download to a printer's memory remain there until you turn off the printer, or in some cases until someone else prints on the printer with a different version of printer software than you use.

Comparing Fixed-Size and TrueType Fonts

Look closely at some text in a TrueType font and at the same text in an equivalent fixed-size font. You'll see differences in letter shape, width, and height that may affect text spacing. The TrueType fonts match the PostScript fonts used in printers better than fixed-size fonts do. Fixed-size fonts display faster, however, and many of them look better onscreen in sizes smaller than 18 points. The following figure illustrates the problem with enlarged type samples of text at display resolution (72 dots per inch).

Today we are on the verge of creating new tools that will empower individuals, unlock worlds of knowledge, and forge a new community of ideas.
TrueType Times
12-point plain

Today we are on the verge of creating new tools that will empower individuals, unlock worlds of knowledge, and forge a new community of ideas.
Fixed-size Times

Today we are on the verge of creating new tools that will empower individuals, unlock worlds of knowledge, and forge a new community of ideas.
Fixed-size Times
12-point bold italic

Today we are on the verge of creating new tools that will empower individuals, unlock worlds of knowledge, and forge a new community of ideas.
TrueType Times
12-point bold italic

Printing fonts on a non-PostScript device

On a printer or other device that doesn't have PostScript, the system software tries to use TrueType fonts. If your Mac doesn't have a needed TrueType font but does have ATM installed, the system software looks for a PostScript version of the font. If neither type of outline font is available, the system software uses a fixed-size font.

If you print on a non-PostScript printer such as a StyleWriter and have both fixed-size and TrueType fonts installed, text may not look quite the same onscreen as it does on paper. Character shapes may be different. More important, the spacing of words in the line may not match. When this happens, the system software has used a fixed-size font for display (at 72 dpi) and a TrueType font for printing (at a higher resolution). You can fix the problem by removing the fixed-size font from your System file. In some programs, you may also be able to set an option that tells the system software to ignore fixed-size fonts.

Understanding Outline Fonts

To understand why TrueType fonts look different from equivalent fixed-size fonts, you need to know how outline-font technology works. Like PostScript fonts and any other outline fonts, a TrueType font defines each character mathematically as a set of points that, when connected, outline the character's shape. The system software can vary the font size by moving the points closer together or farther apart and then drawing the character again.

After scaling the outline to the size you want, the system software fills the outline with the dots that make up the text you see onscreen and on paper. The dot size, which is determined by the resolution of the screen or other output device, governs the smoothness of the result at a given size. Devices with more dots per inch produce smoother results, particularly in smaller point sizes. Figure 13-11 shows how dot size affects smoothness.

At small sizes, however, simply scaling the font outlines results in text that has unpleasant problems, such as gaps in diagonal lines or unwanted dots on the edges of curves. These imperfections occur because the outline does not precisely fit the grid in small point sizes, especially if the dots are relatively large, as they are on the computer's 72-dpi screen. On the display screen, the system software must draw a typical 11-point letter in a space eight dots square. At small sizes and relatively low resolutions, deciding which dots to darken is difficult. The system software reduces the character outline, lays it over the grid, and darkens the dots whose center points fall inside the outline, as shown in Figure 13-12.

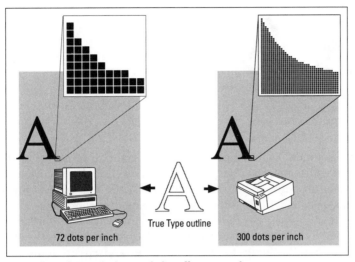

Figure 13-11: Output device resolution affects smoothness.

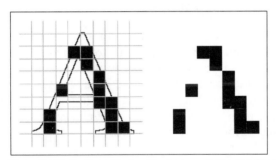

Figure 13-12: Scaling a font outline to a small size may leave gaps.

TrueType and PostScript fonts include a mechanism for adjusting the outline at small sizes on low-resolution devices. The font designer provides a set of instructions (also known as *hints*) that tells the system software how to modify character outlines at small font sizes, as shown in Figure 13-13. This process is called *grid fitting*.

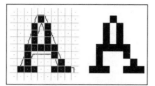

Figure 13-13: Hints modify
outlines at small sizes.

High-resolution devices such as typesetters and film recorders usually don't
need grid-fitting instructions; their grids are so fine that the character outlines
don't need adjusting to get filled with dots. A 300-dpi grid is 4 times finer than
a 72-dpi grid, and a 1,270-dpi grid is more than 16 times finer.

Scaling and grid fitting occur so quickly that you usually don't notice a delay.
TrueType and PostScript fonts are not as fast as fixed-size fonts, however, and
occasionally the lag is perceptible onscreen.

QuickDraw GX Typography

QuickDraw GX, included as an option with system software 7.5 and later,
makes it possible for any application to use some precise typesetting techniques
and achieve special effects that previously were available mainly in specialized
publishing programs. The catch is that you need TrueType GX fonts together
with programs designed to use QuickDraw GX typography. With TrueType
GX fonts and a program that has adopted GX typography, you can have the
following special effects generated automatically:

❖ Fancy swashed initial or final characters in words or lines

❖ Lowercase (or old-style) numerals

❖ Ligatures (linked characters)

❖ Small caps instead of standard caps

You also can type diagonal fractions from the keyboard and format subscript or
superscript in one step. In compatible programs, QuickDraw GX also makes it
possible to customize certain fonts, making them bolder, lighter, skinnier, or
wider. In any QuickDraw GX-compliant program — not just in high-end page-
layout or illustration programs — you easily can control the letter spacing within
words. Not every font will include all the possible GX options. Figure 13-14
shows the pop-up menu from a demonstration program that offers most of the
type options.

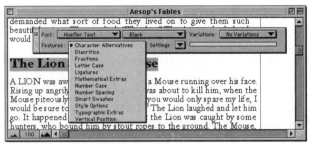

Figure 13-14: Any QuickDraw GX-compliant program can offer a multitude of typography options.

QuickDraw GX comes with a version of Adobe Type Manager (ATM) for smooth scaling.

Keep in mind that QuickDraw GX is not automatically installed when you install the system software. With Mac OS 7.6 and later, you must deliberately select QuickDraw GX in the Install Mac OS program. With Systems 7.5–7.5.5, you must run the separate QuickDraw GX installation software. The typography features described in the rest of this chapter work only if you've installed QuickDraw GX in addition to the basic system software.

PostScript fonts with QuickDraw GX

You can use PostScript Type 1 fonts after installing QuickDraw GX, but you must have Adobe Type Manager (ATM). In addition, you may need to convert your PostScript Type 1 fonts to fonts that are compatible with QuickDraw GX.

ATM for QuickDraw GX

ATM smoothly scales the PostScript fonts so that they look good onscreen — and printed on non-PostScript printers — at any size. A version of ATM comes with QuickDraw GX, although that version of ATM can't substitute multiple-master PostScript fonts for missing PostScript fonts as can some versions of ATM you get from Adobe. (Adobe's ATM versions work fine with QuickDraw GX.)

ATM is installed automatically when you install the version of QuickDraw GX that comes with Mac OS 7.6.1 or earlier. With Mac OS 8, you must do a custom installation of QuickDraw GX to get ATM. When the Installer window for QuickDraw GX comes up during the custom installation (as described in Chapter 28), choose Custom Install from the pop-up menu in the Installer window. The Installer window displays a list of QuickDraw GX modules you can install. Select the ATM for QuickDraw GX module (by clicking its check box) and click the Install button.

Type 1 font conversion

Most PostScript fonts are converted automatically when you install the version of QuickDraw GX that comes with system software 7.6.1 and earlier. Conversion of PostScript Type 1 fonts is not automatic with Mac OS 8, nor for PostScript fonts outside the System Folder with earlier system software versions.

Only PostScript Type 1 fonts are converted to GX versions. Most PostScript fonts are Type 1, but any PostScript Type 3 you may have will not be converted to GX versions.

To convert PostScript Type 1 fonts yourself for QuickDraw GX, you use the Type 1 Enabler program. To get it you must do a custom installation of QuickDraw GX. When the Installer window for QuickDraw GX comes up during the custom installation (as described in Chapter 28), choose Custom Install from the pop-up menu in the Installer window. The Install window displays a list of QuickDraw GX modules you can install. Select the ATM for QuickDraw GX module (Mac OS 8) or the QuickDraw GX Utilities module (Mac OS 7.6.1 and earlier) and click the Install button.

Before you can convert old PostScript Type 1 font files, the fixed-size fonts for each PostScript font family to be converted must be in its own font suitcase. Also, those font suitcases should not include TrueType fonts. The Type 1 Enabler program will not enable multiple PostScript font families whose fixed-size fonts are all in the same font suitcase. Related font families such as Helvetica and Helvetica Condensed are considered separate families and their fixed-size fonts must be in separate font suitcases.

After isolating each fixed-size font family in its own font suitcase, create a new folder named Old Fonts (or another name you like). Move the PostScript Type 1 font files that you want to convert and the matching font suitcase into the Old Fonts folder.

Open the Type 1 Enabler program, and in the Open dialog box that appears, select the Old Fonts folder and click the button labeled Select "Old Fonts." The program inspects the fonts and then displays a dialog box in which you select the destination for the converted fonts. Open your Fonts folder and then click the button labeled Select "New Fonts" to select it as the destination, unless you have a reason for selecting a different destination. (If the program finds a problem with the unconverted fonts, it displays a message in its log window.)

The Type 1 Enabler program converts the fonts to GX versions. Its log window reports the outcome of the conversion process. When it finishes, you may quit.

If you look in your Fonts folder for the converted fonts, you will see a suitcase with the same name as the one containing the original fixed-size fonts. Inside the new suitcase, you will find copies of the fixed-size font files together with new files for the converted PostScript Type 1 fonts. These files look like TrueType font files, but are actually PostScript Type 1 GX fonts.

TrueType GX

Part of QuickDraw GX is an improved kind of fonts called TrueType GX fonts. They work pretty much the way that older TrueType fonts work — but they include additional typographic information that gives QuickDraw GX-compatible programs more convenient access to the fonts' sophistication. TrueType GX fonts should work fine on Macs without QuickDraw GX. Regular TrueType fonts should look fine and print well with QuickDraw GX installed, although application programs will be unable to access special features of the fonts.

Ligature substitution

Some GX fonts (PostScript Type 1 GX and TrueType GX) include linked letter groups as a single character to substitute for individual letters when they fall together in a word — for example, diphthongs such as *ae*, and *ff* or *fi* in words such as *afflicted* and *official*. Ligatures appear automatically as you type if you meet all three of these conditions: (1) you have QuickDraw GX installed; (2) you're running a program that allows you to turn on automatic substitution of ligatures for the traditionally linked letter groups; and (3) you are using a font that contains the ligatures. Figure 13-15 shows examples of QuickDraw GX ligatures.

 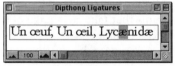

Figure 13-15: With QuickDraw GX and a compliant application, ligatures automatically appear as you type.

Without QuickDraw GX and a compatible program, you'd have to type Option-key combinations to access alternative characters in the font. When you use those alternative, two-letters-in-one characters, you can't select each letter of the ligature separately as you can with QuickDraw GX ligatures. Furthermore, spelling checkers do not recognize one-character ligatures, and hyphenation routines in programs do not properly divide words in the middle of ligatures. QuickDraw GX corrects those problems.

Automatic swashes

Some GX fonts include alternate *glyphs*, or characters, that have fancy tails called *swashes* on some of the strokes, usually on ascenders and descenders. The swashed alternatives are meant to be optional decorative characters, usually for letters that begin or end a line. Programs that take advantage of QuickDraw GX fonts allow you to decide just how swashbuckling you want your type to be (assuming that you have a font that includes alternate swashed glyphs), as shown in Figure 13-16.

Figure 13-16: A QuickDraw GX font with swashes (left) and without swashes (right) at the ends of lines.

Numeral and fraction options

Some fonts offer more than one set of numerals, perhaps both proportional and monospaced numerals, or both uppercase numerals that stand as tall as capital letters and lowercase (or old-style) numerals that dip below the baseline of the type. Programs that take advantage of QuickDraw GX allow you to choose which of a font's number sets to use. Figure 13-17 shows examples of different QuickDraw GX numerals.

Figure 13-17: QuickDraw GX and compliant applications make it easy to choose among a font's numeral sets.

In addition, because QuickDraw GX provides more control of the vertical and diagonal spacing of characters, compatible programs can let you type professional-looking fractions with either diagonal or horizontal lines. You don't need a specialized fractions font. Also, you don't need to remember arcane key combinations to type special fraction characters.

Font variations

If you're familiar with Adobe Systems' Multiple Masters line of fonts, you'll immediately understand the font-weight and width-variation controls that QuickDraw GX makes available in applications that take advantage of them. Here's how they work: a type designer can build into a font some leeway to allow you to change the font's weight (making the characters bolder or lighter) and width (extending or condensing the font characters). A program that includes QuickDraw GX font-variation controls offers a pop-up menu, sliders, or some other simple controls that allow you to modify selected text instantly. Figure 13-18 shows some of the variations you can make to a GX font's weight and width with QuickDraw GX-compatible applications.

Figure 13-18: With an application that takes advantage of QuickDraw GX, you can control the weight and width of some QuickDraw GX fonts.

Letter-spacing controls

Without QuickDraw GX, only programs for publishing and design specialists include decent tools for moving characters closer together or farther apart. With QuickDraw GX, any compatible program can offer simple letter-spacing controls.

Tracking

The overall spacing between letters in an entire document or text selection is called *tracking*. Text with loose tracking has extra space between the characters in words. Text with tight tracking has characters squeezed close together. Figure 13-19 shows examples of tracking from a QuickDraw GX demonstration program.

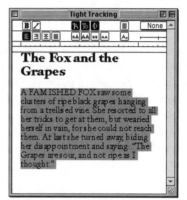

Figure 13-19: Text with loose tracking (left) has more space between characters than text with tight tracking (right).

Changing tracking can come in handy when you're trying to fit text into a space that's a little too big or too small. You also can adjust tracking to improve the appearance of the text in headlines, script typefaces, or logos or to create arty effects.

Kerning

Sometimes, particularly in large sizes, letters that are supposed to look like they're part of the same word have too much space between them. A capital *T* at the beginning of a word may not be close enough to the lowercase *r* that follows, making the word harder to read. Correcting the spacing between letter pairs is called *kerning*.

Many fonts include kerning information for letter pairs that commonly need closer spacing for legibility, but you may find cases that are not covered by a font's built-in kerning. In QuickDraw GX-compatible programs, you can just select the two letters that need closer spacing and adjust the spacing until it satisfies you. Figure 13-20 shows an examples of kerning.

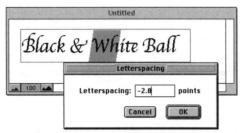

Figure 13-20: Kerning brings together pairs of letters that are too far apart, such as the *W* and *h* in this figure.

Subscript and superscript

Some programs have for years made it possible to insert subscript and superscript numbers and text, such as footnote references in text and elements of formulas. Any program that takes advantage of QuickDraw GX enables you to easily insert subscript or superscript that's properly positioned and in a size that's in scale with the nearby text. Figure 13-21 shows examples of superscript and subscript text from a QuickDraw GX demonstration program.

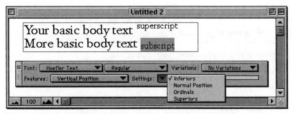

Figure 13-21: With QuickDraw GX and a compliant program, you can format subscripts and superscripts in one step.

Obtaining Fonts

The Mac system software comes with a standard set of TrueType fonts. They include Times, Helvetica, Palatino, Courier, and Symbol, as well as Chicago, Geneva, Monaco, and New York. You can get more fonts from many sources. For example, the Apple Font Pack contains 19 TrueType fonts families, 43 fonts in all, and is distributed by Claris Corp. (800-325-2747 in the United States, 800-361-6075 in Canada, http://www.claris.com).

Non-commercial fonts

You can get additional TrueType and PostScript fonts at nominal cost from sources of shareware and freeware. For information on obtaining freeware and shareware products, see Chapter 24. Figure 13-22 shows examples of freeware and shareware TrueType fonts.

Figure 13-22: Some freeware and shareware TrueType fonts.

Commercial fonts

Many type companies make TrueType and PostScript fonts, including the following companies:

Adobe Systems Inc.
415-961-4400, 800-833-6687
http://www.adobe.com

Alphabets, Inc.
708-328-2733, 800-326-3973
http://www.alphabets.com

Agfa Division, Bayer Corp.
201-440-0111, 800-424-8973
http://www.agfahome.com

Bitstream Inc.
617-497-6222, 800-522-3668
http://www.bitstream.com

Carter & Cone Type Inc.
617-576-0398, 800-952-2129
mailto:70402.155@compuserve.com

Casady & Greene Inc.
408-484-9228, 800-359-4920
http://www.casadyg.com

Castle Systems Design
415-459-6495
http://home.earthlink.net/%7Ecastlesys

Emigre
916-451-4344, 800-944-9021
http://www.emigre.com

The Font Bureau, Inc.
617-423-8770
http://www.fontbureau.com

Fonthaus Inc.
203-367-1993, 800-942-9110
http://members.aol.com/fonthaus/
index.html

Font World, Inc.
716-235-6861
http://www.FontWorld.com

Hoefler Type Foundry Inc.
212-777-6640
http://www.typography.com

Image Club Graphics, Inc.
403-262-8008, 800-661-9410 US
http://www.imageclub.com

International Typeface Corp.
212-371-0699, 800-425-3882
http://www.esselte.com/itc

Letraset
201-845-6100, 800-343-8973
http://www.esselte.com

Linotype-Hell Co.
800-633-1900 US, 800-366-3735
Canada
http://www.linotype-hell.com

Monotype Typography Inc.
847-718-0400, 800-666-6897
http://www.monotype.com

Precision Type
516-864-0167, 800-248-3668

Stone Type Foundry Inc.
415-324-1870, 800-557-8663
mailto:StoneFndry@aol.com

T-26
773-862-1201, 888-T26-FONT
http://www.t26font.com

Treacyfaces, Inc.
203-389-7037, 800-800-6805
http://www.treacyfaces.com

URW America, Inc.
603-664-2130, 800-229-8791
mailto:75054.574@compuserve.com

Summary

In this chapter you learned that fixed-size (bitmapped) fonts look good only at installed sizes, but the system software can smoothly scale TrueType fonts to any size for the display screen or any type of printer. PostScript fonts look good at any size on PostScript printers and with the addition of Adobe Type Manager (ATM) on the display screen and non-PostScript printers as well. You also learned that all three types of fonts are kept in the Fonts folder, although PostScript fonts can also be kept in the Extensions folder or System Folder. For convenience, TrueType and fixed-size fonts are often kept in font suitcases. You can add and remove fonts by dragging their icons to and from the Fonts folder.

This chapter also explained how the system software chooses between fixed-size, TrueType, and PostScript versions of the same font. The priorities are different for the display screen, PostScript printers, and non-PostScript printers.

You also found in this chapter an overview of how outline fonts (TrueType and PostScript) work.

In addition, this chapter described QuickDraw GX typography, which comes as an option with System 7.5 and later. You learned about TrueType GX fonts, ligature substitution, swashes, numeral and fraction options, font variations, letter-spacing controls, and subscript and superscript options.

CHAPTER FOURTEEN

Get Ready to Print

IN THIS CHAPTER

- **Comparing printer driver software** for PostScript printers, non-PostScript printers, and other output devices

- **Using printers with desktop icons:** Creating printer icons; where to put them; making one the default; and changing printer setup

- **Using printers without desktop icons:** Selecting and setting up printers without desktop icons

- **Managing background printing** with and without desktop printers

- **Sharing printers** not connected to a network

W ith the Mac OS, you always set up and control printing the same basic way, regardless of the application you are using or the type of printer you have. The Mac system software enforces this consistency by providing complete printing services to applications. All applications use the same piece of software to prepare the page description for, and communicate with, a particular type of printer. This software, called a printer driver, resides in the Extensions folder inside the System Folder. Compare this uniformity with other types of personal computers, on which you often have to install printer driver software separately for each application, and you see the benefit.

You choose a printer with the standard Chooser desk accessory, which comes with the system software, and that choice persists among all applications and through restarts until you choose again. Apple's Desktop Printing software improves the administration of background printing and allows you to print documents by dragging their icons to a printer icon on the desktop. Desktop printing also allows you to choose a printer from a universal Printer menu or a Control Strip module, bypassing the Chooser and giving you complete control of the printing process without leaving your application.

You control the rest of the printing process with your application's Page Setup and Print commands; the standard options for these commands are the same in all applications. Alternatively, you can select one document or a group of documents (created by one application or several) and then give the command to print the selected documents from the Finder.

You don't have to wait for documents to finish printing before continuing with other work. With many printer models, the system software can manage printing in the background, so you can continue working on other tasks.

337

This chapter tells you how to set up for the specific printer or printers you use and how to manage background printing. You'll learn how to use the desktop printer methods included with recent system software versions, and you'll also find instructions for using printers if your Mac doesn't have desktop printing software installed. Also, this chapter describes how you can share printers among networked computers even though the printers aren't connected to the network. For instructions on setting up and printing documents, see Chapter 15.

The software and methods described here don't apply if you have installed the optional QuickDraw GX software versions 1.0 through 1.1.5. Those versions of QuickDraw GX, which can't be used with Mac OS 8.0 or later, provide alternative printing methods. For a discussion of QuickDraw GX printing, see Appendix A. (If you use QuickDraw GX 1.1.6, which is included with Mac OS 8, then use the printing methods described in this chapter and the next.)

Comparing Printer Driver Software

For each type of printer you use, your computer needs printing software in the Extensions folder. That software is called a *printer driver*. A printer driver prepares a complete description of each page to be printed, in a format that the printer can interpret, and then sends the page descriptions to the printer. Figure 14-1 displays the icons of the printer drivers that come with Mac OS 8.

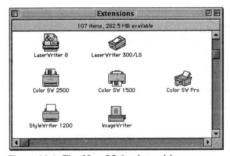

Figure 14-1: The Mac OS 8 printer drivers.

Your application prints by sending a description of your document to the printer driver software. The printer driver translates the description into data that the printer can use.

Many printers work with Macs, and each type of printer requires its own printer driver software. Apple supplies printer drivers for its printers in several ways: with the system software; with Apple printers; from Apple's on-line software library (http://www.info.apple.com); and through Apple dealers.

In general, you should use the latest version available. For example, if you buy an Apple printer after upgrading to Mac OS 8, and you find that the printer comes with older driver software than the driver that came with Mac OS 8, use the driver that came with Mac OS 8.

PostScript printer drivers

Printers that interpret PostScript commands to create printable images are called *PostScript printers*. Examples include most Apple LaserWriter models (but not the Personal LaserWriter LS or 300), the Hewlett-Packard LaserJet series, Texas Instruments' MicroLaser series, GCC Technologies' Elite series, and NEC's SilentWriter and ColorMate series. Although some of these printers come with proprietary driver software, most also work with Apple's LaserWriter drivers or Adobe's PSPrinter drivers.

Apple's LaserWriter drivers

There are two major revisions of Apple's driver for PostScript printers in use. They are LaserWriter 8 and LaserWriter 7, which is usually named simply LaserWriter. You can use either LaserWriter or LaserWriter 8 with printers that have the original version of PostScript, which is called PostScript Level 1. You should use LaserWriter 8 with newer printers that have the newer version of PostScript, known as PostScript Level 2.

Besides taking advantage of PostScript Level 2, the LaserWriter 8 driver provides other enhancements over the original LaserWriter driver. With LaserWriter 8, you can print multiple pages per sheet of paper. You also can see the effect of choosing certain page-size and orientation options in a miniature representation of the page as you make those choices.

LaserWriter 8 version 8.4 introduces many additional improvements to printing on PostScript printers. It's faster than earlier LaserWriter 8 drivers, especially when printing medium to highly complex documents. If you have access to more than one PostScript printer, you can choose the one you want when you print a document; earlier LaserWriter 8 drivers require you to choose the printer before printing. When you print a document you can also schedule when you want it to print, either relative to other documents waiting to be printed or at a specific time. Moreover, with LaserWriter 8 version 8.4 and later you don't have to worry about running out of disk space when printing a large document, as you do with earlier LaserWriter 8 drivers.

Generally you should use the most recent LaserWriter driver available, but that's not always possible. For instance, a computer with a 68000, 68020, 68030, or 68040 processor can't combine LaserWriter 8 version 8.4.3 with Mac OS 7.6 unless the computer also has the CFM-68K Runtime Enabler version 4.0 or later installed. Combinations of earlier versions of those three software components may work, but to reduce the chance of crashing you should install version 4.0 or later of the CFM-68K Runtime Enabler before using LaserWriter 8 version 8.4 or later on any computer without a PowerPC processor regardless of its system software version. CFM-68K is not required with any Power PC computer or with a 68040 computer and Mac OS 8.

If you decide not to use LaserWriter 8 version 8.4 or later, you have a choice of LaserWriter 8 version 8.3.4 (the latest LaserWriter 8 driver prior to version 8.4) or LaserWriter 7.2 (the latest LaserWriter driver prior to LaserWriter 8). Avoid using LaserWriter 8 versions between 8.0 and 8.3.3 or LaserWriter versions earlier than 7.2, because they don't have all the features and bug fixes in LaserWriter 8 version 8.3.4 or LaserWriter 7.2.

If you're not sure which version of the LaserWriter driver you have, select its icon in the Extensions folder and choose Get Info from the Finder's File menu. You then see the driver's Info window, which reports the version number.

Adobe's PSPrinter drivers

Apple developed LaserWriter 8 in collaboration with Adobe Systems (creator of PostScript) to take advantage of PostScript Level 2. Adobe distributes the LaserWriter 8 driver under the name PSPrinter. If you buy a non-Apple printer, it may come with the PSPrinter driver. Adobe has updated PSPrinter since its initial release, adding features and fixing bugs. To get the benefit of the newest features and bug fixes, use the latest version of PSPrinter. Do not use PSPrinter 8.0; instead, use PSPrinter 8.3.1 or later. Adobe does not have a version of PSPrinter equivalent to Apple's LaserWriter 8 version 8.4. Most PostScript printers that work with PSPrinter 8.3.1 also work with LaserWriter 8 version 8.4.3 and later.

Application compatibility

Some applications (notably, PageMaker 5 and later) require LaserWriter 8 or PSPrinter. However, LaserWriter 8 and PSPrinter do not work well with all applications, particularly older applications. If you experience problems printing with LaserWriter 8.4.3 or later, try LaserWriter 8.3.4 or PSPrinter 8.3.1. If you have trouble with LaserWriter 8.3.4 and PSPrinter 8.3.1, use LaserWriter 7.2.

Multiple driver versions on a network

Macs that share a LaserWriter or another PostScript printer on a network need not all have the same version of LaserWriter or PSPrinter driver. All versions of LaserWriter 8, PSPrinter, and LaserWriter 7 coexist peacefully on a network. Networked Macs can use any version of LaserWriter 7 or LaserWriter 8 and be compatible with other Macs on the network.

Although it's OK to mix driver versions on a network, bear in mind that a mixture of driver versions can delay printing. If you use a network printer that was last used by a Mac with a different LaserWriter driver than your Mac has, then your Mac must take extra time to send its version of the driver to the printer. For best efficiency, all Macs on a network should use the same printer driver.

PostScript Printer Description files

The LaserWriter 8 and PSPrinter drivers let you configure specific features of a particular printer, such as its *resolution* (the number of dots it can print per inch) and the size and capacity of its paper trays. These PostScript Level 2 drivers get a printer's optional features from a special file called a *PostScript Printer Description (PPD)* file. A set of PPD files comes with the LaserWriter 8 or PSPrinter driver, and the PPDs reside in a folder named Printer Descriptions inside the Extensions folder (which is in the System Folder). In addition, printer manufacturers include the appropriate PPD with each printer that has PostScript Level 2.

Non-PostScript printer drivers

Many printers do not use PostScript to create page images. Examples from Apple include all the various StyleWriter printers, the ImageWriter II, the Personal LaserWriter 300, and the Personal LaserWriter LS. Non-PostScript printers from other companies include Hewlett-Packard's DeskWriter and DeskJet series, the Epson Stylus models, and GCC Technologies' PLP II.

Each type of non-PostScript printer has its own printer driver software. With few exceptions, your Extensions folder must include a different driver for each non-PostScript printer that you use. Notable exceptions:

❖ StyleWriter (original) can use these drivers: Color StyleWriter 1500, StyleWriter 1200, StyleWriter II, or StyleWriter

❖ StyleWriter II can use these drivers: Color StyleWriter 1500, StyleWriter 1200, or StyleWriter II

❖ StyleWriter 1200 can use these drivers: Color StyleWriter 1500, StyleWriter 1200

❖ Color StyleWriter 2400 can use Color StyleWriter 2500 driver

❖ Color StyleWriter 2200 can use Color StyleWriter 2500 driver

❖ Personal LaserWriter LS can use LaserWriter 300 driver

Other output device drivers

Other types of output devices, although not technically printers, also have printer driver software. These devices include fax/modems, plotters, and portable document makers such as Acrobat and Common Ground. If you have any of these devices, each must have a driver in your Extensions folder.

Using Printers with Desktop Icons

A Mac OS computer can print or otherwise create output from an application on any printer or other output device for which you have a driver in your Extensions folder. The output device could be a personal printer, a network printer, a fax modem, a plotter, and so on. You must designate which device you want to use. For example, if your organization has different printers for different types of printing (letterhead, envelopes, plain paper, and so on), you can change printers based on your need.

The main method for choosing a printer depends on whether you have Apple's Desktop Printing software installed, although the method of choosing each printer you use for the first time is the same with or without Desktop Printing software. You can always choose a printer with the Chooser accessory program, which is normally listed in the Apple menu.

If you have Desktop Printing software installed, you use the Chooser only once for each printer that's compatible with the Desktop Printing software. (All Apple LaserWriter and StyleWriter printers are compatible with Desktop Printing software, as are some printers made by other companies.) With Desktop Printing installed, each time you choose a new printer you create an icon for it on the desktop. Thereafter you can use the desktop printer icons and Finder menu commands to choose and configure a printer. You also have the option of choosing desktop printers from a universal Printer menu or a Control Strip module.

Without Desktop Printing software, or to choose a printer that isn't compatible with it, you always use the Chooser. For information on choosing and configuring a printer without Desktop Printing software, see "Choosing and Configuring a Non-Desktop Printer" later in this chapter.

Desktop Printing is part of a standard installation of Mac OS 7.6 and later, and System 7.5.3 includes it as a custom installation option. Desktop Printing is also available as an add-on for system software versions 7.1 and later from Apple's online software library (http://www.info.apple.com). If you're not sure whether you have Desktop Printing installed, look for the files Desktop Printer Extension, Desktop Printer Spooler, and Desktop PrintMonitor in your Extensions folder.

Desktop Printing generations

There are two generations of Desktop Printing software. The second generation, beginning with version 2.0, introduces a new look for desktop printing windows and controls, allows moving printer icons off the desktop, and lets you turn off notification that a printer is waiting for you to manually feed paper. It also gives you the option of choosing a printer from a universal Printer menu or from a Control Strip module. None of these features is included with the first generation, which includes versions 1.0 through 1.0.3.

The first generation of Desktop Printing software does have a couple of advantages. For one, it works on all Macs, whereas Desktop Printing 2.0 and later don't work on Macs with 68000 processors, such as the Mac Classic, SE, and Plus. Also, Desktop Printing 1.0 through 1.0.3 work with more non-Apple printers than Desktop Printing 2.0 and later.

The procedures described in this chapter apply to both generations of Desktop Printing software unless noted otherwise.

Creating desktop printer icons

If you have Desktop Printing software installed, you should try to create a desktop icon for each printer you use. Don't worry about whether a printer is compatible with the Desktop Printing software. You won't break anything by trying to create a desktop icon for an incompatible printer. You simply won't get a desktop icon for an incompatible printer.

You can try to create icons for a printer connected to your computer and for any other type of printer for which you have a printer driver installed in your Extensions folder. There are several reasons why you might want to create printer icons for printers not connected to your computer. For instance, you might want to create printer icons on a PowerBook for printers that you use at various locations. As another example, you might want to create an icon for an expensive color printer that you use at a service bureau.

You may already have one printer icon on the desktop if you installed the Desktop Printing software on a Mac with System 7.5.5 or earlier, or if you upgraded a Mac from System 7.5.5 or earlier to Mac OS 7.6 or later. During the installation or upgrade process the Installer program attempts to create an icon for the printer most recently chosen before installation. To make sure that icon works properly, you can go through the process of creating an icon for the same printer as if no icon existed.

You cannot create desktop icons for most fax modems, including Global Village fax modems and Apple's Express Modem. To send a fax, you either use the fax modem's keyboard shortcut or you choose the fax modem in the Chooser. If no desktop icon appears when you try to create one for a fax modem, it simply means you can't choose and configure that fax modem with a desktop icon. For information on choosing and configuring output devices that don't have desktop icons, see "Choosing and Configuring a Non-Desktop Printer" later in this chapter.

Selecting a type of printer

To create a desktop icon for a printer, open the Chooser. On the left side of the Chooser window, select the type of printer for which you want to create a desktop icon. Actually, you are selecting a printer driver. You can make the selection by clicking the appropriate icon in the Chooser or by typing the first part of that icon's name. Figure 14-2 shows an example of the Chooser ready for selecting a printer driver in Mac OS 8.

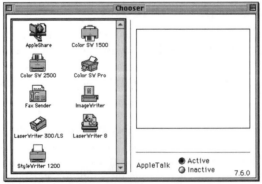

Figure 14-2: Select the type of printer for which you want a desktop icon.

Selecting a networked printer

After selecting a printer driver, you can select a specific printer from the list that appears on the right side of the Chooser window. If you selected a driver for a networked type of printer driver such as LaserWriter 8, the Chooser lists the names of all printers of that type that are currently available. You select the printer for which you want to create a desktop icon by clicking its name. You can also select a listed printer by typing the first part of its name. (To select by typing, the list of printer names must be surrounded by a heavy border; if it isn't, press Tab until it is.) Figure 14-3 shows an example list of PostScript printers in the Chooser.

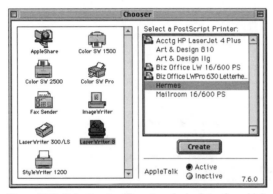

Figure 14-3: Select a specific networked printer for which you want a desktop icon.

If your network has zones, you see a list of network zones in the lower left corner of the Chooser window and the Chooser lists printer names only for the currently selected zone. You can select a different zone to see the printers available in it. (If you don't see a list of zones, your network has no zones.)

If there are no names listed on the right side of the Chooser window when a networked type of printer driver is selected on the left side of the window, then there are no printers of that type available on the network (in the currently selected zone if your network has zones). You can create a desktop icon for the type of printer selected on the left side of the Chooser window without selecting a specific printer on the right side of the window. Naturally, you won't be able to set up that printer icon for a particular printer's installed options (paper trays, memory available, and so on). You can use that icon subsequently to create documents formatted for the type of printer it represents. For example, you might want to prepare a document at home, where you don't have a LaserWriter, to be printed later from a Mac at work that does have access to a LaserWriter.

Selecting a directly connected printer

If you selected a printer driver for a directly connected type of printer such as Color SW 2500, the Chooser lists the ports to which it could be connected (commonly printer and modem). You select a port by clicking it in the Chooser. Figure 14-4 shows an example list of ports for a directly connected printer.

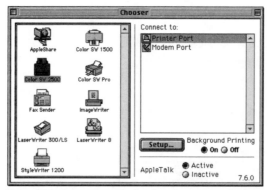

Figure 14-4: Select the port of a directly connected printer for which you want a desktop icon.

You may not be able to select the printer port for a directly connected printer unless you set the AppleTalk option to Inactive in the Chooser. If you don't want to make AppleTalk inactive, you can use the AppleTalk control panel or the Network control panel, whichever your computer has, to set the AppleTalk connection to something other than the printer port. For example, you can select Remote Only if it is installed on your computer. For more information on the Remote Only option, see "Configuring an AppleTalk Connection" in Chapter 17.

Turning off AppleTalk doesn't always release the printer port so you can use the port for a serial printer. If you have trouble printing to a serial printer connected to a port that was used previously for an AppleTalk network, restart the computer after making AppleTalk inactive.

In addition to ports, you may see the names of shared printers on the left side of the Chooser window when you select a directly connected type of printer on the right side. If you want to create an icon for one of those shared printers, select it by clicking or typing its name. For more information on sharing directly connected printers on a network, see "Sharing Printers" later in this chapter.

Setting up the selected printer

Most types of printers have options you can set up as part of creating a desktop printer icon. For example, a printer may have optional paper trays or extra memory installed. You can set up some directly connected printers, such as StyleWriters, for sharing on a network. The process is fully described in "Sharing Printers" at the end of the chapter. With many printer drivers you can turn background printing on and off, as described in "Managing Background Printing" later in this chapter.

In many cases the printer driver can automatically set up a printer's options, and later you can change the setup manually. For example, if you have selected LaserWriter 8 or PSPrinter on the left side of the Chooser window, the printer driver can automatically determine the correct PPD file to use for the specific printer you have selected on the right side of the Chooser window and can automatically determine which optional equipment the selected printer has.

To set up a printer you have selected in the Chooser, click the Create button or the Setup button on the right side of the Chooser window. When you click the Setup or Create button, the printer driver either displays status messages describing its automatic setup process or it displays a dialog box with setup options for you to choose.

If no Setup or Create button appears for the printer you have selected, or if the button is dimmed (grayed out), then there is nothing to set up. This will be the case if you have not selected a printer name on the right side of the Chooser window, perhaps because you're making a desktop icon for a type of printer that doesn't exist at your current location so you can create documents to print later at another location where that type of printer does exist.

Making the new printer icon appear

A printer icon appears automatically on the desktop at the conclusion of the setup process for some types of printers, such as printers that use the LaserWriter 8 driver. If a printer icon does not appear automatically, you can make it appear by closing the Chooser. In some cases you can also make an icon appear by switching to the Finder (click the desktop or choose Finder from the Applications menu) without closing the Chooser. You may have to wait several seconds before the desktop printer icon appears.

Where to put desktop printer icons

You can handle desktop printer icons as you would other Finder icons. You can rename them, drag them to the Trash, and create aliases for them. With Desktop Printing 2.0 and later, you can move printer icons from the desktop to a folder. With Desktop Printing 1.1.3 and earlier, desktop icons must remain on the desktop.

Choosing a default printer

If you have more than one printer icon, you choose one that represents the printer you want to use by default. You can choose the default printer by using a Printing menu in the Finder, and you may be able to use other methods as well.

Printing menu

After creating desktop printer icons for all the printers you use, you must designate which one you want to use by default. First, select the printer's desktop icon; a Printing menu appears next to the Finder's Special menu. Choose Set Default Printer from that menu. The Finder indicates the default printer by drawing a heavy black border around its desktop icon. The Printing menu is only available in the Finder. Figure 14-5 shows a couple of desktop printer icons and the Printing menu.

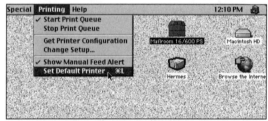

Figure 14-5: Setting a default printer with the Finder's Printing menu.

Printer menu and Control Strip module

You can choose a desktop printer from any program — no need to switch to the Finder and use the Printer menu — if you have Desktop Printing 2.0 or later. If the Control Strip is installed on your computer, you can choose a printer from it. You can also choose a printer from a universal Printer menu with Desktop Printing 2.0, which comes with Mac OS 7.6. The Printer menu isn't available in Desktop Printing 2.0.2, which is part of a standard installation of Mac OS 8. Figure 14-6 shows an example of the Printer Selector module in the Control Strip.

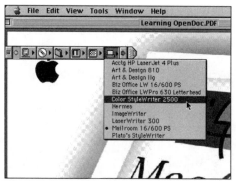

Figure 14-6: Choosing a default printer from the Control Strip.

To get the Printer Selector control panel module, plus the Printer menu if you have Desktop Printing 2.0 (but not 2.0.2), you may need to do a custom installation of the Mac OS module. In the Installer program's Install System Software window, choose a custom installation and select the Desktop Printing component (in the Printing category). Also select the Control Strip component (in the Utility category) if you have a desktop computer, since the Control Strip is installed by default only on PowerBook models. For detailed instructions on doing custom installations, see Chapters 28 and 29.

Chooser

In addition to using the Finder's Printing menu, the Printer menu, or the Printer Control Strip module to designate the default printer, you can use the Chooser. Just select the printer in the Chooser as if you were creating an icon for it. If a printer you select in the Chooser already has a desktop icon, the Chooser makes the selected printer the default printer without creating another icon for it.

Printer status and printer setup

You can use the Finder's Printing menu to check the current status and configuration, see a list of fonts currently installed, and change the setup of a printer whose desktop icon is based on a LaserWriter 8 driver. To display a printer's status and configuration in a printer information window, you select the printer's desktop icon and choose Get Printer Info from the Finder's Printing menu. You can switch between viewing status and configuration information and viewing a list of installed fonts by choosing the view you want from the pop-up menu in the printer information window. (If the Get Printer Info menu command is not in the Printing menu, you can't get status, configuration, and installed fonts for the selected printer.) Figure 14-7 shows examples of both views of the printer information window.

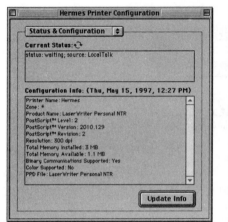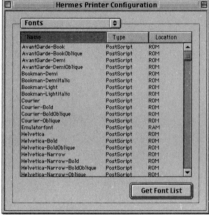

Figure 14-7: Viewing a desktop printer's current status, configuration, and fonts.

Another command in the Finder's Printing menu, Change Setup, lets you change the PPD file and reconfigure any installed options of a printer whose desktop icon is based on a LaserWriter 8 driver. Selecting a printer icon and choosing Change Setup brings up a dialog box that displays the current setup. The dialog box contains a button for changing the PPD file, other controls for changing the settings of options installed in the printer, and an Auto Setup button that has the printer driver interrogate the printer to configure those settings automatically. Figure 14-8 shows an example of the Change Setup dialog box.

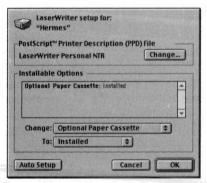

Figure 14-8: Changing a desktop printer's setup from the Finder.

The Change Setup and Get Printer Info commands are only available with Desktop Printing 2.0 and later. You can always change the setup of a desktop printer with the Chooser as described in the next section.

Using Printers Without Desktop Icons

You may have a printer, fax modem, or other output device that can't have a desktop icon, or you may not have Apple's Desktop Printing software installed. In either case you always choose the printer or other output device with the Chooser. You also use the Chooser to change the setup of a non-desktop printer or other output device. The Chooser procedures are basically the same for non-desktop printers as for desktop printers, but no desktop icon is created or reconfigured for non-desktop printers as a result of the procedures.

Selecting a printer

To select a printer or other output device, choose the Chooser from the Apple menu. Each printer or other output device for which you have a driver in your Extensions folder appears as an icon in the Chooser. On the left side of the Chooser window, select the type of printer or other device that you want to use. You are actually selecting a printer driver. You can make the selection by clicking the appropriate icon in the Chooser or by typing the first part of that icon's name. Figure 14-9 shows the Chooser ready for selecting a printer driver.

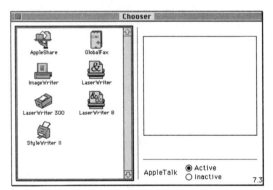

Figure 14-9: Select the type of printer you want to use.

If you select a type of printer or other device that's connected to a network, the Chooser lists the names of all printers of that type that currently are available on your network. You select the printer you want by clicking its name. You can also select a listed printer by typing the first part of its name. (To select by typing, the list of printer names must be surrounded by a heavy border; if it isn't, press Tab until it is.) If your network has zones, you see the names of printers in the currently selected zone. You can select a different zone in the lower-left part of the Chooser. The Chooser does not display a list of zones unless your network has more than one zone. If there are no names listed on the right side of the Chooser window when a networked type of printer driver is selected on the left side of the window, then there are no printers of that type available on the network (in the currently selected zone if your network has zones). Figure 14-10 shows an example list of printers that use the LaserWriter 8 driver and are available in the currently selected network zone.

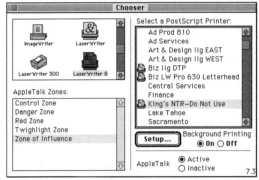

Figure 14-10: Select the specific networked printer you want to use.

If you select a printer or device that connects directly to your Mac, the Chooser lists the ports to which it could be connected. You select a port by clicking it in the Chooser. Figure 14-11 shows an example list of ports for a directly connected printer that uses the StyleWriter II driver.

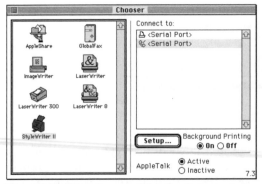

Figure 14-11: Select the port of the directly connected printer you want to use.

SECRETS

Retrofit GrayShare on an Original StyleWriter or a Personal LaserWriter LS

Are you stuck with an original StyleWriter or a Personal LaserWriter LS and wish that it had a newer model's GrayShare technology for printing shades of gray and sharing your printer on a network? All you need is a newer printer driver. Instead of the StyleWriter driver, use the StyleWriter II, StyleWriter 1200, or Color StyleWriter 1500 driver. Instead of the Personal LaserWriter LS driver, use the LaserWriter 300 or LaserWriter 300/LS driver. Suitable drivers come with System 7.5 and later. The latest drivers are also available from Apple's on-line software library (http://www.info.apple.com). Be sure to install the new driver software with the Installer program — don't just drag the driver file to your Extensions folder. The Installer updates the Chooser and other system software if necessary, depending on the model of your Mac and the version of your system software. (Macs that lack Color QuickDraw, including the Plus, SE, Classic, Portable, and PowerBook 100, can't print shades of gray even with the newer drivers.)

Setting up a printer

The Chooser has another function for some printer drivers: setting up printer options such as paper source. You can set up some directly connected printers, such as StyleWriters, for sharing on a network. The process is described fully in "Sharing printers" at the end of the chapter. With many printer drivers you can turn background printing on and off, as described in "Managing Background Printing" later in this chapter.

If the selected printer has options you can set up, a Setup button or Review button appears on the right side of the Chooser window. If no Setup or Review button appears for the printer you have selected, or if the button is dimmed (grayed out), then there is nothing to set up.

The first time you click the Setup button for a particular printer, the printer driver may set up the printer's options automatically by querying the printer for its current configuration. Later you can change the setup manually by clicking the Setup button again.

Managing Background Printing

When you print a document (as described in the next chapter), the printer driver creates page descriptions for each page to be printed. The driver may send the page descriptions to the printer immediately, forcing you to wait until the document finishes printing before you can do anything else. Alternatively, many printer drivers can save the page descriptions in a file for later automatic printing in the background, while you do other work in the foreground. A file of page descriptions is called a *print request*, a *print job*, or a *spool file*.

In the short time it takes to save a print request, the printer driver has control of the computer. You regain control as soon as a driver finishes saving. While you work (or not), the Desktop PrintMonitor application opens automatically in the background and handles the waiting print request by sending the saved page descriptions to the printer a bit at a time during the slices of time it gets to work in the background. (Instead of the Desktop PrintMonitor, the PrintMonitor application handles the waiting print request if you don't have desktop printing installed.) The background printing activity may make the computer feel less responsive, especially on a slower computer.

While a document is printing in the background, you can queue additional print requests by using the Print command in one or more applications. The Desktop PrintMonitor application (or PrintMonitor, if you don't have desktop printing installed) handles the queued print requests in the order they were saved unless you set a specific print time or a special priority for some, as described later in this section. You can also stop and start the print queue whenever you want.

The rest of this section tells you how to turn background printing on and off and then explains how to manage a queue of waiting print requests. You'll find separate explanations for managing a print queue with desktop printing software installed and without it, because the methods are different.

Turning background printing on and off

You can turn background printing on or off separately for each printer driver. With many drivers, you set background printing in the Chooser before you print documents. On the left side of the Chooser window you select the icon of a printer driver, and then on the right side of the Chooser window you set that driver's Background Printing option on or off. Figure 14-12 shows the Background Printing option in the Chooser.

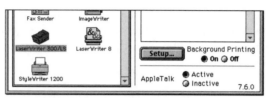

Figure 14-12: With some printer drivers, you turn background printing on or off in the Chooser.

With LaserWriter 8 version 8.4 and later, you do not need to set background printing in the Chooser. Instead you turn background printing on or off whenever you use the Print command to print a document. In the Print command's dialog box, you choose the Background Printing group of options, and set the Print In option for background or foreground printing. Figure 14-13 shows the Print In option of the Print command for LaserWriter 8 version 8.4.3.

Figure 14-13: Turning background printing on or off in the Print dialog box for LaserWriter 8 version 8.4 and later.

Background printing with desktop printers

You can view and manage the queue of waiting print files for each printer individually by using desktop printer icons and the Finder's Printing menu. If your Mac doesn't create desktop printer icons when you choose a printer with the Chooser, then you must use the methods described later for managing background printing without desktop printers.

Viewing the print queue

At any time, you can see the queue of print requests waiting for a particular printer by opening that printer's desktop icon in the Finder. Opening a desktop printer icon brings up its window. At the top of the window are buttons for managing the queue of print requests and general information about the print queue. A box below the buttons identifies the print request now being printed (if any) and reports the status of that print job. Below that is a list of waiting print requests. You can sort the list of waiting print requests by name, number of pages, number of copies, or print time. Choose a sort order by clicking a column heading in the desktop printer's window. With Mac OS 7.6.1 and earlier, you can also choose a sort order from the View menu. Figure 14-14 shows a printer's window.

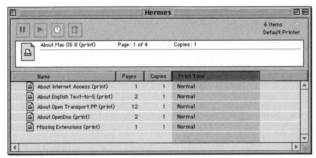

Figure 14-14: View queued print requests in a desktop printer's window.

You can redirect a waiting print request by dragging it from its current desktop printer window to the icon or window of a compatible desktop printer. In general, compatible printers have the same icon in the Chooser (they use the same printer driver).

Changing the order of printing

Print requests in a desktop printer's window print in listed order when the list is sorted by print time. You can change the order of print requests by dragging them up and down in the window. You can drag a print request by its icon, name, or any other text on the same line in the desktop printer's window. Figure 14-15 shows an example of changing print request order.

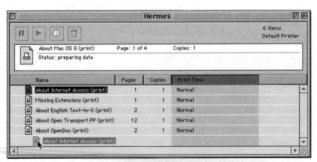

Figure 14-15: Change the order of print requests by dragging them in the desktop printer's queue.

Scheduling print requests

You can also change a print request's place in line by setting its priority to urgent, normal, or scheduled for a specific time and date. To set a print request's priority, select it and click the Set Print Time button (the one with the clock icon) in the desktop printer's window. If the printer window has no such button, your Mac has a version of desktop printing software prior to 2.0; in that case choose Set Print Time from the Printing menu. Figure 14-16 shows the dialog box in which you set a print request's priority with Desktop Printing 2.0 and later.

Click the Schedule button to bring up the Set Print Time dialog box

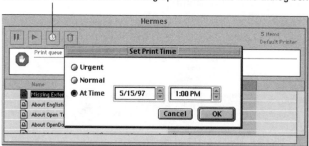

Figure 14-16: Scheduling a priority or a specific time for a print request.

A print request's priority changes automatically if you drag it to a place among print requests of a different priority. For example, dragging a scheduled print request above an urgent print request makes the scheduled print request urgent.

You can postpone a print request indefinitely, even if the print request is currently being printed. Select a print request in the desktop printer's window and click the Hold button (looks like a VCR's pause button with Desktop Printing 2.0 and later). To take a print request off hold, select it and then click the Resume button (looks like a VCR's play button with Desktop Printing 2.0 and later) in the desktop printer's window. Clicking this button displays the Resume Print Request dialog box, in which you can specify the page at which you want printing to resume.

You can also stop a print request by dragging it out of the desktop printer's window. To get rid of a print request altogether, either drag it to the Trash or select it and click the Remove button (with the trash can icon).

Managing multiple print requests

You can schedule or re-sequence more than one print request at a time in a desktop printer's window. To select multiple print requests, press the Shift key while clicking them or drag across them.

Starting and stopping printing

To stop all printing on a particular printer, select its desktop icon and then choose Stop Print Queue from the Printing menu. A small stop sign appears on the printer's desktop icon.

To start printing again, select the printer's desktop icon and then choose Start Print Queue from the Printing menu.

Instant Reprints (Well, Almost)

It takes quite a while to save background print requests for some documents, and that's on top of the time it takes to open the application and the document before you can begin printing. For example, it may take several minutes to save a print request for a Photoshop image to be printed on a Color StyleWriter. You don't have to repeat that wait each time you reprint the image in the future if you can spare the disk space to store a copy of the print request. (Yes, you could print multiple copies of the image at one time and hand them out as needed; it doesn't take any longer to save a print request for multiple copies than for a single copy. But then you may end up with extra copies that you have to throw away, thus wasting ink and expensive special paper.)

Here is a procedure for reprinting without the delay of saving a new print request each time: Before printing a document for the first time, select the desktop printer icon and choose Stop Print Queue from the Finder's Printing menu. Then print the document, causing a print request to be created for the desktop printer. If you forget to stop the print queue before printing, immediately go to the Finder and stop the print queue or open the desktop printer icon and put the print request on hold. Next open the desktop printer icon and drag the print request to any folder. When you're ready to make a print, hold down the option key and drag the print request from that folder to the desktop printer icon. This makes a copy of the print request for the desktop printer and leaves the original print request untouched for future reprints. If necessary, use the Finder's Start Print Queue command to start up background printing. Et voilà! Reprints without saving new print requests or opening a document and its application!

Manual paper feed notification

With Desktop Printing 2.0 and later, the Printing menu makes it easy to turn off notification that the printer is waiting for you to manually feed paper. Just select the relevant desktop printer and choose Show Manual Feed Alert from the Printing menu so that there is no check mark next to it in the menu.

Background printing without desktop printers

If your Mac doesn't have desktop printers (and you can't create them as described in "Choosing and Setting Up a Desktop Printer" earlier in this chapter), you can manage background printing with the PrintMonitor application. The PrintMonitor program handles printing in the background. This program opens in the background automatically whenever there are print requests in the PrintMonitor Documents folder (inside the System Folder), deletes each print request that it prints, and quits automatically when the PrintMonitor Documents folder is empty.

Viewing the print queue

While PrintMonitor is open in the background, you can make it the active application by choosing it from the Application menu. You also can open it at any time by double-clicking its icon, which is located in the Extensions folder. Making Print-Monitor active or opening it brings up its window, which identifies the print request that it is printing, lists the print requests waiting to be printed, and displays the status of the current print job. Figure 14-17 shows the PrintMonitor window.

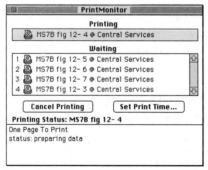

Figure 14-17: View queued print requests in the PrintMonitor window (without desktop printers).

PrintMonitor automatically hides its window when you switch to another program, but the program remains open in the background as long as it has print requests to process.

Changing the order of printing

PrintMonitor ordinarily processes print requests in chronological order, oldest first. You can change the order by dragging print requests in the PrintMonitor window. You drag a print request by its icon, not by its name or sequence number. While you drag, an outline of the print request follows the mouse pointer, as shown in Figure 14-18.

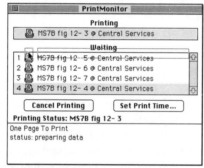

Figure 14-18: Change the order of print requests by dragging them in the PrintMonitor queue (without desktop printers).

Scheduling printing requests

You can schedule when PrintMonitor will process a print request, or you can postpone a print request indefinitely. In the PrintMonitor window, you first select the print request you want to schedule (by clicking it). You can select the print request being printed or any print request waiting to be printed. Then click the Set Print Time button. Figure 14-19 shows the dialog box in which you set a time and date for processing a print request or postpone it indefinitely.

A print request scheduled for later printing appears in PrintMonitor's waiting list with an alarm-clock icon in place of a sequence number. A print request postponed indefinitely appears in the waiting list with a dash in place of a sequence number, and it will not be printed until you schedule a print time for it.

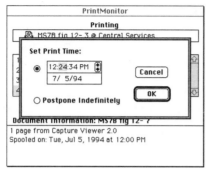

Figure 14-19: Scheduling a specific time for a print request (without desktop printers).

Stopping and starting printing

You can suspend all background printing by choosing Stop Printing from PrintMonitor's File menu. Before PrintMonitor stops printing, it finishes the print request that it is currently printing. To resume printing, choose Resume Printing from the File menu.

QUICK TIPS

Print Later

If your Mac is not attached to a printer and does not have desktop printer icons, but you want to be able to print documents when you finish them, you can delay printing. Turn on background printing in the Chooser and print the desired files. Then open PrintMonitor and use its Stop Printing command to suspend printing. Now any documents that you print wait in PrintMonitor's queue until you connect to a printer and begin printing with PrintMonitor's Resume Printing command. To avoid PrintMonitor's nagging alert messages and blinking icon in the menu bar, use PrintMonitor's Preferences to suppress notification of printing errors.

To shut down your Mac while it is not connected to a printer and background printing is turned on, you must respond correctly to two PrintMonitor alerts that appear during the shutdown process. The first alert tells you that something is being printed and asks whether you want to finish printing or print later; you must click the Print Later button. Then another alert tells you that the printer can't be found; click the Cancel Printing button to conclude the shutdown process without losing any queued print requests. (If you click Try Again instead, you abort the shutdown process, and PrintMonitor tries again to find the missing printer.) This process is somewhat confusing, because clicking Cancel Printing under other circumstances *does* delete the print request that is being printed.

Setting PrintMonitor preferences

PrintMonitor can notify you when something happens that requires your attention during background printing. For example, PrintMonitor can notify you when you need to manually feed paper for background printing. You can be notified by an alert box, a blinking PrintMonitor icon in the menu bar, or both. To specify how you want to be notified, you use the Preferences command in PrintMonitor's File menu. Note that if you turn off notification of manual paper feed and forget to feed paper when the printer needs it, the printer eventually cancels the print request automatically. Figure 14-20 shows the Preferences dialog box for PrintMonitor.

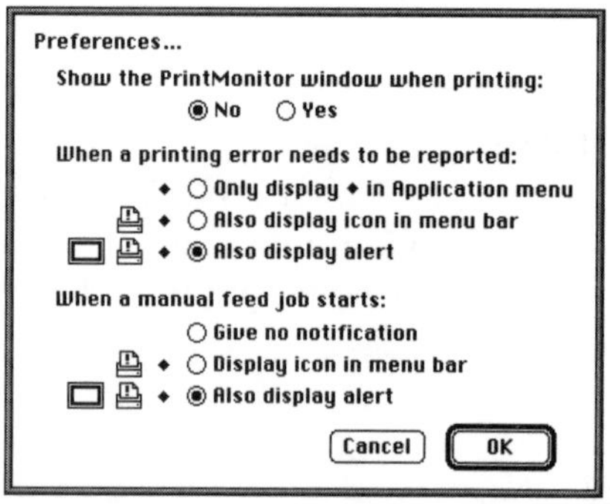

Figure 14-20: Setting PrintMonitor preferences.

You also can use the Preferences command to specify how you want to be notified about printing errors, such as not being able to locate a printer that is supposed to print a print request. PrintMonitor can just display a diamond symbol next to its name in the Application menu at the right end of the menu bar; it can do that and blink its icon in the menu bar; or it can do both of those things and display an alert as well. You can turn off everything except the diamond in the Application menu.

Sharing Printers

When Apple introduced the first LaserWriter in 1985, it was the first printer that came ready for sharing. Because all Macs and most LaserWriters contain LocalTalk ports (and some contain Ethernet ports as well), you can daisy-chain several Macs together with a LaserWriter to create a network. When several people share a printer, it may not always be available when you want to print.

You don't have to wait for a shared printer to become available if you turn on background printing with your Chooser. As you continue working, your documents print in the background when the shared printer becomes available.

Although background printing solves the problem of a busy shared printer, it doesn't enable sharing printers that lack network ports, such as a StyleWriter or LaserWriter Select 300. To enable sharing of a printer that's directly connected to your computer's modem port (or printer port, if it's not being used for a network connection), you can make your computer host the printer on the network. Other computers on the network print through the host computer. Because the host computer provides network services, it's called a *print server.*

There is a catch to sharing a printer that is directly connected to your computer: your hard disk must store all the print requests waiting to be printed by everyone who's using your printer, and your computer must print those files in the background. If you continue working while your computer handles all that background printing, you may notice a performance slowdown.

Making your printer available for sharing

You can share any printer that uses any Color StyleWriter driver, the StyleWriter 1200 driver, the StyleWriter II driver version 1.2 or later, or the LaserWriter 300 driver. To make a printer that uses one of those drivers available to other network computers, open the Chooser on the computer to which the printer is connected. In the Chooser, select the driver's icon and the serial port to which the printer is connected (the modem port, if the printer port is used to connect to the network). Then click the Setup button to bring up the sharing setup dialog box for the printer. Figure 14-21 shows the sharing setup dialog for Color StyleWriter 2500.

Figure 14-21: Setting up a directly connected printer for sharing.

In the printer's sharing setup dialog box, turn on the Share this Printer option. Give the printer a distinctive name by which it will be known on the network. You also can specify a password that anyone who wants to use the printer will have to enter. You have the option of keeping a log of printer activity. Click OK to dismiss the dialog box and close the Chooser.

Using a shared printer on your network

To use a shared printer that's directly connected to another computer on your network, your computer must have the same printer driver as the host computer and Chooser 7.3 or later. When you open the Chooser on your computer and select that driver's icon, the names of the available shared printers are listed on the right side of the Chooser window. Select the shared printer that you want to use. Figure 14-22 shows a shared StyleWriter printer in the Chooser.

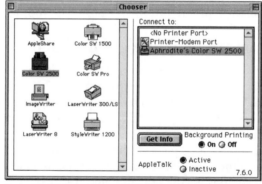

Figure 14-22: Choosing an available shared printer.

Before closing the Chooser, you can get information about the printer that you're sharing by clicking the Get Info button in the Chooser. The dialog box that appears reports the system software version installed on the printer's computer, the name of that computer, and the fonts installed on your computer that are missing on the shared printer's computer. Any documents containing fonts that are not installed on the shared printer's computer print slowly or may not print correctly.

After closing the Chooser, a desktop icon appears for the shared printer, and you can print to it like any other desktop printer. The printer driver takes care of forwarding your print requests over the network to the host computer. (If no desktop printer icon appears, then your computer doesn't have Desktop

Printing software, but you can still print on the shared printer that you selected in the Chooser.)

Summary

In this chapter, you learned that every printer you use must have a printer driver in your Extensions folder. A printer driver prepares a complete description of each page to be printed, in a format that the printer can interpret, and then sends the page descriptions to the printer. To choose a driver and a specific printer that uses it, you use the Chooser. With Apple's Desktop Printing software installed, as it is by default with Mac OS 8 and 7.6, choosing a printer in the Chooser creates a desktop icon for the printer. Once you have created desktop printer icons, you can use the Finder's Printing menu, the optional universal Printer menu, or the optional Printer Selector module in the Control Strip to select a printer you want to use. You don't have to use the Chooser again for printers that have desktop icons.

You can usually continue working while the system software prints in the background. You can view queued print requests by opening desktop printer icons. You can change the order of queued print requests, set their priorities or print times, put them on hold, or delete them. You can also stop and start any printer's queue. If you don't have desktop printer icons, you can manage background printing with the PrintMonitor program.

In addition, you learned in this chapter how to share printers among networked computers even though the printers aren't connected to the network.

Print Your Documents

Almost every Mac OS application has the same commands for printing documents — Page Setup and Print — and those commands are usually in the File menu. Some applications give you other methods of printing, such as a Print button in a toolbar, but the alternate methods are all based on the standard Page Setup and Print commands. Learn how to use the standard commands, and you know how to use the alternate methods as well.

You use the Page Setup command to specify how you want the document pages to be formatted. You need to set the paper size (such as letter or legal size), a page orientation (horizontal or vertical), a reduction or enlargement factor, and other options that affect how the document is arranged on the page. With some printers, you also can turn optional printer effects on and off.

You use the Print command to specify a range of pages, a number of copies, and a paper source. You may have additional options, depending on the type of printer driver you have chosen.

With both the Page Setup command and the Print command you may notice additional options that are not described in this chapter, because some applications and utility software add their own options to those commands. For example, the existence of a Page Setup option labeled ClickBook means the ClickBook utility from ForeFront Technology (713/961-1101, http://www.ffg.com) is installed for printing double-sided pages or booklets on regular printers. For explanations of Print or Page Setup options not described in this chapter, check the documentation for the application you're using and for any printing utility software installed on your computer.

This chapter tells you how to set up and print pages on printers that use the following Apple printer driver software:

❖ LaserWriter 8

❖ LaserWriter versions 7.2 and earlier

❖ Color StyleWriter 2500, 2400, 2200, and 1500; and Color StyleWriter Pro

❖ StyleWriter 1200, StyleWriter II, and the original StyleWriter

❖ LaserWriter 300/LS

❖ ImageWriter

For detailed information about these printer drivers and about setting up printers to use them, see Chapter 14. That chapter also explains how to manage background printing and how to share non-networked printers such as StyleWriters over a network.

The software and methods described here don't apply if you have installed the optional QuickDraw GX software versions 1.0 through 1.1.5. Those versions of QuickDraw GX, which can't be used with Mac OS 8.0 or later, provide alternative printing methods. For a discussion of QuickDraw GX printing, see Appendix A.

Setting LaserWriter 8 Options

This section describes how to set up and print documents on printers that use Apple's LaserWriter 8 printer driver. The LaserWriter 8 driver takes advantage of PostScript Level 2 and provides other enhancements over the original LaserWriter driver, which is described in the next section. You can also use LaserWriter 8 with printers that have PostScript Level 1. All Apple LaserWriter printers with PostScript can use LaserWriter 8, and so can most PostScript printers made by other companies.

LaserWriter 8 Page Setup

When you choose the Page Setup command for a printer that uses the LaserWriter 8 driver, you see a dialog box with settings for page attributes, including paper type, orientation, and scale. You can switch to settings for PostScript Options by choosing that category from the pop-up menu in the dialog box. Figure 15-1 shows the Page Setup page attribute and PostScript option settings for LaserWriter 8 version 8.4.3.

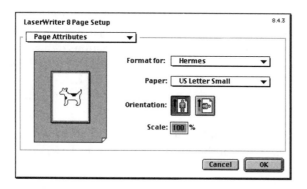

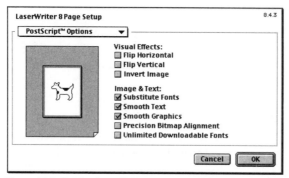

Figure 15-1: Setting LaserWriter 8 page attributes (top) or PostScript options (bottom).

If your computer has LaserWriter 8 version 8.0 through 8.3.4, you use an Options button instead of a pop-up menu to switch from page attributes to PostScript options. The Page Setup dialog box itself looks different for versions of LaserWriter 8 prior to 8.4, but both variations offer similar options.

Page attribute settings

The LaserWriter 8 Page Setup page attribute settings have the following effects:

❖ **Format for** lets you choose which of your Mac OS desktop printers to format. The pop-up menu lists your desktop printers that use the LaserWriter 8 driver. The setup of the printer you choose here (in particular its PPD file) can affect the page format. This setting is not available prior to version 8.4 of LaserWriter 8.

❖ **Paper** lets you choose a paper size such as US Letter (8½ by 11 inches), US Legal (8½ by 14 inches), and A5 and B5 (European standard sizes). LaserWriter 8 version 8.4 and later have two variations of many sizes, such as US Letter and US Letter Small. The Small variation has a larger unprintable area at the edges of the paper; in earlier LaserWriter 8 drivers you get the same effect by turning off the Larger Print Area option in the PostScript options.

❖ **Layout** lets you choose a number of mini-pages to be printed per sheet of paper. This option is part of the Print command with LaserWriter 8 version 8.4 and later.

❖ **Orientation** determines whether the top of the printed page will be on a short edge or long edge of the paper.

❖ **Scale** (called Reduce or Enlarge with LaserWriter 8 version 8.0 through 8.3.4) reduces or enlarges the printed image according to the percentage you enter. Full size is 100%; the minimum reduction is 25%; and the maximum enlargement is 400%.

PostScript options

LaserWriter 8 Page Setup's PostScript options (called LaserWriter 8 Options with LaserWriter 8 version 8.0 through 8.3.4) have the following effects:

❖ **Flip Horizontal** and **Flip Vertical** create mirror images of your document. You can see the result in the illustration in the dialog box when you click the check box. The Flip Horizontal option flips the image right to left, which is useful if you are creating a film image on a Linotronic imagesetter for a transparency or if the pages have to be emulsion side down. Flipping the image vertically (upside down) has no apparent use because turning the paper around has the same effect.

❖ **Invert Image** makes all the black parts of a page print white, and vice versa. You probably won't have much use for this parlor trick unless you create film negatives on a slide printer that has no method of its own for creating negative images.

❖ **Substitute Fonts** substitutes PostScript fonts for any fixed-sized screen fonts for which no PostScript or TrueType equivalent is available (as described in Chapter 13). For example, Geneva becomes Helvetica, Monaco becomes Courier, and New York becomes Times. The one drawback of font substitution is that although the variable-size font is substituted for its fixed-sized cousin, the spacing of letters and words on a line does not change, and the printed results often are remarkably ugly. For best results, do not use fixed-size fonts that lack TrueType or PostScript equivalents (such as Venice or London), and leave the Font Substitution option off.

❖ **Smooth Text** smoothes the jagged edges of fixed sizes for which there are no matching PostScript fonts or TrueType fonts (such as Venice 14 and London 18). For best results, avoid such fonts, and leave the Text Smoothing option off.

❖ **Smooth Graphics** smoothes the jagged edges of bitmapped graphic images created with painting programs such as MacPaint. Smoothing improves some images but blurs the detail out of others. Try printing with Graphics Smoothing set both ways, and go with the one that looks best to you. Notice that this option has no effect on graphics created with drawing programs such as MacDraw, FreeHand, and Illustrator.

❖ **Precision Bitmap Alignment** reduces the entire printed image to avoid minor distortions in bitmap graphics. The distortions occur because of the nature of the dot density of bitmap graphics. For example, 72 dpi (dots per inch), which is the standard screen-image size, does not divide evenly into 300 dpi, 400 dpi, or 600 dpi (the dot density of laser printers). When you are printing to a 300-dpi printer, for example, turning on this option reduces page images by 4 percent, effectively printing them at 288 dpi (an even multiple of 72 dpi). The reductions align the bitmaps properly to produce crisper output.

❖ **Larger Print Area** (available only with LaserWriter 8 version 8.0 through 8.3.4) lets you reduce the unprintable area at the edges of the paper from one-quarter inch to one-eighth inch on many printers. This option may not work on an old printer that has only a small amount of RAM. This option's function is implicit in the Paper option of page attribute settings in LaserWriter 8 versions 8.4 and later, as described previously.

❖ **Unlimited Downloadable Fonts** allows you to use more fonts than your printer's memory can hold at one time by removing fonts from the printer's memory after they are used, making way for other fonts. You can use this option in conjunction with the Larger Print Area option. Be aware that the constant downloading and flushing of font files takes time and thus slows printing. EPS (Encapsulated PostScript) graphics that use fonts that are not present elsewhere on the page will not print correctly because the printer will substitute Courier for those orphan fonts. If you see Courier in a graphic where you did not want it, make sure that this option is turned off.

Saving custom Page Setup settings

If you don't like the Page Setup settings that LaserWriter 8 versions 8.2 or later uses by default, you can have it use your settings instead. After making your changes in the Page Setup dialog box, press Option while clicking OK to dismiss the dialog box. An alert asks you to confirm whether you want to save the current Page Setup settings as the default settings.

You have to perform this exercise separately in each application that has its own Page Setup settings. You may be able to tell whether a particular application has its own Page Setup settings by looking for the application's name in the pop-up menu at the top left of the Page Setup dialog box. If that pop-up menu doesn't list the current application's name, the application may use the generic Page Setup default settings. Changing the generic Page Setup defaults in one application affects all applications that use them (but doesn't affect applications with their own Page Setup settings).

LaserWriter 8 Print

When you choose the Print command for a printer that uses the LaserWriter 8 driver, you see a dialog box with settings for the number of copies, page numbers to print, paper source, output destination, and more. You can switch among several groups of options by choosing a group from the unlabeled pop-up menu near the top of the dialog box. If your computer has versions 8.0 through 8.3.4, you use an Options button instead of a pop-up menu to bring up a secondary Print Options dialog box.

Figure 15-2 shows the pop-up menu for switching among groups of options in the Print dialog box for LaserWriter 8 version 8.4.3. Figure 15-3 shows the main Print and secondary Print Options dialog boxes for LaserWriter 8 version 8.3.4.

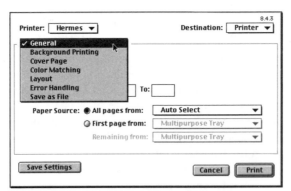

Figure 15-2: Choosing a group of Print options with
LaserWriter 8 versions 8.4 and later.

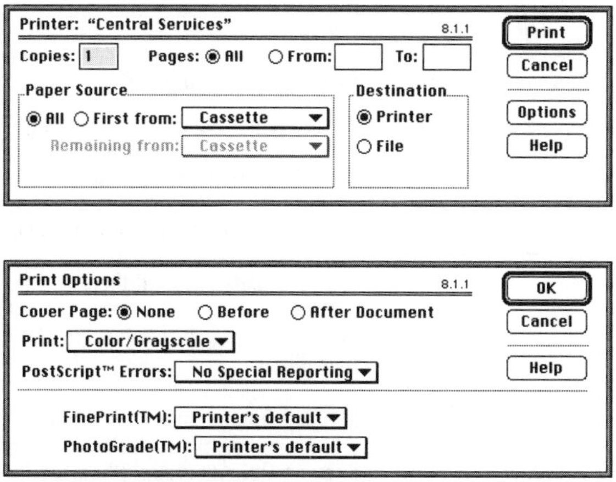

```
Printer: "Central Services"                    8.1.1      [  Print  ]
Copies: [1]        Pages: ⦿ All   ○ From: [    ] To: [    ]   [ Cancel ]
┌─Paper Source──────────────────┐  ┌─Destination─┐
│ ⦿ All ○ First from: [Cassette ▼]│  │ ⦿ Printer   │  [ Options ]
│     Remaining from: [Cassette ▼]│  │ ○ File      │  [  Help  ]
└────────────────────────────────┘  └─────────────┘
```

```
Print Options                                  8.1.1      [   OK   ]
Cover Page: ⦿ None   ○ Before   ○ After Document          [ Cancel ]
Print: [ Color/Grayscale ▼]
PostScript™ Errors: [ No Special Reporting ▼]             [  Help  ]

    FinePrint(TM): [ Printer's default ▼]
  PhotoGrade(TM): [ Printer's default ▼]
```

Figure 15-3: Setting options for printing with LaserWriter 8 versions 8.0 through 8.3.4.

The remainder of this section describes the Print command's options in more detail. The descriptions are organized according to the Print option groups used in LaserWriter 8 version 8.4 and later — all, general, background printing, cover page, color matching, layout, error handling, save as file, imaging options, and printer specific options. Earlier versions of LaserWriter 8 have similar options but organize them differently. For example, in LaserWriter 8 versions 8.0 through 8.3.4, the cover page option is called Print Cover Page and is located in the Print Options dialog box, but in LaserWriter 8 version 8.4 and later, this option is called Cover Page and is located in the Cover Page Group of the Print dialog box.

To help you locate information about Print command options in this section, Table 15-1 cross-references each option in LaserWriter 8 versions earlier than 8.4 with the name of the corresponding LaserWriter 8 version 8.4 group and option.

Table 15-1
LaserWriter 8 Print Options Cross-Reference

Option in versions 8.0–8.3.4 Print dialog box	*Option in version 8.4 Print dialog box*
Copies	General group: Copies
Pages	General group: Pages
Paper Source	General group: Paper Source
Destination	All groups: Destination

(continued)

<table>
<tr><td colspan="2" align="center">Table 15-1 (continued)</td></tr>
<tr><td>Item in versions 8.0–8.3.4 Print Options dialog box</td><td>Option in version 8.4 Print dialog box</td></tr>
<tr><td>Cover Page</td><td>Cover Page group: Print Cover Page</td></tr>
<tr><td>Print</td><td>Color Matching group: Print Color</td></tr>
<tr><td>Printer Profile*</td><td>Color Matching group: Printer Profile</td></tr>
<tr><td>PostScript Errors</td><td>Error Handling group: If there is a PostScript error</td></tr>
<tr><td>Resolution**</td><td>Imaging Options or Printer Specific Options group: Resolution</td></tr>
<tr><td>FinePrint**</td><td>Imaging Options group: FinePrint</td></tr>
<tr><td>PhotoGrade**</td><td>Imaging Options group: PhotoGrade</td></tr>
<tr><td>Tray Switch**</td><td>Error Handling group: If the cassette is out of paper</td></tr>
<tr><td>Paper Type**</td><td>Imaging Options group: Image for Paper Type</td></tr>
<tr><td>Print Quality Mode**</td><td>Imaging Options group: Print Quality Mode</td></tr>
<tr><td>Save**</td><td>All groups: Save Settings</td></tr>
<tr><td>Item in versions 8.0–8.3.4 Save dialog box (for File destination)</td><td>Option in version 8.4 Print dialog box</td></tr>
<tr><td>Format</td><td>Save as File group: Format</td></tr>
<tr><td>(unnamed)</td><td>Save as File group: PostScript Level</td></tr>
<tr><td>(unnamed)</td><td>Save as File group: Data Format</td></tr>
<tr><td>Font Inclusion</td><td>Save as File group: Font Inclusion</td></tr>
<tr><td>Other items in versions 8.0–8.3.4</td><td>Option in version 8.4 Print dialog box</td></tr>
<tr><td>Chooser</td><td>All groups: Printer</td></tr>
<tr><td>Chooser</td><td>Background printing group: Print in</td></tr>
<tr><td>Finder's Printing menu or PrintMonitor's File menu</td><td>Background printing group: Print Time</td></tr>
<tr><td>N/A</td><td>Cover Page group: Cover Page Paper Source</td></tr>
<tr><td>N/A</td><td>Layout group: Layout Direction</td></tr>
<tr><td>N/A</td><td>Layout group: Border</td></tr>
</table>

*versions 8.3–8.3.4 only

**not available on all printers

Options for all groups

No matter which group of options you choose in the Print dialog box for
LaserWriter 8 version 8.4 and later, the following options are always available
at the top and bottom of the dialog box (as previously shown in Figure 15-3):

❖ **Printer** lets you choose which of your Mac OS desktop printers you want to
print your document. The pop-up menu lists your desktop printers that use
the LaserWriter 8 driver. This setting is not available with LaserWriter 8
versions prior to 8.4.

❖ **Destination** specifies whether the driver sends page descriptions to the
chosen printer or to a PostScript file. For a discussion of the latter setting,
see the sidebar "Creating an EPS or PostScript file."

❖ **Save Settings** makes the settings you have made in the Print dialog box the
ones used by default for the currently chosen desktop printer. This option is
not available with Laser Writer 8 versions prior to 8.4.

Creating an EPS or PostScript file

Instead of printing, the Print command can save a document as a PostScript file for later printing on
another system. The Print command also can save one page of a document as an encapsulated
PostScript (EPS) file (like the files saved by Adobe Illustrator and Aldus FreeHand) for placement in a
page-layout program or other program that lets you work with EPS files. This capability is available with
the LaserWriter, LaserWriter 8, or PSPrinter driver.

To create a PostScript file, set the Print command's Destination option to File. The Print button becomes a
Save button, and clicking it brings up a Save dialog box (shown for LaserWriter 8 version 8.4.3 in this
sidebar), in which you name the PostScript file and select the folder where you want to save it.

The Save dialog box includes additional options if you are using LaserWriter 8 versions 8.0 through 8.3.4
(not shown here). With LaserWriter 8 version 8.4 and later, these additional options are part of the Print
dialog box's Save as File group. The options are described in more detail in the nearby section
"LaserWriter 8 Print." (The options are not available with the LaserWriter driver version 7.2 and earlier.)

General group options

When you choose General from the unlabeled pop-up menu near the top of the Print dialog box (LaserWriter 8 version 8.4 and later), the following options are displayed, as shown in Figure 15-4:

❖ **Copies** specifies the number of copies to print.

❖ **Pages** specifies the range of pages to print.

❖ **Paper Source** specifies where the chosen printer should get paper to print your document — multipurpose tray, envelope feeder, paper cassette, manual feed, and so forth. You can choose one paper source for all pages, or a separate source for the first page and for remaining pages.

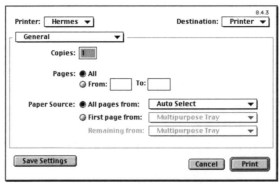

Figure 15-4: Setting General options for the Print command (LaserWriter 8 version 8.4 and later).

Background Printing group options

When you choose Background Printing from the unlabeled pop-up menu near the top of the Print dialog box (LaserWriter 8 version 8.4 and later), the following options are displayed, as shown in Figure 15-5:

❖ **Print in** specifies whether you want your document to print in the foreground or background. Foreground printing requires less disk space than background printing and may cause your document to start printing faster, but does not let you use the computer for anything else until printing stops. Background printing lets you work on other tasks while printing continues, but requires extra disk space for temporary spool (page description) files. (In versions of LaserWriter 8 prior to 8.4, you set background or foreground printing with the Chooser.)

❖ **Print Time** specifies a priority for printing your document in the background — urgent, normal, or hold — or a specific time and day when you want your document printed. You can change this setting for a document waiting to be printed in the background by opening the desktop printer icon as described in "Managing Background Printing" in Chapter 14. The Print Time option is disabled if you set the Print In option for foreground printing, which is always immediate. (This option is not available in versions of LaserWriter 8 prior to 8.4.)

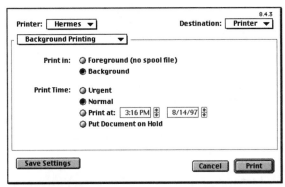

Figure 15-5: Setting Background Printing options for the Print command (LaserWriter 8 version 8.4 and later).

Cover Page group options

When you choose Cover Page from the unlabeled pop-up menu near the top of the Print dialog box (LaserWriter 8 version 8.4 and later), the following options are displayed, as shown in Figure 15-6:

❖ **Print Cover Page** specifies whether to print a cover page before printing your document, after printing your document, or not at all. A cover page reports the document's name, the owner name of the computer that printed it, and when it was printed.

❖ **Cover Page Paper Source** specifies where the chosen printer should get paper to print a cover page. This option is disabled if you set the Print Cover Page option to None. (This option is not available in LaserWriter 8 versions prior to 8.4.)

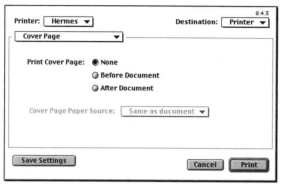

Figure 15-6: Setting Cover Page options for the Print command (LaserWriter 8 version 8.4 and later).

Color Matching group options

When you choose Color Matching from the unlabeled pop-up menu near the top of the Print dialog box (LaserWriter 8 version 8.4 and later), the following options are displayed, as shown in Figure 15-7:

❖ **Print Color** (called Print prior to version 8.4 of LaserWriter 8) lets you choose to print your document in black and white or in color on a color printer or in shades of gray on a monochrome printer. Alternatively, you can choose to have ColorSync or PostScript match printed grays and colors to displayed colors as closely as possible. (Although this option is available in LaserWriter 8 versions prior to 8.4 as the Print option, Apple's ColorSync technology is only available with LaserWriter 8 version 8.3 and later.) The PostScript setting for this option, which is called Calibrated Color/Grayscale prior to version 8.3 of LaserWriter, requires a printer with PostScript Level 2.

❖ **Printer Profile** specifies the color profile to use for color matching. You choose a profile from the pop-up menu, which lists all the appropriate printer profile files in the ColorSync™ Profiles folder (which is in the Preferences folder inside the System Folder). Additionally, if the Print Color setting is PostScript Color Matching, you can choose Printer Default to use the profile currently stored in the printer. The Printer Profile setting is disabled if you set the Print Color option to Black & White or Color/Grayscale. (This option is not available in versions of LaserWriter 8 prior to 8.3.)

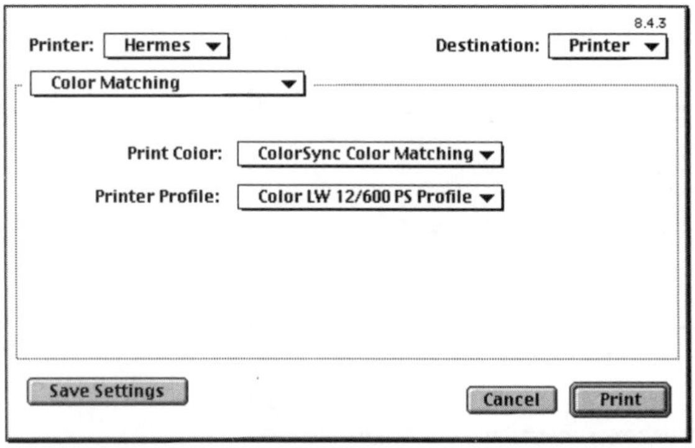

Figure 15-7: Setting Color Matching options for the Print command
(LaserWriter 8 version 8.4 and later).

Layout Group options

When you choose Layout from the unlabeled pop-up menu near the top of the
Print dialog box (LaserWriter 8 version 8.4 and later), the following options
are displayed, as shown in Figure 15-8:

❖ **Pages per sheet** lets you choose a number of mini-pages to print per sheet
of paper. (This option is part of the Page Setup command in versions of
LaserWriter 8 prior to 8.4.)

❖ **Layout Direction** specifies whether to lay out the mini-pages from left to
right or right to left. This option becomes available if you set the Pages Per
Sheet option to more than one mini-page per sheet of paper. (This option is
not available in LaserWriter 8 versions prior to 8.4.)

❖ **Border** lets you choose the type of border line to print around each mini-
page. This option becomes available if you set the Pages Per Sheet option to
more than one mini-page per sheet of paper. (This option is not available in
LaserWriter 8 versions prior to 8.4.)

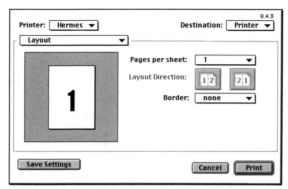

Figure 15-8: Setting Layout options for the Print command
(LaserWriter 8 version 8.4 and later).

Error Handling group options

When you choose Error Handling from the unlabeled pop-up menu near the top of the Print dialog box (LaserWriter 8 version 8.4 and later), one or both of the following options are displayed, as shown in Figure 15-9:

❖ **If there is a PostScript error** specifies how the LaserWriter 8 driver handles PostScript errors: no special error reporting, display a summary of PostScript errors onscreen, or print detailed descriptions of PostScript errors.

❖ **If the cassette is out of paper** specifies what the LaserWriter driver should do if the paper source runs out of paper: either automatically look for the same size paper in another paper tray, or display an alert onscreen. (This option is not available on all types of laser printers and is not available in LaserWriter 8 versions prior to 8.4.)

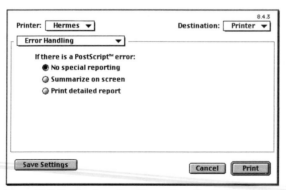

Figure 15-9: Setting Error Handling options for the Print command (LaserWriter 8 version 8.4 and later).

Save as File group options

When you choose Save as File from the unlabeled pop-up menu near the top of the Print dialog box (LaserWriter 8 version 8.4 and later), the following options are displayed, as shown in Figure 15-10:

❖ **Format** specifies the kind of PostScript file to save. Choose PostScript Job to create a standard PostScript file for later printing. Choose one of the three EPS (Encapsulated PostScript) formats to create a one-page graphic for placement in another document. The EPS Mac Standard Preview includes a black-and-white 72-dpi bit-mapped image for previewing onscreen. The EPS Mac Enhanced Preview includes a color PICT preview image, which can be smoothly reduced or enlarged on the screen display. The EPS Mac No Preview takes the least amount of disk space because it has no preview image. Without a preview image, you can't see the file onscreen, but this option prints just like the other EPS formats. (In LaserWriter 8 versions prior to 8.4, this option appears in the Save dialog box.)

❖ **PostScript Level** specifies PostScript compatibility. Choose the Level 1 Compatible option for a file that can be used on printers with PostScript Level 1 or PostScript Level 2. If you are using only PostScript Level 2 printers, choose the Level 2 Only option.

❖ **Data Format** specifies whether to use text characters or binary data in the PostScript file. Choosing the ASCII option creates a more widely compatible PostScript file than the Binary option, but the Binary option can speed printing on a printer that can handle it.

❖ **Font Inclusion** specifies how many fonts to embed in the PostScript file. The None setting, which does not embed any fonts, uses the least disk space but prints correctly only on a system that has all needed fonts. The All option, which embeds every font used in the document, may use a great deal of disk space, but all fonts will print from any system. The All But Standard 13 option embeds all the fonts used except the 13 fonts that commonly are factory-installed in PostScript printers.

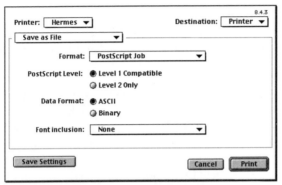

Figure 15-10: Setting Save as File options for the Print command (LaserWriter 8 version 8.4 and later).

Imaging Options group options

When you choose Imaging Options from the unlabeled pop-up menu near the top of the Print dialog box (LaserWriter 8 version 8.4 and later), one or more of the following options are displayed, as shown in Figure 15-11:

❖ **Resolution** specifies the granularity of the printed image in dots or pixels per inch.

❖ **FinePrint,** if on, specifies that the printer should smooth jagged edges of text and graphic objects. Bitmapped images may print better with this option off. This option is only available with printers that have Apple's FinePrint technology.

❖ **PhotoGrade,** if on, specifies that the printer should enhance the shading and contrast of graphics. Text quality may be better with this option off. This option is only available with printers that have Apple's PhotoGrade technology.

❖ **Image for Paper Type** adjusts brightness for the selected type of paper.

The Imaging Options choice does not appear in the pop-up menu if none of these options apply to the current printer.

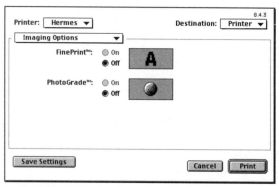

Figure 15-11: Setting imaging options for the Print
command (LaserWriter 8 version 8.4 and later).

Printer Specific Options group options

When you choose Printer Specific Options from the unlabeled pop-up menu
near the top of the Print dialog box (LaserWriter 8 version 8.4 and later),
options that are specific to the current printer appear. For example, a
LaserWriter Pro 630 printer has a Choose Resolution option in the Printer
Specific Options group (rather than a Resolution option in the Imaging
Options group). The Printer Specific Options choice does not appear in the
pop-up menu if the current printer has no special options.

Setting LaserWriter Options

This section describes how to set up and print documents on printers that use
Apple's original LaserWriter printer driver (versions 7.2 and earlier). The
LaserWriter driver has fewer options but is more reliable with older versions of
application programs than the LaserWriter 8 driver described in the preceding
section. Unlike LaserWriter 8, the original LaserWriter does not take
advantage of PostScript Level 2 in printers that have it.

LaserWriter Page Setup

When you choose the Page Setup command for a printer that uses the
LaserWriter driver (versions 7.0 through 7.2), you see a dialog box with
settings for paper size, reduction or enlargement percentage, page orientation,
and printer effects. An Options button gives you access to more printer effects.
Figure 15-12 shows the Page Setup dialog box and the Options dialog box for
LaserWriter version 7.2.

Figure 15-12: Setting LaserWriter 7 page attributes and printer effects (top) and PostScript options (bottom).

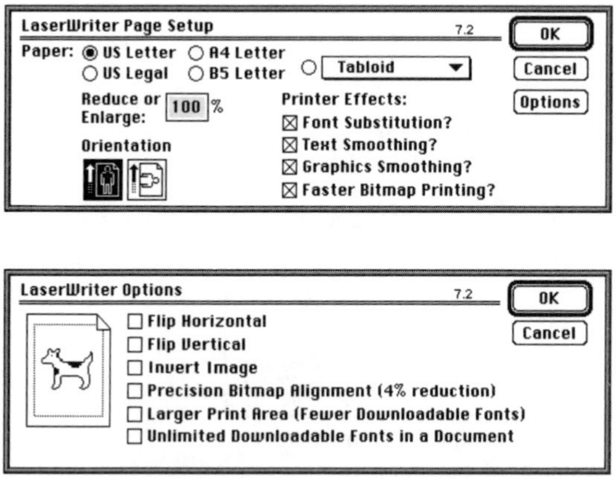

All but one of the settings for LaserWriter driver versions 7.0 through 7.2 are explained fully in the preceding section, "LaserWriter 8 Page Setup." The additional setting is Faster Bitmap Printing, which may speed the printing of bitmapped images, such as those created by a painting program. Paradoxically, setting this option actually slows printing in a few applications. Moreover, most printers made since 1992 are fast enough that you won't notice a difference whether this option is set or not.

LaserWriter Print

When you choose the Print command for a printer that uses the LaserWriter driver version 7.2, you see a dialog box with settings for number of copies, page numbers to print, paper source, and output destination. You can click the Options button to bring up a Print Options dialog box. Figure 15-13 shows the main Print and secondary Print Options dialog boxes for LaserWriter version 7.2.

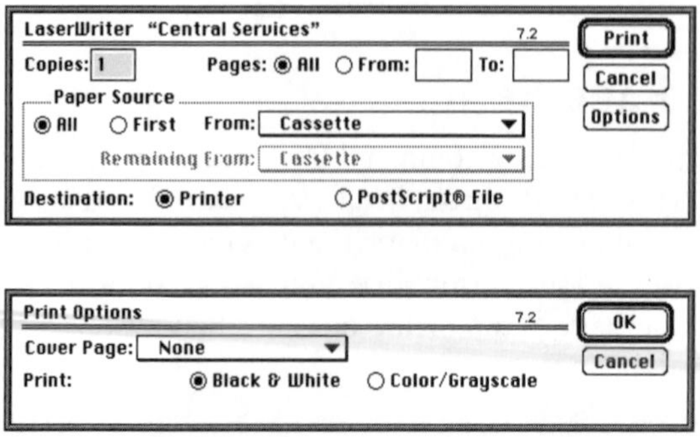

Figure 15-13: Setting Print options with LaserWriter version 7.2.

If your printer has more than one paper source — for example, a multipurpose tray and a paper cassette — you can set all pages to come from one paper source, or you can set the first page (of each copy printed) to come from one source and subsequent pages to come from another source. You choose a paper source from a pop-up menu.

The setting of the Destination option determines whether the LaserWriter 7.2 driver sends page descriptions to the printer or saves them as a PostScript file. If you set the Destination option to PostScript File, the Print button becomes a Save button. Clicking it brings up a Save dialog box, in which you name the PostScript file and select the folder where you want to save the file. Clicking Save in this dialog box creates a file that contains all the PostScript instructions for your document. You then can send the file to a printer by using the LaserWriter Utility. PostScript files are easier to take to service bureaus than actual document files are, because you don't have to worry that the service bureau has the application that created the document.

In the Print Options dialog box, the Cover Page option specifies whether to print a cover page before printing the document, after printing the document, or not at all. A cover page reports the document's name, the owner name of the computer that printed it, and when it was printed. Setting the Print option to Black & White prints colors and shades of gray in black and white. A document that contains colors or shades of gray may print faster when this option is set. Setting the Print option to Color/Grayscale prints colors in a document in color (on a color PostScript printer) or as shades of gray (on a monochrome PostScript printer).

The Print dialog box for versions of the LaserWriter driver earlier than 7.2 contains the same options as the pair of LaserWriter 7.2 dialog boxes, but it looks different. Figure 15-14 shows the Print dialog box for LaserWriter version 7.1.2.

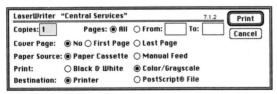

Figure 15-14: Setting Print options with LaserWriter version 7.1.2 and earlier.

Setting Color StyleWriter Options

This section describes how to set up and print documents on printers that use Apple's various Color StyleWriter drivers, including the Color StyleWriter 2500, Color StyleWriter 2400, Color StyleWriter 2200, Color StyleWriter 1500, and Color StyleWriter Pro drivers. In addition, the monochrome StyleWriter 1200, StyleWriter II, and original StyleWriter can use the Color StyleWriter 1500 driver.

Color StyleWriter Page Setup

When you choose the Page Setup command for a printer that uses a Color StyleWriter driver — either the Color StyleWriter 1500, Color StyleWriter 2500, Color StyleWriter 2200, or Color StyleWriter Pro driver — you see a dialog box with settings for page size, scaling, and page orientation. On all but the Color StyleWriter Pro drivers, the dialog box also includes layout and borders options. In addition, a Watermark button in the Color StyleWriter 1500, 2200, and 2500 dialog boxes lets you select a graphic to be printed lightly "behind" the main page image, like a watermark. Figure 15-15 shows the Page Setup dialog box and the Watermark dialog box for Color StyleWriter 2500.

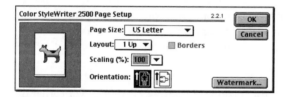

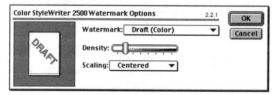

Figure 15-15: Setting Color StyleWriter page attributes (top) and watermark options (bottom).

Page attribute settings

The Color StyleWriter Page Setup's page attribute settings have the following effects:

❖ **Page Size** lets you choose a paper size such as US Letter (8½ by 11 inches), US Legal (8½ by 14 inches), and #10 Envelope.

❖ **Layout** (not present with Color StyleWriter Pro) lets you choose a number of mini-pages to be printed per sheet of paper.

❖ **Borders** (not present with Color StyleWriter Pro) controls printing of borders around mini-pages. This option becomes available if you set the Layout option to print more than one mini-page per sheet of paper.

❖ **Scaling** reduces or enlarges the printed image according to the percentage you enter. You can either type a percentage or choose one from the pop-up menu. Full size is 100%; the minimum reduction is 5%; and the maximum enlargement is 999%.

❖ **Orientation** determines whether the top of the printed page will be on a short edge or long edge of the paper.

Watermark options

The Color StyleWriter Page Setup's Watermark options have the following effects:

❖ **Watermark** specifies the graphic to be printed as a watermark. You choose one of the graphics listed in the Watermark pop-up menu, and a thumbnail preview of the watermark you chose appears in the dialog box. (You choose None if you no longer want a watermark.) The pop-up menu lists all graphics files of type PICT contained in the Printing Prefs folder, which is in the Preferences folder inside the System Folder. You can move files in and out of that folder with the Finder. In addition, you can create and edit watermark images with graphics programs such as ClarisWorks, Claris Impact, Adobe Photoshop, and Macromedia FreeHand. If a watermark file contains text, make sure the fonts it uses are installed in your Fonts folder so the text looks its best.

❖ **Density** adjusts the darkness of the watermark image. The thumbnail preview of the watermark image does not reflect changes to the Density setting.

❖ **Scaling** adjusts the size and placement of the watermark image on the page. You set this option by choosing from the Scaling pop-up menu. Your choices include

- **Centered** resizes the watermark to fill the center of the page without changing the watermark's original proportions.

- **Align Top Left** places the watermark in its original size at the upper left corner of the page.

- **Stretch to Fit** resizes the watermark to fill the page from top to bottom and side to side even if the watermark's proportions change.

Color StyleWriter Print

When you choose the Print command for a printer that uses a Color StyleWriter driver — either the Color StyleWriter 1500, Color StyleWriter 2500, Color StyleWriter 2200, or Color StyleWriter Pro driver — you see a dialog box with settings for number of copies, page numbers to print, print quality, and more. A Color button lets you specify a color blending method and an optional color matching method. A Utilities button lets you specify that you want the printer to clean the ink cartridge or perform other available self-maintenance. Figure 15-16 shows the main and secondary Print dialog boxes for Color StyleWriter 2500.

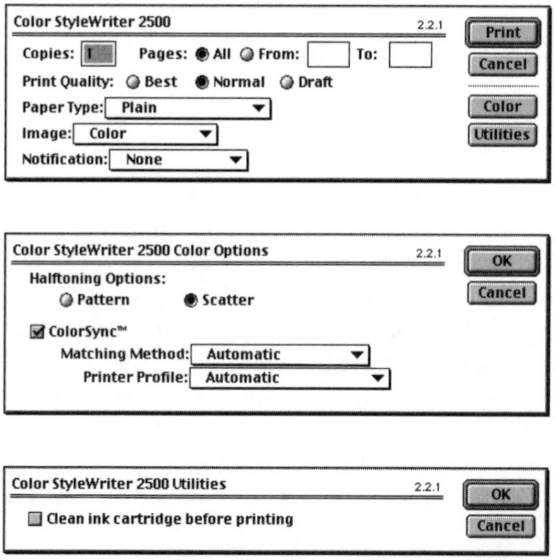

Figure 15-16: Setting options for Color StyleWriter printing (top), color printing (middle), and printer utilities (bottom).

Main print options

The Print dialog box for a Color StyleWriter has the following main options:

❖ **Copies** specifies the number of copies to print.

❖ **Pages** specifies the range of pages to print.

❖ **Print Quality** offers a trade-off between appearance and speed, with Best quality the slowest and best-looking.

❖ **Paper Type** adjusts the printer for the selected type of paper.

❖ **Image** lets you choose the amount of color appropriate for your document. For color graphics or photos, choose Color or Grayscale. For text or line drawings without color or shades of gray, choose Black & White.

❖ **Notification** specifies a sound or message that notifies you when your document finishes printing. You can choose any available system alert sound. (You can add or remove alert sounds with the SimpleSound program, which is described in "Accessory Program Encyclopedia" in Chapter 11.)

Color options

The Color Options dialog box for a Color StyleWriter, which you see when you click the Color button in the Print dialog box, has the following options:

❖ **Halftoning Options** specifies whether to blend colors and gray tones using a pattern of dots or a random scattering of dots.

❖ **ColorSync,** if on, specifies that Apple's ColorSync match printed colors to displayed colors as closely as possible. This option is disabled unless the ColorSync software is installed and you set the Image option in the main Print dialog box to Color.

❖ **Matching Method** lets you choose the color matching method that's best for the content of your document. The Photographic method reduces color saturation, and the Business Graphics method increases color saturation. The Automatic method picks the Photographic method if the page contains mostly bitmapped images or the Business Graphics method if the page contains mostly graphic objects.

❖ **Printer Profile** specifies the color profile to use for color matching. You choose a profile from the pop-up menu, which lists all the appropriate printer profile files in the ColorSync™ Profiles folder (which is in the Preferences folder inside the System Folder). This option is disabled unless the ColorSync option is turned on.

Utilities options

The Utilities dialog box for a Color StyleWriter, which you see when you click the Utilities button in the Print dialog box, has one or more options for cleaning the ink cartridge before printing. With the Color StyleWriter Pro driver, there are also options for preparing a new print head and checking the printer alignment.

Setting StyleWriter Options

This section describes how to set up and print documents on printers using Apple's drivers for monochrome StyleWriters, specifically the StyleWriter 1200, StyleWriter II, and original StyleWriter drivers.

StyleWriter Page Setup

When you choose the Page Setup command for a printer that uses a black-and-white StyleWriter driver — either the StyleWriter 1200, StyleWriter II, or original StyleWriter driver — you see a dialog box with settings for page size, scaling, and page orientation. The Style Writer 1200 driver dialog box also has layout and borders options as well as a Watermark button that lets you select a graphic to be printed lightly "behind" the main page image. (The StyleWriters do not have any visual effect or printer options.) Figure 15-17 shows the Page Setup dialog box and the Watermark dialog box for StyleWriter 1200.

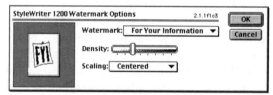

Figure 15-17: Setting StyleWriter page attributes (top) and watermark options (bottom).

All the Page Setup settings for the StyleWriter drivers are explained fully in the preceding section, "Color StyleWriter Page Setup."

StyleWriter Print

When you choose the Print command for a printer that uses a black-and-white StyleWriter driver — either the StyleWriter 1200, StyleWriter II, or original StyleWriter driver — you see a dialog box with settings for number of copies, page numbers to print, print quality, and more. An Options button (not available with the original StyleWriter) lets you specify other options. Figure 15-18 shows the main Print dialog box and the Print Options dialog box for StyleWriter 1200.

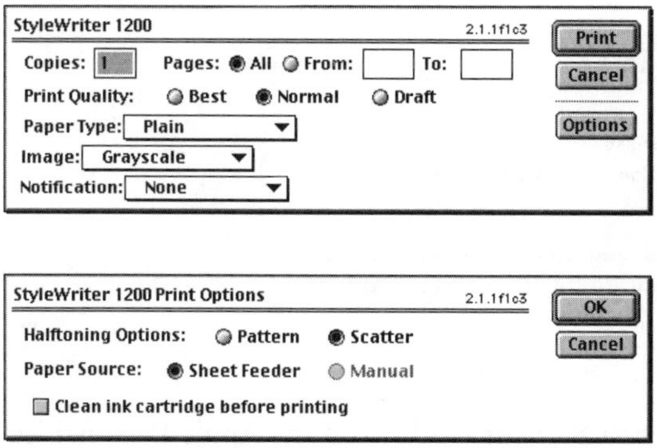

StyleWriter 1200	2.1.1f1c3	Print / Cancel / Options

Copies: 1   Pages: ● All ○ From: [ ] To: [ ]
Print Quality: ○ Best ● Normal ○ Draft
Paper Type: Plain ▼
Image: Grayscale ▼
Notification: None ▼

StyleWriter 1200 Print Options   2.1.1f1c3   OK / Cancel
Halftoning Options: ○ Pattern ● Scatter
Paper Source: ● Sheet Feeder ○ Manual
☐ Clean ink cartridge before printing

Figure 15-18: Setting Print options with StyleWriter 1200.

The Print options for the black-and-white StyleWriter drivers are similar to the options for Color StyleWriter drivers. For descriptions of the options, see the preceding section "Color StyleWriter Print."

Setting LaserWriter 300/LS Options

This section describes how to set up and print documents on printers that use Apple's LaserWriter 300/LS series of drivers. These drivers are for Apple laser printers that don't have PostScript and don't connect to a network, including the LaserWriter 300 and Personal LaserWriter LS.

LaserWriter 300/LS Page Setup

When you choose the Page Setup command for a printer that uses a LaserWriter 300 or Personal LaserWriter LS driver, you see a dialog box with settings for page size, scaling, and page orientation. An Options button gives you access to printer effects. Figure 15-19 shows the Page Setup dialog box and the Options dialog box for LaserWriter 300.

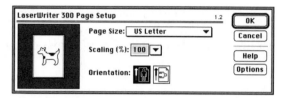

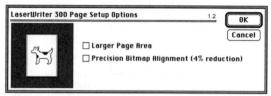

Figure 15-19: Setting LaserWriter 300/LS page attributes (top) and printer effects (bottom).

The LaserWriter 300/LS driver works with the Apple Personal LaserWriter 300 and Personal LaserWriter LS printers. These printers do not prepare their own page images based on PostScript descriptions sent by the printer driver. Instead, the LaserWriter 300/LS driver prepares page images based on QuickDraw graphics that are built into every Mac OS computer.

Page attribute settings

LaserWriter 300/LS Page Setup's page attribute settings have the following effects:

❖ **Page Size** lets you choose a paper size such as US Letter (8½ by 11 inches), US Legal (8½ by 14 inches), and #10 Envelope.

❖ **Scaling** reduces or enlarges the printed image according to the percentage you enter. You can either type a percentage or choose one from the pop-up menu. Full size is 100%; the minimum reduction is 5%; and the maximum enlargement is 999%.

❖ **Orientation** determines whether the top of the printed page will be on a short edge or long edge of the paper.

Page Setup options

LaserWriter 300/LS's Page Setup options have the following effects:

❖ **Larger Page Area** lets you print closer to the edges of legal-size paper.

❖ **Precision Bitmap Alignment** reduces the entire printed image to avoid minor distortions in bitmap graphics. The distortions occur because of the nature of the dot density of bitmap graphics. For example, 72 dpi (dots per inch), which is the standard screen-image size, does not divide evenly into 300 dpi (the dot density of laser printers that use the LaserWriter 300/LS driver). Turning on this option reduces page images by 4 percent, effectively printing them at 288 dpi (an even multiple of 72 dpi). The reductions align the bitmaps properly to produce crisper output.

LaserWriter 300/LS Print

When you choose the Page Setup command for a printer that uses the LaserWriter 300/LS driver, you see a dialog box with settings for number of copies, page numbers to print, paper source, and more. You can click the Options button to bring up a Print Options dialog box. Figure 15-20 shows the main Print and secondary Print Options dialog boxes for LaserWriter 300.

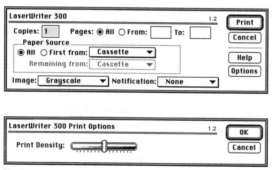

Figure 15-20: Setting Print options with LaserWriter 300.

In the main Print dialog box, you can set all pages to come from one paper source — paper cassette or manual-feed tray — or you can set the first page to come from one source and the remaining pages to come from another source. The LaserWriter 300 and Personal LaserWriter LS drivers are not for PostScript printers, and neither driver can save page descriptions as a PostScript file.

The Image option lets you choose Grayscale for printing shades of gray, Black & White for fastest printing, or PhotoGrade (if the current printer is equipped with it) for enhanced grays. The Notification option specifies a sound or message that notifies you when your document finishes printing. You can choose any available system alert sound. (You can add or remove alert sounds with the SimpleSound program, which is described in "Accessory Program Encyclopedia" in Chapter 11.)

In the Print Options dialog box you can set the print by adjusting a slider. Moving the slider to the left makes printing lighter, thereby saving toner. Moving it to the right makes printing darker and uses extra toner.

Setting ImageWriter Options

This section describes how to set up and print documents on printers that use Apple's ImageWriter drivers, including the ImageWriter I and II.

ImageWriter Page Setup

When you choose the Page Setup command for an ImageWriter II or original ImageWriter printer, you see a dialog box with settings for paper size, orientation, and special effects. Figure 15-21 shows the Page Setup dialog box for ImageWriter.

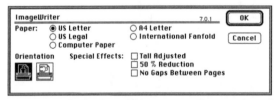

Figure 15-21: Setting ImageWriter page attributes and special effects.

The ImageWriter Page Setup options have the following effects:

❖ **Page Size** lets you choose a paper size: single sheets of US Letter (8½ by 11 inches), US Legal (8½ by 14 inches), or A4 Letter (8½ by 11⅔ inches); or continuous, sprocket-fed International Fanfold (8¼ by 11 inches).

❖ **Orientation** determines whether the top of the printed page will be on a short edge or long edge of the paper.

❖ **Tall Adjusted** correctly proportions graphics or text. Turning on this option prints graphics with correct proportions but widens individual text characters. Turning off this option prints text with correct proportions but elongates graphics.

❖ **50% Reduction** prints page images half their actual size.

❖ **No Gaps Between Pages** eliminates top and bottom margins, primarily for printing continuously on fanfold paper.

ImageWriter Print

When you choose the Print command for an ImageWriter II or original ImageWriter printer, you see a dialog box with settings for print quality, page numbers to print, number of copies, and paper source. Figure 15-22 shows the Print dialog box for ImageWriter.

```
ImageWriter                              7.0.1      [ Print ]
Quality:      ○ Best      ⦿ Faster    ○ Draft
Page Range:   ⦿ All       ○ From: [     ] To: [     ]   [ Cancel ]
Copies:       [ 1 ]
Paper Feed:   ⦿ Automatic  ○ Hand Feed
```

Figure 15-22: Setting ImageWriter Print options.

QUICK TIPS

Hints for Better ImageWriter Printing

If pictures printed on an ImageWriter look vertically stretched, as though El Greco had drawn them, choose the Page Setup command's Tall Adjusted option. This option adjusts the computer output from 72 dpi to the 80-dpi vertical resolution of the printer, thus generating a proportional image.

To avoid the irregular word spacing that occurs in draft mode, change your document's font to a monospaced font, such as Monaco or Courier, for printing out a draft. The fixed-spaced font on the screen then will match the spacing of the printer's internal font, making the draft easier to read. Change your document to a more professional variable-sized font, such as Helvetica or Times, when you are ready to print your final copy.

Always install fonts in pairs — 9 point with 18 point, 10 point with 20 point, and so on — so that the Font Manager portion of the system software has the larger font available for scaling in Best mode. The best way to avoid spacing problems is to use TrueType fonts (or PostScript fonts and Adobe Type Manager software) and let the computer do the scaling for you.

A very clear font for use with the ImageWriter family is Boston II, a shareware font that is available from user groups and online information services.

Best quality looks clearest with a slightly used printer ribbon, not with a brand-new ribbon, because there is less smudging of characters due to high levels of ink on the ribbon.

Do not stockpile ribbons for an ImageWriter; buy them one or two at a time. The ink in the ribbons dries out over time.

Choosing the Best quality option prints your document at 144 dpi, which is twice the screen resolution. Best quality is slower than Faster quality, which prints at 72 dpi. Draft quality prints text only (no pictures) with a font built into the printer. The built-in font's spacing matches the spacing of Monaco 10 and other 10-point monospaced fonts. Printing proportionally spaced fonts in Draft quality results in poorly spaced letters and words that may be hard to read.

Summary

This chapter described how you print a document in almost any application — with the Page Setup and Print commands. You use the same commands for all printers, but the options available in the Print and Page Setup dialog boxes depend on the printer driver for the printer. This chapter detailed the Page Setup and Print options for printers that use the following drivers:

❖ LaserWriter 8

❖ LaserWriter versions 7.2 and earlier

❖ Color StyleWriter 2500, 2400, 2200, and 1500; and Color StyleWriter Pro

❖ StyleWriter 1200, StyleWriter II, and the original StyleWriter

❖ LaserWriter 300/LS

❖ ImageWriter

Manage Your Memory

If you never open more than one program at a time and don't care about your computer's performance or effectiveness (not to mention your own), you can ignore the topic of memory management. But to get the most from your computer, you must pay attention to how you use its memory.

This chapter explains how to find out the amount of memory each open program is using. It tells you how to adjust the amount of memory your application programs use, and how to reduce the amount of memory the system software uses. This chapter also describes several ways to increase the amount of memory available for opening programs.

Gauging Memory Use

Computers use memory like a large company might use office space (though on a very different time scale). Just as each department needs office space, each computer program needs a memory partition. Departments come in all sizes, and so do computer programs. Over the years a company may eliminate some departments and use their space for new ones. Similar events take place on a computer but in a much shorter time. In a matter of hours you may quit some programs and use their memory space to open others. Figure 16-1 diagrams how programs share a computer's memory space at one point in time.

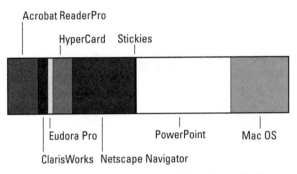

Figure 16-1: Each open program gets a piece of your Mac's memory.

To use your computer's memory most effectively, you need to know the total memory available, which programs are open, how much memory they use, and how much memory is currently unused. You also need to know roughly how much memory each of your programs uses, because you may have to quit one or more open programs to make space for another one that you want to open.

Memory Compared with Hard Disk Space

Note that memory management does not involve disk space. The amount of disk space reported available at the top of your hard disk's window indicates how much space you have to store programs and documents when they are not open. When you open a program, the system software allocates some memory space for the program, copies part of the program into that memory space from disk, and starts running the part copied into memory. Programs usually require much less memory space than they do disk space because the entire program file is not generally loaded into memory all at once. Rather, a program's memory space contains just the portion of the program that you need now.

About This Computer

For information on the condition of your Mac's memory, switch to the Finder and choose About This Computer (Mac OS 7.6 and later) or About This Macintosh (System 7.5.5 and earlier) from the Apple menu. The Finder displays a window that reports the total amount of memory installed in your computer and the largest amount available for opening another program. It also graphs the amount allocated to and currently used by the system software and each open program. Figure 16-2 shows an example of the About This Computer window in Mac OS 8.

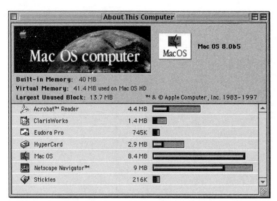

Figure 16-2: Gauging memory usage in the About This Computer window.

To learn the exact amount the system software or an open program is using at the moment, turn on Balloon Help and point at the item's memory-use bar in the About This Computer or About This Macintosh window.

Notice that the About This Computer or About This Macintosh window reports the size of the largest unused block of memory. There may be other unused blocks as well, each smaller than the largest block. This condition, known as *fragmented memory*, can make it difficult to open a large program. You'll find techniques for recognizing fragmented memory and dealing with it in "Adjusting Application Memory Use" later in this chapter.

What's more, the system may not report every bit of memory that's in use. For example, built-in video uses 40K to 600K on various computer models but some versions of the Finder do not include that amount in the system software size. There may be an additional discrepancy of several K (kilobytes) due to rounding errors.

Memory mapping utilities

For a more precise report of memory use than you get from the Finder's About This Computer or About This Macintosh command, use a utility such as Memory Mapper from Street Logic Software (http://www2.connectnet.com/~stlogic/). It shows you not only how much memory each open application uses, but where the applications are in relation to each other and to blocks of unused memory.

Figure 16-3 shows an example of Memory Mapper's window, although the graph it displays is color-coded to the list of programs and is much easier to decipher on a color monitor than in this black-and-white reproduction.

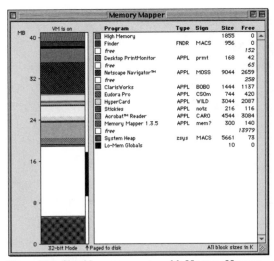

Figure 16-3: Checking memory use with Memory Mapper.

You don't see one number for system software size in the Memory Mapper window. Instead of reporting an aggregate amount as in the About This Computer or About This Macintosh window, Memory Mapper breaks out system software memory use into several individual items, including

❖ **High Memory**, which is used for video, sound, and disk cache

❖ **Finder**

❖ **Desktop PrintMonitor, File Sharing, QuickTime, Speech Recognition,** and other system extensions that are actually programs open in the background

❖ **System Heap**, which is used for fonts, icons, sounds, and other system resources

❖ **Low Memory Globals**, which is used for many system parameters

Adjusting Application Memory Use

Each program you open gets a section of memory called a memory *partition* for its exclusive use. This section tells you how to change the size of an application's memory partition with the Finder's Get Info command, increasing the partition size to help the application perform better or decreasing the size so you can open additional programs. This section also tells you how to avoid fragmenting unused memory as you quit some programs to free up memory for opening others, and how to fix memory fragmentation if it does happen.

Application memory size

You can change how much memory an application program gets by setting the memory sizes in its Info window, which the Finder's Get Info command displays, or with the AppSizer utility program (described in Chapter 24). You must quit an open application before changing its memory size setting. If an application is open, its Info window shows the memory size settings but won't let you change them. You can't ever change the memory size of some kinds of programs, such as desk accessories. If a program's size is permanently set, its Info window doesn't show any memory sizes. Figure 16-4 shows a sample Info window of an application that is not open.

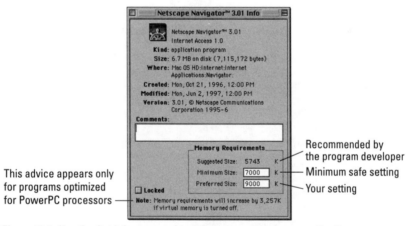

Figure 16-4: Use the Get Info command to set memory sizes for an application.

Suggested, Minimum, and Preferred sizes

An application's Info window shows three memory sizes: Suggested, Minimum, and Preferred. The system won't open a program unless there is a block of available memory at least as large as the Minimum size. The system allocates more memory, if available, but never more than the Preferred size. The Suggested size, which you can't change, is the amount of memory the program's developer recommends for standard program performance.

Setting the Preferred size higher than the Suggested size may improve performance or enable you to open more documents or larger documents. Setting the Preferred size below the suggested size usually has the opposite effect. For example, setting HyperCard's Preferred size below the Suggested size reduces the number of stacks you can have open simultaneously, limits your access to painting tools and scripting, and prevents opening some stacks altogether.

Some programs require more memory with Mac OS 8 than earlier versions of the system software. If a program refuses to open after you upgrade to Mac OS 8, try increasing its minimum memory size by 200K to 300K and opening it again.

CAUTION

Going Below the Minimum

Every application has a memory size that's not listed in its Info window. This fourth memory size, which is set by the program developer, specifies the least amount of memory in which a program will work without crashing. Most programs use this safe minimum size for the initial setting of the Minimum size in the Info window. Setting the Minimum size lower than the safe minimum may cause the program to crash. For example, HyperCard 2.3 does not work properly if you set its Minimum size below Apple's recommended minimum of 800K. The Finder warns you when you close an Info window if you have set the Minimum size lower than the safe minimum recommended by the developer.

You can see the safe minimum size with a resource editing program such as Apple's ResEdit, which is available from Apple's software library (http://www.info.apple.com). Use the resource editor to open the application's SIZE -1 resource. The minimum size listed there is the application's safe minimum size in bytes; divide by 1024 for the size in K (kilobytes).

PowerPC memory sizes

A note at the bottom of some Info windows advises you that turning on virtual memory changes the memory requirements. This note appears only in the Info window of a program that is optimized for the PowerPC processor. This type of program requires less memory when virtual memory is turned on or the RAM Doubler utility software is installed and turned on (as described in the section "Increasing Total Memory" later in this chapter).

Memory fragmentation

As you open and quit a series of programs, the unused portion of your computer's memory tends to become fragmented into several noncontiguous blocks. You may find yourself unable to open a program because it needs a memory partition bigger than the biggest unused block (the Largest Unused Block amount displayed in the About This Computer or About This Macintosh window). The total of all unused blocks may be large enough to open the program, but the Mac system software cannot consolidate fragmented memory nor open a program in multiple blocks of memory. It's like looking for a parallel parking space on a street with several half-spaces between parked cars. A Hyundai wouldn't fit in any of the spaces, but if you could put them together you'd have enough room to park a truck. Figure 16-5 illustrates fragmented memory.

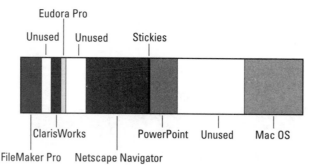

Figure 16-5: Opening and quitting programs haphazardly may fragment unused memory.

Is Your Computer Fragmented?

To check for memory fragmentation, add up the memory sizes of all the open programs and the system software as listed in the About This Computer or About This Macintosh window, and subtract the total from the total memory reported there. Also subtract 300K to 600K (depending on monitor resolution and number of colors) if your computer doesn't have VRAM (video RAM). In this case, your computer uses its main RAM, sometimes called DRAM (dynamic RAM), for the screen image. Examples of Macs that do this include a Power Mac 6100, 7100, or 8100 with a monitor connected to the system board video port. If the number you come up with is substantially less than the largest unused block, your unused memory is probably fragmented into two or more blocks.

Avoiding fragmented memory

You can avoid memory fragmentation by planning the order in which you open and quit programs. First open the programs you're least likely to quit, and then open the programs that are the most expendable in your work session, starting with the most important of them and finishing with the least important. When you need more memory to open another program, quit the most recently opened program. If that doesn't free enough memory, quit the next most recently opened program, and so on. This method frees up a contiguous block of memory. Quitting programs helter-skelter leads to memory fragmentation.

The Finder sometimes hastens memory fragmentation in low-memory situations. If you try to open an application that needs more memory than is available, the Finder suggests quitting all programs with no open windows — or the largest open program, if all have open windows. Accepting the Finder's suggestion can fragment memory. To avoid memory fragmentation, you must quit programs in the reverse of the order in which they were opened.

Hidden Sources of Fragmentation

Sometimes quitting all open applications does not cure memory fragmentation. With Open Transport 1.1, a standard part of Systems 7.5.3 and 7.5.5, memory can become fragmented if the TCP/IP control panel's "Load only when needed" option is turned on, as it is by default. With that option turned on, Open Transport 1.1 allocates a block of memory for TCP/IP networking right after you open the first TCP/IP application (such as a Web browser or e-mail program). If you later quit the TCP/IP application and all other applications you have opened, memory may remain fragmented by the block of memory allocated for TCP/IP networking. Open Transport 1.1 releases the block of memory allocated for TCP/IP networking after about two minutes of no TCP/IP activity, except that Open Transport 1.1 never releases the TCP/IP memory with some types of PPP (dial-up) connections. Once the TCP/IP memory is released, you can quit all open applications to clear up fragmented memory.

Open Transport 1.1.1 and later does not fragment memory on PowerPC Macs. With other Macs and Open Transport 1.1, the best way to avoid memory fragmentation is to turn off the "Load only when needed" option. Mac OS 8 comes with Open Transport 1.2; Mac OS 7.6 comes with Open Transport 1.1.1; and the latest version is available from Apple's software library (http://www.info.apple.com).

Fixing fragmented memory

To consolidate fragmented memory, quit all open programs and then open them again. This method isn't completely foolproof. You may have a program that doesn't release all of its memory when you quit it. This error is called a *memory leak*. A program that makes use of shared library extensions may also leave memory fragmented after you quit it, in this case because the shared library continues to occupy memory after the program has quit. Restarting your computer fixes fragmentation and may reduce the amount of memory used by system software as well.

If you don't want to restart or even quit all open applications, you can use the Memory Mapper utility to identify which applications are open between blocks of unused memory, and quit only those applications to consolidate memory. You can actually send a Quit message from Memory Mapper to any open program. To do that, select the program in Memory Mapper's window and choose Send Quit Event from the File menu.

Adjusting System Memory Use

The system software gives itself a big memory partition when you start up your computer, as you can see by looking at the length of the bar labeled System Software or Mac OS in the About This Computer or About This Macintosh window. This section explains how you can reduce the size of system software by disabling marginally useful system extensions and control panels, turning off expendable system options, reducing the disk cache, and reducing or eliminating a RAM disk.

Minimum system size

Just how small can the system software be? You can reduce the system software's memory size to its minimum by pressing Shift while restarting your computer. Look for the message "Extensions Off" during startup. It confirms that you have suppressed loading of all items in the Extensions folder, Control Panels folder, and System Folder that would increase the system software's memory size. You have also bypassed opening items in the Startup Items folder, reduced the disk cache to 16K, forced virtual memory off, and prevented file sharing from starting.

None of these changes persist when you restart without pressing Shift. To make changes stick, you must remove items from the special folders and change settings in the Memory and other control panels.

Startup items

Many of those lovely little icons that march across your screen during startup are chewing up memory as they go. They're not alone. Lots of other startup software that doesn't display icons also increases the system software memory partition.

Many items identified as system extensions in a list view of the Extensions folder or System Folder increase the system software's memory size during startup. So do some other types of items besides extensions. But some items in the Extensions folder do not increase memory size. Chooser extensions for printers (LaserWriter, StyleWriter, ImageWriter, and so on), communications tools, MNPLinkTool documents, Finder Help, or the PrintMonitor application fall in this category.

Control panels that display an icon at the bottom of the screen during startup (or offer the option of doing so) have system extensions built in and most of them increase the system software's memory size. Control panels that don't display startup icons generally don't increase system software's memory size, though there are exceptions such as Easy Access.

The easiest way to manage extensions and control panels is with the Extensions Manager control panel (see "Control Panels Encyclopedia" in Chapter 10). There are also commercial alternatives that provide more information and control than Extensions Manager. For example, Conflict Catcher 4 from Casady & Greene, Inc. (408-484-9228, http://www.casadyg.com) tells you how much memory each startup item uses.

The key to adjusting memory size is to compare your system software's memory size before and after removing an item and weigh the potential memory savings against the benefit the item provides. It's a trial-and-error process unless you have Conflict Catcher or another utility that can determine the memory sizes of startup items.

Note that you have to restart the computer to see the effect of removing startup items.

Expendable options

You can reduce the system software size by turning off a handful of system options that you might not be using. For example, if you're not using file sharing, you can recover 200K to 300K by turning it off in the File Sharing control panel (Mac OS 8 and later) or the Sharing Setup Control panel (Mac OS 7.6.1 and earlier). If you're not using speech recognition for a while, turn it off in the Speech control panel or the Speech Setup control panel (depending on the version of speech recognition installed on your computer). You can also save some memory by turning off AppleTalk in the Chooser.

Disk cache

A portion of the system software's memory partition always goes to the disk cache, which improves system performance by storing recently used information from the disk in memory. When the information is needed again, it can be copied from memory instead of from disk. Copying from memory is much faster than copying from disk.

You can use the Memory control panel to adjust the amount of memory allocated for the disk cache. Be aware that setting the disk cache very low will degrade performance in many applications, particularly the Mac OS 8 Finder. The usual rule of thumb is to set the disk cache to 32K times the number of megabytes of RAM (random-access memory) in your computer. Virtual memory and RAM Doubler don't count in this calculation. For example, if your computer has 32MB of RAM, try setting the disk cache to 1024K. Figure 16-6 shows an example of the disk cache setting in the Memory control panel.

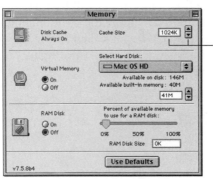

Enter a number or click the arrows

Figure 16-6: Setting the disk cache size.

QUICK TIPS

Disk Cache and IIsi or IIci Performance

If you have a Mac IIsi and you set the number of colors or grays for a monitor attached to the back-panel video port to four or more, you can improve system performance by setting the disk cache to 768K. Then the disk cache and the built-in video circuitry together use up all the memory that's soldered to the main

(continued)

(continued)

circuit board. This forces the system software and your programs into the part of memory in the four SIMM sockets, which may help the programs run much faster than they would if they shared the soldered-on memory with the built-in video circuitry. The same trick works on a Mac IIci with 5MB, 9MB, or 17MB of RAM. To get the performance boost, the 256K SIMMs must be installed in the four sockets nearest the disk drive. (Realizing a performance increase on a IIci with other RAM capacities is not feasible because you would have to set the disk cache so high that it would waste a large amount of memory.)

RAM disk

A RAM disk uses part of RAM as if it were a hard disk. The RAM disk has an icon that appears on the desktop, and you manipulate folders and files on a RAM disk the same as any other disk. A RAM disk works much faster than a hard disk, but only stores items temporarily. The RAM disk feature is not available on all computers. If it is available on your computer, your Memory control panel will have settings for it. The settings will be dimmed if your computer does not have enough unused memory for the minimum RAM disk size or if your computer has less than 6MB of installed RAM. The minimum size for a RAM disk, starting with System 7.5.3, is 416K. Figure 16-7 shows the RAM disk settings in the Memory control panel.

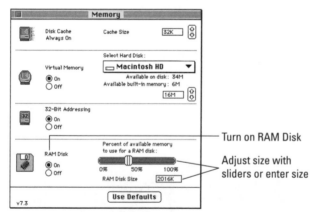

Figure 16-7: Setting up a RAM disk.

The contents of a RAM disk are preserved when you restart most computers, including all PowerBook models. This is true even if you use the emergency restart keys (⌘-Control-power button) or the Reset button.

RAM Disk Not Permanent

You lose the contents of a RAM disk when you shut down the computer unless your computer has Apple's Assistant Toolbox installed. The Assistant Toolbox saves the RAM disk's contents in a file in the Preferences folder and uses that to restore the RAM disk the next time you start up. You also lose the contents of a RAM disk after a power failure, although if you have the Assistant Toolbox installed it will restore the RAM disk to its state the last time you shut down.

Because a RAM disk's contents can easily be lost, you should observe these precautions:

❖ Don't store a file exclusively on a RAM disk. Copy documents from RAM disk to another disk frequently.

❖ Copy files from the RAM disk to another disk before shutting down.

❖ Don't use a program for the first time on a RAM disk. Test it on another disk first.

To resize or remove a RAM disk, first copy the files you want to save from it to another disk. Then drag everything from the RAM disk to the Trash and empty the Trash. Finally use the Memory control panel to turn the RAM disk off or change its size, and restart your computer.

Increasing Total Memory

Enjoy whatever unused memory you have while it lasts. Software developers see unused memory as a vacuum to be filled with new programs and new features for old programs. Before long, you will want and then need more memory for new software and upgrades.

When you find yourself invariably quitting programs in order to open others, it's time to increase your computer's memory. As this section explains, you can increase memory by turning on or increasing virtual memory, by adding more RAM modules, or by using a memory enhancement program such as RAM Doubler 2. In addition, the 32-Bit Addressing option affects how much memory some computer models can access.

Virtual memory

You may be able to increase the total memory available for opening applications without buying and installing more RAM modules. The system software can transparently use part of a hard disk as additional memory. This extra memory, called *virtual memory*, enables you to get by with less RAM. You buy only as much RAM as you need for average use, not for peak use.

Virtual memory has other benefits on computers with PowerPC processors. Turning on virtual memory may help you avoid running out of memory when you use programs that are optimized for the PowerPC processor (programs that use only native PowerPC instructions). Native PowerPC programs need less memory with virtual memory on than off. In contrast, programs written for 68040, 68030, 68020, and 68000 processors, often called *68K applications*, require the same amount of memory whether virtual memory is on or off.

The downside to virtual memory is that it can slow down the system, especially if you set it up wrong.

Configuring virtual memory

To turn virtual memory on and off, you use the Memory control panel. Before turning it on, you can set the size of total memory and select a hard disk (non-removable) that has a block of available space as large as the total amount of memory you want available (RAM plus virtual memory). You must restart your computer for changes to take effect. Figure 16-8 shows the virtual memory options in the Memory control panel.

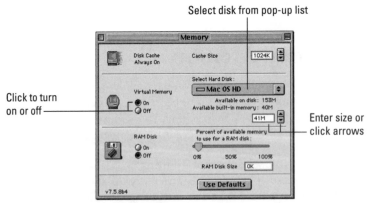

Figure 16-8: Setting up virtual memory.

With virtual memory on, the About This Computer or About This Macintosh window reports the total amount of memory and the amount of built-in memory (RAM). It also tells you how much disk space is used for virtual memory storage.

The higher you set virtual memory in the Memory control panel, the more it slows down the system. If you use virtual memory mostly to reduce the memory requirements of PowerPC applications, set the virtual memory size to 1MB more than the amount of RAM installed. If you use virtual memory to make more memory available for opening programs, set it no higher than double the installed RAM and use it for opening multiple small programs.

The limit on total memory (virtual memory plus RAM) is one gigabyte (1024MB) with Mac OS 7.6 and later. With Systems 7.0–7.5.5 the limit is lower if you turn off 32-Bit Addressing (as described later in this section). With 32-Bit Addressing off, the maximum total memory is 14MB, minus 1MB for each installed NuBus board and minus 1MB more if you use built-in video on your computer.

Virtual Memory Turn-Off

Virtual memory users, do you hate having to open the Memory control panel when you occasionally have to turn virtual memory on and off? For instance, you must turn of virtual memory for maximum performance with QuickTime movies and multimedia applications. Sure, holding down the Shift key during startup turns it off — and all your system extensions as well. But by holding down the ⌘ key during startup, you can disable virtual memory and still keep all your extensions. Restarting without the ⌘ key restores virtual memory with its previous settings. No more trips to the Memory control panel.

How virtual memory works

Virtual memory gives you more memory for opening programs by keeping only the most active program segments in RAM. Less-used segments of open programs are kept in an invisible file named VM Storage on the hard disk. When a program needs a segment not currently in physical memory, the virtual memory system automatically swaps the least-used segment in RAM with the needed segment on disk. For example, a swap might occur when you switch programs. However, no swapping occurs unless you are trying to use more memory than your computer has RAM.

Virtual memory's ability to load program pieces on demand is also responsible for reducing a PowerPC application's memory requirements, as mentioned earlier. What makes PowerPC applications need more memory than 68K applications when virtual memory is off is how the system software loads a PowerPC application into memory. Apple designed the system software to load PowerPC applications in bigger pieces, called *code fragments*, than 68K applications' smaller pieces, called *segments*. Larger pieces should require more memory for the same reason you need a bigger ferry boat to carry busses than cars. That's exactly the case with virtual memory turned off. A PowerPC application needs at least enough space for its largest code fragment, and usually more, when virtual memory is turned off.

In designing the system around large PowerPC code fragments, Apple planned all along to compensate by having the virtual memory system load and unload portions of code fragments on demand. With virtual memory turned on, code fragments don't have to be loaded whole and an application can get by with less memory.

Using virtual memory to manage application code fragments works because of the performance of the PowerPC processor. Virtual memory just isn't fast enough without a PowerPC processor.

How virtual memory affects performance

Because a hard disk is much slower than RAM, using virtual memory can degrade system performance. The performance penalty is barely noticeable if a swap between RAM and disk happens when you switch programs. The slowdown may be severe if you use virtual memory to open a program that's bigger than the amount of RAM left after system software gets its share. The disk may thrash for several minutes as it tries to swap segments back and forth.

The performance of code fragment management on PowerPC computers is actually better than the performance of virtual memory in general. That's because code fragments are never written to the VM Storage file. In fact, the VM Storage file is not involved at all in managing a PowerPC application's code fragments. The application file itself is the storage file. The virtual memory system software loads code fragments directly from the application file into memory, a technique called *file mapping*. This technique eliminates the delay that sometimes occurs when a 68K program's code is loaded into memory and then immediately written out to the VM Storage file. With file mapping, that thrashing never happens.

File mapping benefits performance in another way. The system software never writes code fragments back to the application file as it would if they went through the VM Storage file. The system software assumes code fragments are read-only (never changed). So when part of a code fragment is no longer needed, a needed part can replace it right away. The system doesn't take the time to write the disused piece back to the disk because it can always read an identical copy that's still there (in the application file).

QUICK TIPS

Hiding from Virtual Memory

With virtual memory turned on, you can often improve system performance by using the Hide Others command in the Application menu. Hidden windows of background applications don't need updating, which may require disk access when virtual memory is on. However, some programs continue working in the background even with their windows hidden. For example, a database program might generate a report in the background. But the Hide Others command usually reduces the amount of background work going on.

Which Macs can use virtual memory

Virtual memory works on any computer with a PowerPC, 68040, or 68030 processor. Some Macs with 68020 processors can be upgraded with an MMU (memory-management unit) chip to use virtual memory. A Mac II can be retrofitted with an MMU chip, and an LC can be upgraded with an accelerator card containing an MMU chip. However, Macs with 68000 processors can't use the Mac OS virtual memory even if they have accelerators with MMU chips. The ROM (read-only memory) in those models is missing some information that the system software needs to implement virtual memory. To use virtual memory on those models, install Connectix's utility software Virtual.

Installing more RAM

Virtual memory has its uses, but it can't take the place of built-in RAM. If you're not sure how much RAM your computer has, bring up the About This Computer or About This Macintosh window. In that window, the Built-in Memory is the amount of RAM installed. You won't see an amount labeled Built-in Memory if you use Mac OS 7.6.1 or earlier and virtual memory is turned off. In this case, the amount reported as Total Memory is the amount of RAM installed. If the amount is reported in K (kilobytes), you can convert to MB (megabytes) by dividing the number of K by 1,024. For example, 32768K ÷ 1024 = 32MB.

Do-it-yourself RAM upgrade

If your computer needs more RAM, you may be able to upgrade it yourself. Upgrading involves opening the computer (tricky on a Mac Plus, SE, SE/30, Classic, Classic II, and the PowerBook 100 and 200 series) and either installing or replacing some small, plug-in circuit board modules. You must also cut a resistor on a Mac Plus or an older SE and move a jumper on a newer SE.

Each computer model has specific memory-configuration rules. Some Macs use *DIMMs* (dual in-line memory modules) and some use *SIMMs* (single in-line memory modules). Both DIMMs and SIMMs come in various capacities, measured in MB (megabytes), and speeds, measured in ns (nanoseconds). PowerBooks use special memory modules. You can install RAM modules only in certain combinations on each model. To find out which type of RAM modules your computer uses, consult the latest free GURU (guide to RAM upgrades) application from memory-maker Newer Technology (316-685-4904, http://www.newertech.com). Another source of information is the electronic document Apple Memory Guide from Apple's online software library (http://www.info.apple.com). You can also get advice from dealers and companies that sell RAM.

Although you may be perfectly capable of installing SIMMs or DIMMs in your computer, Apple recommends that only an Apple-certified technician install them. Apple's warranty does not cover any damage that you or a non-certified technician cause when installing or removing SIMMs and DIMMs. Proceed with caution, but know that many computer owners install their own memory boards. The more paranoid owners may also remove what they install before taking their computers in for warranty service. Most technicians won't bother to ask unless they see damage or oddball parts, such as composite SIMMs or DIMMs.

Buying RAM

You can order RAM by mail from a plethora of companies that advertise in *Macworld* and *MacWeek* magazines. Memory prices are highly competitive. As you shop for a memory upgrade, look for a lifetime warranty from a reputable company that as best you can tell will be around to honor the warranty. RAM chips are very reliable, but they can fail.

Buy your RAM from a company that includes illustrated installation instructions for your make and model. Pay a little extra to get the instructions if you have to. A grounding wrist strap is a good precaution against unlikely damage due to static electricity discharge during installation. If the SIMM seller doesn't include one, you can buy one from an electronics store (Radio Shack part 276-2397; $3.99).

Steer clear of composite SIMMs and DIMMs. They may work on one computer, but on another they may cause sporadic startup failures, system errors, or mysterious crashes. You may have no trouble with one composite SIMM or DIMM, but install another and watch your computer have fits. You can spot a composite SIMM or DIMM by the large number of chips on it. For example, a regular 16MB SIMM uses eight 16-megabit chips, but a composite SIMM might use 32 4-megabit chips. The best way to avoid composite SIMMs and DIMMs is to buy from a reputable source.

RAM upgrade by a technician

If you don't want to upgrade the memory yourself, you can take your computer and your mail-order SIMM to an Apple dealer or other computer service center. An experienced technician should be able to install more memory in well under 30 minutes, so you shouldn't have to pay for more than a half hour of labor. Some stores charge less to install RAM they sell to you, so investigate that angle before bringing in your own RAM that you "got for your birthday."

Memory optimizing software

You can get twice as much out of the RAM installed in your computer with very little performance penalty by using one or two software products — RAM Doubler 2 and RAMCharger. You can use either product alone or use them together.

RAM Doubler 2

RAM Doubler 2 from Connectix (800-950-5880, 415-571-5100, http://www.connectix.com) can actually triple the amount of total memory as reported in the About This Computer or About This Macintosh window. If you prefer, you can set RAM Doubler 2 to extend memory by a lesser amount. You can even set RAM Doubler 2 to not extend memory at all, but just to provide file mapping and code fragment management for PowerPC applications.

Compared with virtual memory, RAM Doubler 2 is faster, more efficient, and uses very little hard disk space. It's great for older PowerBooks that can only have 8MB of RAM, because it doesn't use the power-draining hard disk like virtual memory. Virtual memory's strengths are that it's free and is somewhat more reliable.

RAM Doubler 2 accomplishes its magic by reallocating RAM automatically behind the scenes while you continue working. It takes over the RAM reserved but not used by open applications (the lighter portion of the bars graphed by the About This Macintosh command) and temporarily reallocates the unused RAM to applications that need it. RAM Doubler 2 also compresses parts of programs in RAM that probably won't be used again, such as parts that initialize a program when you open it. Also, RAM Doubler 2 may store infrequently used areas of RAM to disk, just like conventional virtual memory, especially if your computer has less than 8MB of RAM. RAM Doubler 2 reduces overall system performance slightly, but you probably won't notice the difference in normal operations. However, it's not suitable for time-critical operations like video digitizing.

Like virtual memory, RAM Doubler 2 works with most but not all Macs. It requires a PowerPC, 68040, or 68030 processor. It doesn't work on a Mac Plus, SE, original Classic, PowerBook 100, or original LC, even if you accelerate them with a 68030 processor. RAM Doubler 2 works on all other Macs that have at least 8MB of RAM installed. In addition, 32-Bit Addressing must be on, and the programs you use must work with 32-Bit Addressing (as described later in this section).

You can't use RAM Doubler 2 in combination with virtual memory (including Connectix's Virtual). You can't set the memory size of any application higher than the amount of physical RAM installed in your computer; Connectix recommends leaving your programs set at their usual memory sizes.

RAMCharger

The benefits of RAMCharger from Syncronys Softcorp (888-777-5600, 213-340-4100, http://www.syncronys.com/ramcharger/) can't be stated precisely. RAMCharger doesn't literally double the total available memory, but it does allow you to keep more programs open at the same time. In addition, it allows open programs to use more memory than the Preferred sizes set in their Info windows.

RAMCharger takes a different approach to memory optimization and has fewer restrictions than RAM Doubler 2. RAMCharger opens a program in its Minimum memory size, not its Preferred memory size, as specified in the program's Info window. If a program needs more memory, RAMCharger gives it more from the unused portion of RAM on your computer. When the program no longer needs the extra memory, RAMCharger reclaims it for future reallocation. You probably won't notice any performance degradation in normal operations.

You can use RAMCharger on a computer with less than 4MB of RAM installed, and there is no RAM maximum. RAMCharger does not require 32-Bit Addressing or an MMU. RAMCharger works with virtual memory on or off.

32-Bit Addressing

If your computer has a 68040, 68030, or 68020 processor and uses Systems 7.0–7.5.5, the Memory control panel may have an option called 32-Bit Addressing. Its setting affects how much memory your computer can access. You won't find this option in the Memory control panel of a PowerPC computer or any type of computer that has Mac OS 7.6 or later. In these cases, 32-Bit Addressing is always turned on.

When the 32-Bit Addressing option is turned off, the computer can only use 8MB of RAM; with virtual memory turned on, the maximum goes up to 14MB. Turning on 32-Bit Addressing lets you use all the RAM installed in your computer and removes the limit on virtual memory. Figure 16-9 shows the 32-Bit Addressing option in the Memory control panel.

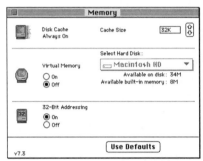

Figure 16-9: Setting the 32-Bit Addressing option.

If you turn off 32-Bit Addressing and your computer has more than 8MB installed, the About This Macintosh command adds the unusable amount to the system software size. On a 20MB Quadra 605, for example, turning off 32-Bit Addressing adds 12,000K (12MB) to the system software size. If 32-Bit Addressing is off, you can only use 8MB of RAM regardless of the amount installed.

32-Bit Addressing doesn't work on Mac SE/30, II, IIx, and IIcx models unless you install the extension MODE32, which is available free from Apple's software library (http://www.info.apple.com). You must use MODE 32 version 7.5 with Systems 7.5 through 7.5.5. If you are using MODE32 version 1.2 or earlier with Systems 7.5 through 7.5.5, you must do a clean installation of the system software (as described in Chapter 30) or you risk serious file corruption.

The Mac Classic, SE, Plus, Portable, and PowerBook 100 models can't use 32-Bit Addressing because their 68000 processors can't access more than 8MB.

Summary

In this chapter, you learned that the About This Computer command (Mac OS 7.6 and later) or About This Macintosh (System 7.5.5 and earlier) shows you the total memory available, which programs are open, how much memory they use, and how much memory is currently unused. The Memory Mapper utility shows you a more detailed picture of that information.

This chapter also told you how to set an application's minimum and preferred memory sizes with the Finder's Get Info command. You learned what causes memory fragmentation, how to fix it, and how to avoid it. You found out how to determine your computer's minimum system software size by holding down the Shift key during startup. You read about four ways to reduce the system memory size: disable nonessential startup items, turn off expendable options, reduce disk cache size, and reduce or eliminate a RAM disk.

In this chapter you also learned how to increase the total memory available for opening programs. Options include turning on virtual memory, installing more RAM, using RAM Doubler 2 or RAMCharger, and turning on 32-Bit Addressing if it's off.

Set Up a Network

IN THIS CHAPTER

- **Hooking up a network** using LocalTalk, PhoneNet, or Ethernet 10Base-T cables

- **Configuring an AppleTalk network connection** with the AppleTalk or Network control panel

- **Making a remote AppleTalk network connection** over a phone line with Apple Remote Access (ARA)

- **Configuring a TCP/IP network connection** with the TCP/IP or MacTCP control panel

- **Making a dial-up TCP/IP network connection** over a phone line with Open Transport PPP's Modem and PPP control panels

If you have more than one computer in your office or home, you can benefit by connecting them in a network. The idea may seem intimidating, but a simple Mac OS network is easy to set up, doesn't cost much, and just look at some of the things you can do with it:

❖ Share printers, including printers without network ports

❖ Share files from other computers in your company or home as if their files were on your desktop, and share files from your computer with other computers

❖ Exchange electronic mail

❖ Browse information on the Internet's World Wide Web

❖ Participate in Internet discussion groups

❖ Transfer files over the Internet to and from any type of computer (not just Macs) anywhere in the world

❖ Access a central database while other computers do likewise

❖ Maintain a group schedule or calendar

❖ Backup hard disks of all networked computers on a central tape drive

❖ Access your hard disk from a remote location over a telephone line

This chapter focuses on setting up a network so you can use some of those services. The first section of this chapter discusses hooking up a local area network (LAN) using either of the two most common types of network wiring for Mac OS computers: LocalTalk and Ethernet. You can skip that section if your computer is already hooked up to a network. The remainder of this chapter tells you how to make a connection to the two most common kinds of Mac OS networks: AppleTalk and TCP/IP.

This chapter does not describe how to use network services once your local network is set up. For information on printers and printing, see Chapters 14 and 15. For information on sharing files with other computers, see Chapter 18. For information on Internet services such as global e-mail and the World Wide Web, see Chapter 20. For information on e-mail and other network services provided by Apple's defunct PowerTalk software, which can't be used with system software version 7.6 and later, see Appendix B.

Hooking Up a Network

The first step in setting up a local network is hooking up lines of communication between the computers and printers that you want on the network. Basically that involves running a cable to each computer and printer. You may also need a cable connector box for each computer and a central junction box. If your computer is already connected to a network, you can skip this section.

This section describes how to hook up a LocalTalk network using inexpensive LocalTalk connector boxes and either Apple's LocalTalk cables or an ordinary telephone cord. This section also describes how to hook up an Ethernet network using 10Base-T parts, which are the lowest in cost of the many Ethernet cabling alternatives. In addition, this section discusses how you can bridge a LocalTalk network and an Ethernet network with Apple's LaserWriter Bridge or LocalTalk Bridge software.

Besides Ethernet and LocalTalk, Macs can be connected with other types of network wiring such as Token Ring. Because Mac OS computers don't come with token ring network ports, one must be added in the form of a network interface card. If your organization has a Token Ring network, you undoubtedly have a network administrator or other expert who has already connected your computer to it or will do so for you. Setting up a Token Ring network or any network other than Ethernet or LocalTalk is not something you want to attempt on your own. At any rate, it's outside the scope of this book.

LocalTalk

The simplest and cheapest type of Mac OS network wiring is LocalTalk. All Mac OS computers have a LocalTalk network port, and so do all printers that can be connected to a Mac OS network. It costs less than $20 per computer and printer (for a network cable and connector box) to set up a small LocalTalk network. All the software you need is built into all versions of the Mac system software. LocalTalk performance is generally suitable for networks of a couple dozen or fewer computers and printers, although performance depends greatly on how much the computers use the network. LocalTalk wiring is primarily for Mac OS-only networks, although it is possible to buy LocalTalk expansion cards for hooking up Windows and DOS PCs. You can also connect Newton portable computers to a LocalTalk network.

To establish a LocalTalk network you simply plug a network connector box into the printer port of each computer and into the LocalTalk port of each network printer or other network device (such as a network modem), and run wires between the boxes. Connector boxes with two modular phone jacks, such as PhoneNet from Farallon Computing (510-814-5000, http://www.farallon.com) are the most common. You link them with an ordinary telephone cord, the kind used to connect a telephone to a modular wall socket. Be sure to use a four-wire cord, not two-wire (look for four colored wires showing through the clear RJ-11 modular plugs). In many homes and small businesses you can use the existing telephone wiring and jacks in the walls to extend your network from room to room. With the four-wire cables common in homes, for example, the telephone uses the red and green wires and the network can use the yellow and black wires.

Instead of phone cords and PhoneNet connector boxes, you can use Apple's proprietary LocalTalk connector boxes and cables. However, this stuff costs more and doesn't offer any advantages over PhoneNet. If you already have some Apple LocalTalk supplies, you can get adapters from Farallon to mix them with phone wiring.

For networking only two devices — for example, two computers or one computer and one printer — you can save money by using Farallon's one-jack PhoneNet pocket connectors. Later you can add to this minimal network with dual-jack connector boxes. An even cheaper alternative is to connect the two devices with a serial printer cable, like the one you would use to connect a StyleWriter to a computer.

Ethernet

A significantly faster (though somewhat costlier) type of network wiring for all kinds of computers is Ethernet. Many newer Mac OS computers and printers have Ethernet ports, especially models intended for businesses as opposed to homes. Ethernet adapters are available for all Mac OS computers that don't have built-in Ethernet ports. The cost to set up a small Ethernet network starts at $20, $50, or $120 per computer or printer, depending on the type of built-in port (if any). The cost and performance of Ethernet scales up to accommodate networks of all sizes. The software for accessing an Ethernet network is included with the Mac system software, although you may have to do a custom installation to get it installed. An Ethernet network can include computers using Mac OS, Windows, Unix, and other operating systems. They can use common software — for example, Internet software — to communicate and share services (see Chapter 20 for more information on Internet software).

Hooking up an Ethernet network is more complicated than hooking up a LocalTalk network. For starters, some computers have Ethernet ports and some don't. Some computers have a built-in port for 10Base-T Ethernet cable, which uses an RJ-45 connector that looks like a big modular phone connector. 10Base-T is by far the most popular of the several kinds of Ethernet cables. Other kinds include thin, thick, and fiber optic.

Many Mac OS computers have an AAUI (Apple attachment unit interface) port to accommodate any kind of Ethernet cable. An AAUI port requires a connector box, called a *transceiver,* designed for the particular type of Ethernet cable in your network.

Computers without built-in Ethernet need an Ethernet adapter to connect to an Ethernet network. There are internal adapter cards for the various kinds of expansion slots found in Mac OS computers: PCI, NuBus slot, Comm, and PDS (processor direct slot). For computers without internal expansion slots, there are external Ethernet adapters that plug into the SCSI port. For PowerBooks that accept PC cards (also known as PCMCIA cards), there are Ethernet adapters on a PC card. All these Ethernet adapters are widely available for 10Base-T and other kinds of Ethernet cables from many manufacturers (including Farallon, Asanté, and Dayna).

You can directly connect two computers equipped with 10Base-T Ethernet ports by using a crossover cable. Global Computer Supplies (800-845-6225) carries these cables in 3-foot, 12-foot, and custom lengths for less than $10. If you use a crossover cable and you shut down both computers, you may have to reset a control panel option on the first one you start up again, as described in the sidebar "Crossover Cable Confusion."

You can connect more than two computers and Ethernet-capable printers by plugging each into the port of an Ethernet hub. The hub is a central junction box that helps route network traffic. Prices start around $50 for a generic 5-port hub and go up for more ports and a name brand. Another option: You can connect up to eight 10Base-T devices without a hub by using Farallon's EtherWave family of transceivers and adapter cards (prices range from $90 to $250).

Crossover Cable Confusion

When using a crossover cable to connect two computers equipped with 10Base-T (RJ-45) Ethernet ports without a hub, you must start up both computers before changing the connection to Ethernet in the AppleTalk control panel or Network control panel. If the Mac OS doesn't see another device on the Ethernet network, it won't let you set the AppleTalk connection to Ethernet. After successfully setting the AppleTalk connection to Ethernet, a similar problem occurs if you subsequently start up one computer while the other is off. An alert explains, "An error occurred while trying to start up your AppleTalk connection. The built-in LocalTalk port will be used instead." If this happens, you have to reset the AppleTalk connection to Ethernet after starting up the other computer. (The AppleTalk and Network control panels are covered in "Configuring an AppleTalk Connection" later in this chapter.)

Bridges

Sometimes a hybrid network, part Ethernet and part LocalTalk, makes sense. For example, you might have a printer with a LocalTalk port (and no Ethernet port) that you want to use with several computers that have Ethernet ports. Or you might have some older computers connected in a LocalTalk network that you'd like to have access to network services on a newer Ethernet network. Fortunately you can interconnect the dissimilar networks with a bridge.

LaserWriter Bridge

Apple's free LaserWriter Bridge 2.1 software lets you use a LocalTalk printer from a computer that's connected to an Ethernet network. In fact, if more than one printer is connected to the LocalTalk network, you can use any of them. The theoretical maximum is 32 printers, but Apple recommends eight or fewer. You install LaserWriter Bridge 2.1 on the computer to which a LocalTalk printer (or a network of printers) is connected. You can allow other computers on the Ethernet network to use the LocalTalk printer or printers, or you can designate the bridge to be private. LaserWriter Bridge is available from Apple's software library (http://www.info.apple.com).

The LaserWriter Bridge works only one way. It allows computers on an Ethernet network to see printers on a LocalTalk network. It doesn't allow computers on a LocalTalk network to see printers or computers on an Ethernet network.

LocalTalk Bridge

Apple's LocalTalk Bridge 2.1 software (order no. M3246Z/A) creates a two-way connection between a LocalTalk network and an EtherTalk network. The LocalTalk computers can use printers, shared files, and other network services on the Ethernet network. Computers on the Ethernet network can use printers, shared files, and other network services on the LocalTalk network. You install LocalTalk Bridge 2.1 on the computer that is connected to both the Ethernet network and the LocalTalk network. If you prefer, you can make the connection private, so that only the computer with the LocalTalk Bridge can use network services on both networks.

Configuring an AppleTalk Connection

To use network services on your computer, the system software must be configured to get network services from the port that is physically connected to the network. You can configure the Mac system software for more than one kind of network, with each kind of network providing a specific set of services. The most common kinds of Mac OS networks are AppleTalk and TCP/IP. Technically, AppleTalk and TCP/IP are networking *protocols*. A networking protocol is a set of rules for exchanging data.

An AppleTalk network provides Mac-oriented services such as printer sharing, file sharing, data sharing, and program sharing. Apple designed AppleTalk to be easy to use and reliable. AppleTalk has been built into every version of the Mac system software. Until the advent of Open Transport networking software in 1995, AppleTalk was the primary kind of Mac OS network and all other kinds of networks were subordinate.

Note that connecting to a network does not necessarily make specific network services available. For example, connecting to an AppleTalk network makes it possible to use a network printer, but you can't actually print to a network printer unless one is connected to the network and set up as described in Chapter 14. Likewise, connecting to an AppleTalk network makes it possible to share files with other computers on the network, but to actually share files the computers must have the file sharing set up as described in Chapter 18.

This section describes how to configure an AppleTalk network connection with the AppleTalk or Network control panel and how to turn an AppleTalk connection on and off.

To use TCP/IP network services such as the Internet, your computer's system software must be configured for a TCP/IP network as described in "Configuring a TCP/IP Connection" later in this chapter.

Specifying an AppleTalk connection

By default, the system software connects to an AppleTalk network at the printer port. If your AppleTalk network is connected to an Ethernet port or the modem port, you need to make that setting in the AppleTalk control panel or the Network control panel, whichever is in your Control Panels folder.

Computers with Mac OS 7.6 and later have an AppleTalk control panel. Computers with PCI expansion slots have an AppleTalk control panel regardless of their system software version. Other computers with Systems 7.1 through 7.5.5 may have either an AppleTalk control panel or a Networking control panel, but not both. Computers with System 7.5.1 and earlier are more likely to have a Networking control panel.

Mac Networking Software

There are two generations of Mac OS networking software. The newer one is Open Transport, and the older one is known as classic networking. You can tell which one your computer is using by looking in the Control Panels folder. If you see an AppleTalk control panel, your computer is using Open Transport. If you see a Network control panel, your computer is using classic networking.

Open Transport is faster than classic networking and makes all kinds of networks equal. With classic networking, AppleTalk is dominant, and other kinds of networks such as TCP/IP are converted to AppleTalk for transmission on the network. A computer with an AppleTalk control panel uses Open Transport, and a computer with a Network control panel uses classic networking.

Open Transport is included and required with Mac OS 7.6 and later. Open Transport is included for optional installation with Systems 7.5.3 and 7.5.5, though it is required on all computers with PCI slots regardless of system software version. Open Transport is available separately for installation with system software version 7.1 or later from Apple's online software library (http://www.info.apple.com). Open Transport works on a computer with a PowerPC, 68040, or 68030 processor and at least 5MB of RAM (68030 and 68040 computers) or 8MB of RAM (PowerPC computers). These RAM requirements are for the total system, not for Open Transport itself, but they don't include RAM used for a RAM disk or disk cache. If you want to use Open Transport on a Performa or Power Mac in the 5200, 5300, 6200, and 6300 series, you must use Open Transport 1.1.1 or later. However, some of these computers have a hardware problem that prevents using Open Transport. If the problem exists, the Installer program notifies you and won't install Open Transport until you replace the computer's Cache/ROM module. You can continue using classic networking. Repairs are free from Apple-authorized service providers under a warranty extension program until 2003.

If your computer can use either Open Transport or classic networking, you can switch between them using the Network Software Selector program in the Apple Extras Folder (located at the main level of your hard disk). You must restart the computer after changing from one to the other.

AppleTalk control panel

If your computer has an AppleTalk control panel, you use it to specify an AppleTalk network connection. The AppleTalk control panel lists the available network ports in a pop-up menu. You choose the one through which your computer connects to an AppleTalk network. If your computer is connected to an AppleTalk network that's divided into multiple zones, the AppleTalk control panel also specifies the zone in which your computer resides. Depending on the characteristics of your computer and network, you may be able to change the network connection port, the zone, or both. If your computer has only one network connection port, you won't be able to change the port. If your computer is connected to a network with only one zone, there won't be any zones available to choose from. If someone else sets up your computer's AppleTalk network connection, the port and zone settings may be locked so you can't change them. Figure 17-1 shows an AppleTalk control panel with several port choices.

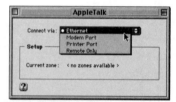

Figure 17-1: Choose a connection port for an AppleTalk network in the AppleTalk control panel.

If you change the connection port in the AppleTalk control panel, a message warns that you'll lose any network services that you're using with your current AppleTalk connection. This is because you can maintain a connection to only one AppleTalk network at a time. When you switch to a different network port, you'll no longer be able to access any printers, shared files, file servers, or other AppleTalk network services on the former AppleTalk connection port. Changing the AppleTalk connection port does not affect network services on other kinds of networks, such as Internet services on a TCP/IP network. (For information on changing the TCP/IP connection, see "Configuring a TCP/IP Connection" later in this chapter.)

You can see and use three groups of settings, or user modes, in the AppleTalk control panel. The Basic mode shows the settings most people need. The Advanced mode shows additional settings for special situations. The Administration mode provides control over which settings can be changed. To change the user mode, choose User Mode from the Edit menu, and select the mode in the dialog box that appears. If you select Administration mode, you can set a password so that only people who know the password can access Administration mode. Figure 17-2 shows the User Mode dialog box.

Figure 17-2: Select a user mode for the
AppleTalk control panel.

In the Advanced mode, you see the network address that was dynamically assigned to your computer when it connected to the network. By selecting the "User defined" check box, you can assign a fixed address to your computer. If you assign a fixed address, you must be sure that no other computer on the network has the same address. Clicking the Options button brings up a dialog box in which you can turn AppleTalk on and off. Figure 17-3 shows the AppleTalk control panel's Advanced mode.

Figure 17-3: The AppleTalk control
panel's Advanced mode.

In the Administration mode, you can assign a fixed network address as in the Advanced mode. In addition, you can lock each of the three settings independently — port, zone, and AppleTalk network address. Locked settings can't be changed in Basic or Advanced modes. Figure 17-4 shows the control panel's Administration mode.

Figure 17-4: The AppleTalk control panel's Administration mode.

You can save the current state of the AppleTalk control panel as a named configuration by choosing Configurations from the File menu to bring up the Configurations dialog box. Your saved configurations are listed in the dialog box, and you can make any one active, import or export them individually, and delete or rename them one at a time.

Network control panel

If your computer has a Network control panel, use it to specify an AppleTalk network connection. The Network control panel displays the available network ports as icons, and you select the one through which your computer connects to an AppleTalk network. Note that the Network control panel shows an EtherTalk port instead of an Ethernet port. *EtherTalk* is Apple's term for an AppleTalk network carried on Ethernet cables. Figure 17-5 shows an example of the Network control panel.

Figure 17-5: Select an AppleTalk network connection in the Network control panel.

If you change the network port, a message warns that you'll lose all network services that you get through your current network connection. This is because the Network control panel can connect through only one network port at a time. When you switch to a different network port, you'll no longer be able to access any printers, shared files, file servers, or other network services through the former network port.

Turning AppleTalk On and Off

If you're not using an AppleTalk network, you can turn it off altogether. Turning off AppleTalk saves power on a PowerBook. Turning off AppleTalk also frees the printer port for another purpose, such as connecting a serial printer. However, it's not necessary to turn off AppleTalk just to free the printer port, as detailed in the sidebar "AppleTalk Without a Serial Port."

To turn off AppleTalk, open the Chooser desk accessory and in the lower right corner of its window set the AppleTalk option to Inactive. If you turn off AppleTalk, it remains off until you turn it on again by selecting the Activate option in the Chooser. Figure 17-6 shows the AppleTalk option in the Chooser.

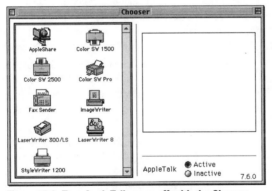

Figure 17-6: Turn AppleTalk on or off with the Chooser.

If you attempt to turn off AppleTalk while you are using a network service, such as file sharing, you get a warning message that current services will be disconnected.

If your computer has an AppleTalk control panel (not a Network control panel), you can use it to turn AppleTalk on and off. With the AppleTalk control panel set to Advanced or Administration mode, click the Options button to bring up the AppleTalk Options dialog box. There you can select Inactive to turn off AppleTalk or select Active to turn on AppleTalk. Figure 17-7 shows the AppleTalk control panel's Options dialog box.

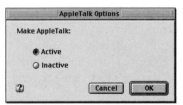

Figure 17-7: Turn AppleTalk on or off with the AppleTalk control panel's Options dialog box.

QUICK TIPS

AppleTalk Without a Serial Port

You may need to turn off AppleTalk so you can print to a StyleWriter or other serial printer through the printer port while using the modem port for a modem. If your computer has only one serial port, you may need to turn off AppleTalk so you can use the port with an external modem. The trouble is, if you turn off AppleTalk, you won't be able to use applications that require AppleTalk, such as NetPresenz. Furthermore, if your computer has Open Transport 1.1.2 or earlier, turning off AppleTalk may cause it to crash.

You can keep AppleTalk turned on and still use a serial printer and a modem by installing the Remote Only extension and then selecting Remote Only in the AppleTalk control panel or the Network control panel, whichever your computer has. The Remote Only extension comes with Open Transport 1.1.2 or later, which is available from Apple's software library (http://www.info.apple.com). Remote Only is also part of the ARA Client software, which is described later in this section.

An Open Transport crash happens when you try to open a PPP connection a second time using FreePPP or other PPP software that is not Open Transport native (in other words, PPP software that also works with MacTCP). The crash doesn't happen when AppleTalk is active, and it shouldn't affect Apple's Open Transport/PPP software, which is Open Transport native (requires Open Transport). Also, America Online 3.0 software includes an extension, OpenOT, designed to prevent the crash whether AppleTalk is active or not.

Making a Remote AppleTalk Connection

Your computer can connect to an AppleTalk network with a phone call, either by calling a computer on the network or by calling a special remote access server if there is one on the network. Your computer needs Apple's ARA (Apple

Remote Access) Client software, which is included for optional installation with Mac OS 7.6 and later. If your computer calls another computer, that other computer must be running Apple's ARA Personal Server software, which is available from software resellers. In addition, your computer and the computer or server it calls must have compatible modems or ISDN adapters.

When connected, you can access shared files on the remote computer or network exactly as though you were connected to the computer or network locally (as described in Chapter 18), but someone using the remote computer or network can't access files on your computer. In addition, you may be able to use other services on the remote network, such as network printers and file servers. However, the ARA server that you call has the ability to restrict your access to certain parts of the remote network.

ARA Client setup

You set up ARA Client software with the Remote Access Setup control panel, specifying the type of modem or ISDN adapter you have and the port to which it's connected. Figure 17-8 shows an example of the Remote Access Setup control panel.

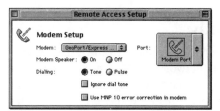

Figure 17-8: Specify a remote AppleTalk connection in the Remote Access Setup control panel.

ARA connection

You connect to a remote AppleTalk network by calling it with the Remote Access Client program. All you need to make a connection is your registered name and password on the remote network (as described in "Sharing Someone Else's Folders and Disks" in Chapter 18) and the phone number of the remote computer or ARA server. You can save this information as a Remote Access Client document, which you can later open to make the same connection again. An Options button in the Remote Access Client window lets you specify how to redial if the number is busy. You have the option of entering an alternate number to call if the main number is busy or doesn't answer. And you have the option of being reminded with a flashing icon in the menu bar or an alert message that you must periodically acknowledge in order to maintain your connection. Figure 17-9 shows an example of the Remote Access Client window and its Options dialog box.

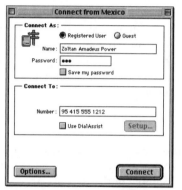
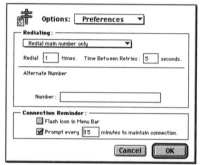

Figure 17-9: Connect to a distant network with the Remote Access Client program (left) and its Options dialog box (right).

Remote network only

While your computer is connected to a remote AppleTalk network, you can disconnect your local AppleTalk network. There are two reasons you may need to do this. For one, you may be unable to see remote printers or file servers that have the same names as printers or file servers on your local network unless you disconnect the local network. (Local services have priority over remote services.) You may also want to disconnect your local AppleTalk network so you can use your serial ports for other purposes. For example, you may want to use the printer port for a StyleWriter printer and the modem port for a modem that connects you to a remote AppleTalk network.

To disconnect your local AppleTalk network, set the AppleTalk connection to Remote Only in the AppleTalk control panel or the Network control panel, whichever your computer has.

ARA speed

The speed of a remote connection depends on the speed of the modem or ISDN connection but is always slower than a local connection. The maximum rate, which requires an ISDN or better telephone line, is 112.5 Kbps (kilobits per second). The built-in serial ports are not capable of that speed on all Mac OS computers. The following Apple computers have built-in serial ports capable of 112.5 Kbps:

❖ Centris and Quadra 660AV and 840AV

❖ Performa 6100 series

❖ Power Mac 6100, 7100, 7200, 7500, 8100, 8500, and 9500 series

❖ Workgroup Server 6150, 7250, 8150, 8550, and 9150

If you choose a modem script in the Remote Access Setup control panel that specifies a speed of 112.5 Kbps (115200 bps) and your computer's serial port is not capable of that speed, Apple Remote Access 2.1 automatically falls back to 56 Kbps (57600 bps).

Configuring a TCP/IP Connection

To use TCP/IP network services such as the Internet, your computer's system software must be configured to connect to a TCP/IP network through one of its ports. Naturally, that port must be physically connected to a network that provides TCP/IP services. The port may be wired to an Ethernet or LocalTalk network, or a modem plugged into the port may provide a dial-up connection.

This section describes how to configure a TCP/IP network connection with the TCP/IP or MacTCP control panel. If you want to set up a TCP/IP network just to access the Internet and you have Mac OS 8 or later, you should consider using the Internet Setup Assistant program instead of the control panels described here. (The Internet Setup Assistant is described in Chapter 20.)

To use Mac OS-oriented network services such as printer and file sharing, you need to configure an AppleTalk network connection as described in the previous section, "Configuring an AppleTalk Connection."

Preparing for a TCP/IP connection

Before setting up a TCP/IP connection, you need to know some facts about the network. You may have to get the facts from an expert such as your local network administrator or your Internet service provider (ISP). Here is what you need to know:

❖ Type of network connection, usually PPP, Ethernet, or MacIP

❖ Your TCP/IP configuration method, such as manual, PPP Server, BootP

Server, DHCP Server, RARP Server, or MacIP Server

❖ Domain name server (DNS) address or addresses, each a set of four numbers separated by periods, like 192.14.59.10 (provided automatically by some configuration methods)

❖ IP address of your computer, a set of four numbers separated by periods, like 192.14.59.35 (provided automatically by most configuration methods)

❖ Subnet mask (provided automatically by most configuration methods)

❖ Router address (provided automatically by most configuration methods, and not applicable for some networks)

❖ Phone number your computer calls to connect to the Internet (needed only for PPP or other dial-up connection)

Specifying a TCP/IP connection

You specify a TCP/IP network connection with the TCP/IP control panel or the MacTCP control panel, whichever is in your Control Panels folder. Computers with Mac OS 7.6 and later have a TCP/IP control panel. Computers with PCI expansion slots have a TCP/IP control panel regardless of their system software version. Other computers with Systems 7.1 through 7.5.5 may have either a TCP/IP control panel or a MacTCP control panel, but not both. Computers with System 7.5.1 and earlier are more likely to have a MacTCP control panel.

The presence of the TCP/IP control panel indicates your computer uses Open Transport networking software. The presence of the MacTCP control panel indicates your computer uses classic networking software. For more information on Open Transport and classic networking, see the sidebar "Mac Networking Software" earlier in this chapter.

TCP/IP control panel

If your computer has a TCP/IP control panel, you use it to specify a TCP/IP network connection. As mentioned at the beginning of this section, you need to get specific configuration information from your Internet service provider or network administrator to properly set up a TCP/IP connection. You enter this information in the TCP/IP control panel. If someone else sets up your computer's TCP/IP network connection, the connection and configuration settings may be locked so you can't change them. Figure 17-10 shows a TCP/IP control panel configured for a typical dial-up (telephone) connection.

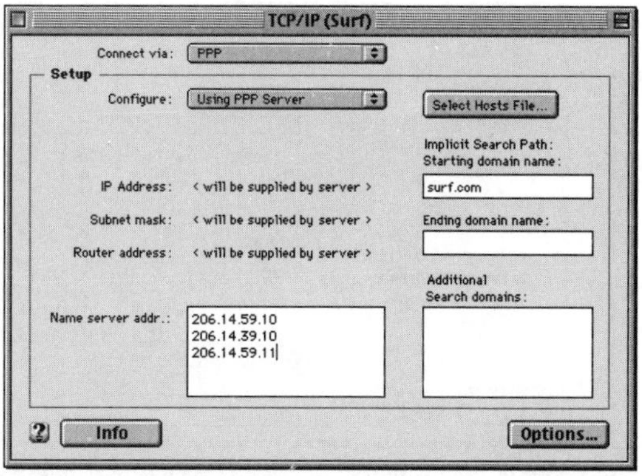

Figure 17-10: Specify a TCP/IP network connection in the TCP/IP control panel.

You can see and use three groups of settings, or user modes, in the TCP/IP control panel. The Basic mode shows the settings most people need. The Advanced mode shows additional settings for special situations. The Administration mode provides control over which settings can be changed. To change the user mode, choose User Mode from the Edit menu, and select the mode in the dialog box that appears. If you select Administration mode, you can set a password so that only people who know the password can access Administration mode. In the Administration mode, you can lock several settings independently. Locked settings can't be changed in Basic or Advanced modes.

You can save the current state of the TCP/IP control panel as a named configuration by choosing Configurations from the File menu to bring up the Configurations dialog box. Your saved configurations are listed in the dialog box, and you can make any one active, import or export them individually, and delete or rename them one at a time.

MacTCP control panel

If your computer has a MacTCP control panel, you use it to specify a TCP/IP network connection. You need to get specific configuration information from your Internet service provider or network administrator to properly set up a TCP/IP connection, as mentioned at the beginning of this section. You enter that information in the MacTCP control panel. In the main MacTCP window you select the icon that represents the type of network connection. Then you click the More button to bring up a dialog box full of additional options, which you set to match the information provided by your network administrator, ISP, or other expert. Figure 17-11 shows an example of the MacTCP control panel and its dialog box.

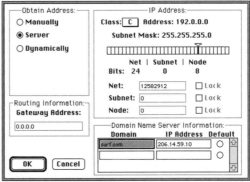

Figure 17-11: Specify a TCP/IP network connection in the MacTCP control panel (left) and its dialog box (right).

Making a Dial-Up TCP/IP Connection

Your computer can connect to a TCP/IP network with a phone call by using PPP (point-to-point protocol) or SLIP (serial line interface protocol) software. The PPP or SLIP software has your computer's modem or ISDN adapter dial the phone number of the TCP/IP network's entry point, which is sometimes called a *point of presence (POP)*. Then the PPP or SLIP software negotiates a connection with the TCP/IP network. Usually that involves identifying you with an ID and password, a process called *authentication*.

This section covers making a dial-up connection to a TCP/IP network with Open Transport PPP software, which is included for optional installation with Mac OS 7.6 and later. Open Transport PPP requires Open Transport networking software, so it works only in conjunction with the TCP/IP control panel, not with the MacTCP control panel.

This section also describes the most common alternative PPP software: MacPPP and FreePPP. They both work with Open Transport or classic networking, so they work in conjunction with the TCP/IP control panel or the MacTCP control panel. However, MacPPP and FreePPP versions 2.5 and earlier do not take full advantage of Open Transport networking.

Open Transport PPP

To take full advantage of Open Transport networking for dial-up connections to the Internet or any TCP/IP network, Apple developed Open Transport PPP. It's part of a standard installation of Mac OS 8 and is included as an option with Mac OS 7.6 and 7.6.1. Open Transport PPP is also available separately from Apple's software library (http://www.info.apple.com). It requires Open Transport 1.1.1 and system software versions 7.1, 7.1.1, 7.1.2, or 7.5.3 or later (it does not work with Systems 7.5, 7.5.1, or 7.5.2).

Setup for Open Transport PPP

Before making a connection with Open Transport PPP, you must set up your modem or ISDN terminal adapter with the Modem control panel. You specify the port to which your modem is connected, the type of modem, and other settings as shown in Figure 17-12.

Figure 17-12: The Modem control panel sets up your modem for making an Open Transport PPP connection to the Internet.

The Modem control panel has two modes, Basic and Administration. The Basic mode shows the settings most people need. The Administration mode provides control over which settings can be changed. To change the user mode, choose User Mode from the Edit menu, and select the mode in the dialog box that appears. If you select Administration mode, you can set a password so that only people who know the password can access Administration mode. In the Administration mode, you can lock several settings independently. Locked settings can't be changed in Basic mode.

You can save the current state of the Modem control panel as a named configuration by choosing Configurations from the File menu to bring up the Configurations dialog box. Your saved configurations are listed in the dialog box, and you can make any one active, import or export them individually, and delete or rename them one at a time.

Making an Open Transport PPP connection

To connect to the Internet or other TCP/IP network with Open Transport PPP, you use the PPP control panel. In the control panel you indicate whether you're connecting as a registered user (with a user name or user ID and a password) or as a guest (anonymously). If you're connecting as a registered user, you type your name or ID, your password, and the phone number provided by your Internet service provider in the spaces provided. You can click the Connect button to make a connection. The PPP control panel is initially configured to connect automatically when an application tries to access something on a TCP/IP network, such as an e-mail program trying to check for e-mail. You can change this behavior by clicking the Options button, as described next. Figure 17-13 shows the PPP control panel.

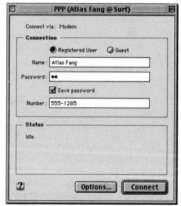

Figure 17-13: The PPP control panel makes an Open Transport PPP connection to the Internet.

Clicking the Options button in the PPP control panel brings up a dialog box in which you can set the following options:

❖ **Redialing.** No redialing when busy; redial the main number only, or redial main and alternate numbers.

❖ **Connection.** Connect automatically when starting TCP/IP applications; use verbose logging.

❖ **Reminders.** Flash an icon in the menu bar while connected; prompt every x minutes to maintain the connection; disconnect if idle for y minutes (you set values for x and y).

❖ **Protocol.** Allow error correction and compression in the modem; use TCP header compression; connect to a command-line host either in a terminal window or with a connect script you specify.

If you're calling from a place where you must dial the number yourself (such as when making an operator-assisted call), don't click the Connect button in the PPP control panel. Instead, choose Dial Manually from the PPP menu and follow the instructions on the screen.

The PPP control panel has two modes, Basic and Administration. The Basic mode shows the settings most people need. The Administration mode provides control over which settings can be changed. To change the user mode, choose User Mode from the Edit menu, and select the mode in the dialog box that appears. If you select Administration mode, you can set a password so that only people who know the password can access Administration mode. In the Administration mode, you can lock several settings independently. Locked settings can't be changed in Basic mode.

You can save the current state of the PPP control panel as a named configuration by choosing Configurations from the File menu to bring up the Configurations dialog box. Your saved configurations are listed in the dialog box, and you can make any one active, import or export them individually, and delete or rename them one at a time.

MacPPP

MacPPP is PPP software that some Internet service providers give to their customers for making dial-up Internet connections. It's reliable but not as fast as Open Transport PPP with a TCP/IP connection configured by the TCP/IP control panel.

After installing MacPPP, you use the Config PPP control panel to configure the dial-up connection. You specify the port to which your modem or ISDN adapter is connected, the type of modem or ISDN adapter, and other settings as shown in Figure 17-14.

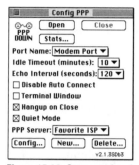

Figure 17-14: Set up and make a dial-up TCP/IP connection with MacPPP's Config PPP control panel.

You can make a connection by clicking the Open button in the Config PPP control panel. You can also set Config PPP to connect automatically when an application tries to access something on the TCP/IP network, such as a Web browser trying to load a Web page or an e-mail program trying to send or receive e-mail.

To disconnect, you click the Close button in the Config PPP control panel.

FreePPP

FreePPP is an enhancement of MacPPP that many Internet service providers give to their customers for making dial-up Internet connections. FreePPP has many more configuration options yet is easier to understand than MacPPP. Like MacPPP, FreePPP is reliable but as of version 2.5v2 is not as fast as Open Transport PPP with a TCP/IP connection configured by the TCP/IP control panel. FreePPP is available from RockStar Studios (http://www.rockstar.com).

After installing FreePPP, you use the FreePPP Setup program to configure the dial-up connection. You specify the port to which your modem or ISDN adapter is connected, the type of modem or ISDN adapter, and other settings as shown in Figure 17-15.

You can make a connection by clicking the Connect button in the FreePPP Setup program or by choosing Open PPP Connection from the FreePPP menu. The FreePPP menu appears as a telephone icon next to the Guide menu at the right end of the menu bar and is available in all applications unless you turn off the FreePPP Menu control panel. You can also set FreePPP Setup to connect automatically when an application tries to access something on the

TCP/IP network, such as a Web browser trying to load a Web page or an e-mail program trying to send or receive e-mail.

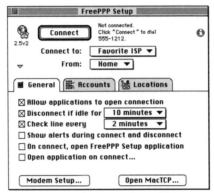

Figure 17-15: Set up and make a dial-up TCP/IP connection with the FreePPP Setup program.

To disconnect, you click the Disconnect button in the FreePPP Setup program or choose Close PPP Connection from the FreePPP menu.

Summary

In this chapter, you learned how to hook up a simple local area network (LAN). You can create a LocalTalk network with inexpensive connector boxes and either Apple's LocalTalk cables or an ordinary telephone cord. For a better performing (though more expensive) LAN, you can create an Ethernet network using the lowest in cost of the many Ethernet cabling alternatives, 10Base-T. You can also create both LocalTalk and Ethernet networks and bridge them with Apple's LaserWriter Bridge 2.1 or LocalTalk Bridge 2.1 software.

This chapter told you how to configure an AppleTalk network connection with the AppleTalk or Network control panel, whichever your computer has. You learned how to turn an AppleTalk connection on and off. And you learned how to connect to a remote AppleTalk network by phone using Apple Remote Access (ARA) Client software.

You read in this chapter about configuring a TCP/IP network connection with the TCP/IP or MacTCP control panel, whichever your computer has. You also learned how to make a dial-up TCP/IP network connection using PPP software such as Open Transport PPP, MacPPP, or FreePPP.

CHAPTER EIGHTEEN

Share Your Files

Similar to a library, *file sharing* allows you to share files, folders, and disks with people whose computers are connected to your computer in a network. You can share items from your computer with other people, they can share their items with you, and they can share their items with one another. In effect, these network users become librarians of their shared information, controlling who has access to shared items and determining what a user can do to files.

All you need to share your files among Mac OS computers in your office or home are the Mac system software and a network. The previous chapter explains how to set up a simple network. This chapter describes how you can connect to other computers on your network and use their shared files. But first this chapter explains the more complicated process of making some of your files available so other people with computers on your network can connect to your computer and use your shared files. First you plan for file sharing and identify your computer on the network. Next you start the file sharing software on your computer and designate which hard disks or folders contain files you want to share. Then you can identify users who you want to let access your shared items. For each of your shared folders you can restrict the type of access some of those users have. At any time you can monitor file sharing activity to see who is connected to your computer and how much of its processing power is consumed by file sharing.

Planning for File Sharing

The personal file sharing capabilities of Mac OS 8 and earlier make sharing items across a network surprisingly easy, but not without some cost. This section discusses the capabilities and limitations of Mac OS file sharing so you can decide in advance whether it meets your network's needs. The alternative to file sharing is a dedicated file server.

Distributed or dedicated file sharing

Your network can implement file sharing in a distributed or centralized fashion. In a distributed file-sharing network, each computer makes files, folders, and disks available to other computers on the network. While your computer shares your files with other computers, you are free to use your computer for other tasks. The price you pay for making files from your computer available for people using other computers to share is reduced performance of your computer while other computers are accessing it. In addition, the file sharing capabilities of Mac system software have some limitations that make file sharing unsuitable for serving files to large numbers of computers on a network.

By contrast, a network with centralized file sharing dedicates one computer (or more) to providing file-sharing services. That computer runs file server software, such as Apple's AppleShare software, which enables the computer to serve files to a large number of other computers. Other computers on the network get shared files from the *dedicated file server* (or file servers) rather than from each other. Usually, a computer that acts as a dedicated file server needs more than minimal processing capabilities and one or more large hard disks. The Mac system software does not include file server software; you must purchase it separately.

Although the system software's file-sharing capabilities are designed for distributed file sharing, you can use file sharing on a dedicated computer to create an ersatz dedicated file server for a small network. Folders or entire hard disks on that file-server computer can be made available to other computers on the network as described in the remainder of this chapter.

The problem with an ersatz file server is its performance. The Mac system software assumes somebody is using the dedicated computer for more than sharing files and reserves about 50 percent of the dedicated computer's processing power for non-file-sharing tasks. A utility called Nok Nok 2.0 from the AG Group (510-937-7900, http://www.aggroup.com), which sells for about $50, can adjust the amount of processing power reserved for file sharing, greatly improving file-sharing performance. Apple's AppleShare IP 5.0 provides even faster file service, and other services to boot, but it costs $800 to $2000, depending on the number of users.

BACKGROUNDER

AppleShare IP 5.0 File Server

A network with more than ten people actively sharing files needs a dedicated file server administered by software such as Apple's AppleShare IP 5.0 software. The AppleShare IP file server extends network file-sharing and background-printing services beyond the system software's capabilities. Installing AppleShare Server software turns a computer into an efficient centralized file server capable of sharing the files and folders on its hard disk (or disks) among up to 250 users of Mac OS, Windows 3.*x*, and Windows 95 computers.

Centralized disk storage reduces the amount of local disk storage required by each networked computer, while providing a way for people who work together to share information. People can store files on the server's disks, where other people can open or copy them. Many people can access the server's disks and folders simultaneously, and new files become available to everyone instantly. Unlike the file sharing provided by the Mac system software, no one uses the server's computer to do personal work because it is dedicated to providing network services. Conversely, your computer is not burdened when someone else on the network accesses one of your shared items on the AppleShare server's disks.

A centralized file server is set up and maintained by a trained person called a *network administrator*. The AppleShare IP software includes organizational, administrative, and security features to manage file access on the network. The network administrator does not control access to folders and files on the server's disks; that is the responsibility of each person who puts items on the disks.

AppleShare's file server is compatible with the Mac system software's file sharing. You use the methods described in this chapter to make your files available for sharing whether those files are on your hard disk or the file server's hard disks. You also access files on the file server's hard disks using the same method as described in this chapter for sharing files from other computers' hard disks.

The AppleShare IP print server supports up to 30 printers, 10 queues, and 32 simultaneous print sessions so users don't have to wait for print jobs to finish or have their computers bogged down by background printing. It can balance the total printing load among all available printers, so that faster printers do more of the work. The printer server is available to Mac OS, Windows 3.*x*, and Windows 95 computers.

In addition to being a Mac OS file and printer server, AppleShare IP 5.0 provides e-mail, Web, and FTP (file transfer protocol) services like those available on the Internet. Any computer on the network that has Internet client software for e-mail, Web, and FTP can access those services. That includes Mac OS, Windows, Unix, OS/2, and Newton computers.

AppleShare IP 5.0 servers run on a computer with a PowerPC 601, 604, or 604e processor (603, 603e, and systems with other processors can't run the server software), 32MB of RAM, at least 10MB of hard disk space, and a CD-ROM drive. It requires Mac system software version 7.6 or later, Open Transport 1.1.2 or later, and OpenDoc 1.2 or later.

Limitations on file sharing

With personal file sharing you can designate up to 10 disks or folders that contain other folders and files that you want to share (see "Designating Your Shared Items" later in this chapter). Only the disks and folders you designate count toward the limit of 10 shared items; folders inside the designated disks and folders don't count toward the limit.

Up to ten other computers can be connected to your computer at one time, but only five can access files at once. (This limit applies only to file sharing, not necessarily to other network activity such as using a multi-user database file located on your computer.)

You can identify registered users and groups of users (see "Identifying Who Can Access Your Shared Items" later in this chapter). You use the users and groups to control who can connect to your computer and to specify special access privileges for any of your shared items (see "Controlling Access to Your Shared Items" later in this chapter).

If you need to exceed the limitations described here, your network needs a file server.

Guidelines for file sharing

You can do several things to optimize file sharing and prevent potential problems. The following are some guidelines and tips for sharing folders and disks:

❖ Share from the highest level of your disk and folder structure. For example, a disk can't be shared if it contains an already-shared folder (no matter how deeply nested in the unshared disk). If you attempt to share a disk or folder that contains an already-shared folder, you get a message telling you that the disk or folder cannot be shared because it contains a shared folder. To work around this situation, identify the shared items (as explained in "Monitoring File Sharing Activity" later in this chapter), unshare it, and then share the enclosing disk or folder.

❖ Share as few folders as possible. The more shared folders being accessed, the greater the memory and processing demands on your computer. Sharing too many folders can slow your system to a crawl.

❖ Check any applicable licensing agreements before sharing folders that contain programs, artwork, or sounds. Often, licensing agreements or copyright laws restrict use of these items to a single computer.

❖ Set up a dedicated computer to act as a dedicated file server for the shared information. This method is often the most efficient way to share numerous files or to share folders with several users simultaneously.

Identifying Your Computer

Before you can begin sharing files, you must give your computer a network identity. Identifying your computer involves entering the name of its owner, a password to prevent other people from connecting to your computer as its owner, and a name for your computer. With Mac OS 8, you specify those facts when you go through the Mac OS Setup Assistant program. The Assistant comes up automatically the first time you restart the computer after installing Mac OS 8. You can run it again at any time; it's located in the Assistants folder on the startup disk.

You can also specify your computer's network identity with the File Sharing control panel or the Sharing Setup control panel, whichever your computer has. The File Sharing control panel is part of Mac OS 8.0, and the Sharing Setup control panel is part of system software versions 7.0 through 7.6.1. Figure 18-1 shows the File Sharing and Sharing Setup control panels.

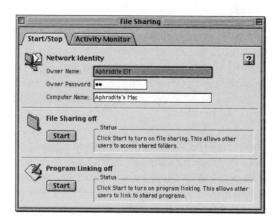

Figure 18-1: Specifying a Mac's network identity in the File Sharing control panel (top) or the Sharing Setup control panel (bottom).

The Owner Password can be up to eight characters long. A password is *case-sensitive*, meaning that if you create a password that includes uppercase and lowercase letters, you must always type that password with the same uppercase and lowercase letters to gain access. Select a password that is easy for you to remember but difficult for others to guess. Mix letters with numbers; try replacing the letters *I* and *O* with the numbers 1 and 0 (for example, "brownie" becomes "br0wn1e"). You must know the Owner Password to access your computer from another computer on the network. For privacy, the system displays bullets in place of the actual password characters in the File Sharing or Sharing Setup control panel.

The computer name that you enter should be one that other people will easily recognize when they see it in the Chooser as they start to share your files. The name must be unique on your network. If you enter a name that another computer is already using, the system displays an alert telling you to use a different name.

Turning File Sharing Off and On

Once your computer's network identity is set in the File Sharing or Sharing Setup control panel, you can use the same control panel to turn file sharing on and off at any time. You must turn on file sharing when you want to make your shared files available to people using other computers on the network. You do not need to turn on file sharing to access shared files from other computers on the network.

Turning on file sharing increases the system software memory size by 200K to 300K. Also, your computer is theoretically more vulnerable to invasion while file sharing is on, although you can institute effective security measures (lock the door, so to speak) as described in "Controlling Access to Your Shared Items" later in this chapter. All in all, it's a good idea to leave file sharing turned off unless other people need to access your shared files over the network.

When you turn off file sharing, other computers on the network cannot access your computer or its shared files. Turning off file sharing does not change which items you have designated for sharing (as described in the next section) or the access privileges you have set for your shared items (as described in the subsequent section "Controlling Access to Your Shared Items"). With file sharing turned off, other computers simply can't connect to your computer for file sharing. (They may still be able to connect to your computer if it provides other network services, such as access to a multi-user database file.)

If your Mac has System 7.5 or earlier, you can share only from disk volumes whose icons are on the desktop when you turn on file sharing. If you plan to share files from a CD-ROM or a removable hard disk, you must insert the disk before turning on file sharing. Conversely, before turning on file sharing you must eject a CD-ROM or removable hard disk that you do not want to share. You cannot eject a CD-ROM or removable hard disk whose icon was on the desktop when sharing started; you have to turn off sharing before ejecting.

With System 7.5.1 and later, file sharing does not exert the grip of death on removable disks and CD-ROMs. You can eject removable disks and CD-ROMs without first turning off file sharing. Also, you can share files from a removable disk or CD-ROM that you insert after turning on file sharing. (Audio CDs are not shared.)

Turning on file sharing

To turn on file sharing, click the Start button in the File Sharing section of the File Sharing control panel or the Sharing Setup control panel, whichever your computer has. The Start button's label changes to Cancel, and the status message next to the button describes what is happening while file sharing is starting up. It may take anywhere from several seconds to several minutes for file sharing to start up, depending on the number of disk volumes and shared items on your computer. You can close the control panel anytime after clicking the Start button, but you won't know precisely when file sharing is enabled if you do. Your computer is ready to share its files when the button's label changes to Stop and the File Sharing control panel reports "File Sharing on" or the Sharing Setup control panel's status message reads "File sharing is now on." Figure 18-2 shows how the File Sharing control panel and the Sharing Setup control look when file sharing is turned on.

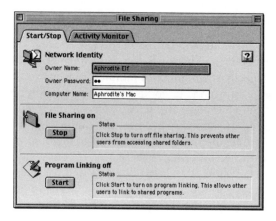

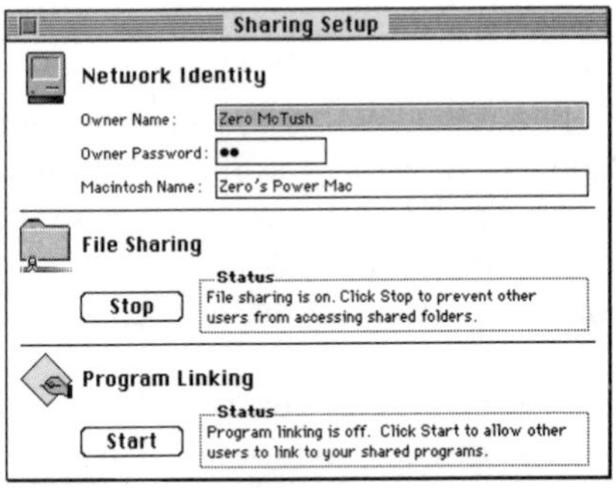

Figure 18-2: Seeing that file sharing is turned on in the File Sharing control panel (top) or the Sharing Setup control panel (bottom).

There are other ways to turn on file sharing. You can use the Control Strip, if it's installed on your computer. Or you can speak the command "Start file sharing" if speech recognition is installed on your computer. (For more information on the Control Strip, see Chapter 10. For more information on speech recognition, see Chapter 21.)

If you shut down or restart your computer after turning on file sharing with the File Sharing or Sharing Setup control panel or by spoken command, the system software automatically starts file sharing the next time the computer starts up. If you turn on file sharing with the Control Strip, the system software does not automatically turn it on again when you restart the computer (unless you had turned on file sharing with one of the other methods since the last time the computer started up). In other words, file sharing status as set by the File Sharing or Sharing setup control panel or by spoken command persists through a system restart.

Turning off file sharing

To turn off file sharing, click the Stop button in the File Sharing section of the File Sharing control panel or the Sharing Setup control panel. A dialog box appears, asking you to specify the number of minutes' warning to be given to anyone who is sharing items from your computer. (Allow enough time for people sharing items from your computer to close any shared items.) Every computer that's connected to yours displays a message indicating that access to your computer is going to be disconnected at the end of the time you specified. The same events happen when you shut down or restart your computer with file sharing on. Figure 18-3 shows the dialog box in which you specify how long until file sharing stops and the message box that appears on other computers that are connected to your computer for file sharing.

What you see

What people who are sharing your folders
and disks see.

Figure 18-3: Messages that appear when you turn off file sharing.

Caution: The notification cycle described here does not occur with some
methods of restarting and shutting down your computer. For example, if you
restart or shut down with the Special menu in some versions of Apple's At Ease
software, other people sharing your items do not receive notification of your
impending shutdown. At Ease can provide a simplified view of the Mac OS
desktop and gives you control over which programs and documents people can
access on your computer. It is not included with the system software; you
purchase and install it separately.

Designating Your Shared Items

After identifying your computer and turning on file sharing, you can designate
the folders and hard disks that contain files you want to share. You can share up
to ten folders and hard disks (including CD-ROMs and removable hard disks) at
a time. To share just one file, you must drag it into a folder and share the folder.

When you share a folder or hard disk, every item it contains is shared, including
enclosed folders. You can't share a document by itself (outside a folder) or an
item located on a floppy disk. After you share a folder or hard disk, you can drag
items into the shared folder or hard disk to share them as well.

Aliases in shared folders or disks are shared, but their original items are shared
only if they are in shared folders or disks. If network users try to use a shared
alias whose original item is not in a shared folder or disk, the system software
tells them the original item can't be found.

Making an item shared

To make a folder or hard disk available for people using other computers to
share, select the item and then choose Sharing from the File menu to display

the item's sharing window, in which you specify access privileges. In the sharing window, turn on the option "Share this item and its contents." Figure 18-4 shows an example of a shared item's sharing window as it looks in Mac OS 8 and in Mac OS 7.6.1 and earlier.

Figure 18-4: A shared item's sharing window in Mac OS 8 (left) and in earlier versions of the system software (right).

The remaining options in the sharing window establish which users can access the shared item and what privileges they have (as explained in "Controlling Access to Your Shared Items" later in this chapter). The initial settings for a shared item depend on the version of system software you're using. With system software version 8.0 and later, a folder's initial settings allow only the item's owner to access the folder; the owner can add items, delete items, and save changes to files in the folder. With system software version 7.6.1 and earlier, a folder's initial settings enable anyone on the network to access the folder and its contents and make any changes he or she wants.

The settings that you make in an item's sharing window persist until you use the Sharing command again to change them. Shutting down or restarting your computer does not affect sharing window settings; neither does turning off file sharing.

Recognizing your shared items by their icons

The icon of a shared folder on your computer appears with network cables, indicating its shared status. When someone is using your shared folder, the folder icon has faces on it. Unlike folder icons, disk icons don't change when you share them. Figure 18-5 shows examples of shared folders as they look in Mac OS 8 and in Mac OS 7.6.1 and earlier.

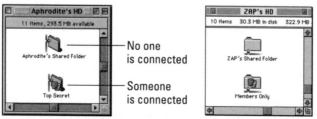

Figure 18-5: Shared folders on your computer in Mac OS 8 (left) and in earlier versions of the system software (right).

You can't rename a shared folder or disk; nor can you drag it to the Trash. Also, you can't eject and put away a removable hard disk or CD-ROM that contains shared folders. To do any of these things, you first must turn off file sharing or turn off the option "Share this item and its contents" in the item's sharing window.

Network Trash

If another user throws away a shared item from your computer, the Finder creates an invisible folder on your computer with the name *Network Trash Folder.* As long as the user doesn't empty the Trash, the items thrown away appear inside the Network Trash Folder in folders labeled *Trash Can #1, Trash Can #2,* and so on — one for each computer with something of yours in its Trash. To restore an item that someone else has trashed, use a utility program such as ResEdit (described in Chapter 24) to make the Network Trash Folder visible. Then find the item that you want to rescue and drag it out of the *Trash Can #* folder it's in. You can set access privileges to prevent others from trashing your shared items (as described in "Controlling Access to Your Shared Items" later in this chapter).

Identifying Who Can Access Your Shared Items

You could let everyone access your shared folders and disks (as happens by default if you're using system software 7.6.1 or earlier) or you could let no one but you access your shared items (as happens by default if you're using Mac OS 8). But you don't have to take an all or nothing approach. This section explains how you use the Users & Groups control panel to identify individual people and groups of people who you want to grant or deny access to your shared items. The next section, "Controlling Access to Your Shared Items," tells you how to specify which of those people or groups has privileged access to a shared folder or disk and its contents.

Users & Groups

The Users & Groups control panel displays named icons for people and groups who can access your shared items. There's always an icon for the computer's owner. The owner icon is marked with a clipboard if you're using Mac OS 8, or it has a bold outline if you're using an earlier version of system software. There's also always an icon for guests — that is, any unidentified person using a computer on your network. The guest icon is marked with a suitcase if you're using Mac OS 8, or its name is enclosed in angle brackets if you're using an earlier version of system software. You create additional icons for registered network users to whom you want to grant greater access privileges than guests have. You can also create groups of registered users. You can create any number of registered users and groups in the Mac OS 8 Users & Groups control panel. With earlier system software you're limited to 100 users and 100 groups, but for optimal performance, you shouldn't name more than 50. Figure 18-6 shows examples of the Users & Groups control panel as it looks in Mac OS 8 and in Mac OS 7.6.1 and earlier.

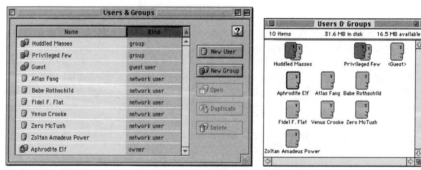

Figure 18-6: The Users & Groups control panel in Mac OS 8 (left) and in earlier versions of the system software (right).

Sorting users and groups

When working in the Users & Groups control panel, it can be helpful to sort the Users & Groups list by kind so that all groups are listed together alphabetically and all network users are listed together alphabetically. If you're using Mac OS 8, click the column heading to sort the list by that heading. If you're using an earlier version of system software, choose the sort order from the View menu.

Selecting multiple users or groups

You can perform some operations in the Users & Groups control panel on more than one user or group at the same time. With Mac OS 8, you ⌘-click to select multiple icons one by one, or Shift-click to select a range of icons. With earlier versions of system software, you Shift-click to select multiple icons one by one, or drag a selection rectangle to select a range.

The owner

The owner icon controls your ability to access your computer when you connect as its owner from another computer. The owner can have the unique ability to access all disks whether they're designated for sharing or not. The owner icon bears the name of the computer's owner and looks different from other icons in the Users & Groups control panel. In Mac OS 8, it looks like a face next to a clipboard. In earlier system software versions, the owner icon has a heavy black outline.

You change the owner's access privileges in the owner window, which you display by opening the owner icon. You can also change the owner's name and password in the owner window if you're using Mac OS 8. With Mac OS 8, the owner name and password in the owner window and in the File Sharing control panel always match; if you make a change one place the system software updates the other place. With earlier versions of the system software, you must use the Sharing Setup control panel to change the owner's name and password. Figure 18-7 shows the two views you can see of the owner window in Mac OS 8 and the one view you see in Mac OS 7.6.

Turning on the "Allow user to connect" option gives you access to your computer from another computer connected to the network. Turning on the "Allow user to change password" option enables you to change your password remotely. The option "Allow user to see entire disk" enables you to see and use any items on any hard disk attached to your computer. This setting gives you access to all disks and folders on your computer (while you are connected to your computer from another computer), whether they are shared or not. When you connect as the owner you have unlimited access whether or not you're named the owner of a shared folder and regardless of the privileges assigned to shared disks and folders.

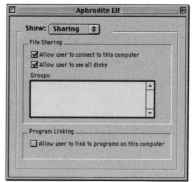

Figure 18-7: Changing the owner's name, password, and file sharing access privileges in Mac OS 8 (top), or the access privileges in earlier versions of the system software (bottom).

Guests

The Guest icon controls the ability of any unidentified network user to access the shared items on your computer. You can deny guests any access or you can allow access to your computer and restrict guest access to shared folders and disks individually (as described in the next section, "Controlling Access to Your Shared Items").

To disable all guest access, open the Guest icon in the Users & Groups control panel to display the Guest window, and turn off the "Allow guests to connect" option. Now only registered users are allowed to share items on your computer. Figure 18-8 shows the two views you can see of the Guest window in Mac OS 8 and the one view you see in Mac OS 7.6.

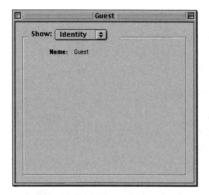

Figure 18-8: Changing guests' file sharing access privileges in Mac OS 8 (top) and in earlier versions of the system software (bottom).

Registered network users

Registering network users helps secure your shared items from unauthorized access. You can specify whether each registered user can connect to your computer for file sharing, as described in this section. You can also give a registered network user special access privileges to shared folders, as described in the next section, "Controlling Access to Your Shared Items."

Creating a new network user

To register a network user, first open the Users & Groups control panel. Next, click the New User button or choose New User from the File menu to create a new user icon in the Users & Groups control panel. (The New User button doesn't exist in system software versions earlier than Mac OS 8.) An icon named New User appears in the Users & Groups control panel, and if you're using Mac OS 8, the icon opens to display the user window for that new network user.

Rather than create a new user, you can duplicate one or more existing users in the Users & Groups control panel by selecting one or more user icons and clicking the Duplicate button or choosing Duplicate from the File menu. (The Duplicate button doesn't exist in system software versions earlier than Mac OS 8.)

Identifying a network user

When you create a new user, the new user name is selected and you can replace it by typing the name of the network user who you want to register. After duplicating a selection of multiple users, you have to select and rename the duplicates one by one.

You should ask a network user what name he or she would like to use when connecting to your computer to share your files, and suggest he or she use the owner name in his or her File Sharing or Sharing Setup control panel. If you devise the name yourself, you must tell the network user his or her registered name on your computer because the user must type the exact name to connect to your computer and share your files. Network user names are not case-sensitive, so a user doesn't have to match your use of uppercase and lowercase letters when connecting to your computer. As soon as you give a network user a name, he or she is registered on your computer.

You can add another level of security by assigning to a registered user a password that he or she needs to type to access your shared items. You assign a password in the user window, which you display by opening the user icon. Enter a password up to eight characters long. Keep in mind that the user must type the password exactly as you type it here, including uppercase and lowercase letters. Figure 18-9 shows the two views you can see of a user window in Mac OS 8 and the one view you see in Mac OS 7.6.

Setting a network user's privileges

Additional options in a user window let you specify whether a registered user can connect to your computer and whether the user can change his or her password. If the "Allow user to connect" option is turned on, the network user name can be used to connect to your computer for file sharing. Turn off that option to deny access to anyone using that registered name. If you want to let this user change the password at will, turn on the "Allow user to change password" option. When you finish setting the registered user's access privileges, close the user window to make your changes take effect.

Keep in mind that access privileges are associated with a registered user name, not necessarily with a particular person. Any person who connects to your computer with a valid user name (and password, if any) has the privileges you set for that registered user name. If you're concerned about the security of your shared items, you can tell your registered users not to divulge their passwords and periodically ask them to change their passwords.

Figure 18-9: Identifying and setting privileges for a registered user in
Mac OS 8 (top) and in earlier versions of the system software (bottom).

Changing a network user

You can modify a registered user's name, password, and access privileges or
remove the user from your set of registered users at any time.

To remove a registered user, drag its icon from the Users & Groups control
panel to the Trash. Alternatively, you can select one or more user icons and
click the Delete button or choose Delete from the File menu. (The Delete
button doesn't exist in system software versions earlier than Mac OS 8.)

Apple Remote Access privileges

If you have installed the Apple Remote Access Personal Server software, the
owner, guest, and user windows include additional options. (These additional
options do not appear if you have installed only the Apple Remote Access Client
software that comes with some versions of the Mac system software.) The remote
access options let you allow or deny remote access to the owner, to guests, and to

each registered user individually. For the owner and for each registered guest, you can specify a call-back phone number. When Apple Remote Access gets a call from a user who has a call-back number, the program hangs up and calls the user back at the specified number. This procedure prevents an unauthorized person from gaining access to your computer by learning a registered user's password and trying to call from an unauthorized location. When you specify a call-back number, you have to pay the cost of the phone call for the connection, but you know that the person accessing your computer has the correct password and is calling from the user's computer. Figure 18-10 shows the remote access privileges as they appear in Mac OS 8 and Mac OS 7.6.

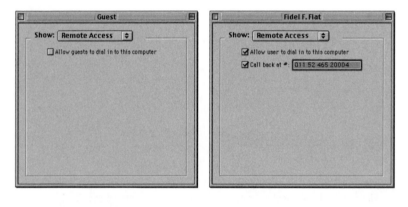

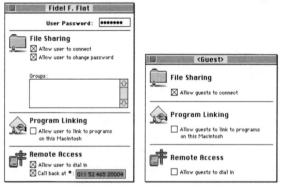

Figure 18-10: Remote access privileges for registered users (including the owner) and guests in Mac OS 8 (top) and in earlier versions of the system software (bottom).

Groups of users

Office or work environments usually consist of groups of people, such as departments or project teams, who need to share certain items. The Mac system software's file sharing enables you to specify special access privileges for groups as well as for individual users. Groups simply are collections of individual registered users, and you can grant specific access privileges for a shared item to a group instead of to a single user. (The procedures for setting access privileges of shared items are covered in the next section, "Controlling Access to Your Shared Items.")

Creating a group

To establish a group of users, open the Users & Groups control panel and click the New Group button or choose New Group from the File menu. (The New Group button doesn't exist in system software versions earlier than Mac OS 8.) An icon named New Group appears in the Users & Groups control panel, and if you're using Mac OS 8, the icon opens to display the group window for that new group. The group icon looks different than a single-user icon.

Rather than create new groups, you can duplicate one or more existing groups in the Users & Groups control panel by selecting one or more group icons and clicking the Duplicate button or choosing Duplicate from the File menu. (The Duplicate button doesn't exist in system software versions earlier than Mac OS 8.)

Right after you create a new group, the new group name is selected and you can replace it by typing a name you make up. If you duplicate a selection of multiple groups, you have to select and rename them one by one.

Don't invent group names that might offend someone who uses your shared files. Your group names are not private if you use them to set specific access privileges of shared items. At least some people who connect to your computer will be able to see some of your group names.

Adding users to a group

To add registered users to a group, drag their user icons to the group icon or group window. You can also add a user to a group by dragging the group icon to the user icon. To speed the process of adding users to groups, select multiple users and then drag them to the group icon together. (You don't need to include the owner icon in groups.)

To see the members of the group, open the group icon. The group window shows a user icon for every user in the group. (If you're using system software

7.6.1 or earlier, user icons look different in group windows than in the Users & Groups control panel.) If you want to see or change information for a registered user, you can open the user icon wherever you see it — in a group window or in the User & Groups window. You cannot create a new user directly in a group window, however. Figure 18-11 shows an example of a group window as it looks in Mac OS 8 and Mac OS 7.6.

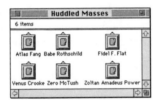

Figure 18-11: Seeing the members of a group in Mac OS 8 (left) and in earlier versions of the system software (right).

Removing users from a group

To remove users from a group, open the group icon to display its window, and drag the user icons that you want to remove from the group window to the Trash. If you're using Mac OS 8, you can also remove users from a group by selecting the user icons in the group window and choosing Remove from the File menu. Users are removed right away; they don't wait in the Trash until you empty it.

Seeing the groups a user belongs to

To see all the groups to which a registered user belongs, open the user icon. If you're using Mac OS 8, you also need to choose Sharing from the pop-up menu at the top of the user window. The user window displays a list of groups to which the registered user belongs, as shown in Figure 18-12.

Figure 18-12: Seeing the groups to which a registered user belongs in Mac OS 8 (left) and in earlier versions of the system software (right).

Controlling Access to Your Shared Items

Even if you allow guests and registered users to connect to your computer, by default Mac OS 8 doesn't permit them to see or change your shared folders and disks. Earlier versions of the Mac system software take the opposite approach, by default letting everyone who connects to your computer see and change your shared items. Besides those extremes, you can grant full or partial access to each shared folder independently. Moreover, each shared folder can have different access privileges for three categories of users: the owner, one user or group, and everyone. For example, you might want to ensure that a user or group of users can access a folder of templates on your computer but not modify them. Access privileges also enable you to selectively share a folder of confidential documents, such as employee performance reviews.

This section explains how you use the Finder's Sharing command to set separate access privileges for the owner, one registered network user or one group, and everyone else. (The previous section, "Identifying Who Can Access Your Shared Items," tells you how to identify network users and groups of users to whom you want to grant or deny access to your shared folders.)

Setting specific access privileges

You set the access privileges of a folder or disk in its sharing window, which appears when you select the folder or disk and choose the Sharing command from the File menu. The access privileges you can set and the methods you use for setting them are different in Mac OS 8 than in earlier versions of the Mac system software.

Access privileges in Mac OS 8

With Mac OS 8, a sharing window displays icons to indicate the access privileges of each user category, and you set access privileges by choosing from pop-up menus. Figure 18-13 shows a pop-up menu for setting access privileges in Mac OS 8.

Figure 18-13: Setting access privileges with pop-up menus in Mac OS 8.

You can set one of the following four privilege levels for each user category in the sharing window displayed by Mac OS 8:

❖ **Read & Write** lets users open the folder and see enclosed folders; see, open, and copy enclosed files; and create, delete, move, and change enclosed files and folders.

❖ **Read only** lets users open the folder and see enclosed folders, and see, open, and copy enclosed files.

❖ **Write only** lets users drag files and folders into the folder, but not open the folder. Note that this privilege makes sense only for folders enclosed by a shared folder or disk. Users can't access any write-only disk or a write-only folder that's not enclosed in a shared folder.

❖ **None** denies users access to the folder.

Access privileges in Mac OS 7.6 and earlier

In system software versions earlier than Mac OS 8, a sharing window displays access privileges of each user category with check boxes, and you set access privileges by turning the check boxes on or off. Figure 18-14 shows the check boxes you use to set access privileges in Mac OS 7.6.1.

Figure 18-14: Setting access privileges with check boxes in system software 7.6.1 and earlier.

In this sharing window, you can grant or deny any combination of the following three access privileges for each user category:

❖ **See Folders** lets users open the folder and see folders inside it.

❖ **See Files** lets users see, open, and copy files inside the folder.

❖ **Make Changes** lets users create, delete, move, and change files (if the See Files privilege is granted) and folders (if the See Folders privilege is granted) that are inside the folder. By itself (without See Files or See Folders), Make Changes lets users drag files and folders into the folder, but not open the folder.

Correlation of old and new access privileges

Each access privilege level in Mac OS 8 corresponds to a combination of access privileges in earlier versions of the Mac system software. For example, setting the Read Only privilege in Mac OS 8 corresponds to the See Folders and See Files privileges in Mac OS 7.6. Table 18-1 lists all the newer privilege levels and the equivalent combinations of older privilege settings.

Table 18-1 Mac OS 8 Privileges Compared with Privileges in Earlier Systems	
Privilege set in Mac OS 8	*Privileges set in earlier versions of system software*
Read & Write	See Folders, See Files, and Make Changes
Read Only	See Folders and See Files
Write Only	Make Changes
None	None

Not all combinations of access privileges in system software 7.6.1 or earlier correspond to privilege levels in Mac OS 8. Mac OS 8 honors all combinations of access privileges set on computers that use earlier versions of the system software. Mac OS 8 displays a question mark in a sharing window for a combination of privileges that doesn't match one of the privilege levels it knows about. These are the combinations of access privileges that have no corresponding privilege level in Mac OS 8:

❖ See Folders and Make Changes

❖ See Files and Make Changes

❖ See Folders alone

❖ See Files alone

Selecting specific or adopted access privileges

By default, folders inside a shared disk or shared folder adopt the access privileges of the enclosing folder or disk. Instead, you can set specific access privileges for any enclosed folder. An option in an enclosed folder's sharing window controls whether the folder has specific access privileges or adopts the privileges of its enclosing folder. The option is labeled "Use enclosing folder's privileges" in Mac OS 8. With earlier versions of the system software, the option is labeled "Same as enclosing folder." This option appears only for folders that are inside a shared folder or shared disk.

If you move a folder with adopted privileges, it takes on the privileges of its new enclosing folder. In contrast, a folder with specific access privileges keeps its specific privileges if you move it to a different enclosing folder.

Setting specific privileges for an enclosed folder

To set specific access privileges for an enclosed folder, display the enclosed folder's sharing window, turn off the option labeled "Use enclosing folder's privileges" or "Same as enclosing folder," and set the specific access privileges you want the enclosed folder to have. Figure 18-15 shows an example of an enclosed folder's sharing window with specific, not adopted, privileges set in Mac OS 8 and in Mac OS 7.6.1.

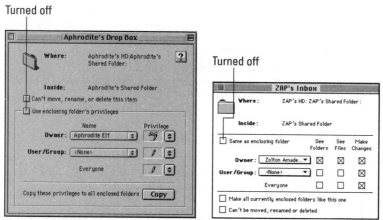

Figure 18-15: Setting specific access privileges for an enclosed folder in Mac OS 8 (left) and in earlier versions of the system software (right).

Adopting the enclosing folder's privileges

To make an enclosed folder adopt the access privileges of its enclosing folder, bring up the enclosed folder's sharing window and turn on the option labeled "Use enclosing folder's privileges" or "Same as enclosing folder." When you turn on that option, the system software dims the controls for setting access privileges. Figure 18-16 shows an example of an enclosed folder's sharing window with adopted privileges set in Mac OS 8 and in Mac OS 7.6.1.

Changing all enclosed folders' privileges

In Mac OS 8, if you change a folder's privileges and want to force all enclosed folders to have the same privileges, click the Copy button in the enclosing folder's sharing window. In earlier system software versions (which don't have the Copy button), you turn on the option "Make all currently enclosed folders like this one" and close the sharing window. Folders inside enclosed folders are also affected.

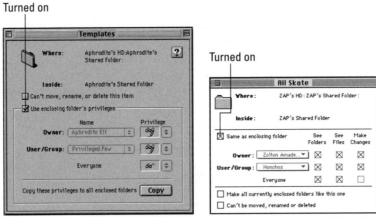

Figure 18-16: An enclosed folder with adopted access privileges in Mac OS 8 (left) and in earlier versions of the system software (right).

Caution: Forcing enclosed folders to use the privileges of their enclosing folder turns off the option labeled "Use enclosing folder's privileges" or "Same as enclosing folder" in all enclosed folders. Henceforth none of the enclosed folders will be updated automatically when you change the enclosing folder's privileges. You'll have to click the Copy button or turn on the option "Make all currently enclosed folders like this one" every time you change the enclosing folder's privileges, or else laboriously go through all enclosed folders and turn on the option labeled "Use enclosing folder's privileges" or "Same as enclosing folder."

You don't need to (and generally shouldn't) click the Copy button or turn on the option "Make all currently enclosed folders like this one" when you first make a disk or folder available for sharing. At that time all the enclosed folders automatically adopt the privileges of the enclosing folder or disk. Any new enclosed folders that you create also automatically adopt the privileges of the enclosing folder.

Specifying who has access privileges

The sharing window displays the following three categories of users for whom you can set access privileges:

❖ **Owner** names the owner of the computer from which the folder was created (not necessarily your computer), or a registered user or group to whom the current owner assigns ownership.

❖ **User/Group** names one registered user or one group of users with special access privileges to the shared folder or disk.

❖ **Everyone** refers to anyone who connects to the computer as a guest or as a registered user.

The three categories of users are dimmed if the "Share this item and its contents" option is off, or for enclosed folders, if the option labeled "Use enclosing folder's privileges" or "Same as enclosing folder" is on.

Owner privileges

Ownership of a folder or disk gives you the right to modify its access privileges. You can transfer ownership of a folder or disk to a registered user, to a group, or to all network users that you allow to connect to your computer. If the folder or disk is on your computer, you choose a new owner from the Owner pop-up menu in the folder or disk's sharing window. If the folder or disk you own is on someone else's computer, you type the name of the new owner in the space provided. Figure 18-17 shows both procedures in Mac OS 8 (the only differences in earlier versions of the system software are cosmetic).

On your own computer, use the pop-up menu.

On someone else's computer, type the new owner's name.

Figure 18-17: Changing the owner of a shared folder or disk.

The Owner pop-up menu lists the registered users and groups to whom you can transfer the ownership of the folder. If you have added a new user or group that doesn't appear in the pop-up menu, close the sharing window and then reopen it to make the new name appear.

No pop-up menu appears for a shared folder or disk that you own on someone else's computer, so you must type the new owner's name. The name you type must match the name of a registered user or a group in the Users & Groups control panel of the computer where the folder or disk is located. Leave the Owner name blank if you want to transfer ownership to any user.

Keep in mind that after you transfer ownership of a folder or disk, the new owner can restrict your access to that item and its contents — but only when you try to access the folder from another computer on the network. Giving away ownership of a folder or disk on your computer doesn't take away your ability to open, use, or modify it from your own computer. In effect, an item can have dual ownership, giving two users ownership privileges. If you make another user the owner of an item on your computer, both you and that other user have ownership privileges. You can reclaim sole ownership at any time by making yourself the owner in the item's sharing window.

User/Group privileges

You can give one registered user or a group of registered users greater access privileges than other network users to a shared folder or disk. If the folder or disk is on your computer, you choose a registered user or group from the User/Group pop-up menu in the folder or disk's sharing window. If the folder or disk you own is on someone else's computer, you type the name in the space provided. Figure 18-18 shows both procedures in Mac OS 8 (the only differences in earlier versions of the system software are cosmetic).

On your own computer, use the pop-up menu.   On someone else's computer, type the name of the new registered user or group.

Figure 18-18: Changing the user or group that has special access privileges to a shared folder or disk.

The User/Group pop-up menu lists all the registered users and groups in your Users & Groups control panel. If you have added a new user or group that doesn't appear in the pop-up menu, close the sharing window and then reopen it to make the new name appear.

The pop-up menu doesn't appear for a shared folder or disk that you own on someone else's computer, so you must type the name of a registered user or group in the space provided. The name you type must match the name of a registered user or a group in the Users & Groups control panel of the computer where the folder or disk is located. If you want to change the User/Group to none, delete the User/Group name and leave it blank.

Everyone category

The Everyone category includes all registered users that you let connect to your computer. This category also includes guests (unregistered users) if you let them connect. If you want registered users but no one else to have access to the shared folders on your computer, disable Guest access in the Users & Groups control panel (as described in "Identifying Who Can Access Your Shared Items" earlier in this chapter). Then set the Everyone category to the privileges you want all registered users to have.

Note that a registered user or group of users specified for the User/Group or Owner category can have greater privileges than granted by the Everyone category.

QUICK TIPS

Giving Rank Its Privileges

If you're using Mac system software 7.6.1 or earlier, you should make Everyone's access privileges less than or the same as those of the User/Group category. Likewise, you should make the User/Group privileges less than those of the Owner. Mac OS 8 won't let you do otherwise, but earlier versions of the system software will. No one can actually get lesser privileges than the Everyone category, because everyone who connects is part of that category. Even registered users designated as the User/Group or the Owner are part of the Everyone category. Just remember: rank hath its privileges.

Common Access-Privilege Scenarios

Controlling who can do what with files in shared areas opens new possibilities for working in groups. Using access-privilege settings, you can keep folders private between two users, make the folders accessible to everyone on the network, or assign combinations between these extremes. The remainder of this section describes setting access privileges for five interesting file-sharing scenarios.

Universal access

Allowing everyone on the network access to a shared item and its contents is easy: just set the Everyone category to Read & Write in Mac OS 8 or grant the Everyone category the See Files, See Folders, and Make Changes privileges in earlier system software versions. You don't actually have to set the User/Group and Owner categories. Figure 18-19 shows the access privileges for universal access in Mac OS 8 and in earlier versions of the system software.

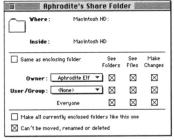

Figure 18-19: Access privileges for universal access in Mac OS 8 (left) and earlier system software (right).

Restricted access

If you want to give one registered user or one group access to a shared item but deny access to guests, name that user or group in the User/Group category and set the User/Group privileges as you like. Be sure the Everyone category has no privileges (you'll have to turn them all off if you're using system software version 7.6.1 or earlier). Figure 18-20 shows the access privileges for restricted access in Mac OS 8 and in earlier versions of the system software.

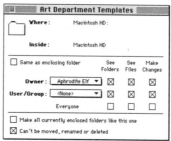

Figure 18-20: Access privileges for restricted access in Mac OS 8 (left) and earlier system software (right).

Private access

If you own a folder on someone else's computer, you can keep that folder private by setting the User/Group and Everyone categories to have no privileges. Only you and the user of that computer can access your folder. Figure 18-21 shows the necessary settings in Mac OS 8 and in earlier versions of the system software.

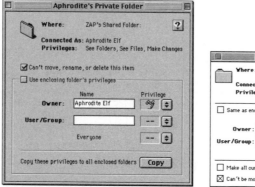

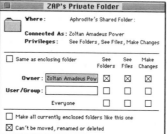

Figure 18-21: Access privileges for private access in Mac OS 8 (left) and earlier system software (right).

To keep a folder or disk on your own computer private, make sure that its "Share this item and its contents" option is off; use the Finder's Sharing command to verify its status. You'll still be able to access that folder when you use another computer to connect to your computer as its owner. Remember, a computer's owner always has full access privileges to every disk and folder when connecting over the network.

A private in-box folder

Setting up a folder to act as an in-box (or in-basket) enables other network users to deposit documents, folders, and other items in that folder. In-box folders sometimes are referred to as *drop boxes*, meaning that other users can drop in items, but only you can take those items out. A drop box must be inside another shared folder to enable network users to access it.

You prevent all other people from seeing, removing, or changing your folder's contents by setting the User/Group and Everyone categories to Write Only in Mac OS 8 or granting only the Make Changes privilege in earlier system software versions. Figure 18-22 shows the privilege settings for a private in-box in Mac OS 8 and in earlier versions of the system software.

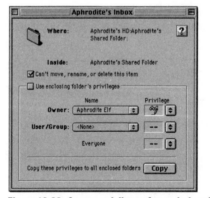
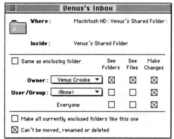

Figure 18-22: Access privileges for an in-box folder in Mac OS 8 (left) and earlier system software (right).

A user or group bulletin board

Another useful configuration of access privileges is setting up a folder to act as a bulletin board, enabling other users to open and read documents but preventing them from adding or changing documents. They could submit items for posting to the bulletin board by dropping them in an in-box folder (as described previously).

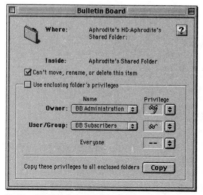

Figure 18-23: Access privileges for a bulletin-board folder in Mac OS 8 (left) and earlier system software (right).

To establish a bulletin-board folder, create and name an empty folder. Select the folder, and choose Sharing from the File menu. If you don't want to share your bulletin-board folder with everyone, set the Everyone category to have no privileges. Then name a user or group for the User/Group category and set the User/Group access privileges to Read Only in Mac OS 8 or to see folders and files in earlier versions of system software. You might want to name a small group as the owner of the folder so that members of the owner group could help with bulletin-board administration. Figure 18-23 shows the settings for a bulletin board in Mac OS 8 and in earlier versions of the system software.

Controlling Security Risks

File sharing poses a security risk, especially if you make your entire hard disk available for sharing and if you allow guests to connect to your computer. When you make an entire hard disk available for sharing, you either have to trust everyone you let access your computer or you have to go to a lot of trouble setting specific access privileges for various folders that you want to keep network users out of. There's always the risk of forgetting to deny access to a folder that you don't want network users to share.

Guests pose a particular security risk because they can connect without a password. If you disable guest access in the Users & Groups control panel, you can require everyone who connects to your computer to enter a password. Although passwords can be shared, stolen, or guessed, they are still more secure than no passwords.

Controlling access to disks, folders, and files

Here are some ways you can improve file sharing security:

❖ Share folders, not entire hard disks.

❖ Register users and give them passwords.

❖ Organize registered users into groups. Make a folder for each group, and in it put files and folders for group members to share. Keep in mind that you can make a registered user a member of every group whose folder you want that user to share.

❖ For each group folder you create, set the User/Group to be the group for which you created the folder. Also set the User/Group privilege level that you want group members to have. Be sure to set the Everyone privileges to none. If you want group members to have less access to some items, put those items in a folder inside the group's folder, and set specific lesser privileges for that enclosed folder.

❖ If you decide to allow guests to connect to your computer, make a folder (or folders) for guests and in it put files and folders you want them to share. Your registered users will also have access to this folder.

❖ Set a privilege level for your guest folder's Everyone category. If you want guests to have less access to some items, create a folder inside your main guest folder and set specific access privileges for that enclosed folder. For all shared folders outside your guest folder, make sure that the Everyone category has no privileges.

Locking folders

To prevent anyone from renaming a folder, deleting it, or moving it into another folder, bring up the folder's sharing window and turn on the option labeled "Can't move, rename, or delete this item" (in Mac OS 8) or "Can't be moved, renamed, or deleted" (in earlier system software). This option works like the Locked option in the Info windows of files. It affects you or anyone else using your computer as well as network users who access the folder from another computer. This option affects a folder even if you don't make the folder available for sharing. This option is not available for disks, although they are always locked when they are shared.

Coping with Network Insecurity

Can crackers invade your network? The Mac system software's file sharing puts your hard disks at risk if your computer is connected to a network. The risk of invasion exists even if you normally have file sharing turned off. Someone who spends 40 seconds at your keyboard can open your File Sharing control panel or Sharing Setup control panel, change your owner password (without knowing your current password), start file sharing, and close the control panel, leaving no sign of these activities. Then, at his or her leisure, the cracker can use another computer on the network to connect to your computer as its owner and snoop through everything on your hard disks without leaving any electronic footprints.

You eventually would notice if someone changed your files, of course, and you would see that your password had been changed if you tried to connect to your computer from another computer. But a less easily detectable invasion involves altering access privileges with the Users & Groups control panel and the Finder's Sharing command; this procedure could take less than 10 minutes.

Apple could make your system more secure by adding password access to the File Sharing control panel and the Users & Groups control panel. In the meantime, you can password-protect your disks or folders by using software such as Folder Bolt from Kent-Marsh. Another approach is to encrypt sensitive files with Private File from Aladdin Systems (408-761-6200, http://www.aladdinsys.com). If you want to go to great lengths, you can encrypt your entire hard disk with PGPdisk from Pretty Good Privacy (415-572-0430; http://www.pgp.com) or the CryptDisk shareware by Will Price. Otherwise, you must either remove the File Sharing extension from your Extensions folder or trust everyone who has access to a Mac on your network.

Monitoring File Sharing Activity

When file sharing is on, you can view who is connected to your computer and list which of your folders and disks you are sharing. To monitor file-sharing activity, open the File Sharing control panel and select its Activity Monitor view (in Mac OS 8) or open the File Sharing Monitor control panel (in earlier system software). You see a list of the folders and disks you have made available for sharing (enclosed folders are not listed). You also see a list of the network users currently connected to your computer. An activity indicator shows you how much of your computer's total processing time is being spent handling file sharing. Figure 18-24 shows how all this looks in Mac OS 8 and in earlier versions of the system software.

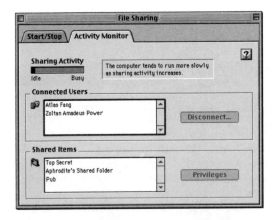

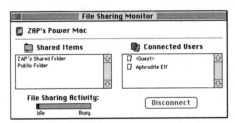

**Figure 18-24: Seeing who is connected and what you are
sharing in Mac OS 8 (top) and in earlier system software (bottom).**

If any guests are connected to your computer, each one that is currently
connected is listed as <Guest>. Because guests are anonymous, there's no way
to tell which guest is which.

You can disconnect one or more users by selecting them in the list of
connected users and clicking the Disconnect button. You select multiple users
by ⌘-clicking or Shift-clicking in Mac OS 8, or by Shift-clicking in earlier
versions of system software. When you click the Disconnect button, the system
asks you to specify the number of minutes you want to elapse before the
disconnection occurs. It's good networking etiquette to give people enough
time to save any changes they have made to the files before you disconnect
them. To disconnect a user immediately, specify 0 minutes. This disconnection
doesn't turn off file sharing.

Bear in mind that this procedure disconnects a user only temporarily. The same
user can connect again and access your shared folders. To keep a user from
connecting again, use the Users & Groups control panel to deny that user
access to your computer.

You can also review and change the access privileges of items in the shared items list of the File Sharing control panel in Mac OS 8. You select one or more items in the list and click the Privileges button to bring up the sharing windows of the selected items. (The Privileges button does not exist in the File Sharing Monitor control panel of system software 7.6.1 and earlier.)

Sharing Someone Else's Folders and Disks

So far, you have created and set access privileges for items that you're sharing with other network users. Other users on the network who are sharing their items have performed similar tasks to make folders or disks available to you and to other network users. Before you can access another user's shared items as a guest, you need to know the name of the computer you want to access. To access the shared items as a registered user, you must also know your registered name and password on the other computer. In addition, if your network has zones, you need to find out the name of the zone in which the other computer is located.

Connecting to another computer

To make a connection to another computer, open the Chooser. Make sure that AppleTalk is active (so that you can connect to another computer on the network), and click the AppleShare icon. If your network contains zones, click the zone in which the other computer to which you want to connect resides. The Chooser then displays a list of computers that you can connect to for file sharing. From the list, select the name of the computer you want to connect to, and click the OK button. A dialog box appears, allowing you to identify yourself as a registered user or guest. Figure 18-25 shows an example of the connection dialog box in Mac OS 8.

Figure 18-25: Connecting to another computer.

QUICK TIPS

Mac and Windows File Sharing

If use a Mac and a Windows computer, you probably need to transfer files back and forth. For small files you can use floppy disks, but for large files it would make sense to connect the computers in a network and use file sharing.

To use Mac file sharing from a Windows computer you need software that adds AppleTalk protocols to Windows. PC MacLAN for Windows 95 lets a PC access a Mac's drives and printers, and lets a Mac access a PC's drives and printers; it's from Miramar Systems (805-966-2432, http://www.miramarsys.com). COPSTalk 2.0 for Windows 95 lets a PC see Mac devices but not vice versa; it's from CoOperative Printing Solutions (770-840-0810, http://www.copstalk.com).

For the network connection between the machines, Ethernet works great. Many Macs have built-in Ethernet capability and need only a transceiver for a particular type of Ethernet cable, with 10Base-T cable the most popular by far. The newest Macs have built-in 10Base-T ports. Macs without built-in Ethernet need an Ethernet adapter, and a variety are widely available from many manufacturers. Most PCs need an Ethernet network interface card (NIC). You have several options for connecting computers with Ethernet (as discussed in "Hooking Up a Network" in Chapter 17).

Connecting as a registered user

To connect as a registered user, select the Registered User option, and enter your registered name and password in the spaces provided. This name and password must have been assigned by the owner of the computer that you want to access. If you're accessing your own computer from another computer, you enter the owner name and password. Type your password exactly as it was assigned, including uppercase and lowercase letters, and then click the OK button.

Connecting as a guest

If you're not a registered user and the Guest option isn't dimmed, you can access the other computer as a guest. If the Guest option is dimmed, guests are not permitted access to the selected computer.

Changing your password

Before connecting to another computer, you may be able to change your password. Click the Set Password button, and a series of dialog boxes leads you through the process of changing your password. If you get a message saying your password couldn't be changed, you probably don't have permission to change your password on the computer you're about to connect to. Contact the owner of that computer to find out.

Selecting disks and folders

After connecting you as a registered user or guest of another computer, the Chooser displays a dialog box that names the other computer and lists its shared folders and disks. You select the names of items you want to use now and the check boxes of items you want to use every time you start up your computer, and then click the OK button. To select more than one item name, Shift-click each name. You can scroll through the list or type the first few letters of a shared item's name to find it. If a listed item is dimmed, either you're already using that folder or disk or the owner of that folder or disk hasn't granted you access privileges to see it. Figure 18-26 shows an example of the Chooser's dialog box that lists shared items from a computer you're connected to in Mac OS 8.

If you mark a check box and are a registered user, two options appear in the dialog box below the list of items. Select the option "Save My Name Only" if you want the system to ask for your password before opening the shared folder or disk during startup. Use this option to prevent unauthorized people from accessing the shared folder or disk from your computer by restarting it. If you select the "Save My Name and Password" option, your computer automatically supplies your password when it opens the checked items during startup.

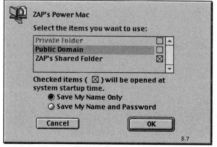

Figure 18-26: Selecting folders and disks to use from a computer you are connected to.

An icon appears on your desktop for each item you're using from another computer. Your computer treats a shared volume like a disk, no matter whether it's a folder or a disk on the other computer.

Sharing with aliases

Fortunately you don't have to go through the Chooser to use a shared folder or disk again. Connect and select once as described previously, and while the shared item's icon is on your desktop, make an alias of it. You can also make an alias of a file or folder contained in the shared folder or disk. If you open the alias of something from another computer on the network, the system software connects to the other computer and opens the alias's original item for you. You have to enter your password again unless you were connected as a guest when you made the alias.

Recognizing your access privileges

You use the items shared from another computer in the same manner that you use items on your own computer. Of course, what you can do with a shared item depends on the access privileges that its owner has granted you. You can recognize your access privileges from a shared folder's icon, from small icons in the window of a shared folder or disk, or by viewing the shared item's sharing window.

Icons of shared folders you're using

Often you can ascertain your privileges for a folder by looking at the folder's icon. A folder icon with a belt around it indicates that you don't have any access privileges. A belt-strapped folder icon with an accompanying down arrow is a drop box; you can drop items into the folder but cannot open it or use anything inside it. Only folders enclosed in a shared folder or disk have these special icons. You won't see a special icon for an enclosed folder that has a custom icon. Figure 18-27 shows examples of the special folder icons in Mac OS 8 and in Mac OS 7.6.1.

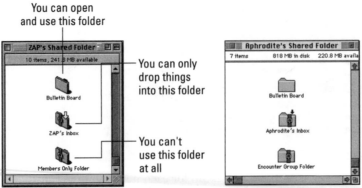

Figure 18-27: Interpreting access privileges from special folder icons in Mac OS 8 (left) and earlier system software versions (right).

Privilege icons in window headers of items you're using

When you open a folder that belongs to someone else, look for one or two small icons just below the window's close box. The icons indicate any privileges that the folder's owner has denied you. A pencil with a line through it means that you can't make changes to items in the window. A document with a line through it means that you can't see files in the window. A folder with a line through it means that you can't see folders in the window. Figure 18-28 shows examples of the privilege icons in a Mac OS 8 window.

Figure 18-28: Identifying denied privileges in windows: can't see folders (left), can't see files (middle), and can't make changes (right).

The sharing windows of items you're using

In addition to interpreting access privileges from icons, you can look at the sharing window of a shared folder or disk you're using. With the shared item's icon selected, choose the Sharing menu command. For an item shared from another computer, the sharing window tells where the item is, the name under which you're connected, and your access privileges for that item. Unless you're the owner of the item, you can only view the privileges. Table 18-2 shows the access privileges that you need in order to perform common tasks with a shared folder or disk.

An owner's special privileges

If you connect to a computer as its owner, you can see and use everything on that computer. In other words, you have full access privileges to all items, whether or not they have been designated for sharing. This feature is handy if you need copies of files from your computer while you're not in your office. By connecting to your computer over the network, you can copy those files to the computer at which you're working and then read, change, or print them. However, other people can also access all your hard disks if they learn your owner name and password.

Table 18-2
Access privileges for common tasks

To do this with shared folder or disk *XYZ*:	You need these privileges:	
	Mac OS 8	Earlier system software
Open a file from *XYZ*	Read Only or Read & Write	See Files
Save changes to a file in *XYZ*	Read & Write	See Files, Make Changes
Drag something to *XYZ*	Write Only or Read & Write	Make Changes
Copy a file from *XYZ*	Read Only or Read & Write	See Files
Copy a folder from *XYZ*	Read Only or Read & Write	See Folders
Discard a file from *XYZ*	Read & Write	See Files, Make Changes
Discard a folder from *XYZ*	Read & Write	See Folders, Make Changes
Create a file in *XYZ*	Read & Write	See Folders, See Files, Make Changes
Create a folder in *XYZ*	Read & Write	See Folders, Make Changes

It's possible to remove the owner's special access to all hard disks, essentially treating the owner like an ordinary registered user. This makes your computer more secure. This also makes file sharing less convenient because you have to assign access privileges to the owner for every disk or folder that you want to access (as owner) over the network. To remove the owner's special access privileges, open the owner window in the Users & Groups control panel and turn off the option labeled "Allow user to see all disks" (in Mac OS 8) or "Allow user to see entire disk" (in earlier system software versions).

For even greater security, you can also prevent anyone from connecting to your computer as the owner. To do this, open the owner window in the Users & Groups control panel and turn off the option labeled "Allow user to connect to this computer" (in Mac OS 8) or "Allow user to connect" (in earlier system software versions). If you turn off this option yet still want to connect to your computer over the network, you must create a secret identity for yourself as a registered user and assign this user the necessary access privileges.

Transferring items between computers

The most common use of file sharing is to transfer items from one computer to another. For the most part, you transfer items between computers just as you would copy files to a floppy disk. If you try to move a folder or file from a shared folder or disk to the desktop, a message asks whether you want to copy the item to your startup disk. If you click OK, a copy of the item appears on your desktop.

Opening items shared from another computer

When you open a shared document, the Finder searches your local disks for the application needed to open the document. If the application isn't found, the Finder tries to find it on the computer from which you're sharing the file and to open it across the network. Running applications over a network is considerably slower than running an application on your computer. To give you a rough idea of network activity, the system software displays a small double-arrow in the upper left corner of the menu bar while it is sending or receiving anything over the network.

Disconnecting from another computer

You can disconnect from another computer in three ways:

❖ You can select the icons of all items that you're sharing from that computer and then choose Put Away from the File menu.

❖ You can drag those file-server icons to the Trash.

❖ If you're done working on your computer, you can choose the Shut Down command from the Finder's Special menu; you disconnect from the other computer while shutting down.

Summary

In this chapter, you learned that Mac system software's distributed file sharing is great for a small group, but a dedicated file server like AppleShare IP is generally better for a large group. You read about file sharing's limitations: 10 shared items, 10 computers connected to yours, 5 computers accessing your files, and with system software versions earlier than Mac OS 8, 100 registered users and 100 groups. You also read some guidelines for file sharing.

You learned how to use the File Sharing control panel in Mac OS 8 or the Sharing Setup control panel in earlier system software to identify your computer with a name, an owner, and an owner password; and to turn file sharing on and off.

You found out how to use the Finder's Sharing command to designate which folders and disks are available for sharing. This chapter also told you how to use the Users & Groups control panel to register network users with names and passwords; how to create groups of registered users; and how to set general access privileges for each registered user, the owner, and guests.

Then you learned how to set access privileges for your shared folders and disks. You set privileges separately for three categories of network users: all network users (everyone), one registered user or group of your choosing, and the owner. The owner can be any registered user or group you choose. You can set specific privileges for an enclosed folder, or it can adopt the privileges of the folder that encloses it.

Although file sharing poses risks to your computer's security, you learned some strategies for controlling the risks. You also found out how to monitor the file sharing activity on your computer.

Finally, this chapter told you how to connect to someone else's computer and use its shared folders and disks. You learned how to recognize your access privileges to shared items you're using. And you learned how to disconnect your computer from another computer when you're done sharing its folders and disks.

CHAPTER NINETEEN

Enjoy Multimedia

IN THIS CHAPTER

- **Watching QuickTime movies** with Movie Player and other programs

- **Viewing QuickTime VR** panoramas and objects

- **Manipulating QuickDraw 3D graphics**

- **Hearing and recording audio CDs** with the AppleCD Audio Player

- **Watching and capturing video input** with the Apple Video Player

The Mac OS gives you many ways to enjoy audio and video on your computer. The QuickTime system extension lets you watch digital movies, including MPEG video. With QuickTime VR, you can view "virtual reality" panoramas and objects interactively. The QuickDraw 3D system extension enables you to display and manipulate three-dimensional objects. The AppleCD Audio Player program lets you control playback of audio CDs from your computer's CD-ROM drive, using simple push buttons or sophisticated programming of tracks by name. The Apple Video Player program enables you to view videos from video equipment such as a camcorder, VCR, or television, and to capture that video input digitally on disk.

This chapter explains how to use all this audio and video software, which comes with Mac OS 8 as well as some earlier system software versions. QuickTime works with all Macs that are capable of displaying color (even if they have monochrome monitors). QuickTime 2.5 comes with Mac OS 7.6 and 8, and earlier QuickTime versions come with Mac OS 7.1 through 7.5.3. In addition, Apple distributes a QuickTime plug-in for Web browsers so you can watch QuickTime movies on the Internet (as described in Chapter 20). All the QuickTime software is available for separate installation from Apple's QuickTime site on the Web (http:// quicktime.apple.com).

QuickTime Movies

Apple's QuickTime software not only makes it possible to watch movies on your computer, QuickTime makes movies ubiquitous! You don't need a special program to watch QuickTime movies. Most applications let you copy and paste movies as easily as you copy and paste graphics, and you can play a QuickTime movie wherever you encounter one. For starters, you can watch QuickTime movies from — and paste them into — SimpleText and the Scrapbook.

But there's more to QuickTime movies than a motion picture and a soundtrack. Recent versions of QuickTime expand the definition of *movie* considerably to include all kinds of interesting data that changes or moves over time. With QuickTime 2.5 and later, "movies" can include any of the following:

❖ Motion pictures — like what you watch on TV or at the movies

❖ Digital audio recordings — music and other sounds — that play in CD-quality sound (44.1 KHz, 16 bit, stereo) on PowerPC computers

❖ MIDI soundtracks, which take far less disk space to store than digital audio, yet sound realistic and play in CD-quality sound on PowerPC computers

❖ Text for closed-caption viewing, karaoke sing-a-longs, or text-based searches of movie content

❖ Sprites, which move independently like actors moving on a stage with a motion-picture backdrop

❖ Panoramas and objects that you can view in 360 degrees using QuickTime VR methods

❖ Three-dimensional graphics, drawn by QuickDraw 3D and composited in real time with other elements of the movie's picture

BACKGROUNDER

What's in a Movie?

In a QuickTime movie, the video, sound, and other types of media exist in separate tracks. A simple movie might consist of one video track and one sound track. A more complex movie may have several video tracks, several audio tracks, and closed-caption text tracks for text subtitles. Each video track could be designed specially for playback with a certain number of available colors (for example, 256 colors, thousands of colors, and millions of colors), each audio track could provide dialog in a different language (English, Spanish, Japanese, and so on), and each closed-caption text track could provide subtitles in a different language.

If a QuickTime movie contains MIDI sound, sprites, QuickDraw 3D graphics, or a QuickTime VR scene or object, each one is in a separate track. QuickTime takes care of synchronizing all the tracks so they play at the right time.

This section explains how to watch QuickTime movies wherever you find them. It also explains how to use Apple's MoviePlayer application to play and edit movies.

Compressed Images

QuickTime not only handles time-based and interactive media, but also extends the standard graphics format, PICT, to handle compressed still images and image previews. An application that recognizes QuickTime can compress a graphic image using any QuickTime-compatible software or hardware compressor that is available on your computer. All applications that can open uncompressed PICT images are also capable of opening compressed PICT images. QuickTime automatically decompresses a compressed PICT image without requiring changes to the application program.

QuickTime Magic

A computer shouldn't be able to play digital movies any more than a bumblebee should be able to fly. A single full-screen color picture on a 14-inch monitor takes a megabyte of disk space. To get 30 pictures per second, which is what you see on TV, the computer would have to store, retrieve, and display 30MB per second. Dream on, right? Right!

QuickTime pulls every trick in the book to play movies. Most movies are considerably smaller than the full 640 by 480 pixels available on a 14-inch color monitor. Although QuickTime 2.0 and later can play back full-screen movies from a hard drive on PowerPC computers, quarter-screen movies (320 by 240 pixels) are the largest that play back well from CD-ROM drives. With older versions of QuickTime, the optimum movie size is smaller.

Furthermore, QuickTime movies may play back fewer frames per second than TV or movies. Whereas TV shows 30 *fps* (frames per second) in the United States and other countries that use the NTSC standard (25 fps in Europe and other places that use the PAL or SECAM standards), QuickTime movies may play at 15 fps on slower computers. QuickTime 2.0 is the earliest version that can achieve 30 fps at a useful movie size (320 by 240) without special hardware, and it can achieve that playback rate only from a hard disk on a computer that has a 68040 or PowerPC processor.

Showing smaller pictures at slow frame rates reduces the amount of data to be stored, retrieved, and displayed, but not nearly enough. So QuickTime compresses movies, throwing out the redundant parts.

Watching QuickTime Movies

In addition to playing movies on your computer, QuickTime defines a standard controller (like the one on a VCR) that you use to start, stop, and control the movie playback in other ways. An application can suppress the movie controller, and there are standard methods for controlling playback when the controller is absent.

The movie controller

You usually control playback of a QuickTime movie with a standard collection of buttons and sliders along the bottom edge of the movie. With this controller, you can play, stop, browse, or step through the movie. If the movie has a sound-track, you can use the controller to adjust the sound level. The controller also gauges where the current scene is in relation to the beginning and end of the movie. By pressing certain keys while operating the controller, you can turn the sound on and off, copy and paste parts of the movie, play in reverse, change the playback rate, and more. Figure 19-1 shows a QuickTime movie with a standard controller. (Some applications have variants of the standard controller and may put the controller in a palette that floats above the document window.)

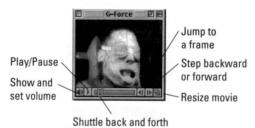

Figure 19-1: Controlling movie playback.

Clicking the volume control (labeled with a speaker) in the movie controller pops up a slider that you can use to adjust the volume. Clicking the play button (labeled with a right-pointing triangle) next to the volume control plays the movie. While the movie is playing, the play button becomes a pause button. The gray play bar in the middle of the movie controller shows the position of the currently playing frame relative to the beginning and end of the movie. To go to a different place in the movie, you can drag the frame marker in the play bar, or simply click the play bar. The two step buttons at the right of the play bar step backward and forward one frame per click. You can change the size of the movie window by dragging the size box at the right end of the movie controller.

In addition, the standard movie controller has several hidden capabilities. You can turn the sound off and on by Option-clicking the speaker button. You can set the sound volume louder than its normal maximum by holding down the Shift key while adjusting the volume with the slider. You can select part of a movie by pressing the Shift key while dragging or clicking in the play bar, and then using the Cut, Copy, or Clear command in the Edit menu. After cutting or copying part of a movie, you can paste it anywhere in the same movie or another movie. To deselect, ⌘-click anywhere in the gray bar. ⌘-click the reverse-step button to play the movie backward. Control-click either step button to reveal a slider that controls the direction and playback rate. Option-click a step button to jump to the beginning or end of the movie, as indicated by the direction of the step button. (If part of the movie is selected, Option-clicking the step button also jumps to the end of the selection.) To make the movie an optimal size, press the Option key while dragging or clicking the size box.

Playback without controllers

Applications may display movies without controllers. In this case, a badge in the lower-left corner of the movie distinguishes it from a still graphic. To play a movie that has a badge and no controller, you double-click the movie. Clicking a playing movie stops it. You can also display a standard movie controller by clicking the badge. Figure 19-2 shows a QuickTime movie with a badge.

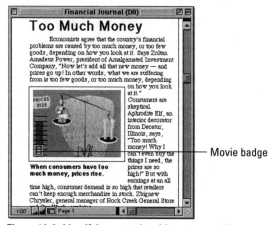

Movie badge

Figure 19-2: Identifying a movie without a controller.

QuickTime also extends the directory dialog box that appears when you use the Open command (and similar disk-related commands) to show what a movie or PICT contains before you open it. (Figure 19-3 shows an Open dialog box with a QuickTime movie preview.)

Figure 19-3: Previewing movies with the Open command.

The MoviePlayer application

Although you don't need a special application to view QuickTime movies, newer versions of the Mac OS include one called MoviePlayer. With the MoviePlayer menu commands, you have more control over playing a movie. For example, there are commands that let you do the following:

❖ Set the movie to play in a continuous loop, either always playing forward or playing alternately forward and backward.

❖ Play only the currently selected frames or all frames.

❖ Set the frame size to normal, half size, double size, or full-screen size.

❖ Center a movie presented at normal size on a completely black screen.

❖ Select the language sound track, if a movie has multiple language soundtracks.

❖ Display a movie's copyright information.

❖ Go to the movie's *poster frame*, set the current frame to be the poster frame, and see the poster frame in an Open dialog box that shows previews.

There are also MoviePlayer menu commands that let you edit parts of movies:

❖ The Enable Track command lets you turn tracks on and off. For example, you could turn off a movie's video and just hear the audio, or vice versa.

❖ The Delete Track command lets you delete tracks altogether, and the Extract Track command lets you extract individual tracks as new movies.

❖ The Get Info command displays a window in which you can see and in some cases change various attributes of each track in a movie. One pop-up menu lists the tracks, and another pop-up menu lists categories of attributes for the currently chosen track. Figure 19-4 shows a Get Info window for a movie.

Figure 19-4: Viewing and changing movie information.

Working with QuickTime Movies

It's easy enough to drag (or copy and paste) a movie into a document, but it's harder to figure out what to do with movies in an application such as a word processing program, which seems to exist for creating static printed documents.

WordPerfect was one of the first general productivity applications to include QuickTime movie capabilities. It's not immediately obvious how you can use movies in a word processing document, but WordPerfect has demonstrated several examples. One example is an interactive newspaper whose static illustrations of movie reviews become movie trailers when you double-click them. Imagine seeing an interactive newspaper in a kiosk at the front of a movie-theater complex.

In another example, a business letter describes a new helmet design and includes an animated 360-degree view of the helmet (see Figure 19-5). You can use the movie controller to look at the helmet from any angle. The letter and the animation fit onto a 50-cent floppy disk and can be read by anyone who has a QuickTime-equipped Mac OS computer. Larger documents — such as a student's report about travel to the moon, illustrated with movies of NASA space missions — could be delivered via the Internet.

Storing movies uses a great deal of disk space, but some documents are short-lived. For example, a TV news director could review several clips pasted into a memo and make comments on them in the same document, as shown in Figure 19-6. This document probably would exist (and occupy disk space) only for a day. (The alternative would be to hand the director a stack of videotapes and scrawled notes — not a pretty sight.)

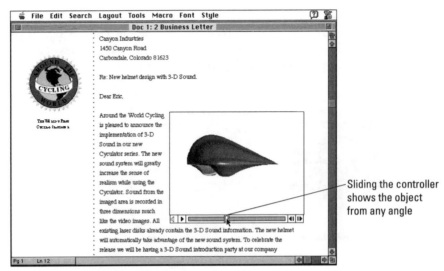

Sliding the controller shows the object from any angle

Figure 19-5: An interactive letter using QuickTime.

Clicking a movie badge displays a movie controller   Double-clicking a movie plays it

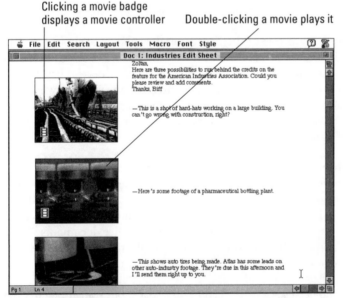

Figure 19-6: A document containing temporarily stored QuickTime movie clips and accompanying commentary.

QuickTime VR

QuickTime VR lets you view panoramas and objects in 360 degrees. When you view a panorama, you can look up, look down, turn around, zoom in to see detail, and zoom out for a broader view. When you view an object, you can manipulate it to see a different view of it.

If you have QuickTime 2.5 or later installed, you can view a QuickTime VR panorama or object anywhere you can view a linear QuickTime movie. For example, you can use SimpleText, the Scrapbook, or MoviePlayer. With earlier versions of QuickTime, you need to use the QuickTime VR Player application or Cyberdog to view VR content. You can also view QuickTime VR scenes embedded in Web pages if you have installed the QuickTime plug-in version 1.1 or later in your Web browser's plug-ins folder.

QuickTime VR 2.0 comes with Mac OS 8 and later. You can get the latest version of it, the QuickTime VR Player, and the QuickTime plug-in for Web browsers from Apple's QuickTime VR site on the Web (http://qtvr.quicktime.apple.com).

VR Panoramas

You change the view in a QuickTime VR panorama by clicking the picture and dragging left, right, up, or down. When viewing a panorama, press the Option key to zoom in, or press the Control key to zoom out. The pointer shape changes when you use it to change the view of a QuickTime VR scene, and the shape suggests the effect of dragging. In addition, if you have QuickTime VR 2.0 or later installed, a VR controller appears across the bottom of the window.

Figure 19-7 shows a QuickTime VR panorama being panned to the right. The pointer in the center foreground indicates the direction of the pan.

Pan

Show hot spots

Zoom in and out

Go back

Show and set volume

Drag mouse pointer

Figure 19-7: Panning a QuickTime VR panorama (to the right).

You can use the VR controller displayed at the bottom of the VR window to zoom in and out and adjust the sound level (if the panorama has sound). As you move the pointer over each control, a text description of its function appears in the VR controller.

Several buttons in the VR controller help you interact with VR *hot spots* — places in a panorama that you click to go to another panorama or object. One way to tell where hot spots are is by moving the pointer around. When the pointer is over a hot spot, it changes to a large white arrow pointing up. You can also have QuickTime VR show the hot spots in the current view. To outline the hot spots, click the VR controller button labeled with an up arrow and question mark. Figure 19-8 shows an example of an outlined hot spot in a QuickTime VR panorama.

Figure 19-8: Hot spots revealed in a QuickTime VR panorama.

After clicking a hot spot, you can go back to your previous location by clicking the Back button, which is labeled with a left arrow in the VR controller. If you've progressed through several hot spots, you can retrace your steps by clicking the Back button repeatedly.

VR Objects

You manipulate a QuickTime VR object by clicking it and dragging left, right, up, or down. As you drag, the object or some part of it moves. For example, it may turn around so you can see all sides of it, or it may open and close. The effect is determined by the author of the VR picture.

When viewing a QuickTime VR object, you can also place the pointer near an inside edge of the VR window and press the mouse button to move the object continuously. Figure 19-9 shows several views of a QuickTime VR object.

With QuickTime VR 2.0 and later, you can also zoom an object in and out by pressing the Shift or Control keys or by clicking the Zoom buttons in the VR controller. While zoomed in, you can pan to another part of the object by Option-dragging.

Figure 19-9: Manipulating a QuickTime VR object.

QuickDraw 3D

QuickDraw 3D makes it easy to view three-dimensional images. You can view and manipulate QuickDraw 3D graphics in any application designed to take advantage of it, such as SimpleText 1.3.1 or later, and Scrapbook 7.5.1 or later. In participating applications, QuickDraw 3D provides a viewer with buttons for changing the view of the image, as shown in Figure 19-10.

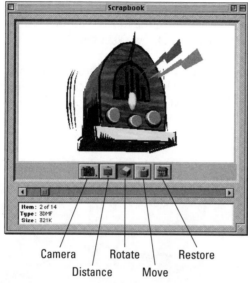

Camera

Distance

Rotate

Move

Restore

Figure 19-10: A QuickDraw 3D viewer has buttons for changing the view.

The QuickDraw 3D viewer's buttons let you move the image closer or farther away, rotate and tilt the image, move the image in the viewer frame, and restore the original view. QuickDraw 3D 1.5, which is included with Mac OS 8, provides five buttons. Earlier QuickDraw versions supply four buttons. Here's how the buttons work:

❖ **Camera**. Choose a view from the menu that pops up when you click this button. Choices typically include Fit To View, Front view, Back View, Left View, Right View, Top View, and Bottom View.

❖ **Distance.** Click inside the frame and drag toward the bottom of the frame to move the image closer, or drag toward the top of the frame to move the image farther away.

❖ **Rotate**. Click the image and drag to rotate it, or click outside the image and drag to tilt it.

❖ **Move**. Drag the image to move it vertically or horizontally in the frame.

❖ **Restore.** Click the button to restore the initial viewing distance, rotation, and position in the frame. This button is present only with QuickDraw 3D 1.5.

QuickDraw 3D also establishes a common file format for 3D graphics, called 3DMF (for "3D metafile"). The 3DMF format for 3D graphics is analogous to the PICT format for 2D graphics.

You don't always interact with QuickDraw 3D graphics. For example, with QuickTime 2.5 and later, movie authors can composite animated QuickDraw 3D graphics with other movie tracks.

Mac OS 7.6 and 8 include QuickDraw 3D as an optional part of a standard installation. System 7.5.3 CD-ROMs include QuickDraw 3D as a bonus. The latest version of QuickDraw 3D is also available from Apple's QuickDraw 3D site on the Web (http://quickdraw3d.apple.com).

Audio CDs

If your computer has a CD-ROM drive, you can listen to audio CDs with it. This section tells you how to control the playing of audio CDs with the AppleCD Audio Player application, explains the cable connections and control panel settings you might have to adjust to hear audio CD sound on your computer, and how to have a CD play automatically when you insert it or when you start up your computer. This section also describes how you can record passages from audio CDs as sound files.

If you play an Enhanced CD from your CD-ROM drive and open a program, access a file, or use the Finder, the Enhanced CD may stop playing. Enhanced CDs contain audio and other types of media such as text, movies, or multimedia software. This problem does not occur when playing regular audio CDs, which contain only audio.

AppleCD Audio Player

The AppleCD Audio Player application plays audio CDs from your CD-ROM drive. It has buttons that correspond to all the tangible push-button controls you'd expect to find on a machine that plays CDs. Many of the Audio Player's onscreen buttons have keyboard equivalents. What sets the Audio Player apart from an ordinary CD player is its program mode. You can program a custom play list for every CD, and Audio Player remembers each play list you create. You can also enter CD and track titles, which Audio Player remembers as well.

Figure 19-11 shows the AppleCD Audio Player and identifies its basic controls.

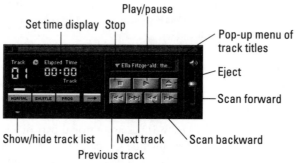

Figure 19-11: The AppleCD Audio Player program.

The Audio Player program has an Options menu that you can use to change the window color and the number-display color. You also can use this menu to play back the left channel or right channel only. In addition, if your computer has more than one CD-ROM drive, the Startup CD Drive submenu lets you choose the drive you want the Audio Player to control by selecting its SCSI ID number. After changing the Startup CD Drive, you have to quit the Audio Player and open it again to enforce the change.

Using control panel buttons

You can play, pause, stop, skip back, skip forward, scan back, and scan forward by clicking the buttons on the right side of the control panel. Here's how the buttons work:

❖ Clicking the Normal button plays the CD tracks sequentially.

❖ Clicking the Shuffle button plays the tracks in random order. Each time you click Shuffle, the order changes.

❖ Clicking the Prog button plays the tracks in an order that you specify (as described in "Programming CD playback," later in this section).

❖ Clicking the arrow button next to the Prog button alternates between playing the CD one time or continuously in the mode that you've selected (normal, shuffle, or program).

❖ Clicking the small down arrow above the Stop button triggers a pop-up menu that lists the tracks on the CD. Use this menu to play a specific track.

❖ Clicking the clock icon near the time display also triggers a pop-up menu. Use this menu to set the display to show elapsed or remaining time on the current track or on the entire disc.

Using keyboard controls

You can also operate many of Audio Player's controls from the keyboard. The following keyboard shortcuts work when the Audio Player is the active application:

❖ Press the left-arrow and right-arrow keys to scan backward or scan forward track by track.

❖ Press the space bar or the Enter key to alternately play and pause the CD.

❖ Press the Delete key or the Clear key to stop playing the CD.

❖ Press ⌘-E to eject the CD.

❖ Press the up-arrow and down-arrow keys to operate the volume control, if the Audio Player includes one. (The presence of a volume control depends on the capabilities of the CD-ROM drive.

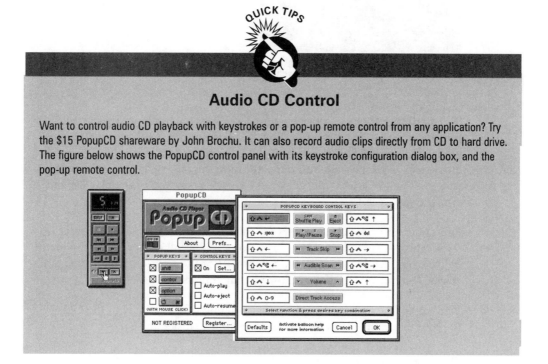

Audio CD Control

Want to control audio CD playback with keystrokes or a pop-up remote control from any application? Try the $15 PopupCD shareware by John Brochu. It can also record audio clips directly from CD to hard drive. The figure below shows the PopupCD control panel with its keystroke configuration dialog box, and the pop-up remote control.

Naming CDs and tracks

When you insert an audio CD, the Audio Player pulls the track times off the CD, but not the track titles. It displays generic titles (Track 1, Track 2, and so forth), but you can replace them with the real track and CD titles. It takes only a couple of minutes to enter the titles for a typical CD, and you only have to do it once — the Audio Player remembers the titles permanently. Once you enter the titles, they reappear every time you pop the CD back into the CD-ROM drive. Figure 19-12 shows an example of track titles in the Audio Player.

Figure 19-12: The AppleCD Audio Player remembers track titles you enter for each CD.

To enter titles, the Audio Player must be in Normal mode or Shuffle mode (not Prog mode). Click the tiny Edit List button (the small triangle located below the Normal button) to show the CD title and below it a track list. To enter track titles, press Tab to move through the track list, typing the titles as you go. To enter a CD title, click the CD title at the top of the play list and type the new title.

You can enter up to 62 characters for each track title. Although the track list itself can't display full titles that long, you can see full titles in a pop-up menu by clicking the CD title in the top right part of the Audio Player. To see more tracks, you can enlarge the window by dragging its size box.

The Audio Player stores the titles that you enter for each CD in the CD Remote Programs file in the Preferences folder (inside the System Folder).

Programming CD playback

To program the order in which the AppleCD Audio Player plays the tracks of a CD, click the Prog button. Then click the Edit List button (the small triangle below the Normal button) to display the track list and play list at the bottom of the Audio Player window. The track list appears on the left side of the window and lists all tracks sequentially. The play list appears on the right side of the window and you build it by dragging tracks from the track list to slots in the play list. The play list can include up to 99 tracks.

You can mix up the order of tracks on the play list any way you like, put the same track on the play list more than once, and leave tracks out of the play list altogether. You can rearrange tracks in the play list on the right by dragging them up or down. You can remove a track from the play list by dragging it back to the track list.

The Audio Player stores all your custom play lists in the CD Remote Programs file together with the CD and track titles you have entered. Figure 19-13 shows an example of a custom play list being built.

Figure 19-13: Drag track titles to program a play list in the AppleCD Audio Player.

Hearing Audio CD Sound

To hear audio CDs on your computer, you may need to set some sound input options in the Monitors & Sound control panel or the Sound control panel. If you want to play audio CDs from an external CD-ROM drive, you first need to connect the drive's sound output either to the computer's input, to amplified speakers, or to a stereo system.

Playing CDs from an external CD-ROM drive

You may be able to play audio CDs from an external CD-ROM drive through your computer's low-fi internal speaker or through external powered speakers connected to the computer's sound output port. Be sure to use magnetically shielded speakers near a monitor or disk. If you want to hear the computer's sounds and the audio CD sound through the same speakers, get a pair of powered speakers with mixed dual inputs (one input for the computer and the other for the CD-ROM drive), such as the AppleDesign Powered Speakers I or II.

External speakers are easy to hook up to an external CD-ROM drive, but you can't control their volume with the Audio Player or your computer's control panels. Furthermore, connecting external speakers to an external CD-ROM drive precludes recording CD sound from the drive (as described later in this section). To control the volume of an external CD-ROM drive from your computer or record sound from the external drive, you need to connect the external drive's sound output jacks to your computer's sound input port with a stereo patch cord (available wherever stereo accessories are sold). Your patch cord must have a plug or plugs that fit the sound output jacks on your CD-ROM drive, as well as a plug or plugs that fit the microphone port on your computer. Most external CD-ROM drives have a headphone jack on the front, and many drives also have RCA-style jacks on the back. Your computer probably has a stereo mini-jack for its microphone input, like the kind used for cassette player headphones. Some computers also have RCA-style jacks for alternate sound input. By examining the output jacks on your CD-ROM drive and the input port on your computer, you should be able to figure out the kind of patch cord plugs that are required for your equipment.

With some Mac models and versions of the Mac OS, you must also move the External CD Sound file from the Apple Extras folder to the Extensions folder. According to Apple, the only Macs that require that extension are the 630 series and the Power Mac and Performa 5200 and 6200 series. If your Apple Extras folder doesn't contain the External CD Sound extension, you probably don't need it. Apple includes the extension with all computers that need it. Apple doesn't distribute the extension through its online software updates library or on system software CDs. If you use powered speakers or a stereo system, you don't need the External CD Sound file.

The Power Mac Microphone Port

Although a Power Mac's microphone port is designed for the extra-long plug of Apple's PlainTalk speech recognition microphone, you can use an ordinary patch cord to connect an audio source to the microphone port. The PlainTalk microphone's plug reaches deep inside the Power Mac's microphone port to draw power for the microphone's internal preamplifier. A patch cord doesn't need electricity, so its regular ⅛-inch stereo mini-plug need not reach the port's power lead. The Quadra 660AV and 840AV have the same type of microphone port.

Sound Input Levels

When you connect an audio source such as an external CD-ROM drive to your computer, you must make sure it delivers a signal at the right level. If the level is too high, you will hear distorted sound. If the level is too low, the sound may be noisy or inaudible. You can connect a line-level audio source such as a VCR, cassette deck, or audio CD player to any of the following Macs, which have a line-level sound input (2 volts maximum, 8 KΩ impedance): all Power PC computers; the Quadra 605, 630, 660AV, and 840AV; the LC 475, 575, and 630; and the PowerBook 500 series. All other Macs have a microphone-level sound input (20 millivolt, 600 Ω). To avoid overloading the microphone-level sound circuitry with a line-level source — which would probably distort recorded sound but cause no damage — you should use a special cable that attenuates the high-level signal (for example, Sony part number RK-G128 or Radio Shack part number 42-2461-A).

Changing sound input options

To hear an audio CD, you may need to change a couple of sound input settings in the Monitors & Sound control panel (in Mac OS 8 and later) or in the Sound control panel (in earlier system software versions). You may have to make these changes whether you're using an internal CD-ROM drive or an external drive whose sound output is connected to your computer's microphone port (as described previously). You'll also probably have to turn off speech recognition, as described in Chapter 21. However, if you're playing audio CDs on an external CD-ROM drive that's connected to powered speakers or a stereo system, you can play and listen to audio CDs without making any of the control panel changes described here. In this case, you can even listen to an audio CD and use speech recognition at the same time, as long as the CD sound doesn't confuse the speech recognition software.

If you're using Mac OS 8 or later and an internal CD-ROM drive or an external drive connected to the computer's microphone port, open the Monitors & Sound control panel and click the Sound button to see the sound options. Set the Sound Input option to Microphone for an external CD-ROM drive or Internal CD for an internal drive, and turn on the Listening option. While looking at the Sound options, make sure the Sound Out Level and Computer Speaker Volume options are not turned all the way down or muted. You should now hear the audio CD through the computer's speakers or through external speakers if you have them plugged into your computer.

If you're using Mac OS 7.6.1 or earlier, open the Sound control panel and turn on the Playthrough option by clicking the Options button in the Sound In section of the Sound control panel. On Macs that normally use the Monitors & Sound control panel with Mac OS 7.6.1 and earlier, such as Macs with PCI slots, the Sound control panel is in the Apple Extras folder, not the Control Panels folder. Also, make sure the levels are not turned all the way down or muted in the Volumes section of the Sound control panel. You should now hear the audio CD through the computer's speakers or through external speakers if you have them plugged into your computer.

On some older computers, such as the Mac LC III, you must use the free PlayThrough application by Andreas Pardeike to hear audio CDs from an external CD-ROM drive that's connected to the computer's microphone port. You enable play-through by launching PlayThrough and leaving it open, but to put it in the background you must click outside its window (for some reason the Application menu doesn't work). To disable play-through, choose Ablage, which is German for Quit, from PlayThrough's File menu. This menu also contains German commands for setting the volume (Lautstärke 0 through 7).

Recording Audio CD Sound

You can record sound from an audio CD using the SimpleSound application, newer versions of the Monitors & Sound control panel, or the Sound control panel. In all cases, you control the CD with the AppleCD Audio Player program. For more control over recording short segments from an audio CD, use the freeware utility program GrabAudio by Theo Vosse. You can record long segments of an audio CD as a sound-only movie by using QuickTime.

Before you can record from an audio CD, you may have to set the computer's sound input source using the Monitors & Sound control panel or the Sound control panel (as described previously).

Some older Macs can't record directly from an audio CD in the internal CD-ROM drive if anything is plugged into the sound input (microphone) port. Affected models include Quadra or Centris 610 or 650, Quadra 800, Mac IIvx or IIvi, and Performa 600CD.

Using the Monitors & Sound or Sound control panel

If you're tired of the standard system alert sounds, you can record a new alert sound from your own audio CD using the AppleCD Audio Player program and the Sound control panel. First you observe the Audio Player while listening to the passage you want to record and note the track and time where the passage starts. Then use the Audio Player's controls to pause the CD a few seconds before the start of the passage. Make sure the Audio Player's volume control is all the way up. Next open the Sound control panel and display its Alert Sounds settings. (If you're not familiar with the controls for recording a new alert sound, click the Add button to see them, and then click Cancel to put them away for now.) Switch back to the Audio Player, start the CD playing and without hesitation switch back to the Sound control panel and click the Add button. Click the Record button a split-second before the beginning of the passage you want to record, and click the Stop button when you want it to finish (a second or two for an alert sound). Finally you save the sound with a name you want.

Figure 19-14 shows the controls for recording sound as they look in Mac OS 8.

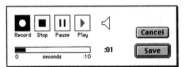

Figure 19-14: Recording sound with standard controls.

If your Control Panels folder doesn't contain a Sound control panel, see if you have a Monitors & Sound control panel with an Add button in the Alerts settings (which newer versions of Monitors & Sounds have). If there's no Add button here, look for the Sound control panel in the Apple Extras folder on your startup disk or use the SimpleSound program.

Using the SimpleSound program

The SimpleSound program can copy sound from an audio CD to a disk file. And like the Sound control panel and newer versions of the Monitors & Sound control panel, SimpleSound can record new alert sounds. SimpleSound comes with Mac OS 8 and some earlier system software versions. You set the sound quality with SimpleSound's Sound menu. The better the quality, the more disk space per second is required.

To capture part of a CD as a digital sound file, use the AppleCD Audio Player program to start the CD playing about 15 seconds before the start of the section you want to capture. Without hesitation switch to SimpleSound and choose the New command (or press ⌘-N) to bring up the system software's standard sound recording controls. Click the Record button a split-second before the beginning of the passage you want to record, and click the Stop button when you want it to finish. Then click the Save button to save the digital sound file in the AIFF format.

To record a new alert sound, choose Alert Sound from SimpleSound's Sound menu. This brings up the Alert Sounds window. Then use the Audio Player to start the CD playing a few seconds before the start of the sound you want to record. Immediately switch back to SimpleSound and click the Add button in the Alert Sounds window to display the controls for recording sound. Click the Record button a split-second before the beginning of the passage you want to record, and click the Stop button when you want it to finish. Then click the Save button to save the new alert sound.

Playing Audio CDs Automatically

You can have your computer play an audio CD when the computer starts up. Putting an alias of Track 1 from any audio CD into the Startup Items folder has the Finder automatically launch AppleCD Audio Player during startup and begin playing whatever CD is in the drive. The Track 1 alias works with any audio CD, not just the one used to make the alias. If there's no CD in the drive, the Mac OS requests one during startup. To make the alias, insert any audio CD, open its icon, select Track 1, and use the Make Alias command.

If you have QuickTime 2.5 installed, you can have the Mac automatically play an audio CD not only during startup but any time you insert one. Just turn on the Enable Audio CD AutoPlay option in the AutoPlay section of the QuickTime Settings control panel. This feature starts playing the CD earlier during startup than the Startup Items method and doesn't require the AppleCD Audio Player application. However, you do have to open AppleCD Audio Player (or its equivalent) if you want to control playback of an autoplaying CD while it's playing. (Of course, you can always just stop the autoplaying CD by ejecting it.)

Apple Video Player

If your computer has video inputs, chances are you can use the Apple Video Player application to play video and audio from a VCR, camcorder, or other video equipment on your computer screen. If your computer has a TV tuner installed, you can use the Video Player to tune in and watch TV shows. In addition, the Video Player can capture the video and audio and save it in a movie file on disk. You can use the Apple Video Player with the following Apple video input equipment:

❖ Built-in video ports on Power Mac 7500, 7600, 8500, and 8600 computers

❖ Apple Video System card or Apple TV/Video System card in these series of computers:

  • Power Mac and Performa 5200, 5300, 5400, 5500, 6300, 6400, and 6500

  • Quadra and Performa 580 and 630

❖ Power Mac AV card in Power Mac 6100AV, 7100AV, and 8100AV computers

If your computer doesn't have video input capability, you may be able to add it by installing a video card made by Apple or another company such as ATI Technologies (905-882-2600, http://www.atitech.ca), IXmicro (408-369-8282, http://www.ixmicro.com), or Radius Inc. (408-541-6100, http://www.radius.com). If you get a video card made by a company other than Apple, the card may use its own video player application instead of the Apple Video Player. For example, video cards from ATI Technologies use the Xclaim Video Player.

You can also buy more sophisticated video software that works with most major brands of video input equipment, including the Apple video input equipment listed previously and video cards from ATI Technologies, IXmicro, and Radius. Video editing and composing software such as Adobe Premiere and Avid Cinema can not only capture movies like Apple Video Player, they can also slice, dice, chop, mix, combine, and bake new movies from pieces of captured movies.

This section doesn't get into the complicated subject of video editing, but it does explain how to connect your video source to your computer and watch and capture video input with the Apple Video Player.

Connecting a video source

Before you can watch or capture video from a VCR or other video equipment outside your computer, you need to connect the video equipment to your computer. This involves connecting a cable from the video output jack of the video source to the video input port on your computer, and connecting another cable from the audio output jack (or jacks, for stereo) of the video source to the computer's audio input port or microphone port.

The type of video cable you use depends on the type of output jack on the VCR or other video equipment. If the video equipment has an S-video output jack (which looks like a keyboard or serial port on your computer), use an S-video cable. If the video equipment has a *composite* output jack (which looks like the RCA jacks on many stereo components), use a composite cable. Most consumer grade camcorders, VCRs, and TVs have composite output jacks. High-end video equipment has S-video jacks.

You can use an adapter to connect a composite cable to an S-video port on your computer. If your computer has only an S-video input port, it probably came with a composite cable adapter.

The video cable doesn't carry sound, so you have to connect a separate audio cable from the VCR or other video equipment to your computer. The plug at one end of the audio cable must fit the type of audio output jack on the video equipment, which is usually one or two RCA jacks. The plug at the other end of the audio cable must fit the computer's audio input port. Your computer may have a pair of RCA jacks for audio input or a stereo mini-jack (the microphone port).

Because the details of connecting video equipment to a computer vary according to the type of video input, you should consult the manual that came with your computer or video card for specific instructions.

Watching video

The Apple Video Player has a window for viewing video from an external video source or an internal TV tuner (if your computer has one). You select the video source and adjust the picture with controls in a separate Controls window. To see the video source and picture controls, click the video screen icon on the left side of the Controls window. Figure 19-15 shows the main Video Player window and the Controls window.

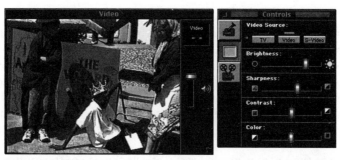

Figure 19-15: Selecting a video source and adjusting the picture in the Apple Video Player.

Capturing video

While watching video through the Apple Video Player, you can save a single frame as a picture file, copy a frame to the Clipboard, or save a video sequence as a QuickTime movie. You capture a single frame with the Copy Video Display command in the Edit menu, and you capture SimpleText picture files or QuickTime movie files with controls in the Controls window. To see the capture controls, you click the video camera icon on the left side of the Controls window. Figure 19-16 shows the capture controls.

Figure 19-16: Capturing
single-frame or movie files
with the Apple Video Player.

To successfully capture a still picture or a movie, you may need to increase the memory size of the Apple Video Player using the Get Info command in the Finder. The memory requirements depend on the size of the Video window and on the complexity of the image. If the Video Player runs out of memory while attempting to capture an image, it displays a vaguely worded alert notifying you that an error occurred.

Capturing a still picture

To capture a still picture, click the Freeze button in the Controls window when you see an image in the Video window that you want to save. The picture in the video window stops (although the video input continues unseen unless you pause or stop the VCR or other video source). If you like the still picture in the Video window, you can save it as a SimpleText picture file (a PICT file) by clicking the Save button in the Controls window. If you don't like the still picture, click the Freeze button again to resume viewing the video input.

The size of the Video window directly affects the size of the captured picture. Making the window smaller reduces the amount of disk space required to store the picture. For the smallest amount of disk space, choose Smallest Size from the Video Player's Window menu.

Capturing a movie

To capture a video sequence as a movie, click the Record button in the Controls window as you see the sequence begin in the Video window. Recording begins, the Record button changes to a Stop button, and the Pause button becomes functional. Click the Pause button if you want to suspend the recording process while the incoming video continues playing. When you click the Pause button, it changes to a Resume button, and clicking the Resume button resumes recording with the sequence then playing in the Video window. To end the recording, click the Stop button. The Video Player then uses QuickTime to compress the movie so it takes up less disk space (unless you turned off compression as described later), and displays a Save As dialog box so you can name the movie file and select a folder for it.

While recording is in progress, the motion you see in the Video window may become more jerky than usual. This does not mean the recorded movie will be as jerky. The computer optimizes the number of video frames it can record per second by devoting less processing power to displaying the incoming video. You want the computer to record as many frames per second as it can, because a higher frame rate produces smoother motion. The computer can record video at a higher frame rate if you eliminate background processing tasks that sap its performance. For example:

❖ Turn off virtual memory and the menu bar clock (restart the computer to make virtual memory changes take effect).

❖ If you use RAM Doubler instead of virtual memory, turn it off.

❖ Make sure file sharing is off, and make AppleTalk and TCP/IP inactive.

❖ Insert a floppy disk, a CD-ROM, and any other type of removable disk you have so the computer doesn't have to periodically check to see if you've inserted one.

Another factor that affects frame rate is the size of the Video window. The window size also affects the picture quality and file size of a captured movie. For the best quality movie in the smallest amount of disk space, choose Smallest Size from Video Player's Window menu. This sets the movie frame size to 160×120 pixels. Choosing Normal Size from the Windows menu sets the frame size to 320×240 pixels.

You can also increase a movie's frame rate and reduce its file size by having the movie compressed. Unfortunately video compression degrades picture quality. You can adjust the amount of compression or completely turn off compression by choosing Preferences from the Video Player's Setup menu and setting the Movie Compression option to None, Normal, or Most. The Normal setting reduces file size by 12% to 50%. The Most setting reduces file size up to 50% more than the Normal setting. The compression method that the Video Player uses, known as Apple Video, works best when the number of colors is set to thousands (not 256 or millions) in the Monitors & Sound control panel or the Monitors control panel (whichever your computer has).

Frame rate is also affected by the speed of the hard disk. You need a fast hard disk to record at high frame rates. To achieve the optimum frame rate of 30 fps (frames per second) with a normal frame size (320×240), your hard disk should be capable of sustained writes at 5MB per second or more. That rate is the maximum throughput of a regular external SCSI port, so you should connect your fast hard disk to a SCSI-2 port (10MB per second) or SCSI-3 port (20MB per second). Some Macs, such as the Power Mac 8500 and 8600, come with internal SCSI-2 ports. You can also install expansion cards with fast SCSI ports.

Frame rate and picture quality are irrelevant if your hard disk doesn't have enough space to record the movie. Capturing a normal frame size (320×240) requires 2MB to 4MB per second, depending on the frame rate. That much disk space must be available to initially capture the movie, when the Video Player automatically saves the uncompressed captured video in a temporary file. This temporary file is normally on the same disk as the Video Player program. If that disk becomes full and your computer has other hard disks, the Video Player looks for more temporary storage space on them. After recording the movie, the Video Player has QuickTime compress it and then releases the temporary storage space.

CAUTION

Can You Copy That?

Be careful what you copy. Video and sound are protected by copyright just like printed materials. Before capturing part of a videotape, videodisc, television program, or other recorded pictures and sound, you may need to get the copyright owner's permission. It's best to get permission in writing. You don't need permission to copy from works in the public domain, such as works of the United States government. (Works of state and local governments, as well as other national governments, may be protected by copyright.) You also don't need permission if your copying comes under the doctrine of *fair use* as defined by the US Copyright law. The law doesn't precisely define fair use, but does specify four criteria that must be considered:

1. The purpose and character of the use, including whether such use is of commercial nature or is for nonprofit educational purposes

2. The nature of the copyrighted work

3. The amount and substantiality of the portion used in relation to the copyrighted work as a whole

4. The effect of the use upon the potential market for or value of the copyrighted work

Summary

In this chapter, you learned that QuickTime pulls every trick in the book to play digital movies on your computer. It plays movies at reduced frame sizes and slower than normal frame rates, and it decompresses movies to reduce the amount of data it has to transfer from disk. You also learned how to control the playback of a QuickTime movie with and without the VCR-like movie controller.

This chapter told you how to interact with QuickTime VR panoramas and objects. You can change your view of a VR panorama by panning, tilting, zooming, and clicking hot spots. You can manipulate a VR object to see a different view of it. You also learned how to manipulate 3D graphics displayed by the QuickDraw 3D system extension.

This chapter also explained how to play audio CDs with your computer's CD-ROM drive. You can use the AppleCD Audio Player to control playing with all the push-button controls you'd expect to find on a CD player, and to program playback in ways few (if any) CD players can match. To hear audio CD sound on your computer, you may have to set some options in the Monitors & Sound control panel or the Sound control panel. To use an external CD-ROM drive, you have to connect it to your computer with an audio patch cord. You can also use the control panels, the SimpleSound application, and the Audio Player to record parts of CDs as sound files.

Finally, this chapter described how you watch video on a computer with video input equipment, and how you can capture still pictures or QuickTime movies from incoming video. You have to connect cables from the video equipment to your computer's video and audio ports. Then you can use the Apple Video Player application (if your computer has Apple video input) to watch and capture incoming video.

CHAPTER TWENTY

Explore the Internet

IN THIS CHAPTER

- **Setting up an Internet connection** with the Internet Setup Assistant, Internet Config, and various control panels

- **Connecting to and disconnecting from the Internet** manually or automatically

- **Sending and receiving e-mail** with Claris Emailer or Cyberdog

- **Browsing the World Wide Web** with Netscape Navigator or Cyberdog

- **Sharing your own Web site** with the Web Sharing control panel

- **Running Java applets** in a Web browser or independently

- **Transferring files** over the Internet

- **Participating in newsgroups**

The Internet is an amazing resource that's just become popular in the past few years. Using the Internet, you have access to an incredible variety of information and entertainment resources, from online newspapers and encyclopedias to the latest research data to stage and film reviews, and much more. Electronic mail (e-mail) connects people all around the world, bringing words from far away lands to your screen just seconds after they're sent. Mac OS 8 makes it easy to get on the Internet; it includes setup assistants to get you connected easily and many applications that help you surf the Net.

Setting up an Internet Connection

Before you can tap the wealth of information and services on the Internet, you need to set up your computer so it can make an Internet connection. To assist you in setting up an Internet connection, Mac OS 8 includes a special program aptly named the Internet Setup Assistant. If necessary, you can fine-tune the connection (or set up a connection from scratch with system software earlier than Mac OS 8) with the Internet Config utility and several control panels.

Using Internet Setup Assistant

In the dark ages, say in the first half of 1997, it could be very difficult to set up your computer to connect to the Internet. People often needed to learn arcane settings and deal with terminology best left to the hard-core geeks among us. The Internet Setup Assistant that's included with Mac OS 8 is a program that goes a long way toward easing the pain of getting connected. It leads you step-by-step through a series of decisions and questions to get your Internet information from you, and it enters that information into the various control panels and applications that the Mac OS uses for Internet access. You'll find an alias to the Internet Setup Assistant in the Assistants folder on your startup disk.

Getting started

You can use the Internet Setup Assistant any time you want to set up a new Internet connection or change an existing connection. You automatically get an opportunity to use the Internet Setup Assistant when you first start up your computer after installing Mac OS 8. At other times, you can double-click the Internet Setup Assistant's alias to begin the setup process. The Internet Setup Assistant window displays some introductory information and the first decision you need to make. You have to decide whether to click the Register button or the Update button. Figure 20-1 shows the Internet Setup Assistant's introductory information.

Figure 20-1: The first Internet Setup Assistant screen.

If you don't already have an *Internet Service Provider* (*ISP*), which is the company that gives you access to the Internet with your modem, you can find one by clicking the Register button. This makes a toll-free call to a registration service and gives you the opportunity to sign up with an ISP. You'll need a credit card to use this service, and it's only available in the United States and Canada.

If you already have an ISP account or an account on a local area network (LAN), and you just need to set up Mac OS 8 for that account, click the Update button. You'll get an introduction that explains what you need to know to set up an Internet configuration. Read the information and then click the right arrow button in the window to go to the next step. In this step, you tell the Assistant whether you want to add, modify, or remove an Internet configuration. Figure 20-2 shows the add, modify, and remove settings.

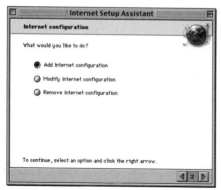

Figure 20-2: Tell the Internet Setup Assistant what you want to do.

To add an Internet configuration, select the "Add Internet configuration" setting and then click the right arrow. In the next step, you give the configuration a name. The name of your ISP is a good choice. If you're going to connect via a modem, select the Modem setting at the bottom of the window and continue at the next heading, "Internet setup through a modem." If you have a connection through a LAN, select the LAN setting and skip to the subsequent heading, "Internet setup through a local area network (LAN)." Figure 20-3 shows the settings for a configuration name and type of connection.

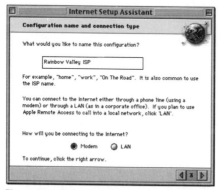

Figure 20-3: Tell the Internet Setup Assistant the name and type of connection.

Internet setup through a modem

The next step asks what kind of modem you're using. Scroll through the list until you find your modem model, and then click it to select it. Select the port to which your modem is connected (probably the modem port). You'll most likely want to change the Phone Line setting to Tone (used in most parts of the United States and Canada). Figure 20-4 shows the modem settings.

Figure 20-4: Specify your modem.

The next step is especially important because it's where you enter the phone number for your ISP, your account name, and your password. Your account name is usually the same as the first part of your e-mail address. Figure 20-5 shows these settings.

Figure 20-5: Enter your phone number, account name, and password.

You'll be asked in the next step if you have been assigned your own IP address, which is a numerical address like 206.117.213.011 that identifies one machine on the Internet. Because you're connecting by modem, you probably don't have a permanent IP address; instead, your ISP assigns you an IP address dynamically, which is to say, temporarily, and only for the length of time you're connected. Don't confuse IP addresses, which identify machines, with e-mail addresses, which identify people. If you don't have a permanent IP address, select the No setting and click the right arrow button to move on.

The remaining steps in setting up an Internet connection are the same for a modem connection and a LAN connection. Skip the next heading, which describes the initial steps for setting up a LAN connection, and continue at the subsequent heading, "Domain Name Server setup," to finish setting up your Internet connection.

Internet setup through a local area network (LAN)

If you'll be connecting to the Internet over a LAN instead of a modem, you probably have an Ethernet connection and will be connecting via a high-speed link of some sort. The first part of the setup is described under the heading "Getting Started" earlier in this section. When you come to the step where you indicate how you'll be connecting to the Internet, click the LAN button and forge on by clicking the right arrow button.

You've probably been assigned your own IP address. If so, select the Yes setting at the IP address step. Click the right arrow button and in the next step, enter the numerical IP address that your LAN administrator gave you. Figure 20-6 shows the IP address setting.

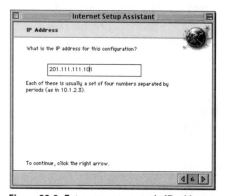

Figure 20-6: Enter your computer's IP address.

The next step asks for your subnet mask and router address. You don't need to know what these settings mean; just enter the numbers exactly as your LAN administrator gives them to you. Figure 20-7 shows the subnet mask and router address settings.

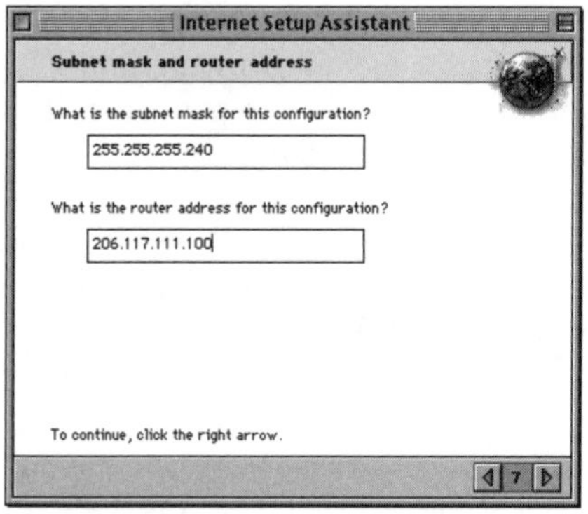

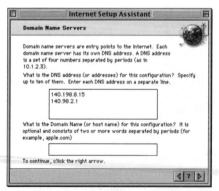

Figure 20-7: Entering the mysterious subnet mask and router numbers.

Domain Name Server setup

The remaining steps are the same for setting up a modem connection or a LAN connection to the Internet. The next information you must supply is the addresses of your Domain Name Service (DNS) server. A DNS server converts the hard-to-remember numerical IP addresses like 17.254.3.62 into something easier for humans to remember like www.apple.com. Every ISP or LAN has a DNS server, and whenever you enter any kind of Internet address, the DNS server converts it into its numerical equivalent and sends the address on its way (and in the right direction, too). Your ISP or LAN administrator will probably give you the IP addresses of two DNS servers (primary and secondary). Enter these numerical addresses in the space provided, pressing the Return key after each address to separate them. You can skip the host name for this configuration. Figure 2-8 shows the DNS settings.

Figure 20-8: Enter your DNS servers' IP addresses.

Click the right arrow button to get to the next step. Enter your e-mail address (as given to you by your ISP or LAN administrator) and your e-mail password. Figure 20-9 shows the e-mail address and password settings.

```
┌─────────────────────────────────────────────┐
│ ▣        Internet Setup Assistant          ▤ │
│ ╔═══════════════════════════════════════════╗│
│ ║ E-mail address and password          ╭───╮║│
│ ║                                      │ ⊕ │║│
│ ║ What is the e-mail address for this c╰───╯║│
│ ║ This address is where people send you e-mail (for example: ║│
│ ║ chris@isp.com or pat@company.com or kelly@school.edu) ║│
│ ║  ┌──────────────────────────────────┐    ║│
│ ║  │ ffflat@rainbowvalley.com         │    ║│
│ ║  └──────────────────────────────────┘    ║│
│ ║                                           ║│
│ ║ What is the e-mail password for this configuration? ║│
│ ║ You can leave this blank, but you will have to enter your password ║│
│ ║ when you want to receive mail.            ║│
│ ║  ┌──────────────────────────────────┐    ║│
│ ║  │ pellucidar!                      │    ║│
│ ║  └──────────────────────────────────┘    ║│
│ ║                                           ║│
│ ║ To continue, click the right arrow.       ║│
│ ║                              ┌─┬─┬─┐      ║│
│ ║                              │◁│8│▷│      ║│
│ ║                              └─┴─┴─┘      ║│
│ ╚═══════════════════════════════════════════╝│
└─────────────────────────────────────────────┘
```

Figure 20-9: Enter your e-mail address and password.

Click the right arrow button to get to another e-mail setup step, where you put in the e-mail account (sometimes called the POP account). This is different from your e-mail address in that it includes both your user name and the name of the mail server, as in ffflat@mail.rainbowvalley.com. You also need to enter the mail server name (also known as the SMTP host), as in mail.rainbowvalley.com. Figure 20-10 shows the e-mail account and mail server settings.

```
┌─────────────────────────────────────────────┐
│ ▣        Internet Setup Assistant          ▤ │
│ ╔═══════════════════════════════════════════╗│
│ ║ E-Mail account and host computer     ╭───╮║│
│ ║                                      │ ⊕ │║│
│ ║ What is the e-mail account for this c╰───╯║│
│ ║ joe@pop.isp.com or pat@mail.company.com)  ║│
│ ║ This account, also called your POP (Post Office Protocol) ║│
│ ║ account, is where you receive your e-mail. ║│
│ ║  ┌──────────────────────────────────┐    ║│
│ ║  │ ffflat@mail.rainbowvalley.com    │    ║│
│ ║  └──────────────────────────────────┘    ║│
│ ║                                           ║│
│ ║ What is the e-mail host for this configuration? (for example: ║│
│ ║ smtp.isp.com or mail.company.com)         ║│
│ ║ Usually called the SMTP (Simple Mail Transfer Protocol) host, this ║│
│ ║ computer is where your outgoing e-mail is processed. ║│
│ ║  ┌──────────────────────────────────┐    ║│
│ ║  │ mail.rainbowvalley.com│          │    ║│
│ ║  └──────────────────────────────────┘    ║│
│ ║                                           ║│
│ ║ To continue, click the right arrow.       ║│
│ ║                              ┌─┬─┬─┐      ║│
│ ║                              │◁│9│▷│      ║│
│ ║                              └─┴─┴─┘      ║│
│ ╚═══════════════════════════════════════════╝│
└─────────────────────────────────────────────┘
```

Figure 20-10: Enter your e-mail (POP) account and e-mail server (SMTP host).

The next step asks you to specify the name of the host computer for newsgroups (also known as the Usenet host). This is almost always your ISP's domain name preceded by the word "news," as in news.rainbowvalley.com. Figure 20-11 shows the newsgroup host setting.

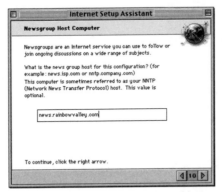

Figure 20-11: Enter your news server address.

Clicking the right arrow button brings you to the last step in setting up a connection to the Internet. You can review the settings you've made by clicking the Show Details button. If any of the connection settings are wrong, you can click the left arrow button to go back to the steps where you entered them, make corrections, and then click the right arrow button to get back to this step. To make the settings effective, click the Go Ahead button and wait a few minutes while your settings are stored in the various control panels. You also have the option of clicking the Cancel button to quit the Internet Setup Assistant without making any of your settings effective. Figure 20-12 shows the last step in setting up a connection to the Internet.

Figure 20-12: Decide whether to make the settings effective.

After finishing the last step in the Internet Setup Assistant, you can make a connection (as described later in "Your Internet Connection").

Internet Config

Internet Config is an application that makes your life easier by keeping track of your personal Internet information for many of the different applications you may use to access Internet services. Other applications, including Claris Emailer, Cyberdog, Netscape Navigator, and NewsWatcher, can all get your e-mail address from the same place: Internet Config. The makers of these applications have agreed to get the information they need from Internet Config so you don't have to enter it in each application separately. Likewise, if you change any of your information (such as your ISP), you only need to make the change in Internet Config.

In addition to your e-mail address and mail server information, Internet Config lets you specify your Usenet news server, the default home page for your Web browser, and the folder on your hard disk where any files you get from the Internet will go. Internet Config also lets you assign helper applications. These helpers open files specified by URLs, and you can have Internet Config direct a particular kind of URL to a particular application. In applications that use Internet Config settings, you can ⌘-click a URL to have the assigned helper application automatically access that URL. For example, if a friend sends you an e-mail containing the URL of a great new Web page, you open the e-mail in Claris Emailer, ⌘-click the URL in the e-mail, and your Web browser opens and goes to that URL.

Understanding URLs

You've probably seen World Wide Web addresses in advertisements — they're the ones that look like http://www.paramount.com. These Web addresses are one example of a type of address called a *URL*, which stands for Universal Resource Locator. The nice part about URLs is that they can point you directly to any Web page, or any file on an FTP site. In fact, there's a URL for everything you can get to on the Internet. A URL begins with a code that specifies a kind of Internet location. The remainder of the URL specifies a location in terms of a server or account name, a *domain name* (the name of the organization or company that owns the server), and in some cases a file directory. In the http://www.paramount.com example, the http:// part specifies that the address is for a Web page, the www portion is the name of a computer that serves Web pages, and Paramount.com is the domain name.

Internet Config is part of a standard installation of Mac OS 8. After installation, you'll find it in the Internet Utilities folder (inside the Internet folder on the startup disk). You can also get Internet Config separately from software sources on the Internet (see "Where to Get Utility Software" in Chapter 24 for more information).

Setting Internet Config preferences

To set a preference in Internet Config, launch the program. Then click one of the category buttons in the Internet Preferences window to get the settings window for that category. Figure 20-13 shows the Internet Preferences window and one of its settings windows.

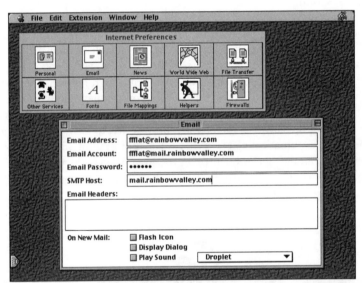

Figure 20-13: Enter your Internet user information in one place — the Internet Config application.

For example, to set your e-mail information for all compliant applications to use, click the Email button in the Internet Preferences window. This brings up the Email settings window, where you can enter your e-mail address, account, password, and so on.

You don't have to set all or even most of the Internet Config preferences at once. Set the ones you need now, and return to set more another time. When you have set all of the Internet preferences you need for now, quit the Internet Config program, saving the changes you made when asked if you wish to do so.

Setting applications to use Internet Config preferences

After you have set your Internet preferences in Internet Config, you'll need to tell your Internet applications to use those settings. The procedure varies among different applications. For example, in Netscape Navigator 3.0 you choose Mail and News Preferences from the Options menu, click the Identity tab, and turn on "Use Internet Configuration System" option. You have to quit Navigator and open it again for the information in Internet Config to take effect. Figure 20-14 shows the Netscape Navigator 3.0 dialog box where you choose the Internet Config settings.

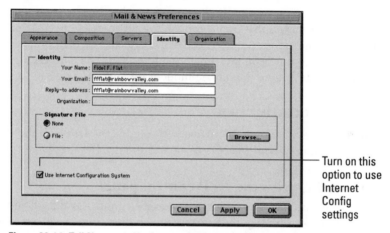

Turn on this option to use Internet Config settings

Figure 20-14: Tell Netscape Navigator whether to use Internet Config settings.

The TCP/IP, PPP, and Modem control panels

Some of the settings you make in the Internet Setup Assistant are saved in the TCP/IP control panel, and if you're using a modem, in the Modem and the PPP control panels. If you have trouble connecting to the Internet after setting up with the Internet Setup Assistant, you may have to change the settings in those control panels. For example, if you connect to the Internet through an Ethernet LAN and you have added an Ethernet card to your computer, you may need to open the TCP/IP control panel to make sure the settings are correct. If you're using System 7.5.5 or earlier, you may have a MacTCP control panel instead of a TCP/IP control panel. With any system software version, your ISP may have you use the MacPPP or FreePPP control panel instead of the Modem and PPP control panels. (For detailed information on all these control panels, see "Configuring a TCP/IP Connection" and "Making a Dial-Up TCP/IP Connection" in Chapter 17.)

Your Internet Connection

Setting up your computer to connect to the Internet makes it ready to access e-mail, Web pages, and other Internet services. If you have a LAN connection to the Internet, you can access its services any time you want by using the applications described in subsequent sections of this chapter. A LAN connection gives you full-time access to the Internet.

A modem connection generally does not give you full-time access to the Internet. When you want to use Internet services through a modem, you must make a connection to your ISP. You can make a manual connection or an automatic connection. When you finish using Internet services, you can disconnect from the ISP. You'll probably want to disconnect if your ISP charges for the amount of time you are connected or the phone company charges for the time you use the phone line. You'll have to disconnect if you need to use the phone line or the modem for something else.

Manual connection

You can connect to your ISP manually through a modem with the PPP control panel. In addition, with Mac OS 8 you can use the Internet Dialer program.

Connecting with the PPP control panel

To make an Internet connection with the PPP control panel, all you need to do is open it, make sure that the information entered there is correct, and then click its Connect button. Your modem will dial your ISP and the control panel will negotiate a connection with your ISP by supplying your account name and password. When a message tells you the connection is OK, you can use an Internet application such as Netscape Navigator or Claris Emailer (as described later in this chapter). Figure 20-15 shows the PPP control panel.

Connecting with the Internet Dialer

If you have Mac OS 8, you can use the Internet Dialer program to connect to your ISP for Internet access. The Internet Dialer has a Connect button for initiating a connection and a timer that shows how long you have been connected. Internet Dialer also has a pop-up menu that lists all the ISP accounts you have configured using the Internet Setup Assistant or the TCP/IP, Modem, and PPP control panels. You'll find an alias of the Internet Dialer in the Internet folder on the Mac OS 8 startup disk. Figure 20-16 shows the Internet Dialer window.

531

Figure 20-15: Manually connecting to
the Internet with the PPP control panel.

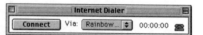

Figure 20-16: Manually connecting to the
Internet with the Internet Dialer.

For the Internet Dialer to use configurations you have made directly in the TCP/IP, Modem, and PPP control panels, each of the three control panels must have a configuration with the same name. For example, if you have a configuration named Rainbow Valley in the PPP control panel, there must also be a configuration with that name in the Modem and the TCP/IP control panels. These naming requirements are taken care of automatically when you use the Internet Setup Assistant to set up an Internet configuration.

Automatic connection

You can have the PPP control panel automatically dial and connect to the Internet whenever you open an application that requires an Internet connection. For example, when you open Netscape Navigator and it looks for the home Web page, PPP will dial the modem and connect to your ISP; then Navigator can go to the Web page. To make automatic connections happen, you turn on the "Connect automatically when starting TCP/IP applications" option in the Connection panel of the PPP control panel's Options dialog box. You get at that dialog box option by clicking the Options button in the PPP control panel. Figure 20-17 shows the Connection panel of the PPP Options dialog box.

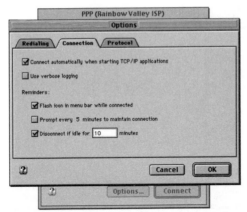

**Figure 20-17: Turn on automatic Internet connection
in the PPP Options dialog box.**

Disconnecting from the Internet

To disconnect from your Internet Service Provider, click the Disconnect button
in the PPP control panel or the Internet Dialer program. After a moment, your
modem will hang up and the connection will end.

You can also set the PPP control panel to disconnect automatically. You can
have it disconnect after a period of inactivity you specify. In addition, you can
have the control panel prompt you periodically with a dialog box and
disconnect if you fail to respond to the dialog box (because you have left your
computer and forgotten to disconnect manually). You set up these options in
the Connections section of the PPP control panel's Options dialog box (review
Figure 20-17).

Using Connect To

In Mac OS 8, the Connect To application is installed in the Apple menu. It's a
simple little application that brings up a dialog box where you enter the URL of
an Internet location you want to access. Connect To then routes your request to
the application that best handles that kind of URL. For example, if it's a Web
URL (that is, a URL beginning with http://), Connect To sends the URL to
Netscape Navigator, which launches and opens that Web page. If it's an e-mail
URL (that is, a URL beginning with mailto:), Connect To sends the address to
Claris Emailer Lite, which enters it in the address field of a new message.

Connect To determines which application to use for each kind of URL by looking at the preferences set in the Helpers section of Internet Config. Those preferences are preset during the installation of Mac OS 8, but you can change them at any time.

Sending and Receiving E-mail

Electronic mail is the most popular reason people use the Internet. With e-mail, you can communicate with people all over the world and keep in touch with family and friends. Unlike regular mail, your correspondents can be reading your messages within minutes after you send them, no matter if the recipients are across the street or halfway around the world. Mac OS 8 gives you three programs for handling your e-mail. The best is Claris Emailer Lite, but you can also use Apple's Cyberdog or the mail program built into Netscape Navigator.

Using Claris Emailer Lite

Claris Emailer is a terrific e-mail program, and a lite version is included with Mac OS 8. Actually, it's both a lite and an older version, as Emailer has since been updated to version 2.0. (Unfortunately, the 2.0 Lite version wasn't ready in time for the Mac OS 8 shipment date.) The Lite version of Emailer handles only one Internet e-mail account, where the full version can get e-mail from any number of Internet, America Online, CompuServe, and Radiomail accounts. The real advantage of the full version is that if you have more than one e-mail account, you can manage all of your e-mail with one program, with one unified address book, and you can even pick up all of your mail from all of your accounts with a single phone call. Another feature the full version sports that is missing in the lite version is the ability to set up Mail Actions, which automatically process your mail according to rules you set up. For example, you can set up a mail action that looks at the sender of a message and assigns the message a priority, files it in a specific mail folder, and sends a reply, all automatically.

Emailer setup

When you first open Claris Emailer Lite, you'll be presented with a personalization dialog box. Enter your name and optionally your company name. (You don't need a serial number.) Click the OK button to display Internet Service Entry dialog box. Figure 20-18 shows this dialog box.

Figure 20-18: Set up your e-mail account in Emailer Lite's Internet Service dialog box.

If you've already entered your e-mail information in the Internet Setup Assistant or directly into Internet Config (as described earlier in this chapter), the information appears in this dialog box, and all you need to do is enter the account name (usually the name of your Internet Service Provider). If you haven't entered your e-mail information in the Internet Setup Assistant or Internet Config, you'll need to enter the following information in Emailer's dialog box:

❖ **User name** is your name as you wish it to appear in the header of your e-mail messages. (It's usually better to put your real name in here, rather than a handle like "Galactic Hero.")

❖ **Email address is** the address assigned to you by your ISP, in the form name@domain (for example, ffflat@rainbowvalley.com).

❖ **Email account** may be the same as your e-mail address, or may require a slightly different form of address. Your ISP will tell you what information goes here when you sign up for your Internet account.

❖ **Email password** is the secret password that you gave your ISP when you signed up. It's best to use some combination of letters and numbers, and you should make your password more than five characters long. (Don't use easily guessed passwords like your name, your spouse's or kids' names, your dog's name, or the words "secret," "password," or any other obvious password.) You should also consider changing your password from time to time.

❖ **SMTP host** is the name of the mail server machine at your ISP. This is usually the word "pop" or "mail," followed by a period, then followed by your ISP's domain name (as in "mail.rainbowvalley.com"). Again, your ISP should tell you this information.

When you've entered the required information, click the Save button. A dialog box appears that asks if you want to connect now to your ISP and pick up your mail. Unless there is some reason you don't want to get your mail, click the Yes button. Emailer will connect to your ISP (dialing the modem and opening a PPP session if necessary) and get your incoming mail, displaying it in the Browser window. Emailer can connect automatically through a modem only if you have set the PPP control panel to make automatic connections (as described in "Setting Up an Internet Connection" earlier in this chapter). Figure 20-19 shows a sample Browser window with received mail.

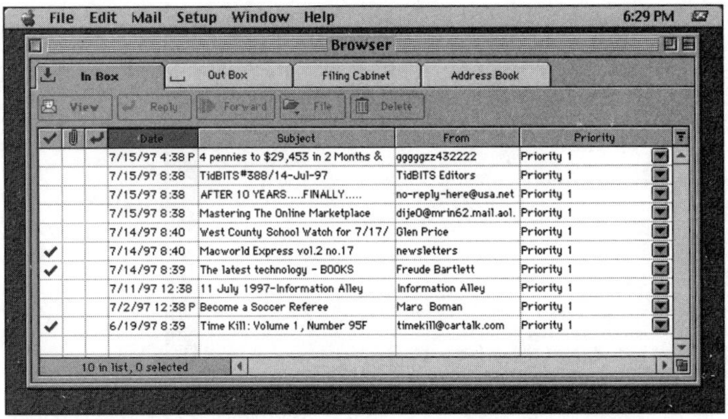

Figure 20-19: Viewing the list of received e-mail in Emailer's In Box.

As you can see, the Browser has four tabs, representing the In Box for received mail, the Out Box for mail you have written, the Filing Cabinet where you can store mail in folders you create, and the Address Book for keeping the e-mail addresses of your correspondents.

Receiving mail

To get your mail, choose Connect Now from the Mail menu. A dialog box appears with options for sending mail, receiving mail, or both. Make sure the Get option is turned on and click the Connect button to have Emailer retrieve your mail from your Internet mail server. The Connect Again command in the Mail menu repeats the mail connection without bringing up the dialog box again. If you connect to the Internet through a modem and have set the PPP control panel for automatic connection, Emailer's Connect Now and Connect Again commands make an automatic Internet connection. If you haven't set the PPP control panel for automatic connection, you have to connect to the Internet manually (as described earlier in this chapter) before using Emailer's Connect Now or Connect Again commands. Either way, you'll have to disconnect manually after receiving your mail, because Emailer can't tell PPP to disconnect. You can use AppleScript to automate connecting, getting and sending mail, and disconnecting (as described in "Using AppleScript with Applications" in Chapter 22).

Received mail appears in the Emailer In Box. To sort messages by any of the columns, click the column name (most people prefer to have mail sorted by Subject or Date). To read a message, double-click it in the In Box, or select it and click the View button. Figure 20-20 shows an example of an e-mail message window.

Figure 20-20: Viewing an e-mail message in Emailer.

In the message window, you can see a row of buttons that let you act on the message; a header where the sender's name and e-mail address is displayed; and the message body. The buttons are self-explanatory, except for the File button, which is a pop-up menu that lets you put the message in a folder after reading into any of your mail folders. The other button that might puzzle you is the button with a plus sign next to the sender's e-mail address. Clicking this button lets you easily add the sender to Emailer's Address Book.

Emailer has keyboard equivalents for many of its buttons. To see the keyboard equivalents displayed on the buttons, hold down the ⌘ key for a few seconds.

Replying and sending mail

Clicking the Reply button in a message window brings up a new message window with the subject and the recipient already entered. If you select some text in the message window before you click Reply, Emailer copies the text into the new message window with a > symbol at the beginning of each line. This is the standard e-mail convention for marking quoted text. Figure 20-21 shows an example of the Emailer reply message window.

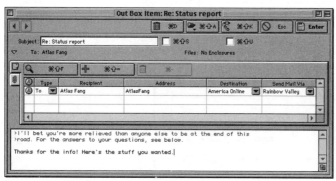

Figure 20-21: Replying to an e-mail message.

Type in your message, then click the Save button or press the Enter key to put the message in your Out Box for later transmission. You can then continue working your way through your received messages, replying as needed.

To start an entirely new message, choose New from the Mail menu, or use its keyboard equivalent, ⌘-N. For a new message, you have to type a subject and specify one or more recipients in the spaces provided.

When you're ready to send all of your replies and new messages, choose Connect Now from the Mail menu. In the Connect Now Setup dialog box, be sure the Send option is turned on before clicking the Connect button. If this option was turned on the last time you connected to your Internet mail server, you can use Emailer's Connect Again command instead of its Connect Now command. If you connect to the Internet through a modem, you must either make a manual connection or set the PPP control panel to make automatic connections before using Emailer's Connect Now or Connect Again commands. Furthermore, you must manually disconnect your modem from the Internet after Emailer has sent your outgoing mail. (See "Your Internet Connection" earlier in this chapter for more information on modem connections.)

Using Cyberdog

You can use Cyberdog to work with your e-mail, though it isn't as full-featured as Emailer. Setup is easy, however. Just choose Mail & News Setup from the Mail/News menu. If you've previously entered your mail information in the Internet Setup Assistant or Internet Config, it will automatically be set up in

Cyberdog. Both Cyberdog and the OpenDoc software it requires come with Mac OS 7.6 and later, and are available separately through Apple's Cyberdog Web site (http://cyberdog.apple.com). Figure 20-22 shows Cyberdog's Mail & News Setup dialog box with the preferences provided by Internet Config.

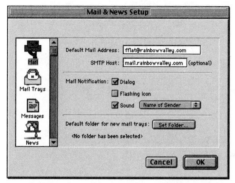

Figure 20-22: Setting your mail preferences in Cyberdog.

If you haven't already set your mail preferences in the Internet Setup Assistant or Internet Config, you can enter them in this dialog box. Select the Mail icon in the scrolling list on the left and enter in your e-mail address and SMTP host (mail server) information. You can set preferences in the other areas of this dialog box by clicking the other icons, but all that's strictly required is the address and host. Feel free to explore the rest of the icons, especially the Handlers icon, which is similar to the Mail Actions in the full version of Emailer. Also check out the Mail Trays icon, which allows you to set up multiple mail accounts if you have them. Click the OK button when you're done setting preferences.

Checking mail

To get your mail, choose Check Mail in the Mail/News menu and enter your mail password when prompted to do so. Cyberdog connects and gets your incoming mail, and displays a list of received messages in a Mail Trays window. Double-click a listed message to open it. Like any other address in Cyberdog, you store your mail addresses in the Notebook, and you can drag e-mail addresses from incoming messages to the Notebook.

Creating and sending mail

To make a new message, choose New Message from the Mail/News menu. A dialog box appears, asking which letterhead you want to use. If you choose one of the supplied letterheads that includes a picture, be aware that recipients will only be able to see the picture if they too are using Cyberdog; most other people will get an annoying file enclosure with your message. For maximum readability, it's best to choose the "Blank Document - Plain Text" letterhead. In the message form that appears, fill in the Subject line and then press the Tab key to get to the To: field. You can type in the recipient's address, or you can click the Addresses button on the form to use an address from your Notebook. When you're done writing your message, click the Send Now button to dispatch your mail immediately or the Send Later button to schedule delivery for a later time.

Browsing the World Wide Web

The World Wide Web is the 800-pound gorilla that shook the Internet into prominence with the public, so much so that many people think that the Web is the Internet. Not so; the Web is just one of the many services available over the Internet. It happens to be the most interesting because it lets you easily access text and pictures from places all over the world. You access the Web with a program called a *Web browser*, and there are three of them included with Mac OS 8. The most popular is Netscape Navigator 3.01; Apple's Cyberdog has a browser component; and you also get Microsoft's Internet Explorer 3.01.

To use the Web, you'll first have to know a bit of the terminology. Web browser programs display information in Web *pages*, which can contain text, pictures, animation, and even audio and video clips. On a Web page, there is usually underlined text known as *links* or *hyperlinks*. When you click one of these links, you are taken to another page. Out there on the Internet, the machines that store all of this information, and serve it up to you upon request, are called *Web servers*. The intriguing thing about hyperlinks is that the page that they take you to can be another page on that same server, or a page on any other Web server on the planet. So it's entirely possible to click your way around the world and not even know it!

Using Netscape Navigator

Netscape Navigator 3.01 is included on the Mac OS 8 CD-ROM. (Newer versions of Netscape Navigator are available separately or as part of a package called Netscape Communicator, and you can get them at http://www. netscape.com.) When you open Netscape Navigator, it displays a browser window and goes to a Web page that has been previously designated as the *home* page. With Mac OS 8, the home page is initially designated to be the Apple Live page (http://livepage.apple.com). You can change the home page in the Appearance section of Navigator's General Preferences dialog box (accessed from the Options menu). Figure 20-23 shows the Apple Live home page in Navigator 3.01.

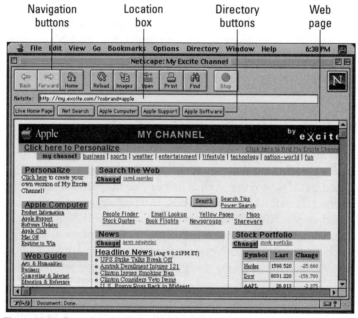

Figure 20-23: Browsing the Web with Netscape Navigator (*courtesy of Apple Computer, Inc.*)

From the Apple Live home page, you can go to other places on the Web by clicking one of the underlined links on the page. Graphics on the page can also be links. To determine if something is a link on a Web page, move the mouse over the area, and if the pointer turns from an arrow into a pointing hand, it's a link.

Clicking links is a good way to get used to browsing the Web, but you should also know how to use Netscape Navigator's other navigation features. These include navigation buttons, location box, directory buttons, Bookmarks menu, Go menu, and multiple browser windows.

Navigation buttons

At the top of the browser window is a set of buttons called the navigation buttons. These buttons help you move from one page to the next, move to your home page, or get around on the Web page that you're currently viewing. Here's what each button does:

❖ **Back** takes you to the page you were just viewing. You can keep clicking the Back button to go to previous pages. This is useful when you're browsing and want to get back to a place that you want to read again.

❖ **Forward** returns you to a subsequent page after you've used the Back button. Most times, this button is grayed out (which means it's unavailable) because you are at the front of your browsing session.

❖ **Home** takes you back to the home page — the page that loads automatically when Navigator starts up.

❖ **Reload** tells Navigator to get the current Web page from the Internet again and redisplay it. This reloading is useful with pages that have constantly changing content, such as online news.

❖ **Images** tells Navigator to reload all the graphics on a page (unlike Reload, which reloads the entire page). People with slow connections seem to use this the most, because they don't always let all the graphics from a page finish loading before they press the Stop button.

❖ **Open** displays a dialog box in which you can type a URL.

❖ **Print** prints the current Web page on the printer you have selected. Be aware that many Web pages are wider or taller than real sheets of paper, so one Web page may take any number of pages to print out. You may be able to make a Web page fit on one sheet of paper by using the Page Setup command to change the page orientation or reduction factor.

❖ **Find** pops up a dialog box that lets you search for text on the current page. This is really useful if you're on a long page that's packed with words and you just want to find where one word is.

❖ **Stop** tells Navigator to stop loading a page and display as much of the page as it has loaded.

Tip: As useful as the navigation buttons are, they take up a fair amount of space. You can make them smaller by eliminating their icons and displaying just their text labels. To make that happen, set the Show Toolbar As option to Text in the Appearance section of the General Preferences dialog box, which you display by choosing General Preferences from the Options menu. You can hide the navigation buttons altogether by choosing Show Toolbar so that there is no check mark next to it in the Options menu.

Location box

Below the navigation buttons is the location box. You can use it to identify the URL of the current page and to enter the URL of a page you want to see. To go to a page whose URL you know, click the location box to select it, type the

URL, and press the Return key. You can hide the location box by choosing Show Location so that there is no check mark next to it in the Options menu.

In Netscape Navigator, you don't have to type in the entire URL of a site you want to visit. You can omit the http:// part of the URL, because Navigator assumes it and puts it in for you when you press the Return key. In fact, you don't even have to type in the www. or .com parts of a URL that has them. Because most of the places on the Web start with www. and end with .com, if you type a one-word URL in the location box, Navigator adds www. to the beginning and .com to the end. For example, if you type *apple* into the location box and press Return, you'll end up at http://www.apple.com, the main Apple Web site.

Directory buttons

Below the location box are the directory buttons, which take you to pre-determined Web sites. These buttons are specially configured in the Netscape Navigator you get with Mac OS 8 to take you to the main Apple home page, a page with technical support information for Apple products, and Apple's software library. You can hide the directory buttons by choosing Show Directory Buttons so that there is no check mark next to it in the Options menu.

Bookmarks menu

Rather than remembering the URL for a page, you can add a *bookmark* for it to the Bookmarks menu. A bookmark keeps track of the URL and the name of a Web page.

To create a bookmark for the current Web page, choose Add Bookmark from the Bookmarks menu. Navigator adds the name of the page to the bottom of the Bookmarks menu. You can go back to that Web page later by choosing its name from the Bookmarks menu.

Go menu

The Go menu keeps a list of the recently visited pages in the current browsing session. To go back to a page, choose it from the Go menu.

Opening multiple browser windows

You can have more than one browser window open at a time. This is useful because sometimes you want to have one page available and read another page in another window. Browser windows are independent, and you can have as many Web pages open as Navigator has the memory to handle. To open another browser window, choose New Web Browser from the File menu. If you regularly keep many browser windows open, it's a good idea to increase

Navigator's memory size by 2000K or more with the Finder's Get Info command (see "Adjusting Application Memory Use" in Chapter 16).

Using Cyberdog

Cyberdog includes a Web browser, but you don't always see a Web browser window when you open Cyberdog as you do with conventional Web browsing applications such as Netscape Navigator. What you see are the unique contents of a Cyberdog document, which can include *cyberbuttons* that you click to go to Web sites, one or more Web browsers displaying live Internet pages, *notebooks* that list favorite Web sites, and other Internet items as well as ordinary contents such as text, graphics, movies, and sound. You always open Cyberdog documents, never the Cyberdog application, because there is no Cyberdog application icon to open. Cyberdog is not a conventional application. It is a collection of OpenDoc plug-in software components that you can mix and match any way you like in documents. Unfortunately Apple has decided not to develop Cyberdog beyond version 2.0. That doesn't mean you can't take advantage of it in its current incarnation, but don't expect it to get any better than it is. Figure 20-24 shows an example of a Cyberdog document that contains cyberbuttons, a Web browser, and a notebook that lists favorite Web sites as well as some text and graphics.

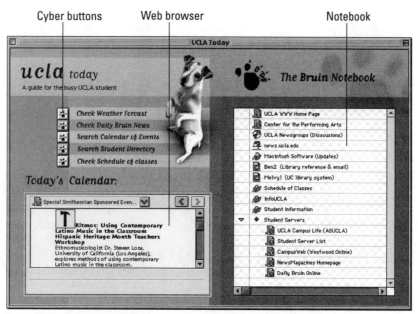

Figure 20-24: A Cyberdog Web browser can appear in a document with other items.

You can create Cyberdog documents by double-clicking the Cyberdog DocBuilder stationery pad. (You'll find it on a Mac OS 8 startup disk by opening the Internet folder, the Internet Applications folder, the Cyberdog 2.0 folder, and finally the Samples & Tools folder.) When you open the Cyberdog DocBuilder stationery pad, you get an empty Cyberdog document. You then add content to it as you would add content to any OpenDoc document, by dragging in Cyberdog objects (cyberbuttons, a Web browser, and so on) or other OpenDoc objects (text, graphics, and so on). For more information on working with OpenDoc documents, see "OpenDoc Compound Documents" in Chapter 23.

Although Cyberdog as a whole is decidedly unconventional, browsing the Web with it isn't too much different from using a conventional application such as Netscape Navigator. One difference is that you use a Cyberdog notebook instead of a menu (such as Navigator's Bookmarks menu) to keep track of your favorite Internet locations. Each entry in a Cyberdog notebook consists of an address icon and a name. A notebook can be in a window by itself or it can be embedded in a larger document. Figure 20-25 shows an example of a Cyberdog notebook in a window by itself (review Figure 20-24 for an example of a notebook in a larger document).

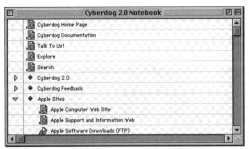

Figure 20-25: Keep favorite Internet locations in a Cyberdog notebook.

You go to a Web page listed in a Cyberdog notebook by double-clicking the address icon of that page. Cyberdog displays the page in a separate Web browser window.

You can also have Cyberdog go to a Web page and display it in a separate browser window by clicking a cyberbutton or by choosing Connect To from the Cyberdog menu and typing a URL in the resulting dialog box. Figure 20-26 shows a sample Cyberdog Web browser window.

Cyberdog's Web browser has a number of navigation features. They include the current page's address icon, navigation buttons, and a location box.

Current page's address icon   Location box   History button   Forward and Backward buttons   Web page

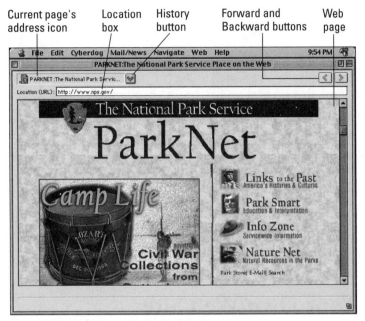

Figure 20-26: Browsing the Web with Cyberdog.

Current address icon

In Cyberdog, you can drag the address icon of the current Web page from the upper left corner of the browser window to a notebook, making it easy to keep track of places you like. If you prefer, you can add the page location to your notebook by choosing Add Window to Notebook from the Cyberdog menu. This is especially useful if you happen to have more than one notebook open because a dialog box appears in which you can choose the notebook to use. Figure 20-27 shows the Add to Notebook dialog box.

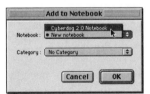

Figure 20-27: Choose the notebook where you want to keep a Web page's address.

Navigation buttons

Here's how the Cyberdog navigation buttons work:

❖ **History,** which is labeled with a large down arrow, keeps a running log of the pages that you've visited in the current surfing session. It displays a pop-up menu that lets you easily return to a prior page.

❖ **Back,** which is labeled with a large left arrow, brings you back to the page you were last viewing.

❖ **Forward,** which is labeled with a large right arrow, returns you to the page you came from if you've used the Back button.

Location box

The location box tells you the URL of the page you're currently viewing. You can also use the location box to go to a different URL. Simply type the URL in the location box and press the Return key.

Sharing Your Own Web Site

Ever wanted to host your own Web site? With Mac OS 8, a Web server is built in. The Web Sharing control panel is a snap to set up and use and lets you put a Web site on the Internet or on your company's intranet in about a minute (not counting the time it takes you to actually create your Web pages). There are some limitations, however.

A Web server needs a fixed IP address and name, so that people can point their browser to the Web site. If you connect to the Internet by modem, your ISP assigns your computer a temporary IP address (also called a dynamic address), which isn't very useful for a Web server. Because a dynamic address changes every time you connect to the Internet, other people won't be able to find the address of your Web server. But if your computer happens to have a fixed IP address, which is likely if you connect to the Internet through a LAN, then you can take advantage of Web Sharing to make Web pages and files on your computer available to any other computer with a Web browser and an Internet connection. (Other computers connecting to your Web site do not need fixed IP addresses.)

Because Web Sharing is intended for personal use, it's not especially high-powered. On the one hand, you shouldn't try to use Web Sharing to host a Web site getting thousands of hits per day. On the other hand, it's perfect for sharing information within your company with your coworkers. And it can even run CGIs, which are scripts (usually written in AppleScript or UserLand Frontier) that can do things like take the output from a Web form and send it to a database like FileMaker Pro.

You use the Web Sharing control panel to specify which folder contains your Web pages and to specify which of those pages is your site's home page. You also use the control panel to select the type of security you want and to start or stop Web sharing. Figure 20-28 shows the Web Sharing control panel.

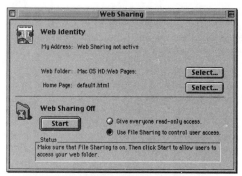

Figure 20-28: Set up your Web site and start Web sharing in the Web Sharing control panel.

In the control panel, you use the first of two buttons labeled Select to specify the folder that contains your Web pages. Initially this is set to the Web Pages folder on the startup disk. You use the second Select button to bring up a dialog box that lists the Web pages in that folder, and you select one to be your Web site's home page. Figure 20-29 shows the dialog box in which you select a home page.

Figure 20-29: Choosing your home page.

In the home page dialog box, you can click on the None button (instead of selecting a home page and clicking the Select button). This turns on an interesting feature called Personal NetFinder. When Personal NetFinder is active, visitors to your Web site don't see a regular home page; instead, they see a listing of the files and folders in the Web Pages folder (similar to the list views in the Finder's folder windows). Figure 20-30 shows a sample of a Personal NetFinder listing as viewed in Netscape Navigator.

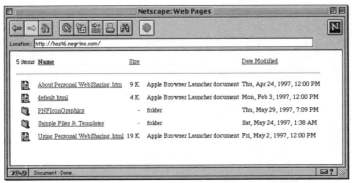

Figure 20-30: If your Web site has no home page, visitors see a listing of files in your Web Pages folder.

After specifying the folder that contains your Web pages and selecting a home page (or not), all you need to do to get your server on the air is to click the Start button. You can also use the two radio buttons to the right of the Start button to allow all users read-only access, or to have Web Sharing apply the security and require passwords that you've set up using the Users & Groups control panel.

When Web Sharing is on, your Web site's address appears in the Web Sharing control panel next to the heading My Address. Your Web site has a numeric IP address like http://192.0.0.2. Depending on the type of Internet connection you have, your Web site may also have a name address like http://host6.domain.com. Give this name or number to people who want to connect to your Web site, and they can type the name into their Web browsers.

Tip: If your network only assigns numeric IP addresses, put a note on your home page telling people who connect to add a bookmark for your page, so they never have to type in those numbers again.

Running Java Applets

Java is a relatively new programming language that has been getting a lot of interest. The reason for this is that Java makes it easy to create small applications, called applets, that can be automatically received by your browser from a Web page, and that extend the functionality of the page. For example, if you have a Java-enabled browser (Netscape Navigator 3.0 or later, Microsoft Internet Explorer 3.0 or later, and Cyberdog 2.0 are all Java-enabled) you could go to a stock page and have continually updated stock quotes scroll in ticker-tape fashion across your screen. Netscape and Microsoft provide their own implementations of Java along with their browsers. Cyberdog uses the Mac OS Runtime for Java (MRJ), a system component which is installed with Mac OS 8. Optionally, Microsoft Internet Explorer can use MRJ instead of its own version of Java.

Okay, so being able to run applets inside Web pages is a nice feature, but other than that, how important is Java? For the near term, not very. Sun Microsystems, the company that invented Java, is still inventing it, and as the language changes, it is moving away from its original selling point to software developers, which was that it was completely cross-platform. This meant that a programmer using Java could theoretically write a program once, then run it on Macs, Windows machines, or even UNIX systems. But as Sun has released new versions of Java that are incompatible with previous versions, and Microsoft has created other incompatible Java versions, that dream seems to be fading.

In the meantime, Apple has committed to supporting Java in its system software, both on Mac OS 8 and in the forthcoming Rhapsody operating system. But aside from running applets for Web pages, there isn't much you can do with Java at this time. If you want to try out some Java applets, you can do it with the Apple Applet Runner, a program that lets you run Java applets outside of a browser. You'll find the Apple Applet Runner and a folder of sample applets inside the Mac OS Runtime for Java folder, which is installed inside the Apple Extras folder when you do a standard installation of Mac OS 8. Just double-click the Apple Applet Runner to open it, and then choose one or more of the sample applets from the Applets menu. Figure 20-31 shows some sample Java applets in the Apple Applet Runner.

You can also include Java applets in an OpenDoc document by using the Apple Applet Viewer, which is part of the Mac OS Runtime for Java package installed with Mac OS 8. You'll find OpenDoc stationery for the Apple Applet Viewer in the Stationery folder on the startup disk. This folder has an alias named OpenDoc Stationery in the Apple menu. You won't get the Apple Applet Viewer if OpenDoc is not installed when you install Mac OS Runtime for Java. After installing OpenDoc, reinstall MRJ to get the viewer part.

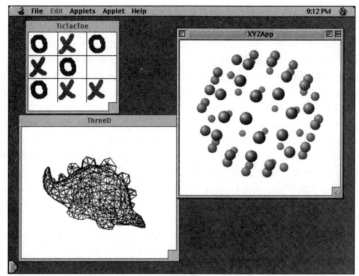

Figure 20-31: Three Java applets running in the Apple Applet Runner.

In Case You've Heard of JavaScript

Despite the similar names and the fact that they're both associated with Web browsers, Java and JavaScript are almost completely unrelated. JavaScript is a scripting language developed by Netscape to help Web page developers automate the Netscape Navigator browser. JavaScript was originally called LiveScript, but when Java became "The Next Big Thing," Netscape changed LiveScript's name to try to ride Java's marketing coattails.

Transferring Files

One of the best things about the Internet is the easy access to useful (and sometimes, absolutely frivolous) files that you can copy to your computer from other computers anywhere in the world. This transfer process is called *downloading*. Similarly, if you send a file from your computer to another, you are *uploading* the file to that computer.

On the Internet, files are sent using a *protocol* (an agreed-upon standard for data communications to ensure that the computers on both ends of the phone lines are talking the same language) called *FTP* (File Transfer Protocol). The computer that has the file on it runs a program called an *FTP server*, and the computer requesting the file uses a program called an *FTP client*. There are FTP clients built into Netscape Navigator and Cyberdog, and there are also independent FTP client programs. You may sometimes hear people refer to an *FTP site*, which is a collection of files on an FTP server available for downloading.

Getting ready to download

Before downloading any files, you should specify where to put them. The best place to do this is in the Internet Config program. You click the File Transfer button in Internet Config's Internet Preferences window to bring up the File Transfer window. At the bottom of this window, click the button next to the label Download Folder. This brings up an Open dialog box, in which you select the folder you want to use for downloaded files. Finally, quit Internet Config, saving the changes you made when asked if you wish to do so. Figure 20-32 shows the File Transfer window in Internet Config.

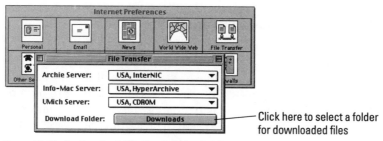

Figure 20-32: Setting the folder for downloaded files with Internet Config.

If you don't use Internet Config, you should set the destination folder in your browser or FTP client. Using Netscape Navigator 3.01 as an example, choose General Preferences from the Options menu, click the Applications tab in the resulting dialog box, and then click the Browse button next to the text that begins Downloads Directory. This brings up an Open dialog box, in which you select the folder you want to use for downloaded files. After selecting a downloads folder, the path to it appears in the General Preferences dialog box.

Downloading files

Here's how most file transfers work: while browsing a Web page, you come across a description of a file that interests you, with a link to download the file. You click the link, and the browser opens a file transfer progress window and downloads the file to your hard disk. Pretty easy, right? That's because browsers understand how to handle URLs that begin with ftp://, and they route it to their built-in FTP client programs. Figure 20-33 shows how this works in Netscape Navigator 3.01.

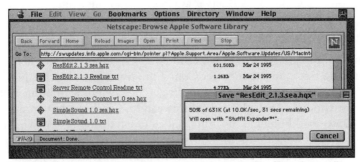

Figure 20-33: Using Netscape Navigator to download a file. Note the small progress window at the lower right.

FTP client programs

Sometimes you want to download a file from an FTP site, and you don't want or need to fire up a Web browser. Or perhaps you want to upload a file, which most browsers can't do. Instead, you can use one of the independent FTP client programs available for the Mac OS. Of these, the two most popular are the shareware Anarchie and the freeware Fetch. (For more information on shareware and freeware, see "Where to Get Utility Software" in Chapter 24.)

Anarchie

Anarchie is a terrific FTP program written by the Australian author Peter Lewis, who is also one of the people behind Internet Config. Anarchie's claim to fame is that it lets you access and work with files on FTP servers in much the same way that you work with files in the Finder. Some other FTP programs make you deal with files in directory dialog boxes (similar to the Open and Save dialog boxes). With Anarchie, if you want to download a file from an FTP server, you go to that server and double-click a folder icon that represents one of the file directories on the FTP server. A window opens with the contents of the directory (as it might if you had a Finder window open to a list view). To download a file or group of files from the open directory, you can simply select them and drag them to your Mac OS desktop. Uploading is as simple as dragging files from your desktop to a directory window. Anarchie also keeps a handy set of bookmarks with pointers to useful FTP sites of interest to Mac OS users. Figure 20-34 shows the Mac OS desktop with an FTP server's Internet folder open to display the Anarchie files.

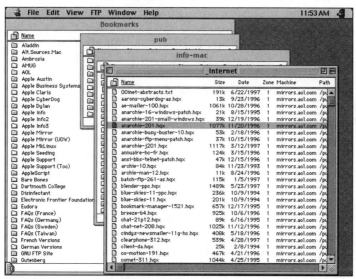

Figure 20-34: Anarchie makes browsing and downloading files from FTP servers easy.

Fetch

The freeware Fetch was developed by Dartmouth University and was one of the earliest FTP programs available for the Mac OS. It's a perfectly fine FTP program, except that it isn't as easy to work with as Anarchie. Unlike Anarchie, Fetch makes you access files in directory windows. If you want to download a file from an FTP server, you open the directory by double-clicking it, which brings up a dialog box with a list of all the files in the directory. Then you must select a file and click the Get File button in the dialog box. This isn't exactly hard physical labor, but it also isn't as fluid as working with Anarchie. On the other hand, Fetch is free. Let your conscience decide.

Decoder programs

Decoding programs, sometimes called *helper applications*, take data (usually files) that you download from the Internet and convert it into a form that your computer can use. The reason that this is necessary partly has to do with the

Internet and partly with the Mac OS. First, the Internet is pretty much a plain-text environment; it sends streams of text across the phone lines. But application programs, pictures, sounds, and Mac OS files aren't plain-text files; they're a kind of file called a *binary file*. In order for binary files to be sent over the Internet, they must be converted into text files. There's a standard for doing this called the BinHex standard. *BinHexing* a file, therefore, is the process of converting a binary file into a plain text file so that it can be sent over the Internet. When you receive a BinHexed file, your software must decode it back into a binary file before you can use it. The decoding process reads the BinHex file, converts it, and writes out a decoded version of the file. You'll end up with two files, and you'll probably want to throw away the encoded version once you have the decoded binary file.

The other type of file that needs decoding is the type that has been compressed. This is a scheme where a binary file is run through a compression program before it is BinHexed. The resulting compressed binary file is considerably smaller in size than the uncompressed file, and as a result, it takes less time to upload and download. With the Mac OS, the most common compression program is StuffIt Deluxe from Aladdin Systems (408-761-6200, http://www.aladdinsys.com).

You can usually tell what type of file you're downloading by the file's extension, a series of letters tacked on to the end of the file's name, separated by a period. Table 20-1 shows the encoded file extensions you're likely to encounter while cruising the Internet and what they mean.

Table 20-1
Encoded File Extensions

File Extension	What It Means
.bin	MacBinary file (also known as BinHex5)
.gz	Compressed with Unix *GNU Zip* program
.hqx	BinHex4 file
.sea	Self Extracting Archive — compressed with StuffIt, but no separate decompression utility needed
.sit	Compressed with StuffIt
.tar	Archived with Unix *tar* program
.uue	UUEncode file
.z or .Z	Compressed with Unix *compress* program
.zip	Compressed with the DOS or Windows PKZip Program

Decoding helper applications have the benefit of working transparently when used with a Web browser. When the browser needs to decode or decompress a file, the browser calls the helper, which opens (usually into the background), does its decoding job, and quits. Often, you won't even be aware that the process has taken place. Browsers aren't the only Internet programs that benefit from helper applications. E-mail, FTP clients, and Usenet news readers can benefit from helper applications that decode and decompress files.

StuffIt Expander

There's a pair of helper applications included with Mac OS 8 that will handle virtually all of your compressing, encoding, decoding, and decompressing needs. The first member of this matched pair is called StuffIt Expander, and it's free from Aladdin Systems (408-761-6200, http://www.aladdinsys.com), the people who make StuffIt Deluxe. By itself, StuffIt Expander can decompress StuffIt (.sit) and Compact Pro (.cpt) archives, and files encoded in BinHex (.hqx or .hex) and MacBinary (.bin) formats. StuffIt Expander is incredibly easy to use; you either configure it to be automatically opened by your Internet applications, or you simply drag and drop files onto the StuffIt Expander icon.

A $30 shareware package called DropStuff with Expander Enhancer, also from Aladdin, completes the decoding duo. DropStuff enables you to compress and encode files. You can have your Internet applications open it automatically, and you can compress and encode files by dragging them to the DropStuff icon.

Expander Enhancer enables StuffIt Expander to expand files compressed with virtually every compression format found on Mac OS, Unix, Windows, and DOS computers. These include ZIP (.zip), ARC (.arc), gzip (.gz), Unix Compress (.Z), UUencode (.uu), and StuffIt SpaceSaver files. It will also join files that were segmented with another StuffIt product. The programs are accelerated on Power PC computers, though they'll work fine (albeit a bit slower) on other Macs.

The really great thing about the StuffIt Expander package is that it operates completely transparently. When you click an FTP link in your Web browser, the browser downloads the file from the FTP server, then hands the file off to StuffIt Expander, which decodes the file (converting it back into a binary file), decompresses the file further if necessary, and automatically quits. StuffIt Expander can also handle batches of files to be decoded and decompressed at the same time, and (if you prefer) it's smart enough to automatically delete the BinHexed files once it finishes decoding them.

BinHex 5.0

This program is still in use by some people, but it's not nearly as capable as StuffIt Expander. All that this program can do is encode and decode BinHex and MacBinary files. But considering that it was written in 1985, it's amazing that it still works at all on modern computers.

uuUndo

What BinHex is to Mac OS users, UUEncode/UUDecode is to the rest of the people on the Internet. It's the Unix standard way of converting a binary file into text for transmission.

UUencoding is a bit more efficient than BinHex, and it's more widely used because most of the computers hooked up to the Internet (or anywhere, for that matter) don't use the Mac OS. To decode a uuencoded file, you can use StuffIt Expander; however, it has problems with some files and doesn't always decode them properly. For example, in decoding some JPEG files, the bottom part of the picture may turn out garbled. Switching to uuUndo (a free utility from Aaron Giles) as the uudecoding helper application cures most of the problems. The program is shipped as a fat binary, which means that it's accelerated for PowerPC computers and decodes files very quickly.

Participating in Newsgroups

Besides e-mail, the Web, and file transfers, there's another part of the Internet called Usenet. You can think of Usenet as a world-wide bulletin board system, where people from everywhere can post messages and join discussions about subjects that interest them. Each subject is called a *newsgroup*. At last count, there were more than 25,000 newsgroups, covering virtually every subject you can imagine. To find a newsgroup that interests you, you'll have to know a little about the structure of newsgroup names. There is a hierarchy of names, akin to domain names, within Usenet. Table 20-2 shows the most common top-level newsgroup names.

Below these top-level identifiers, there can be any number of qualifying names that narrow down the subject, separated by periods. Examples of a few newsgroups are listed in Table 20-3.

Table 20-2
Common Top-Level Newsgroup Names

Identifier	Included Subjects
alt	Subjects that don't fit into one of the other, "official" categories
biz	Business
comp	Computers
news	News and other topical information
rec	Recreational hobbies and arts
sci	Scientific
soc	Social
talk	Debates
misc	Miscellaneous subjects

Table 20-3
Sample Qualifying Newsgroup Names

Newsgroup Name	Subject
alt.fan.gillian-anderson	The pictures are out there
comp.sys.lang.java	Java programming language
rec.arts.music.folk	Folk music and musicians
sci.nanotech	Nanotechnology discussions

Using Netscape Navigator to read news

To find the newsgroup of your dreams, choose Netscape News from the
Window menu in Netscape Navigator. You'll get a window with three panes;
the top left pane lists your news server. Double-click the server's icon to open it
and download a list of the available newsgroups. The first time you do this,
don't be surprised if it takes several minutes (Netscape Navigator will
subsequently remember the groups). The list will appear as an expandable
outline (somewhat like the Finder's list views). You can expand groups as
needed to find the ones that interest you, and when you see a likely group, click
in the column to the right of the group to subscribe to that group (a blue check

mark appears next to the newsgroup). After you check off all of the groups that look good to you, choose Show Subscribed Newsgroups from the Options menu to display only your groups.

To read newsgroup messages, double-click one of the newsgroup names in the top left pane of the news window. Netscape Navigator will download a list of messages from that newsgroup and display them in the top right pane of the news window. Clicking a message title will display the message in the large pane covering the bottom half of the news window. If the message is part of a string of messages about the same subject (known as a *thread*), then you can choose Next Message from the Go menu to read the next message in the thread. You can also use the navigation buttons to move through threads or from one newsgroup to the next.

If you wish to reply to a message and join the discussion, choose Post Reply from the Message menu, and type your message in the new message form that appears. Click the Send Now button to post your message.

Tip: Usenet can be a wild place, and old-timers can be merciless to new people who ask what seem to be foolish questions. Be sure to read the Web pages under Netscape Navigator's Help menu called On Usenet News before you post your first message in a newsgroup. You may save yourself a lot of grief and avoid many nasty messages (called "flames"). Never forget that your messages can be potentially read by millions of people worldwide.

Other news clients

You can also use Cyberdog to read and post Usenet messages, and there are several other Usenet client programs available. The best of them all (even better than Netscape Navigator) is NewsWatcher, a free program that you can download from many FTP sites. NewsWatcher gives you many tools to easily subscribe to newsgroups as well as read and reply to messages. It is much more flexible than the other programs. If you get serious about Usenet, be sure to check NewsWatcher out.

Summary

After reading this chapter, you know how to set up an Internet connection using the Internet Setup Assistant program that comes with Mac OS 8. You can set additional Internet configuration options with the Internet Config program and the TCP/IP, PPP, and Modem control panels.

You know how to connect to and disconnect from the Internet. While connected, you can send and receive e-mail with Claris Emailer, Cyberdog, or another e-mail program. You know how to browse the Web with Netscape Navigator or Cyberdog, and how to set up your own Web site with the Web Sharing control panel. You can run Java applets in a Web browser or use the Java Applet Runner. In addition, you know how to transfer files over the Internet, encoding and decoding them as necessary. Finally, you know how to participate in Usenet newsgroup discussions.

Master Speech and Languages

21

Keyboarding and mousing are not particularly natural ways to communicate. For years, computer designers have looked for a more natural way to operate computers. One of the most compelling ways to work with a computer is simply to talk to it. Present-day Mac OS computers have taken the first steps toward achieving the science fiction of *Star Trek*, when people of the future speak naturally and conversationally with their computers. When the crew of the spaceship *Enterprise* traveled back in time to a mid-1980s San Francisco in the movie *Star Trek IV*, chief engineer Scotty tried to use a Mac SE by speaking into the mouse. Of course it was a big joke. Macs have been able to speak text out loud since 1985, but it wasn't until 1993 that Apple introduced speech recognition.

Apple calls its speech technology PlainTalk. You don't always see that name in Apple's documentation or product descriptions because the company now distributes the text-to-speech and speech recognition parts of PlainTalk separately. Apple generally identifies the separate parts of PlainTalk as English Text-to-Speech, Mexican Spanish Text-to-Speech, and English Speech Recognition.

This chapter describes how to use the speech software that may be installed on your computer, beginning with a discussion of speech software versions and requirements. After that, the chapter tells you how to use text-to-speech capabilities and speech recognition capabilities.

This chapter concludes by discussing a topic that's related to speech, namely language. Although the Mac can speak only a couple of languages, people can write and edit on Mac OS computers in a multitude of languages. This globalization of the Mac OS, as Apple puts it, is made possible by the WorldScript system extensions, language kits for various languages, and multilingual application software.

Speech Requirements and Sources

This section tells you which processor your computer must have for various levels of speech software. This section also tells you where to find speech installation software.

Speech requirements

All Macs OS computers from the Mac Plus on up are capable of basic speech. Computers with 68030 processors running at 33MHz or better are capable of more sophisticated speech. Computers with 68040 and PowerPC processors have the power to synthesize quite natural sounding speech.

Listening is harder than talking, both for people and for computers. Speech recognition requires extra computing power. Computers with PowerPC processors have the power to recognize speech while you do other work. The computer must be capable of 16-bit sound input and must be equipped with a PlainTalk microphone, the microphone built into Apple audiovisual displays, or another microphone capable of 16-bit sound input. Early production models of the Performa 5200 and 5200 LC have 8-bit sound input and can't use speech recognition software. You can determine whether a 5200 has 16-bit sound input by looking at the Sound Out settings in the Sound control panel. If the 16-bit option is grayed out, the 5200 has 8-bit sound and speech recognition won't work.

Among the Macs that don't use PowerPC processors, only the Centris and Quadra 660AV and the Quadra 840AV have sufficient processing power to recognize speech while you continue working. The 660AV and 840AV have a special coprocessor, an AT&T 3210 digital signal processor (DSP), that handles speech recognition; therefore, speech recognition does not burden the 68040 central processor in the 660AVs and 840AVs. The DSP handles speech recognition while the 68040 does other work.

Speech sources

Apple includes English Text-to-Speech software with System 7.5.3 and later, though installation is optional. In addition, system software installation packages on CD-ROM (but not on floppy disks) include extra installation software for Mexican Spanish Text-to-Speech. Apple also generally includes North American English speech recognition software on the CD-ROM that comes with a Power Mac capable of using it. Apple's speech software is also available separately from its PlainTalk Web site (http://www.speech.apple.com/ptk/).

The version of PlainTalk speech software you get varies with the version of Mac system software. With Mac OS 8, 7.6.1, and 7.6 you get PlainTalk 1.5. With Systems 7.5.3 through 7.5.5 you get PlainTalk 1.4 or 1.4.1. And with Systems 7.5 through 7.5.2 you get PlainTalk 1.3.

It's generally OK to upgrade the speech software without upgrading the system software, but PlainTalk 1.5 requires System 7.5 or later. A few Mac models also have specific speech software version limitations. The Power Mac and Performa 5200, 5300, 6200, and 6300 series require Speech Recognition 1.5 or later regardless of the system software version installed. And a Quadra or Centris 660AV or 840AV can't use anything higher than Speech Recognition 1.3.

Because speech software uses a lot of system resources, your computer may not have it installed. In particular, your PowerPC computer may not have speech recognition software installed. If your computer does not have speech software installed and you need installation instructions, see the sections of Chapter 28, 29, or 30 (depending on your version of system software) about custom installation and about installing additional software.

Text-to-Speech

There are several ways to get a Mac OS computer to speak. You can use an application that has commands for speaking the text in a document. You can program the computer to speak. And with Text-to-Speech 1.5 you can have the computer automatically read out the text of alert messages. Regardless of what your computer speaks, it can speak in different voices, and with later versions of speech software you can choose the voice. This section tells you how to choose a voice and make your computer speak. There's also a discussion of speech quality at the end of the section.

Choosing a voice

The PlainTalk Text-to-Speech software can talk in different voices. With PlainTalk 1.4 and later you can choose a voice for the system as a whole. Each application can use the system voice, pick its own voice, or let you choose a voice for that application's speech. However, not all applications give you a voice choice.

Choosing a system voice

You can choose your computer's voice and set a speaking rate with the Speech control panel that's included with Text-to-Speech 1.4 and later. A pop-up menu lists the available voices, a slider adjusts the speaking rate, and a button lets you hear a sample using the current settings. Figure 21-1 shows the Speech control panel's Voice settings.

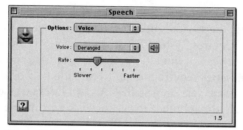

Figure 21-1: Set the computer's speaking voice and speaking rate.

Choosing an application voice

The method for choosing an application's speaking voice varies among applications. For instance, in SimpleText you choose a voice from the Voices submenu of the Sound menu. Figure 21-2 shows an example of SimpleText's Voices submenu.

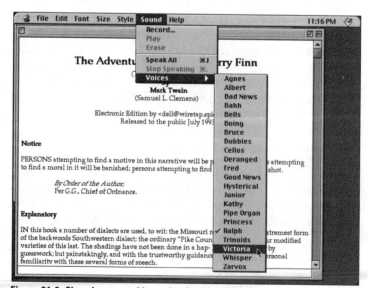

Figure 21-2: Choosing a speaking voice for SimpleText.

Where voices are installed

For each speaking voice available on your computer there is a voice file in the Voices folder, which is inside the System Folder. (With Mac OS 7.6.1 and earlier, the Voices folder is in the Extensions folder.) You get several male, female, and robotic voices when you install English Text-to-Speech. The exact assortment depends on the capabilities of your computer model, as explained in detail at the end of this section.

You can remove voices by dragging their files out of the Voices folder. If you obtain additional voices from a source such as Apple's Speech Web site (http://www.speech.com), you can make them available by dragging them into the Voices folder.

Talking alerts

With Text-to-Speech 1.5, you can use the Speech control panel to set up the manner in which the computer announces its alert messages. There's an option for having the computer read the text of alert messages aloud, a slider for adjusting how long the computer waits after it displays an alert message before it speaks, and an option for having the computer speak a phrase such as "Excuse me!" when it displays an alert. There's also a button that lets you hear a sample alert using the current settings. Figure 21-3 shows the Speech control panel's Talking Alert settings.

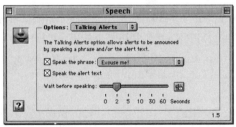

Figure 21-3: Set the computer to announce alert messages.

If you select the option to have the computer speak a phrase when it displays an alert, you choose the phrase you want from a pop-up menu. The pop-up menu includes a choice that tells the computer to use the next phrase listed in the menu each time it speaks an alert. The pop-up also includes a choice that tells the computer to pick a phrase at random from the list each time it speaks an alert. There's also a choice that lets you edit (change, add, or delete) phrases.

If you set the time the computer waits before speaking an alert to more than two seconds, the computer plays the alert sound as soon as it displays an alert and then waits to speak. If you set the time to wait before speaking to less than two seconds, the computer does not play the alert sound when it displays an alert message.

Reading documents aloud

To have your computer speak the text in a document, you need one of the many applications that include commands for speaking. SimpleText is one, and ClarisWorks, FileMaker Pro, and WordPerfect are others. Various applications have different methods for initiating speech. For example, SimpleText has a Speak command in its Sound menu, whereas ClarisWorks has a Shortcut button that looks like a pair of lips. Most applications that can speak text will speak the currently selected text or all text in the active document if no text is selected.

Text-to-speech also augments other types of software. Here are some examples:

❖ outSPOKEN by Berkeley Systems (510-540-5535, http://access.berksys.com) uses text-to-speech software to read out the text and the graphics of standard Mac OS applications such as word processors, spreadsheets, communications programs, and more.

❖ Talk:About by Don Johnston Inc. (http://www.execpc.com/~labres/dj.html) lets individuals who don't speak participate in conversations.

❖ eText by META Innovation (61 3 9439 6639, http://www.meta-inn.com) uses text-to-speech to teach typing for computers (not for typewriters).

❖ NetMeter by The AG Group, Inc. (510-937-7900, http://www.aggroup.com) monitors network traffic and can vocally announce network traffic conditions and warnings.

❖ Storybook Weaver Deluxe by MECC (612-569-1500, http://www.mecc.com) can read aloud storybooks that kids write in English or Spanish.

❖ Hollywood by Theatrix Interactive (http://www.theatrix.com) lets kids become screenwriters and have their written dialogue, character actions, and stage directions performed on screen by any of ten characters.

❖ MacYack Pro from Scantron Quality Computers (800-966-1508, http://www.lowtek.com/macyack/) lets you add speech to any word processor, hear dialog boxes, see and hear customized messages at startup and shutdown, hear calculations instantly, correct pronunciation errors, create double-clickable speech files, have speaking alert sounds, add speech to HyperCard stacks, and use AppleScript to add speech to other programs.

Speaking on command

In addition to having documents and alerts read to you, you can program your computer to speak on command. One way to accomplish this is with AppleScript (which is described in Chapter 22). Alternatively you can use a macro utility such as QuicKeys 3.0 from CE Software (515-221-1801, http://www.cesoft.com). The QuicKeys Speak Ease shortcut speaks text you enter in its text window or text you copy from a document (up to 32K) to the Clipboard. Whenever you type the shortcut's keystroke, the computer speaks the text that you entered or copied. You also can set up a timer so that the computer speaks the text at specified intervals. Figure 21-4 shows the QuicKeys dialog box in which you specify text-to-speech.

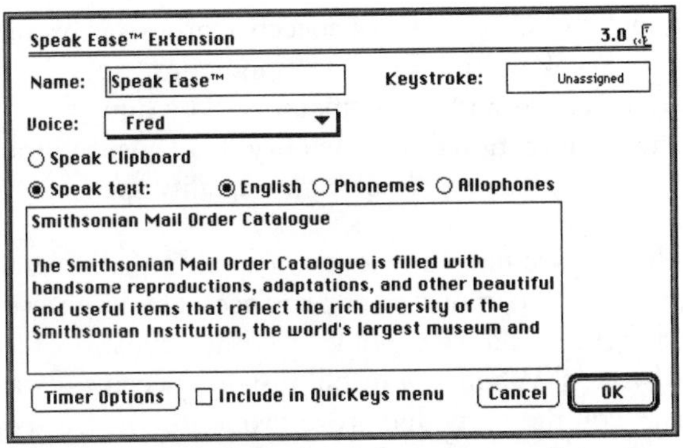

```
Speak Ease™ Extension                                    3.0

Name:    Speak Ease™              Keystroke:      Unassigned

Voice:   Fred                  ▼

○ Speak Clipboard
● Speak text:      ● English ○ Phonemes ○ Allophones

Smithsonian Mail Order Catalogue

The Smithsonian Mail Order Catalogue is filled with
handsome reproductions, adaptations, and other beautiful
and useful items that reflect the rich diversity of the
Smithsonian Institution, the world's largest museum and

( Timer Options )  ☐ Include in QuicKeys menu   ( Cancel )  [ OK ]
```

Figure 21-4: The QuicKeys Speak Ease shortcut allows you to enter text you want spoken.

Speech quality

Several factors affect the quality of computer-generated speech. Clarity of intonation obviously affects how easily you can understand your computer's speech. Less obvious factors include handling contractions, sequencing words idiomatically, avoiding robotic cadence, and generating the sounds of speech.

For natural-sounding speech, the text-to-speech system needs to compensate for idiomatic differences between written and spoken text. This includes expanding contractions, changing word order, and making substitutions. For example, when the system sees "$40 billion" it should not say "dollars forty billion." The system also has to deal with ambiguous abbreviations such as "St. Mary's Church is on St. Mary's St."

Besides saying the right words in the right order, the text-to-speech system has to pronounce them correctly. Consider how many ways "ough" is pronounced in the words enough, ought, slough, dough, through, and drought. Pronunciation also depends on sentence structure, as in "A strong wind can wind a kite string around a tree." Moreover, the system has to avoid putting the emPHASis on the wrong sylLAble. Names pose a special problem because their spelling is even less reliable a guide to pronunciation than ordinary English words.

Getting the words and pronunciation right isn't enough. Without the right cadence, spoken words may sound robotic. Beyond just sounding unnatural, the wrong phrasing may convey the wrong meaning. Compare the meaning of "Atlas already ate, Venus" to "Atlas already ate Venus."

The most computationally intensive part of speech synthesis is producing the sound of a human voice speaking the text. Each moment of speech requires many mathematical calculations and ample memory. The higher the quality of speech, the greater the computational and memory demands. In other words, a higher-performance computer is capable of higher quality speech.

Apple's text-to-speech software has three levels of speech quality, each demanding a different level of computer performance. The levels are known as MacinTalk 2, MacinTalk 3, and MacinTalk Pro. Each consists of a system extension and a set of voices. When you install text-to-speech software, the Installer program gives you the parts that are appropriate for your computer. For example, a PowerPC computer gets MacinTalk Pro and MacinTalk 3. (You can get MacinTalk 2 on a PowerPC computer by doing a custom installation of the text-to-speech software.)

MacinTalk 2

The least demanding speech synthesizer is MacinTalk 2. It generates an audio signal the same way as music synthesizers, with a technique known as wave table synthesis. MacinTalk 2 has ten voices that you can use on any Mac OS computer from a Mac Plus up.

MacinTalk 3

The mid-level speech synthesizer, MacinTalk 3, sounds less robotic than MacinTalk 2 because it's based on an acoustic model of the human vocal tract. MacinTalk 3 has 19 voices, including several novelty voices (robots, talking bubbles, whispering, and singing) that you can use on a computer with a 33MHz 68030 processor or better.

MacinTalk Pro

The best synthesizer, MacinTalk Pro, bases its audio signal on samples of real human speech. It sounds more like a human voice than the other synthesizers, especially when synthesizing a female voice. To assist with pronunciations, MacinTalk Pro has a dictionary of 65,000 words plus 5,000 common U.S. names. To generate cadence, it uses a sophisticated model of the acoustic structure of human speech that resulted from many years of research. MacinTalk Pro has three English voices that require a 68040 or PowerPC processor. It also has two Mexican Spanish voices that require a 68020 processor or better. All the voices are available in three quality levels, with each level striking a different balance between memory requirements and speech quality.

Speech Recognition

Apple made headlines in 1992 when it began touting its speech recognition technology, then called Casper. Now called English Speech Recognition, the technology enables computers that have enough processing power and can input high-quality sound to take spoken commands from anyone who speaks North American English. You don't have to train the computer to recognize your voice. You just speak normally, without intense pauses, unnatural diction, or special intonation.

English Speech Recognition is designed to understand a few dozen commands for controlling your computer. You can add to and remove some of the commands that the speech recognition system understands, but you can't turn it into a general dictation system.

This section explains how to configure speech recognition and how to speak commands. It tells you what commands the speech recognition system understands and how you can add your own speakable commands. The section concludes by describing some applications that make special use of speech recognition.

Configuring speech recognition

You configure speech recognition with the Speech control panel if you have speech software versions 1.4–1.5, or with the Speech Setup control panel if you have speech software version 1.3 or earlier. You can turn speech recognition on and off, make limited adjustments to what is recognized, and specify the kind of feedback you get when you speak commands.

On and off

You turn speech recognition on or off in the Speakable Items section of the Speech control panel (for Speech Recognition 1.4 and later). You can also specify whether the computer should listen for the names of buttons such as OK and Cancel when speech recognition is on. Figure 21-5 shows the Speakable Items section of the Speech control panel.

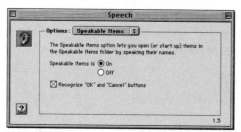

Figure 21-5: Turn speech recognition on and off and set it to listen for button names (Speech Recognition 1.4 and later).

With Speech Recognition 1.3 or earlier, you turn speech recognition on and off at the top of the Speech Setup control panel. There is also a slider for adjusting the sensitivity of recognition. Move the slider to the left to accept a wider range of accents, grammatical rules, and vocabulary words. When the slider is at its most tolerant setting, speech recognition is very sensitive to ambient noise; in fact, it sometimes mistakenly interprets room sounds as commands. Figure 21-6 shows the on–off and sensitivity settings in the Speech Setup control panel.

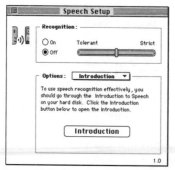

Figure 21-6: Turn speech recognition on and off and adjust its sensitivity (Speech Recognition 1.3 and earlier).

Feedback

Turning on speech recognition brings up a feedback window, which floats above all other windows. At the left side of the feedback window, an animated cartoon character indicates whether the computer is standing by, is listening for a command, is hearing sounds, recognizes your spoken words as a command, or doesn't recognize your spoken words. Beneath the character, some italicized text reminds you what you must do to make the computer listen for a command: press the named key or speak the indicated code name (as described later in this section). The feedback window can also display your voice commands in writing along with a written response. You can hide and show the text by clicking the feedback window's zoom box. Figure 21-7 shows an example of the speech recognition feedback window.

Figure 21-7: Getting feedback on your spoken commands.

You determine how the computer lets you know whether it heard and recognized your spoken commands by setting options in the Feedback section of the Speech control panel (for Speech Recognition 1.4 and later). You can choose the feedback window's cartoon character from a pop-up menu. You can turn the "Speak text feedback" option on or off to control whether the computer speaks its response to your commands in addition to displaying them in writing in the feedback window. You can also choose a sound from a pop-up menu that lists the sounds in the System file, and the computer will play that sound when it recognizes what you said. Figure 21-8 shows the Feedback section of the Speech control panel for Speech Recognition version 1.4 and later.

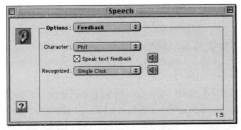

Figure 21-8: Specify how you want the computer to respond to your spoken commands (Speech Recognition 1.4 and later).

With Speech Recognition 1.3 or earlier, the Feedback section of the Speech Setup control panel has options for sounds that speech recognition uses to provide feedback on your spoken commands. You can set the voice to be used in spoken messages, the sound that the computer makes when it responds to a spoken command, and the sound that the computer makes when it completes a command. Figure 21-9 shows the Feedback section of the Speech Setup control panel for speech recognition version 1.3 and earlier.

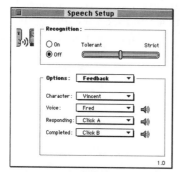

Figure 21-9: Specify how you want the computer to respond to your spoken commands (Speech Recognition 1.3 and earlier).

Speaking commands

You don't want the computer listening to every word you say, or it might try to interpret conversational remarks as commands. There are basically two ways of controlling when the computer listens for commands: the push-to-talk method and the code-name method. The push-to-talk method, which is only available with Speech Recognition 1.4 and later, is the most reliable method because the computer listens for commands only while you are pressing a key you designate. With the other method, the computer listens for its code name and tries to interpret the words that follow it as a command.

Push-to-talk method

To use the push-to-talk method of signaling the computer that you are speaking a command, bring up the Listening section of the Speech control panel and set the Method option to "Listen only while key(s) are pressed." The Key(s) option specifies the key or keys you must hold down to make the computer listen for a spoken command. You can change the setting of the Key(s) option by pressing a different key or combination of keys. Generally you must use the Esc key, Delete key, a symbol key, or any key on the numeric keypad either alone or together with any combination of the Shift, Option, and Control keys. You can't use letter keys or number keys on the main part of the keyboard. Figure 21-10 shows the Speech control panel set for the push-to-talk method with the Esc key, which is the initial setting for Speech Recognition versions 1.4 through 1.5.

Figure 21-10: Setting speech recognition for push-to-talk listening (Speech Recognition 1.4 and later).

Code name method

If you prefer to have the computer listen for a code name that you say before speaking a command, bring up the Listening section of the Speech control panel and set the Method option to "Key(s) toggle listening on and off." Then you can type a name for the computer in the space provided, and you can choose from the nearby pop-up menu to specify if and when you must speak the name. You can make the code name optional, but not without risk: the computer could interpret something you say in conversation as a voice command. Figure 21-11 shows the Speech control panel set for the code-name method.

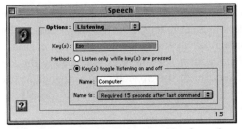

Figure 21-11: Setting speech recognition for code name listening (Speech Recognition 1.4 and later).

With Speech Recognition 1.3 and earlier, you always use the code-name method. You set it up in the Name section of the Speech Setup control panel. Keep in mind that if you make the code name optional, the computer could interpret a conversational remark as a spoken command. Figure 21-12 shows the code-name settings in the Speech Setup control panel for Speech Recognition 1.3 and earlier.

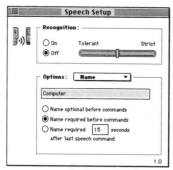

Figure 21-12: Setting the speech recognition code name (Speech Recognition 1.3 and earlier).

You can configure all Speech Recognition versions so that you don't have to speak the code name if you spoke the last command less than 15 seconds ago (or another interval that you specify). The idea is that when you have the computer's attention, you shouldn't have to get its attention all the time. You can tell whether you need to speak the code name by looking at the speech recognition feedback window. If you see the code name beneath the feedback character, you have to speak the name before the next command.

Attention key

When you set speech recognition to listen for its code name, you can press a key or a combination of keys to turn listening on and off. Turning listening off puts speech recognition on standby, which may improve the performance of the computer. With Speech Recognition 1.4 and later you specify the key or keys at the top of the Listening section of the Speech control panel. With Speech Recognition 1.3 and earlier, you specify the key or keys in the Attention Key section of the Speech Setup control panel.

Speakable commands

After setting up and turning on speech recognition, you are ready to speak commands (such as "Make this speakable"), expecting the computer to carry out your order. But what commands will the computer obey? With Speech Recognition 1.4 and later the answer is pretty simple: items in the Speakable Items folder and some buttons in dialog boxes. Earlier Speech Recognition versions can also recognize some menu commands.

Speakable Items folder

Speech recognition (all versions) recognizes the names of items in the Speakable Items folder (which you can access from the Apple menu) as commands. Saying the word "open" before the name of an item in the Speakable Items folder is generally optional unless the item name begins with the word "open." For example, if you had a speakable item named "ClarisWorks," you could open it by saying "open ClarisWorks" or "ClarisWorks."

Speech recognition is similarly liberal about the use of *a, an, the, and*, and *or* in spoken commands. For instance, you can say "close window" or "close the window." Moreover, you can often substitute *these* for *this*, as in "Make this speakable" and "Make these speakable." The computer is somewhat more likely to recognize a phrase that exactly matches a speakable item. If the computer has trouble recognizing a spoken command, try saying the exact name of the speakable item.

When speaking a command, you should not pause between words, but you should pause slightly when saying a command with initials or an acronym, as if you were spelling it out for someone. For example, if you had a speakable item named "open PPP control panel" you should say "open P P P control panel."

If a name includes an ampersand, a slash, or another symbol, speech recognition ignores it. For example, if you had a speakable item named "open Monitors & Sound" you could say "open Monitors Sound" or "open Monitors and Sound."

In addition, Speech Recognition 1.4.1 and earlier ignore numbers in a speakable item name unless they are spelled out. Speech Recognition 1.5 recognizes numbers, so if you had a speakable item named "Web Browser 3.1" you could say "Open Web Browser three point one," or "Open Web Browser three one," or simply "Open Web Browser."

Menu items

Speech Recognition 1.3 and earlier can recognize the names of menu items in any application that creates its menus with standard Mac OS programming practices. (A program must use MENU resources to define its menus.)

If you want Speech Recognition 1.4 or later to recognize menu commands, you will have to create an AppleScript application for each menu command. This works only for scriptable applications. (For more information on AppleScript, see Chapter 22.)

More speakable commands

You make the computer understand more spoken commands by adding items to the Speakable Items folder. Anything that you can open in the Finder becomes a speakable command when you add it to the Speakable Items folder.

Aliases

If there are documents, applications, folders, control panels, or any other items that you want to open by spoken command, simply put aliases of them in the Speakable Items folder. You can do this very easily by selecting the items in the Finder and speaking the command "Make this speakable." The result is an alias in the Speakable Items folder for every item you originally selected, and the aliases have exactly the same names as the original items. If the computer doesn't recognize the name of an item you add to the Speakable Items folder, try restarting the computer.

You can change the speakable command that opens an alias by editing the name of the alias. You should remove the word *alias* from any alias names that include it, although speech recognition usually ignores *alias* at the end of a speakable item's name. If the computer doesn't respond when you say "open" before saying the name of a speakable item, change the item's name so that it begins with "open."

If speakable items have names that sound similar, the computer may have trouble distinguishing them. If the computer frequently mistakes one speakable item for another, try changing the name of one or both so they don't sound alike. Also, the computer has more trouble identifying short names than long ones. To prevent these problems, make the names of your speakable items as long and unique sounding as possible.

AppleScript or Speech Macro Editor

To make a multistep speakable command, you can use the Script Editor program to create an AppleScript application that you put in the Speakable Items folder. If you have Speech Recognition 1.3 or earlier, you use the included Speech Macro Editor to create a speech macro instead. With some applications you can record an AppleScript application or a speech macro of a procedure while you carry it out. Another way to create your own AppleScript application or speech macro is to use an existing one as a basis. However, you can create AppleScript applications and speech macros only to control applications that respond to Apple events. (For more information on AppleScript and Apple events, see Chapter 22.)

Speech recognition applications

It would be very difficult if not impossible to add enough items to the Speakable Items folder to gain anything approaching complete control of an application. Yet applications have access to the speech recognition infrastructure behind the Speakable Items folder, and an application developer can use that infrastructure to give you extensive spoken control of an application. Here are some applications that offer enhanced control through speech recognition:

❖ SurfTalk by Digital Dreams (http://www.surftalk.com) is an add-on for Netscape Navigator or Microsoft Internet Explorer that lets you control the Web browser with spoken commands. You can follow hot links on a Web page, go to bookmarks, and use common navigational commands such as "Go back," "Reload," and "Add Bookmark."

❖ Speech Typer by Michael F. Kamprath (http://www. kamprath.net/claireware/) takes speech recognition beyond speakable commands into the realm of data entry. It lets you type any predefined phrase into any application you may be using. Because you must predefine spoken phrases, Speech Typer doesn't turn speech recognition into a full-fledged dictation system, but it does allow you to dictate commonly used words and phrases.

❖ MT-NewsWatcher by Simon Fraser (http://www.santafe.edu/~smfr/mtnw/) is a speech-controlled Internet newsreader.

❖ Dynamic English by DynEd International (650-578-8067 http://www.dyned.com) teaches English as a second language, using speech recognition to improve articulation and fluency and to reinforce language structure and vocabulary.

❖ Hearts Deluxe 4.4 by Free Verse Software (212-929-3549, http://www.freeverse.com) lets you play the classic card game of hearts against Winston Churchill, Alice in Wonderland, or a bunch of dogs, using only your voice.

❖ IndyCar Racing II by Sierra On-Line (425-649-9800, http://www.sierra.com) is a car racing game in which you can call out commands to your crew over your radio so they'll be ready for time-critical servicing as soon as you roll into the pits.

WorldScript

Mac system software enhanced its position as an international operating system with the inclusion of WorldScript software in System 7.1. WorldScript puts Asian, Middle-Eastern, and other non-Roman languages on an equal footing with English and other Roman languages. WorldScript deals with differences in language structure, writing direction, alphabetical sorting, calendar, date and time display, and currency. Prior to WorldScript, Apple had to laboriously revise the system software's Roman base for each non-Roman language. WorldScript makes the system software's language base nonspecific and modular, so it works equally well with any language plugged into it.

WorldScript consists of two system extensions that handle all the requirements of various human languages. The WorldScript I extension handles bidirectional and contextual languages, and the WorldScript II extension handles languages with large alphabets. Both extensions are included with Mac OS 8 and other system software versions as far back as System 7.5.3. However, they are not part of a standard installation of the system software. You can get them by doing a custom installation of the Mac OS module — select the International component group in the Custom Install section of the Installer program (as described in Chapters 28–30).

The WorldScript extensions give the system and applications the ability to work with any language, but the extensions don't translate text into multiple languages or even provide the specifications of any language. You install additional software that provides the specifications for displaying and inputting a language, and you use applications and system software whose menus and other text are written in one of the languages installed on your computer. Some applications let you create multilingual documents if your computer has multiple languages installed. For example, if you have English, Spanish, and Hebrew installed on your computer, your system software might be in English and some applications might be in Spanish or Hebrew. You might use a word processor that has menus in English but lets you write documents in any or all of the languages.

The Mac OS comes with the necessary software for at least one language — English and several European languages with the U.S. version of the system software — and you work in additional languages by buying and installing language kits.

This section describes the additional software you need and how you work with multiple languages.

Language script systems

With WorldScript installed, the Mac OS works with multiple languages and methods of writing (vertical or horizontal, left to right, or right to left). The software that defines a method of writing is called a *language script system*, or simply a script. Do not confuse this kind of script with the kind of script you create with AppleScript (as described in Chapter 22).

A language script system tells the system software which character in the specified language every keystroke produces, as well as how the characters should behave — for example, the direction in which text flows. The script also specifies sort order, number and currency formats, and date and time formats.

One language script system can be used by multiple languages. For example, the Roman script is used in most Western languages, such as English, French, Italian, Spanish, and German.

Each language has its own rules of behavior, even though it may use the same script as another language. You teach the Mac OS the rules to use by setting the language behavior in the Text control panel. The options in this control panel tell the Mac OS how to produce text from characters. For languages that flow right to left, the control panel provides additional options. You can split the caret insertion point so that you can see where your next typing will next appear for left-to-right writing as well as for right-to-left. Figure 21-13 shows the Text control panel options for the Roman and Hebrew scripts.

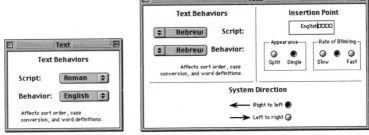

Figure 21-13: Set behavior options for each installed language.

The Mac OS can handle more than one language script system at a time. The system-level script is called the *primary script*. If you are working on a computer that is set up for English, Roman is your primary script; your secondary script can be any other installed language's script, such as Japanese.

Keyboard layouts

Associated with each language script system are one or more keyboard layouts. A keyboard layout defines the relationship between keys you press and characters entered. For example, the keyboard layout for U.S. English produces a # symbol when you press Shift-3, but the same keystroke produces a £ symbol with the British English keyboard layout. The U.S. system software includes a set of keyboard layouts similar to the following (there are some minor differences depending on the version of system software): Australian, Brasil, British, Canadian - CSA, Canadian - ISO, Canadian French, Danish, Dutch, Español ISO, Finnish, Flemish, French, French-numerical, German, Italian, Norwegian, Spanish, Swedish, Swiss French, Swiss German, and U.S.

There are several ways to designate which keyboard layout you want to use of the ones installed on your computer. You can use the Keyboard control panel, a keyboard shortcut, or the Keyboard menu. Keep in mind that only one keyboard layout matches the printed key caps on your keyboard. If you change to a different layout, some keys will no longer generate the characters printed on the keyboard.

Keyboard control panel

You can select a keyboard layout by opening the Keyboard control panel and clicking the name of the layout you want to use. With Mac OS 8, you can select more than one keyboard layout and you can choose a language script system in the Keyboard control panel. If you select more than one keyboard layout, the Keyboard menu appears near the right end of the menu bar (as described later). Figure 21-14 compares the Keyboard control panel from Mac OS 8 with the Keyboard control panel from Mac OS 7.6.

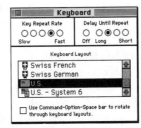

Figure 21-14: Selecting a keyboard layout in Mac OS 8 (left) and in earlier system software versions (right).

Keyboard layout shortcut keys

The Keyboard control panel includes an option for enabling a keyboard shortcut. When you turn on the option, you can cycle through the available keyboard layouts by pressing ⌘-Option-spacebar while working in any application. (The option is not included in the Keyboard control panel that comes with System 7.5 and earlier.)

Whether the keyboard shortcut option is selected or not, you can cycle through the installed script systems on your computer by pressing ⌘-spacebar.

Keyboard menu

If you regularly switch keyboard layouts with Mac OS 8, you can list the layouts you use in the Keyboard menu. You can then choose the layout from this menu while working in any application. To make the Keyboard menu appear, you select more than one keyboard layout in the Keyboard control panel that comes with Mac OS 8, and then close the control panel. The Keyboard menu is located near the right end of the menu bar next to the Application menu. The Keyboard menu's icon is a flag that indicates which keyboard layout is currently selected. Figure 21-15 shows an example of the Keyboard menu in Mac OS 8.

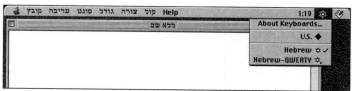

Figure 21-15: Switch keyboard layouts with the Keyboard menu.

If your computer has more than one language script system, switching keyboards may also change script systems. Each keyboard implicitly designates a script system because a keyboard layout can only be part of one script system. For example, if you switch from the U.S. keyboard layout to the Hebrew keyboard layout, you implicitly switch from the Roman script system to the Hebrew script system.

The keyboard menu always appears if your computer has more than one language script system installed, because there must be at least one keyboard layout selected for each script system.

English and other Western languages typically provide only one way to enter text, and U.S. keyboards are based on that text input method. But in languages that are based on ideograms, such as Japanese and Chinese, text can be input in multiple ways. The Japanese Language Kit comes with an input method called Kotoeri that enables entering Kanji, Katakana, Hiragana, and Romaji. Other input methods are available. (Input methods are listed in the Keyboard menu.) The Chinese language kit comes equipped with Pinyin, Zhuyin, Cangjie, and Wubi input-method software, as well as two character sets: simplified and traditional.

Language Kits

If you want to write in a language that uses a different script system than your system's primary language, you need to install additional software. Apple sells complete packages called Language Kits for several script systems, including

❖ Arabic & Persian

❖ Chinese

❖ Cyrillic — Bulgarian, Russian, Ukrainian, Belorussian, Macedonian, and Serbian

❖ Hebrew — Hebrew and Yiddish

❖ Indian — Hindi, Sanskrit, Gujarati, Marathi, Punjabi, and Nepali languages using the Devanagari, Gujarati, and Gurmukhi script systems

❖ Japanese

❖ Korean

Each Language Kit includes a Language Register utility. You use this utility to designate a language script system to be used with each individual application. Registered applications use the correct fonts for menus, dialog boxes, buttons, and so on. You can store two copies of the registered applications so that one application can open in the primary script and the other in a secondary script. Figure 21-16 shows the Language Register utility.

Figure 21-16: Registering an application tells the Mac OS which language the application uses.

Apple's Language Kits require an updater for full functionality with Mac OS 8. You can get an updater from Apple's online software library (http://www.info.apple.com). If you can't get the updater right away, try the following procedure to improve compatibility. First, use the Mac OS 8 Installer program to do a custom installation of the Mac OS 8 module, and select the International component group in the Custom Install section of the Installer program (as described in Chapter 28).Then reinstall your Language Kit. If the Language Kit installer asks about installing older or newer files, always choose newer.

Foreign-language software

By using an application that takes advantage of WorldScript, you can write in any language for which you have the necessary script system and keyboard layout. These are some applications that take advantage of WorldScript to let you write in multiple languages:

❖ ClarisWorks from Claris Corporation (408-987-7000, http://www.claris.com)

❖ HyperCard from Claris Corporation (408-987-7000, http://www.claris.com)

❖ WordPerfect from Corel (613-761-9176, http://www.corel.com)

❖ Nisus Writer from Nisus Software, Inc. (619-481-1477, http://www.nisus-soft.com)

❖ WorldWrite from WorldSoft (801-350-9490, http://www.worldsoft.com)

❖ WinText from WinSoft S.A. (+33-76-875601)

❖ LightningDraw GX from Lari Software, Inc. (919-968-0701, http://www.larisoftware.com)

❖ Ready, Set, Go! GX from Daiwan Software, Ltd. (http://www.diwan.com)

❖ Eudora from QUALCOM, Inc. (800-238-3672, http://www.qualcomm.com)

Many software developers have also used WorldScript to localize some of their products for one or more languages besides English. In localized programs, the menus, dialog boxes, help messages, and other elements appear in the localized language. For example, Nisus Writer and WordPerfect have been localized for Japanese; both word processing programs use correct Japanese for menus, dialog boxes, and toolbars. Other developers, such as Claris and Adobe, offer versions of some of their products in several languages. For lists of localized applications, check Apple's Language Kit Web page (http://www.macos.apple.com/multilingual/).

Apple has used WorldScript to localize the Mac system software for 35 languages: Arabic, British, Bulgarian, Croatian, Czech, Danish, Dutch, English (International version), English (U.S. version), Faroese, Finnish, French, French Canadian, German, Greek, Hangul (Korea), Hebrew, Icelandic, Italian, Japanese, Magyar, Norwegian, Persian, Polish, Portuguese, Romanian, Russian, Simplified Chinese, Spanish, Swedish, Swiss French, Swiss German, Thai, Traditional Chinese (Taiwan), and Turkish. For some languages the Mac system software is not available in the latest version.

Summary

In this chapter you learned the requirements and sources for Apple's PlainTalk text-to-speech and speech recognition software. You found out there are several ways to get a Mac OS computer to speak. You can use an application that has commands for speaking the text in a document. You can program the computer to speak. And with Text-to-Speech 1.5 you can have the computer automatically read out the text of alert messages. Regardless of what your computer speaks, it can speak in different voices, and with later versions of speech software you can choose the voice. The quality of the speech depends on which speech synthesizer your computer has the power to use: MacinTalk 2, MacinTalk 3, or MacinTalk Pro.

You also learned how to use speech recognition software. You use the Speech or Speech Setup control panel, whichever your computer has, to turn recognition on and off and to specify how you want the system to respond when it recognizes a spoken command. You learned the push-to-talk method of speaking commands and the code-name method. You found out what spoken commands the computer understands and how you can add more with aliases and AppleScript.

Finally, you learned how the WorldScript system extensions make it possible for you to work in several languages. Language script systems define language structure, writing direction, alphabetical sorting, calendar, date and time display, and currency. Keyboard layouts define the relationship between keys you press and characters entered. You choose a keyboard layout and script system if you have more than one by using the Keyboard control panel, Keyboard menu, or keyboard shortcut. You can use multiple languages in any application that takes advantage of WorldScript.

CHAPTER TWENTY-TWO

Automate with Scripts

Peple have worked together for thousands of years, but personal computer programs have just begun to do so. Why? People have been talking (or otherwise communicating), but programs have not — at least, not aside from the limited communication that the Copy and Paste commands provide.

The technology that enables programs to work together, called *interapplication communication* (IAC), was first implemented system-wide in System 7.0. The publish and subscribe capabilities described in the next chapter, together with the Copy and Paste commands, are one part of IAC. The other part of IAC enables programs to share services.

Apple Events

Programs can share services behind the scenes by sending and receiving messages called *Apple events.* When an application receives Apple event messages sent by another program, the receiving application, also known as the *server application,* does something. The action that the server application takes depends on the contents of the Apple event messages. This action can be anything from executing a particular command to taking some data, working with it, and then returning a result to the program that sent the Apple events, known as the *client application.*

When you choose Shut Down or Restart from the Special menu, for example, the Finder sends the Apple event Quit to every open program. When you drag and drop icons into an application, the Finder sends the Apple event Open Documents, which includes a list of all the items that you dragged into the icon. You may have seen programs that make aliases or shut down your machine for you. These programs accomplish these tasks by sending Apple events to the Finder.

A program, however, does not automatically send or receive Apple events; the developer must build in the capability to receive and act on Apple events. More and more developers are putting Apple-event capability in their applications. Most applications introduced or revised since the middle of 1991 can receive and act on at least the four basic Apple events: Open Application, Open Documents, Print Documents, and Quit Application, all of which are defined in Table 22-1.

Table 22-1 Basic Apple Events Messages	
Message Sent to Application	*What Happens*
Open Application	The application opens
Open Documents	The application opens the specified documents
Print Documents	The application prints the specified documents
Quit Application	The application quits

The Finder uses the basic Apple events messages to open programs, open documents, print documents, and quit programs. When you double-click a program icon, the Finder sends the program an Open Application message. When you double-click a document, the Finder sends the program that created the document an Open Application message and an Open Documents message with the name of the document you double-clicked. When you select one or more documents and choose Print from the Finder's menu, the Finder sends the application an Open Application message, a Print Documents message with the names of the documents you selected, and a Quit Application message. When you choose the Shut Down or Restart command, the Finder sends a Quit Application message to each open program. For programs that don't understand the basic Apple events, the Finder uses its traditional means of opening, printing, and quitting.

Programs that go beyond the four basic Apple events messages understand another two dozen messages. These messages encompass actions and objects that almost all programs have in common, such as the close, save, undo, redo, cut, copy, and paste commands. Programs with related capabilities recognize still more sets of Apple events messages. Word processing programs understand messages about text manipulation, for example, and drawing programs understand messages about graphics manipulation. Program developers also can define private messages that only their own programs know.

The Mac OS provides the means of communicating Apple events messages between programs. The programs can be on the same computer or on different computers connected to the same network. A program doesn't have to be open or even accessible to receive messages; the system software stores messages and forwards them when the program becomes available. Only application programs can send and receive Apple events; "true" control panels and desk accessories cannot. Control panels that are actually applications (they are listed in the Applications menu when open) are not subject to this limitation. And a desk accessory can work around this limitation by sending and receiving through a small surrogate application program that is always open in the background. This background application does not have to appear in the Application menu, and the computer user does not have to know that the application is open.

To understand how Apple events work, think of them as a telephone system. The Mac OS furnishes a "telephone" and "voicemail" for each program, as well as the wires that connect them. For messages sent across a network, the Mac OS uses the built-in AppleTalk networking software and LocalTalk, Ethernet, or other networking connectors and cables (described in Chapter 17). Application programs talk on the telephones and leave Apple events messages for each other. Desk accessories aren't capable of talking on the phone, but some of them have agents that forward incoming and outgoing messages.

Apple events offer many intriguing possibilities for the world of personal computing. No longer does an application need to handle every possible function; instead, it can send messages to smaller, more specialized, applications and use the information that those applications provide. Your word processing program, for example, may be able to communicate with a small, very good spell checker. The developer doesn't have to spend time working on a spell checker, and you don't have to worry about the poor performance of the spell checker that the developer may introduce.

Introducing AppleScript

Apple events aren't just for professional software engineers. Everyday users can use Apple events to control applications by writing commands in the *AppleScript* language. For example, suppose you want to quit all open applications so you can open one really big application. The Mac OS doesn't have a Quit All command, but you can create one with an AppleScript command. You can use AppleScript commands to automate simple tasks such as this one, as well as more complex tasks, as you'll see in the following sections.

AppleScript language

AppleScript is a user-oriented programming language that allows end users to send Apple events to programs. With AppleScript, you can write your own programs, called *scripts*, to perform complex tasks easily. You can use AppleScript to move data between applications. You can develop your own tools to accomplish exactly what you need.

Because AppleScript is aimed at users, Apple has made the scripting language as easy as possible to understand and use. The language is very natural and English-like. You can look at scripts and know right away what they're supposed to do. Also, AppleScript removes the need for you to decipher the four-letter codes that make up Apple events. Instead, you get information from the application itself about what words to use to represent the Apple events that the program understands. Inside an application, a Get Data event is represented by codes like "core" and "getd," but with AppleScript you may see only "get." This way, even novice users can understand AppleScript. Finally, AppleScript can actually watch you as you work with an application and write a script for you behind the scenes. This process is called *recording* a script.

Although AppleScript is designed for end users, it offers all the capabilities of a traditional programming language and won't frustrate programmers and more advanced users. You can store information in variables for later use; write if-then statements to execute different commands, depending on some condition that you specify; or repeat a set of commands as many times as you want. AppleScript also offers error checking and even enables you to do object-oriented programming.

AppleScript pieces

Several pieces make up a complete AppleScript setup. Perhaps most noticeable is the Automated Tasks folder listed in your Apple menu. Initially this folder contains sample scripts that Apple includes with the Mac OS. You can add and remove scripts from the Automated Tasks folder as you wish. It's located in the AppleScript folder (inside the Apple Extras folder on your startup disk). The AppleScript folder also contains additional sample scripts from Apple in the More Automated Tasks folder.

In addition to the sample scripts, there are several AppleScript items in the System Folder or the Extensions folder. Chief among these is the AppleScript extension, which contains the actual AppleScript language. Another important

AppleScript item is a folder named Scripting Additions. This folder contains special files, called *scripting additions*, that add commands to the AppleScript language, much as plug-in files add capabilities to Photoshop or a Web browser. In Mac OS 8, there can be two Scripting Additions folders: one in the System Folder and another in the Extensions folder. However, if there are any duplicate items in the two Scripting Additions folders, the one in the System Folder takes precedence. Prior to Mac OS 8, the Scripting Additions folder must be in the Extensions folder.

AppleScript also includes a simple application, Scrip Editor, for creating and editing scripts. You can use the Script Editor to record, write, and edit scripts for any application that is compatible with AppleScript. A prime example of a scriptable application (an application that you can control with AppleScript) is the Finder. In Mac OS 7.6.1 and earlier, the Finder is only scriptable if the Finder Scripting Extension file is in the Extensions folder. The Finder in Mac OS 8 does not require or use the Finder Scripting Extension.

If you do a lot of scripting, you may want to replace the Script Editor with a more capable application such as Scripter from Main Event Software (202-298-9595, http://www.mainevent.com) or Script Debugger from Late Night Software (604-929-5578, http://www.latenightsw.com).

Introducing the Script Editor

The program that you probably will use the most when you use AppleScript is Script Editor. This simple program allows you to write and run scripts. Find the Script Editor icon on your hard drive and open it.

When you open Script Editor, an empty window appears. This window, called the *script window*, can contain one script. The bottom pane of the script window is the *script editing area*, where you type and edit the text of the script. The top pane of the window is the *script description area*. You use this area to type a description of what the script does. Figure 22-1 shows an empty script window.

The middle area of the window contains four buttons. The first button puts you in Record mode. When you click this button, AppleScript begins watching you as you work with applications. If you are working in an application that accepts recording, AppleScript writes out the script commands that correlate to the things you do with that application. Pressing ⌘-D also starts recording.

Clicking the Stop button takes you out of recording mode or stops a script that is running, depending on which action is relevant at the time. Pressing ⌘-period (.) is the same as clicking the Stop button.

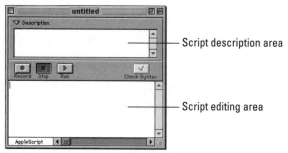

Figure 22-1: A new script window.

The Run button starts running the script in the script editing area. You also can press ⌘-R to run the script.

Finally, the script window contains a Check Syntax button. Clicking this button compiles the script. *Compiling* a script means putting it in a format that AppleScript recognizes as a script. While AppleScript compiles your script, it checks your script for things that it doesn't understand. For example, if you forget a parenthesis where AppleScript expects to find one, it lets you know. After you fix any syntax errors, AppleScript compiles the script.

Recording a Script

One of the easiest ways to see how AppleScript looks is to record your actions and let AppleScript write a script for you. You cannot record scripts for every scriptable program because software developers must do more work to make an application recordable than to make it scriptable.

One recordable application is the Finder. You can experiment with it to see how script recording works. To do this, open the Script Editor and click the Record button in a new script window. Notice that a tape cassette icon flashes over the Apple menu while you are recording a script. This reminds you that AppleScript is recording your actions. Now switch to the Finder, make a new folder, set its label, open it, move its window, and set its view options. When you finish, switch back to Script Editor and click the Stop button. AppleScript displays a script that mimics all your actions. (Some Finder actions can't be recorded in Mac OS 7.6.1 and earlier.) Figure 22-2 shows an example of a script you might record in the Mac OS 8 Finder.

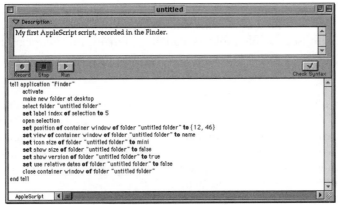

Figure 22-2: A sample script recorded in the Finder.

To test the script, go back to the Finder and delete the new folder you created. (This ensures that the Finder starts out the same way as when you recorded your script.) Now switch back to Script Editor and click the Run button in your recorded script's window. AppleScript plays back everything you did. When the script finishes running, there should be a new folder set up exactly the same as when you finished recording your script. Now switch to Script Editor again and examine the script. You'll find the script to be fairly understandable — it may not be perfectly fluent English, but many of the commands will make sense as you read them.

Analyzing a Script

Having looked through the script that AppleScript wrote in the previous Finder example, you may be surprised to learn that AppleScript doesn't know anything about Finder operations. AppleScript doesn't know how to set an icon's label, how to move windows, or how to do any of the things that your script did in the Finder. In fact, AppleScript knows how to perform only five commands: Get, Set, Count, Copy, and Run. AppleScript learns how to perform other commands in a script from the application controlled by the script. Each scriptable application contains a dictionary that defines procedures for performing additional AppleScript commands that work with it.

Look at the sample script you recorded. The first line says "tell application 'Finder'." To AppleScript, this means "start working with the application named Finder." When a script is compiled, AppleScript looks at the application you specified. By looking at the program's dictionary, AppleScript figures out what Apple events the program understands. AppleScript learns, for example, that Finder understands the "make" Apple event. The dictionary also tells AppleScript what kind of information, or *objects*, the application knows how to work with, such as files, folders, and disks. Finally, the dictionary tells AppleScript what words to use as AppleScript commands instead of the four-letter codes that the application understands.

When you run your sample script and AppleScript reaches the "tell application 'Finder'," AppleScript starts sending Apple events to the application program named in that line. AppleScript translates every command it encounters in your script into a four-letter Apple event code based on the program's dictionary, and it sends that code to the application. The application receives the Apple event and takes the appropriate action.

When AppleScript hits the "end tell" that appears at the bottom of the script you recorded, it stops sending messages to the Finder. If you are working with several applications, you may have another "tell" statement; AppleScript starts talking to that application, translating the commands into their four-letter equivalents.

You can look at the dictionary of an application to see what commands the application understands. In Script Editor, choose Open Dictionary from the File menu. A standard Open dialog box appears. Select the Finder, and click the Open button. The Script Editor displays a dictionary window for the Finder, as shown in Figure 22-3.

Lists suite names in bold, commands in plain, and object classes in italics

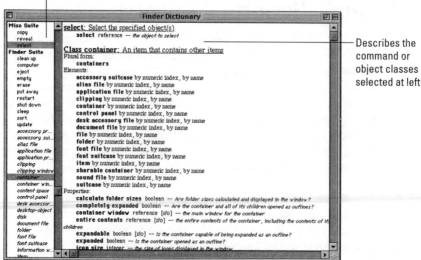

Describes the command or object classes selected at left

Figure 22-3: A scriptable application's AppleScript dictionary.

The left side of the dictionary window displays a list of commands, classes of objects, and suites that the application recognizes. A *suite* is a group of commands and other items for a related activity, but you don't have to worry about suites when you're scripting.

You can select one or more terms listed on the left side of a dictionary window to see detailed descriptions on the right. Just as you can get more information about a command from a program's dictionary, so can AppleScript.

Because AppleScript gets all the relevant information from the application itself, you never have to worry about controlling a new application. As long as the application has a dictionary, AppleScript can work with it.

Tip: Scripting additions also have dictionaries, which you can open the same way as you open applications' dictionaries. In fact, in the Open Dictionary dialog box, Script Editor provides a button that takes you directly to the Scripting Additions folder.

Saving Your Script

The Script Editor allows you to save your scripts in three distinct forms. You choose the form from a pop-up menu in the Script Editor's Save dialog box, as shown in Figure 22-4.

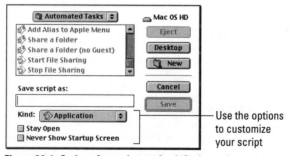

Figure 22-4: Options for saving an AppleScript script.

The pop-up menu contains three options:

❖ **Application** saves the script as an application, complete with an icon. Opening the icon (by double-clicking it, for example) runs the script. You must have AppleScript installed to open a script application.

❖ **Compiled Script** saves the script in a compiled form that you can open with the Script Editor and run or change from there.

❖ **Text** saves the script as a plain text document, which you can open in Script Editor, any word processing program, and many other applications.

If you choose Application from the pop-up menu in the Save dialog box, two check boxes appear in the dialog box. The Stay Open check box, if checked, causes the script application to stay open after its script finishes running. If the Stay Open check box is not checked, the script application quits automatically after running its script. Checking the Never Show Startup Screen check box suppresses the display of an identifying "about" window when the script application is opened.

Creating a Script from Scratch

You know how to use Script Editor to record your actions and write an AppleScript script for you. This type of script, however, has limited value. A recorded script is not much more intelligent than a simple macro, because the script doesn't take advantage of the fact that AppleScript is a full programming language. Furthermore, not all applications that work with AppleScript permit recording, so you can't always rely on being able to record.

More frequently, you'll use AppleScript to create complex scripts from scratch. This section shows that you can create a full-blown script quickly and use the resulting custom utility to augment a program's capabilities.

Making a Finder utility

One of the nice features of the Mac OS is that it enables you to drag files into the System Folder and have the Finder figure out where those files should go. Control panels are stored in the Control Panels folder, Fonts go in the Fonts folder, Desk Accessories are placed in the Apple Menu Items folder, and so on.

This capability, however, is limited to whatever the people at Apple provide. If you drag an After Dark module into the System Folder, for example, the Finder won't put the module in the After Dark Files folder. If you drag a scripting addition into the System Folder, the Finder won't put it in the Scripting Additions folder. You must dig your way through the System Folder hierarchy to get to the relevant folders.

You can, however, write a simple script that uses the Finder and mimics the System Folder's behavior, but moves the files you want to move to the folders in which you want those files to go. As you'll see, the script is more powerful than the System Folder, because the target folder can be anywhere. For example, you can make your QuickTime movies find their way into a folder that's nowhere near your System Folder.

Beginning the script

Open Script Editor, or create a new window if Script Editor already is open. This blank window is where you'll write your script.

Tip: You can change the default size of a new script window. Make the script window the size you want and then choose Set Default Window Size from the File menu in Script Editor.

The first thing this script must do is provide a way to select the file you want to move. One of the scripting additions that comes with AppleScript, Choose File, allows you to bring up a dialog box for selecting a file from within the script.

In the script editing area of the window, type

```
choose file
```

Then click the Check Syntax button. AppleScript changes the text fonts as it compiles the script, using different type styles to show different kinds of words. Geneva 10 Bold, for example, represents words that are native to AppleScript, whereas Plain Geneva 9 represents words that come from another application.

Tip: If you don't like these typestyles, you can change them via the AppleScript Formatting command in Script Editor's Edit menu.

Click the Run button to run the script you wrote, selecting any type of file and clicking the Open button. AppleScript shows you the result of the script in a window named, appropriately enough, "the result." (If this window isn't open, choose Show Result from the Controls menu.) The window contains the word "alias" and the path through your folders to the file you selected. Notice that this word does not mean that the file is an alias, however; in the context of a script, *alias* means the same thing as *file path*. Figure 22-5 shows an example of the result window.

Figure 22-5: Checking a file specification in Script Editor's "the result" window.

The result of the Choose File command is called a *file specification*, or *file spec*. A file spec tells the system software exactly where to find a file or folder. You will need the file spec later in the script, so you must put it in a *variable*, which is a container for information. You can place data in a variable and then retrieve it whenever you want before the script finishes running. You also can place new data in a variable during the course of the script.

On the next line of the script, type the following:

```
copy the result to filePath
```

This line places the result of the Choose File command in a variable named filePath. To access the information, type the name of the variable in your script; AppleScript understands this name as a representation of the file spec you got from the first command.

When you run the script, you'll see that the "copy" command doesn't change the result of the script. The result of copying information to a variable is the information itself.

Working with the Finder

Ultimately, the script you are creating decides where to move a file you select, based on the file's four-letter file type. That means you have to get the file type of the file you selected. You can use the Finder to get this information. Enter the following commands in the script, starting on the third line of the script:

```
tell application "Finder"
copy the file type of file filePath to fileType
end tell
```

The first of these lines tells AppleScript to start using the Finder. Remember that after encountering this "tell" command, AppleScript knows all the commands and objects from the Finder's AppleScript dictionary.

The second line asks the Finder for the file type of the file you selected and then copies that information into the variable named fileType. Even though the word "Finder" doesn't appear in this line, the "tell" command in the preceding line tells AppleScript to direct these requests to the Finder.

Finally, the "end tell" command tells AppleScript to stop working with the Finder for now.

Run the script, select a file, and look at the result. The result window contains the four-letter file type of the file you selected, displayed as a piece of text.

Executing Script commands conditionally

For the next part of the script, you have to provide the information; you can't get it from the Finder. You need to write the commands that will move the file to the folder you want, based on the file type of the file (stored in the variable fileType).

To accomplish this task, you write a series of conditional statements, or *conditionals* for short. A conditional is a command or set of commands that AppleScript runs only when a certain condition is met. AppleScript evaluates the condition you set forth, and if the condition is true, AppleScript runs the specified commands.

The condition you will set up for each conditional is whether the information in the variable fileType is equal to a four-letter string that you will provide. You attach to the conditional a command that moves the file to a designated folder. In other words, if the information in the variable fileType is equal to a particular four-letter string, AppleScript moves the file to a certain folder. In AppleScript, the conditional looks like this:

```
if fileType is "sfil" then move file filePath to folder "Mac
OS HD:Sounds:"
```

In this example, the condition is whether the information in fileType is "sfil," which is the four-letter type of sound files. If it is, AppleScript moves the file specified by the variable filePath to the folder named Sounds on the hard drive named Mac OS HD.

Include as many of these conditionals as you want. In each conditional, use a different four-character file type for the type of file you want to move, and specify the path of the folder to which you want AppleScript to move files of that type. A quick way to enter several conditionals is to select one conditional, copy it, paste it into the script, and change the relevant pieces of information. You can repeat this for each conditional you want to include.

When you type a long command, notice that the Script Editor never breaks it automatically (as a word processor would). You can break a long line manually by pressing Option-Return. (Do not break a line in the middle of a quoted text string, however.) AppleScript displays a special symbol (¬) to indicate a manual line break. Here's an example:

```
if fileType is "sfil" then move file filePath
to folder "Mac OS HD:Sounds:"
```

Figure 22-6 shows an example of a script with three conditional statements that move a selected file depending on its file type.

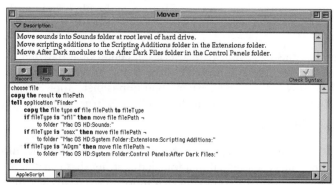

Figure 22-6: A sample script with conditional statements.

Trying out your script

After creating a new script, you must run it and test it thoroughly. To test the script that moves files according to their type, run the script. When the dialog box appears, select a file that is of a type your script should recognize but that is not in the destination folder, and click the Open button. Switch to the Finder, and make sure that the file you selected moved from the source folder to the destination folder. Then repeat the test, selecting a different file type that your script should recognize.

Finding a Folder Path

If you don't know the full path of a folder, you can use a script to get this information. Open a new window in Script Editor and type the following script in the script editing area:

```
choose folder
```

Run the script, and select a folder. The result is a file spec for the folder you selected. You can copy only the text and paste it in any script.

Finding a File's Type

You may not know the file type of the files that you want to move. For example, you may know that you want to put After Dark modules in the After Dark Files folder, but you may not know that the four-letter file type of After Dark modules is "ADgm." To make the process easy, copy the following five-line script into a new Script Editor window:

```
choose file
copy the result to filePath
tell application "Finder"
copy the file type of file filePath to fileType
end tell
```

Run this five-line script, and select a file whose four-character file type you need to learn. If the result window is not visible, choose Show Result from the Controls menu. The result of the script is the file type of the file you selected. You can copy and paste the result from the Result window into a conditional statement in any script window.

Creating a drag-and-drop script application

Although the sample script you created is useful, it would be more useful as an icon on your desktop to which you could drag files and have them move to their appropriate spots, just as you can with the System Folder. You wouldn't have to run Script Editor every time you want to move files, and you could move more than one file at a time. AppleScript gives you this capability.

You know that AppleScript can make stand-alone applications from your scripts. With a little extra work, you can make an application with drag-and-drop capability so that you can simply drag files to it.

Remember that when you drag and drop a set of icons into an application on the desktop, the Finder sends that application an Open Documents message that includes a list of the files that you dragged to the icon. This message is sent to all applications, even ones that you make with AppleScript.

You need to tell your script to intercept that Apple event and run the appropriate commands. Place the following line at the beginning of your script:

```
on open (itemList)
```

Now enter the following line at the end of your script:

```
end open
```

The first line tells the script to intercept the Open Documents message and to put the list of files in a variable named itemList. The End Open command helps AppleScript know which commands to run when the open message is received. Any lines between the first and second lines are run when the script receives an Apple event Open Documents.

Save this script by choosing the Save As command from the File menu. From the pop-up menu in the Save As dialog box, choose the Application option. If you switch to the Finder and look at the icon of the application you just created, you'll notice that the icon contains an arrow on it, showing you that this application is a drag-and-drop application. Script Editor knows how to use this kind of icon, because it sees that the application's script intercepts the Apple event Open Documents. (You can give the application a custom icon, as described in "Appearance and Behavior Modification" in Chapter 5.)

The script won't be fully operational until you make a couple more changes. As the script stands, it places the list of files in a variable, but it doesn't do anything with that information. If you dragged several files to the application now, the script would merely bring up a dialog box asking you to pick a file, and then quit, having accomplished nothing.

First, delete what now are the second and third lines of the script (the ones beginning with the words "choose" and "copy"), and replace them with the following:

```
repeat with x from 1 to the number of items in itemList
copy item x of itemList to filePath
```

Between the End Tell and End Open commands, enter the following:

```
end repeat
```

Figure 22-7 shows the complete sample script modified for drag-and-drop operation.

In the modified script, AppleScript repeatedly executes the commands between the Repeat and End Repeat commands for the number of times specified in the Repeat command. This arrangement is called a *repeat loop*. The first time AppleScript executes the Repeat command, it sets variable x to 1, as specified by "from 1." When AppleScript encounters the End Repeat command, it loops back to the Repeat command, increments the variable x by 1, and compares the new value of x with the number of items that were dragged to the icon ("the number of items in itemList"). If the two values are not equal, AppleScript sequentially executes the command following the Repeat command. If the two values are equal, AppleScript goes to the command immediately following End Repeat. The End Open command ends the script.

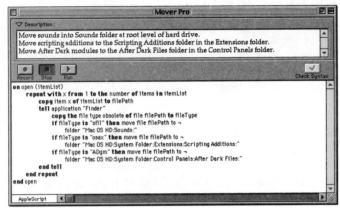

Figure 22-7: A sample script ready to be saved as a drag-and-drop script application.

The first command in the repeat loop that you just created takes item x of the variable itemList (where once again, x is a number ranging from 1 to the number of items in itemList), converts it to a string, and then copies that information to the filePath variable. (The list that comes with the Open Documents message is a list of file specs, so you need to convert each item to a string before the Finder can use it.)

Save the script, and switch back to the Finder. You now have a drag-and-drop application that you can use to move certain types of files to specific folders. Anytime you want to add a file type, use Script Editor to open the script, add a conditional that covers that file type, and save the script. You can place several different files in a single folder, if you want, but you can't place files of the same type in different folders.

Tip: If you want to edit a script application, you can drag its icon to the Script Editor icon, and Script Editor will open the script for you. (Keep in mind that double-clicking a script application runs it.)

Using AppleScript with Applications

The Finder is only one application that you can use with AppleScript; more and more vendors are including AppleScript capability in their applications. This section provides a few examples of scripts that use some popular scriptable programs. These scripts are reasonably small, so you can type them quickly. The scripts also give you an idea of other things that AppleScript can do.

ShrinkWrap and a Web browser

Many people find that a Web browser performs better if its cache is on a RAM disk. But if you use the Memory control panel to create the RAM disk, it's always there using up memory even if you're not browsing the Web. One solution is to use the ShrinkWrap utility from Aladdin Software (originally distributed as shareware by its author, Chad Magendanz) to create a RAM disk.

ShrinkWrap can create a file that contains an image of the browser's cache disk. You can mount the disk image file as a RAM disk on demand, and you can put away the RAM disk whenever you want, freeing the memory it used. You can put an alias of the disk image file into the Startup Items folder so that ShrinkWrap will mount the disk image as a RAM disk at startup, making the cache files available then, or you can double-click the disk image file to mount the RAM disk just before you open the browser.

A more elegant solution is to create a small script application that mounts the RAM disk and opens the browser. You would open this script application in lieu of opening the browser directly. For quick access to this script application, you could name it Browser RDC (where *RDC* stands for "RAM disk cache") and put it or an alias of it in the Apple menu. The script requires ShrinkWrap 2.0 or later, because earlier versions do not allow setting ShrinkWrap preferences with AppleScript commands. Figure 22-8 shows the script.

Before creating the script application, you must open ShrinkWrap and create the Internet Cache disk image file or you won't be able to save the script application successfully. Before running the script application for the first time, you must mount the disk image, open your Web browser, and change the location of its cache to the mounted disk image. If you open the Web browser directly, without first mounting the disk image, the browser resets the cache to its default location and you have to set it back to the mounted disk image again.

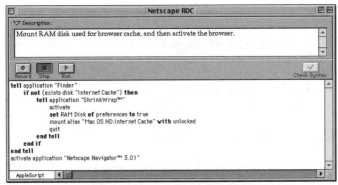

Figure 22-8: A script application that mounts a RAM disk used for a browser cache and then activates the browser.

When you type the script from Figure 22-8 into a Script Editor window, be sure you replace "Internet Cache" with the actual name of your RAM disk, and replace "Mac OS HD:Internet Cache" with the path to your ShrinkWrap disk image file. Also, put the exact name of your browser in the last statement of the script.

Another short script application can automate the process of quitting the Web browser and putting away the RAM disk. The same script can also disconnect a dial-up Internet connection. For easy access to this script application, you could name it Quit Browser RDC and put it or an alias of it in the Apple menu. Figure 22-9 shows this script.

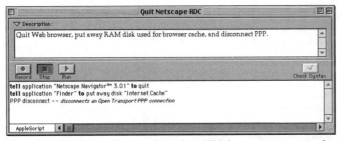

Figure 22-9: A script application that quits a Web browser, puts away the RAM disk used for its cache, and disconnects the dial-up Internet connection.

When you type the script from Figure 22-9 into a Script Editor window, be sure you replace "Internet Cache" with the actual name of your RAM disk. Also, put the exact name of your browser in the first statement of the script.

The last statement disconnects a dial-up Internet connection made with Open Transport PPP, which is a standard part of Mac OS 8. If you use MacPPP or FreePPP for dial-up Internet connections, replace the last statement with "closePPP". To control MacPPP or FreePPP with AppleScript, you must put the scripting addition file MacPPP Control in your Scripting Additions folder. MacPPP Control is available from sources of freeware and shareware, as described in Chapter 24. If you use MacPPP or FreePPP version 2.5 or later, you must also use MacPPP Control version 1.5 or later. (Open Transport PPP does not require a scripting addition file.)

Notice that the script in Figure 22-9 does not modify the browser's Quit command so that it also removes the RAM disk. Unfortunately, very few applications allow attaching an AppleScript script to their menu commands. There is a way to seamlessly integrate an AppleScript script that automatically puts away the RAM disk when you quit the browser. You can do this by modifying the AppleScript application that mounts the RAM disk and launches the browser in the first place. You add some script commands that periodically check to see if the browser is still open and put away the RAM disk if it's not. To make the AppleScript application stay open in the background so it can monitor the browser's status, you must turn on the Stay Open option when you save it. Figure 22-10 shows an example of this script with Netscape Navigator as the browser.

Figure 22-10: The last nine lines of this stay-open script application put away the RAM disk used for a Web browser's cache after you quit the browser.

This script could also include a command that disconnects your PPP connection after you quit the browser. For example, inserting the command "PPP disconnect" before the "put away" command would disconnect an Open Transport PPP connection before putting away the RAM disk. If you use the Control PPP for AppleScript control of FreePPP or MacPPP, the disconnect command is ClosePPP.

Claris Emailer and a PPP dialer

Claris Emailer sends and receives e-mail, but like many Internet applications, it relies on other software such as Open Transport PPP, MacPPP, or FreePPP to open and close dial-up Internet connections. You can fully automate your Internet e-mail by scheduling Emailer or Emailer Lite versions 1.0v2 and later to run an AppleScript script that dials through Open Transport PPP or through MacPPP/FreePPP, accesses your mail through Emailer or Emailer Lite, and hangs up through Open Transport PPP or through MacPPP/FreePPP.

Emailer 1.0v2 and later come with an AppleScript script and instructions for using it, but Emailer Lite does not. Moreover, the included script does not work reliably unless you bring Emailer or the AppleScript script to the front while PPP is making a connection. You can get improved AppleScript scripts from the Fog City Web site (http://www.fogcity.com).

To schedule your Internet mail connection (and disconnection), open Emailer or Emailer Lite and choose Schedules from the Setup menu. Click the Add button (Emailer 1.1v4 and earlier) or the New button (Emailer 2.0 and later) to set up a new schedule. In the Schedule Entry dialog box that appears, choose AppleScript from the Execute pop-up menu and choose the script by name from the AppleScript pop-up menu. Enter an appropriate schedule name, and set the schedule times or interval as documented in the Emailer manual. (Don't forget, Emailer makes scheduled connections only when it's open.)

Emailer 2.0 is not only scriptable but also attachable. This means that you can execute AppleScript scripts directly from the application itself; you don't have to switch to Script Editor or choose script applications from your Apple menu. With Emailer 2.0, you can access your scripts from an AppleScript menu. This feature is very handy for small utility scripts that augment Emailer's capabilities. For example, you can get scripts that change the status of currently selected incoming or outgoing messages, forward all selected messages to a single address, save the currently selected messages in a text file, permanently delete the selected messages and move their enclosures to the Trash, and so on. Check for scripts at the Fog City Emailer 2.0 Utilities page on the Web (http://www.fogcity.com/em_utilities2.0.html).

QuarkXPress

QuarkXPress guides are great, but that doesn't mean you want them around forever. You could delete the guides manually, page by page, but it's easier to run the script shown in Figure 22-11.

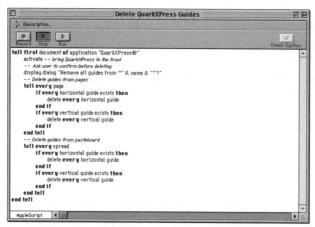

Figure 22-11: This script deletes all guides in the frontmost QuarkXPress document.

When you run this script, you will be asked to locate your copy of QuarkXPress if its name does not exactly match the name in quotes in the first line of the script.

Linking Programs

You have seen how AppleScript can automate tasks on your own machine. You also can send Apple events to open applications on other machines in a network. As a result, you can use AppleScript to control applications on other people's machines. Sharing programs by sending and receiving Apple events across a network is called *program linking*.

Program linking adds tremendous potential to AppleScript. If you are in charge of a network, you can use AppleScript to perform network installations or backups. If you have a script that uses many applications, you can speed up the script by sending a command to a remote application and retrieving the data later. You send only a blip across the network; the remote application does the work while other parts of your script are running, and you get the results later. In addition, this capability can help you get around possible memory problems that might arise from opening several applications from a script.

Setting up program linking

Program linking can be controlled much like file sharing. You can turn program linking on and off, can control who on the network is allowed access to your programs, and can deny access to specific programs.

Starting and stopping program linking

If you want to allow other network users to link to programs on your computer, you must activate program linking. To do this, click the Start button in the Program Linking section of the File Sharing control panel (Mac OS 8 and later) or the Sharing Setup control panel (Mac OS 7.6.1 and earlier). Your computer is ready for program linking when the button's label changes to Stop and the File Sharing control panel reports "Program Linking on," or the Sharing Setup control panel's status message reads "Program linking is on." Figure 22-12 shows how the File Sharing control panel and the Sharing Setup control look when program linking is turned on.

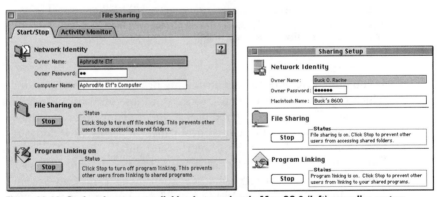

Figure 22-12: Seeing that program linking is turned on in Mac OS 8 (left) or earlier system software versions (right).

To turn off program linking, click the Stop button in the File Sharing section of the File Sharing control panel or the Sharing Setup control panel, whichever the computer has. Clicking the Stop button prevents all programs on the computer from receiving Apple events from any other computer on the network.

Authorizing access to shared programs

You control which network users can link to programs on your computer with the Users & Groups control panel. To allow everyone on the network to link to your programs, open the Guest icon in the Users & Groups control panel, and turn on the "Allow guests to link to programs on this computer" option. (This option is called "Allow guests to link to programs on this Macintosh" in Mac OS 7.6.1 and earlier.) To prevent unidentified network users from linking to your programs, turn off this option. Figure 22-13 shows the guest window as it looks in Mac OS 8 and Mac OS 7.6.

Figure 22-13: Setting guests' program linking privileges in Mac OS 8 (left) or earlier system software versions (right).

If you don't give guests program-linking privileges, you need to designate which registered users in your Users & Groups control panel can link to your programs. To allow a registered user to link to your programs, open that user's icon in your Users & Groups control panel. In the user's window, turn on the "Allow user to link to programs on this computer" option ("Allow guests to link to programs on this Macintosh" in Mac OS 7.6.1 and earlier). (For information on registering users, see "Identifying Who Can Access Your Shared Items " in Chapter 18.) Figure 22-14 shows a user window as it looks in Mac OS 8 and Mac OS 7.6.

You can block any registered user from linking to your programs by turning off that user's "Allow user to link to programs on this computer" option ("Allow guests to link to programs on this Macintosh" in Mac OS 7.6.1 and earlier).

Figure 22-14: Setting a registered user's program linking privilege in Mac OS 8 (left) or earlier system software versions (right).

Denying access to specific programs

Even though you may allow certain network users to link to your programs, you may want to specifically deny access to a particular application, just as you may want to prevent someone from seeing a particular folder inside a shared folder. You control program linking for each application in its sharing window, which appears when you select the program in the Finder and choose Sharing from the File menu.

To prevent an application from receiving Apple events sent by another computer, turn off the "Allow remote program linking" option in its sharing window, and then close the window. If the option is dimmed, the program is open; you must quit a program before changing its program-linking option.

Figure 22-15 shows an example of a program's sharing window as it looks in Mac OS 8 and Mac OS 7.6.

Figure 22-15: Preventing other users from sharing a specific program in Mac OS 8 (left) or earlier system software versions (right).

Scripting across a network

Using AppleScript to run a program across the network doesn't take much more work than writing a script to use a program on the same computer. Start program linking on a networked computer. Now go to another computer on the network. Open the Script Editor, and type the following command:

```
choose application
```

This command brings up a dialog box in which you select an application on your computer or on the network. On the left side of this dialog box, select the computer you set up (you may need to select a zone if your network has zones and the computer is in a different zone). The applications that are running on the selected computer are displayed on the right side of the dialog box. One application is the Finder. Select it and click OK. Figure 22-16 shows the dialog box with a computer and its Finder application selected.

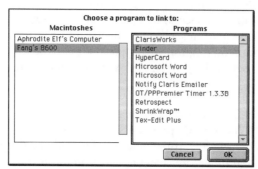

Figure 22-16: Choosing a program to link to.

Open the result window in Script Editor, if it's not open already. You see that the result of this short script is the network path of the application you selected: the name of the application, the name of the computer, and the name of the zone (if your network has more than one zone).

Enter the following line below the first one and then run the script, selecting the same application on the same computer:

```
copy the result to netpath
```

This script places the path to the application in a variable named netpath. To send Apple events to this application, enter the next two lines in the script:

```
tell netpath
end tell
```

This "tell" command specifies the name of the application with the netpath variable instead of with the word "application" and the literal name of the application. The effect is the same: AppleScript starts sending Apple events to the application, which in this case happens to be on a different computer.

Enter the following command lines between the "tell" and the "end tell" command lines, except that if the target computer doesn't have text-to-speech software installed, don't enter any of the "say" statements:

```
activate
beep
say "Your computer is under my control. Resistance is
futile."
set nbrWindows to number of windows
if nbrWindows > 0 then
        say "I will now close all your windows."
        set windowList to windows
        set openItemsList to item of every window
        close windowList
        say "I will now open them again."
        if nbrWindows > 1 then open reverse of
openItemsList
        if nbrWindows = 1 then open openItemsList
end if
get count of every item of font
set fontCount to count of items in font
set half to round (fontCount / 2)
open font
say "You have " & fontCount & ¬
        " fonts. That is too many. Get rid of " & half & ¬
        " or I will call the font police."
say "I now return control to you. Have a nice day."
```

Run the script. As before, the script displays a dialog box in which you select the Finder that is running on the other computer. Before the script can send Apple events to that application, however, the script must connect your computer to the other computer. To do this, the script displays a connection dialog box like the ones you use to connect to other computers for file sharing, as shown in Figure 22-17.

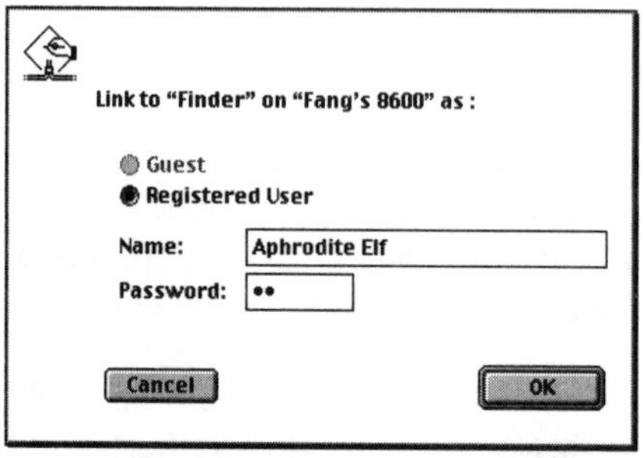

Figure 22-17: Linking to another machine as a registered user.

In the connection dialog box, you specify whether you want to connect as a guest (if the other computer allows guests) or as a registered user. To connect as a registered user, enter your name and password as they were set up in the other computer's Users & Groups control panel. If you connect successfully, the script runs.

Before going over to the other computer to check the results, try running the script again. This time, you don't have to go through the log-on process. Once you connect to another application, you don't have to go through the connection dialog every time you want to send an Apple event. You have to re-enter your password if someone quits the application you're linked to or turns off program linking on the target computer.

Now go over to the other computer, and look at the Finder. You should see the Fonts folder opened, as your script directed.

That's all the work you have to do if you want to script a remote application. You don't have to use the choose application command, either. You can simply write the network path of the application, as in this example:

```
tell application "Finder" of machine "Fang's 8600"
...
end tell
```

Program linking offers many possibilities for scripters. For example, you could use a script to create a large catalog by farming out different sections of that catalog to several networked computers. Each machine could work on its section, and the script could pick up the resulting file via file sharing from the computers as they finish their individual sections. As another example, a network administrator could back up crucial documents from computers across the network onto a central tape drive and then shut down the individual computers.

QUICK TIPS

Working Around Program-Linking Barriers

One of the biggest problems with using Apple events over a network is the fact that some applications do not accept Apple events that come from a remote computer. There is a way around this problem, however. *Script applications* — that is, scripts you save as applications from the Script Editor — accept Apple events from across a network. When a script application runs a script, the application acts as though the script is on the local computer. If you're trying to control a remote application that does not allow networked Apple events, you can send a message to a script application on the remote computer. The script application in turn executes a script to control other applications on the same computer. To see how this process works, create the following simple script application on a networked computer:

```
on netMessage()
tell application "Finder"
   open about this computer
end tell
end netMessage
```

This script has a handler for netMessage, just as the earlier drag-and-drop script had a handler for open. This netMessage handler tells the Finder to display the About this Computer window. (If you create this script on a computer with Mac OS 7.6.1 or earlier, replace the second line with "open about this macintosh".) This script has no problem sending Apple events to the Finder on the same computer, because no network is involved.

When you save this script as a script application, be sure to turn on the Stay Open option in the Save dialog box. With this option checked, the script stays open once you open it, rather than quitting after the script runs.

Open the script application and go to another networked computer that has AppleScript installed. On that computer, write the following script:

```
choose application
copy the result to netPath
tell netPath to netMessage()
```

Run the script, and use the dialog box to select the name of the script application that you left open on the other computer. The script gets the result and tells the script application to "netMessage." The script application on the other computer receives this message and runs the commands in the netMessage handler, showing the About this Computer window on that computer. (If the other computer has Mac OS 7.6.1 or earlier and you modified the script running on it as instructed in the previous paragraph, that computer displays the About This Macintosh window.)

Summary

In this chapter, you learned how applications can communicate by sending each other messages called Apple events. When an application receives an Apple event, it performs a task specified by the event. You can use the Apple event mechanism to automate tasks involving one or more applications. You do this with AppleScript scripts. AppleScript is a programming language designed with everyday users in mind, but with enough power for advanced users and programmers.

You learned how to create scripts with the Script Editor application. An easy way to create scripts for some applications is to have AppleScript record your actions as a script. Then you can save the recorded script and run it again to repeat the same actions.

You also learned that a recorded script has limited value. To take full advantage of AppleScript, you use the Script Editor or another script editing program to create scripts from scratch. You type AppleScript statements into a new Script Editor window, check the syntax for errors, and run the script to test it. Your script might use conditional statements to perform some operations only when the conditions you specify are met. You'll probably use repeat loops to execute a group of statements over and over. When you're done, you may save the script as a script application.

This chapter described several examples of how you can use scripts to control applications other than the Finder. A script can mount a RAM disk and then the Web browser that uses the RAM disk for its cache. Another script can dial-up a PPP connection to the Internet and then send and receive e-mail with Claris Emailer. Yet another script can remove all guides from a QuarkXPress document automatically, saving the drudgery of doing the job with the mouse.

And finally, this chapter showed how AppleScript can control applications over a network on computers that have program linking set up and turned on. You turn on program linking with a computer's File Sharing or Sharing Setup control panel. You use the Users & Groups to designate which users can link to programs on your computer. And you use the Finder's Sharing command to designate which programs other computers can link to. Once your computer is connected to another computer for program linking, you can use AppleScript to control applications on the other computer.

CHAPTER TWENTY-THREE

23 Create Compound Documents

IN THIS CHAPTER

- Introducing **OpenDoc parts, editors, and stationery**

- **Creating OpenDoc documents** from stationery and from existing documents

- **Creating new OpenDoc stationery** based on your own documents

- **Working with OpenDoc parts:** adding parts; adding and editing content; and selecting, moving, resizing, copying, and deleting parts

- **Using publish and subscribe:** creating publishers, subscribing to editions, setting publisher and subscriber options, making changes to publishers, and updating editions

D on't inflexibly limit yourself to copy and paste whenever you want to create a compound document containing various types of material or material from several sources. The Mac OS offers two more-powerful methods: one is OpenDoc, the other is publish and subscribe.

The first method, OpenDoc, makes it possible for you to include any type of material in a document. Unlike copy and paste or publish and subscribe, you're not limited to the types of material allowed by the application you're using. Every OpenDoc document can contain not only standard text and graphics but spreadsheets, graphs, database records, QuickTime media, sounds, styled text, live Web pages, and so forth. It may sound like OpenDoc is a super-integrated, does-it-all behemoth, but it's not. OpenDoc by itself can't work with any kind of material. Instead it provides an endless number of software sockets for a new kind of general-purpose plug-in software, and each plug-in software part gives you the ability to work with a particular type of material.

The second method for creating compound documents, publish and subscribe, is like copy and paste, but where the latter is static the former is dynamic. Copied material that you paste into a document doesn't change unless you replace it by pasting a newer copy. Compare that to publish and subscribe, which places a dynamically linked copy of material from one document into another document, so that if the material changes in the source document, the linked copy changes automatically.

617

This chapter describes OpenDoc and publish and subscribe in more detail. You'll learn how to create and work with OpenDoc documents. And you'll find out how to create publishers, subscribe to editions, set publisher and subscriber options, update editions, and more.

OpenDoc Compound Documents

OpenDoc lets you create documents an old-fashioned way. Rather than emphasizing applications, as personal computers have always done, OpenDoc puts the focus where it was before personal computers came along — on documents. With OpenDoc you don't have to switch applications to work on a different kind of content. You just select the content you want to work on and the appropriate menus appear automatically in the menu bar, and you use the menu commands to work with the selected content.

The OpenDoc 1.2 system software is part of a standard installation of Mac OS 8, and a standard installation of Mac OS 7.6 includes OpenDoc 1.1. The System 7.5.3 CD-ROM includes OpenDoc 1.0.4, but you must install it separately. You can also get the OpenDoc system software from Apple's OpenDoc site on the Web (http://opendoc.apple.com). OpenDoc works with System 7.1.1 and later on a computer with a 68030, 68040, or PowerPC processor.

Although OpenDoc is an interesting technology with a lot of promise, Apple has decided not to develop it any further. You should not expect to see any OpenDoc improvements in the Mac OS after Mac OS 8.

Introducing OpenDoc parts

An OpenDoc document can include any kind of content for which an appropriate OpenDoc plug-in software component, called a *part*, is installed on your computer. In general, each OpenDoc part lets you work on one type of document content — text, graphics, spreadsheets, charts, database information, sound, movies, Web pages, e-mail, and so on. You can drag any combination of OpenDoc parts into an OpenDoc document. Mix and match OpenDoc parts to create any document you can think of. If you want to use a new kind of content, you simply plug in an OpenDoc part that can handle it. Figure 23-1 shows an OpenDoc document with several parts.

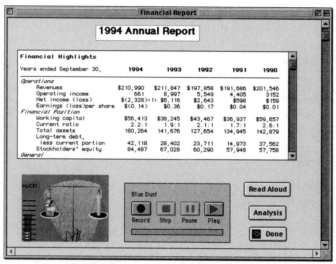

Figure 23-1: OpenDoc documents can include all kinds of content.

Parts can't function independently like applications and desk accessories. Parts rely on an infrastructure that OpenDoc provides. When you install OpenDoc system software, you get the infrastructure. To do anything with the OpenDoc infrastructure, you have to install parts. OpenDoc is like the electrical sockets in a new house. They make it possible to have light, music, TV shows, hot and cold food, and so forth, but the appliances you plug in actually provide those things.

When you give your OpenDoc documents to other people, they need OpenDoc parts that handle the kinds of content in your document. That doesn't mean another person's OpenDoc parts have to be exactly the same as yours. For example, you might use the Brand X graphics part while someone else uses the Brand Y graphics part. As long as other people have OpenDoc graphics parts with the same basic capabilities as yours, those people will be able to view graphics in OpenDoc documents you send them. If you don't have the necessary OpenDoc part for a kind of content in an OpenDoc document you receive, OpenDoc displays a gray box in place of the content and tells you the name of the missing part.

Cyberdog

One source of OpenDoc parts is the Mac OS installation software. Mac OS 8 and Mac OS 7.6 include Cyberdog, which is a collection of OpenDoc parts, for optional installation. In addition to parts for accessing Internet services such as the Web and e-mail, Cyberdog has parts for basic text editing, viewing graphics, and viewing QuickTime movies. (For specific information on using Cyberdog to access the Internet, see "E-mail" and "World Wide Web" in Chapter 20.) You can also get Cyberdog from Apple's Cyberdog Web site (http://cyberdog.apple.com).

OpenDoc Essentials Kit

In addition to Cyberdog, Apple distributes a collection of basic OpenDoc parts known as the OpenDoc Essentials Kit. It contains the following:

❖ **Apple Draw** for creating and editing basic graphics

❖ **Apple 3DMF Viewer** for viewing and manipulating 3D shapes created with QuickDraw 3D (does not work with QuickDraw 3D version 1.5 or later)

❖ **Apple Audio** for recording and playing back sound or playing a sound file saved in a variety of formats

❖ **Apple Button** for adding buttons that can play sounds, start AppleScripts, or take you to an Internet location

❖ **Apple Image Viewer** for viewing pictures saved in GIF, TIFF, JPEG, or PICT format

The OpenDoc Essentials Kit comes with Mac OS 7.6 for optional installation. The OpenDoc Essentials Kit is not included with Mac OS 8, but you can get it from Apple's OpenDoc DR Live site on the Web (http://www.opendoc.apple.com/dr-live/OpenDocParts/byName.html).

Apple QuickTime Viewer

Another OpenDoc part from Apple, the Apple QuickTime Viewer, plays QuickTime movies and QuickTime VR panoramas and objects. It's available separately from Apple's online software library (http://www.info.apple.com).

Introducing OpenDoc editors

Installing OpenDoc parts puts items called *editors* in an Editors folder, which is in the System Folder. You can think of an OpenDoc editor as a small, focused application that specializes in a particular kind of data. Editors are like the items in the Extensions folder in that you don't open or use an editor directly. You can get access to a part editor's functionality through the corresponding stationery files (described later).

Some editors, called viewers, allow you to see, hear, or otherwise experience a type of content, but do not allow you to change the content. For example, the

Apple QuickTime Viewer lets you watch QuickTime movies and manipulate QuickTime VR panoramas and objects, but the viewer does not let you change the movies, panoramas, or objects. Figure 23-2 shows the contents of the Editors folder after installing Mac OS 8, Cyberdog, the OpenDoc Essentials Kit, and the Apple QuickTime Viewer.

Name	Size	Kind
▽ 🗀 Cyberdog Libraries	–	folder
🖼 Cyberdog Data	33K	library
🖼 Cyberdog DocBuilder Editor	462K	library
🖼 Cyberdog Editors	3.8 MB	library
▽ 🗀 OpenDoc	–	folder
▽ 🗀 OpenDoc Shell Plug-Ins	–	folder
🖼 AppleGuidePlugIn	83K	library
🖼 About the ShellPlugins Folder	33K	SimpleText read-only document
🖼 OpenDoc Editor Setup	99K	library
▽ 🗀 OpenDoc™ Essentials Kit	–	folder
🖼 Apple 3DMF Viewer	396K	library
🖼 Apple Audio	413K	library
🖼 Apple Button	413K	library
🖼 Apple Draw	693K	library
🖼 Apple Image Viewer	545K	library
🖼 Apple QuickTime™ Viewer	611K	library
🖼 ODFLibrary	561K	library
🖼 About the Editors Folder	33K	SimpleText read-only document

Figure 23-2: Some part editors, part viewers, and other OpenDoc items in an Editors folder.

Some editors exist as separate files, and other editors exist together in a conjoint file. The Editors folder contains items that OpenDoc uses besides editors.

You should leave all OpenDoc editors, including viewers, in the Editors folder, and leave the Editors folder in the System Folder, so that OpenDoc can find the editors. Editor files do not have to be directly in the Editors folder; they can be in folders within the Editors folder. But Apple warns that if you move an editor file so that it is no longer contained within the Editors folder, OpenDoc will not be able to find it.

Introducing OpenDoc stationery

You don't open an OpenDoc editor to create a new document. Instead, you open a stationery document. OpenDoc stationery works much like stationery documents of conventional applications. When you open a stationery document, you get a new document. With OpenDoc, you also get the functionality of an OpenDoc editor. For example, if you open an AppleDraw stationery document, you get a new document and the ability to create and edit basic graphics in it.

Besides opening stationery to create a new document, you can drag OpenDoc stationery to an existing OpenDoc document to add a new part to the document.

There's a Stationery folder at the root level of the startup disk, where stationery may be installed initially when you install OpenDoc parts. But some part installers don't put stationery in the Stationery folder. For example, Cyberdog puts stationery in a Samples & Tools folder inside the Cyberdog folder. You can move stationery anywhere you like; it doesn't have to remain where you initially find it. In fact, you can create your own OpenDoc stationery (more on that later). Figure 23-3 shows the contents of the Stationery folder after installing the OpenDoc Essentials Kit.

Figure 23-3: OpenDoc part stationery in the Stationery folder.

Creating an OpenDoc document

You can create an OpenDoc document from stationery or from another OpenDoc document. Regardless of the method you use to create an OpenDoc document, OpenDoc opens the new document and immediately saves the document on disk with a temporary name. You can change the name and location when you save the document. In addition, the new document is listed in the Applications menu at the right end of the menu bar.

Creating a document from stationery

To create a document from stationery, find the stationery for the part that you want to use as your document's root part and open the stationery. OpenDoc creates a new copy of the stationery and opens this new copy. OpenDoc gives the new document a temporary name based on the stationery name and initially saves the new document in the same folder as the stationery. The new document may be empty, or it may have some initial content. Figure 23-4 shows a new empty document created from the Apple Draw stationery that's part of the OpenDoc Essentials Kit.

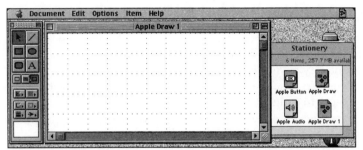

Figure 23-4: A new OpenDoc document has a temporary name and is saved on disk automatically.

Creating a document from another document

There are several ways to create a new document from an existing OpenDoc document. You can create a new document based on parts in the existing document or on the part that contains all the other parts, which is called the *root part*.

To create a new document based on the root part of an existing document, open the document and choose New from the Document menu. OpenDoc gives the new document a temporary name based on the name of the root part and initially saves the new document in the same folder as the existing document.

To create a new document based on a part in an existing document, first select the part and then choose New from the Document menu. You can create a new document by dragging a part from an existing document to the desktop, a folder, or a disk. You can also create a new document by selecting multiple parts, content from a part, or content that includes one or more parts, and dragging the selection to the desktop, a folder, or a disk.

Note that some OpenDoc documents (notably Cyberdog documents) have a File menu instead of a Document menu. In those documents, the New command is in the File menu.

Saving a document

Anytime after making changes to a new document you can save it. Use the Save command (not Save a Copy) in the Document menu or File menu, whichever exists. The Save command displays a standard Save dialog box, in which you can specify a name and location for the document if you don't want to use the ones proposed by OpenDoc.

Creating new OpenDoc stationery

After creating a new document, you can make changes to it, and if you'd like to be able to create more documents like the changed one, you can make your own stationery from the changed document. To make new stationery from an open document, use the Save a Copy menu command to bring up the standard Save dialog. In addition to typing a name and selecting a location for the stationery, select the Stationery option. Figure 23-5 shows the Save a Copy command's dialog box with the Stationery option selected.

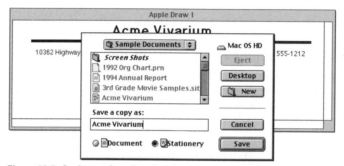

Figure 23-5: Saving an OpenDoc document as new stationery.

Introducing the Document and Edit menus

When working on most OpenDoc documents, you see Document and Edit menus next to the Apple menu instead of the File and Edit menus you see when working in conventional applications. The Document menu contains commands that affect the whole document. The Edit menu contains commands that you can use to change a document's contents. OpenDoc provides the Document and Edit menus and most of the commands in them. The part editor provides the rest of the menus. Figure 23-6 shows examples of the Document and Edit menus.

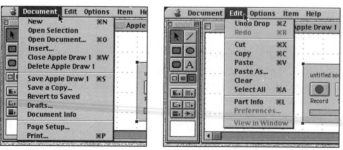

Figure 23-6: Most OpenDoc documents have similar Document and Edit menus.

Notice that the Document menu has no Quit command. None is needed, because OpenDoc automatically quits an editor when you switch to another editor. When you close the last OpenDoc window, OpenDoc itself quits automatically.

The Document menu isn't universal. When working with some OpenDoc documents, notably Cyberdog documents, there is a File menu with a Quit command. Cyberdog has added this command so it looks more like a conventional application.

Adding parts to OpenDoc documents

You can add parts to some OpenDoc documents and to some parts inside OpenDoc documents. To add a part to an OpenDoc document, you can drag the part's stationery icon into the document window, or you can drag a part from one OpenDoc document to another. Either way, a copy of the part you dragged is placed in the destination window. To add a part to another part that's inside an OpenDoc document, drag the part you want to add to the part inside the document window. Figure 23-7 shows part stationery being dragged into an OpenDoc document.

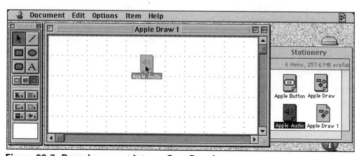

Figure 23-7: Dragging a part into an OpenDoc document.

You can also add a part to a document or to a part in a document with the Insert command in the Document menu. First you make the document active (bring its window to the front). If you want to add a part to a part that's already in the document, select the part you want to add to. Then choose Insert from the Document window. In the Open dialog that appears, select the stationery for the part you want to add. For example, to add a drawing part, you could select the Apple Draw stationery.

Instead of adding a part directly, you can add a part indirectly by adding a file whose content the part handles. Either drag the file to the OpenDoc document window, or use the Insert command and select the file. For example, you could add an Apple Audio part to an OpenDoc document by dragging a sound file to the document window or by choosing the Insert command and selecting a sound file.

Not all OpenDoc documents and parts can contain other parts. A part that can contain other parts is called a *container*. An OpenDoc document can contain other parts only if its root part (the part you used to create the document) is a container. You don't do anything to make a part a container or not. Software engineers determine whether a part is a container when they design it. For example, Apple engineers made the Apple Draw part a container but did not make the Apple Button part a container.

Working with parts

Once a part is in an OpenDoc document, you can edit its content, move it, resize it, copy it, delete it, or get information about it. Before moving, resizing, copying, deleting, or getting information about a part, you must select it.

Adding content

You can add content to a part in an OpenDoc document by dragging a file onto the part. The file must contain something the part can handle. If a file's content is compatible with a part, the part becomes highlighted when you drag the file to the part. Some parts can handle more than one type of content. For example, you can drag a sound file or a QuickTime movie but not a text file to an Apple Audio part because a sound file and a QuickTime movie contain sound but a text file does not. Figure 23-8 shows a sound file being added to an Apple Audio part.

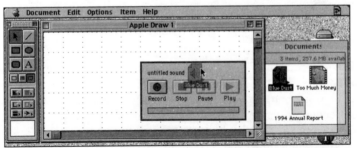

Figure 23-8: Adding content to an OpenDoc part by dragging a compatible file to it.

Editing content

If a part has content, you can edit the content by making the part active and making your changes. To make a part active, you click anywhere inside it. There can be only one active part, and the active part has a distinctive border made of two dotted lines. Clicking the background of the document window makes the document's root part active, although no border appears around the root part when it is the active part. Figure 23-9 shows the border around an active part in an Apple Draw container.

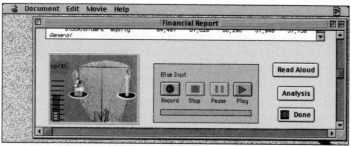

Figure 23-9: A distinctive border made of two dotted lines indicates the active part (here, the QuickTime movie on the left).

When you activate a part, the part editor's menus appear in the menu bar. You can use the menu commands to edit the part.

Selecting a part

Before you can move, resize, copy, delete, or get information about a part, you must select it. Remember that clicking a part makes it active so you can work with the part's content. When you want to work with a whole part and not its content, you must select the part, not activate it. Where the active part has a dotted-line border, a selected part has small, black square handles at its corners. Figure 23-10 shows a selected part in the Apple Draw container.

You can't select a part while another part is active. First you must click the background of the document window, making the root part active. Then you can press the Shift key or the ⌘ key and click the part you want to select. To select more than one part in the same container, click the container's background to make the container active and press the Shift key while you click each part. Some kinds of containers also allow you to select one or more parts by dragging a selection rectangle around the part or parts.

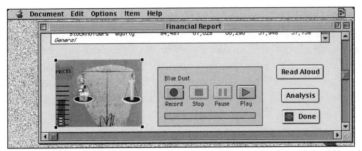

Figure 23-10: Small black handles at the corners of a part indicate it is selected.

If you want to select the active part, you don't have to make it inactive first. You can just click its border. In a container where the active part has a dotted-line border, such as the Apple Draw container, you should be able to tell where to click by watching for the pointer to change to a hand as you place it on the border. However, not all containers change the pointer to a hand when you place it on the border.

When you select a part, the part's container becomes active. You will see the menus change when the container becomes active (unless the selected part and the container are the same kind of part).

You can deselect a selected part by Shift-clicking it. If more than one part is selected in a container, you can deselect them all by clicking the background of the container.

Some parts can only be selected by pressing the Shift key or the ⌘ key and clicking the part while it is inactive. For example, an Apple Button part might play a sound when clicked unless you Shift-click or ⌘-click it to select it for editing.

Moving a part

You can move a part by selecting it and dragging it to a new location in the document. To move the selected part to another OpenDoc document, press the Control key and drag. (If you drag to another document without pressing the Control key, you add a copy of the selected part to the other document.) You can also use the Cut and Paste commands to move the selected part to another document.

In some types of OpenDoc containers you can move the selected part by pressing the arrow keys. The characteristics of the container part determine whether the arrow keys work. For instance, the arrow keys work in a document whose root part is an Apple Draw part.

Resizing a part

You change the size or shape of a part by selecting it and dragging one of its small black handles. Some kinds of containers do not allow resizing of parts in them.

Copying a part

You can make a copy of a part in the same document by selecting the part and pressing the Option key while dragging the part. To copy the selected part to another OpenDoc document, simply drag it without pressing any keys. You can also use the Copy and Paste commands to copy the selected part.

Deleting a part

You delete a part by selecting it and dragging it to the Trash, choosing Clear from the Edit menu, or pressing the Delete key.

Getting part information

You can get information about a part and change some of its properties by selecting it and choosing Part Info from the Edit menu. In addition to the standard properties shown in the Part Info window, some editors make additional properties accessible through a Settings button at the bottom of the Part Info window. Figure 23-11 shows an example of a Part Info dialog box.

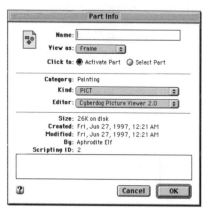

Figure 23-11: Getting information about an OpenDoc part.

The standard properties you can change include the following:

❖ **Name** can be anything you want to type, but it's not displayed for many parts (the Apple Audio part is one that does display its name).

❖ **View as** can be Frame (a bounded rectangle, oval, or irregular shape that contains the part), Large Icon or Small Icon (like in the Finder, but not named), or Thumbnail (usually a miniature picture that represents the part). To view or edit a part represented by an icon or a thumbnail, you double-click the icon or thumbnail.

❖ **Click to** can be Activate Part, meaning the part becomes active when you click it (as described previously), or Select Part, meaning the whole part is selected when you click it (you don't have to Shift-click as described previously).

❖ **Kind** is the format of the part's content. The pop-up menu lists different formats that the part may be able to use, but the part's editor can't necessarily work with all the choices listed in the pop-up menu.

❖ **Editor** is the software you use to view the part's content and edit the content if the editor allows editing. If more than one editor is available for the kind of data specified by the Kind property, a pop-up menu lists all the editors in your Editors folder that can handle the kind of data specified by the Kind property. But if only one editor can handle the part's kind of data, the Editor pop-up is replaced by the name of the editor as static text. Sometimes changing the Kind property makes more editors available.

In addition to these standard properties, the editor for the part may add more properties such as a script or a printing option. Other properties may be accessible through a Settings button at the bottom of the Part Info window. Clicking the Settings button brings up a dialog box that contains the additional properties. You may also be able to bring up the same Settings dialog box for a part by activating the part and choosing a Settings command from one of the part editor's menus. Figure 23-12 shows the Settings dialog box for the Apple QuickTime Viewer part.

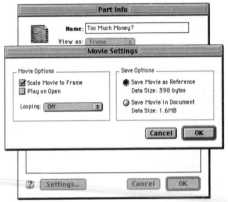

Figure 23-12: Some parts have additional settings accessible through the Part Info dialog box.

You can also get product information about a part by activating it (not selecting it) and choosing the first command in the Apple menu, which begins with "About."

Setting document memory size

Each OpenDoc document has a memory size, much the way conventional applications have memory sizes. If you get a message saying memory is running low, you can increase the document's memory size. To change the active (frontmost) document's memory size, you choose Document Info from the Document window. The Document Info dialog box appears, and in it you click the Size button to bring up the Memory Requirements dialog box. In that dialog box you select the option Use Document Preferred Size and click the nearby up arrow or down arrow to increase or decrease the amount of memory the document uses. Then click OK to dismiss the Memory Requirements dialog box, and click OK again to dismiss the Document Info dialog box. Finally, close the document and reopen it. The new memory size takes effect when you reopen the document. Figure 23-13 shows the Memory Requirements and Document Info dialog boxes.

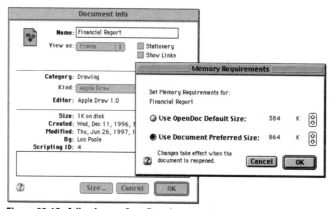

Figure 23-13: Adjusting an OpenDoc document's memory size.

Setting up editors

It's very likely you have two or more OpenDoc part editors that handle a particular kind of content, yet it's possible you may receive an OpenDoc document that someone else created with a different part editor for the same kind of content. To cope with those situations, you use the Editor Setup control panel to specify a preferred editor for each kind of content. If you open a document that contains a part created by an editor you don't have, OpenDoc uses the preferred editor for the kind of content in that part.

To specify a preferred editor for a kind of content, open the Editor Setup control panel. In its list select a kind of content and click the Choose Editor button (or double-click the kind) to see a list of editors available on your computer for that kind of content. Select an editor to be the preferred editor for that kind of content and click OK (or simply double-click the editor). Figure 23-14 shows the Editor Setup control panel with the Choose Editor dialog box open.

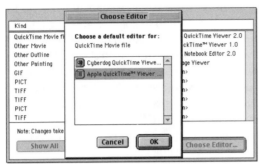

Figure 23-14: Use the Editor Setup control panel to set your preferred editor for a kind of content.

Publish and Subscribe

The United States Constitution is often referred to as being a living document because it has the capability to change with the times. You can create your own living documents, albeit of a type different from the U.S. Constitution, using applications that have adopted the publish and subscribe capabilities of the Mac OS. The Create Publisher and Subscribe To commands enable you to share information between documents dynamically.

Think of the Create Publisher and Subscribe To commands as being live Copy and Paste commands. You can use these commands to copy a group of cells or a chart from a spreadsheet and paste it into a word processing report. Anytime the selected information in the spreadsheet changes, the report is updated automatically.

In this section, you'll learn how to breathe life into your documents by using the Create Publisher, Subscribe To, and other related commands.

Introducing publishers, editions, and subscribers

The Mac OS borrows concepts and terminology from the publishing industry for its publish and subscribe technology. A selected area of a document becomes a *publisher* when you make a live copy of it available to other documents. The publisher can include any information that you can select within a document.

Publishing material from a document creates a live copy of the material in a separate file, which is called an *edition*. You include a copy of an edition in another document by subscribing to the edition. The area of the document that contains a copy of an edition is called a *subscriber*. A document can contain any number and combination of publishers and subscribers. Figure 23-15 diagrams the relationship between publisher, edition, and subscriber.

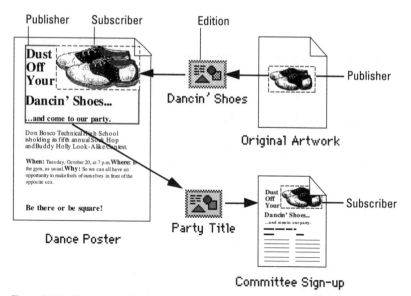

Figure 23-15: The relationship between publisher, edition, and subscriber.

Saving a document after changing a publisher in it can update the publisher's edition automatically (or you can update the edition manually). When an edition is updated, the Mac OS notifies all subscribers to that edition that a new edition is available. The subscriber can automatically reflect the latest information from the edition, or you can update it manually.

Documents containing subscribers do not have to be open for the subscribers to receive edition updates. The Mac OS stores notices of edition updates destined for closed subscribers. When you open documents containing subscribers, most applications automatically check for notices of new editions. Some applications make you choose a command to update subscribers. Information always flows from the publisher to an edition and then to the edition's subscribers.

Publish and subscribe work across a network just as well as they work locally on your computer. You can subscribe and get updates to editions that are on any disk or folder that you are sharing from someone else. Likewise, other people can subscribe and get updates to editions on disks or folders that those people are sharing from you. If you update an edition that someone has subscribed to on another computer, their subscriber will be updated the next time they mount your disk or folder that contains the updated edition. (For more information on file sharing, see Chapter 18.)

The publish and subscribe process works only in programs that are designed to take advantage of it. Such programs contain publishing commands in the Edit menu or in a submenu of the Edit menu. If you have a program that lacks those commands, check with the program's developer to see whether an upgraded version is available.

Creating a publisher

You create a publisher by selecting the information that you want to share and then choosing Create Publisher from the Edit menu of your program. Many programs put the Create Publisher command in a Publishing submenu or an Editions submenu of the Edit menu. Figure 23-16 shows an example of creating a publisher.

In most programs, you need to select text or graphics in your document to create a publisher. If you haven't selected anything, the Create Publisher command is dimmed. In a few programs, such as Adobe Photoshop, you can publish an entire document by choosing Create Publisher without selecting anything.

After you choose the Create Publisher command, the Publisher dialog box appears. A thumbnail view of the material that you selected appears in the Preview area of the dialog box. Figure 23-17 shows an example of the Publisher dialog box.

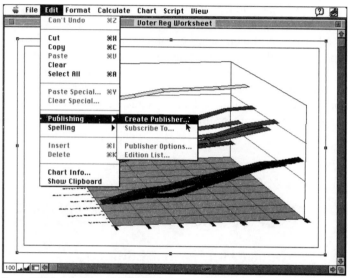

Figure 23-16: Creating a publisher.

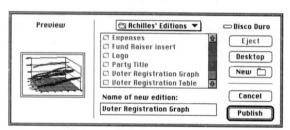

Figure 23-17: Saving an edition.

Usually, the folder in which you saved the last edition is open in the dialog box. The Mac OS knows which folder to open because it keeps an alias of the most recently saved edition in the Preferences folder inside the System Folder. You can go to a different folder by using the same methods you would use with the Save As command. If you want to make the edition available to other users on your network, be sure to save the edition in a folder or disk that you allow those users to share.

To keep a new publisher, you must save the document that contains it. If you close the document without saving, the program asks whether you want to save changes. You lose the publisher if you decline to save.

You can create as many independent publishers in a document as you want. Some programs permit publishers to overlap partially or completely; one publisher can include all or part of the information contained in another publisher. Apple's guidelines suggest that word processing programs permit nested publishers but not overlapping publishers. Spreadsheet programs and graphics programs should permit both nesting and overlapping publishers. A program that does not allow overlapped or nested publishers dims the Create Publisher command when you select any part of a document that already is part of an existing publisher.

Smart Multiformat Editions

An edition's format — plain text, styled text, paint-type picture, object-type graphic, and so on — is determined by the program that created the publisher. Some programs save information in several formats in an edition file. When you have a program subscribe to a multiformat edition, the program uses the most appropriate format for its documents. Microsoft Excel, for example, saves spreadsheet cells as a picture, as a text table, and as a range of formatted Excel cells. A graphics document subscribing to an Excel edition uses the picture format; a word processor probably uses the text table (although Microsoft Word uses the formatted cells to create a formatted Word table); and another Excel worksheet uses the formatted cells.

Subscribing to an Edition

You subscribe to an edition to incorporate live information from another document into the document on which you're working. To subscribe to an edition, select a place in your document for the edition and then choose Subscribe To from the Edit menu. Some programs put the Subscribe To command in a Publishing submenu of the Edit menu. Figure 23-18 shows an example of subscribing to an edition.

The place you select for the edition depends on the type of document that's subscribing to it. In a word processing document, you click an insertion point. In a spreadsheet document, you select a cell or range of cells. You do not have to select a place in most graphics documents, because you can move the subscriber after placing it in the document.

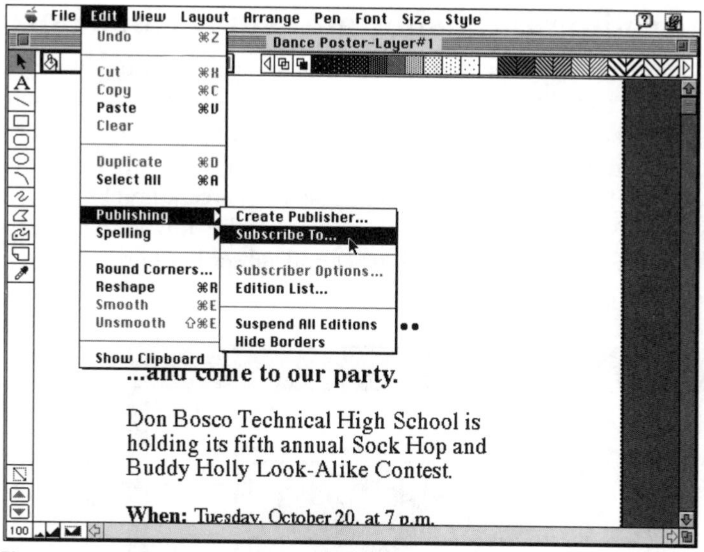

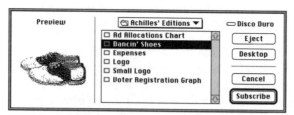

Figure 23-18: Subscribing to an edition.

Choosing Subscribe To from the Edit menu displays the Subscribe To dialog box. The dialog box displays the highlighted name of the last edition that you published or subscribed to, and you can select a different edition as though you were using an Open command. When you select an edition, a thumbnail view of its contents appears in the Preview area of the dialog box. Clicking the Subscribe button places a copy of the selected edition in your document. Figure 23-19 shows an example of the Subscribe To dialog box.

Figure 23-19: Selecting an edition to subscribe to.

A document can subscribe to any number of editions. The editions can be on a disk directly connected to your computer, or on a disk or folder that you're sharing from another computer on the same network.

Controlling publisher and subscriber borders

Most programs display a gray border around a publisher or subscriber when you click or select something inside the publisher or subscriber. The border also appears if you select part of a document that contains a publisher or subscriber. The standard border lines, which are three pixels thick, are medium gray (50 percent gray) for publishers and dark gray (75 percent gray) for subscribers. Clicking outside the publisher or subscriber makes the border disappear. Figure 23-20 shows examples of the publisher and subscriber borders.

Figure 23-20: Borders around publishers and subscribers.

An optional Edit menu command, Show Borders, displays borders around all publishers and subscribers in the active document. After you choose the Show Borders command, it becomes the Hide borders command, which (surprise!) hides all borders except the one for the subscriber or publisher that you clicked.

Some programs, including Microsoft Excel 4 and 5, don't show publisher or subscriber borders. Excel's Links command can select a publisher's range of cells (but not a chart, another type of publisher, or a subscriber). In the Links command's dialog box, you select the name of the publisher that you want from a list of publishers in the document, and then you click a Select button. Excel selects the range of cells and scrolls the document window so that you can see it.

Setting publisher and subscriber options

The Mac OS provides several options for working with publishers and subscribers. You can *adorn* a subscriber (change its formatting), locate and open a subscriber's publisher, control edition updates, and cancel or suspend a publisher or subscriber.

Application programs use different methods to make publisher and subscriber options available. Some programs place a Publisher Options command in the Edit menu when a publisher is selected in the active window, and they place a Subscriber Options command in the menu when a subscriber is selected. Choosing one of those commands brings up a dialog box in which you set the publisher or subscriber options. Figures 23-21 and 23-22 show examples of the Publisher Options and Subscriber Options dialog boxes.

Figure 23-21: A Publisher Options dialog box.

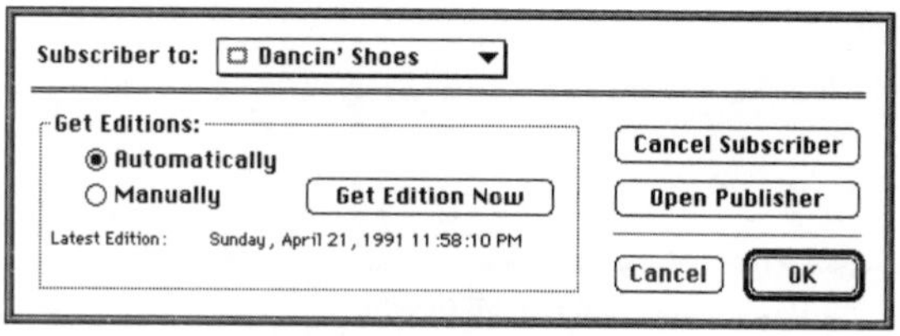

Figure 23-22: A Subscriber Options dialog box.

Other programs put the Publisher Options and Subscriber Options commands in a Publishing submenu or an Editions submenu of the Edit menu. As a shortcut, many programs bring up the appropriate options dialog box when you double-click a publisher or subscriber while pressing Option.

Microsoft Excel 4 and 5 have their own eccentric methods. In Excel, you choose the Links command from the File menu to display the Links dialog box. In that dialog box, you choose Publisher or Subscriber from the Link Type pop-up menu to see a list of the publishers or subscribers that are in the document. Then you select the one whose options you want to see, and click an Options button. Excel's eccentric methods for publish and subscribe have their origins in Microsoft's own data sharing technology called OLE (Object Linking and Embedding). Excel has a hybrid of OLE and publish and subscribe.

Adorning a subscriber

Most programs do not permit you to change the contents of a subscriber directly, because your changes would disappear the next time the subscriber was updated. Many programs, however, permit you to adorn a subscriber in ways that the program can reapply to a new edition. For example, you may be able to resize or crop an entire subscriber as you would resize or crop a graphic in a word processing document. You may be able to change all the text in a subscriber to a different font, style, or size.

Programs that allow adornment generally have an option in the Subscriber Options dialog box that you can set to maintain or cancel adornments. When this option is on, the program reapplies the changes that you made to the subscriber the next time the subscriber is updated. Figure 23-23 shows an example of a Subscriber Options dialog box with an option for maintaining subscriber adornment.

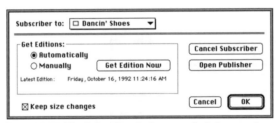

Figure 23-23: The Subscriber Options may include an option that maintains subscriber adornment.

Opening a subscriber's publisher

Generally, you make changes to a subscriber by opening its publisher and changing the publisher. To help you open a publisher, the Subscriber Options dialog box includes an Open Publisher button. Clicking this button is supposed to open the document that contains the subscriber's publisher (and the program that created the publisher's document, if it's not already open), scroll the publisher into view, and select the publisher. Some programs also open a publisher when you press Option while double-clicking a subscriber. In practice, however, clicking the Open Publisher button and Option-clicking the subscriber do not always open the publisher.

Sometimes you can open a publisher by opening its edition icon in the Finder. When you do, an edition window appears. The window contains a miniature view of the publisher and an Open Publisher button. Clicking this button is supposed to open the publisher's original document, just as the Open Publisher button does in the Subscriber Options dialog box, but the Open Publisher button doesn't always work. Figure 23-24 shows an example of an edition window.

Figure 23-24: You may be able to open a publisher from its edition window.

You can see the last edition that you used by opening the Preferences folder in the System Folder. Opening the alias named Last Edition Used displayed the edition window of the last edition you saved.

QUICK TIPS

Suspend Before You Amend

In programs that permit you to modify a subscriber, you should suspend or cancel automatic edition updating before you begin editing the subscriber. This action preserves your changes until you update the subscriber manually by clicking the Get Edition Now button in the Subscriber Options dialog box. When a subscriber is updated, changes you have made directly to it (not to the corresponding publisher) may be lost. Some programs warn you before automatically updating a subscriber that you have modified, but many automatically update without warning.

Making changes to a publisher

Because a publisher is just part of an ordinary document, you can modify a publisher within a document the way you would any other part of a document. You can add material to a publisher or delete material from it, making the publisher larger or smaller. You can cut an entire publisher and paste it in a different place in the document. Copying and pasting or otherwise duplicating a publisher, however, isn't a good idea. If you do, all duplicates of the publisher share one edition, making the contents of subscribers to that edition seem to be unpredictable. (The edition reflects the contents of the most recently updated duplicate publisher.)

Each time you save a document that contains a revised publisher, the application program automatically updates the publisher's edition. You can turn off automatic updating and update only manually, however, as described in the following section.

Updating editions

The Subscriber and Publisher Options dialog boxes enable you to control whether edition updates are sent or received automatically or manually. Various programs label these dialog-box options differently. You can set update options individually for each publisher and subscriber. For example, you may want one subscriber in a document (such as a logo) to be updated on request and another subscriber (such as daily sales figures) to be updated automatically.

A publisher's Publisher Options dialog box (refer to Figure 23-21, shown previously) controls when new editions of the publisher are sent. When you activate the standard setting, On Save, the program automatically sends a new edition the next time you save the document (if you modified the publisher). Setting the Manually option suspends sending new editions of the publisher until you click the Send Edition Now button in the Publisher Options dialog box.

The subscriber can receive new editions automatically or manually. If the Automatically option is set in the subscriber's Subscriber Options dialog box (refer to Figure 23-22, shown previously), the subscriber gets updated as soon as the program receives a new edition. You can suspend automatic subscriber updating by setting the Manually option in the subscriber's Subscriber Options dialog box. To get a manual update, click the Get Edition Now button in the Subscriber Options dialog box.

You can cancel a publisher or subscriber by clicking the Cancel Subscriber or Cancel Publisher button in the Publisher Options or Subscriber Options dialog box. Canceling a publisher or subscriber permanently breaks the link between the publisher and the subscriber.

Some programs enable you to suspend all updating activity temporarily by providing a Suspend All Editions command (or its equivalent) in the Edit menu. When this command is activated, a check mark appears next to it in the menu, and the program blocks all publishers from sending new editions and all subscribers from receiving new editions. Turning off the command removes the check mark from the menu and updates, with any new editions, all subscribers that are set to receive new editions automatically. The Stop All Editions command affects only publishers and subscribers in documents created by the program in which you use the command.

Summary

In this chapter, you learned that OpenDoc provides an infrastructure for plug-in part software, and each plug-in part gives you the ability to work with a particular type of content. Installing parts puts editors in the Editors folder. Editors are like small, focused applications that specialize in particular kinds of data. You don't open an OpenDoc editor to create a new document. Instead, you open a stationery document. You can also create a new OpenDoc document from an existing document by using the New command or by dragging parts to the desktop. To create your own stationery, you can use the Save a Copy command.

Some OpenDoc parts can contain other parts. You can add a part by dragging its stationery to a container. Another way to add a part is to drag a file whose content the part can handle. Once a part is in an OpenDoc document, you can edit its content, move it, resize it, copy it, delete it, or get information about it. To view or work with the content of a part, you make the part active. To work with the part itself, you select the part as a whole.

Another way to create compound documents is with publish and subscribe. They're a dynamic alternative to copy and paste. You select part of a document that you want to include in another document, but instead of copying it to the Clipboard, you publish a live copy of the selection in an edition file. Then in the other document, you subscribe to the edition. Thereafter, the subscriber is updated automatically whenever the publisher changes. (You usually have the option of making the updates happen manually instead of automatically.)

You want to avoid making substantive changes to subscribers, because your changes would disappear the next time the subscriber was updated. But many programs let you resize or otherwise adorn a subscriber in ways that the program can reapply to a new edition.

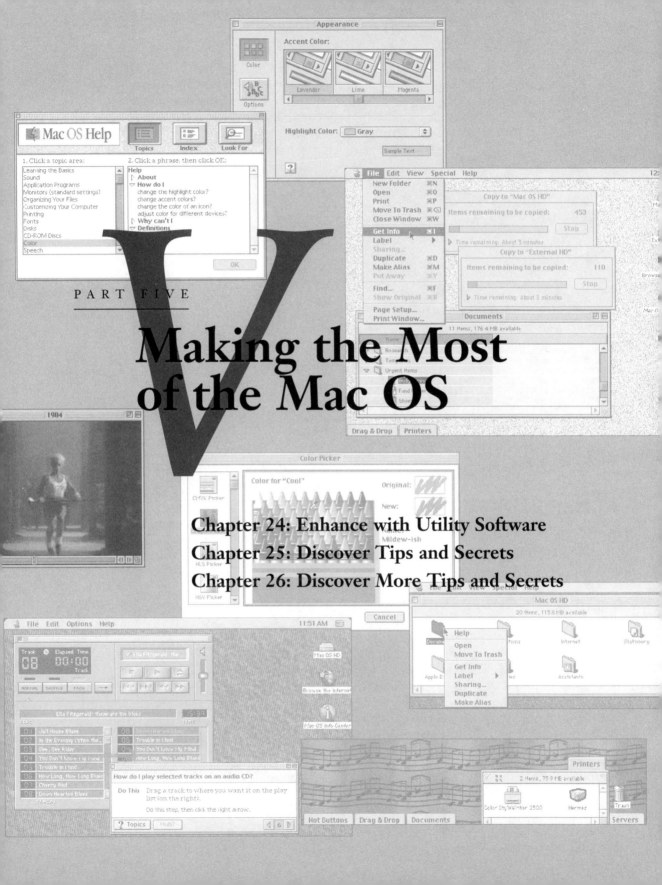

CHAPTER TWENTY-FOUR

Enhance with Utility Software

Every system software upgrade, including Mac OS 8, offers significant enhancements in performance and ease of use over older Mac system software. However, even Mac OS 8 can stand some assistance in performing its disk and file management, alias management, networking, and other duties. Software that enhances the Mac system software to even further increase your productivity is the subject of this chapter.

Many programmers have developed small accessory applications, control panels, and system extensions that enhance the performance of the Finder and other system software. Mac OS users are an idiosyncratic lot and like to personalize their systems. These shareware, freeware, and commercial software utilities personalize the activities of the Finder and other system software so that the computer does exactly what you need it to do, when you need it to. With these programs, you can open specific files directly without having to know where they are located. You can also throw away files while using an application without going to the Finder, create aliases in new ways, and make using your Mac much more fun.

The software items described in this chapter are listed alphabetically, with a short description of each of their features, the names of their authors, their system requirements, and prices. Software is updated often, especially noncommercial software, and you may find that newer versions of programs have features not described here.

648   Part V: Making the Most of the Mac OS

Where to Get Utility Software

You can use several avenues to acquire the software listed in this chapter. It's all available from some software library on the Internet or a commercial online information service. Much is available on CD-ROM from user groups. And some is available from Apple. Start with these sources:

❖ **Macworld Online** software library (http://www.macworld.com) has most if not all of the software listed in this chapter, plus many more shareware, freeware, and Apple utilities. All are available for the cost of downloading.

❖ **America Online** (800-827-6364) has a large collection of shareware, freeware, and Apple utility software, all available for the cost of downloading.

❖ **Filez** (http://www.filez.com), **Shareware.com** (http://www.shareware.com), **HyperArchive** (http://hyperarchive.lcs.mit.edu/HyperArchive.html), and other **Internet sites** too numerous to mention have extensive, searchable collections of shareware and freeware utilities.

❖ **Berkeley Macintosh Users Group (BMUG)** (510-549-2684, http://www.bmug.org), **Arizona Macintosh Users Group (AMUG)** (602-553-8966, http://www.amug.org), and other **user groups** sell collections of shareware and freeware on CD-ROM. Apple will refer you to the user group nearest you (800-538-9696).

❖ **Apple Software Library** (http://www.info.apple.com) has all Apple utility software and much but not all Mac system software. Everything in the library is available for the cost of downloading.

❖ The **Apple Order Center** (800-293-6617) supplies some Apple utility software on floppy disk and CD-ROM for a nominal fee, usually $10 to $20.

How to use utility software

This chapter describes utility software but does not include detailed operating instructions. Because noncommercial software is usually distributed online or on disk, it doesn't come with printed manuals. Instead, noncommercial software usually comes with a documentation file, frequently called "Read Me." You also should check for onscreen help in the Help menu or at the top of the Apple menu.

About shareware and freeware

The software described in this chapter is not available in any store. This noncommercial software is distributed on the Internet, through online information services, by user groups, and person-to-person. Whatever you pay for an online connection or a user group's CD-ROM goes strictly to the online service or user group; none of that money goes to the authors of the noncommercial software. That's fine with some authors, who distribute their products as *freeware* and don't expect to be paid.

Authors of *shareware* encourage you to try their software and to share copies with friends and coworkers. Each person who decides to keep a shareware product sends payment directly to the author. Many shareware authors also accept payment through a clearinghouse on the Internet, Kagi Software (http://www.kagi.com).

It's important to understand that freeware and shareware are not in the public domain. Most freeware authors and all shareware authors retain the copyrights to their work. You can use it and you can generally pass it around, but you can't sell it.

Shareware and freeware programs typically are written by enthusiasts who can't afford to provide technical support by telephone, as the developers of commercial programs can. Moreover, shareware and freeware authors can't afford to thoroughly test their software with many combinations of computer models, system software versions, and other software. All the programs listed in this chapter worked on a Power Mac 7500 with Mac OS 7.6.1, but this does not mean that they will work on other computer models, with other system software versions, or even on differently configured Power Mac 7500s.

Noncommercial software, on the whole, is not as stable as commercial programs. Be sure to follow the instructions and discussions provided by the authors in their ReadMe or Help files before using any of these programs. You use shareware and freeware at your own risk.

QUICK TIPS

Support Shareware Authors

Shareware depends on the honor and honesty of the people who use it. If you decide to keep shareware installed on your disk, the *Honorable Society of Civilized People* politely insists that you immediately send payment to the author. The $5 to $50 that you pay for the shareware you use today helps fund development of more great shareware. For detailed information about the amount of payment requested for a particular shareware product and where to send payment, check the product's ReadMe file, About command (in the Apple menu), or onscreen help.

System Utilities Listing

Apple, commercial developers, and shareware and freeware authors offer thousands of utility programs. Many new programs become available each day. The software listed in this chapter has been culled from the pack based on its usefulness, ease of use, completeness, and reliability. This list is not meant to be all-inclusive, but rather to be an example of the types of software that are available to enhance the performance of your computer with Mac system software.

All of the software listed in this section can be used with System 7.5–Mac OS 7.6.1, and you should be able to use most of it with Mac OS 8. A few of the programs listed here are redundant or partially redundant with Mac OS 8 features, but are still beneficial to users of earlier system software versions. The individual program descriptions in this section tell you about Mac OS 8 redundancies.

The compatibility of each program with Mac OS 8 was unknown when this book went to press. Authors of noncommercial software don't typically have the facilities to test their programs with a variety of software combinations and computer models. Instead they fix problems reported by people who try out the utility programs. If you decide to try a program, check the Read Me file or other included documentation for compatibility information of the version you get. If the compatibility information doesn't assure you that the utility program you want to try is compatible with your computer model and system software version, you should take the precaution of making a backup of your disk before trying the utility program.

Many of the programs listed here have been around for several years and are compatible with system software versions earlier than System 7.5. Because this book does not specifically cover those earlier system software versions, the program descriptions in this section do not tell you about compatibility with System 7.1.2 and earlier.

Aaron

Aaron gives a Mac OS 8 look to earlier system software versions by replacing dialog boxes, pop-up menus, scroll bars, folders, windows, and other interface elements. This extension by Gregory Landweber and Edward Voas requires a color-capable computer and costs $10.

Agent Audio

Agent Audio lets you replace the "snd" resources (sounds) of any file or application that already contains them. Select the program you wish to customize, and Agent Audio lets you view and edit the available sounds, or extract and archive the sounds into playable "snd" files. This application by Clixsounds requires a color monitor and 2MB of RAM and costs $12.

a.k.a.

Drag a file onto a.k.a. to create or rename aliases, and place the newly created aliases anywhere on any mounted volume, or in user-specified folders. This extension by Fred Monroe is free.

Alias Crony

Alias Crony can scan all of your online volumes to create lists of attached and unattached aliases; retrieve aliases and originals; and link, update, delete, and move aliases. It also creates "SuperAliases" of applications which can reside on separate volumes and still possess drag-capability, enabling you to drag items onto the alias to launch the application. This application by Rocco Moliterno costs $5.

AliasZoo

AliasZoo is a quick and easy way to get control over the mountain of alias files living on your hard drive. It searches a hard drive or folder and displays a report listing details on the aliases it finds, deletes orphaned aliases quickly and easily, and includes Apple Guide support. This application by Blue Globe Software costs $15.

AppDisk161

AppDisk creates a RAM disk on your desktop which you can copy files to. Since AppDisk gets the RAM for this disk from its own application memory, you get all your memory back from the RAM disk when you quit AppDisk. AppDisk also provides an option to save its contents to your regular hard drive. This application by Mark Adams costs $15.

AppSizer

AppSizer enables you to change the amount of memory allocated to applications (the suggested size in the Info window) as you launch them. This control panel by Michael Peirce costs $19.95.

ARACommander

The ARACommander control panel is an adjunct to the Apple Remote Access software provided by Apple. ARACommander automates dialing into remote networks by creating connectors that contain the telecommunications and network configuration information necessary to complete the transaction.

The device requires less disk space and less RAM than the Apple Remote Access client and server software (see "Making a Remote AppleTalk Connection" in Chapter 17). This control panel by Trilobyte Software requires Apple Remote Access and costs $25.

Auto Menus Pro

Auto Menus Pro provides easier access to hierarchical menus by enabling menus to drop down and stay down when the pointer is placed in the menu bar, or after a click of the mouse. Depending on your settings, the menus close automatically or with a click of the mouse. This control panel by Night Light Software costs $15.

BatteryAmnesia

BatteryAmnesia provides a safe, fast, and automatic way to deep discharge a PowerBook's (NiCad) or nickel-hydride (NiMH) battery, bypassing the low battery warning messages, and preventing the sleep state normally brought on by those messages. It runs your PowerBook's battery down until a hardware shutdown occurs, which is at a lower voltage, providing the best discharge possible without an expensive external battery conditioner. This application by Jeremy Kezer requires a PowerBook and costs $10.

BatteryMinder

BatteryMinder is a comprehensive PowerBook toolbox that includes controls for brightness and contrast; a backlight toggle depending on charger status; AppleTalk automation and toggling; sound and modem on/off with button control; monitoring of battery voltage, watts, and battery life; and easy toggling of screen color depth. This application by Randall Voth requires a PowerBook and costs $15.

Blitz

The Blitz file management utility can catalogue hard disks and large removable drives like CD-ROMs when volumes are dragged and dropped onto its application. Blitz records large catalogues using very little disk space, while providing extremely fast search functionality. This application by Matthew Bickham requires a computer with a color monitor (256 colors or better) and costs $10.

BunchOApps

BunchOApps lists your most recently run applications and installed applications and launches them when selected. You can specify how many applications to remember (up to 25). This Control Strip module by Patrick McClaughry requires Apple's Control Strip or Men & Mice's Desktop Strip and is free.

Carpetbag

Carpetbag allows various system resources, such as fonts, sounds, and FKeys, to be kept outside your System file. Place PostScript fonts in one specified folder outside the System Folder and ATM and the LaserWriter driver will see them. This may still be useful with newer system software versions in the case of system sounds. This control panel by James W. White costs $5.

Clock Synch

Clock Synch synchronizes the clocks between two or more computers on an AppleTalk network, by setting the clocks of the servant computers to that of a master computer. This application by Jeremy Kezer requires an AppleTalk network and costs $5 for a three-user license.

CopyPaste

CopyPaste enhances the Mac OS clipboard functionality by remembering the last ten items copied and keeping them accessible via menu or key commands and includes hot keys for switching between applications you're copying and pasting between. It can also append the Clip Sets to text files or save the clipboards on shutdown or restart. This extension by Peter Hoerster costs $20.

Default Folder

Default Folder enhances Open and Save dialog boxes, making file management easier by letting you specify where files should always be saved by certain applications, providing a pop-up menu of recently used folders, moving items to the Trash from within dialog boxes, and adjusting multiple save options. This control panel by St. Clair Software costs $25.

Discolour

Discolour enables your computer to display full-color floppy disk icons instead of the black and white system default. This extension by Ambrosia Software requires a color computer and is free.

Disk Copy

Disk Copy will mount disk images on your desktop, make exact copies of floppy disks from a disk image, convert disk images from one format to another, and create a disk image from a mounted volume or individual folder.

In conjunction with DiskScripts and AppleScript, it can be used to automate software installations and disk image manipulation. This application by Apple Computer is free.

Disk Rejuvenator

Disk Rejuvenator addresses problems of hard disks becoming inaccessible from the standard Open dialog boxes and custom icons disappearing (which can be caused by the Finder information for the root of the disk getting corrupted). It corrects the problems by examining attributes of your disk and correcting those that are in need of correction. This application by Aladdin Systems is free.

DiskSurveyor

DiskSurveyor provides a graphical display of files and folders residing on your hard drive and shows the amount of space these individual items are taking up. You can open and manage folders from within the display and create DiskSummary files that list all the files found on CD-ROMs or any other volume. This application by Tom Luhrs, Twilight Software requires a monitor set to display at least 256 colors or grays and costs $10.

DragThing

DragThing is an application dock designed to tidy up the icons littering your desktop. Simply drag an application from the Finder onto an empty square in a dock and then drag documents onto the application to open them. Double-click a docked application to launch it or bring it to the front. In addition, the docks can contain files, folders, disks, and servers, and there is also an option to display the name of the active application in a special dock. This program by James Thomson requires a 68020, 68030, 68040, or PowerPC processor and costs $15.

Drive Setup

Drive Setup scans for SCSI devices, and initializes and formats Apple hard disk drives for Macs. This application by Apple Computer requires an Apple hard disk drive and is free.

Drop Slot

Drag and drop unsorted files onto the Drop Slot application icon and they will be automatically stored in folders on your hard drive in the same way the System Folder automatically moves its items to the correct folder. Drop Slot stores files by type, prompting you for destinations and storing types it recognizes in folders you designate. This application by Rick Christianson costs $10.

DropPS

DropPS sends text files containing PostScript code to any PostScript printer, independently of installed printer drivers. This application by Bare Bones Software is free.

Drop-Rename

Drop-Rename enables you to search for and rename files or folders with a variety of options, like changing name-cases and file extensions, changing specified search strings under certain conditions, and more. Multithreading lets it run easily in the background. You can also create "Renamelets," customized self-running applications for operations you perform regularly. This application by SouthSide Software costs $10.

DropStuff with Expander Enhancer

DropStuff with Expander Enhancer creates compressed StuffIt archives when you drag your files and folders onto the DropStuff icon. With Expander Enhancer installed, the StuffIt Expander program is able to decompress archived files in a wide variety of formats. DropStuff with Expander Enhancer by Aladdin Systems is included with Mac OS 8 in the Internet Utilities folder (inside the Internet folder on the startup disk) and has a shareware fee of $30.

Duo Extension Picker

Duo Extension Picker loads one set of extensions if you start your PowerBook Duo while docked and a different set if you start when not docked. This application by Alan Steremberg is yours to use for the cost of a postcard sent to the author.

Easy Errors

Easy Errors enables you to quickly access the meanings of particular errors reported by the Mac system software (or the Newton system software, if you happen to have a Newton device) by selecting the appropriate system and entering the error number. Easy Errors displays a result code and, in most cases, a more useful description. This application by Dave Ribinic is free.

EMMpathy

EMMpathy fixes PowerBook 520 and 540 Smart Battery memory-related errors and includes VST's Smart Battery Probe, an advanced smart battery diagnostic. This application by VST Technologies/Billy Steinberg is free.

Fat Cursors

Fat Cursors installs slightly larger arrow and I-beam pointers and features a "find pointer" function. This is particularly handy for PowerBook users. Control panel by Robert Abatecola costs $10.

File Buddy

File Buddy enhances file management. You can obtain a wide set of file and folder information using extensive search criteria; find files containing specified resources and delete or modify these resources; modify batches of file names and extensions; create aliases; find and delete duplicates, unattached aliases, and old preferences files; rebuild the desktop; and more. This application by Laurence Harris costs $35.

File eXpress

Drop files on the File eXpress FXPackager's mailbox icon, and you can send them to any other machine running File eXpress on your AppleTalk network. The program places a FXInBox folder on your desktop for your incoming files. This application by Ruskin Group, Inc. requires a TCP/IP connection and is free.

FileLock

Big Al FileLock is a simple password protection program that lets you place a password on any file. Users will then be forced to enter the correct password to open the file. This application by Al Staffieri, Jr. costs $10.

FileTyper

Drop files on FileTyper's icon to quickly change types, creators, attribute flags, and date stamps on files. It also supports processing batches of files, filtering, and directory searches. This application by Daniel Azuma costs $10.

FinderNote

FinderNote is a simple text editor whose documents are saved as clippings and can be read in the Finder (on the Desktop) without needing to run any application. This application by Jae Ho Chang, eMusicas Software is free.

Finder Options

Finder Options lets you selectively enable the following hidden options: Control-drag to make aliases; add a Reveal Original item (⌘-R) to the File menu for finding an alias's original item; ⌘-Delete to move to the Trash; disable zoom rectangles; and disable translucent dragging. Most of these features are redundant with Mac OS 8. This control panel by Rolf Braun is free.

Folder Icon Cleaner

Folder Icon Cleaner lets you scan a folder or an entire disk and delete all custom icons and their corresponding Icon files. An Erase Unused option annihilates empty Icon files that are left over when you remove custom icons using the Finder. This application by Fabrizio Oddone costs $5.

Folder Icon Maker

Folder Icon Maker creates folders with custom icons when you drag an application or document onto the FIM application. A new folder will be created in the same directory as the file is in. It also supports PICT data as a source for custom folders and works with folder resource files. This application by Greg Robbins requires a Mac Plus or later and is free.

!ForceQuit

!ForceQuit enhances the conventional Force Quit (Option-⌘-Escape) feature of the Mac OS. You can either totally enable or disable forced quits or disable forced quits only for selected applications. This extension by Daffy Software is free.

GoMac

GoMac behaves like the Windows 95 task bar, including a Program Bar displaying open applications and a Start menu listing all installed applications, recently accessed servers, files and folders, other easy navigation tools, and a small pop-up calendar. Control panel by Proteron, L.L.C is free.

GrabAudio

GrabAudio lets you record any part of an audio CD quickly and easily using simple digital audio marking features. This application by Theo Vosse requires an Apple CD300 CD player or better and the Apple CD software (which is included with the system software). GrabAudio is free.

GURU

GURU provides you with information concerning memory upgrades for every model of Mac OS computer ever made by Apple and other companies and is updated regularly. It also includes memory information on all Apple

LaserWriter printers. Memory information includes RAM, DRAM, VRAM, EDO, SDRAM, PSDRAM, Static RAM, and FRAM. This application by Craig Marciniak, Newer Technology is free.

Helium

Helium enhances the Mac OS balloon help feature, enabling you to use key commands to make help balloons appear and disappear automatically or toggle balloon help on and off, as well as setting a more legible font size for the help text. This control panel by Tiger Technologies requires a color-capable computer and costs $12.

Icon Archiver

The Icon Archiver is a database utility that can quickly scan whole disks or folders for icons and icon archives and can create archives of compressed icons. It filters icons by size and color depth, provides a wide variety of icon views, removes duplicate icons, and sorts icons using multiple criteria. This application by Alessandro Levi Montalcini costs $25.

I Love Native!

I Love Native! enables you to check whether an application, control panel, system extension, shared library, or code resource file is written in PowerPC, 68K, or fat (both PowerPC and 68K) code. It allows you to create either a PowerPC-only or a 68K-only application from a fat application to reduce application size. It also allows you to combine a PowerPC-only and a 68K-only application into a fat application (both 68K and PowerPC applications must be the same program). This application by Jerry Du is free.

The Informinit

The Informinit is a regularly updated guide for information on extensions and control panels, listing almost every system extension Apple has ever produced, with information on what they do, who needs them, version numbers, RAM consumption, and tips and tricks. This application by Dan Frakes costs $10.

Kaleidoscope

Kaleidoscope completely overhauls the Mac OS interface using plug-in Color Scheme files that are fairly simple to create using another program called "Kaleidoscope for Laymen." It includes an Aaron plug-in (described earlier in this chapter), a WindowShade widget, dynamic draggable windows, customizable Finder Window backgrounds, and much more. This control panel by Greg Landweber costs $20.

KeyQuencer

KeyQuencer is a powerful keyboard-shortcut utility with several dozen ready-to-play macros. One keystroke flips your monitor to a different color setting. Another lets you take a screen shot (a captured PICT file) of anything you rope off with the selection rectangle. Other KeyQuencer macros do things like type the date, move a window, adjust the speaker volume, or switch to the next open program. You must build every KeyQuencer macro manually; however, the task is made simpler with built-in menu commands. This control panel by Alessandro Levi Montalcini costs $10.

KillFinderZooms

KillFinderZooms performs a simple hack on your Finder, which removes the zoom-animation the Finder draws each time you open or close a window or perform desktop clean-up operations (things you do quite often). KillFinderZooms will only hack a copy of your Finder to ensure an unhacked copy is saved (in case you want to reinstall your old Finder again). This application by Jonathan Jacobs is yours to use for the cost of a postcard sent to the author.

Mac Identifier

When the Mac OS is unable to provide model or icon information about the computer it is running on, Mac Identifier provides the information from a special database of stored model names. This is useful for network administrators and users who need to share other's disks. This control panel by Maurice Volaski costs $5.

Mac OS Purge

Mac OS Purge optimizes the system software memory very quickly. It's especially useful under tight memory conditions, such as when running with small amounts of RAM or when run between launching memory intensive applications. It runs, purges, and returns to the Finder. This application by E. Kenji Takeuchi is free.

Memory Minder

Memory Minder's interface lets you examine how much memory your open applications are actually using, and lets you adjust the preferred memory size while an application is open (changes take effect the next time you launch the application). This type of management should enable you to keep more applications open simultaneously. This application by Andrew S. Downs costs $10.

Mt. Everything

The Mt. Everything enhanced hard disk management application is most beneficial for users with multiple drives. It displays the types, manufacturers, and partition maps of devices connected to your SCSI bus; mounts partitions and drives without the necessity to restart; supplies its own driver software; and supports removable media. This control panel by Horst H. Pralow requires a 68020, 68030, 68040, or PowerPC processor and is yours to use for the cost of a postcard sent to the author.

MultiTimer

MultiTimer compiles auto-saved data logs of the time you spend on your computer, including time spent in specific applications, online time, and other tasks. MultiTimer lets you create special modules representing each project, which ensures accurate records of your sessions. You can record multiple projects simultaneously using MultiTimer, and you can paste log files with MultiTimer module data into spreadsheets. This application by Karl Bunker costs $15.

MyBattery

MyBattery shows the voltage levels for three different PowerBook batteries. The program also lets you enable and disable AppleTalk and turn your modem on and off. This application by Jeremy Kezer costs $10.

MyEyes

MyEyes draws a pair of eyes on the menu bar that constantly follow the pointer's movement. MyEyes helps PowerBook users who have trouble seeing the pointer hunt it down more quickly. This extension by Federico Filipponi requires a color-capable computer and costs $10.

Natural Order

Natural Order improves the sorting order that your computer uses when it displays lists of items by overriding the system's comparison of the numerical portions of strings and by sorting them by numerical value instead of alphabetically. Natural Order only overrides the sorting of the numeric parts of strings and still honors foreign sorting orders. This extension by Stuart Cheshire is free.

Net-Print

Net-Print allows you to print or save a portion of a Netscape Navigator, Internet Explorer, or Mosaic document rather than saving or printing the entire thing. The extension places a small icon in your menu bar. You use this icon to print or save your selections. This extension by John Moe is free.

NetStickies

NetStickies adds AppleTalk network functionality to the Stickies application that comes with System 7.5 and later. You can send and receive stickies from other users that have NetStickies installed, send text clippings from a text drag and drop, and send clipboard text. The target user will receive the text as a sticky note, immediately visible on their screen. This extension by Ron Duritsch is free.

Network Reporter

Network Reporter acts as an "information agent" for a network administrator, periodically scanning an AppleTalk network and building a database of all devices it can locate. Using that database, more than 20 types of reports can be compiled and viewed online, e-mailed to one or more addresses, or exported to a text file. This application by Mr. Mac Software costs $429.

Newer Technology Gauge Series

The Gauge Series profiles and measures the performance of various hardware components in your computer, including level-2 cache, CPU, RAM, SCSI devices, and PCI Slots. This set of applications by Newer Technologies, Inc. is free.

Pattern Manager

Pattern Manager provides storage for desktop patterns in simple palettes, which allows for one-click viewing and installation of patterns. It includes a powerful PICT importer and features a toggle preference for automatically changing desktop patterns over specific periods of time. Pattern Manager 1.5 and earlier do not work with Mac OS 8. This application by Sterling Augustine is free.

PlugAlert

PlugAlert detects when the power adapter has become unplugged from the wall or your PowerBook and also indicates when the wall outlet isn't supplying electricity. This extension by Sean Hummel is free.

PopChar Lite

PopChar Lite simplifies "typing" of unusual characters. Pull down the PopChar menu, select the character you want, and PopChar automatically inserts it in the current document as if you had typed the proper key combination on the keyboard. This control panel by Gunther Blaschek requires a 68020 , 68030, 68040, or PowerPC processor and is free.

PopupCD

PopupCD provides a pop-up remote control for quick and easy access to your audio CDs through your CD-ROM drive. The remote control has all the functions normally used with conventional CD players, as well as a playing time indicator and a pop-up track menu. You can access all functions with configurable keyboard hotkeys as well through the onscreen remote. If you're tired of launching or switching applications just to control your CDs, PopupCD can be an elegant and unobtrusive alternative. PopupCD can also record audio clips directly from CD to hard drive. This control panel by John Brochu requires a color-capable computer and the Apple CD-ROM software version 5.0.1 or later, which is included with the Mac OS. It costs $15.

PortShare Pro

PortShare Pro enables you to share serial devices (including fax modems, printers, and plotters) over your AppleTalk (LocalTalk, Ethernet, or Token Ring) network and achieve remote access for data, faxing (Class 2), ARA, e-mail, and BBS sessions with password protection. Any Mac OS computer can operate as a PortShare Pro server and as a PortShare Pro client at the same time: when somebody is working with devices connected to your serial ports, you can use devices attached to other networked computers' serial ports. This control panel by Stalker Software, Inc. requires a Mac SE or better and a LocalTalk or Ethernet network, and costs $149.

PowerBar Pro

PowerBar Pro is an application launcher featuring handy Finder-action tiles, such as Move to Trash, Empty Trash, and Restart. Tiles can launch QuicKeys macros, Control Strip modules, or other PowerBar palettes. When you hold the mouse down on a folder tile, a pop-up menu shows everything inside. This application by Scott Johnson, Trilobyte Software costs $25.

PowerSaver Tweak

PowerSaver Tweak provides more control over the power conservation settings than the standard Energy Saver and PowerBook control panel. It lets you configure the conservation settings for specific applications, screen dimming, drive spindown, system sleep, and CPU cycling for up to fifty applications (unregistered copies allow four). For example, you can prevent your PowerBook from cycling while you are playing a particular game. Or use

PowerSaver Tweak so that your hard drive never spins down while using Microsoft Word. This control panel by Jeremy Kezer requires a PowerBook or a computer with PCI expansion slots and costs $10.

Power Speed Mouse

Power Speed Mouse allows you to speed up your mouse. It's particularly beneficial if you're using a large monitor, since the mouse speeds up over long distances but otherwise moves normally. The application has options for speeding up the mouse and returning the mouse to normal, and speeds must be reset across restarts. This application by Alamo Computer is free.

PrintChoice

The PrintChoice extension is designed to bypass the Chooser. You can choose a printer from the Printer menu it adds to the menu bar, and you can use PrintChoice to create desktop printer icons for drag-and-drop printing. This extension by Kerry Clendinning costs $14.

Program Switcher

Program Switcher allows you to switch between the running programs on your computer via a simple two-key keystroke. You can also assign keystrokes to Finder-related functions for rapid desktop shortcuts, like showing and hiding applications. This control panel by Michael F. Kamprath costs $10.

Recent Additions

Recent Additions is a system enhancement that creates aliases for recently created documents and applications and displays them in a hierarchical menu inside the Apple Menu (like Recent Applications and Recent Documents). This extension by Andrew Downs is free.

ReminderPro

ReminderPro lets you schedule one-time or repeating reminders as you work on your computer. The package includes a Control Strip module for scheduling reminders instantly, and the ReminderPro system extension, which works continuously in the background to display reminders at the appropriate times as well as automating tasks like scheduled launching of applications, opening of documents, and automatically running AppleScripts at designated times. This extension by Manoj Patwardhan, Crystal Software, Inc. requires a 68020, 68030, 68040, or PowerPC processor and costs $18.

ResEdit

Apple's ResEdit enables you to edit system and application resources, such as icons, menus, and the text of alert messages. You can do many fun things with ResEdit, but beware — only work on copies of the files you are editing. This application by Apple Computer is free.

SerialSpeed 230

SerialSpeed 230 works with the Geoport enhanced serial ports of most PowerPC computers and Quadra and Centris 660AV and 840AV computers to boost serial port speed up to 230 Kbps. The port speed determines the rate at which the computer and modem communicate. A fast port speed is especially beneficial when used with a high-speed modem that has hardware compression. This control panel by Brookline Software requires a V.34 or V.FC modem and application software that is normally used at 57.6 Kbps. It costs $25.

Sesame

Sesame prevents unauthorized access to your computer by requesting a password whenever the Sesame application is running. This application by Bernard Frangoulis costs $10.

ShrinkWrap

ShrinkWrap creates disk image files like Disk Copy (described earlier in this chapter) when you drag and drop floppy drive icons onto the ShrinkWrap icon. It also opens DiskCopy disk images and will automatically compress and decompress archived image files on-the-fly with Aladdin's StuffIt Expander (described in "Transferring Files" in Chapter 20). ShrinkWrap 3.0 is distributed commercially by Aladdin Systems (408-761-6200, http://www.aladdinsys.com) for $29.95. ShrinkWrap 2.1 may still be available as shareware from its author, Chad Magendanz, for $20.

Shutdown Delay

Shutdown Delay displays a dialog box at restart or shutdown time, allowing you to complete the original command, return to the desktop, restart, shut down, or force quit and return to the Finder. This control panel by Alessandro Levi Montalcini costs $10.

Sleeper

Conserve energy when you're away from your computer and quiet your disk drive with Sleeper. After periods of inactivity, Sleeper will dim the screen on your desktop computer and spin down SCSI disk drives, at separate times if you prefer. Sleeper will also let your current screen saver work while handling the disk drives. This control panel by St. Clair Software costs $20.

Sloop

Sloop adds pointer focusing to the Mac system software: whatever window the pointer is over automatically moves to the front (acquires focus) — a navigational strategy popular in X Windows, which provides windows for the Unix OS. You can configure Sloop to operate exclusively in specific applications or as a general desktop feature. This extension by Graham Herrick costs $20.

SoftwareFPU

SoftwareFPU allows most applications expecting an FPU to work properly on a computer that does not have one (as is the case on many older models and some Power Macs and PowerBooks). Because of a bug in the 68LC040 chip, this program may or may not work with individual applications running on these machines; more information is provided in the program's documentation. The author also makes PowerFPU, a commercial version with twice the performance on PowerPC computers. This control panel by John M. Neil requires a 68020, 68030, or 68LC040 processor without FPU (floating-point unit), or a PowerPC processor and costs $20.

SoundApp

SoundApp is a sound playback and conversion utility for the Mac OS. Use it as a sound-playing helper application with Web browsers. In addition to managing a collection of play lists, SoundApp can play files or convert files dropped onto it into a variety of formats and sample rates. This application by Norman Franke III is free.

SoundMaster

SoundMaster makes your computer play sounds when you perform various tasks on your system, such as inserting a disk, emptying the trash, shutting down, or performing keyboard functions such as tabbing, deleting, and scrolling. This control panel by Bruce Tomlin costs $15.

StickyClick

StickyClick simulates the sticky menus feature of Mac OS 8 on computers that have an earlier system software version. This extension by Steve Zellers is free.

Super Comments

Super Comments permits comments to be viewed in Open dialog boxes and edited in Save dialog boxes. It can also save Get Info comments when you rebuild the desktop; this feature is redundant with Mac OS 8. This control panel by Maurice Volaski costs $10.

SuperTools

SuperTools is a series of three applications that speed the launching, printing, and erasing of documents. SuperPrint is a drop-box desktop printer that prints a document on a currently selected printer when you drag and drop the document's icon onto SuperPrint. SuperLaunch lets you bundle a series of documents to create workbooks by dragging the collection on top of the SuperLaunch icon. SuperTrash permanently erases a document by writing zeroes on top of its data before deletion. This application by Pascal Pochet costs $25.

SwitchBack

SwitchBack synchronizes two folders on the same volume, on two different volumes, or on two different computers connected by a network to contain copies of the most recent versions of files in both places. It works with all Mac OS computers and also backs up DOS disks. This application by Glendower Software Ltd. costs $30.

System Picker

System Picker lets you choose the folder that will be the active System Folder upon restart. It scans all volumes to create a list of usable System Folders, accessible via a pop-up menu. System Picker 1.1 or later is required for Mac OS 8. This application by Kevin Aitken requires Mac Plus or better and is free.

TattleTech

TattleTech provides hundreds of details about your computer and its system-related software, generating reports by category and output to the screen, printer, text file, or a tab-delimited text file. Report data includes "bug" and "unit" information as well as a complete summary of your system configuration. Tech-support people sometimes request such profiles of your system in order to help you troubleshoot problems. This application by John Mancino costs $15.

TechTool

TechTool performs various simple diagnostic and repair operations, such as analyzing your system file for damage, cleaning the floppy drive, deleting and rebuilding the desktop, resetting PRAM, and displaying the date the computer was manufactured and the number of hours it has been used. This application by Micromat Computer Systems is free.

TimeSlice

The TimeSlice time-tracking program logs timed tasks you perform on your computer, including time spent in particular applications. You can use it to run multiple time sessions at once; search and sort time records; set time and money budgets; and start, stop, pause, resume, and restart time records. This application by MauiSoft costs $49.

TitlePop

The TitlePop extension turns a document window's title into a pop-up menu, listing items for windows belonging to the current program and an item for background programs, which are shown in hierarchical menus below their respective program items. You can bring any window to the front by selecting it from the TitlePop menu. This extension by Jouko Pakkanen is free.

Trash It!

The Trash It! Control Strip module can empty the trash without warnings about locked or busy files. It accepts drag and drop multiple file and folder deletions and can delete the desktop on mounted volumes and floppies. This control Strip module by Ammon Skidmore, Skidperfect Software requires a Mac Plus or later or a PowerBook and the Extensions Strip, Control Strip, or Desktop Strip software. It is free.

TypeIt4Me

TypeIt4Me works inside any application that allows text-entry, letting you type small abbreviations for predefined strings like names, addresses, and difficult-to-type phrases. It's similar to the commercial program QuicKeys; however, instead of assigning key-commands, you assign your own special abbreviations. This control panel by Ricardo Ettore costs $30.

UltraFind

UltraFind quickly searches any mounted media on your desktop or network, including remote volumes via modem using ARA, providing detailed information about items, copying or moving them across the network, performing backups, or deleting selected items. It can also extract information from damaged files. This application by UltraDesign Technology costs $39.

Virtual

Virtual, an adaptation of Sun Microsystems' window manager olvwm, enables you to simulate more than one monitor on your desktop, drawing as many virtual screens as you like, as well as the windows of open applications inside them. You can create windows' representations in Virtual, place them in different virtual screens to organize them in workgroups, make some windows sticky, or assign whole applications in a particular virtual screen. This application by Pierre-Luc Paour requires a color-capable computer and costs $10.

WrapScreen

WrapScreen implements a wrap-around mouse-pointer: instead of stopping at the right edge of the screen, for example, the pointer appears at the left edge. This control panel by Eric Arbourg is yours to use for the cost of a donation.

Yank

Yank uninstalls an application and files created by the application by moving them to the Trash. It also detects and moves outdated preferences folders, also moving them to the Trash. Yank does not automatically delete anything. This application by Maui Software costs $15.

Summary

In this chapter, you found out that noncommercial software is available from many Internet sites, user groups, and Apple Computer. You can distribute copies of shareware and freeware, but authors generally retain copyrights to their software. Shareware authors ask you to send them payment for products you decide to keep, but freeware authors don't ask for payment. The 90-plus utilities listed in this chapter are a representative sample of the noncommercial software that's available for enhancing the Mac system software.

Discover Tips and Secrets

S cattered throughout the previous chapters of this book are scores of tips and secrets for getting more out of Mac OS 8. For your convenience, the next two chapters contain a digest of the most useful tips and secrets plus some tips that don't appear elsewhere in this book. In this chapter you'll find tips for the desktop: icons, folders and windows, the Trash, the Apple Menu, and fonts. The next chapter concentrates on system-related tips: dialog boxes, file sharing, system utilities, control panels and extensions, applications, and memory and system performance.

To use some of these tips, you'll need a copy of ResEdit, Apple's no-cost resource editor. You can get ResEdit from Apple's online software library (http://www.info.apple.com), online services like America Online (keyword: filesearch), and Macintosh user groups. You can also get a copy of ResEdit, as well as the many shareware and freeware programs mentioned in these two chapters from the Macworld Online Web site (http://www.macworld.com).

Icons

This section contains tips for saving time and effort while editing icon names, making and using aliases on the desktop, and getting icons to look the way you want.

Spotting a name selected for editing

For a visual cue that you have selected the name of an icon on a color or
grayscale monitor, use the Appearance control panel to set the text-highlight
color to something other than black and white. Then you'll know that a name
highlighted in color (or gray) is ready for editing, whereas a name highlighted
in black and white is not. Figure 25-1 shows an example of a file name
highlighted in gray and ready for editing and a file that has been merely
selected and is therefore uneditable.

**Figure 25-1: A distinctive highlight
color makes it easy to spot an icon
whose name is ready for editing (left).**

Edit, don't open

If you have trouble editing icon names without opening the item, remember to
click on the item *name*, not the icon. Keep the cursor over the item name and
wait for the name to highlight automatically. (The lag time between your click
and the name highlighting depends on the Double-Click speed you've chosen
in the Mouse control panel: a slower Double-Click speed means a longer wait
for the name to highlight.)

Undoing an accidental name change

If you rename an icon by mistake, choose Undo from the Edit menu (or press
⌘-Z) to restore the original name. Another way to restore the icon's original
name is to press Backspace or Delete until the name is empty and then press
Return or click outside the icon. (You cannot undo your changes to a name
after you finish editing it, only while it is still selected for editing.)

Copy/Paste icon names

While editing a name, you can use the Undo, Cut, Copy, Paste, and Select All
commands in the Edit menu. You can also copy the entire name of any item by
selecting its icon (or its whole name) and then choosing the Copy command
from the Edit menu. This capability comes in handy when you're copying a
disk and want to give the copy the same name as the original.

You can copy the name of a locked item — select the item and use the Copy command but you can't change the name of a locked item. (Unlock an application or file by using the Get Info command (⌘-I) or, if the item is a disk, by sliding its locking tab.)

The Mac OS doesn't limit you to copying one icon name at a time. If you select several items and then use the Copy command, the names of all the items are put on the Clipboard (up to 256 characters in all), one name per line.

Removing the alias from aliases

When you use the Finder's Make Alias command, the resulting alias has the word *alias* at the end of its name. To remove the word *alias* from the end of an icon name, select the name for editing, press the right-arrow or down-arrow key to move the insertion point to the end of the name, and press Delete six times (five times, if you want to leave a blank space at the end of the alias name to distinguish it from the original name) and ⌘-Option-drag it to a new folder, volume, or the desktop.

Permanently Removing *alias*

If you always remove the word *alias* from the end of new alias names, you may prefer never to have the word appended to file names at all. You can make a change with ResEdit so that the Finder never appends *alias* to the names of new aliases. Follow these steps:

1. Make an alias of ResEdit and place it on the desktop.

2. Open the system folder and Option-drag the Finder onto the desktop, which creates a duplicate Finder. Drag this duplicate Finder onto the ResEdit icon to open it.*

   You see a window full of icons, each icon representing a different type of resource in the Finder.

3. Double-click the STR# resource type, opening a window that lists all the Finder's string-list resources by number.

4. Locate STR# resource number 8200, and double-click it to open it. In system software versions earlier than Mac OS 8, open STR# resource number 20500.

   The *alias* suffix is in string #1. This is the text that the Finder appends to the original file name to make up the alias name.

5. Change the string to one blank space rather than making it completely empty, so that the names of original files and their aliases will be different.

(continued)

(continued)

6. To finish, close all the ResEdit windows or simply quit ResEdit. Answer Yes when you are asked whether you want to save changes.

7. To see the results of your work, drag the original Finder into a folder outside the system folder, then drag the altered Finder into the system folder and restart your computer.

*Always work on a copy of the original file when using ResEdit. You might think ResEdit keeps your changes only in the computer's memory until you save them to disk, because the program asks whether you want to save changes before closing a file or quitting the program. But that alert is some kind of a cruel joke. As you make changes to a file, ResEdit actually updates the file on disk. If you get the alert and answer no, ResEdit reverses the changes and your file is safe. But if your computer crashes (does anyone have a computer that does not crash?) or ResEdit quits unexpectedly before you have the opportunity to reverse your ResEdit changes, you'll find the changes in place when you restart your computer and reopen the file with ResEdit. Be aware, and may the power of ResEdit be with you.

Desktop Aliases

Rather than drag frequently used programs, control panels, documents, and folders themselves onto the desktop, make aliases of those items and place the aliases on the desktop. You get quick access to the original items through their desktop aliases. Also, you can open several related items at the same time by opening aliases on the desktop, even if the original items happen to be in different folders or on different disks.

If your desktop becomes too cluttered with aliases, you can store related aliases together in a desktop folder, and tuck the folder conveniently out of the way at the bottom of your screen by using the Finder's Pop-up Window View command. Figure 25-2 shows aliases on the desktop and in a pop-up window.

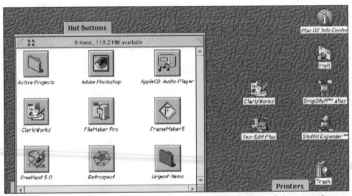

Figure 25-2: Keep frequently used items handy with aliases of them on the desktop or in pop-up windows.

Express access to CD-ROMs

Cut through the drudgery of wading through folders on a CD-ROM by making aliases of items inside the CD-ROM folders. Because CD-ROMs are permanently locked, you must put the aliases on your hard disk (or a floppy disk). Opening an alias makes a beeline to the original item on the CD-ROM.

Cataloging items on floppy disks

You can use aliases to keep track of, and quickly open, items on floppy disks — even floppies that aren't inserted into your computer. Make aliases of the items on a floppy disk by selecting them and ⌘-Option-dragging them to your startup disk. (If you use the Make Alias command to make the aliases, you'll have to copy the aliases to the startup disk and then delete the aliases from the floppy disk.) When you need the item again, the system software tells you the name of the disk to insert so that it can open the alias's original item. If you change your mind or can't find the needed disk, click the Cancel button. Figure 25-3 shows an example of a disk insert message.

Figure 25-3: If you open an alias whose original item is on a disk that's not inserted, the Mac OS prompts you to insert the specific disk.

Making many aliases

To make aliases for several items in the same window at the same time, select all the items and then use the Make Alias command (⌘-M). An alias appears for every item that you selected. All the new aliases are selected automatically so that you can drag them to another place without having to manually select them as a group. If you accidentally deselect the items, you can easily group them together for reselecting by arranging or sorting the window by kind or date created.

Reverting to standard icons

You can revert to an item's standard icon after replacing the icon with custom graphics. Just select the item, choose Get Info (⌘-I) from the Finder's File menu, select the icon in the Info window, and choose Clear or Cut from the Edit menu.

Fixing blank icons

Sometimes, a file that you copy onto your disk ends up with a generic (blank) icon. You really don't want to rebuild your desktop files just to fix one icon (especially if you have a large disk). Instead, open the icon's Info window (⌘-I) and select the icon in the Info window. A box appears around the icon, indicating that you have selected the icon. Now copy, paste, and cut the icon — in that order. If you are lucky, the correct icon shows its face.

Here's how it works: copying the icon makes it possible to paste; pasting the icon causes the Finder to internally mark the file as one that has a custom icon; and cutting the icon causes the Finder to unmark the file and restore its standard icon. You can't do the cutting step unless you have done the pasting step, and you can't do the pasting step unless you have done the copying step.

Custom floppy icons

If you've customized your desktop icons and long to do the same to the icons of any disk inserted into the floppy drive, use Andrew Welch's freeware extension Discolour (or CD Discolour for CD-ROMs). It gives all floppy disk icons a colorful, three-dimensional look and only increases system software memory size by 1K. (You can't permanently edit the floppy disk icons — even with ResEdit — because the floppy disk icon the system software uses is built into the computer's ROM.)

If the icons that come with Discolour and CD Discolour aren't quite what you want, you can edit them with ResEdit (follow the instructions located in the Read Me files that accompany the extensions).

Customizing Folder Icons

If you think you have too many boring, look-alike folders cluttering your desktop, you can enliven those folders by superimposing relevant application icons. Follow these steps:

1. Copy a folder icon from its Info window (which you display by choosing the Finder's Get Info command), and paste the icon into a color paint program.

2. Open the folder that contains the application whose icon you want to use, view the folder window by Small Icon, and take a screen snapshot (press ⌘-Shift-3).

(continued)

(continued)

3. Open the screen-snapshot file (named Picture 1 on your startup disk) with the color paint program or with SimpleText, copy the small application icon from the snapshot, and paste it over the pasted folder icon.

4. Copy the composite icon from the paint program, paste it into the folder's Info window, and close the Info window.

Tip: When you select the custom icon in the paint program, you must take care to select a rectangular area no larger than 32 by 32 pixels (the maximum size of an icon). If you select a larger area, including lots of white space around your custom icon, the Finder shrinks the selection to 32 by 32 when you paste it into the folder's Get Info window, and your custom icon ends up shrunken. If you select an area smaller than 32 by 32, the Finder centers the selection in the folder's icon space, and the custom icon will not line up horizontally with a plain folder icon (which is flush with the bottom of its icon space).

You can avoid this rigmarole by using the freeware utility Folder Icon Maker by Gregory Robbins. Just drag a great-looking application or document icon to Folder Icon Maker, and presto — Folder Icon Maker creates a new folder with a small version of that icon superimposed on it.

The custom icons obscure any subsequent changes that you make to the folder's color (with the Finder's Label submenu, under the File menu) or to the folder's file-sharing status (with the Finder's Sharing command).

Aliases where you want them

When you make an alias of an item on one disk with Mac OS 7.6.1 and earlier and want to move the alias to another disk, the Finder copies the alias to the new volume. But you then have to tidy up by trashing the original alias. A better way is to make an alias exactly where you want it in the first place — no bothersome copying and deleting the alias from the folder of its original item. Add Rolf Braun's freeware Finder Options to the Extensions folder and restart. You can then make an alias by pressing the Control key and dragging the original item where you want an alias of it. You don't need to use this extension with Mac OS 8, because you can ⌘-Option-drag an item to another disk to make an alias of it there.

Bad disk icon

If you have problems with a custom disk icon — for instance, if your hard disk icon appears as a generic document icon — try the freeware utility Disk Rejuvenator from Aladdin Systems (which is also handy if you have a problem accessing your hard disk from standard Open dialog boxes). If you have problems with a custom folder icon, drag the folder's contents to a new folder and then drag the troublesome, now-empty folder to the Trash.

Desktop and Startup

This section covers tips for customizing your desktop, as well as the sights and sounds that you see and hear during and after startup.

Rebuilding the desktop

To rebuild the desktop of any disk whose icon normally appears on the desktop after startup, press ⌘-Option while starting your computer. For each disk in turn, the Finder asks whether you want the disk's desktop to be rebuilt. (Rebuilding the desktop with System 7.5.2 and earlier erases all comments in Info windows, but later system software versions leave them intact.) To rebuild the desktop of a floppy disk or another removable disk whose icon is not on the desktop, press ⌘-Option while inserting the disk. Figure 25-4 shows an example of a rebuild confirmation dialog box.

Figure 25-4: You must confirm rebuilding each disk's desktop individually.

Desktop by name

If your desktop gets so cluttered that you can hardly find the icon for an inserted floppy disk, you may wish that you could use the Finder's View menu to arrange items on the desktop as a list, as you can in individual windows. You can't do that, but you can get a similar effect through a little icon voodoo.

First, make sure the Icon Arrangement option of the View Options command (located in the Finder's View menu) for the desktop is set to None. Next, open an empty folder and take a picture of a small area of white space by pressing Control-⌘-Shift-4 and dragging a small selection in the folder window's white background. (If you have System 7.5.5 or earlier, you'll have to press ⌘-Shift-3 to take a picture of the whole screen, open the screen picture in SimpleText, select a small area of white space, and copy it.)

With your white space copied to the Clipboard, use the Finder's Get Info command (⌘-I) on each desktop item that you want to view by name, and paste the white space over the icon in each item's Info window. Pasting the white space leaves only the item's name visible, and six items without icons fit into the space previously occupied by two items with icons, as shown in Figure 25-5.

Figure 25-5: Items on the desktop take less space if you "white out" their icons.

Custom startup screen

Instead of the plain old "Welcome to Mac OS" startup screen, your computer can display a special picture. If your system folder contains a file named StartupScreen that contains a PICT resource with ID 0, the graphic image in that resource replaces the standard startup screen. You can use any of several programs to create such a startup screen for your computer, or you can create one using just ResEdit and the Scrapbook (see the sidebar "Creating Your Own Startup Screen"). Figure 25-6 shows an example of a custom startup screen.

Figure 25-6: You can make a custom startup screen to replace the "Welcome to Mac OS" message.

If you use a graphics program to create your custom startup screen, save the file as Startup Screen or StartupScreen as the file type (generally by choosing it from a pop-up menu in the Save As dialog box). In some graphics programs, you choose Resource File as the type of file to save and then specify a resource ID of 0 instead.

Startup movie

If you have QuickTime installed, you can have a movie play during startup by naming it Startup Movie and placing it in the System Folder. (To halt the Startup Movie, press ⌘-period or any other key.)

Startup sounds

You can put a sound file in the Startup Items folder (inside the System Folder), and that file will be played when you start your computer.

Creating Your Own Startup Screen

If you don't have a graphics program that can save a startup screen but you do have ResEdit, you can use it and the Scrapbook to create your own startup screen file. Follow these steps:

1. Paste the image that you want to use as a startup screen into the Scrapbook.

2. Close the Scrapbook and use ResEdit to open a copy of the Scrapbook file (located in the System Folder).

   ResEdit displays a window containing icons that represent different types of resources in the Scrapbook file.

3. Open the Scrapbook file's PICT-resources icon and scroll through the images until you see the one that you want for your startup screen.

4. Copy the PICT resource that you want to use.

5. Create a new document in ResEdit and paste the PICT resource you just copied. Save it with the name "StartupScreen" in the System Folder.

6. Open the PICT-resource icon in the new document, select the image that you just pasted, and choose Get Resource Info (⌘-I) from the Resource menu. In the Resource Info window that appears, change the ID number to 0.

7. Quit ResEdit, clicking the Yes button when you are asked whether you want to save changes.

8. Restart your computer to see the custom startup screen.

If your computer has a microphone, you can use the SimpleSound program or the Sound control panel to record a message for the next person who uses the computer, or just for fun. (To halt startup sounds, press ⌘-period.)

Squelching startup sounds

Have you ever wanted to silence the computer's startup chime? On some Mac models, you can't quiet the startup chime by turning down the volume level in the Monitors & Sound control panel. If you want to eliminate the computer's startup chime, plug an earphone or headphones into the sound output port — you don't have to wear them.

Bigger pointers

If your computer's pointer is just too small for you to comfortably keep track of in its travels around your desktop, try out Robert Abatecola's shareware Fat Cursors. Fat Cursors enlarges both the arrow pointer and the I-beam-shaped text pointer.

Several utilities just make it easier to locate a normal-sized pointer. Eyeballs installs a pair of eyes that watch your pointer from the menu bar. FindCursor, ZoomToCursor, and CursorBeacon each create a different type of visual commotion around the pointer when you press a specified key combination.

Start-up booby trap

Don't hold down the Power-on key on the keyboard for more than a second or two when starting up a Power Mac, or else you set the stage for an unexpected appearance of the mysterious programmer's window (a dialog box — containing only a greater-than symbol — that provides access to a limited set of program debugging tools known as the Mini Debugger). This baffling window appears sometime later, seemingly unbidden and definitely unwanted, when you press the ⌘ key. (You can make the programmer's window appear at will by holding down the ⌘ key and pressing the Power-on key on the keyboard.)

If the programmer's window appears on your screen, you can usually resume work without restarting by typing the letter G (short for Go) and pressing Return. If you type anything else and press Return, you may have to restart, losing all unsaved work.

If you hold down the Power-on key too long when starting up and later press Control-⌘, the computer restarts as if you switched the power off and on. In this case, you have inadvertently invoked the emergency restart sequence, which normally involves holding down Control-⌘ and pressing the Power-on key. Warning: Don't use this technique as a shortcut for the Restart command. Use it only in lieu of restarting with the power switch, for example, if your computer crashes.

Custom System Beeps

You can create your own custom system alert sounds on your computer from any audio CD. Follow these steps:

1. Using the AppleCD Audio Player, play the audio CD from which you want to make the alert sound and note the track and time where the passage you want to record starts. Pause the CD a few seconds before the start of the passage.

2. Open the Monitors & Sound control panel and click the Sound button. Set Sound Input to Internal CD and turn on Listen, and turn up the volume control all the way. Switch to the Alert view by pressing the Alert button.

3. Switch back to the AudioCD Player and click or press the Play button (or the spacebar). Immediately switch back to the Monitors & Sound control panel and click the Add button, then the Record button (the timing can be tricky). Click the Stop button to finish your new alert sound — a second or two at most is plenty. The figure below shows this step in progress.

4. Name and save your new alert sound.

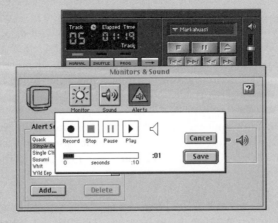

Tip: If you want more control over recording short segments from an audio CD, try Theo Vosse's freeware utility GrabAudio (described in Chapter 24).

Better file-sharing startup

Although you can have AppleShare servers and file-sharing servers mounted automatically at start-up, doing so can really slow down network performance (especially if everyone on the network does it). To reduce network traffic while keeping servers conveniently accessible, use aliases to mount network volumes whenever you need them. To set up the aliases, use the Chooser to mount the network volumes. Then select the network volumes and make aliases. Put copies of the aliases on the desktop, in the Apple Menu Items folder, and anywhere else you want quick access to the network volumes.

When you open the alias of a network volume, or drag something to the alias, your computer automatically asks you for a password and then mounts the network volume. Similarly, you can make aliases of folders on network volumes and use those aliases to simplify accessing the original folders on the servers.

Thawing a frozen program

Applications sometimes freeze up and don't respond to ordinary controls such as Cancel buttons or pressing ⌘-period. When this happens use the Force Quit command (⌘-Option-Escape). This combination brings up a dialog box with a Force Quit button and a Cancel button. Clicking Cancel (not Force Quit) sometimes seems to act like a whiff of ammonia for a program that has passed out. It doesn't often work, but when it does it beats the alternatives. Be sure to save your work and restart the computer right away after reviving a frozen program.

First or last in a hurry

In most folder and disk windows, you can highlight the item that comes first alphabetically by pressing any number key or the spacebar. In most cases you can highlight the item that comes last alphabetically by pressing the Option key along with any number key.

These tricks (which stem from the ability to select an item by typing the first part of its name) work fine unless you have many item names that come after a bullet (•), including names beginning with most accented capital letters, most symbols you type with the Option and Shift keys, and some symbols you type with the Option key alone.

If nothing is selected in the active Finder window (or on the desktop, if no window has racing stripes to indicate it is the active one), you can highlight the first or last item by pressing Tab or Shift-Tab. With an item highlighted, pressing Tab or Shift-Tab highlights the item that follows or precedes it alphabetically, and pressing an arrow key highlights the closest item on the desktop in the direction of the arrow.

Start-up messages

Do you like to have reminders at start-up, but don't want to use Stickies? Create a clipping file of your notes, and place an alias of it in the Startup Items folder. Rename it to be alphabetically last, so it opens after other start-up items. At start-up, the Finder does not have to launch an application to display the note, which you can easily dismiss with ⌘-W. If you keep the clipping on your desktop, you will be able to view it anytime you want within seconds.

To edit a clipping file directly (without dragging it to the Note Pad or some other application), get the freeware Finder Note by Jae Ho Chang, eMusicas Software (described in Chapter 24).

Futuristic Finder

Want to glimpse the future, when Web browsers may usurp the Finder's role? If you drag a folder into a browser window of Netscape Navigator 2.0 or later, Netscape Navigator lists the folder contents. You can even save the catalog as a file. Files and nested folders become clickable links, and if you click an HTML file (a Web page), a text file, a JPEG graphic file, or another file format that Netscape Navigator can handle, it displays the file's contents. Figure 25-7 shows an example of a "futuristic Finder."

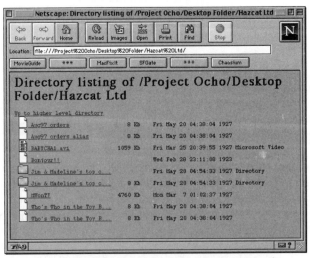

Figure 25-7: Use Netscape Navigator 2.0 or later to browse the contents of a folder dropped onto the Navigator window.

You can also view files for which you have configured Netscape Navigator to use a plug-in or a helper application. For instance, you can view a QuickTime movie by clicking its file name in the browser window if you have configured Netscape Navigator to use the QuickTime plug-in or the MoviePlayer application. It's a perfect way to catalog and browse clip art.

Folders and Windows

The tips in this section involve customizing and manipulating Finder windows and folders.

Locking folders

Everyone knows how to lock a file with the Finder's Get Info command, but how do you lock a folder? Just select the folder that you want to lock, choose Sharing from the Finder's File menu to bring up the folder's file-sharing privileges window, and check the box labeled "Can't move, rename, or delete this item." For this trick to work, file sharing must be turned on in the File Sharing or Sharing Setup control panel, whichever your computer has. (You don't have to actually share the folder or change any other setting in the privileges window.) Figure 25-8 shows the Sharing window for a locked folder.

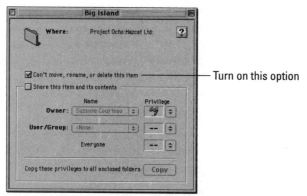

Figure 25-8: The Sharing window is the only way to lock a folder without third-party software.

Special folder replacement

Should you happen to discard one of the special folders inside the System Folder, you can make a replacement by using the Finder's New Folder command (File menu). After creating a new folder, change its name to that of the special folder you want: Apple Menu Items, Control Panels, Extensions, Fonts, Preferences, or Startup Items. Close the System Folder, wait a few seconds and reopen it, and you'll see its icon get the distinctive appearance of the special folder that you're creating.

Window arranger

If you're tired of dragging a window created on a big screen back to center when you open the folder on a smaller monitor, try Allesandro Levi Montalcini's DragAnyWindow shareware utility. Not only can you use it to center a window onscreen, but DragAnyWindow also moves dialog boxes (such as Save and Open).

Special folder mistakes

The Finder sometimes makes mistakes when it puts items in the System Folder's special folder for you. The Finder may put some items in the correct places and incorrectly leave others in the System Folder itself. For example, it may put a control panel in the Control Panels folder but leave that control panel's auxiliary folder in the System Folder. That control panel won't work right because it expects to find its auxiliary folder in the same folder that it occupies. To correct this problem, you must open the System Folder and drag the auxiliary folder to the Control Panels folder yourself.

Abridged System Folder

Does finding the Apple Menu Items folder, Startup Items folder, or some other item in your System Folder take too long? Make aliases for the System Folder items that you access often — including an alias of the System Folder itself — and consolidate the aliases in a new folder. You can open and find an item in that folder faster than you can in the System Folder.

To make the new folder look like a System Folder, copy the icon from the System Folder's Info window and paste it into the new folder's Info window.

Labeling System Clutter

Installer programs simplify the process of updating or installing software, but too many of these programs rudely scatter files all over the System Folder without so much as a by-your-leave. Some installers even commit the unforgivable offense of overwriting your existing control panels and extensions with older versions. Although you may be able to limit this subterranean mischief by doing a custom installation, there's an easy method for keeping tabs on the changes. Follow these steps:

(continued)

(continued)

1. Before running an installer program, label every System Folder file you want to keep track of, using the Label command under the Finder's File menu, as shown in the figure below. Then restart.

   Tip: If you label the contents of your System Folder after a clean install — say, of Mac OS 8 — you'll start off on the right foot when it comes to resolving conflicts and crashes. In the Finder, open Preferences, located under the Edit menu, and designate a label as Mac OS 8 files only.

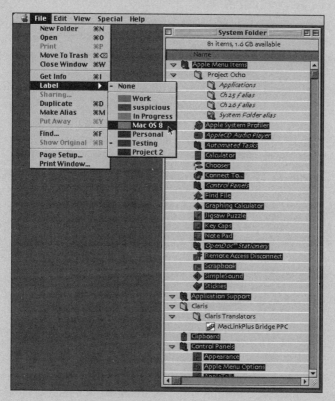

2. Back up your hard disk and run the installer. If the installer forces you to restart the computer but you don't want new extensions loaded until you see what they are, disable extensions (by holding down the Shift key during the restart).

3. To locate the new items, select the System Folder and choose Find. Set it to search for any item in the Find selection whose label is *none*. When Find File displays its list of found items, you can select all, copy it, and paste the list into the Scrapbook or any text document for later reference. You can also select any number of found items quickly and change the label using Find File's Open Enclosing Folder (⌘-E).

At best, labeling system files can help you reduce System Folder clutter and save RAM and hard disk space. At the very least, you know exactly which files the installer added. All else being equal, knowledge is always better than ignorance.

Removing items from the System Folder

Be sure to put items that you drag from the System Folder's special folders in the Trash, on the desktop, or in an ordinary folder. If you merely drag items from the Control Panels folder or Extensions folder to the main level of the System Folder, those items may still be effective.

Easy startup items

If you want an item to open at startup time, put an alias of it in the Startup Items folder. Don't put original items there because returning them to their original locations when you no longer want them opened at startup time can be a drag.

When you finish using an alias, you can drag it to the Trash or use the Finder's Move to Trash File command (⌘-Delete).

Seeing desktop items

If the windows of open programs obscure desktop icons, you can hide those windows by choosing Hide Others from the Application menu while the Finder is active. If Finder windows cover desktop icons, you can close all the windows at the same time by pressing Option while clicking the close box of any Finder window. Or with Mac OS 8, collapse all of the active application's windows by Option-clicking the active window's collapse box.

Drag to scroll

You can scroll a window without using the scroll bars. Simply place the mouse pointer in the window, click the mouse button, and drag toward the area that you want to view. Drag the pointer up, down, left, or right past the window's active area, and scrolling begins. Dragging past a window corner scrolls diagonally.

To scroll slowly, drag just to the window's edge (and continue holding down the mouse button). Increase scrolling speed by dragging beyond the window's edge.

Manipulating background windows

Sometimes you need to get at something in a background window that's covered by a window in front, but you don't want to bring the background window forward. For instance, you might want to drag some carefully selected icons from the frontmost Finder window to a folder in a background window. If you can see any part of the background window, you can move it without bringing it to the front by ⌘-dragging the background title bar or window frame. If you're using a system software version earlier than Mac OS 8, you can only drag a window by its title bar (not by its frame).

Copy Fitting

When you copy batches of files from your hard disk to floppies, you must do some arithmetic beforehand so that the Finder won't tell you that there's not enough room on the disk. To have the Finder help you figure out how many files will fit on a floppy, follow these steps:

1. Create a new folder on the hard disk.

   The new folder must be in a window, not directly on the desktop.

2. Use the Finder's Get Info command (⌘-I) to bring up the folder's Info window.

3. Begin dragging files into the folder.

   As you drag, the Finder updates the folder's size in its Info window.

4. When the size approaches 1.4MB for a high-density floppy or 800K for a double-sided floppy, stop dragging files into the folder; the disk will be nearly full.

If the Trash is empty, you can collect items in it instead of a specially created folder. This method has two advantages: You can quickly return all items to their original places by choosing the Put Away command from the File menu (⌘-Y), and you don't have to wait for the Finder to make copies of items that come from several disks. (The Finder doesn't copy items to the Trash, but it must copy items that you drag from one disk to a folder on another disk.) The Get Info command reports the size of the Trash only to the nearest K; however, it gives you the exact number of bytes in a folder.

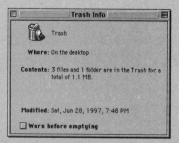

If you have a large hard disk, you may notice some space left over on the floppy disk after you copy the files there. This is because the smallest possible file takes less space on a floppy disk than on a hard disk, and the difference increases as the capacity of the hard disk increases. For example, on a 2GB hard disk each file uses a minimum of 32K and your average error per file copied will be 16K. This can add up pretty quickly. An alternative method that avoids this problem is to use the ShrinkWrap program (described in Chapter 24) to create an unlocked 1400K disk image, mount that on the desktop, and then copy stuff to it. When it's full, you can copy from it to a floppy. The extra copying to and from the disk image doesn't take very long because ShrinkWrap keeps the disk image contents on the hard disk (or in RAM, which is even faster).

Also, you can collapse a window in the background without bringing it to the front by ⌘-double-clicking it. (These tricks only work with background windows that belong to the active application.)

If you've selected some icons to drag to another folder but you discover that you need to scroll a background window to bring the destination folder into view, you won't disturb the selection if you click in the scroll bar or information header areas of the windows. Clicking anywhere else in a window, including the title bar, cancels the selection. This trick doesn't work with Mac OS 8.

When windows open unbidden

Many CD-ROMs are set up to open windows automatically when you insert them. Some of these windows are full of custom icons and can take an inordinately long time to display. To keep windows from opening, simply hold down the Option key while inserting the CD. The same trick works for other types of removable disks.

Expanding multiple folders

You can use keyboard commands to see the contents of multiple folders in a window that's set to list view. Select the folders (press ⌘-A to select all) and press ⌘-right arrow to expand the selected folders and see their contents. To also expand all folders contained in the selected folders, press ⌘-Option-right arrow. Pressing ⌘-left arrow collapses all selected folders, and pressing ⌘-Option-left arrow collapses all selected folders and all folders in them.

Finding empty folders

You can force empty folders to the bottom of a window. With Mac OS 8, just turn on the Calculate Folder Sizes options with the View Options command in the View menu, and then choose the "by Size" item from the Sort List or Arrange submenu of the View menu. With earlier system software versions, use the Views control panel and the Finder's View menu.

If you want to find all the empty folders on your disk, use the Find File program. Set it to find items whose folder attribute is empty. Find File's ability to search for folders that are or are not locked, shared, or empty is not very well known but can be extremely useful. After using Find File to find all shared folders, you can select some or all of the found folders and use Find File's Sharing command to change the access privileges of all the selected folders at once. Figure 25-9 shows the Find File program set to find empty folders.

Figure 25-9: To find empty folders, set up Find File as shown here.

The Trash

This section's tips are all about throwing stuff away and retrieving it from the Trash if you change your mind.

Stop all Trash warnings

The next time you empty the Trash you can skip the standard Trash warning (for example, "The Trash contains 104 items, which use 3.9MB of disk space. Are you sure you want to remove these items permanently?"). First select the Trash icon, and then choose the Get Info command (⌘-I). In the Trash Info dialog box that appears, turn off the "Warn before emptying" option — you'll never see the Trash warning again. Figure 25-10 shows the Trash Info dialog box with the warning option turned off.

Figure 25-10: Use the Get Info command to disable the warning that appears when you empty the Trash.

Discarding locked items

When you use the Empty Trash command, the Finder normally doesn't discard locked items that you dragged to the Trash. Instead of unlocking each locked item with the Finder's Get Info command (⌘-I), you can simply press Option while choosing Empty Trash from the Special menu.

Retrieving Trash

To put items that are currently in the Trash back where they came from, open the Trash, select the items, and choose Put Away (⌘-Y) from the Finder's File menu. The Finder returns each selected item to its previous folder although not necessarily to the same place in the folder window.

Rescuing items

Sometimes, the Trash contains a folder named Rescued Items. This folder usually contains formerly invisible temporary files that were found when you started your computer. The Rescued Items folder may appear after a system crash, and you may be able to recreate your work up to the time of the system crash from the contents of the Rescued Items folder.

Apple Menu

Use the tips in this section to get more organized with the Apple menu.

Apple-menu organization

After you add more than a few items to the Apple Menu, it becomes a mess. You can group different types of items by prefixing different numbers of blank spaces to their names — the more blank spaces, the higher on the Apple menu.

Prefixing a name with (Control-T in the Chicago or Charcoal fonts) or a ◆ (Control-S) makes the name appear below names that are prefixed with a space but above names that have no prefixes. To make items appear at the bottom of the Apple menu, prefix them with a ◊ (Option-Shift-V) or • (Option-8).

If you have a hard time remembering what all the special symbol keyboard commands are, try Günther Blaschek's excellent shareware program PopChar Lite (or PopChar Pro), which automatically pops up a list of all letters, numbers, and symbols available in the current font when you move the pointer to a pre-designated hot spot.

Fast Apple-menu changes

To add or remove Apple-menu items quickly, list the Apple Menu Items folder in the Apple menu. How? Make an alias of the Apple Menu Items folder and put the alias in that folder.

Apple-menu separators

A long Apple menu — even one that's organized by type of item as described previously — can be hard to scan quickly. Visually separating the different types of items helps.

You can make a separator by making an alias of anything and giving the alias a name composed of hyphens. Prefix the name with blank spaces so it comes alphabetically where you want it in the Apple menu. An alias of the Finder works well as a separator because accidentally opening it (by choosing it from the Apple menu) results in a message saying the item can't be opened. You also can use ordinary folders instead of aliases to create separators in the Apple menu.

To further refine your Apple menu, you can hide the icons of the separators that you make using the method described in the "Desktop by name" tip in the "Desktop and Startup" section earlier in this chapter.

Too-full Apple menu

If your Apple menu contains so many items that you must scroll to see them all, consider organizing them in folders within the Apple Menu Items folder. The contents of each folder appear in hierarchical submenus if the Submenus option is turned on in the Apple Menu Options control panel. Figure 25-11 shows an example of Apple-menu subfolders.

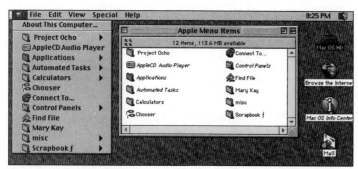

Figure 25-11: Keep your Apple menu short by putting items in folders inside the Apple Menu Items folder.

Universal Show Clipboard

Some application programs lack a Show Clipboard command; others that do have such a command use a private Clipboard whose contents may look different when pasted into another program. Put a Show Clipboard command in your Apple menu and then use the command to review the standard Clipboard contents from any application program.

First, make an alias of the Clipboard file, which is in the System Folder. Then place the alias in the Apple Menu Items folder and rename the alias Show Clipboard. Now choose Show Clipboard from the Apple menu; your computer switches to the Finder and opens the Clipboard.

The Non-ABCs Approach to Arranging Menu Items

Forcibly reordering items in the Apple menu by placing spaces or special symbols at the beginning of the items' names has side effects that you may not like. The spaces or symbols visibly alter the names, and they conspicuously shift the names to the right. To invisibly force the order you want, follow these steps:

1. Open the Note Pad or a new document in SimpleText or a word processor.

2. Press Return to create a blank line, select the blank line, and copy it to the Clipboard.

3. Switch to the Finder.

4. In the Apple Menu Items folder, select the name of the item that you want to appear at the top of the Apple menu.

5. Press the up-arrow key to move the insertion point to the beginning of the selected name and then paste.

6. The entire name goes blank, but don't fret — just press Return or click outside the name, and the name springs back into view.

    The renamed item jumps to the top of the window if you're viewing by list. To increase an item's alphabetic buoyancy, paste the blank line two or more times at the beginning of the item's name.

Caution: Some programs don't work properly with documents or folders whose names contain blank lines. If you have trouble after pasting a blank line into the name of a file or folder, remove the item from the Apple Menu Items folder and replace it with an alias, then try this naming trick on the alias.

Invisible file aliases

Do you crave the convenience of accessing items stored in the invisible Desktop Folder from the Apple Menu? Because the Desktop Folder *is* invisible, alias-creating utilities are of no help.

STEP-BY-STEP

Hierarchical Information Manager

You can turn your Apple menu into a contact database. By treating folder names as single-line entries in a database, you easily can create an elegant hierarchical database of often-used addresses, phone numbers, client contacts, and other information that you are tired of fumbling for on your crowded desktop or hard disk.

You can access the data instantly from the Apple menu and its submenus, and view the data by traversing the menu structure without actually choosing any menu item. (When you finish viewing the data, just drag the mouse pointer away from the menus and release the mouse.) For a persistent display, choose the menu item whose submenu contains the data that you want to see; the Finder opens the folder that contains the data.

Adding, deleting, and modifying data is a snap. Follow these steps:

1. Choose the menu item whose submenu you want to change and open the folder in which you need to make changes.

2. To add a line of data, use the Finder's New Folder command (⌘-N) and type the data as the new folder's name (up to 31 characters).

3. To change data, edit the corresponding folder names.

4. To remove a line of data, drag corresponding folders to the Trash.

5. To add a submenu, open a folder and add folders to it.

Because items appear alphabetically by name in the submenus, you may have to put extra spaces or other special characters at the beginning of folder names to arrange the names in the order you want. (You usually have to do this with a multiple-line address, for example.)

Another neat trick: Use aliases to duplicate data if you want that data to appear in several places in the database. After making an alias of the folder that you want to clone, simply drag the alias to the folder that represents another location in the database where you want the information to appear. Cloned parts of your hierarchical database stay up to date, because aliases don't contain any duplicate data that can get out of sync; the aliases simply point to the folders that contain the actual data.

No matter how large your database of folders becomes, the Finder always calculates its size on disk as zero K! Yes, this *is* too good to be true. In fact, your data, consisting only of nested named folders, is kept in the startup disk's invisible catalog file, which contains information about the hierarchical organization of fields and folders on that disk. The Finder reports only the sizes of aliases and other actual files that you may have in your hierarchical folders.

Keeping contact information in a hierarchical Apple menu has two advantages over using contact-database software such as Now Contact: You can always locate your contacts without opening (or keeping open) another program, and you can find any contact quickly without typing or even remembering a name. Managing hundreds of contacts is easier with contact-database software, though.

The trick is to access your computer via file sharing. When you access your computer from another machine via file sharing, the Desktop Folder becomes visible at the root level of your hard disk. Create an alias of the Desktop Folder (be sure to lock that Desktop Folder alias in its Info window to prevent it from becoming invisible) and transfer the alias to your computer. If you're using Mac OS 7.6.1 or earlier, don't try to find the original item of a Desktop Folder alias by clicking the Find Original button in the alias's Info window unless you want to crash your system. Using the Show Original command in Mac OS 8 does not seem to cause a crash.

If your computer isn't on a network, you'll have to borrow a computer and temporarily network it to your computer by connecting the two computer's printer ports with LocalTalk connectors or a serial printer cable. Alternatively, you can buy a disk utility such as File Buddy (described in Chapter 24) to make an alias of the invisible Desktop Folder.

Apple menu options

If you use the Apple Menu Options control panel to list recently used documents, applications, and servers but don't necessarily want all three submenus active, set the number to zero in the Apple Menu Options control panel for those submenus you don't want to activate. The items with a zero value disappear.

Fonts

This section deals with tips on working with and modifying the System Folder's Fonts folder. When making changes to the Fonts folder, keep in mind that any fonts you add aren't available to open programs until you have quit them and opened them again. Moreover, you must quit all open programs before removing fonts from the Fonts folder.

Duplicating fonts

Because you can't rename individual fixed-size or TrueType fonts with the Finder, you can't duplicate them in the same folder (you can't have two items with the same name in the same folder). However, you can rename or duplicate PostScript fonts and font suitcases.

To duplicate a fixed-size or TrueType font, press Option and then drag the font to another folder or to the desktop. (Dragging to another disk automatically makes a copy of the font on the target disk.)

You can create a new, empty font-suitcase file by duplicating an existing font suitcase file, opening the duplicate, and dragging its contents to the Trash. Figure 25-12 shows a duplicated font suitcase.

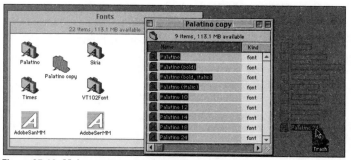

Figure 25-12: Make a new, empty font suitcase by duplicating an existing font suitcase and dragging its contents to the Trash.

Personalized Sample Text

You don't have to read about "cozy lummoxes" in their "job pens" (or "razorback frogs and piqued gymnasts" if you use Mac OS 7.6.1 or earlier) when you open a TrueType or fixed-size font file in the Finder. Use ResEdit to change the sample text as follows:

1. Open your System Folder, and press Option as you drag a copy of the Finder to the desktop.

2. Open this duplicate Finder with ResEdit.

3. Open the Finder's STR# resource icon, and then open the STR# resource whose ID is 5816. With System 7.5–Mac OS 7.6.1, open STR# resource ID 14516.

   A window appears that displays the sample text.

4. Edit the text to your liking.

5. Quit ResEdit, answering Yes when you are asked whether you want to save your changes.

6. Drag the original Finder from your System Folder to a folder outside the System Folder, and drag the modified Finder from the desktop to the System Folder.

7. Restart your computer, and test the results of your modifications.

Deleting a damaged font

If you somehow manage to damage a font suitcase, you may not be able to delete it simply by opening the Fonts folder and dragging the suitcase to the Trash. Try dragging the Fonts folder from the System Folder to the desktop first. Then open the Fonts folder and drag the damaged suitcase to the Trash. Empty the

Trash, and put the Fonts folder back in your System Folder. If you can't drag the damaged suitcase to the Trash, try this: With your original Fonts folder still sitting on the desktop, create a new folder named Fonts inside the System Folder. Drag everything except the damaged suitcase from the old Fonts folder (on the desktop) to the new Fonts folder. Restart the computer and then drag the old Fonts folder (which still contains the damaged suitcase) to the Trash.

Summary

In this chapter, you learned some tips for the desktop, and how to organize the Mac OS virtual desktop for better efficiency. You also learned that you don't have to use the same, boring (even if they are 3-D) icons everybody else uses. Customizing icons, either by altering the default icon, using a custom icon, or removing the icon completely is easy with ResEdit.

In this chapter, you picked up some tips on enlivening the startup process. You can change the look of your startup screen. You can also have your computer play a QuickTime movie, display a message, or a play a sound during startup.

This chapter also gave you several ideas for working with folders and windows. You can lock folders with the Sharing command. You can also scroll windows without using the scroll bars and move background windows without making them active. You can also prevent windows from opening automatically when you insert a CD-ROM. In addition, you can use the View menu to spot empty folders.

You also got some tips on working with the Trash. You can stop Trash warnings with the Get Info command, and you can remove locked items by pressing the Option key. And the Put Away command makes it easy to retrieve items from the Trash.

This chapter gave you some tips for organizing your Apple and some ideas for adding items to it. You can change the order of items by prefixing their names with blank space and other special characters. You can separate items in the Apple menu with dashed lines that you make from aliases. You can add a universal Show Clipboard command to the Apple menu, and you can access the entire contents of your desktop from the Apple menu.

Finally, this chapter told you how to create new font suitcases and how to delete damaged font suitcases.

CHAPTER TWENTY-SIX

Discover More Tips and Secrets

This second chapter of tips and tricks covers shortcuts and productivity boosters for your system in general: Open and Save dialog boxes, file sharing, Mac OS extensions and control panels, using the Mac OS with your applications, and memory and performance issues. Finally, the tips section ends with a few of Mac OS 8's "Easter eggs."

Open and Save dialog Boxes

The tips in this section will help you zoom through the dialog boxes that appear when you choose Open, Save, Save As, and other disk-related commands.

Find an alias's original item

You can go quickly to an alias's original item in an Open and Save dialog box by pressing Option while opening the alias (by double-clicking it, for example). Alias names appear in italics in Open and Save dialog boxes, just as they do in Finder windows.

Folder switching

If you find that you frequently go back and forth between two folders, put an alias of each folder in the other. Whichever folder you are in, you can go to the other in one step by opening its alias.

Aliases for favorite folders

Putting aliases of your favorite folders on the desktop or inside disk windows enables you to open a favorite folder quickly from an Open and Save dialog box. Instead of working your way down through one branch of your folder structure and then working you way up another branch to the folder that you want, you zip to the desktop level or the disk level, and then open the alias of the folder that you want. This process is like jumping from one branch of a tree to the root level and then jumping to a spot on another branch without crawling up the trunk and along the other branch.

You can get to aliases of favorite folders on the desktop quickly by clicking the desktop button. Get to aliases at the disk-window level by choosing the disk from the dialog box's pop-up menu.

Sidestepping a double-click

As usual, you can open an item in the directory window by double-clicking it. If, before you release the mouse button, you realize that you double-clicked the wrong item, continue holding down the mouse button and drag the pointer to the item that you want to open. When you release the mouse button, the currently selected item opens.

Canceling a double-click

To cancel a double-click in an Open and Save dialog box, hold down the mouse button on the second click and drag the pointer outside the dialog box before releasing the mouse button.

Server access from the Save dialog box

Don't you hate it when you get into a Save dialog box only to find that you aren't connected to the server volume you want to save to? Just make an alias of the Recent Servers folder and put it on the desktop. Now you can connect to any server in that folder by opening the server in a Save dialog box. Beats a trip to the Chooser any day. (If you don't have an alias of the Recent Servers folder on the desktop, you can open the folder from the Apple Menu Items folder. Still beats a trip to the Chooser.) Figure 26-1 shows an example of getting to the server via an alias in the Save dialog box.

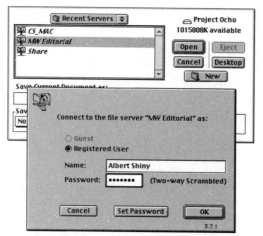

Figure 26-1: Save yourself a trip to the Chooser by placing an alias of the Recent Servers folder on the desktop.

File Sharing and Networking

This section describes tips for easier networking, plus ins and outs for file sharing under Mac OS 8.

Reducing network cabling costs

For a less expensive network, use Farallon's PhoneNet connectors (510-814-5100, http://www.farallon.com) or the equivalent and ordinary telephone cables instead of Apple's LocalTalk connectors and cables. Not only does PhoneNet cost less, but it also works with greater cable lengths than LocalTalk connectors do.

Picking a secure password

Pick a password that is easy for you to remember but difficult for other people to guess. For better security, mix letters with numbers; try replacing the letters *I* and *O* with the numbers 1 and 0. Don't use birthdates, anniversaries, or family members' names.

Want to make sure you haven't chosen a too-obvious password? Ask a good friend, relative, or coworker to play spy: have them try to guess your password, writing down their guesses on a piece of paper. If your password is on the list, or is very similar to one on the list, choose a less-obvious password.

Sharing disks or outer folders

When you share a folder, Mac OS 8 won't let you share the outer folder or the disk that contains it. You have to drag the shared folder to another place or unshare it before you can share the outer folder or disk. To avoid this situation, share from the highest level of your disk and folder structure.

Improved file-sharing performance

For best performance of your computer, share as few of your folders as possible. The more items that others can access on your computer, the greater the demands on your computer's performance. Sharing too many folders can slow your system to a crawl. When you need to share numerous files or to share a folder simultaneously with several users, consider setting up a dedicated computer to act as a centralized file server for the shared information. (A great way to recycle older computers.)

Cutting file-sharing red tape

Getting access to shared items involves wading through a fair amount of Chooser-related bureaucracy. Aliases cut through the red tape.

First, access a shared disk or folder one time, using the Chooser. Next, select the shared item, or any folder or file in it; then choose Make Alias from the File menu (⌘-M). Finally, copy the alias to your desktop or hard disk. An alias keeps track of its original item even if the original item is on another networked computer.

After you make an alias of a shared item, you can access the shared items by opening the alias either from the Finder or from an Open command's dialog box. Dragging something to the alias of a shared disk or folder also accesses that shared item automatically. You still must enter a password unless you initially accessed the original item as a guest. If the shared item is not available (when, for example, the computer where the item resides is turned off), a message tells you so.

Office on a disk

Because aliases can give you nearly automatic access to items on a networked computer via file sharing, take the previous tip a step further.

To access files on your computer from another computer on the network, open the File Sharing control panel or Sharing Setup control panel, whichever you have, and check the status of File Sharing. If File Sharing is off, click the Start button and wait until it is on (the Start button changes into a Stop button).

Next, select all your hard-disk icons and choose Sharing from the File menu to open a sharing window for each disk. In each window, turn on the "Share this item and its contents" option. Also set the privileges for the User/Group and Everyone categories to None. (If you're using Mac OS 7.6.1 or earlier, turn off the See Folders, See Files, and Make Changes options for User/Group and Everyone.) These settings restrict access to your disks so that only you can make changes or see files or folders. Make an alias of each disk on your computer's desktop, copy the aliases to a floppy disk, and lock the floppy.

As long as file sharing is active on your computer, you can use that floppy disk to access your hard disk from any other computer on your network. Simply insert the disk, open the alias for the disk that you want to use, and enter your password when asked. Correctly entering your password gives you access to all applications, folders, and documents on your disk from any remote Mac OS computer. You don't have to bother with opening the Chooser, selecting AppleShare, selecting your computer, and typing your name as the registered user.

What people have trashed

Items from your shared disk or folder that someone has dragged to the Trash — but not yet permanently removed — on another computer do not appear in your Trash. Mac OS 8 puts those items in folders whose names begin Trash Can #. You cannot see these folders with the Finder because they are in an invisible folder inside the shared folder or disk. To see the Trash Can # folders, use a utility program such as Norton Utilities for Macintosh from Symantec (408-253-9600, http://www.symantec.com) or File Buddy (described in Chapter 24).

Trouble renaming hard disks

Are you stymied because you're unable to change the name of your computer's hard disk? Make sure file sharing is turned off in the File Sharing control panel or the Sharing Setup control panel, whichever you have. While file sharing is on, you can't change the name or icon of an item that's available for network access.

Server log-in shortcuts

When connecting to an AppleShare server or a file-sharing server through the Chooser, you can press ⌘-R for Registered User or ⌘-G for Guest. By eliminating an extra trip to the mouse, this shortcut is especially nice for keyboard-oriented folks.

Extensions, Control Panels, and Accessories

This section includes the what, where, and why of extensions and control panels, along with tips on how to get the most out of them.

Scripted Calculator

You can copy the text of a calculation — for example, 69.65+26.98+14.99*.0725 — and paste it into the standard Calculator control panel. Be sure to use the asterisk symbol (*) for multiplication and the slash (/) symbol for division.

Alternative Scrapbooks and Note Pads

After extensive use, your Scrapbook may become cluttered with old clippings. If you can't bear to throw them out, make a copy of the Scrapbook File in your System Folder (use the Finder's Duplicate command) before you start weeding. Later, you can use the old copy that you made by double-clicking it.

In fact, you can extend this idea to make any number of Scrapbook Files that you keep in a folder somewhere (perhaps in the Apple menu). Naturally, you'll have to give each file in the folder a unique name. To make an empty Scrapbook File, just duplicate an existing Scrapbook File, open the duplicate, and delete everything in it.

The same technique works with the Note Pad file, which is also located in the System Folder. You can make copies of it, rename the copies, and keep them in any folder. To open a copy, double-click it or put it in the Apple menu and choose it from there.

The Note Pad and Scrapbook can only have one file open at a time. If you open a Note Pad file while the Note Pad is already open, or open a Scrapbook File while the Scrapbook is already open, the currently open file closes automatically.

Easy Access shortcuts

Instead of using the Easy Access control panel to turn Mouse Keys, Slow Keys, or Sticky Keys on and off, you can use the keyboard. (To get Easy Access, you must do a custom installation of the system software, as described in Chapters 28 and 29.)

Mouse Keys allows control of the pointer from the keyboard. To turn Mouse Keys on or off, press ⌘-Shift-Clear. Mouse Keys requires a numeric keypad to work.

Slow Keys guards against accidental keystrokes by requiring that a key be held down for a second or two before the keystroke is entered. To turn Slow Keys on or off, hold down the Return key for about 10 seconds. After 5 seconds you'll hear a beep; 5 seconds after that you'll hear an ascending tone (on) or a descending tone (off).

Sticky Keys lets you type keyboard combinations such as ⌘-S one key at a time. To turn Sticky Keys on or off, press the Shift key five times in a row without moving the pointer.

Big Map

You can enlarge the world map in the Map control panel by pressing Option while opening the control panel. To magnify more, press Shift-Option while opening the map. Figure 26-2 shows the world map at various sizes.

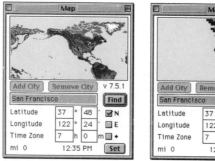

Figure 26-2: You can zoom in on the Map control panel to get more detail (sort of).

Color Map

If you use System 7.5.5 or earlier, your Map control panel may display a black-and-white world map on your color or grayscale monitor. You can colorize the map. First, look, through your Scrapbook for a color version of the world map used in the Map control panel. If you find one, copy it, open the Map control panel, and paste.

If you tossed your color map picture from your Scrapbook, you can get it by reinstalling the Scrapbook from your system disks or CD. Temporarily move your current Scrapbook File from you system folder to the desktop. Next, do a custom installation of the system software, selecting Scrapbook in the Apple Menu section of the Install System Software window (see Chapters 28–30 for detailed instructions on doing a custom installation). This should install a new

Scrapbook File. Open the new Scrapbook File. Copy and paste the color map as described in the previous paragraph. Finally, select the Scrapbook File on the desktop, choose Put Away from the Finder's file menu, and click OK when the Finder asks whether it's OK to replace the Scrapbook File in the system folder with the one that you're moving (putting away) from the desktop.

Time zone tracking

If you regularly contact people in multiple time zones, you can use the Map control panel to keep track of local times for those people. With the Map control panel open, type the name of the city and click the Find button. Then type the person's name over the city name and click the Add City button. Now you need only type a person's name in Map and click the Find button to find his or her time zone.

If you want Map to remember a person whose city isn't on the map, you can substitute a known city in the same time zone or add the unknown city. Whenever you add a new place or person to Map, verify the time zone and correct it, if necessary.

Hidden free beep

The Scrapbook includes an extra system alert sound that you can paste into the Alert Sounds section of the Sound control panel. If the Sound control panel is not in your Control Panels folder, you'll find it in the Apple Extras folder on your startup disk. You can't paste alert sounds into the Monitors & Sound control panel, which replaces the Sound control panel in the Control Panels folder with Mac OS 8.

If you threw away the extra system alert, you can get it by installing a new copy of the Scrapbook file. For instructions on getting the standard Scrapbook File, refer to "Color Map" earlier in this section.

Find file improvements

By pressing one key you can extend Mac OS 8's Find File window to find files and folders that are invisible, have custom icons, contain text you specify, or have names and icons that can't be changed. You expand the leftmost pop-up menu in the Find File window (which defaults to "name") to include these four additional choices by pressing the Option key when you first click the pop-up. Figure 26-3 shows these additional Find File search criteria at the bottom of the pop-up menu.

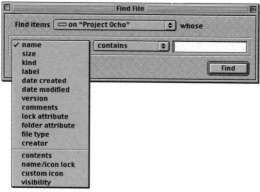

Figure 26-3: Reveal four hidden search criteria by Option-clicking the leftmost pop-up menu in Find File.

Virtual memory turn-off

Instead of opening the Memory control panel on those occasions when you need to turn virtual memory on or off, restart your computer while holding down the ⌘ key. Holding down the ⌘ key at startup automatically disables virtual memory; restarting without pressing ⌘ restores virtual memory to its previous settings. Holding down the Shift key during startup also disables virtual memory along with all extensions, whereas ⌘ does not disable all extensions. However, some third-party extensions or control panels may be disabled individually by a ⌘ key restart. If you have a startup file that's sensitive to the ⌘ key, check its documentation or Read Me files to see if you can change the key that acts as a disabler during startup.

Stuck in the past

If your Time and Date control panel insists that it's really 1956, you aren't stuck in a time warp — you just need to replace the lithium battery on the system board. When the computer is off, the battery keeps the clock ticking and powers the parameter RAM (PRAM), which stores settings for many control panels, including Mouse, Keyboard, and Startup Disk. You could get the battery from an Apple dealer and replace it yourself, but you should consider having a technician do the work because the system board can easily be damaged by static electricity or incorrect handling.

Batch copy or delete

Have you ever heard this jibe from a Windows user? "At least in Windows you can delete or copy a batch of files by typing a command such as Copy C:\draw*.eps D:." Ever since System 7.5, Mac OS users have had the same functionality through Find File. Use Find File to find a batch of files from multiple folders on one disk or on multiple disks. You can then select all or any part of the found items and drag the batch from the Find File window to the Trash or to any disk or folder.

Timeless

Sometimes when you're on a deadline, the last thing you want to know is the date and time. Instead of going to the Date & Time control panel to shut off the menu-bar clock, Option-click the clock and it disappears. It reappears if you Option-click the space again.

Close a Stickies note without warning

When you click a Stickies note close box, a dialog box pops up asking you to confirm that you want the note deleted. To skip the warning, Control-click the note's close box.

Autoclosing Find File

You can quit Find File while opening a found item by holding down the Option key and double-clicking the item in Find File's Items Found window. This trick saves you the trouble of reactivating Find File in order to quit it. The Option-key shortcut also works with Find File's Get Info, Sharing, Open Enclosing Item, and Print commands.

PowerBook airport security

When you take a PowerBook through airport security and are asked to turn it on, the last thing you want to do is wait through a lengthy start-up. Waking a sleeping PowerBook is fast enough, but who wants to waste battery power while the PowerBook sleeps through check-in? Instead, use the Password Security control panel. The Password Security dialog box comes up quickly on start-up and proves that you have a computer, not a bomb. Then press the Cancel button to shut down quickly so you can make your plane. Whatever you do, don't forget your password, because you can't bypass the Password Security dialog box by starting up with the Shift key pressed or by starting up from a Disk Tools floppy disk — the password control is handled at the disk-driver level. You'll have to take your PowerBook with proof of purchase to an authorized service center, where a technician can bypass the security dialog box.

If you have an older-model PowerBook, you can't use the Password Security control panel. In this case, either hold down the Shift key for a fast startup at the airport, or download one of the many quick-start extensions available online. John Bullock's Scout's Honour, John Bascombe's Airport Quickstart, and Jon

Wind's Zorba are all freeware extensions designed to provide quick start-up and shutdown for airport security agents. And they work on any model PowerBook.

Note Pad notetaker

The next time you need to look through a plain text document — especially if you want to find specific text in it — try the Note Pad. Although the Note Pad has no Open command in its File menu, it can display the contents of a plain text document, including SimpleText documents and text clipping files. To view a text file, you simply drag its icon to the open Note Pad. Even better reasons for using the Note Pad are that it opens instantly and ordinarily uses less than half the memory of SimpleText and other text editors such as BBEdit Lite and Tex-Edit Plus. Moreover, the Note Pad can search read-only SimpleText documents (the kind with a "newspaper" icon), which SimpleText itself can't do.

Audio CD AutoPlay

With QuickTime 2.5, which installs as part of Mac OS 8, you can have your computer automatically play an audio CD not only during startup (by placing an alias of Track 1 from any audio CD into the Startup Items folder) but any time you insert an audio CD into the CD-ROM drive. Turn on the Enable Audio CD AutoPlay option in the AutoPlay section of the QuickTime Settings control panel. This feature starts playing the CD earlier during start-up than the Startup Items method and doesn't require the AppleCD Audio Player application. You have to open that application or its equivalent if you want to control playback of an autoplaying CD while it's playing. Your computer may handle playthrough automatically; if it doesn't, you must click the Sound button in the Monitors & Sound control panel, then change the Sound Input from its default (microphone) to Internal CD. Figure 26-4 shows the QuickTime Settings and Monitors & Sound control panels.

Turn on this option

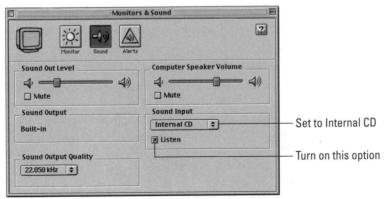

Figure 26-4: Set your computer to automatically play an audio CD inserted in the CD-ROM drive.

STEP-BY-STEP

Audio-Only QuickTime Movies

It's easy to record a passage from an audio CD as a sound file — the QuickTime system extension makes it possible. (Keep in mind that many uses of sounds copied from a CD constitute a violation of copyright law unless you first obtain permission from the copyright holder.) You just need SimpleText and an audio CD. Then follow these steps to record the CD passage:

1. Insert the audio CD you want to use for your clip.

2. Open SimpleText and choose Open from SimpleText's File menu (⌘-O).

3. In the Open dialog box that appears, open the audio CD, select the track you want to record, and click the Convert button to bring up a Save dialog box.

4. In the Save dialog box, name the sound-only movie and select a folder location for it.

5. Still in the Save dialog box, click the Options button to bring up QuickTime's Audio CD Import Options dialog box. Adjust the slider controls to specify which part of the audio track to include, set the sound-quality options, and close the Audio CD Import Options dialog box. The following figure shows this dialog box.

6. Back in the Save dialog box, click the Save button.

   QuickTime copies the audio data from the CD to the movie file. The following figure shows an example of an audio-only movie open in Simple Text and the movie file's icon in the Finder.

(continued)

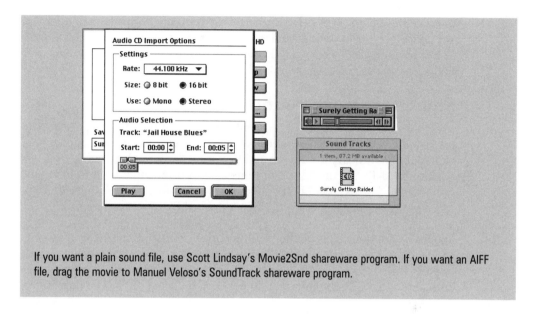

If you want a plain sound file, use Scott Lindsay's Movie2Snd shareware program. If you want an AIFF file, drag the movie to Manuel Veloso's SoundTrack shareware program.

Applications

In this section, you'll find tips for using Mac OS 8 features while working with your applications.

Canceling an opening

If you have really fast fingers, you can cancel the accidental opening of an application. You must press ⌘-period within a few seconds of opening the application.

Hiding windows while switching

To hide the active program's windows as you switch to a particular program, press Option while choosing the other program from the Application menu, or press Option while clicking another program's window. You hide windows and switch to the Finder by pressing Option while clicking the desktop or a Finder icon.

Hide windows to boost performance

When you have several programs open, you can spend a great deal of time waiting while inactive programs redraw portions of their windows as dialog boxes come and go. This delay is particularly protracted when you're using virtual memory, because the window redrawing may require disk access. Eliminate the delay by choosing Hide Others from the Application menu. Hidden windows don't require updating.

Stationery workaround

With Mac OS 7.6.1 and earlier, you can work around the Finder's prompt to name and save a new document every time you open a particular stationery pad. Make an ordinary document, and lock it by using the Finder's Get Info command (⌘-I). You don't have to name a new document created from a stationery pad of an application that knows how to open stationery itself. And Mac OS 8 always names a new document created from a stationery pad.

You may want to use this method with templates for printing single envelopes and mailing labels, for example. Then you can open the locked template, type or paste the recipient's address, print, and close without saving. (This method does not work with programs that do not permit changes in locked documents.)

Fix unreadable floppies

Getting the dreaded message "This disk is unreadable by this Macintosh. Do you want to initialize the disk?" after inserting a once-good floppy disk? Possibly the floppy was formatted or written on a different computer, or is an old archive disk with essential data. A trick with the Disk First Aid utility works in most cases to read and repair floppies that have become unreadable. Disk First Aid is included with the Mac OS installation software.

When you get "This disk is unreadable" message, immediately eject the disk and open Disk First Aid. With Disk First Aid as the active application, insert the problem floppy again. In Disk First Aid's window, select the floppy's icon and click the Verify button. When Disk First Aid finishes verification, it should tell you the disk needs repairs. Click the Repair button, and when Disk First Aid finishes, it will probably tell you that it successfully repaired the disk.

This trick works only if you insert the floppy while Disk First Aid is the active application and if you have it verify before you have it repair. If you skip the verify step, the repair step ends unsuccessfully.

Placing Graphics in SimpleText

How do people get graphics into a Read Me file or other SimpleText document, and how do they give it the special newspaper-style icon that designates a read-only SimpleText document? As you may know, the obvious methods — pasting graphics into the text and locking the file with the Finder's Get Info command — don't work. You need a secret keystroke and a resource editor such as Apple's ResEdit. Here is the procedure:

1. Open the SimpleText document you want to enrich with graphics. Place the insertion point wherever you want to insert a graphic, and type Option-spacebar, followed by several blank lines to leave space for the graphic. (The number of lines isn't critical; you can adjust it later.)

2. Paste the graphics into the Scrapbook.

3. Use ResEdit to open a copy of the SimpleText document.

   If ResEdit tells you that opening the document will add a resource fork (where SimpleText stores graphics) and asks if you want to do that, answer OK. (If ResEdit doesn't ask about adding a resource fork, then the document already has one.)

4. One by one, in the order of their intended appearance, copy each graphic from the Scrapbook and paste it into the SimpleText document's ResEdit window.

(continued)

(continued)

When you paste the first graphic, a PICT resources icon appears in the window.

5. Open the PICT resources to see the individual PICT graphics you pasted. Select each graphic and choose Get Resource Info from ResEdit's Resource menu (or press ⌘-I). In the Resource Info window that appears, change the ID number. Make the ID number 1000 for the graphic you want placed first, 1001 for the graphic to be placed second, and so on.

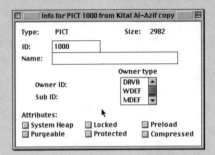

6. Close all the ResEdit windows, saving changes when asked.

7. Open the edited document file using SimpleText.

You should see a graphic in each place you inserted an Option-space. The graphics are always centered in the document window. If a graphic overlaps text, simply add blank lines for additional space.

Sometimes graphics seem to vanish after you add or remove a line. To display the images, scroll the document or collapse and expand the window to refresh it.

8. To prevent other people from changing the document and give it the newspaper-style icon, close it and use ResEdit's Get File/Folder Info command to change the document type to ttro.

Cookie blocker

Web-browser "cookies" are files created by browsers and placed in your Preferences folder in the System Folder. Each cookie contains information about how you access a particular Web site. The server for that site generally uses the cookie information to help you access the site, but you never really know what's in a cookie or how it's used. If the unknown and intrusive aspects of cookies bother you enough to forgo their benefit, you can block them. Because a folder can't replace a file, and vice versa, the easiest way to eliminate a cookie is to copy the name of the cookie file (MagicCookie in Netscape Navigator; cookies.txt in Internet Explorer), delete the file, make a new folder in the same place, and rename the folder by pasting the copied name.

Memory and Performance

The tips in this section help you make the most of your computer's memory and increase its performance.

Quitting startup programs

If you have several programs opening during startup, you may have to quit some of them later to free memory for opening another program. Naturally, you want to quit the programs that are the least important to you. You'll get maximum benefit from quitting those programs if they were the last items opened during startup. To make that happen, rename the items in your Startup Items folder so that the most important item comes first alphabetically, the next most important comes second, and so on. Better yet, you can avoid renaming original items by placing aliases in the Startup Items folder.

Reducing system memory size

You can reduce the system software's memory size (as reported by the About This Computer menu item or the About This Macintosh menu item in the Apple menu) to its minimum by pressing Shift while restarting your computer. Look for the message "Extensions Off" during startup. This message confirms that you have suppressed loading of all items in the Extensions folder, the Control Panels folder, and the System Folder that would increase the system software's memory size. You have also bypassed opening items in the Startup Items folder, reduced the RAM cache to 16K, forced virtual memory off, and prevented file sharing from starting.

None of these changes persists when you restart without pressing Shift. To make persistent changes, you must disable items with the Extensions Manager control panel (or drag items out of the special folders) and then change settings in the Memory and File Sharing control panels.

You can also save memory by turning off file sharing if you're not using it. Reducing the RAM cache size reduces the system software's memory size K for K — but slows system performance.

An Extra Maintenance Disk

If you want to fix or optimize your only hard disk with a utility program that can't be run from the disk it's fixing (and the program won't fit on a floppy, and you don't have a high-capacity removable disk such as a Zip disk), use a RAM disk as follows:

1. Use the Memory control panel to create a RAM disk just the size of the application you need to use. After you restart the computer, the RAM disk will use part of the computer's RAM as if it were a disk.

2. Restart, copy the utility program you need from the hard disk to the RAM disk, and open the program from the RAM disk.

3. If you can't work on your hard disk because it's the startup disk, restart from a Mac OS installation CD.

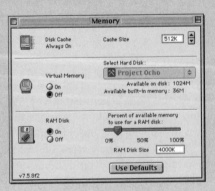

Fragmented memory

To check for fragmented memory, add up the memory sizes of all the open programs and the system software as listed in the About This Computer or About This Macintosh window, and subtract the total from the total memory reported there. Also subtract 300K to 600K (depending on monitor resolution and number of colors) if your Mac has built-in video (doesn't use a display adapter card) and doesn't have VRAM (video RAM) that's separate from the main RAM, sometimes called DRAM (dynamic RAM). Examples of Macs in that category include a Power Mac 6100, 7100, or 8100 with a monitor connected to the system board video port. If the number you come up with is substantially less than the largest unused block, your unused memory is probably fragmented into two or more blocks.

To consolidate fragmented memory, quit all open programs and then open them again. Restarting your computer also fixes fragmentation and may reduce the amount of memory used by system software as well.

You can avoid memory fragmentation by planning the order in which you open and quit programs (see "Quitting startup programs" earlier in this section). First, open the programs that you're least likely to quit first; and last, open the programs that you're most likely to quit last. When you need more memory to open another program, quit the most-recently opened program. If that doesn't free enough memory, quit the next most recently opened program, and so on. This method frees a contiguous chunk of memory. Quitting programs helter-skelter leads to memory fragmentation.

Best partition sizes

If you work with many small files, you can save a significant amount of disk space by partitioning a large hard disk into several smaller volumes. The Mac OS file system allocates a minimum amount of disk space for each file, regardless of its actual contents. The minimum file size for a particular disk is set when it is formatted (or when it is partitioned, if it has multiple partitions) and increases incrementally as disk (or partition) capacity increases. For example, a short memo that takes up 16.5K on a 1GB hard disk would take only 4K on a 230MB partition, saving 12K per small file.

Most formatting programs set a minimum file size of 4K on disks with capacities between 224MB and 255MB, 8K on disks with capacities between 480MB and 511MB, 16K on disks between 992MB and 1023MB, and so on.

If you work mostly with large files, large volumes are more efficient.

Shortcuts to sleep

A computer that's capable of sleep will go to sleep from a number of shortcuts other than the Sleep command in the Finder's Special menu or the Control Strip:

❖ Press the power key to bring up the Restart/Sleep/Shut Down alert box and click the Sleep button. This method requires System 7.5.1 or later.

❖ Control-click the menu-bar battery icon to put the PowerBook in sleep mode. The battery icon is a feature of the menu-bar clock, which you set up with the Date & Time control panel. This method does not work with Mac OS 8.

❖ Press ⌘-Shift-0 (zero) if you're more of a keyboard person and use Mac OS 7.6.1 or earlier.

❖ Press ⌘-Option-Power with System 7.5.1 or later.

Sleeping desktop computers

Some Macs can't be put to sleep with the Energy Saver or PowerBook control panels. If you have one of these Macs, you can use the shareware control panel Sleeper from St. Clair Software to make some parts of your system sleep. Sleeper spins down hard disks and dims the display after periods of inactivity. You can use Sleeper's screen dimming in conjunction with another control panel that reduces power on an Energy Star monitor, such as Apple's Energy Saver control panel, and you can have Sleeper bring up a screen saver, such as After Dark, instead of dimming the display. Sleeper does not affect CD-ROM drives, tape drives, or the processor and other system-board circuitry, all of which remain fully active.

RAM disks

You can speed up surfing the Internet's World Wide Web by putting your Web browser program's disk cache on a relatively small RAM disk. With its cache on a RAM disk, the Web browser reloads pages it has saved to the cache more quickly, accesses the hard disk less frequently, and cleans up its cache almost instantaneously. To get set up, use the Memory control panel to create a RAM disk of 1MB to 5MB. After restarting to mount the RAM disk, set the Web browser to use the RAM disk for its cache. For example, in Netscape Navigator 3.01 (the version that comes with Mac OS 8), you make this setting in the Cache section of the Network Preferences dialog box (which you access through the Options menu). Note that the memory you allocate to a RAM disk is reported as part of the system software by the Finder's About This Computer or About This Macintosh command.

To reclaim the memory used by a RAM disk, you must turn off the RAM disk feature and restart your computer. You can avoid this hassle by creating a RAM disk with the ShrinkWrap or AppDisk program (described in Chapter 24). They all create a RAM disk as an application (sounds weird, but it's true), and you get your memory back as soon as you quit or drag the RAM disk icon to the Trash. You can even automate mounting the RAM disk before opening the Web browser (see "Using AppleScript with Applications" in Chapter 22).

Download to RAM disk

When using an online service like America Online or CompuServe, download files to a RAM disk rather than to your hard disk to save on download time. This can be especially useful when downloading the latest multidisk system software update from Apple. Just make sure that you don't forget to save your RAM disk contents before shutdown.

Cables in a pinch

If you ever need to replace your ADB keyboard cable but can't find one at the local computer shop, head to a store that sells video gear and buy an S-video cable of the desired length instead. You can get a cable that's longer than the original, but Apple recommends that ADB cables be no longer than 5 meters. If your monitor cable needs an extension, you may be able to use an IBM PC Joystick Extender cable, which you should be able to pick up at a computer store for about $5. This cable works with most Mac OS monitors, but causes ghosting with some combinations of monitor and computer.

Eggs and Hacks

Apple's software engineers, true to their kind, have sprinkled Easter eggs — cute or funny animations or other surprising actions — in their work. To finish things off, here's a list of some of the treasures you can find hidden within Mac OS 8.

About the Finder

In the Finder, pressing Option changes the first command in the Apple menu to About the Finder. Choose this command, and instead of the usual memory-usage chart, you see a mountain-range picture like the one that adorned Finder 1.1 in 1984. (With Mac OS 7.6.1 and earlier, you see the original black-and-white picture. Mac OS 8 substitutes a 3-D color picture.) Wait about ten seconds, and credits start scrolling up the screen. Figure 26-5 shows the About the Finder window.

Figure 26-5: The credits are rolling for Mac OS 8.

Finder Hacks

If you have itchy fingers and an idle copy of ResEdit, you can put a personal stamp on your Mac's Finder. This sidebar lists some interesting changes, or *hacks*, that you can make to the Finder. (Be sure to always work on a copy of the Finder.)

The basic procedure is the same for all the hacks listed below. As a rule, always use ResEdit on a copy of the original file instead of the original file itself. (For the reasons why, see "Permanently Removing *alias*" in the "Icons" section of Chapter 25.)

❖ Change the suffix for an alias as follows:

1. Open STR# resource.

2. Open resource 8200 (Mac OS 8) or 20500 (Mac OS 7.6.1 and earlier).

3. Change the alias suffix in string #1 to something else (up to 31 characters).

❖ Change the initial name of a new folder as follows:

1. Open STR# resource.

2. Open resource 4500 (Mac OS 8) or 11250 (Mac OS 7.6.1 and earlier).

3. Alter string #3 to change *untitled folder* to something else (up to 31 characters).

❖ Change the sample text displayed when you open a TrueType or fixed-size font as follows:

1. Open STR# resource.

2. Double-click resource 5816 (Mac OS 8) or 14516 (Mac OS 7.6.1 and earlier).

3. Edit the custom phrase in string #1.

Successfully performing any of these hacks gains you membership in the Loyal Order of the DogCow ("All hail Clarus — aya, aya, moof!"), which entitles you to wear an extra-large T-shirt and sneakers to work and to litter your workspace with candy-bar wrappers and empty cola cans!

Tell me a joke

If you have Speech Recognition 1.4.1 or later installed and turned on, you can get your computer to tell you knock-knock jokes. You say, "Tell me a joke." The computer responds, "Knock, knock." You reply, "Who's there?" The computer answers with a name or some word, such as "orange." You repeat the word and then say "who?" (For more information, see "Speech Recognition" in Chapter 21.) Figure 26-6 shows a transcript of one of these jokes in the speech feedback window.

Figure 26-6: Get Speech Recognition 1.4.1 and later to tell you a joke.

Summary

In this second chapter of system-related tips and tricks, you found ways to navigate through Open and Save dialog boxes more efficiently. You can use the keyboard instead of the mouse. You can use folder aliases to jump from one folder directly to another. And you can side step or cancel a misplaced double-click.

File sharing is very handy, especially when you know a few tricks. You can improve performance by sharing fewer folders. Cut file-sharing red tape with aliases. Carry around replicas of all your hard disks on a single floppy disk; they're fully functional as long as you're near your network.

Perhaps the area most full of useful, hidden shortcuts is located under the Apple menu. You can build multiple Scrapbooks and Note Pads, if that's your fancy. You can magnify the Map control panel. Set your computer to automatically play any audio CD that you insert in the CD-ROM drive, or make an audio-only QuickTime movie. Quickly hide the menu-bar clock. Copy or delete a batch of items (without typing a DOS-style command). And if you're tired of waiting for your PowerBook to start up when you take it through airport security, use a utility to avoid the wait.

This chapter also gave you some tips on managing applications and memory. If you have a fast reaction time, you can cancel a program that you opened by mistake. You can hide a program's windows while switching to another program. In addition, you can boost performance by hiding windows. If your memory isn't what it should be, use the tips in this chapter to reduce system memory size and relieve fragmented memory. If you have a lot of memory, use part of it for a RAM disk. With a RAM disk, you can accelerate your Web browser's handling of its cache, speed up downloading of files, or even run a utility program to perform maintenance on your hard disk. Sleep won't help your computer's memory, but tips in this chapter tell you several ways to put your computer to sleep quickly.

In conclusion, this chapter revealed a couple of Easter eggs that still work in Mac OS 8 and disclosed a list of Finder hacks.

Installing the
Mac OS

CHAPTER TWENTY-SEVEN

Get Ready to Install

IN THIS CHAPTER

- **Obtaining installation software:** CD-ROMs and online sources
- **Preparing for installation:** Backing up disks, verifying disk directories, updating hard disk driver software, configuring Extensions, tracking installer actions, installing on a PowerBook
- **Doing a clean installation**
- **Troubleshooting** installation problems

As the Mac OS has become more complex over the years, the process of installing and upgrading it has become increasingly automated. Where once you dragged a handful of icons from an installation disk to your startup disk, you now run an installer program named the Installer. Its actions are directed by a script that Apple engineers carefully wrote to copy the pieces of system software you're installing from the installation disk or disks to the correct places on your startup disk, and remove outdated software from your startup disk as necessary. The installer script typically offers you a few simple choices, such as whether to install all of the system software or just the pieces you select from a list, and then the Installer takes care of the nitty-gritty.

Obtaining Installation Software

Installation software — the Installer program, installer script, and pieces of software to be installed — comes on several forms of media. You may install from a set of floppy disks, in which case the Installer asks by name for each disk it needs and ejects the disk it no longer needs. As an alternative to floppy disks, you can put the installation software on a hard disk or removable hard disk as described in the sidebar "Net Install." But you're most likely to install from a CD-ROM.

STEP-BY-STEP

Net Install

Installing software from a set of floppy disks is considerably slower than installing from a hard disk or CD-ROM, and you have to pay attention so you know when the Installer needs the next floppy disk. Moreover, installing from floppies is a huge inconvenience if you have to install the same software repeatedly (for example, on a number of networked computers). Rather than installing from floppy disks, you can use them to create an installation folder on a hard disk and install from there. Here's the simplest method:

1. Create a new folder on the hard disk that you want to use for installation. If you need to install the same software on several networked computers, create the new folder on a network file server or a shared hard disk.
2. Copy each floppy disk to the new folder. To copy a floppy, insert it and drag its icon to the new folder's icon.
3. For convenience, make an alias of the Installer in the first installation folder and put the alias in the same folder as the set of installation folders.

You end up with a set of installation folders having the same names as the installation floppy disks. It's important to keep all of the installation folders in the same folder on the hard disk and not to change their names. The Installer won't work if you relocate or rename any folders.

To install from the set of installation folders, you simply start the Installer program in the first installation folder by double-clicking its icon or an alias of it. If you have trouble installing from a set of installation folders — for example, the Installer asks you to insert a floppy disk when it should use the next installation folder — try putting a copy of the Installer program and the Installer script file into the same folder as the set of installation folders, and start the installation with that copy of the Installer. (To copy the Installer and the script file, open the first installation folder and press the Option key while dragging the Installer and the script file to the folder that contains the set of installation folders.)

An alternative method of putting installation software on a hard disk involves creating a disk image file for each floppy disk. This method requires more effort, but it works in cases when the simpler method described above fails. You create the disk image files with a utility program such as Apple's Disk Copy or Aladdin's ShrinkWrap (originally distributed as shareware by its author, Chad Magendanz). For more information on disk image files, see the sidebar "Disk Image Files."

Installation CD-ROMs

When more than a few floppy disks are involved in the installation process, Apple generally makes a CD-ROM equivalent. It's not unusual for an installation CD-ROM to include extra software that won't fit on the equivalent installation floppy disks. Some versions of the Mac OS are available *only* on CD-ROM. Major releases of the Mac OS, such as Mac OS 7.6 and Mac OS 8, are sold in stores and catalogs. Apple usually makes upgrades to the latest major release available at lower cost to Mac OS owners through the Apple Order Center (800-293-6617). The Apple Order Center also distributes minor releases of the Mac OS and some updates to individual Mac OS pieces for a shipping fee.

You may use an installation CD-ROM in your computer directly, or you may access it over a network. Using installation software over a network is pretty much the same as using it from a CD-ROM in your computer's CD-ROM drive.

Disk Image Files

Software you obtain from the Internet, America Online, CompuServe, or other online sources may come in the form of disk image files. These are files from certain utility programs that you can use to create a set of installation floppy disks. Two such utilities are Apple's free Disk Copy and the ShrinkWrap program Alladin Systems (for availability, see "ShrinkWrap" in Chapter 24). With ShrinkWrap or Disk Copy 6.1 or later, you don't have to make floppy disks to install from the disk image files. ShrinkWrap and Disk Copy 6.1 and later can mount any number of disk image files directly onto your desktop. It's as if you had inserted a whole bunch of floppy disks simultaneously. Because you can mount all of the "disks" needed for installation, you don't have to sit in front of your computer to swap floppies. Once you start the installation process, it proceeds without further attention from you. Disk Copy 6.1.2 comes with Mac OS 8.

Online installation software

Apple maintains a library of system software on America Online, CompuServe, and the Internet, and you can copy software from those sources to your hard disk. New versions of individual Mac OS pieces show up in Apple's online software library before they're available on CD-ROM or floppy disk. The library also contains older versions of many Mac OS pieces, including System 7.0.1 complete (other versions of system software are not available from the library). Here's how to access Apple's software:

❖ On the Internet, point your Web browser to http://www.info.apple.com and follow the links to the software library or a featured item. For premium access, check out Apple Club at http://www.club.apple.com.

❖ On America Online, use the keyword **applecomputer** to go directly to the Apple Computer window. All software is located in the software area of that window.

❖ On CompuServe, use the Go word **APLSUP** to take you to the Apple Computer Support forum, where you can find Apple USA SW Updates, or use the Go word **APLWW** to access the Apple Worldwide Software Updates Forum.

Note that major upgrades to the operating system, such as Mac OS 7.6 and Mac OS 8, are not available for free downloading online. These must be purchased from a software retailer, as mentioned previously. However, incremental updates (such as the updater to change Mac OS 7.6 into 7.6.1) are available.

Preparing for Installation

Before installing new Mac OS software — whether that means upgrading to the latest version of the Mac OS, installing a new Mac OS technology, or installing Mac OS 8 to replace System 7.5 (or something even older) — you need to determine whether the new software will work with the software you already have. Ideally you would make a list of every piece of software that's not part of the Mac OS and check with the software publishers or distributors to make sure the versions you have are compatible with what you're about to install. If you have the time and patience to do that — great. If not, at least do the following to minimize the risk of incompatibilities:

❖ Make a backup of your hard disk and of any RAM disk you have.

❖ Verify the directories of all your hard disk volumes.

❖ Update hard disk driver software.

❖ Turn off any security, virus protection, and screen saver software.

❖ Turn on standard extensions.

❖ Look in the SimpleText installation file for known incompatibilities and disable, remove, or upgrade any incompatible software that you have.

❖ Optionally label all items in your System Folder with the Labels menu (after installation, the new items will be the unlabeled ones).

❖ If you are installing on a PowerBook, make sure it's plugged in.

❖ If you're installing on a computer that can go to sleep, make sure it won't go to sleep during installation.

The remainder of this section discusses these tasks in more detail.

Backing up disks

If you use more than one hard disk, or if your hard disk is partitioned into multiple volumes, make backups of all of them. Making backups is like buying car insurance — it's a terrific imposition and you hope it's a total waste of effort. Do it anyway.

If you have a RAM disk, copy its contents to another disk before upgrading or installing any version of system software. The RAM disk may be turned off and its contents lost during the installation process.

Backing up today's large hard disks onto floppy disks is impractical. You need some type of high-capacity backup storage device, either another hard disk of equal or greater capacity, a tape drive, a Zip drive, or a hard disk with removable cartridges. If you have a second hard disk, you can back up your main hard disk by simply dragging its icon to the backup disk's icon. That method isn't very efficient if you want to keep your backup up-to-date on a regular basis, but it's adequate for pre-installation purposes.

You could back up onto removable hard disk cartridges by dragging folder icons, but it's simpler to use a special backup utility such as DiskFit from Dantz Development (510-253-3000, http://www.dantz.com). It automates the process of backing up a large hard disk onto several smaller disk cartridges. DiskFit also makes it easy to keep your backup files current. Each time you back up, it copies only the files and folders that have changed since the last backup. That minimizes the amount of time and number of disk cartridges you need for backup.

The Iomega Zip drive is a popular choice for backup and archival needs. The Zip has become nearly ubiquitous over the past few years; a few Mac OS computers even come configured with internal Zip drives. It uses 100MB floppy-like cartridges and comes with a free program called Personal Backup that, while not the top-rate, meets the backup needs of most.

If you have a tape drive, you must use backup software such as Dantz's Retrospect. You can't back up folders to a tape by dragging icons in the Finder.

Verifying disk directories

It's important to check the condition of a disk before installing new system software on it. The installation software checks the disk you're installing on when you install Mac OS 8 or Mac OS 7.6 normally.

You can check disks any time with Apple's Disk First Aid utility, which comes with the system software. Disk First Aid checks the condition of a disk's directory, which keeps track of where files are stored on the disk and can often repair any problem it finds. The Mac OS maintains each disk directory automatically, updating it every time you save changes to a file or create a new file. The directory can become damaged when the computer freezes or crashes, when an application quits unexpectedly, and so on. The damage may be so slight that you don't notice a problem, but over time the damage can grow and become irreparable. Disk First Aid is easy to use: you simply select one or more disks in its window and click the Verify or Repair button. Figure 27-1 shows an example of the Disk First Aid window.

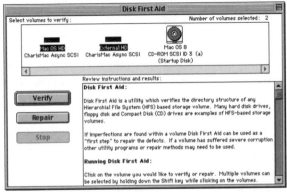

Figure 27-1: Disk First Aid verifies and repairs disk directories.

Disk First Aid has a limitation that you can avoid by starting up your computer from a Disk Tools floppy disk or a Mac OS CD-ROM and opening the copy of Disk First Aid from there. You see, Disk First Aid can't repair problems it finds on the current startup disk or on the disk that contains the running Disk First Aid program. This limitation doesn't get in your way if you start up from a Disk Tools disk or a CD-ROM and run Disk First Aid from it. A Disk Tools floppy disk comes with every set of installation floppy disks for a major release of the Mac OS, including Mac OS 8, Mac OS 7.6, System 7.5.3, and System 7.5, but not with installation floppy disks for minor Mac OS releases such as 7.6.1 or 7.5.5. The Disk Tools floppy may come as a disk image file on CD; use Apple's Disk Copy utility or Aladdin's ShrinkWrap to make a real floppy that you can start your computer from. Similarly, you can start up a computer and run Disk First Aid from any CD-ROM that contains a major release of the Mac OS as well as from the CD-ROM that comes with a Mac OS computer. You cannot start up from a CD-ROM that contains a Mac OS update or minor release, such as System 7.5 Update 2.0.

Some disk problems are beyond Disk First Aid's restorative powers. If Disk First Aid says it can't fix a problem, put the problematic disk through the repair process several more times anyway. The problem may be one that Disk First Aid can fix bit by bit. If after several repair attempts Disk First Aid doesn't tell you the disk appears to be okay, you need to bring in a high-priced disk mechanic — Norton Utilities from Symantec (408-253-9600, http://www.symantec.com). Norton Utilities can detect and fix significantly more problems than Disk First Aid. If it can't repair the disk, it may be able to recover individual files that the Finder can no longer access. After recovering lost files and copying them to another disk together with other files that haven't been backed up, you can resurrect the disk by formatting it.

Updating hard disk driver software

The driver software that resides on every hard disk and removable hard disk cartridge must be compatible with the Mac OS version in use or problems can result. For example, old driver software made by Transoft (805-897-3350, http://www.transnet.net/transoft/) causes a problem with the Mac OS. The old Transoft driver considers the startup disk to be ejectable, and this causes the Mac OS to display a message asking you to insert the startup disk when you shut down the computer, although the startup disk was never ejected. To check whether your startup disk has a Transoft driver, select the disk's desktop icon and choose Get Info from the Finder's File menu. If the Info window's "Where" information contains "NS-SCSI" or "NS-ACAM" then the disk contains a Transoft driver. Transoft drivers were distributed with various brands of hard disks, notably APS Technologies, as well as with Transoft's SCSI Director formatting utility. The problem does not affect APS hard disks with Power Tools software versions 3.0 and later, nor does it affect Transoft SCSI Director version 3.0.9 and later.

Updating disk driver software takes just a minute and in most cases doesn't affect disk contents in any way. (To update the driver on an old hard disk formatted with Apple's HD SC Setup version 2.0, you must reformat the hard disk, erasing the disk contents in the process.)

If you're installing Mac OS 8, the Installer program will update the driver for you; there's no need to run a separate program. If you're not, you need to use the most recent version of the formatting utility program last used on the disk.

Mac OS 8 Driver Compatibility

The hard disk driver software installed with Mac OS 8 is not compatible with computers that have 68000 processors. If a hard disk that uses Apple driver software is connected when you install Mac OS 8, you won't be able to use that hard disk subsequently with a Mac Plus, SE, original Classic, Portable, or PowerBook 100 computer.

Apple hard disk utilities

You update the driver software of an Apple-brand hard disk with one of three formatting utility programs from Apple: Drive Setup, Apple HD SC Setup, and Internal HD Format. The one to use depends on the make and model of your computer and the Mac OS version you're installing, as follows:

❖ **Drive Setup.** Use this utility to update the hard disk driver before installing System 7.5.3 or Mac OS 7.6 on any Apple Power Macintosh or any Apple Macintosh computer that has an IDE (not SCSI) internal hard disk, except a PowerBook 150. Apple Macintosh computers with IDE hard disks include the PowerBook 190, 1400, 2300, and 5300; the Performa and LC 580 series; the Performa, LC, and Quadra 630 series; and the Performa 5200, 5300, 5400, 6200, and 6300 series.

You can also use Drive Setup to update the hard disk driver on any computer before installing Mac OS 8. However, you don't need to do this because the Installer program for Mac OS 8 updates the driver for you.

❖ **Apple HD SC Setup.** Use this utility to update the hard disk driver before installing Mac OS 7.6.1 or earlier on a Quadra (except 630 series), Centris, LC (except 580 and 630 series), Mac II, Classic, SE, or PowerBook with a SCSI internal hard disk. Also, use this utility to update the hard disk driver before installing Systems 7.5.2, 7.5.1, 7.5, or 7.1.2 on a Power Macintosh that can use those versions of the Mac OS. This utility does not work with any IDE hard disks.

The Apple HD SC Setup program is obsolete after installing Mac OS 8. To test, format, partition, mount, or update the driver software of a disk with Mac OS 8, use the Drive Setup program in the Utilities folder on the Mac OS 8 startup disk.

❖ **Internal HD Format.** This utility is for formatting the internal IDE hard disk on an Apple Macintosh that originally shipped with System 7.5.1 or earlier. To update the hard disk driver on any of those computers except a PowerBook 150, use the Drive Setup utility. You do not need to (and in fact cannot) update the driver of a PowerBook 150's internal hard disk, because the driver is in the PowerBook 150's ROM.

Other hard disk utilities

You can't use an Apple hard disk utility on a disk made by another company. In addition, you can't use an Apple hard disk utility to update the driver on an Apple hard disk whose driver has been updated by another company's disk utility.

If you have an internal or external hard disk from another company, contact the company for the latest version of its hard disk formatting utility. If that version is more recent than the one you have, use the more recent version to update your non-Apple hard disk's driver.

You can also switch to a different brand of driver software, such as Hard Disk Toolkit from FWB Software (415-463-3500, http://www.fwb.com). However, once you switch from an Apple driver to another brand, you generally can't switch back. Before switching to another brand of driver software, keep in mind that Apple always updates its hard disk driver software to be compatible with the latest Mac OS. Other companies sometimes take longer than Apple to update their hard disk drivers for the latest Mac OS. The startup disk is particularly susceptible to incompatibilities between disk driver software and the Mac OS, so don't switch the startup disk from an Apple driver to another brand without good reason.

Configuring extensions

Some system extensions and control panels can interfere with installing or upgrading Mac OS 8 or other system software versions. To avoid problems caused by anti-virus, security, screen-saver, or energy-saver software, be sure to do the following before you begin the installation process:

❖ Disable At Ease or other security software that locks or restricts access to files, folders, or disks.

❖ Disable software that protects against viruses.

❖ Turn off screen-saver software.

❖ Deactivate all but the standard set of extensions and control panels for your version of the Mac OS, plus any other extensions and control panels required for installation, as follows:

- If you're upgrading from System 7.5 through Mac OS 7.6.1, open the Extensions Manager control panel and from its pop-up menu, choose the extensions set named System 7.5 Only, System 7.5.2, System 7.5.3, System 7.5.5, or Mac OS 7.6 All. Figure 27-2 shows this setting in System 7.5.5.

- If you're reinstalling Mac OS 8, choose "Mac OS 8 all" from the Extensions Manager's pop-up menu.

Figure 27-2: Activate only the standard extensions and control panels (plus any required for special equipment).

- If you have special equipment that requires extensions or control panels to start up, turn them back on in the Extensions Manager.
- If you are upgrading from System 7.0 through 7.1.4, turn off all extensions by holding down the Shift key while restarting your computer.

❖ Make sure the computer is not set to go to sleep or shut down automatically.

Tracking Installer actions

When you update the Mac OS or reinstall it, the Installer program not only adds entirely new items, it also removes existing items from the startup disk (for which the installation software includes replacements), and then copies the replacements into the correct places on the startup disk. But the Installer gives you no record of what it has done. You can use the Labels menu to keep tabs on the changes by following these steps:

1. Print a report of the System Folder contents before running the Installer. To do that, open the System Folder, use the View menu to view the window contents as a list, choose Select All from the Edit menu, and press ⌘-Option-Right Arrow to expand all folders within the System Folder. Then choose Print Window from the File menu to print the hierarchical list of System Folder contents.

   If you have System 7.5 or later installed, you can use its Find File utility to make a document containing an alphabetical list of everything in the System Folder. Start by opening the startup disk icon and selecting the System Folder icon. Next open Find File and set it to find items in the current Finder selection whose name is not "????" (or any other name you know doesn't exist). When Find File displays its list of found items you can select all, copy, and paste into the Scrapbook, the Note Pad, or any text document for later reference. Figure 27-3 shows an alphabetical list of System Folder items in the Note Pad.

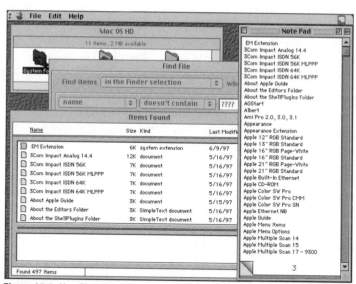

Figure 27-3: Use Find File to make a list of all System folder items in the Note Pad.

2. Use the Label menu to label every item you want to keep track of in the System Folder. The simplest method is this: after expanding all folders as described in Step 1, choose Select All from the Edit menu and choose one of the labels from the Label submenu of the File menu (Mac OS 8) or the Label menu (Mac OS 7.6.1 and earlier). Alternatively, you can use multiple labels to categorize items. For example, you could label all items that are

part of the Mac OS with one label and all items you have added with a different label. Use the Finder's Preferences command (Mac OS 8) or the Labels control panel (Mac OS 7.6.1 and earlier) if you want to change label names or colors (see "Labeling Items" in Chapter 7).

3. Install or upgrade the system software as described later in Chapters 28, 29, or 30. The installation process removes some of the items you labeled and adds other items, which are all unlabeled.

4. To see which items are new or replacements, look in the System Folder for unlabeled items. You can search for unlabeled items in the System Folder using the Find File feature in System 7.5 and later. Start by selecting the System Folder icon or folders inside it if you want to look for new items only in them. Next open Find File and set it to search for items in the Finder selection whose label is None (or is not the label you applied in step 2). You can label items listed in the Found Items window by selecting any number of them and using Find File's Label menu.

To determine which items are completely new and which have been deleted, print another report or make another alphabetical list of the System Folder contents following the procedures described in step 1. Compare the newer and older reports or the newer and older alphabetical lists. Brand-new items appear in the newer list but not in the older list. Deleted items appear in the older list but not in the newer list.

The one thing this procedure does not tell you is which unlabeled replacement items are newer versions of the items they replaced and which replacements are the same versions as the items they replaced. Because there's a rough correlation between an item's version and its modification date, you can get a rough idea of which items are new versions by using Find File to find the unlabeled items and then viewing the found items by date. Items at the top of the list are more likely to be new versions than items at the bottom of the list.

Installing on a PowerBook

Although you can install or upgrade the system software on a PowerBook under battery power, it's better to have the PowerBook plugged in, especially if you're installing from a set of floppy disks. If you are called away during installation, the PowerBook could go to sleep if it's operating on batteries.

You cannot install or upgrade the system software correctly on a PowerBook's hard disk when it is in SCSI disk mode. A PowerBook is in SCSI disk mode when it is connected with a SCSI adapter cable to another computer, and that computer is using the PowerBook as an external hard disk. In this scenario, you would be running the Installer on the other computer, not on the PowerBook, and the Installer would not install the pieces of the Mac OS specifically designed for PowerBooks.

To install or update the system software correctly on a PowerBook, you must run the Installer on the PowerBook. You can use a set of floppy disks, a CD-ROM (in a drive connected to the PowerBook or in a shared drive you access over a network), and so on.

Performing a Clean Installation

Ordinarily, Apple's installation software upgrades the Mac OS that already exists on a computer, merging the new with the old. You get some entirely new items and some replacements for existing items that haven't changed, but preference files and files that contain your data are not replaced. For example, installing Mac OS 8 replaces the Scrapbook program but not items you have added to the Scrapbook file. That is the right thing to do unless your system has become unreliable and you can't seem to resolve its problems.

You can usually eliminate nagging system problems by installing a pristine copy of the Mac OS. This is known as a *clean installation*, and it's a favorite tonic of telephone technical support personnel because it's so effective. The trouble is, a clean installation of the Mac OS forces you to laboriously re-install all of the control panels, extensions, fonts, Apple menu items, Startup items, and anything else that you have added to your System Folder since you started using your computer. You'll also have to reconfigure your control panels and reset options in most of your application programs because all of their settings are kept in preference files in the System Folder. And that's not all. You'll also need to reinstall application programs that keep auxiliary files and folders in the System Folder, such as most Claris and Adobe applications. Sure, you could simply copy files from the old System Folder to the new one, but that defeats the purpose of a clean installation, which is to stop using old, possibly damaged files. Performing a clean installation of the Mac OS is like moving to a new apartment because your old one smells bad. It might be easier to figure out what's causing the stink and fix it. (See "Troubleshooting Installation Problems" at the end of this chapter.)

Still, there are times when a clean slate is the simplest cure, or at any rate a useful diagnostic tool, because a computer clearly doesn't have a hardware malfunction if it works reliably with a cleanly installed System Folder. Apple's installation software makes it easy to do a clean installation of Mac OS 8, Mac OS 7.6, System 7.5.3, or System 7.5. For specific instructions, see Chapter 28, 29, or 30, depending on the system software version you're installing.

Troubleshooting Installation Problems

If your computer will not restart after you install new Mac OS software, try restarting while holding down the Shift key until you see the message "Extensions Disabled." Then follow the instructions in the sidebar "Resolving a Conflict" to resolve a possible conflict among your system extensions. When you find an incompatible extension, disable it and contact its publisher about an upgrade.

If you don't want to troubleshoot an extension conflict, you can try doing a clean installation of the system software as described in the previous section. If a clean installation clears up the problem, you can begin adding other items such as fonts, sounds, control panels, and extensions to the new System Folder. To keep the System Folder as clean as possible, you should install the additional items from their original installation disks. If you don't have the installation disks, you can move items from your old System Folder, which was renamed Previous System Folder. Look for items to move from the old Fonts folder, Apple Menu Items folder, Preferences folder, Extensions folder, Control Panels folder, System File, Startup Items folder, and the Previous System Folder itself. Move only a few items at a time, and make sure they do not cause a problem before moving more. You can use the Labels submenu (Mac OS 8) or the Labels menu (Mac OS 7.6.1 and earlier) to categorize old items before you move them into the new System Folder. While moving items from the Previous System Folder or from folders inside it you may get a message asking if you want to replace items that already exist in the new System Folder. If you get a message like that, click Cancel unless you are very sure you want to replace items in the new System Folder with items from the Previous System Folder.

Sometimes problems occur after a clean installation that don't occur after upgrading the existing system software. For example, a PowerBook or other computer with an internal Express Modem and a Power Macintosh with a GeoPort Telecom Adapter will lose modem services after a clean installation because the Apple Telecom software that's required for modem services with those devices is not included in a clean installation. To troubleshoot problems with a clean installation, try moving items from the old System Folder (now named Previous System Folder) into equivalent places in the new System Folder as described in the previous paragraph. Alternatively, you can deactivate the new System Folder by opening it and dragging the System file into the Startup Items folder. This should activate the old System Folder, now named Previous System Folder, and you can restart the computer to use it. Make a backup copy of the old System Folder, and then install the new system software without doing a clean installation.

If problems arise after installing new Mac OS software and they only affect a few application programs, contact the affected applications' publishers or developers for assistance. They may know about incompatibilities between their software and the new system software you just installed.

Resolving a Conflict

If items you add to the System Folder, Extensions folder, or Control Panels folder don't work, if your computer refuses to start up, or if you start experiencing system crashes or freezes, then some of the system extensions in those places may be in conflict during startup. The easiest way to resolve an extension conflict is with Conflict Catcher from Casady & Greene, Inc. (408-484-9228, http://www.casadyg.com), or the Now Startup Manager from Now Software (503-274-2810, http://www.nowsoft.com). Those utilities take the place of the Extensions Manager control panel. Conflict Catcher and Now Startup Manager walk you through a diagnostic procedure that finds incompatible System Folder items in the least possible amount of time.

You can also troubleshoot a conflict between system extensions and control panels with the Extensions Manager control panel (see Chapter 10), but it is not nearly as convenient or foolproof as Conflict Catcher or Now Startup Manager. If you want to try Extensions Manager, start by disabling half of the extensions and control panels and restart. If this solves the problem, the offending item is among the disabled half of the extensions, so write down all of their names and enable half of them. If disabling half of the items did not cure the problem, the offending item is among the half you did not disable, so write down all of their names and disable half of them. In either case, you leave only half the group containing the offending item (one quarter of all extensions and control panels) enabled, and then restart. If the problem occurs again, the offender is among the group still enabled; if not, it is among the group you just disabled. Continue halving the offending group until you reduce it to a single item (the troublemaker).

Sometimes changing the order in which the Mac OS loads system extensions during startup resolves a conflict. You can make an extension load before others by adding one or more blank spaces to the beginning of its name. You can make an extension load after others by adding a tilde (~) or diamond (◊) to the beginning of its name.

Regardless of their names, all items in the Extensions folder load before items in the Control Panels folder, and the control panels load before items directly in the System Folder. To have a control panel whose name begins with blank spaces load before items in the Extensions folder, put that control panel in the Extensions folder. To have a control panel whose name starts with a tilde or diamond load last during startup, put that control panel in the System Folder. For convenient access to the control panels you move out of the Control Panels folder, make aliases of them and put the aliases in the Control Panels folder.

To have a system extension whose name begins with a tilde or diamond load last during startup, drag that extension from the Extensions folder to the System Folder. Leave system extensions whose names begin with blank spaces in the Extensions folder so they will be installed first during startup.

(continued)

(continued)

As a last resort, remove all system extensions and control panels to the desktop. Then put them in the System Folder (not the Extensions or Control Panels folder) one at a time, from most important to least. Restart your computer each time you add another item to the System Folder. When you find an item that causes a conflict, discard it and try the next item you previously moved to the desktop. You may be able to resume using the items you discarded when they are next upgraded.

(If a conflict prevents starting up from your hard disk, start from a floppy or Zip disk with any version of system software. Make a change to the System Folder on the hard disk and try restarting from it.)

Summary

In this chapter, you read that major releases of the Mac OS are sold on CD-ROMs and floppy disks. You can get system software updates from Apple's online software library.

This chapter recommended that before installing a new version of the system software, you back up your disks, verify disk directories, update hard disk driver software, and turn off all but the standard Apple extensions and control panels, plus any that are required for any special equipment on your computer. This chapter also explained how you can track installation activity with the Labels menu. In addition, this chapter made suggestions for trouble-free installation on PowerBooks.

Also covered in the chapter were the pros and cons of a clean installation. Although a clean installation prevents the carrying over of damaged files from the previous system software, a normal installation is usually quite effective and not nearly as much work.

In conclusion, this chapter described how you can troubleshoot installation problems by checking for extension conflicts with Conflict Catcher, Now Startup Utility, or Extensions Manager.

CHAPTER TWENTY-EIGHT

Install Mac OS 8

28

IN THIS CHAPTER

- **Checking for compatibility** with Mac OS 8
- **Installing** a standard, custom, or universal copy of Mac OS 8

Ever since the earliest days of the Macintosh, installing system software has been easy. Mac OS 8 makes it even simpler with its improved super-installer, Mac OS Install, which coordinates the installation of not only the basic system software, but a host of other choice items like OpenDoc, CyberDog, QuickDraw 3D, and more. Instead of figuring out all by yourself which installation programs you need to run (and in what order), Mac OS Install lets you choose which modules you need, and then automatically runs individual installation programs for those modules. In fact, if you just perform a standard installation, you won't need to make any decisions — Mac OS Install can handle the entire process for you!

Compatibility

Unfortunately, Mac OS 8 isn't for everybody. Some Macs can't use it at all and you must work around problems to install it on some other Macs, as detailed in this section.

Core requirements

Apple recommends using a PowerPC computer with Mac OS 8 — in fact, many of Mac OS 8's best features, such as the native Finder, benefit PowerPC computers the most — but Mac OS 8 works on computers with 68040 processors as well.

Many older Macintosh models don't work with Mac OS 8. Specifically, the computers that Mac OS 8 *won't* run on include

❖ 68000 Macs, such as the original 128k Mac, the 512k Fat Mac, Mac Plus, Portable, PowerBook 100, and Classic

739

❖ 68020 Macs, such as the Mac II, LC, and LC II

❖ 68030 Macs, such as the Mac SE/30, IIx, IIcx, IIci, PowerBook Duo 210 and 230

The oldest computers that can run Mac OS 8 are Quadra and Centris systems. Computers older than these can't use Mac OS 8 — not even a Mac that has an upgrade card with a 68040 or PowerPC processor. For these systems, the latest system software you can use is Mac OS 7.6.1. However, if your Mac came from the factory with a 68040 processor, you can install Mac OS 8.

Mac 5200, 5300, 6200, and 6300 computers

Some Performa and Power Macintosh computers in the 5200, 5300, 6200, and 6300 series can't use Mac OS 8 until a hardware problem is fixed. The problem does not affect the 5260, 6320, or 6360 models. You can test for the problem by using the 5xxx/6xxx Tester utility in the Utilities folder on the Mac OS 8 CD-ROM. In addition, the Mac OS 8 installation software checks for the problem and alerts you if repairs are needed. The repairs are covered under an Apple warranty extension program that's in effect until 2003.

Accelerated 6100, 7100, 8100, and 9150 computers

The Mac OS 8 Install program may not recognize a Power Mac or Performa 6100, 7100, 8100, or 9150 computer whose clock speed has been boosted with an accelerator. If this happens to you, remove the accelerator while installing Mac OS 8. If that's not feasible, you can install each software module individually by running its Installer program. For a description of the basic procedure, see "Installing Additional System Software" in Chapter 30. You'll find the individual Installer programs in folders inside the Software Installers folder on the Mac OS 8 CD-ROM.

400K floppy disks

Mac OS 8 can't use 400K floppy disks. If you have information on 400K floppies, copy it to another disk before installing Mac OS 8.

Installing Mac OS 8 — Standard

The Mac OS Install program leads you through the four steps necessary to install Mac OS 8. The first three steps are selecting a destination disk, reading a document about installing Mac OS 8, and agreeing to a software license. In the fourth step, you select the software modules you want installed. When you finish these four steps, the Mac OS Install program checks the condition of your hard disk's directory, updates your hard disk driver software (if you have an Apple hard disk), and then automatically runs the subordinate Installer program for each system software module you selected. This section describes the installation process.

Starting the Mac OS Install program

To start the Mac OS Install program, insert the Mac OS 8 CD-ROM disc or the Mac OS 8 Install Me First floppy disk, find the Mac OS Install program, and double-click its icon. After a few seconds, the Install Mac OS 8 window appears, displaying some introductory information. Click the Continue button to begin installation. Figure 28-1 shows the introductory information in the Mac OS 8 window.

Figure 28-1: Read the introductory information in the Install Mac OS 8 window.

Selecting a destination

The first step to installing the Mac OS is to choose which disk you want the software to go on. A pop-up menu lists the available disks. When you choose a disk from the pop-up menu, the installer reports that disk's system software version and the amount of free space available. You also have the option in this step of selecting a clean installation. (For advice on doing a clean installation, see "Performing a Clean Installation" in Chapter 27.) Figure 28-2 shows this first step in the Install Mac OS 8 window.

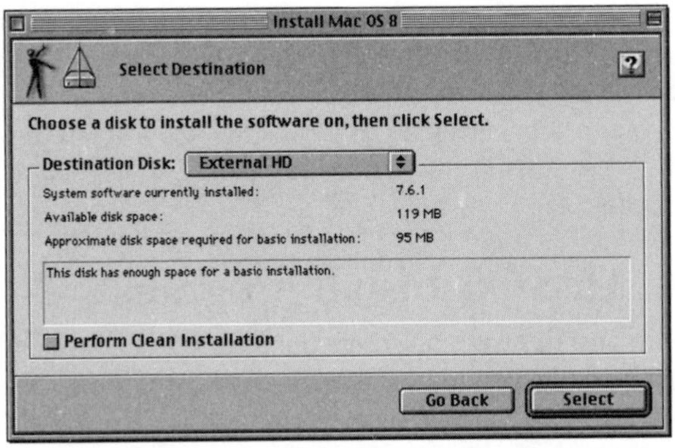

Figure 28-2: Choose a hard disk and optionally select a clean installation.

A standard installation of Mac OS 8 requires about 95MB of free space, the exact amount depending on your computer model. If you elect to install more or fewer software modules than are included in a standard installation, you will need more or less free disk space. Unfortunately, the Mac OS Install program does not help you figure out how much more or less disk space you will need for a non-standard installation. If you want to make more space available on the hard disk you've chosen, you can switch to the Finder, delete some files from that disk, and then switch back to the Mac OS Install program. (Use the Application menu at the right end of the menu bar to switch to and from the Finder.)

After choosing a destination disk and deciding whether to perform a clean installation, click the Select button at the bottom of the Install Mac OS 8 window to go to the second step. You can also go back to the introduction by clicking the Go Back button.

If you chose a destination disk that already has Mac OS 8 installed, the Mac OS Install program displays an alert box explaining the situation and giving you three choices: Reinstall, Add/Remove, or Cancel. If you click the Reinstall button, continue at the next heading, "Reading installation information." If you click the Add/Remove button, skip to the subsequent heading "Selecting modules and options." If you click the Cancel button, you get another chance to choose a destination disk.

Reading installation information

In the second step, the Install Mac OS 8 window displays a document containing last-minute installation information for Mac OS 8. It's tempting to skip over this document, but the information provided actually is important, and you should at least skim it for the mention of your computer model, printers you use, and software you use. You can print the document by clicking the Print button at the bottom of the window. You can also save the document on disk, but there's no need to since it's already available on the installation CD or floppy disk.

After reading the installation and compatibility document, click the Continue button at the bottom of the window to go to the third step. You can also go back to the previous step by clicking the Go Back button.

Agreeing to the software license

In the third step, the Install Mac OS 8 window displays a license agreement. The license agreement is filled with lawyer-speak, but you should look through it so you know what you're agreeing to. For example, one provision states that you can only install the software on one computer at a time. You can print the license agreement or save a copy on disk by clicking the Print or Save buttons at the bottom of the window.

Click the Continue button when you're ready to go to the last step. A small dialog box appears, asking if you agree or disagree with the terms of the license. You cannot continue with the installation unless you click the Agree button!

Selecting modules and options

In the last installation step, the Install Mac OS 8 window displays a checklist of software modules, and you select the ones you want to install. You also have the option of turning off the updating of Apple hard disk driver software. In addition, you can do a custom installation instead of a standard installation (see "Installing Mac OS 8 — Custom" later in this chapter). You click a button to start installation, and under the control of the Mac OS Install program, each selected module is installed by a separate Installer program. During a standard installation, the individual Installer programs do not require any response from you unless you are installing from floppy disks or a problem occurs. Figure 28-3 shows the last step of the Mac OS 8 Install program configured for a standard installation.

Figure 28-3: Select the optional modules you want installed.

Hard disk driver option

The Mac OS Install program normally updates the driver software on Apple hard disks. If you don't want this to happen, click the Options button at the bottom of the Install Mac OS 8 window and in the dialog box that appears, turn off the Update Apple Hard Disk Drivers option. (For more information on updating hard disk drivers, see "Preparing for Installation" in Chapter 27.)

Standard modules

A standard installation of Mac OS 8 always includes four modules not shown on the checklist for a standard installation. The following unlisted modules are part of every standard installation:

❖ **Mac OS 8** includes the core system software (described in detail throughout Chapters 5–19, 21, 22, and 23).

❖ **Mac OS Info Center** provides an overview of system software features, some troubleshooting pointers, and a list of places to start exploring the Internet; you view all this with a Web browser after installation.

❖ **Internet Access** includes Netscape Navigator, Claris Emailer Lite, Internet Dialer, Internet Setup Assistant, Connect To, Internet Config, StuffIt Expander, and Installer for DropStuff with Expander Enhancer (all described in detail in Chapter 20).

❖ **Open Transport PPP** lets you connect your computer by modem to remote TCP/IP networks such as the Internet (for details, see "Making a Dial-Up TCP/IP Connection" in Chapter 17).

These four modules are listed if you click the Customize button (as explained in the next section). These four modules are also listed if the destination disk already has Mac OS 8 and you previously chose (in the second step) to add or remove software on it.

Optional modules

There are ten optional modules in the checklist of the Install Mac OS 8 window. The following five modules on the checklist are initially selected for a standard installation, although you can easily exclude them individually.

❖ **Mac OS Runtime for Java** lets you run Java applets and applications on your computer (see "Java" in Chapter 20 for more details).

❖ **Personal Web Sharing** lets your computer host a Web site (see "Web Sharing" in Chapter 20 for more details).

❖ **QuickDraw 3D** makes viewing and manipulating 3D models and objects just as easy as watching QuickTime movies (see "QuickDraw 3D" in Chapter 19 for more details).

❖ **OpenDoc** provides the underlying foundation for creating compound documents using diverse plug-in software components instead of conventional applications (see "OpenDoc Compound Documents" in Chapter 23 for details).

❖ **MacLink Plus** can translate between Windows and Mac OS files (see "Translating Documents" in Chapter 8 for details).

You also have the option of installing five additional software modules. None of the following modules is initially selected for installation, but you can easily select the ones you want installed:

❖ **Apple Location Manager** assists you in switching groups of control panel settings all at once, typically when you move your computer from one place to another (see "Control Panels Encyclopedia" in Chapter 10 for details).

❖ **Cyberdog** is Apple's ground-breaking software (based on OpenDoc) for incorporating live Web pages and other Internet content into documents together with ordinary text, pictures, movies, sound (see "E-mail" and "World Wide Web" in Chapter 20 for details).

❖ **QuickDraw GX** provides extensive typography enhancements (see "QuickDraw GX Typography" in Chapter 13 for details).

❖ **Text-to-Speech** lets your computer speak text aloud (see "Text-to-Speech" in Chapter 21 for details).

❖ **Apple Remote Access Client** lets your computer connect to a remote AppleTalk network by modem (see "Making a Remote AppleTalk Connection" in Chapter 17 for details).

Installation begins

To begin the installation, click the Start button. The Mac OS Install program checks the destination disk's directory to ensure that files can be written to the disk properly. Next, the Mac OS Install program updates the drivers of Apple hard disks unless you have turned off the Update Apple Hard Disk Drivers options, as described above. These procedures in no way affect the contents of your disk.

After checking the disk directory and updating Apple hard disk drivers, the Mac OS Install program gives control to a succession of subordinate Installer programs, one for each Mac OS 8 module to be installed. Each Installer program briefly displays the message "Preparing to install." Then the Installer displays the folders (or disks) it will need and begins installation.

A standard installation proceeds automatically unless you are installing from floppy disks or a problem occurs. The individual Installer programs do not display welcome messages or offer installation options. If you are installing from a CD-ROM, a standard installation doesn't require more of your attention until it finishes. If you are installing from floppy disks and the Installer needs a different disk, the Installer ejects the disk that it is using and asks you to insert the disk it needs.

You can always cancel an installation that's underway by clicking the Cancel button. If you cancel an installation in progress, the Mac OS Install program displays an alert asking how you want to proceed. You can stop installation, skip installation of the module currently being installed, or try installing the current module again.

When you restart the computer after a successful installation, the Finder may automatically rebuild the desktop database of all inserted disks (see "Maintaining the Desktop Database" in Chapter 8).

Installing Mac OS 8 — Custom

A custom installation of Mac OS 8 gives you the opportunity to select the individual components of Mac OS 8 modules. For example, you must do a custom installation to install the Easy Access and CloseView control panels, which are part of the Mac OS 8 module. A custom installation also gives you the opportunity to remove all or part of a module. Do a custom installation only if you are sure that you know which individual items must be present for a module to work properly.

To do a custom installation of Mac OS 8, follow the same four-step procedure that you use for a standard installation (as described in the previous section, "Installing Mac OS 8 — Standard"), but in the last step click the Customize button. Clicking the Customize button expands the list of available software modules by adding the four that are not listed in a standard installation. They are Mac OS 8, Mac OS Info Center, Internet Access, and Open Transport PPP.

In a custom installation, you must interact with the subordinate Installer program for each module you have selected. This interaction gives you the opportunity to select specific components you want installed or removed. The Mac OS Installer program gives control to the Installer program for each selected module in turn. Some of the Installers display an initial welcome message that you must dismiss to see the Installer's main window, which describes what will be installed. Figure 28-4 shows the Installer for the main Mac OS 8 module.

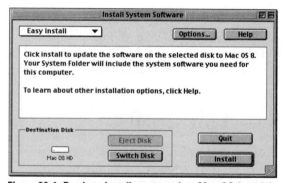

Figure 28-4: Ready to install one complete Mac OS 8 module.

To install a complete module, choose Easy Install from the pop-up menu in the Installer's main window and click the Install button in that window. (If the Installer has no pop-up menu, simply click the Install button.)

To selectively install portions of the module, choose Custom Install from the pop-up menu in the Installer window. The Installer lists components, and in some cases groups of components that you can install. To expand a component group, click the triangle next to it. You can get information about a component by clicking its information button at the right side of the Installer window. Select the components that you want to install by clicking the appropriate check boxes, and then click the Install button. Figure 28-5 shows the Custom Install section of the Installer for the main Mac OS 8 module.

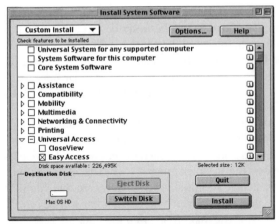

Figure 28-5: Select components to be installed from one Mac OS 8 module.

To selectively remove portions of the module, choose Custom Remove from the pop-up menu in the Installer window. Select the components or groups of components that you want removed, and click the Remove button.

Install Mac OS 8 — Universal

When you perform a standard installation, the Installer programs install the correct files and resources for the computer model you're using. This is very handy, as it keeps your System Folder from becoming bloated with unnecessary files. However, it makes life difficult if you're installing Mac OS 8 on a different computer than it will be used on. For instance, if you install Mac OS 8 on a PowerPC computer's external hard disk and then move that drive to a Quadra, the disk won't be able to start the Quadra.

To get around this problem, you need to perform a universal installation. This places all of the files for all computer models onto the selected hard disk. The resultant System Folder is much larger, but it will be able to start up any kind of computer that can use Mac OS 8. If you're creating an emergency startup Zip disk for use with Norton Utilities, for instance, you'll probably want to do a universal installation so you can use it on any kind of computer.

To create a universal installation of Mac OS 8 you must do a custom installation (as described in the previous section). In the last step of the Mac OS Install program, be sure to select the Mac OS 8 module. You don't have to select the other modules (Mac OS Info Center, Internet Access, and so on) if you know you're not going to need them with this disk. When the Installer for the Mac OS 8 module displays its main window, choose Custom Install from the pop-up menu and then select the "Universal System for any supported computer" Component from the checklist of installable components. Then click the Install button to proceed with installation. You should be able to use the resulting disk to start up any computer that can use Mac OS 8.

Install Mac OS 8 — Minimal

Note that unlike previous Mac system software versions, there is no option for a minimal floppy installation. You can't install Mac OS 8 onto a floppy disk. The only way to get Mac OS 8 on a floppy disk is to copy the 1MB System Folder from a Disk Tools floppy to another floppy. The resulting system software looks and works more like Mac OS 7.6 than 8.0, but it does start up a computer that requires Mac OS 8. (You can make Disk Tools floppies from the image files in the Disk Tools folder on the Mac OS 8 CD-ROM.)

It is possible to squeeze a standard installation of Mac OS 8 on a 94MB Zip cartridge or an 88MB SyQuest cartridge. Mac OS 8 seems to fit on these disks even though Apple says you need 95MB of hard disk space.

The smallest System Folder you can install with the Mac OS Install program takes about 11.5MB. To get this, do a custom installation, selecting only the Mac OS module in the last step of the Install Mac OS 8 window. When the Installer for the Mac OS 8 module displays its main screen, choose Custom Install from the pop-up menu and select only the Core System Software component from the checklist of installable components. The resulting svelte System Folder starts up really fast and uses about 3MB less RAM than a standard System Folder, but includes only one control panel (Memory) and one extension (Appearance).

Summary

In this chapter you learned how to install the Mac OS 8. You learned which computer models are compatible with it and what to do if yours isn't. You saw how to perform a standard installation, and how to customize that installation to suit your needs. You also learned how to do a universal installation on an external disk, so that it can start up any computer capable of using the Mac OS. Finally, you learned how to create a minimal Mac OS 8 startup disk.

Install Mac OS 7.6.1 and 7.6

Because some computers can't use Mac OS 8, you may find yourself wanting to or needing to install the next most recent version, Mac OS 7.6.1. If your computer now has Mac OS 7.6, you can upgrade it to version 7.6.1 from a set of floppy disks or a folder of installation software downloaded from Apple's online software library. If your computer has System 7.5.5 or earlier, you will probably install Mac OS 7.6 from a CD-ROM and then upgrade to Mac OS 7.6.1. This chapter tells you how to upgrade from 7.6 to 7.6.1 and how to install 7.6 in the first place.

Upgrading to Mac OS 7.6.1

Mac OS 7.6.1 can be installed as an upgrade to Mac OS 7.6. There are two versions of the upgrade installation software. The Mac OS 7.6.1 Update works with all computers that can use Mac OS 7.6 except PowerBook 3400s. The Mac OS 7.6.1 Update for PowerBook 3400 upgrades a PowerBook 3400 from Mac OS 7.6 to 7.6.1. Both of these upgrades are available from the Apple online software library (http://www.info.apple.com).

Neither of those upgrades works with computers that can't use Mac OS 7.6 but can use 7.6.1, including a Power Mac 4400, 5500, 6500, 7300, 7600, 8600, and 9600. To upgrade any of these computers, you must use the Mac OS 7.6.1 CD that is distributed only through the Mac OS UpToDate program (800-335-9258, http://www.macos.apple.com/releases/fulfillment.html).

The following instructions tell you how to upgrade to Mac OS 7.6.1 using the Mac OS 7.6.1 Update installation software or the Mac OS 7.6.1 Update for PowerBook 3400 installation software. Follow these steps:

1. If your Mac has System 7.5.5 or earlier, install Mac OS 7.6 by following the instructions in "Installing Mac OS 7.6" later in this chapter.

2. Insert the first Mac OS 7.6.1 floppy disk or open the Mac OS 7.6.1 Update folder and start the Installer program by double-clicking its icon.

3. The Installer program displays an Apple license agreement for you to read and optionally print. Click the Agree button to continue.

   The Installer's main window appears. This window identifies the disk on which the software will be installed and describes what will be installed, as shown in Figure 29-1.

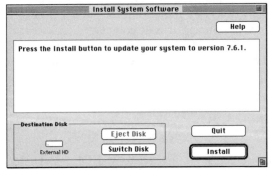

Figure 29-1: The main window for the Mac OS 7.6.1 Update Installer.

4. Make sure the destination-disk name is the one on which you want to install the software. If you have more than one hard disk, you can switch disks by clicking the Switch Disk button.

5. Click the Install button in the main Installer window to begin installation.

   The Installer briefly displays the message "Preparing to install." If you are installing onto the startup disk and other programs are open (such as SimpleText), the Installer displays an alert message advising you that it can't continue while other applications are open. You can click a Cancel button to cancel installation or click a Continue button to have the Installer quit the other open applications. (The Installer also turns off file sharing if it is on.) As each application quits, it may come to the front and ask whether you want to save any changes that you haven't yet saved. After quitting the other open applications, the Installer displays the folders (or disks) it will need and commences installation, as shown in Figure 29-2.

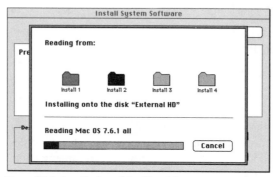

Figure 29-2: Installation of the Mac OS 7.6.1 upgrade is under way.

If you are installing from floppy disks and the Installer needs a different disk, the Installer ejects the disk it used and asks you to insert the next disk it needs. You can always cancel an installation by clicking the Cancel button.

When the Installer finishes upgrading to Mac OS 7.6.1, it tells you to restart the computer to use the new system software.

After upgrading to Mac OS 7.6.1, you can still install individual components of Mac OS 7.6 such as desktop printing or the Control Strip. You can use the Mac OS 7.6 CD-ROM or floppy disks as described in "Installing Mac OS 7.6 — custom."

Installing Mac OS 7.6

Mac OS 7.6 has a simplified installation program called Install Mac OS. You can use this program to install some or all Mac OS 7.6 modules, and you have the option of performing a clean installation (see "Performing a Clean Installation" in Chapter 27). The Install Mac OS program will help you update the disk driver software on most Apple-brand hard disks you have, and you can have it check the condition of the hard disk on which the Mac OS 7.6 modules will be installed (see "Preparing for Installation" in Chapter 27). The modules you can install include the following:

❖ Mac OS 7.6 core software

❖ OpenDoc 1.1.2

❖ OpenDoc Essentials Kit 1.0.1

❖ QuickDraw 3D 1.0.6

❖ MacLinkPlus 8.1

❖ Apple Remote Access Client 2.1

❖ Cyberdog 1.2.1

❖ Open Transport PPP 1.0

❖ English Text-to-Speech 1.5

❖ QuickDraw GX 1.1.5

The section tells you how to use the Install Mac OS program to prepare for installation and then to install standard or custom Mac OS modules for one computer, or to install a universal Mac OS for starting up any computer capable of running Mac OS 7.6.

Installing Mac OS 7.6 — compatibility

Several of the Mac OS 7.6 modules are not compatible with every Mac model and with all Mac software, as detailed in the following paragraphs.

Core requirements

The Mac OS 7.6 core software requires a Mac that was originally equipped with a 68030, 68040, or PowerPC processor and has a 32-bit clean ROM. The following models can't use Mac OS 7.6: Plus, SE, SE/30, II, IIx, IIcx, Portable, PowerBook 100, original Classic, and original LC. System 7.5.5 is the latest version those models can use. Those models cannot be made eligible for Mac OS 7.6 by installing software for 32-bit addressing (for details, see "Increasing Total Memory" in Chapter 16) or by installing hardware accelerators. (Models older than a Plus can't use System 7.0 or later.)

QuickDraw 3D

QuickDraw 3D requires a PowerPC processor. You can't install it on a computer with a 68030 or 68040 processor.

OpenDoc, Cyberdog, and LaserWriter 8.4

OpenDoc, Cyberdog, and the LaserWriter 8.4 printer driver use a common piece of software that has a problem on computers without PowerPC processors. The software, called the CFM 68K Runtime Enabler, is not included with Mac OS 7.6 but is available separately and is included with the

Mac OS 7.6.1 Update. You cannot use Install Mac OS to install OpenDoc, OpenDoc Essentials, Cyberdog, or LaserWriter 8.4 on a computer with a 68030 or 68040 processor. (You can install those items on a computer with a PowerPC processor.) A few application programs also require the CFM 68K Runtime Enabler, including Apple Telecom 3.0, Apple Games Sprockets, and the Apple Media Tool.

Mac 5200, 5300, 6200, and 6300 series

Some Performa and Power Macintosh computers in the 5200, 5300, 6200, and 6300 series can't use Mac OS 7.6 until a hardware problem is fixed. The problem does not affect the 5260, 6320, or 6360 models. You can test for the problem by using the 5xxx/6xxx Tester utility in the Utilities folder on the CD-ROM. In addition, the Mac OS 7.6 installation software checks for the problem and alerts you if repairs are needed. The repairs are covered under an Apple warranty extension program that's in effect until 2003.

Open Transport

If you have installed Open Transport 1.1.2 or newer, it will be replaced with an older version when you install Mac OS 7.6. After installing Mac OS 7.6 you must reinstall your newer version of Open Transport.

AppleShare Workstation software

If your computer has AppleShare Workstation software installed, you must make sure it is version 3.6.3 or later before installing Mac OS 7.6 over a network. Apple Workstation 3.6.3 is included in the Utilities folder of the Mac OS 7.6 CD-ROM. To install it, drag its icon to the System Folder icon of the startup disk.

QuickDraw GX drivers

If you have a printer that doesn't use LaserWriter 8 or another Apple printer driver software, and you want to install QuickDraw GX, you need to get a QuickDraw GX driver for your printer. Once QuickDraw GX is installed, you will not be able to print without a GX driver. Mac OS 7.6 includes GX printer drivers for Apple printers. Contact the maker of your printer for assistance.

Adobe Acrobat

If your computer has Adobe Acrobat installed and you use the Mac OS 7.6 installation software to install or remove QuickDraw GX, Acrobat will display a message about missing fonts each time you start up the computer. Reinstall Acrobat to stop the message — simply disabling QuickDraw GX with the Extensions Manager control panel does not stop the message.

Apple Remote Access

If you install Apple Remote Access Client software after installing Open Transport PPP, an Installer tells you that a more recent version of Open Transport PPP is already installed. Respond that you want to use the newer version of Open Transport PPP.

System 6

You can't install Mac OS 7.6 directly over System 6. You must either install System 7.0 or later, or do a clean installation of Mac OS 7.6.

Installing Mac OS 7.6 — setup

The Install Mac OS program begins by leading you through some of the preparatory tasks that ensure a successful installation of Mac OS 7.6. To prepare for installing some or all Mac OS 7.6 modules, be sure to read Chapter 27, and then follow these steps:

1. Insert the Mac OS 7.6 CD-ROM disc or the Mac OS 7.6 Install Me First floppy disk and find the Install Mac OS program.

2. Start the Install Mac OS program by double-clicking its icon.

   After a few seconds, the Install Mac OS window appears, as shown in Figure 29-3.

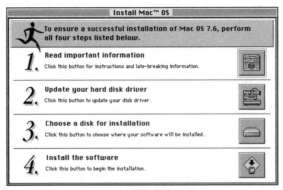

Figure 29-3: The Install Mac OS window.

3. Click the button for task 1 in the Install Mac OS window. The SimpleText program displays a document containing last-minute installation information for Mac OS 7.6. After reading, attending to, and optionally printing that document, close its window and switch back to the main Install Mac OS window.

You can skip step 3 if you have already read the last-minute installation information.

4. Click the button for task 2 in the Install Mac OS window. An alert gives you the opportunity to skip this task if none of your hard disks have Apple drivers. If you click the Continue button, the Drive Setup or HD SC Setup program opens, whichever is appropriate for your computer. Select each Apple hard disk and click the Update Driver button or the Update button to update its driver software. Then quit the Drive Setup or HD SC Setup program and switch back to the main Install Mac OS window.

   To update the driver software of hard disks that have non-Apple driver software, see "Preparing for Installation" in Chapter 27. You can skip this step if you have already updated the driver software on your hard disks.

5. Click the button for task 3 in the Install Mac OS window. A dialog box appears in which you choose the disk on which you want to install the Mac OS 7.6 modules. Choose the disk by name and click the Select button.

   If you skip this task, then in task 4 the Install Mac OS program will display a dialog box that asks you to specify the disk on which to install Mac OS 7.6.

6. Click the button for task 4 in the Install Mac OS window when you are ready to select the Mac OS 7.6 modules you want installed.

7. Do one of the following:

   ❖ Use the procedure in "Installing Mac OS 7.6 — standard" if you want to install the basic Mac OS 7.6 modules plus some or all additional modules, each in its entirety.

   ❖ Use the procedure in "Installing Mac OS 7.6 — custom" if you want to install any of the Mac OS 7.6 modules partially or completely.

   ❖ Use the procedure in "Installing Mac OS 7.6 — universal" if you want to install a Mac OS that can start up any computer capable of running Mac OS 7.6.

Installing Mac OS 7.6 — standard

A standard installation of Mac OS 7.6 always includes the Mac OS core module and the OpenDoc and OpenDoc Essentials modules if they will work on your computer. Other modules you can optionally install are QuickDraw 3D, MacLinkPlus, Apple Remote Access Client, Cyberdog, Open Transport PPP, English Text-To-Speech, and QuickDraw GX. Use the Install Mac OS program to select the optional modules you want to install, and under the control of the Install Mac OS program, each selected module is installed by a separate Installer program. The individual Installer programs do not require any response from you unless you are installing from floppy disks or a problem occurs.

The following steps explain how to do a standard installation of Mac OS 7.6, optionally doing a clean standard installation:

1. Start the Install Mac OS program and go through its four numbered tasks as previously described in steps 1 through 6 in "Installing Mac OS 7.6 — setup."

   After you complete all of the numbered tasks, a dialog box appears in which you can select the Mac OS 7.6 modules you want installed, as shown in Figure 29-4.

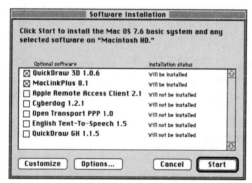

Figure 29-4: The standard Software Installation dialog box in the Install Mac OS program.

2. Select the modules of Mac OS 7.6 that you want installed by clicking the appropriate check boxes.

   The Install Mac OS program may select some modules by default, depending on the type of computer you're installing on. The three basic modules — Mac OS, OpenDoc, and OpenDoc Essentials — are not shown because they are always included in a standard Mac OS 7.6 installation. (OpenDoc and OpenDoc Essentials are included only if they will work on your computer.)

3. To perform a clean installation, click the Options button in the standard Software Installation dialog box. A dialog box appears in which you select the option "Create new System Folder (clean installation)" and then click OK.

4. Verify that the disk named at the top of the standard Software Installation dialog box is where you want the software installed (click the Cancel button and go back to step 1 if it isn't), and click the Start button in the standard Software Installation dialog box to begin installation.

The Install Mac OS program checks the condition of the disk on which it's going to install the software and tries to fix any problems it finds. While checking, it displays a progress gauge. If you want to stop the installation at this point, click the Stop button and go back to step 2.

5. The Install Mac OS program gives control to a succession of subordinate Installer programs, one for each Mac OS 7.6 module to be installed. The first Installer program displays an Apple license agreement for you to read and optionally print. If you agree to its terms, click the Agree button and installation begins.

   Each Installer program briefly displays the message "Preparing to install." If you are installing onto the startup disk and other programs are open (such as SimpleText), the Installer displays an alert message advising you that it can't continue while other applications are open. You can click a Cancel button to cancel installation or click a Continue button to have the Installer quit the other open applications. (The Installer also turns off file sharing if it is on.) As each application quits, it may come to the front and ask whether you want to save any changes that you haven't yet saved. After quitting the other open applications, the Installer displays the folders (or disks) it will need and begins installation, as shown in Figure 29-5.

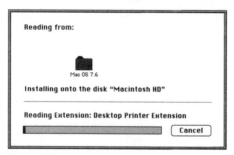

Figure 29-5: Installation is under way.

A standard installation proceeds automatically unless you are installing from floppy disks or a problem occurs. The individual Installer programs do not display welcome messages or offer installation options. If you are installing from a CD-ROM, a standard installation doesn't require more of your attention until it finishes. If you are installing from floppy disks and the Installer needs a different disk, the Installer ejects the disk that it is using and asks you to insert the disk it needs.

You can always cancel an installation that's under way by clicking the Cancel button. If you cancel an installation in progress, the Install Mac OS program displays an alert asking how you want to proceed. To stop installation, click the alert's Stop button and go back to step 2. To skip installation of the module currently being installed, click the alert's Skip button. To try installing the current module again, click the alert's Try Again button.

6. When the last Installer finishes, the Install Mac OS program asks whether you want to continue to install additional Mac OS 7.6 modules. If your answer is yes, click the Continue button to repeat steps 2 through 5 to install the modules. Otherwise quit the Install Mac OS program and restart the computer to use the new system software.

As the startup disk and any other hard disks appear on the desktop during the first restart after installation (or later, in the case of removable hard disk cartridges), the Finder may automatically rebuild the desktop database files (see "Maintaining the Desktop Database" in Chapter 8).

Installing Mac OS 7.6 — custom

A custom installation of Mac OS 7.6 gives you the choice of installing any of the following modules: Mac OS, OpenDoc, OpenDoc Essentials, QuickDraw 3D, MacLinkPlus, Apple Remote Access Client, Cyberdog, Open Transport PPP, English Text-To-Speech, and QuickDraw GX. In addition to installing complete modules, you can selectively install portions of each module. For example, the following are some of the components you can selectively install from the Mac OS module:

❖ Printer driver software for a kind of printer you haven't used before

❖ Control Strip, which provides quick access to various control panel settings

❖ Easy Access, which lets you move the pointer with the numeric keypad, type a key combination one stroke at a time, and so on

❖ Close View, which can magnify the entire display image

Do a custom installation only if you are sure that you know which individual items must be present for a module to work properly. If you're not sure, do a standard installation as previously described in "Installing Mac OS 7.6 — standard."

In a custom installation, you use the Install Mac OS program to select the modules you want installed, and the Install Mac OS program has individual Installer programs install the modules you select. You must interact with each Installer program to specify whether you want it to install all or part of its module.

The following steps tell you how to custom install Mac OS 7.6, optionally doing a clean custom installation:

1. Start the Install Mac OS program and go through its four numbered tasks as previously explained in steps 1 through 6 in "Installing Mac OS 7.6 — setup."

   After you complete all of the numbered tasks, the standard Software Installation dialog box appears, in which you can select modules to be installed and indicate that you want to do a custom installation (review Figure 29-2).

2. Click the Customize button in the standard Software Installation dialog box to change to the Custom Software Installation dialog box, as shown in Figure 29-6.

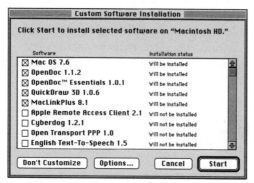

Figure 29-6: The Custom Software Installation dialog box in the Install Mac OS program.

3. Select the modules of Mac OS 7.6 that you want installed by clicking the appropriate check boxes.

   Only the selected modules will be installed. You will have an opportunity later to selectively install portions of each module as it is installed.

4. Click the Options button in the Custom Software Installation dialog box if you want to do a clean installation or disable checking of the destination disk's condition.

   A dialog box appears in which you can turn on or off the options "Create new System Folder (clean installation)" and "Check Destination Disk." If the disk checking option is absent then you are doing a standard installation, which always includes the disk check.

5. Verify that the disk named at the top of the Custom Software Installation dialog box is where you want the software installed (click the Cancel button and go back to step 1 if it isn't), and click the Start button in the Custom Software Installation dialog box to begin installation.

   Unless you disabled the Check Destination Disk option in step 4, the Install Mac OS program checks the condition of the disk on which it's going to install the software and tries to fix any problems it finds. While checking, it displays a progress gauge so you can monitor its progress. If you want to stop the installation at this point, click the Stop button and go back to step 3.

6. The Install Mac OS program gives control to a succession of Installer programs, one for each Mac OS 7.6 module you selected in step 3.

   Before displaying its main window, each Installer except the one for the OpenDoc Essentials module first displays a welcome message. After you dismiss that, some Installers display an Apple license agreement for you to read and optionally print. You must agree to its terms to continue installation. The Installer displays its main window, which describes what will be installed (see Figure 29-7).

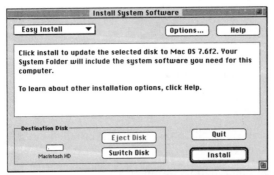

Figure 29-7: Ready to install one complete Mac OS 7.6 module.

7. Do one of the following:

   ❖ To install a complete module, choose Easy Install from the pop-up menu in the Installer's main window and click the Install button in that window. (For the OpenDoc Essentials module, simply click the Install button, because its Installer has no pop-up menu.)

   ❖ To selectively install portions of the module, choose Custom Install from the pop-up menu in the Installer window. The Installer lists components, and in some cases groups of components that you can install. To expand a component group, click the triangle next to it. You can get information about a component by clicking its information button at the right side of the Installer window. Select the components that you want to install by clicking the appropriate check boxes, and then click the Install button (see Figure 29-8).

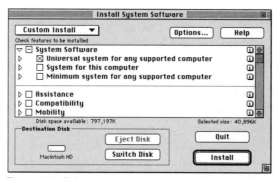

Figure 29-8: Select components to be installed from one Mac OS 7.6 module.

After you click the Install button, the Installer briefly displays the message "Preparing to install." If you are installing onto the startup disk and other programs are open (such as SimpleText), the Installer displays an alert message advising you that it can't continue while other applications are open. You can click a Cancel button to cancel installation or click a Continue button to have the Installer quit the other open applications. (The Installer also turns off file sharing if it is on.) As each application quits, it may come to the front and ask whether you want to save any changes that you haven't yet saved. After quitting the other open applications, the Installer displays the folders (or disks) that will be needed and commences installation. If you are installing from floppy disks and the Installer needs a different disk, the Installer ejects the disk that it is using and asks you to insert the disk it needs.

You can always cancel an installation that's under way by clicking the Cancel button and quitting the Installer program. If you cancel an installation in progress, the Install Mac OS program displays an alert asking how you want to proceed. To stop installation, click the alert's Stop button and go back to step 3. To skip installation of the module currently being installed, click the alert's Skip button. To try installing the current module again, click the alert's Try Again button.

8. When the last Installer finishes, the Install Mac OS program asks whether you want to install additional Mac OS 7.6 modules. Click the Continue

button if you want to repeat steps 3 through 7 to install additional modules, otherwise quit the Install Mac OS program and restart the computer to use the new system software.

Installing Mac OS 7.6 — universal

Normally the Install Mac OS program installs only the Mac OS software for the type of computer it's running on. For example, Install Mac OS installs mobility software only on portable Mac OS computers such as Apple's PowerBooks. If you want to install the Mac OS software needed to start up any type of Mac OS computer — a universal Mac OS — you must do a distinct type of custom installation. Perform steps 1 through 8 as previously outlined in "Installing Mac OS 7.6 — custom," with the following particulars:

❖ In step 3, be sure to select the Mac OS module.

❖ In step 7, as each Installer program takes its turn, specify the following conditions:

- Mac OS 7.6 Installer — choose Custom Install from the Installer's pop-up menu and select either "Universal system for any supported computer" or "Minimum system for any supported computer." You may also select other listed components that you want installed by clicking their check boxes.

- OpenDoc — choose Easy Install from the Installer's pop-up menu.

- OpenDoc Essentials — nothing to specify.

- QuickDraw 3D — choose Easy Install.

- MacLinkPlus — choose Easy Install.

- Remote Access Client Install — choose Easy Install.

- Cyberdog Installer — choose Easy Install.

- Open Transport PPP — choose Custom Install and select all components if the universal Mac OS is to be used with PowerPC processors and 68030 or 68040 processors. Easy Install is OK if it is to be used with only one type of processor.

- English TTS Installer — choose Easy Install.

- QuickDraw GX Installer — choose Custom Install and preferably select all components; at least select the "Base QuickDraw GX Software for any Macintosh" component.

Summary

This chapter told you how to upgrade from Mac OS 7.6 to Mac OS 7.6.1. It also told you how to install Mac OS 7.6 on a computer that's using an earlier system software version. You can install Mac OS 7.6 in its entirety, or you can selectively install portions of any module.

Install Other System Software

Although Apple's latest system software is great, you may prefer to use or have to use an older version. For instance, Mac OS 8 doesn't work on Macs with 68030, 68020, or 68000 processors. Mac OS 7.6 doesn't work on Macs originally equipped with 68020 or 68000 processors, or on some 68030 Macs. Furthermore, Mac OS 8 and Mac OS 7.6 require significantly more RAM and hard disk space than System 7.5.5 and earlier. If your computer has 8MB of RAM or less, a hard disk smaller than 500MB, or less than a 68030 processor, System 7.5.5 may be your best (or only) choice.

This chapter explains how to install System 7.5.5, 7.5.3, and 7.5. It also tells you how to subsequently install individual add-on software modules such as QuickDraw GX and PowerTalk.

Installing System 7.5.5

System 7.5.5 can be installed as an upgrade to System 7.5.3 or 7.5.4. It works on all Mac OS computers from the Mac Plus to the latest models shipping at the end of 1996, except the PowerBook 1400, all Motorola computers, all APS Technologies computers, and all Apple Workgroup Server computers. System 7.5.5 is the latest version of the Mac OS you can install on the following models: Plus, SE, SE/30, II, IIx, IIcx, Portable, PowerBook 100, original Classic, and original LC.

Problems can occur when installing System 7.5.5 on a computer that has the Energy Saver control panel version 1.2 and earlier. Look in the Control Panels folder for Energy Saver. If you find it, use the Finder's Get Info command to determine its version number. If the version number is 1.2 or lower, drag the

Energy Saver from the Control Panels folder to the desktop before installing System 7.5.5. After installing System 7.5.5, you can drag the Energy Saver back to the Control Panels folder.

To upgrade to System 7.5.5, follow these steps:

1. If your Mac has System 7.5.2 or earlier, upgrade it to System 7.5.3 by following the instructions in "Installing System 7.5.3 or 7.5" later in this chapter.

2. Insert the first System 7.5.5 floppy disk or open the first System 7.5.5 installation folder and start the Installer program by double-clicking its icon.

3. The Installer program displays an Apple license agreement for you to read and optionally print. Click the Agree button to continue.

   The Installer's main window appears. This window identifies the disk on which the software will be installed and describes what will be installed, as shown in Figure 30-1.

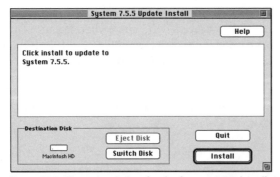

Figure 30-1: The main window for the System 7.5.5 Installer.

4. Make sure the destination-disk name is the one on which you want to install the software. If you have more than one hard disk, you can switch disks by clicking the Switch Disk button.

5. Click the Install button in the main Installer window to begin installation.

   The Installer briefly displays the message "Preparing to install." If you are installing onto the startup disk and other programs are open (such as SimpleText), the Installer displays an alert message advising you that it can't continue while other applications are open. You can click a Cancel button to cancel installation or click a Continue button to have the Installer quit the other open applications. (The Installer also turns off file sharing if it is on.) As each application quits, it may come to the front and ask whether you want to save any changes that you haven't yet saved. After quitting the other open applications, the Installer displays the folders (or disks) it will need and commences installation, as shown in Figure 30-2.

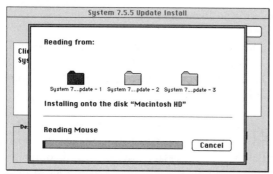

Figure 30-2: Installation of the System 7.5.5 upgrade is under way.

If you are installing from floppy disks and the Installer needs a different disk, the Installer ejects the disk it used and asks you to insert the next disk it needs. You can always cancel an installation by clicking the Cancel button.

When the Installer finishes upgrading to System 7.5.5, it tells you to restart the computer to use the new system software.

After upgrading to System 7.5.5, you can still install individual components of System 7.5.3 such as desktop printing or the Control Strip. You can use the System 7.5 Version 7.5.3 installation CD-ROM or floppy disks as described next in "Installing System 7.5.3 or 7.5 — custom." You can also use System 7.5 Update 2.0 to install individual components of System 7.5.3 onto System 7.5.5, but only if you obtain a special installer script from Apple. The regular installer script that comes with System 7.5 Update 2.0 will not allow you to install individual components into System 7.5.5. The special installer script, named Sys 7.5 Upd 2.0 Custom Install, is available from the Unsupported folder of Apple's online software library (http://www.info.apple.com). Apple does not provide any support for the special installer script, so you can't call 800-SOS-APPLE if you have trouble with it.

Installing System 7.5.3 or 7.5

Installing all of the software that comes with System 7.5.3 or its predecessor System 7.5 involves using several Installer programs. There is one Installer for the basic system software, a second Installer for the optional QuickDraw GX software, and a third Installer for the optional PowerTalk software. System 7.5.3 on CD-ROM includes Installers for additional optional software including QuickDraw 3D and PlainTalk.

This section tells you how to install all or part of the basic System 7.5.3 or System 7.5 software. To install additional system software such as QuickDraw GX, PowerTalk, or OpenDoc, follow the instructions in "Installing Additional System Software" later in this chapter.

Before installing or upgrading to a new version of system software, be sure to back up the startup disk, verify the disk directories, update the hard disk driver software, and turn off all but the necessary extensions and control panels (see "Preparing for Installation" in Chapter 27). If you have a RAM disk smaller than 416K, you must move its contents to another disk prior to installing or upgrading to System 7.5.3. Effective with System 7.5.3, the minimum RAM disk size is 416K. A smaller RAM disk will be turned off and its contents lost when you restart your computer after installing System 7.5.3.

Installing System 7.5.3 or 7.5 — standard

The following steps tell you how to install all the basic components of System 7.5.3 or 7.5, optionally doing a clean installation:

1. Locate the Installer program for the basic system software. On a System 7.5 Version 7.5.3 CD-ROM, the Installer has an alias in the System Software Installers folder. On a System 7.5 CD-ROM, the Installer is in the System Install folder inside the Installation folder. On a set of floppy disks for System 7.5.3 or 7.5, the Installer is on the disk labeled Install Disk 1.

2. Start the Installer program. After a few seconds, the Installer displays a welcome message. When you dismiss the welcome message, the Installer's main window appears. This window identifies the disk on which the software will be installed and describes what will be installed, as shown in Figure 30-3.

3. Make sure that the destination disk name is the one on which you want to install the software. If you have more than one hard disk, you can switch disks by clicking the Switch Disk button.

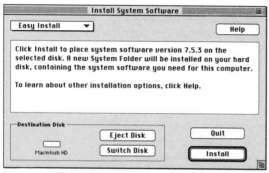

Figure 30-3: The main window of the System 7.5.3 Installer.

4. Do one of the following:

- Click the Install button in the main Installer window to begin installation.

- Perform a clean installation by pressing ⌘-Shift-K. This brings up a dialog box in which you indicate the type of installation you want. Select the Install New System Folder option, and then click OK. Back in the main Installer window, click the Clean Install button to begin installation.

5. The Installer briefly displays the message "Preparing to install."

   If you are installing onto the startup disk and other programs are open (such as SimpleText), the Installer displays an alert message advising you that it can't continue while other applications are open. You can click a Cancel button to cancel installation or click a Continue button to have the Installer quit the other open applications. (The Installer also turns off file sharing if it is on.) As each application quits, it may come to the front and ask whether you want to save any changes that you haven't yet saved. After quitting the other open applications, the Installer displays the folders (or disks) that will be needed and commences installation, as shown in Figure 30-4.

   If you are installing from floppy disks and the Installer needs a different disk, the Installer ejects the disk that it used and asks you to insert the next disk it needs. You can always cancel an installation by clicking the Cancel button.

6. When the Installer finishes, it asks whether you want to continue doing installations. Click the Continue button if you want to repeat steps 3 through 5 to install on other disks. Otherwise quit the Installer and restart the computer to use the new system software.

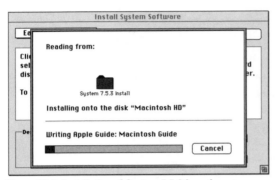

Figure 30-4: Installation of System 7.5.3 is under way.

Installing System 7.5.3 resets the Apple Menu Options and Views control panels to their original factory settings. If you had changed settings in either of those control panels, you will need to reset them after installing System 7.5.3.

After performing a clean installation of System 7.5.3 on a Mac OS computer with PCI slots, virtual memory will be turned on. You can turn off virtual memory in the Memory control panel.

After performing a clean installation of System 7.5, the About This Macintosh command (in the Apple menu when the Finder is active) no longer reports a specific Macintosh model name. Instead it displays a generic name such as Macintosh, Macintosh PowerBook, or Power Macintosh. If you upgrade to System 7.5 without doing a clean installation, the About This Macintosh command continues reporting the specific model name.

Installing System 7.5.3 or 7.5 — custom

In a custom installation of System 7.5.3 or 7.5, you can select the individual components you want installed. The following are some of the components you may need to install using the Custom Install option:

❖ Printer driver software for a kind of printer you haven't used before

❖ Control Strip, which provides quick access to various control panel settings

❖ Easy Access, which lets you move the pointer with the numeric keypad, type a key combination one stroke at a time, and so on

❖ Close View, which can magnify the entire display image

Do a custom installation only if you are sure that you know which individual items must be present for the software to work properly. If you're not sure, do a standard installation as previously described in "Installing System 7.5.3 or 7.5 — standard."

To perform a custom installation, and optionally do a clean custom installation, follow these steps:

1. Locate the Installer program for the basic system software.

   On a System 7.5.3 CD-ROM, the Installer program has an alias in the System Software Installers folder. On a System 7.5 CD-ROM, the Installer is in the System Install folder inside the Installation folder. On a set of floppy disks for System 7.5.3 or 7.5, the Installer is on the disk labeled Install Disk 1.

2. Start the Installer program.

   After a few seconds, the Installer displays a welcome message. When you dismiss the welcome message, the Installer's main window appears. This window identifies the disk on which the software will be installed and describes what will be installed.

3. Choose Custom Install from the pop-up menu.

   The Installer lists groups of components that you can install, as shown in Figure 30-5.

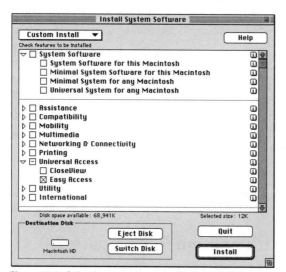

Figure 30-5: Selecting components of System 7.5.3 to be installed.

4. Select the components that you want to install by clicking the appropriate check boxes. To expand a component group, click the triangle next to it. You can get information about a component by clicking its information button at the right side of the Installer window.

5. Do one of the following:

- When you finish making your selections, click the Install button to begin the installation process.

- Perform a clean installation by pressing ⌘-Shift-K. This brings up a dialog box in which you indicate the type of installation you want. Select the Install New System Folder option, and then click OK. Back in the main Installer window, click the Clean Install button to begin installation.

The Installer briefly displays the message "Preparing to install." If you are installing onto the startup disk and other programs are open (such as SimpleText), the Installer displays an alert message advising you that it can't continue while other applications are open. You can click a Cancel button to cancel installation or click a Continue button to have the Installer quit the other open applications. (The Installer also turns off file sharing if it is on.) As each application quits, it may come to the front and ask whether you want to save any changes that you haven't yet saved. After quitting the other open applications, the Installer displays the folders (or disks) that will be needed and commences installation.

If you are installing from floppy disks and the Installer needs a different disk, the Installer ejects the disk that it used and asks you to insert the next disk it needs. You can always cancel an installation by clicking the Cancel button.

6. When the Installer finishes, it tells you to restart the computer to use the new system software.

After performing a clean installation of the Custom Install component "Minimal System for any Macintosh" or "Universal System for any Macintosh" for System 7.5.3, virtual memory will be turned on. You can turn off virtual memory in the Memory control panel.

Installing System 7.5.3 resets the Apple Menu Options and Views control panels to their original factory settings. If you had changed settings in either of those control panels, you will need to reset them after installing System 7.5.3.

Upgrading with System 7.5 Update 2.0

You can use System 7.5 Update 2.0 to upgrade to System 7.5.3 from System 7.5, 7.5.1, or 7.5.2. To upgrade from an earlier version of System 7, use the System 7.5 Version 7.5 CD-ROM or disks, as previously described in "Installing System 7.5.3 or 7.5 — standard."

To use System 7.5 Update 2.0, follow these steps:

1. Insert the System 7.5 Update 2.0 CD-ROM or the first floppy disk, and start the Installer program by double-clicking its icon.

2. The Installer program displays a welcome message. When you dismiss the welcome message, the Installer's main window appears. This window identifies the disk on which the software will be installed and describes what will be installed, as shown in Figure 30-6.

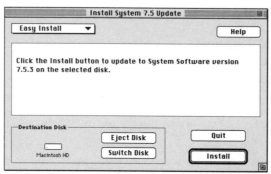

Figure 30-6: The main window for the System 7.5 Update 2.0 Installer.

3. Make sure that the destination disk name is the one on which you want to install the software. If you have more than one hard disk, you can switch disks by clicking the Switch Disk button.

4. Click the Install button in the main Installer window to begin installation.

The Installer briefly displays the message "Preparing to install." If you are installing onto the startup disk and other programs are open (such as SimpleText), the Installer displays an alert message advising you that it can't continue while other applications are open. You can click a Cancel button to cancel installation or click a Continue button to have the Installer quit the other open applications. (The Installer also turns off file sharing if it is on.) As each application quits, it may come to the front and ask whether you want to save any changes that you haven't yet saved. After quitting the other open applications, the Installer displays the folders (or disks) it will need and commences installation.

If you are installing from floppy disks and the Installer needs a different disk, the Installer ejects the disk that it used and asks you to insert the next disk it needs. You can always cancel an installation by clicking the Cancel button.

5. When the Installer finishes upgrading to System 7.5.3, it tells you to restart the computer to use the new system software.

Installing Additional System Software

Apple periodically releases new or upgraded system software modules that you can add to existing versions of the system software. Examples from the past include QuickTime, QuickDraw GX, QuickDraw 3D, AppleScript, OpenDoc, PlainTalk, and PowerTalk. You install most add-on system software with an Installer program, and the following steps usually apply:

1. Locate the Installer program for the add-on software, and start the Installer by double-clicking its icon.

2. If the Installer displays a welcome message, dismiss it to proceed with the installation.

3. If the Installer displays a license agreement, you must agree to its terms to continue installation.

4. When the Installer's main window appears, confirm that the destination disk is correct. If you have more than one hard disk, you can switch disks by clicking the Switch Disk button (see Figure 30-7).

Figure 30-7: An Installer's main window.

5. Do one of the following:

   • To install the complete add-on software module, choose Easy Install from the pop-up menu in the Installer's main window and click the Install button in that window. If there is no pop-up menu in the Installer window, simply click the Install button.

- To selectively install portions of the add-on software module, choose Custom Install from the pop-up menu in the Installer window. The Installer lists components, and in some cases groups of components that you can install. To expand a component group, click the triangle next to it. You can get information about a component by clicking its information button at the right side of the Installer window. Select the components that you want to install by clicking their check boxes, and then click the Install button (see Figure 30-8).

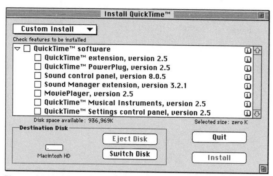

Figure 30-8: Selecting components to be installed from an add-on software module.

The Installer briefly displays the message "Preparing to install" and then commences installation. If you are installing from floppy disks and the Installer needs a different disk, the Installer ejects the disk that it used and asks you to insert the next disk it needs. You can always cancel an installation by clicking the Cancel button.

When the Installer finishes, it may ask if you want to quit or continue doing installations. Quit unless you want to repeat steps 4 and 5 to install the module on other disks. Alternatively, the Installer may tell you to restart the computer to use the new system software.

Summary

This chapter described how to install older system software versions on older computers with RAM, hard disk, or processor limitations. You can upgrade to System 7.5.5 from an earlier version of System 7, and you can install System 7.5.3 or System 7.5. You can install all of a system software version, or you can do a custom installation of selected components. In addition, you can install add-on software such as QuickDraw GX and PowerTalk.

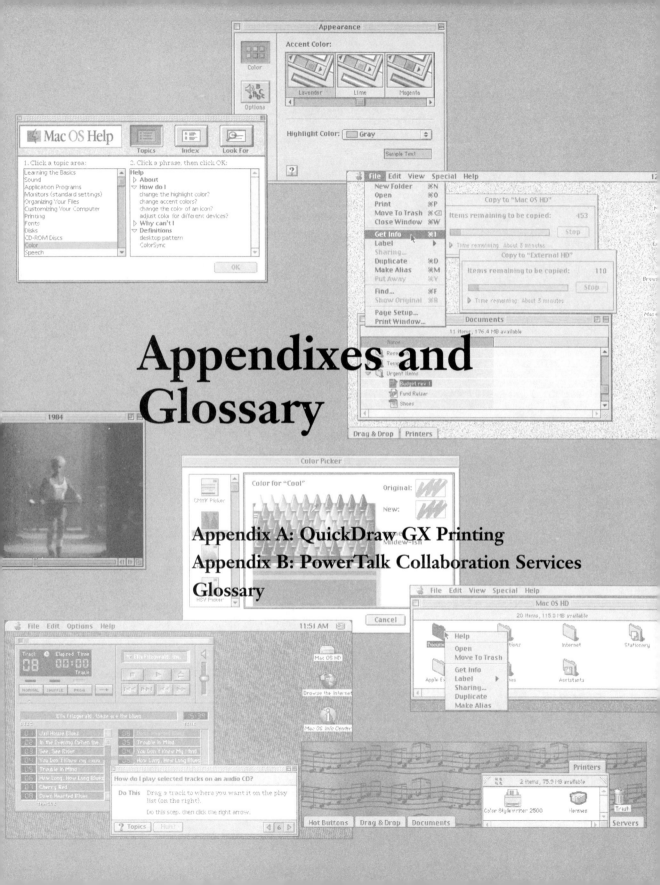

Appendixes and Glossary

Appendix A: QuickDraw GX Printing

Appendix B: PowerTalk Collaboration Services

Glossary

QuickDraw GX Printing

If you choose to install QuickDraw GX with Mac OS 7.6.1 or earlier, you get not only advanced typography (described in Chapter 13) but an enhanced printing system as well. Why are you reading about an enhanced printing system in an appendix? Despite GX printing's benefits, it has not been popular. Apple decided to remove the printing enhancements from QuickDraw GX beginning with Mac OS 8 and standardize on non-GX printing.

These are the main features of QuickDraw GX printing in system software versions 7.5 through 7.6.1:

❖ **Desktop printer icons** give you drag-and-drop printing and improved management of background printing, including the ability to redirect a print job from one printer to another. This feature is similar to the desktop printing described in Chapter 14.

❖ **Simplified Page Setup and Print commands** offer simple options, or at the click of a button they offer expanded options in participating applications — options such as choosing a printer at print time and combining multiple page sizes and margins in a single document. In addition, you can drag the Page Setup and Print dialog boxes around the screen.

❖ **Printer extensions** add special effects such as watermarks and multiple pages per sheet of paper to every participating application.

❖ **Portable Digital Documents** allow you to view and print fully formatted documents without the applications that created them and without the fonts used to create them.

❖ **Printer sharing** enables you to share printers that themselves don't connect to a network and (optionally) to secure any shared printer with a password. This feature is similar to the printer sharing described in Chapter 14.

As with non-GX printing, you set up and control printing the same basic way, regardless of the application you are using or the type of printer you have. All applications use the same printer driver software to prepare the page image for, and communicate with, a particular type of printer. For each printer you use, you select a driver and set up a desktop icon with the Chooser.

To print documents, you use standard Page Setup and Print commands that are enhanced in applications designed to take full advantage of QuickDraw GX printing. In applications that are merely compatible with GX printing, you use Page Setup and Print commands that are similar to the commands without GX printing (described in Chapter 15).

All GX printing occurs in the background, so you don't have to wait for documents to finish printing before continuing with other work. If several documents are waiting to be printed on a particular printer, you can use its desktop icon to manage the queue of waiting print requests.

This appendix describes the software you need and the methods you use with QuickDraw GX-enhanced printing. If your Mac uses Mac OS 7.6.1 or earlier and has QuickDraw GX installed, this appendix is for you. If your Mac does not have QuickDraw GX installed or it uses Mac OS 8.0 or later, refer to Chapters 14 and 15.

Checking for GX Printing

Your Mac may have the QuickDraw GX printing enhancements if it uses Mac OS 7.6 or 7.6.1 or Systems 7.5 through 7.5.5. If your Mac uses a version of System 7 earlier than 7.5, it most likely does not have QuickDraw GX at all. QuickDraw GX is included with complete installation packages for system versions 7.5 through 7.6.1 but is not part of the core installation. The QuickDraw GX installers that come with System 7.5 and Mac OS 7.6 will not install QuickDraw GX on a version of System 7 older than 7.5, although in theory, QuickDraw GX works with System 7.1 and later.

If you're not sure whether your Mac has QuickDraw GX with enhanced printing, you can tell for sure by opening the Chooser and looking for printer icons whose names end with GX. Looking in the Extensions folder (inside the System Folder) for printer driver files whose names end with GX is not a foolproof method, because those files can be present even if the rest of QuickDraw GX is absent. Likewise checking for the QuickDraw GX extension file is inconclusive because QuickDraw GX 1.1.6 and later do not include printing enhancements. Also, the presence of desktop printer icons does not guarantee that you have GX-enhanced printing, because desktop printing software is available without QuickDraw GX.

Comparing GX Printer Driver Software

QuickDraw GX with printing enhancements needs its own printer driver software for each type of printer you use. A GX printer driver prepares an image of each page to be printed, in a format that the printer can interpret, and then sends the page descriptions to the printer. The printer drivers used by non-GX printing do not work with GX-enhanced printing. Installing QuickDraw GX with printing enhancements adds the following printer drivers to the Extensions folder, as shown in Figure A-1:

❖ **LaserWriter GX** for printing on PostScript printers, such as Apple's LaserWriter Plus, II, IINT, IINTX, IIf, and IIg; Personal LaserWriter IINT, IINTR, and 320; LaserWriter Select 360; and LaserWriter Pro 600, 630, and 810. LaserWriter GX takes the place of LaserWriter, LaserWriter 8, and PSPrinter, but it can coexist on a network with those non-GX drivers. LaserWriter GX does not use PPD files.

❖ **Color StyleWriter 2400 GX** for printing on a Color StyleWriter 2200 or 2400.

❖ **Color StyleWriter Pro GX** for printing on a Color StyleWriter Pro.

❖ **StyleWriter GX** for printing on a StyleWriter 1200, StyleWriter II, or original StyleWriter.

❖ **PDD Maker GX** for creating portable digital documents as described in "Using Portable Digital Documents (PDDs)" later in this appendix.

❖ **LaserWriter 300 GX** for printing on a LaserWriter Select 300 or Personal LaserWriter LS.

❖ **ImageWriter GX** for printing on an ImageWriter or ImageWriter II.

❖ **ImageWriter LQ GX** for printing on an ImageWriter LQ.

❖ **LaserWriter IISC GX** for printing on a LaserWriter IISC.

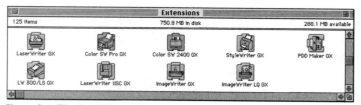

Figure A-1: The QuickDraw GX printer drivers.

Non-GX drivers remain in the Extensions folder after the installation of QuickDraw GX, but you can't use any of those drivers for GX-enhanced printing. You may be able to print with a non-GX driver by using Apple's GX Helper software (as described in "Bypassing GX printing" later in this appendix). For best results with GX-enhanced printing, you should get GX drivers from the makers of devices such as fax/modems, non-Apple printers, and portable document makers.

Extending GX Printing Capabilities

You can add to the basic functions of a printer driver by installing printing-extension software in the Extensions folder. Some printing extensions give you access to a particular printer's features, such as its resolution and the size and capacity of its paper trays. Other printing extensions modify the appearance of a document during the printing process. For example, a printing extension could provide the option of watermarking every page with a light-gray text message (such as *Draft*) or a faint picture (such as a company logo); the ordinary contents of each page would print over this "watermark."

Apple includes a GX printing extension with some versions of QuickDraw GX for printing multiple mini-pages per sheet of paper. Additional printing extensions are available from other companies, such as Peirce Print Tools from Peirce Software (408/244-6554, http://www.peircesw.com). Peirce Print Tools adds nine new printing capabilities to every application (even if the application hasn't been updated to use GX print dialog box) including double-sided printing, multiple pages per side, and watermarks.

Using GX Desktop Printer Icons

With QuickDraw GX 1.1.5 and earlier installed, you do not use the Chooser to choose an output device for printing; instead, you use the Chooser to create desktop printer icons for each printer, fax/modem, or other output device that you use. After creating the desktop printer icons, you use the Finder, not the Chooser, to choose and set up a printer. Background printing is always on for all devices; you cannot turn it off with the Chooser.

Creating desktop printer icons

Installing QuickDraw GX 1.1.5 or earlier creates a desktop printer icon for the printer that was selected in the Chooser before installation. If you use more than one printer, or if you had not selected a printer in the Chooser before installing QuickDraw GX, you use the Chooser to create desktop printer icons. Each printer must have its own icon. If you use three LaserWriters, for example, you need three LaserWriter GX desktop icons. You cannot print to a printer until you create a desktop icon for it.

Selecting a type of printer

To create a desktop printer icon for any device, open the Chooser. Each printer or other output device for which there is a GX driver in the Extensions folder appears as an icon in the Chooser. On the left side of the Chooser window, select the icon of the driver that you want to use. If you see a list of network zones in the lower left corner of the Chooser window, select the zone of the printer for which you want to make a desktop icon. (If you don't see a list of zones, your network has no zones.) Figure A-2 shows an example of the Chooser ready for selecting a GX printer driver.

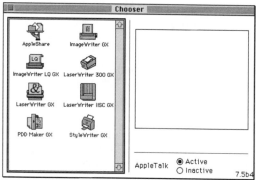

Figure A-2: Selecting a printer driver for GX desktop printer icon.

Selecting a networked printer

After selecting a printer driver, you can select a specific printer (or a specific printer connection) on the right side of the Chooser window. If there is a Connect Via pop-up menu at the top of the Chooser window, use it to choose the type of connection for the type of printer or other output device that you're setting up. Choose AppleTalk for a device connected to a LocalTalk or EtherTalk network; choose Servers for a shared device (described in "Sharing printers under QuickDraw GX" later in this appendix); choose Serial for a device connected without a network adapter box to the Mac's modem or printer port; or choose SCSI for a device connected to the Mac's SCSI port. The pop-up menu lists only relevant choices for the selected driver; it does not list all choices for all drivers. The pop-up menu does not appear for drivers that have no connection options.

If you chose AppleTalk as the Connect Via option for the selected printer, you see a list of the names of all printers of that type that currently are available on your network. You select the specific printer that you want by clicking its name. You can also select a listed printer by typing the first part of its name. (To select by typing, the list of printer names must be surrounded by a heavy border; if it isn't, press Tab until it is.) Figure A-3 shows an example list of printers that use the LaserWriter GX driver.

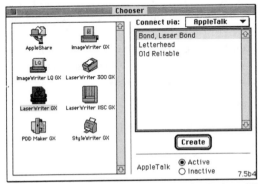

Figure A-3: Selecting a PostScript printer for the LaserWriter GX driver when the Chooser's Connect Via option is AppleTalk.

If your network has zones, you see the names of printers in the currently selected zone. You can select a different zone in the lower-left part of the Chooser. The Chooser does not display a list of zones unless your network has more than one zone.

Selecting a directly connected printer

If you choose Serial as the Chooser's Connect Via option for the selected GX printer driver, the Chooser lists the ports to which the printer can be connected. You select a port by clicking it in the Chooser. Figure A-4 shows an example list of ports for a directly connected printer.

Creating the printer icon

After selecting a specific printer or other device, click the Create button to create a desktop icon for that printer or device. This icon refers only to the printer or device that was selected when you clicked the Create button. If you need a desktop icon for another printer or device of the same type, you must select it and click Create again.

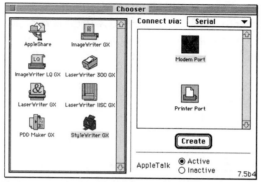

Figure A-4: Selecting a port for a directly connected printer when the Chooser's Connect Via option is Serial.

Choosing the default printer

After creating desktop printer icons for all the printers you use, you must designate which one you want to use by default. First, select the printer's desktop icon; a Printing menu appears next to the Finder's Special menu. Choose Set Default Printer from that menu. The Finder indicates the default printer by drawing a heavy black border around its desktop icon. The Printing menu is only available in the Finder. Figure A-5 shows a couple of desktop printer icons and the Printing menu.

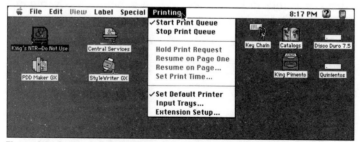

Figure A-5: Setting a default GX printer with the Finder's Printing menu.

Changing printer setup

The Finder's Printing menu contains commands not only for designating the default printer, but also for changing the setup of any printer that has a desktop icon. The Input Trays command specifies the type of paper present in the paper trays of the printer whose desktop icon is selected. Your options vary according to the number of and types of trays installed in the currently selected printer. The paper tray settings are used by the Print command of applications that have adopted GX printing (see "Using the GX Print command" later in this appendix). Figure A-6 shows an example of the dialog box in which you specify the type of paper in a printer's paper tray.

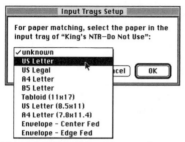

Figure A-6: Specifying the type of paper in a printer's input tray or trays.

The Extension Setup command specifies which of the available GX printing extensions (installed in the Extensions folder) to use with the printer whose desktop icon is selected. The active extensions are applied in the order listed, from top to bottom. You can change the order of printing extensions by dragging them up or down the list in the Extension Setup dialog box. Figure A-7 shows an example of the dialog box in which you set up GX printing extensions.

The other commands in the Finder's Printing menu are covered in "Managing GX Printing" later in this appendix.

Figure A-7: Specifying which GX printing extensions are active for a printer and the order in which they apply.

Using the GX Page Setup Command

Before printing a document, you need to format the document pages. You must specify the type of paper, page orientation, reduction or enlargement factor, and other formatting options. The exact options available depend on the type of printer you are using and on whether the application in which you choose the Page Setup command (usually from the File menu) has adopted GX printing. The following section describes the GX Page Setup command in applications that have adopted GX printing; the section after that one describes the GX Page Setup command in applications that have not adopted GX printing.

In addition to the options described in these sections, you may encounter options added by printing extensions or by individual application programs. For information on these options, see the documentation for the software that is responsible for them.

GX Page Setup in participating applications

Applications that take full advantage of GX printing offer the same general Page Setup options for every type of output device. These applications display a simple Page Setup dialog box that you can drag to a different location by its title bar. Figure A-8 shows an example of the simple GX Page Setup dialog box displayed by applications that have adopted GX printing.

Figure A-8: Setting basic LaserWriter GX page attributes in applications that have adopted GX printing.

In the simple GX Page Setup dialog box, the Paper Type pop-up menu lists the paper sizes that are available on the selected printer. (For example, tabloid size — 11 by 17 inches — is available on LaserWriters but not on StyleWriters.) You also can choose one of three page orientations and enter a reduction or enlargement percentage.

Clicking the More Choices button in the simple Page Setup dialog box expands the dialog box. The expanded Page Setup dialog box includes all the basic options of the simple dialog box. In addition, you can choose a printer from a pop-up menu. The Format For pop-up menu lists every type of printer for which the Extensions folder contains a GX printer driver; the menu also lists the name of every printer with a desktop icon. Choosing a printer from this pop-up menu does not change the default printer; use the Finder's Set Default Printer command for that purpose. Figure A-9 shows an example of the expanded GX Page Setup dialog box displayed by applications that have adopted GX printing.

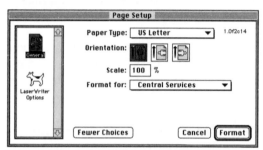

Figure A-9: Setting all LaserWriter GX page attributes in applications that have adopted GX printing.

The icons on the left side of the expanded GX Page Setup dialog box represent panels of options. Many printers, including all StyleWriters and ImageWriters, have only the General panel of options.

The LaserWriter GX dialog box has a LaserWriter Options panel for setting a few PostScript options. LaserWriter GX has fewer PostScript options than the non-GX LaserWriter Page Setup dialog boxes described in Chapter 15. LaserWriter GX sets the missing options automatically for best results. Figure A-10 shows the LaserWriter Options panel of the LaserWriter GX Page Setup dialog box displayed by applications that have adopted GX printing.

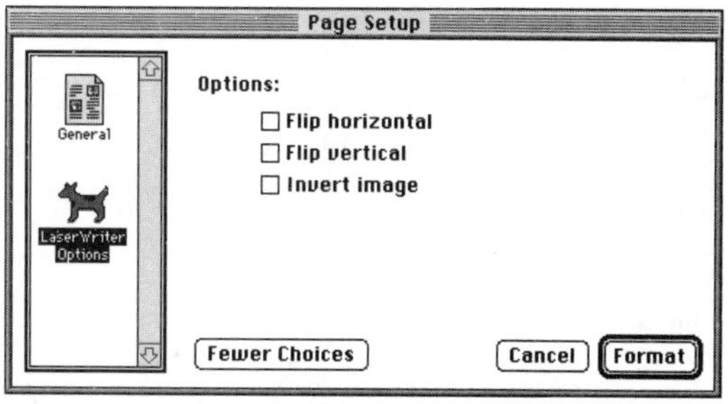

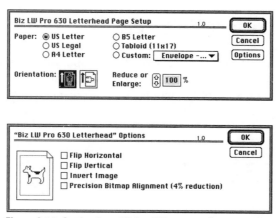

Figure A-10: Setting LaserWriter GX PostScript options
in applications that have adopted GX printing.

GX Page Setup in nonparticipating applications

When QuickDraw GX printing is active, you still can use the Page Setup
command in applications that have not been updated to take full advantage of
GX printing. These Page Setup options are similar to the options offered when
GX is inactive (for details, refer to Chapter 15). Notably you cannot choose a
printer in the Page Setup dialog box of an application that has not been updated
for GX printing. Before using the Page Setup command in such an application,
you must be sure to choose the printer by selecting its desktop icon and using the
Finder's Set Default Printer command (as described in "Choosing the default
printer" earlier in this appendix). Figures A-11 and A-12 show examples of the
Page Setup options offered for a couple of printers in applications that have not
adopted GX printing.

Figure A-11: Setting LaserWriter GX page attributes and PostScript
options in applications that have not adopted GX printing.

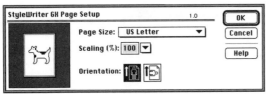

Figure A-12: Setting StyleWriter GX page attributes in applications that have not adopted GX printing.

Using the GX Print Command

After setting page-formatting options with the Print command, you can print a document by choosing the Print command (located in the File menu of most applications). In the Print dialog box, you can specify the range of pages, the number of copies, and a paper source. You may have additional options, depending on the type of printer and on whether the application in which you choose the Print command has adopted GX printing. The following section describes the GX Print command in applications that have adopted GX printing; the section after that one describes the GX Print command in applications that have not adopted GX printing.

In addition to the options described in these sections, you may encounter options added by printing extensions or by individual application programs. For information on these options, see the documentation for the software that is responsible for them.

GX Print in participating applications

Applications that take full advantage of GX printing offer the same general Print options for every type of output device. These applications display the simple Print dialog box that you can drag to a different location by its title bar. Figure A-13 shows an example of the simple GX Print dialog box displayed by applications that have adopted GX printing.

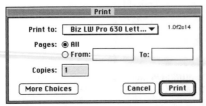

Figure A-13: The simple GX Print dialog box displayed by applications that have adopted GX printing.

In the simple GX Print dialog box, you can choose the printer you want to use from the Print To pop-up menu. The initial choice for a new document is the default printer (as designated by the Finder's Set Default Printer command), but you can choose any printer that has a desktop icon. You also can specify a range of pages and a number of copies to print.

Clicking the More Choices button in the simple Print dialog box expands the dialog box. The expanded Print dialog box includes all the general options of the simple dialog box. You also can specify a paper source — automatic or manual paper feed — and whether multiple copies will be collated as they are printed. Figure A-14 shows an example of the expanded GX Print dialog box displayed by applications that have adopted GX printing.

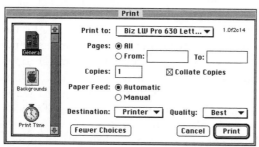

Figure A-14: The expanded GX Print dialog box displayed by applications that have adopted GX printing.

You have additional Print options with some printers. With PostScript printers, you can choose to have the page images saved as a PostScript file by choosing PostScript from the Destination pop-up menu. With a StyleWriter, you can choose one of three print qualities from the Quality pop-up menu.

You can access still more Print options by clicking one of the icons on the left side of the expanded Print dialog box. All printers have the General panel of options; most printers have the Print Time and Paper Match options as well. Still more panels of options may be provided by GX printing extensions in the Extensions folder (inside the System Folder).

The Print Time options determine when your document will be printed. You can elect to have the computer notify you when printing starts, when printing ends, or at both times. Figure A-15 shows the Print Time options of the GX print dialog box displayed by applications that have adopted GX printing.

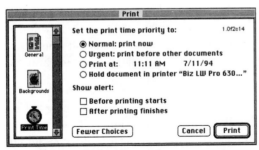

Figure A-15: The GX Print Time options.

The Paper Match options set the type of automatically fed paper and its source. One option is to have the printer driver deduce the type of paper and its source based on the information you specified with the Finder's Input Trays command (described in "Setting up a printer" earlier in this appendix). Alternatively, you can select a different type of paper (which you have put or intend to put temporarily in the paper tray). If you select a particular tray or paper, you can specify how you want the printer driver to handle pages that are too large. You can have the excess portion cropped at the left and bottom margins; you can have pieces of the page printed full-size on multiple sheets of paper that you later tape together; or you can have the page scaled to fit the paper. Figure A-16 shows the Paper Match options of the GX print dialog box displayed by applications that have adopted GX printing.

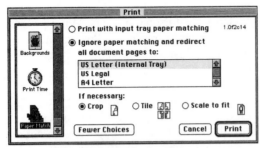

Figure A-16: The GX Paper Match options.

GX Print in nonparticipating applications

In an application that has not been updated to take full advantage of QuickDraw GX, choosing the Print command displays a dialog box similar to the one that appears when QuickDraw GX is inactive (for details, refer to Chapter 15).

Notably you cannot choose a printer in the Print dialog box of an application that has not been updated for GX printing. Before using the Print command in such an application, you must be sure to choose the printer by selecting its desktop icon and using the Finder's Set Default Printer command (as described in "Choosing the default printer" earlier in this appendix). Figures A-17 and A-18 show the Print options for a couple of printers in applications that have not adopted GX printing.

```
Printer "Biz LW Pro 630 Letterhead"          1.0      [ Print ]
Copies: [1]          Pages: ● All ○ From: [    ] To: [    ]   [ Cancel ]
Cover Page:    ● No ○ First Page ○ Last Page
Paper Source: ● Paper Cassette ○ Manual Feed
Destination:  ● Printer          ○ Disk File
```

Figure A-17: Setting LaserWriter GX Print options in applications that have not adopted GX printing.

```
StyleWriter GX                               1.0      [ Print ]
Copies: [1]    Pages: ● All ○ From: [    ] To: [    ]   [ Cancel ]
                                                       [ Help ]
Print Quality:   ○ Best  ● Normal   ○ Draft          [ Options ]
Paper Source:  ● Sheet Feeder  ○ Manual
```

```
StyleWriter GX Print Options                 1.0      [ OK ]
☐ Clean ink cartridge before printing                [ Cancel ]
```

Figure A-18: Setting StyleWriter GX Print options in applications that have not adopted GX printing.

Managing GX Printing

When you click the Print button in a GX Print dialog box, the GX printer driver and any GX printing extensions create page descriptions for the pages to be printed, saving the page descriptions in a file for later printing. Normally, these files are printed in the background automatically, while you continue working. You can view and manage the queue of waiting print files for each printer individually by using the desktop printer icons and the Finder's Printing menu.

The Finder controls background printing for QuickDraw GX. As long as the Finder is open (even in the background), printing proceeds normally. If the Finder is not open, nothing prints. The Finder normally is not open when At

Ease (version 2 and earlier) is present. It's best not to use At Ease 2 and earlier versions with QuickDraw GX.

Viewing a print queue

At any time, you can see the queue of files waiting to be printed on a particular printer by opening that printer's desktop icon in the Finder. Opening a desktop printer icon brings up its window. A desktop printer's window identifies the file that it is printing, reports the status of that print job, and lists the files that are waiting to be printed. You can sort the list of waiting print files by name, number of pages, number of copies, or print time. Choose a sort order from the View menu, or click the column heading in the desktop printer's window. Figure A-19 shows a GX printer's window.

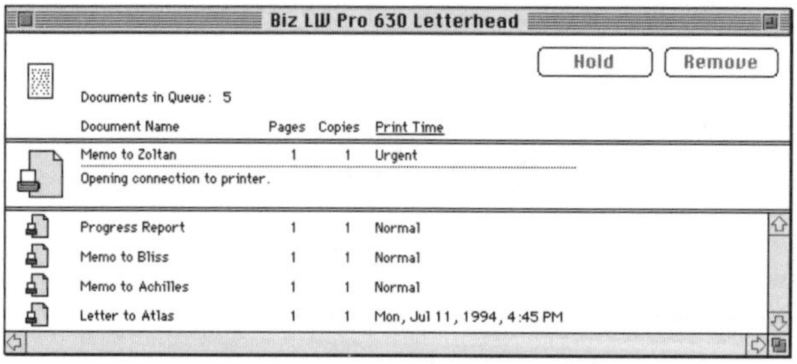

Figure A-19: Viewing queued print files in a GX desktop printer.

You can preview any print file onscreen by simply double-clicking the file's icon. The SimpleText application opens the file and displays one page. Use the Next Page and Previous Page commands in SimpleText's Edit menu to see other pages.

Redirecting a print file from one printer to another is quite easy. Simply drag the printer file from its current location to the desktop icon or window of another printer.

Changing the order of printing

Files in a desktop printer's window print in listed order when the list is sorted by print time. Urgent files are listed first, followed by normal files and files with specific print times. You can change the order of urgent files and the order of normal files by dragging them up and down in the window. You cannot drag an urgent file below the first normal file, and you cannot drag a normal file above the lowest urgent file. You can, however, change a normal file to an urgent file (and vice versa) by selecting the file and choosing Set Print Time from the Finder's Printing menu. You also can use the Set Print Time command to schedule a file to print at a specific time and date.

You can postpone printing a file indefinitely. Select the file in the desktop printer's window and click the Hold button or choose Hold Print Request from the Finder's Printing menu.

To resume printing a file that is on hold, select it and then click the Resume button in the desktop printer's window. Clicking this button displays the Resume Print Request window, in which you can specify the page at which you want printing to resume. (Instead of clicking the Resume button, you can choose Resume on Page One or Resume on Page from the Printing menu.)

Starting and stopping printing

To stop all printing on a particular printer, select its desktop icon and then choose Stop Print Queue from the Printing menu. A small stop sign appears on the printer's desktop icon.

To start printing again, select the printer's desktop icon and then choose Start Print Queue from the Printing menu.

Sharing GX Printers

Beginning with the first Apple LaserWriter, it has always been possible to share printers that connect directly to a network. QuickDraw GX extends printer sharing in two ways: it enables sharing most printers that connect directly to computers (as opposed to networks), and it can limit access to a networked printer. In both cases, the printer must have a desktop icon (which means that it must have a GX printer driver in the Extensions folder). For details on creating a desktop printer icon, refer to "Using GX Desktop Printer Icons" earlier in this appendix.

To share a directly connected printer or to restrict access to a networked printer, select the printer's desktop icon and then choose Sharing from the Finder's Sharing menu. A printer-sharing window appears, as shown in Figure A-20.

Figure A-20: Setting up sharing of a directly connected printer.

In the printer-sharing window, turn on the "Share this printer" option. If you want people who do not have QuickDraw GX to be able to share this printer, turn on the "Non-QuickDraw GX systems may also use this printer" option. (This option is not available for all types of printers.) From the User/Group pop-up menu, choose a registered user or group to which you want to give special access. Use the Guests pop-up menu to specify whether you want to allow all network users, or only users in your zone, to access the shared printer as guests. Unlike registered users and members of groups, guests do not have to enter a password to access a shared printer. (For information on creating registered users and groups, see "Identifying Who Can Access Your Shared Items" in Chapter 18.)

Turn on and off the various access privileges for guests and for the designated user or group. The May Print privilege allows printing on the printer. The See Files privilege allows display of all the waiting print files for the shared printer. The Change Files privilege allows changing the sequence of print files and removing print files.

There is a catch to sharing a printer that is directly connected to your computer: your hard disk must store all the print files waiting to be printed by everyone who's using your printer, and your computer must print those files in the background. If you continue working while your computer handles all that background printing, you may notice a performance slowdown.

Using Portable Digital Documents (PDDs)

QuickDraw GX's print files actually are portable digital documents (PDDs). PDDs are document files that anyone who has QuickDraw GX can view and print without the applications and fonts that were used to create them. One of Apple's GX drivers, PDD Maker GX, facilitates creating PDDs from any application. PDDs can be sent to other QuickDraw GX users for viewing and printing with SimpleText. A PDD retains all its text formatting and graphics.

Creating a PDD is as easy as printing. If you want to create a PDD with an application that has not been updated to use QuickDraw GX printing, you must select the PDD Maker GX's desktop icon and then choose Set Default Printer from the Finder's Printing menu. You also can choose PDD Maker Setup from the Printing menu to select a folder in which to save PDDs by default. (You can always select a folder other than the default folder at the time you actually create a PDD.) Then you can switch to the application in which you want to create a PDD and use the Page Setup and Print commands as though you were printing to a printer.

When you create a PDD, the Print dialog box has a Save button instead of the usual Print button. Clicking the Save button brings up an ordinary Save dialog box, in which you select a folder and type a name for the PDD file. This Save dialog box also has a pop-up menu from which you choose the fonts that you want to include in the PDD. Your choices are to include all fonts used in the document, all fonts except the standard 13 found on most PostScript printers, or no fonts. Fonts included in a PDD work only with that PDD, and they cannot be extracted and installed in anyone's system. Figure A-21 shows the dialog box for saving a PDD file.

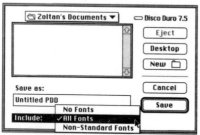

Figure A-21: Saving a portable digital document (PDD).

Bypassing GX Printing

Printing with QuickDraw GX requires a GX driver, but you may be able to bypass QuickDraw GX to use a printer, fax modem, or other output device that has no GX driver. Installing Apple's QuickDraw GX Helper system extension, which requires a custom installation with some versions of QuickDraw GX, enables you to turn off GX printing for applications individually. Installing QuickDraw GX Helper in the Extensions folder adds the command Turn Desktop Printing Off near the top of the Apple menu in applications that allow bypassing GX printing.

Non-GX Drivers Without GX Equivalents

If you want to use a non-GX driver for which no equivalent desktop printer exists, you may have to resort to a bit of chicanery. You will need a copy of Chooser version 7.0 or 7.1, which come with System 7.0.1 and System 7.1, respectively. When you have one of these Choosers, follow these steps:

1. In the Finder, select a LaserWriter desktop printer, and choose Set Default Printer from the Finder's Printing menu.

   If you don't have a LaserWriter desktop printer, use the Chooser to create one.

2. Switch to the application in which you want to use the non-GX driver, and choose Turn off Desktop Printing from the Apple menu.

   A message appears, advising you that QuickDraw GX Helper has selected the (non-GX) LaserWriter driver as a substitute for the current default printer.

3. Click OK to dismiss the message.

4. Open Chooser version 7.0 or 7.1, and select the non-GX driver's icon on the left side of the Chooser window.

   You must use one of these Chooser versions; version 7.3 and later versions do not work.

5. On the right side of the Chooser window, select the port (for nonnetwork devices) or the specific device (for network devices).

6. Click OK to dismiss the Chooser.

7. Use the Page Setup and Print commands to output documents with the selected non-GX driver.

If you use the Finder's Set Default Printer command again, you must repeat steps 4 through 6 to reselect the non-GX driver.

When you choose Turn Desktop Printing Off from the Apple menu, QuickDraw GX Helper tries to find a non-GX printer driver that is equivalent to the current default desktop printer. For example, if the currently selected desktop printer uses the LaserWriter GX driver, then QuickDraw GX Helper tries to find the original LaserWriter driver (version 7.2 or earlier). If the original LaserWriter driver is not in your Extensions folder, then QuickDraw GX Helper tries to find the LaserWriter 8 driver. (Thus, if you want QuickDraw GX Helper to use the LaserWriter 8 driver, make sure the original LaserWriter driver is not in your Extensions folder.)

If QuickDraw GX Helper successfully substitutes a non-GX driver for the current default desktop printer, you can use the Page Setup and Print commands as though QuickDraw GX were not installed (as described in Chapter 15). To choose a different non-GX driver, select an equivalent desktop printer and then choose Set Default Printer from the Finder's Printing menu.

When GX printing is turned off in one application, you still can use GX printing in other applications.

Summary

In this appendix, you learned that on a computer with QuickDraw GX version 1.1.5 and earlier, you use the Chooser to create desktop printer icons and the Finder's Printing command to select a printer.

You use an application's Page Setup command to format the printed page, and use the application's Print command to print pages. The Page Setup and Print commands are different in applications that have adopted GX printing than in applications that have not.

You also learned in this appendix how to manage background printing with GX desktop printer icons. The print files inside GX printer icons are portable digital documents (PDDs) that anyone can see and print with SimpleText.

Although GX printing requires GX printer drivers, by installing QuickDraw GX Helper you can bypass GX printing in individual applications.

PowerTalk Collaboration Services

To provide collaboration services such as e-mail on local area networks, Apple developed PowerTalk system software and PowerShare server software. Both are based on Apple's collaboration technology called Apple Open Collaboration Environment (AOCE). PowerTalk is included for optional installation with complete installation packages of System 7 Pro (a special edition of System 7.1.1) and with Systems 7.5 through 7.5.5 (but not with upgrade packages). PowerTalk does not work with Mac OS 7.6 or later. PowerShare is not part of any system software package.

This appendix describes AOCE, PowerTalk, and PowerShare.

Apple Open Collaboration Environment (AOCE)

Much as your telephone company uses wires, poles, and circuit switching equipment to provide telephone services, PowerTalk uses the Apple Open Collaboration Environment (AOCE) infrastructure to provide collaboration services. AOCE is an infrastructure for the following services:

❖ **Mail and messaging** allow applications and people to send and receive messages and documents over a network whether or not the sender and receiver are available at the same time. Messages and documents can be stored until the recipient is ready to receive them.

❖ **Catalogs** store information about people and network services needed for effective collaboration.

❖ **Authentication and privacy** verify the identity of the sender and receiver, protect messages against snooping while en route, and simplify access to multiple file servers and network services.

❖ **Digital Signature** allows you to add a unique electronic signature to electronic documents, guaranteeing that a document has not been altered since you "signed" it and that you are who you say you are.

Some of those services, such as catalog and mailbox management, are provided through new features of the Finder. Many others of those services could be made available in any application, much like printing and file access. It's up to an application to include menu commands and other means of accessing the collaboration services, just as applications must include Print and Page Setup commands to access printing and Open and Save commands for file access. For example, a spreadsheet program that has a Send command in its File menu can send any spreadsheet as e-mail — no need to attach the spreadsheet file to an e-mail message created in an e-mail program.

The Send command attaches a *mailer*, which like a paper envelope lists the address of the sender and recipient, to the spreadsheet. Your address is added to the mailer automatically. Even better, you can place the recipient on the mailer by dragging the recipient's icon from an open catalog on your desktop to the mailer at the top of the open spreadsheet. As another example, you can get a file from an online service such as CompuServe, open the file in your word processing program, add comments, and send the amended file by e-mail to someone else. If you have the appropriate software installed, you can send a fax or e-mail message from within any application.

Mail and messaging infrastructure

Just as file sharing (described in Chapter 18) enables you to share files with anyone on your network, the AOCE infrastructure enables you to exchange e-mail with anyone on the network. Without AOCE, exchanging e-mail requires that everyone on the network have a special e-mail application. In addition, one computer on the network has to run a program called an e-mail server, which manages e-mail exchanges like the post office manages paper mail. AOCE makes the e-mail server optional and does more than provide the mail transport infrastructure (analogous to the trucks, planes, and postal clerks of the U.S. Mail service).

The mail and messaging infrastructure of AOCE also provide a consistent interface so that you have to learn only one method for sending mail. Every application that takes advantage of AOCE's mail and messaging infrastructure can attach a standard mailer to a document, causing the document to be sent as e-mail. Sending documents by e-mail becomes as easy and consistent as printing. Figure B-1 shows an example of universal mailer in an application that takes advantage of AOCE's mail and message infrastructure.

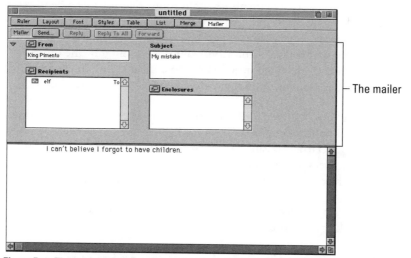

Figure B-1: The universal mailer attachment in an AOCE-compliant application.

The mailer isn't the only standard interface item that AOCE provides. It also puts a universal mailbox for receiving or sending mail on your desktop.

Although AOCE doesn't require an e-mail server on the network, there are advantages to having one. An AOCE e-mail server can store messages sent to you while your Mac was not connected to the network (perhaps it was turned off) and forward them to you the next time you connect to the network. Likewise, the AOCE server can store and forward messages you send to other people. It makes sure that the message gets through, even when the recipient resides on a remote network.

In addition, you can send messages at stated times by using an *agent*. Agents are software entities that manage the flow of messages between computers. You can write your own agents with AppleScript (described in Chapter 22) serving as your front-end for message management. Your agent filters incoming messages and prioritizes them according to criteria that you set. Because Apple events are heavily involved with agents, you can send messages to perform work in your applications if these programs respond to Apple events.

Catalog infrastructure

AOCE organizes your personal and network addresses into *catalogs*. You can move and copy items from one catalog to another by dragging, just as you move items between folders in the Finder. You can also drag items from catalogs to open documents of applications that include a Send command in the File menu or are otherwise designed to take advantage of AOCE's catalog infrastructure. For example, you can easily send e-mail to a team member by dragging that person's icon from your open catalog to the open e-mail. (The e-mail must be created by an AOCE-compliant program such as AppleMail, the AOCE mail program that Apple includes with PowerTalk.)

Catalogs can hold other information, such as phone numbers, Internet addresses, and CompuServe numbers. Thus catalogs act like contact management programs, creating electronic business cards that can be enclosed in other messages or sent by themselves over the network. Workgroups can share catalogs to maintain common contact information, joint calendars, and so on.

The catalog infrastructure also manages AppleTalk network devices and network zones more efficiently than the Chooser.

Authentication and privacy infrastructure

With many messages flying through the ether, a collaboration infrastructure must be able to ensure that communications remain private while in transit. AOCE can encrypt and decrypt messages, making them unrecognizable to someone who manages to tap your network. AOCE can also use an encryption method to authenticate the identities of a message's sender and receiver.

AOCE can also supply the correct passwords automatically when you access file servers (including shared disks and folders) or other password-protected services on your network. Instead of entering passwords individually for each file server or network service you use, you enter a single access code once. The access code verifies that you are who you say you are. After the verification process, AOCE automatically supplies passwords as needed so file servers and network services no longer interrupt you with password requests.

Digital signatures infrastructure

Digital signatures serve the same function as handwritten signatures, namely identifying the person who vouches for the accuracy of the signed document.

Signatures make documents legally binding and trustworthy. Anyone can compare the document's signature with a sample signature and verify that the so-signed document is authentic. Digital signatures perform exactly the same function, providing a way to verify the authenticity of an electronic document.

PowerTalk

PowerTalk software is Apple software that delivers collaboration services based on the AOCE infrastructure. It runs on individual Macs to provide a consistent interface to AOCE's mail and messaging, catalogs, authentication and privacy, and digital signature. In other words, PowerTalk provides the icons, windows, menu commands, and other means to manipulate the AOCE infrastructure. It consists of several system extensions, as well as the AppleMail and DigiSign Utility applications, and requires the Finder that comes with System 7.1.1 (System 7 Pro) through System 7.5.5.

Installing PowerTalk inserts two new commands in the Finder's Special menu and places several new icons on your desktop as well as inside the PowerTalk folder and the Mail and Catalogs folder. Figure B-2 shows the PowerTalk commands and icons.

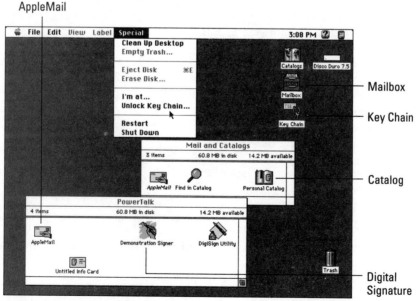

Figure B-2: PowerTalk at a glance.

The PowerTalk icons provide access to collaboration services as follows:

❖ **Key Chain** keeps track of the passwords and other information (the "keys") you must supply to gain access to file servers and other network services. It automatically provides the correct password and other necessary information when you begin using a file server or network service.

❖ **Catalogs** keep track of information about individual people, groups, file servers and other network devices, and so on. This information simplifies sending e-mail, connecting to file servers, and using other cataloged items.

❖ **Mailbox** accumulates incoming and outgoing messages, faxes, e-mail, and voice mail.

❖ **AppleMail** creates and manages e-mail messages and files attached to them.

❖ **Digital Signature** applies an electronic signature to a document so that anyone with PowerTalk can verify who signed the document and can confirm that it has not been changed since that person signed it.

Installing PowerTalk adds services based on AOCE to the Finder and enables you to create e-mail with the AppleMail application, but it does not add services based on AOCE to other applications. It's up to the developers of other applications to add the menu commands necessary to take advantage of the AOCE infrastructure that supports PowerTalk. Developers must upgrade old applications to work with PowerTalk, and you must obtain and install the upgraded applications if you want to create e-mail and use other PowerTalk services from within your applications.

To gain any value from the PowerTalk collaboration services, you must network your computer with other computers that have PowerTalk installed. PowerTalk works on all types of AppleTalk networks — LocalTalk (using either Apple cabling or phone-type cabling), EtherTalk (using any type of Ethernet cabling), Apple Remote Access (using modems and telephone lines), and TokenTalk (using Token Ring cabling).

The following sections describe the PowerTalk collaboration services in more detail.

Key Chain

Some of the most visible symbols of PowerTalk's presence on your desktop are its three new desktop icons that sit on the right side of your computer screen. The Key Chain is a powerful mechanism for automatic access to file servers and other network services that require a password to connect. In Systems 7.5 through 7.5.5, you can also have the Key Chain prevent unauthorized startup of your computer. Using the Key Chain requires entering an *access code* (also called your Key Chain password or key). This access code protects your correspondences, because without knowledge of your password, no one can open your desktop mailbox.

Setting up your Key Chain

You set up the Key Chain access code by choosing Unlock Key Chain from the Finder's Special menu. A dialog box appears and welcomes you to PowerTalk. When you click the Proceed button, another dialog box appears asking whether you have a PowerShare account. If you click the Yes button, the computer searches the network for all available PowerShare services and displays a list of them in yet another dialog box, asking you to select your PowerShare service from the list. The computer does not search for PowerShare services if you click the No button.

Next, another dialog box appears in which you must enter the Key Chain owner's name and access code. You do not have to enter your real name or the Owner name entered in the Sharing Setup control panel (see "Identifying Your Computer" in Chapter 18). Your access code must be at least six characters long and should be easy for you to remember but hard for others to guess. Don't use your name or the name of a close relative. Longer access codes are harder to guess, as are access codes that combine two unrelated words, include punctuation and numbers, and mix uppercase and lowercase letters, such as "D1G+b0z0." When you finish setting up your access code, PowerTalk gives your Mailbox the name you entered. Figure B-3 shows an example of the dialog box in which you enter your PowerTalk access code.

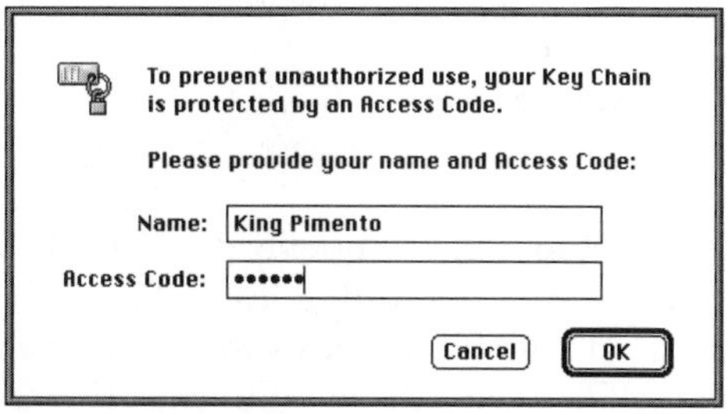

To prevent unauthorized use, your Key Chain is protected by an Access Code.

Please provide your name and Access Code:

Name: King Pimento

Access Code: ••••••

Cancel   OK

Figure B-3: The dialog box displays all the setup information for the Key Chain.

Setting Your Clock and Computer Name

When setting up PowerTalk, it's a good idea to check the accuracy of your system clock. PowerTalk uses the system clock to stamp your outgoing correspondence with the time and date. To check the clock and adjust it if necessary, you can use the Date & Time control panel. If you have not already done so, use the Sharing Setup control panel to set your computer's name (see "Identifying Your Computer" in Chapter 18). The name you set is the "address" to which other PowerTalk users can send you mail. Give your computer a name that makes it easy for others to find you. Consider including your name in the name of your computer: for example, "Biff's Power Mac."

Changing Key Chain services

Your Key Chain always includes at least one service, the AppleTalk network mail service. You can add or remove file servers and other network services at any time. To see the network services that your Key Chain offers, double-click its icon. A list of services appears in the Key Chain window, as shown in Figure B-4.

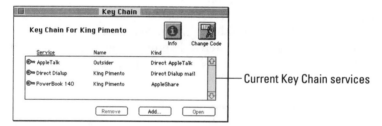

Figure B-4: The Key Chain window lists network services.

To add a file server, simply connect to it as you usually do. Immediately after you enter the server's correct name and password, PowerTalk displays a dialog box asking whether you want to add the file server to your Key Chain. Click the Yes button to connect to the file server and add it to your Key Chain, click the No button to connect to the server without adding it to your Key Chain, or click the Cancel button to neither connect to the file server nor add it to your Key Chain. For details about connecting to a file server, see "Sharing Someone Else's Folders and Disks" in Chapter 18.

To add another type of service, open your Key Chain icon and click the Add button in the Key Chain window.

To remove a service from your Key Chain, select the service in the Key Chain window and click the Remove button there. You cannot remove your AppleTalk network mail service.

Changing the Key Chain name or access code

You can change the Key Chain owner's name or Key Chain access code at any time. Simply open the Key Chain icon on your desktop and click the Change Code button in the Key Chain window. If you try to open your Key Chain while it's locked, PowerTalk asks you to enter the correct Key Chain access code. Figure B-5 shows an example of the Key Chain window and its Change Code button.

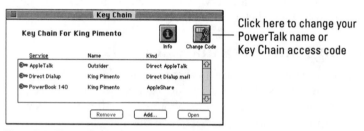

Click here to change your PowerTalk name or Key Chain access code

Figure B-5: The button in this Key Change window will allow the user to change the access code.

When you change the name in the Key Chain window, PowerTalk changes the name of the desktop Mailbox icon to match. You cannot change the name of the Mailbox icon by using normal methods for editing icon names in the Finder (as described in "Icons" in Chapter 5). You can change the name of the Key Chain icon by using normal icon name-editing methods, however.

Locking your Key Chain

The Key Chain access code provides the first line of defense against snooping eyes. You can lock your catalog and mailbox information by choosing Lock Key Chain from the Finder's Special menu. Choosing this command lets you walk away from your computer while restricting access to your data until you re-enter your access code. You can also set PowerTalk to lock your Key Chain after a certain period of inactivity. Use the PowerTalk Setup control panel, shown in Figure B-6.

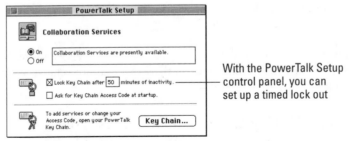

With the PowerTalk Setup control panel, you can set up a timed lock out

Figure B-6: The PowerTalk Setup control panel.

You can also use draconian methods and turn off your collaboration services by clicking the Off option in the PowerTalk Setup control panel. When you restart your computer, no mailbox or catalog appears on the desktop. Your Key Chain icon appears when PowerTalk is off, but you can't open it. To regain access to your collaboration services, you have to go back into the PowerTalk Setup control panel, click On, and restart your computer.

Catalogs and information cards

PowerTalk organizes information about people, shared network devices, and services such as file servers. You can use catalogs to access these people and things quickly and find information about them. All computers with PowerTalk have at least two catalogs, one shared and one personal.

Shared catalogs

Every computer with PowerTalk has an AppleTalk catalog, which contains information about each PowerTalk computer and file server on the network. To see the AppleTalk catalog, open the Catalogs icon on the desktop and then open the AppleTalk icon, as shown in Figure B-7.

The Catalogs icon contains shared catalogs. If you have other shared catalogs on your network, you see their icons when you open the Catalogs icon. You cannot actually move catalogs out of the Catalogs window, but you can make aliases of icons in the Catalogs window and place them anywhere you like. To make an alias of a catalog in the Catalogs window, simply drag the catalog's icon to the desktop or any folder window. The Finder automatically makes an alias; you don't have to use the Make Alias command.

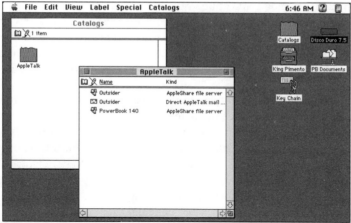

Figure B-7: Access the AppleTalk catalog via the Catalogs icon.

Personal catalogs

The other catalog on every computer with PowerTalk is called the Personal Catalog. It resides on your computer, so you can use your personal catalog even when you are not connected to a network. Initially, your personal catalog is in the Apple Menu Items folder or in the Mail and Catalogs folder inside the Apple Menu Items folder. Either way it is easy to open from the Apple menu. You can move your personal catalog anyplace you like and make aliases of it as needed. Figure B-8 shows how you open you Personal Catalog from the Apple menu.

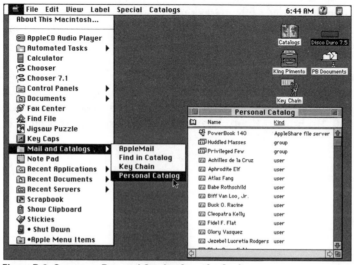

Figure B-8: Open your Personal Catalog from the Apple menu.

Your personal catalog starts out empty. You add information about the individuals and groups with whom you work and about the file servers and network services you use. You can use your personal catalog to create a personal information management system, recording business or pleasure contact information that you can use to contact people by e-mail, fax, telephone, or postal mail.

If one personal catalog is not enough, you can create more. You can name them anything you want and place them anywhere on your hard disk for easy access. To create a new personal catalog, first open your main Personal Catalog (in the Apple menu) or open the Catalogs icon (on the desktop). A Catalogs menu appears next to the Finder's Special menu. Choosing New Personal Catalog from the Catalog menu creates a new personal catalog on the desktop. You can change its name by using normal icon-editing methods (see "Renaming Icons" in Chapter 6). Figure B-9 shows two personal catalogs.

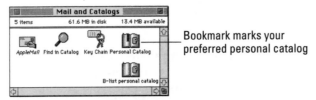

Figure B-9: You can create more than one personal catalog.

When you have more than one personal catalog, you can designate one as your preferred catalog. Applications that take advantage of PowerTalk services can always find items in your preferred personal catalog, no matter where it is on your hard disk. PowerTalk marks the icon of your preferred personal catalog with a bookmark. Initially, your preferred personal catalog is the one in the Apple menu.

To designate a preferred personal catalog, select its icon and choose Get Info from the Finder's File menu to bring up the catalog's Info window. In the Info window, click the Set Preferred button, and then close the Info window. Figure B-10 shows the button you click to designate your preferred personal catalog.

```
┌──────────────────────────────────┐
│ ▣▣ B-list personal catalog Info ▣▣│
├──────────────────────────────────┤
│   ┌──┐                            │
│   │  │  B-list personal catalog   │
│   └──┘                            │
│   Kind : personal catalog         │
│   Size : 8K on disk (6,682 bytes used) │
│                                   │
│  Where : Disco Duro 7.5 : System Folder : │
│          Apple Menu Items : Mail and │
│          Catalogs :               │
│ Created : Mon, Jul 25, 1994, 6:48 AM │
│ Modified : Mon, Jul 25, 1994, 6:48 AM │
│ Version : 1.1b4, ©Apple Computer, Inc. │
│          1989-1994. All rights reserved. │
│ Comments :                        │
│  ┌──────────────────────────┐    │
│  │                          │    │
│  │                          │    │
│  │                          │    │
│  └──────────────────────────┘    │
│                                   │
│ ┌─────────────┐ ┌──────────────┐ │
│ │Set Preferred│ │Find Preferred│ │
│ └─────────────┘ └──────────────┘ │
│ ☐ Locked                          │
└──────────────────────────────────┘
```

Click here to make this your
preferred personal catalog

Figure B-10: A personal catalog's Info window.

Catalog items

PowerTalk represents each person, group, file server, network service, or other catalog item with an information card. Opening an information card (for example, by double-clicking it) brings up a window that contains information about the catalog item in a window. The content and appearance of an information card window depend on the kind of item the card represents.

❖ **User information cards** include a person's name, postal addresses, electronic addresses, telephone numbers, and any other pertinent details you want to record, such as hobbies and spouse's name. Cards that contain electronic addresses simplify addressing e-mail to individuals, as described in the section "AppleMail and the Mailer" later in this appendix. To create a new user information card, open a personal catalog and choose New User from the Finder's Catalog menu. Figure B-11 shows an example of a user information card.

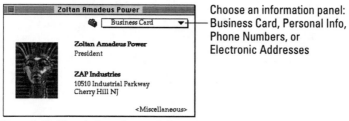

Choose an information panel:
Business Card, Personal Info,
Phone Numbers, or
Electronic Addresses

Figure B-11: The window of a user information card.

❖ **Group information cards** contain aliases that point to user information cards. You can use group information cards to address e-mail to groups, as described in the section "AppleMail and the Mailer" later in this appendix. To create a new group information card, open a personal catalog and choose New Group from the Finder's Catalog menu. To add a user to a group, drag the user's card from a personal catalog to the group's card. To add one group to another group, drag the first group's card to the second group's card. Figure B-12 shows an example of a group information card.

Figure B-12: The window of a group information card.

❖ **File server information cards** contain the information you need to connect to the file servers (usually a registered user name and password) and a list of volumes that are available on the server. Opening a volume listed in a server information card connects you to the server, puts the volume icon on your desktop, and opens the volume. Your AppleTalk catalog (in the Catalogs icon) automatically lists each file server to which you have access. You can copy a file server from the AppleTalk catalog to a personal catalog by dragging the server's card. Figure B-13 shows an example of a file server information card.

Figure B-13: The window of a file server information card.

Browsing and searching catalogs

While browsing a catalog, you can use the Finder's View menu to choose the order in which the catalog window lists items — by name or by kind. Alternatively, you can sort catalog items by clicking a column heading in the catalog window. The Finder underlines the heading of the column by which catalog items are currently sorted.

You can also use the View menu to list only file servers, only users (including groups), or only miscellaneous items in the catalog.

You use the Catalogs icon on the desktop to search for network catalogs and copy addresses from network-based catalogs to your information cards and catalogs. You can also locate shared catalogs over the network by using the Find in Catalog command from the Apple menu. This utility lets you search specific servers as well as search by type of information (for example, file servers or user information cards) and then copy found items to the location you choose.

If you're not sure which catalog contains an item you need, choose Find in Catalog from the Mail and Catalogs submenu of the Apple menu. Use the pop-up menus in that window to tell the Finder which kind of item you are looking for and where to look. Type at least the first part of the item's name and click the Find button to begin the search. A list of matching items appears in the Find in Catalog window. You open a found item by double-clicking it, or you can drag a copy to the desktop or a personal catalog. Figure B-14 shows the Find in Catalog window.

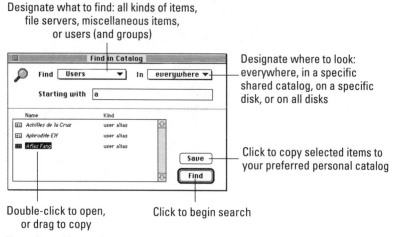

Designate what to find: all kinds of items, file servers, miscellaneous items, or users (and groups)

Designate where to look: everywhere, in a specific shared catalog, on a specific disk, or on all disks

Click to copy selected items to your preferred personal catalog

Double-click to open, or drag to copy

Click to begin search

Figure B-14: Choose Find in Catalog from the Apple menu to search for a forgotten catalog item.

Messaging and mail

One exciting thing about PowerTalk is that it brings consistent e-mail services to both your desktop and to applications designed (or upgraded) to take advantage of PowerTalk. E-mail services, such as sending and receiving messages, enclosing documents, and sending carbon copies, are included with Systems 7.5 through 7.5.5, extending the reach of your computer. PowerTalk's mail services are compatible with third-party e-mail systems, existing beside these stand-alone products to provide a standard interface throughout all applications.

With PowerTalk, you can perform the following mail activities:

❖ Send documents, applications, and folders by dragging them onto a user or group information card containing the recipient's electronic address.

❖ Centralize all your incoming and outgoing e-mail in one place in your desktop mailbox. It has an In Tray that lists all incoming mail, regardless of its origin, and an Out Tray showing mail that has been sent, regardless of its destination.

❖ With a PowerShare server on your network, you can send mail to workgroup members who are not logged onto the network. Likewise, you can receive mail even if your computer was not connected to the network when the e-mail was sent. You can also check for PowerShare mail from another computer on the network.

QUICK TIPS

Sending Files and Folders as E-Mail

To send files, folders, or information cards as e-mail, drag them to a user or group information card icon. You can drag one item at a time or select several items and drag them together. After you drag items to a user or group information card, PowerTalk asks you to confirm or cancel the sending operation. Usually, you keep information cards in your personal catalogs, but you can also keep information cards or their aliases on the desktop or in a folder.

Note that you cannot send user information cards to a group by dragging the user information cards directly to a group information card icon. When you do so, the Finder assumes that you want to add the users to the group. To work around this situation, put the user information cards in a folder and drag the folder to the group information card icon.

By installing additional software called a *personal gateway*, you can extend
PowerTalk to handle other communications. You may install personal gateways
to handle e-mail from other sources such as the Internet. Other personal
gateways can send and receive faxes and take phone messages. Apple didn't
include gateways with System 7.5, but the System 7.5.3 CD's CD Extras folder
includes gateways for the Internet, CompuServe, Microsoft Mail, QuickMail,
faxes, pagers, and voicemail.

Checking your mailbox In Tray

The mailbox icon that appears on your desktop after you install PowerTalk is your
file cabinet for incoming and outgoing mail. Your mailbox contains PowerTalk
e-mail, which may include many different types of materials, such as documents,
information cards, letters, application programs, fonts, and movies. Your mailbox
may also contain e-mail from other sources, faxes, voice mail, and other
communications if you have installed the appropriate personal gateway software.

When you open your mailbox, the first thing you see is your In Tray window.
As you can probably guess, your In Tray lists mail that you have received. You
can also gain access by selecting the In Tray from the Mailbox menu that
appears in the menu bar when you open the mailbox. Figure B-15 shows an
example In Tray window.

Opening your mail is as easy as double-clicking. You can also select a piece of
mail and use the Open command to perform the same function. Delete mail by
dragging its icon from the In Tray to the Trash. To copy a piece of mail, select
and drag it to the desktop or a folder. The In Tray operates exactly like any
window in the Finder, providing all the Finder's file management tools for your
use with mail items.

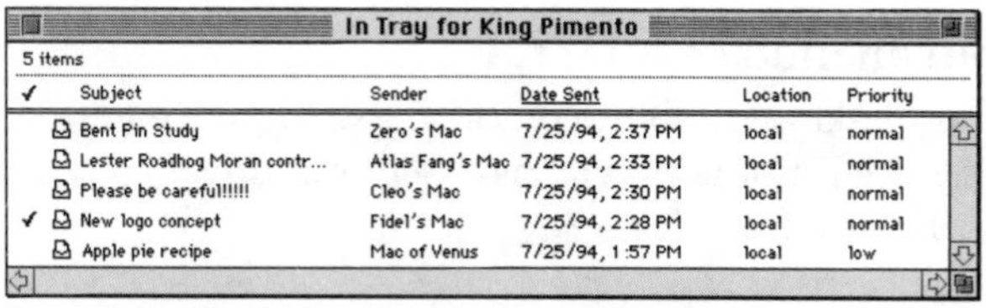

Figure B-15: The In Tray lists your incoming mail.

You can categorize items in your In Tray by attaching tags to them. Select one or
more items and choose Tags from the Finder's Mailbox menu (which appears to
the right of the Special menu when the In Tray is the active window). The Tags
window appears, in which you can either type a tag or choose one from the pop-
up menu that lists previously used tags. To attach multiple tags to an item, use
the Tags command repeatedly, specifying a different tag each time. To remove

tags from the list that appears in the pop-up menu, use the Preferences command in the Mailbox menu.

The In Tray is designed for easy viewing of your mail from many vantage points. The View menu provides six views: by whether or not you have read your mail (indicated by a check mark next to the item), by subject, by sender, by date sent, by location, and by priority. You can also use the View menu to filter your mail to show only those items you have read or not read. Alternately, you can click a column heading in the In Tray to sort the window's contents by that heading. The View menu also lets you filter your mail by tags you have previously attached to mail items, showing only those pieces of mail labeled with specific tags. You can edit tags in the Preferences dialog box, as well as add to or delete them as needed. Figure B-16 demonstrates the view options for your In Tray window.

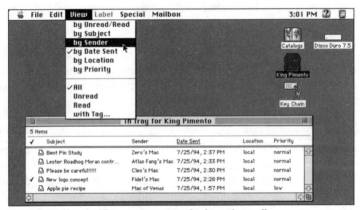

Figure B-16: Use the View menu to organize incoming mail.

Checking your mailbox Out Tray

After opening your desktop mailbox, you can choose Out Tray from the Mailbox menu to see a list of items you have sent recently. Figure B-17 shows an example Out Tray window.

	Out Tray for King Pimento			
3 items				
	Subject	Date Sent	Status	Mail Connection
	Steering Committee Meeting	7/25/94, 3:40 PM	sending	Direct AppleTalk
	Vasquez Promotion	7/25/94, 3:37 PM	waiting	Direct AppleTalk
	New Executive Assistant	7/25/94, 3:35 PM	waiting	Direct AppleTalk

Figure B-17: Review outgoing mail in the Out Tray.

The Out Tray window shows you the status of any message that you have sent. The status possibilities are as follows:

❖ **Sending** means that PowerTalk is in the process of sending out this mail.

❖ **Waiting** means that PowerTalk has not yet sent the mail.

❖ **Done** means that PowerTalk has delivered the mail from your computer to its next destination (or has given up after repeated attempts).

You can't tell by looking in your Out Tray if a recipient has read or even received mail you sent. All you know is that PowerTalk has sent mail marked Done over the network. If your network has a PowerShare server, you know that mail marked Done arrived at the server for forwarding.

Items marked Done are complete copies of the sent items. By default, PowerTalk stores Done items on your hard disk for 14 days. You can change how long PowerTalk retains sent mail by using the Preferences command in the Mailbox menu.

You can sort the Out Tray contents by various criteria. Use the View menu or click the column headings in the Out Tray window.

AppleMail and the Mailer

You probably don't want to send all your mail from the Finder (by dragging documents to user and group information cards) any more than you want to print all your documents from the Finder. You want to be able to send documents as e-mail from the applications in which you create the documents. You can do so in applications that incorporate the PowerTalk Mailer. The Mailer is like an address label for a document. It specifies the sender, lists the recipients, states the subject, and lists enclosed files. You use the Mailer the same way in every application that includes it. Figure B-18 shows an example of the PowerTalk mailer.

You get one application that incorporates the PowerTalk mailer, AppleMail, when you install PowerTalk. You can use AppleMail to write, send, read, reply to, and forward electronic letters and memos. AppleMail includes a pretty powerful text editor that lets you use multiple fonts, styles, and formats in your e-mail. You can also paste pictures, sounds, and QuickTime movies into e-mail that you create with AppleMail.

AppleMail is not the only application that incorporates the Mailer. QuickMail AOCE, for example, is an alternative e-mail application with the same basic capabilities as AppleMail. ClarisWorks 2.1 through 4.0 also lets you attach a mailer to any ClarisWorks document.

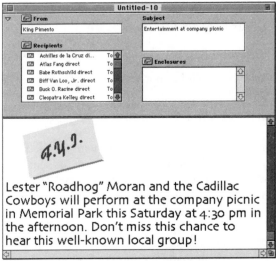

Figure B-18: The PowerTalk Mailer on an AppleMail letter.

QUICK TIPS

Typing Addresses Directly

To type an address directly in a mailer, click the Recipient button to bring up the Mailer's panel for locating and adding recipients. In the Recipients panel, click the button labeled with a picture of a pencil to display the panel for typing an address. As you type, keep the following guidelines in mind:

❖ Pay strict attention to capitalization, spelling, and punctuation. Type the address correctly or the mail will not reach the addressee.

❖ If your network does not have a PowerShare server, PowerTalk assumes that you are sending the mail to a recipient located in your zone. If the recipient is not located in your zone, specify the zone in the following format: *name@zone* (where *name* is the recipient's name and *zone* is the recipient's zone). For example, if the recipient's name is Zoltan Amadeus Power and his zone is Pellucidar, then the complete address is Zoltan Amadeus Power@Pellucidar.

❖ Be as complete as possible when typing PowerShare addresses to speed up sending. Enter zones and folder names where appropriate. Use the @ symbol between the recipient's name and the catalog name, and put colons between folder names, as in Aphrodite Elf@Laconia:Sparta.

❖ When you finish typing an address, you can add it to the list of recipients by clicking the To button or the CC button in the Type-In Addressing panel. You can also designate this address to receive a blind copy by pressing Option, which changes the CC button to a BCC button, and clicking that button. Other recipients don't see addresses that receive blind copies.

The Mailer is linked to your preferred personal catalog, your shared catalogs, and your Key Chain, making addressing as easy as clicking or dragging. You can also search catalogs from the Mailer and type addresses directly if necessary. If you want to enclose files or folders with a message, you can select them from an Open dialog box and drag their icons from folder windows or the desktop to the Mailer.

Sending e-mail

After filling out a mailer, you send it and its contents with the Send command, whose menu location varies from one application to the next. In AppleMail, the Send command is in the Mail menu. In ClarisWorks, the Send command is in the Mail submenu of the File menu. Choosing the Send command brings up a Send dialog box, as shown in Figure B-19.

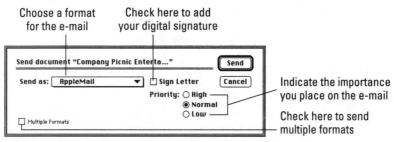

Figure B-19: Set Options for sending e-mail in the Send dialog box.

In the Send dialog box, you can use the pop-up menu to choose a format for e-mail to which the Mailer is attached. The choice of formats is not the same in every application. In AppleMail, you can choose the AppleMail format or the Snapshot format. When you choose the AppleMail format, the recipient is able to read and edit the e-mail by using AppleMail or an application that understands the AppleMail format.

The recipient can copy text, pictures, sounds, and movies that you included in the e-mail. When you choose the Snapshot format, the recipient gets a picture of the e-mail and cannot copy individual parts of it. The Snapshot format creates a PICT file that many applications can read, including SimpleText. In applications other than AppleMail, you may not be able to choose the AppleMail format, but you probably can choose a proprietary format that works with the application you're using. ClarisWorks, for example, gives you a choice of ClarisWorks, AppleMail, and Snapshot formats (and offers other formats if you have translators installed in the Claris folder in your System Folder). You can also elect to use multiple formats to ensure that the recipients can open the letter even if they do not have AppleMail installed. Click the Multiple Formats check box to turn on this option. Note that sending e-mail in multiple formats takes up more disk space, but it is good insurance if you do not know which applications the recipients have. Your choice of format does not affect enclosed files, whose formats were established when they were created.

You can set a priority in the Send dialog box, but it has no effect on how PowerTalk handles e-mail. The priority you set only indicates to recipients of the e-mail how important you consider it to be.

Using PowerTalk with a PowerBook

PowerTalk provides special tools just for PowerBook users. Installing PowerTalk adds the I'm At command to the Finder's Special menu. This command lets you activate and deactivate individual electronic addresses based on your location. For example, you can directly connect your PowerBook to an AppleTalk network when you're at work, but you can use Apple Remote Access to connect to the network by modem and phone lines from home.

Choosing the I'm At command brings up the dialog box shown in the figure. In that dialog box, you choose your location from a pop-up menu, and then you select the PowerTalk services available at that location. Your service options depend on what you have installed, such as the following:

❖ **Direct AppleTalk Mail**, which uses the AppleTalk catalog to send mail.

❖ **PowerShare Server Mail**, which uses the shared catalogs and PowerShare to manage mail.

❖ **Direct Dialup Mail**, which uses Apple Remote Access to connect to a network by modem and phone lines.

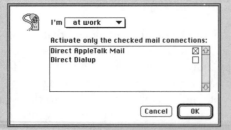

If you choose Off-Line as your location, PowerTalk disconnects you from all service options. You can still create and send e-mail and read e-mail in your In Tray. Items you send while off-line go into your Out Tray, and PowerTalk delivers them later when you connect with the appropriate service.

Setting the Sign Letter option in the Send dialog box puts your digital signature on the e-mail item to ensure its authenticity. To use this option, you must have a DigiSign Signer file, which is described in the section "Digital Signatures" later in this appendix. You do not need to sign a letter digitally to ensure its authenticity if you have a PowerShare account. PowerShare guarantees that the source of every piece of e-mail its servers handle is genuine.

Reading e-mail

E-mail sent to you by someone using AppleMail, QuickMail AOCE, ClarisWorks, or another application that incorporates the PowerTalk Mailer appears in your In Tray. To read e-mail, double-click its icon. The e-mail opens in the application that created it. If the e-mail has enclosures, you can open them by double-clicking them or by dragging them to the desktop or a folder.

You can reply to received e-mail by using the Reply command, and you can forward e-mail by using the Forward command. The menu location of these two commands varies from one application to the next. In AppleMail, they are in the Mailer menu. In ClarisWorks, the Reply and Forward commands are in the Mail submenu of the File menu.

Digital signatures

With a PowerTalk digital signature, you can vouch for the content of an electronic document just as you vouch for the content of paper mail by signing your name to it. Anyone can use a computer with PowerTalk installed to verify a digital signature. You don't have to apply a digital signature to items you send electronically with PowerTalk software. A document sent without your digital signature is like a memo or letter sent without your handwritten signature — the recipient can't verify that it truly came from you. A digital signature goes a step further than a handwritten signature, guaranteeing that the document has not been altered since you applied the digital signature.

Before you can apply a digital signature to any document, you must obtain a special file called a Signer. You create an unapproved Signer with the DigiSign utility program that comes with PowerTalk. When DigiSign creates an unapproved Signer, it also creates an approval request form that you submit to an agency or person authorized to issue you an approval file. The approval file contains the information the DigiSign program needs to change your unapproved Signer into an approved Signer. Once you have an approved Signer, you can apply digital signatures in the Finder, AppleMail, and other applications that incorporate the PowerTalk mailer.

To apply your digital signature to a file in the Finder, drag the file to your Signer. PowerTalk asks you to enter your DigiSign identification code. (You specify your code when you create your unapproved Signer, and you can change your code with the DigiSign program.) To apply your digital signature in AppleMail or another application that incorporates PowerTalk Mailers, set the Sign Letter option in the Send dialog box (as described in the section "Sending E-mail" earlier in this appendix). Figure B-20 shows the dialog box in which you enter your DigiSign identification code.

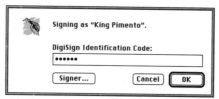

Figure B-20: Use your secret Signer code to set up a digital signature for a document.

Don't tell anyone your DigiSign identification code. Anyone who knows your code can use your Signer to forge your digital signature. PowerTalk cannot prevent this type of forgery or other intentional misuse (such as obtaining a Signer with false ID).

When you apply a digital signature to a document, it does not show up on the document like a handwritten signature does. The digital signature appears as a button in the document's Info window (you display a document's Info window with the Finder's Get Info command). Clicking this verification button brings up a dialog box that asks whether you want to verify or remove the signature. After you click Verify, a dialog box appears, displaying information about the signature and either verifying or not verifying the digital signature. PowerTalk is unable to verify a digital signature if it has been tampered with or if the document has been altered since it was signed. Figure B-21 shows the button you click to verify a document's digital signature.

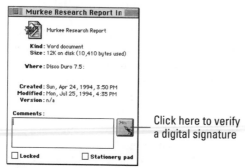

Click here to verify a digital signature

Figure B-21: Verify a digital signature in the signed document's Info window.

PowerShare Servers

PowerShare servers augment the collaboration services provided by PowerTalk. Installing PowerShare software on a computer being used as a server on the local network adds the following collaboration services to every PowerTalk user on the network:

❖ **Shared catalogs** let network users share a common pool of information cards.

❖ **Authentication and privacy** automatically authenticate the addresses of a message's sender and receiver and guarantee the security of e-mail.

❖ **Store-and-forward messaging** lets you send mail to people who are not currently connected to the network and lets other people send you e-mail when you are not connected to the network.

In addition, PowerShare servers can provide central access to collaboration services outside the local network — external e-mail, file servers, and so on.

These additional services are managed by two PowerShare servers, the Catalog server and the Mail server. They can reside on one computer or two and can reside on the same computer as an AppleShare server (described in Chapter 18) or not.

PowerShare catalogs

As with PowerTalk, the basic foundation of PowerShare is the catalog. On PowerShare, catalogs store information about the different members of a network, be they approved users, groups, file servers, other shared devices, administrative materials such as forms, or planning materials such as calendars and project management tools. PowerShare catalogs help locate shared items on the network and assist in managing information about these networked items.

A person acting as system administrator sets up PowerShare's Catalog server, making its catalogs available through the Catalogs icon located on each networked computer. The administrator decides which catalogs can be shared and who can share them. The Catalogs icon is the doorway to PowerShare resources, such as AppleShare file servers, shared printers, fax modems, and data modems. In addition, PowerShare catalogs list user and group information in the same fashion as Personal catalogs, letting users share addresses and data about network members.

Authentication and privacy

The Catalog server acts as a trusted third party, vouching for the authenticity of users who share information over the network. Authentication of users prevents unauthorized access to catalogs and files. Each user or group recorded in a catalog has an authentication key. These keys, managed on individual computers by the PowerTalk Key Chain, serve to verify approved use of collaborative services located on the PowerShare system, such as the sending of e-mail to workgroup members. When an authenticated session is established, data transmitted across the network is encrypted to thwart network crackers.

PowerShare e-mail

PowerShare Mail servers route and store e-mail sent between network users. The Mail server stores e-mail and forwards it when its destination becomes available. Mail sent to users who are not currently connected is not lost, but is held and delivered as soon as they connect.

Summary

In this appendix, you learned that PowerTalk provides collaboration services through AOCE's infrastructure much as your phone company provides phone service through its wires, poles, and switching equipment. You learned how to use and configure your PowerTalk key chain to access any file server or other network service with a single access code. You found out how to keep track of contact information such as phone numbers, e-mail addresses, and postal addresses with PowerTalk's catalogs. You also saw how some applications have taken advantage of PowerTalk's mailer to let you send documents directly from the application. Finally, you learned that PowerShare software running on a computer on your network enhances PowerTalk with shared catalogs, automatic authentication and privacy, and store-and-forward messaging.

Glossary

32-Bit Addressing
A system software capability that increases the amount of RAM that most Macintosh models can use. Without 32-Bit Addressing, a Mac can only take advantage of 8MB of RAM, even if more is installed, and virtual memory is limited to 14MB. With 32-Bit Addressing, a Mac can make use of RAM beyond 8MB.

32-Bit Clean
Describes software that works with the 32-Bit Addressing option turned on (in the Memory control panel). Using software that is not 32-Bit Clean restricts the amount of memory a Mac can use to 8MB.

68K applications
Programs written for 68000, 68020, 68030, and 68040 processors. These programs require the same amount of memory whether virtual memory is on or off.

active program
The program whose menus are currently displayed in the menu bar.

adorn
The process of changing the formatting of a *subscriber*.

alias
A stand-in or agent for a real program, document, folder, or disk. The alias does not duplicate the item it represents; the alias points to the item it represents.

allocation block size
The smallest amount of space that can be allocated to a file on a volume. Larger volumes have a larger allocation block size.

Apple events
The system software language for *IAC*. Applications can send Apple events messages to one another. When an application receives an Apple event, it takes an action according to the content of the Apple event. This action can be anything from executing a particular command to taking some data, working with it, and then returning a result to the program that sent the Apple event.

Apple Guide
A help system that provides step-by-step interactive instructions for completing certain tasks.

AppleScript
An English-like programming language that you can use to send *Apple events* to programs. With AppleScript you can write your own programs, called *scripts*, to perform complex tasks easily. For example, you can use AppleScript to move data between many applications.

AppleTalk
The networking protocol built into all Mac OS computers and most LaserWriter printers for passing messages and information to each other. The content that is passed back and forth could be *Apple events*, page images to be printed, e-mail, file contents, or any other kind of information. The content and the protocol can be transmitted through *LocalTalk* cabling, *Ethernet* cabling, or other media.

applets
Small Java programs embedded in Web pages to make them more interesting or useful.

authentication
The process of identifying a user's ID and password in order to make a network connection.

autoscrolling
The process of scrolling through a window without using the scroll bars by placing the pointer in the window, pressing the mouse button, and dragging toward the area you want to view.

background program
A program that runs during the intervals, typically less than ⅛ of a second long, when the active program isn't using the computer. It usually works while the active program waits for you to do something.

balloon help
A help system that makes a cartoonlike balloon appear when you drag the mouse slowly over a standard object in the Mac OS interface. The balloon may tell you what the object is, what it does, or what happens when you click it.

binary file
A file of formatted text, pictures, sound, movies, other data, or program code.

BinHex
A file transmission program that converts a *binary file* into a plain text file so it can be sent over a network. A BinHexed file must be decoded back into a binary file before it can be used on the receiving computer.

bit
A single binary digit.

bitmapped font
Same as *fixed-size font.*

blessed
A term used for the active System Folder.

bookmark
A way to store *Web page* locations (*URLs*) that you want to remember and/or go to frequently.

case-sensitive
Describes a password in which capitalization matters. For instance, capital *A* is not the same as lower case *a*.

character
A written representation of a letter, digit, or symbol; a basic element of a written language.

Clarus
See *DogCow.*

click-and-a-half
A gesture used to make a disk or folder spring open. It is performed by beginning to double-click the disk or folder but not releasing the mouse button after the second click.

clean installation
This type of installation deactivates your old System Folder and installs a new one with new copies of Mac OS software. You must then reconfigure control panels, reinstall application programs, and reset preferences in them.

client
A program that requests and receives information or services from a server.

clipping file
A file created by the Finder to hold material that has been dragged from a document to the desktop or a folder window.

codec
Compressor-decompressor software or hardware. (See *compressor.*)

color picker
The dialog box in which you specify a custom color either by clicking a color wheel or by entering color values.

compile
To put a *script* in an internal format that *AppleScript* can run. Before compiling a script, AppleScript checks it for things that AppleScript doesn't understand. For example, if you forget a parenthesis where AppleScript expects to find one, it lets you know.

compression algorithm
A method for compressing and decompressing data. Each compression algorithm generally works best with one type of data, such as sound, photographs, video or motion pictures, and computer-generated animation. Three characteristics of a compression algorithm determine how effectively it compresses: compression ratio, image fidelity, and speed.

compression ratio
Indicates the amount of compression and is calculated by dividing the size of the original image by the size of the compressed image. Larger compression ratios mean greater compression and generally mean poorer image quality.

compressor
Something that compresses data so that it takes less space to store, and decompresses compressed data back to its original form for playing or changing. A compressor may consist of software, hardware, or both. Sometimes also called *codec*, a shortened form of "compressor-decompressor."

conditional
A programming command that evaluates a condition (stated as part of the conditional) to determine whether another command or set of commands should be performed. (Also referred to as a *conditional statement.*)

container
An OpenDoc part that can contain other parts.

contextual menu
A menu that lists commands relevant to an item that you Control-click.

control panel
A small program that you use to set the way some part of the system looks and behaves.

custom installation
You can selectively install portions of the Mac OS modules. Do this only if you are sure that you know which individual items must be present for the software to work properly.

dead keys
The keys that generate accented characters when typed in combination with the Option key and in proper sequence. For example, typing Option-E followed by O generates ó. The Key Caps desk accessory outlines the dead keys when you press the Option key.

dedicated file server
A computer that is dedicated to providing *file-sharing* services.

desk accessory
A type of program that doesn't have documents and can't receive Apple events.

desktop database
Used by the Finder to keep track of the location, icon, and Info window comments for every file, folder, and disk. The Mac OS keeps it hidden because you don't use it directly.

digital signature
Functions as a handwritten signature, identifying the person who vouches for the accuracy and authenticity of the signed document.

DIMMs
Dual in-line memory modules.

disk cache
Improves system performance by storing recently used information from disk in a dedicated part of memory. Accessing information in memory is much faster than accessing information on disk.

DogCow
Also known as *Clarus*, the official mascot of Mac hackers is pictured in many Page Setup Options dialog boxes.

domain name
The part of the URL that identifies the organization or company that owns the Internet server.

double-click speed
The rate at which you have to click so that the Mac OS perceives two clicks in a row as a single click.

download
The process of receiving software or other computer files from another computer, over a network, generally through a modem and telephone lines.

dpi (dots per inch)
A measure of how fine or coarse the dots are that make up a printed image. More dots per inch mean smaller dots, and smaller dots mean finer (less coarse) printing.

drag-and-drop editing
To copy text, graphics, and other material within a document, between documents, or between applications. This capability works only with applications that are designed to take advantage of it (such as versions of SimpleText, Stickies, Note Pad, the Scrapbook, and Finder that are included with System 7.5 and later).

drag-and-drop open
To place the mouse pointer over an object (such as a document icon), hold down the mouse button, and move the mouse until the pointer is over another object that can open the first object (such as a compatible application).

The pointer drags the first object along, and the second item becomes highlighted when the pointer is on it. Releasing the mouse button drops the first object onto the second object, which opens the first object.

drop box
A shared folder in which network users may place items, but only the folder's owner can see them.

easy installation
Installs all of a module's components that are recommended for your computer model.

edition
A file that contains a live copy of the material in a *publisher*. When the publisher changes, the edition is updated. *Subscribers* contain copies of editions.

enclosing folder
The folder that contains another folder.

encryption
The process of making messages or files unrecognizable, for example to someone who taps into your network without authorization.

Ethernet
A high-speed standard for connecting computers and other devices in a network. Ethernet ports are built into many newer Mac OS computer and LaserWriter models. Its connectors and cabling cost more than *LocalTalk* equivalents.

EtherTalk
A type of network that uses *AppleTalk* software and communications protocols over *Ethernet* cabling.

extension
A software module that is loaded during startup and adds features or capabilities to the system software.

fair use
Defines the criteria which must be considered before using another person's copyrighted work (printed or recorded materials).

file ID number
The number that the system software uses internally to identify the original item to which an alias is attached even if you have renamed or moved that original item.

file mapping
A technique used by the virtual memory system software to load code fragments directly from the application file into memory.

file name suffix
The three characters following the period at the end of a file name. The file-name suffix indicates the kind of file on a DOS or Windows computer. (Also referred to as a *file name extension*.)

Glossary

file server
A computer running a program makes files centrally available for other computers on a network.

file sharing
Allows you to share files, folders, and disks with people whose computers are connected to yours in a network.

file spec (specification)
Tells the system software exactly where to find a file or folder.

fixed-size font
Contains exact pictures of every letter, digit, and symbol for one size of a font. Fixed-size fonts often are called *bitmapped fonts* because each picture precisely maps the dots, or *bits*, to be displayed or printed for one character.

font
A set of *glyphs* that have a common and consistent design.

font family
A collection of differently styled variations (such as bold, italic, and plain) of a single *font*. Many *fixed-size*, *TrueType*, and *PostScript* fonts come in the four basic styles: plain, bold, italic, and bold italic. Some PostScript font families include twenty or more styled versions.

Fonts folder
Located in the System Folder, this folder includes all *fixed-size*, *PostScript*, and *TrueType* fonts in System 7.1 and later.

font suitcase
A folder-like container specifically for *fixed-size* and *TrueType* fonts. With QuickDraw GX, font suitcases can also contain GX-enabled *PostScript* Type 1 fonts. You can create a new font-suitcase file by duplicating an existing font-suitcase file, opening the duplicate, and dragging its contents to the Trash.

fps (frames per second)
Measures how smoothly a motion picture plays. More frames per second means smoother playback.

fragmented memory
See *memory fragmentation*.

frame
One still image that is part of a series of still images, which, when shown in sequence, produce the illusion of movement.

frame rate
The number of frames displayed in one second. The TV frame rate is 30 fps in the United States and other countries that use the NTSC broadcasting standard; 25 fps in countries that use the PAL or SEACAM standard. The standard movie frame rate is 24 fps. (See also *fps*.)

freeware
Free software distributed through user groups and online information services. Most freeware is copyrighted by the person who created it; few freeware programs are in the public domain.

FTP (File Transfer Protocol)
The data communications *protocol* used by the Internet to send and receive files.

FTP site
A collection of files on an FTP server available for downloading.

full motion
Video displayed at frame rates of 24 to 30 fps. The human eye perceives fairly smooth motion at frame rates of 12 to 18 fps. (See also *fps* and *frame rate*.)

gamma correction
A method the computer's video circuitry uses to balance color on a video display. Color balancing is necessary because the intensity of color on a video display does not correspond uniformly to the intensity of the electron beam that traces the video picture on the phosphor coating inside the video display tube.

glyph
A distinct visual representation of one character (such as a lowercase *z*), multiple characters treated as one (such as the ligature æ), or a nonprinting character (such as a space).

grid fitting
The process of modifying characters at small point sizes so they fit the grid of dots on the relatively coarse display screen. The font designer provides a set of instructions (also known as *hints*) for a *TrueType* or *PostScript* font that tells the system software how to modify character outlines to fit the grid.

groups
Collections of individual registered users. You can grant specific access privileges for a shared item to a group instead of to a single user.

guest
A network user who is not identified by a registered name and password.

hack
A programming effort that accomplishes something ingenious or unconventional.

hacker
A person who likes to tinker with computers, and especially with computer software code. Some Hackers create new software, but many Hackers use programs such as ResEdit to make unauthorized changes to existing software.

handler
A named set of *script* commands that you can execute by naming the handler elsewhere in the same script. Instead of repeating a set of commands several times in different parts of a script, you can make the set of commands a handler and invoke the handler each place you would have repeated the set of commands.

helper application
A program that handles a particular kind of data encountered on the Internet.

hot spots
Places in a QuickTime VR panorama that you can click to go to another scene in the panorama or to a QuickTime VR object.

hyperlink
Underlined text on a *Web page* that, when you click it, takes you to another page on the same or a different Web site.

initialization
A process that erases a disk and creates a blank disk directory. It wipes out the means of accessing the existing files on the disk without actually touching the content of files.

insertion point
A blinking vertical bar that indicates where text will be inserted if you start typing.

installation
Places a new or updated version of software on your disk.

interapplication communication (IAC)
The technology that enables programs to send each other messages requesting action and receiving the results of requested actions. The Mac system software's IAC is called *Apple events* and is the basis of *AppleScript*.

Internet
A worldwide network that provides e-mail, Web pages, news, and file storage and retrieval.

Internet Service Provider (ISP)
The company that gives you access to the Internet via your modem.

kerning
Adjusting the space between pairs of letters so the spacing within the word looks consistent.

label
A means of categorizing files, folders, and disks. Each label has its own color and text, which you can change with the Labels control panel.

language script system
Software that enables the Mac OS to use an additional natural language such as Japanese. One language script system can be used by multiple languages (for example, the Roman script is used for English, French, Italian, Spanish, and German).

ligature
A glyph composed of two merged characters. For example, *f* and *l* can be merged to form *fl*.

link
See *hyperlink*.

live object
An *OpenDoc* plug-in that has been through a certification process to ensure that it works and plays well with others.

localization
The development of software whose dialog-box messages, screens, menus, and other screen elements use the language spoken in the region in which the software is sold.

LocalTalk
A relatively low-speed standard for connecting computers, printers, and other devices to create an *AppleTalk* network. LocalTalk uses the built-in printer ports of Mac OS computers and the LocalTalk ports of many LaserWriter printers.

lossless
A type of compression algorithm that regenerates exactly the same data as the uncompressed original and has a relatively low compression ratio.

memory fragmentation
The condition wherein available memory has become divided into multiple disjointed blocks, with each block separated by an open program. The Mac OS cannot automatically consolidate fragmented memory nor open a program in multiple blocks. You can fix memory fragmentation by quitting all open programs.

memory-management unit (MMU)
A part of the 68030, 68040, or PowerPC processor chip, the MMU is required for virtual memory.

Minimum memory size
The smallest amount of memory in which the system will open a program. The Mac OS displays and lets you change a program's Minimum memory size in its Info window and warns you if you try to set it below the minimum safe size determined by the program's developer.

modem
A device that connects a computer to telephone lines. It converts digital information from the computer into sounds for transmission over phone lines and converts sounds from phone lines to digital information for the computer. (The term *modem* is a shortened form of *modulator-demodulator*.)

movie
1. Any time-related data, such as video, sound, animation, and graphs that change over time. 2. Apple's format for organizing, storing, and exchanging time-related data.

mount
To make a disk's contents available to the computer. In the case of hard disks, this happens every time you start up the computer. You can also use the Drive Setup utility program or a similar disk utility to mount disks.

multimedia
A presentation combining text or graphics with video, animation, or sound, and presented on a computer.

multitasking
The capability to have multiple programs open simultaneously.

navigate
1. To open disks and folders until you have the one open that contains the item you need. 2. To go from one *Web page* to another.

network
A collection of interconnected, individually controlled computers, printers, and other devices together with the hardware, software, and protocols used to connect them. A network lets connected devices exchange messages and information.

network administrator
Someone who sets up and maintains a centralized file server and other network services. The network administrator does not control access to folders and files on the server's disks; that is the responsibility of each person who puts items on the disks.

networking protocol
A set of rules for exchanging data over a *network*.

newsgroup
One of the subjects on the Internet's *Usenet*. It is a collection of people and messages pertaining to that particular subject.

object
A kind of information, such as words, paragraphs, and characters, that an application knows how to work with. An application's *AppleScript* dictionary lists the kind of objects it can work with under script control.

online information service
A source that provides shareware and freeware directly to your computer through telephone lines and modems. Examples include America Online (800-827-6364), CompuServe (800-800-2222), and various *Internet* sites. Except for the Internet, online information services charge access fees and retrieval fees.

OpenDoc
System software that makes it easy to work on many types of data in a single document without switching applications.

OpenDoc editor
Software that lets you view and perhaps edit a particular kind of data (such as graphics, audio, or video) in an OpenDoc document.

original item
A file, folder, or disk to which an alias points. The file, folder, or disk that actually opens when you open its alias. (Same as *target*.)

orphaned alias
An *alias* that has lost its link with its original item (and therefore, the system software cannot find it).

outline font
A font whose *glyphs* are outlined by curves and straight lines that can be smoothly enlarged or reduced to any size and then filled with dots.

owner
1. A registered user or group that can assign access privileges to a shared folder. 2. The person who can access all disks and folders (even those not explicitly shared with the Sharing command); this owner's name and password are set in the File Sharing or Sharing Setup control panel.

package
A logical grouping of items that are related, such as all of the items that make up fax software, or all of the parts of Open Transport.

part
An *OpenDoc* plug-in component that lets you work on a particular kind of content, which could be text, graphics, sound, movies, spreadsheets, charts, databases, Web pages, e-mail, or something else.

partition
To divide a hard drive into several smaller volumes, each of which the computer treats as a separate disk. Also, another name for any of the volumes created by dividing a hard drive.

password
A combination of letters, digits, and symbols that must be typed accurately to gain access to shared items on a file server (including another Mac that is sharing its folders).

PhoneNet
An inexpensive LocalTalk cabling system for connecting computers, printers, and other devices to an *AppleTalk* network.

pixel
Short for picture element, a pixel is the smallest dot that the computer and monitor can display.

pixel depth
The number of colors available for each *pixel* of a displayed image. This also refers to the number of memory bits used to store each pixel's color. The number of colors available depends on the number of bits. For example, 256 colors require 8 bits per pixel, and 32,768 colors require 16 bits per pixel.

platinum appearance
A sleek redesign of the menu bar, menus, windows, and icons introduced with Mac OS 8. The new appearance includes 3D shading and color accents.

point of presence (POP)
A TCP/IP network's entry point.

PostScript font
An outline font that conforms to the specifications of the PostScript programming language. PostScript fonts can be smoothly scaled to any size, rotated, and made to follow a curved path. Originally designed for printing on Laser-Writers and other PostScript output devices, the ATM software makes PostScript fonts work equally well on-screen and with non-PostScript printers.

PostScript printers
Printers that interpret PostScript commands to create printable images.

PPD (PostScript Printer Description)
A file that contains the optional features of a PostScript printer such as its resolution and paper tray configuration.

PRAM (parameter RAM)
A small amount of battery-powered memory that stores system settings such as time, date, mouse tracking speed, speaker volume, and choice of startup disk.

Preferences folder
Holds files that contain the settings you make in control panels and with the Preferences commands of application programs.

Preferred memory size
The maximum amount of memory the system allocates to a program. A program's Info window displays and lets you change the Preferred memory size.

primary script
The *language script system* used by system dialog boxes and menus. If you are working on a computer that is set up for English, Roman is your primary script; your secondary script can be any other installed language script, such as Japanese.

printer driver
Software that prepares pages for, and communicates with, a particular type of printer. This software resides in the Extensions folder inside the System Folder.

print job
A file of page descriptions. Also called a *print request* or *spool file*.

print request
See *print job*.

print server
A computer that is dedicated to managing one or more shared printers.

program linking
The process of sharing programs by sending and receiving *Apple events* across a network. You must turn on program linking in the File Sharing or Sharing Setup control panel, and you can use the Finder's Sharing command to enable or prevent linking to individual programs.

protocol
See *networking protocol*.

publisher
A section of a document, a copy of which has been saved as an *edition* for other documents to subscribe to.

RAM disk
RAM that is set aside to be used as if it were a very fast hard disk.

registered user
Network users who must enter their names and any passwords you've assigned them before they can connect to your computer to share files or programs.

repeat loop
An arrangement of *AppleScript* commands that begins with a Repeat command and ends with an End Repeat command. AppleScript executes the commands between the Repeat and End Repeat commands for the number of times specified in the Repeat command.

resolution
The perceived smoothness of a displayed or printed image. Printed resolution is measured in dots per inch (*dpi*). A high-resolution printed image has more dots per inch than a low-resolution printed image.

resolve an alias
What the system software does to find the original item represented by an *alias*.

resources
Information such as text, menus, icons, pictures, or patterns used by the system software, an application, or other software.

ROM
Read-only memory.

root level
The main level of a disk.

root part
The part (or the part whose stationery) you use to create a new *OpenDoc* document.

script
1. A collection of *AppleScript* commands that performs a specific task. 2. Short for *language script system*, which is software that defines a method of writing (vertical or horizontal, left to right, or right to left). A script also provides rules for text sorting, word breaks, and the formats of dates, times, and numbers.

script applications
AppleScript scripts saved as applications.

scripting additions
Files that add commands to the *AppleScript* language, much as plug-in filters add menu commands to Photoshop or the contents of the Word Commands folder add various features to Microsoft Word. Scripting additions reside in a folder called Scripting Additions, which is in the System Folder.

script recording
A process in which *AppleScript* watches as you work with an application and automatically writes a corresponding *script*.

selection rectangle
A dotted line box that you drag around items to select them all.

server
A program that provides information or services to clients on demand.

shareware
Low-cost software distributed through user groups and online information services. Shareware depends on the honor and honesty of people who use it. You're expected to pay the author a small fee if you plan to use the software.

Shift-click
Holding down the Shift key while clicking the mouse to select multiple items or a range of items.

SIMMs
Single in-line memory modules.

spool file
See *print job*.

spooling
A printer-driver operation in which the driver saves page descriptions in a file (called a *spool file*) for later printing.

standard installation
For Mac OS 8 and 7.6, this type of installation installs the basic modules — Mac OS, OpenDoc, and OpenDoc essentials — plus any additional modules you select. Each module is installed in its entirety. For System 7.5.3 or 7.5, a standard installation installs the basic system software components appropriate for your computer.

startup disk
A disk with the Finder and System files in its System Folder, which allows the computer to begin operation.

Startup Items folder
Items you place here are opened automatically in alphabetical order when you start up your Mac.

stationery pad
A template document that contains preset format and contents.

subdirectories
The equivalent in other operating systems to folders in the Mac OS.

submenu
A secondary menu that pops out from the side of another menu. A submenu appears when you place the pointer on a menu item that has an arrowhead at the right side of the menu.

subscriber
A copy of an *edition* that has been placed in a document and can be updated automatically when the edition is updated by its *publisher*.

Suggested memory size
The amount of memory the program's developer recommends for standard program performance. A program's Info window displays, but does not let you change, the Suggested memory size.

swash
The fancy tail on an alternate, decorative form of a character, or the character with its fancy tail. To use swashes, you need QuickDraw GX, a GX font that includes swashes, and an application that lets you set the text style to show swashes.

system enabler
A plug-in software component that modifies the system software to work with a particular computer model.

system extension
See *extension*.

System file
Contains sounds, keyboard layouts, and language script systems as well as the basic system software.

System Folder
Stores the essential software (including the Finder, the System file, control panels, and extensions) that gives the Mac OS its unique appearance and behavior.

thread
A string of messages about the same subject.

track
One channel of a QuickTime movie, containing video, sound, closed-captioned text, MIDI data, time codes, or other time-related data.

tracking
The overall spacing between letters in an entire document or text selection. Text with loose tracking has extra space between the characters in words. Text with tight tracking has characters squeezed close together.

tracking speed
The rate at which the pointer moves as you drag the mouse.

transceiver
A connector box designed for a particular type of Ethernet cable in a network.

translator
A program that translates your documents from one file format, such as Word for the Mac, to another, such as Word for Windows.

TrueType
The outline font technology built into the Mac OS. TrueType fonts can be smoothly scaled to any size on-screen or any type of printer.

Type 1 font
A PostScript font that includes instructions for grid fitting so they can be scaled to small sizes with good results.

universal installation
Yields a version of the system software that can be used by any Mac OS computer model.

UNIX
An operating system (system software) popular on computers of the workstation class and larger.

unmount
To remove a disk's icon from the desktop and make the disk's contents unavailable without deleting the items in that disk permanently.

upload
The process of sending files from your computer to another computer.

URL (Universal Resource Locator)
An *Internet* address. This can be the address of a *Web page*, a file on an *FTP* site, or anything else you can access on the Internet.

Usenet
A worldwide *Internet* bulletin board system, where people can post messages and join discussions about subjects that interest them.

user group
An organization that provides information to people who use computers. Many user groups, such as BMUG (510-549-2684), have extensive libraries of *shareware* and *freeware*, which they distribute on floppy disk for a nominal fee. For the names and phone numbers of user groups near you, call Apple's referral line (800-538-9696).

variable
A container for information in a *script*. You can place data in a variable and then use it elsewhere in the script.

virtual memory
Additional memory made available by the system software, treating part of a hard disk as if it were RAM.

volume
A disk or a part of a disk that the computer treats as a separate storage device. Each volume has a disk icon on the desktop.

Web browser
A program that enables you to access the World Wide Web.

Web page
A basic unit that the World Wide Web uses to display information (including text, pictures, animation, audio, and video clips). A Web page can also contain *hyperlinks* to other Web pages (on the same or a different Web server).

write protect
The process of locking a disk so it cannot be erased, have its name changed, have files copied onto it or duplicated from it, or have files or folders it contains moved to the desktop or trash.

Index

(continued)

my2cents.idgbooks.com

IDG BOOKS WORLDWIDE REGISTRATION CARD

Visit our Web site at http://www.idgbooks.com

ISBN Number: 0-7645-4036-X

Title of this book: MacWorld® Mac® OS 8 Bible

My overall rating of this book: ❏ Very good [1] ❏ Good [2] ❏ Satisfactory [3] ❏ Fair [4] ❏ Poor [5]

How I first heard about this book:

❏ Found in bookstore; name: [6]   ❏ Book review: [7]

❏ Advertisement: [8]   ❏ Catalog: [9]

❏ Word of mouth; heard about book from friend, co-worker, etc.: [10]   ❏ Other: [11]

What I liked most about this book:

What I would change, add, delete, etc., in future editions of this book:

Other comments:

Number of computer books I purchase in a year: ❏ 1 [12]   ❏ 2-5 [13]   ❏ 6-10 [14]   ❏ More than 10 [15]

I would characterize my computer skills as: ❏ Beginner [16] ❏ Intermediate [17] ❏ Advanced [18] ❏ Professional [19]

I use ❏ DOS [20] ❏ Windows [21] ❏ OS/2 [22] ❏ Unix [23] ❏ Macintosh [24] ❏ Other: [25]_____

(please specify)

I would be interested in new books on the following subjects:

(please check all that apply, and use the spaces provided to identify specific software)

❏ Word processing: [26]   ❏ Spreadsheets: [27]

❏ Data bases: [28]   ❏ Desktop publishing: [29]

❏ File Utilities: [30]   ❏ Money management: [31]

❏ Networking: [32]   ❏ Programming languages: [33]

❏ Other: [34]

I use a PC at (please check all that apply): ❏ home [35] ❏ work [36] ❏ school [37] ❏ other: [38] _____

The disks I prefer to use are ❏ 5.25 [39] ❏ 3.5 [40] ❏ other: [41]_____

I have a CD ROM: ❏ yes [42]   ❏ no [43]

I plan to buy or upgrade computer hardware this year: ❏ yes [44]   ❏ no [45]

I plan to buy or upgrade computer software this year: ❏ yes [46]   ❏ no [47]

Name: _____ Business title: [48] _____ Type of Business: [49] _____

Address (❏ home [50] ❏ work [51]/Company name: _____)

Street/Suite# _____

City [52]/State [53]/Zip code [54]: _____ Country [55] _____

❏ **I liked this book!** You may quote me by name in future IDG Books Worldwide promotional materials.

My daytime phone number is _____

IDG
BOOKS
WORLDWIDE

THE WORLD OF
COMPUTER
KNOWLEDGE®

❏ YES!

Please keep me informed about IDG Books Worldwide's World of Computer Knowledge. Send me your latest catalog.

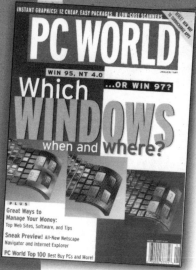

Every issue of PC WORLD is packed with the latest news and information to help you make the most of your PC.

- Hot PC News
- Top 100 PC & Product Ratings
- Applications Tips & Tricks
- Buyer's Guides
- Consumer Watch
- Hardware and Software Previews
- Internet & Multimedia Special Reports
- Problem-solving Case Studies
- Monthly @Home Section

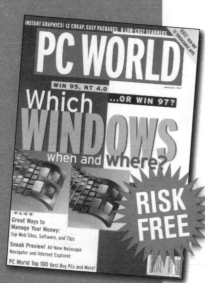

YOUR FREE GIFT!

As a special bonus with your order, you will receive the IDG Books/PC WORLD CD wallet, perfect for transporting and protecting your CD collection.

Send Today for your sample issue and FREE CD wallet.

Plug into PC WORLD Online now!
http://www.pcworld.com